THE WOMAN'S DICTIONARY
OF SYMBOLS
AND SACRED OBJECTS

THE WOMAN'S DICTIONARY
OF SYMBOLS
AND SACRED OBJECTS

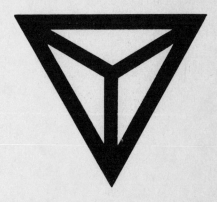

BARBARA G. WALKER

Illustrated by the Author

1817

Harper & Row, Publishers, San Francisco

New York, Grand Rapids, Philadelphia, St. Louis
London, Singapore, Sydney, Tokyo, Toronto

GUIDE FOR USE: Symbols are arranged into sections by shape or type of symbol. Within each section, entries are alphabetical. Words printed in the text in boldface type indicate main–entry treatment of these subjects elsewhere. Index contains alphabetical listing of all symbols.

Illustrations are by Barbara G. Walker.

THE WOMAN'S DICTIONARY OF SYMBOLS AND SACRED OBJECTS. Copyright © 1988 by Barbara G. Walker. All rights reserved. Printed in the United States of America. No part of this book may be used or reproduced in any manner whatsoever without written permission except in the case of brief quotations embodied in critical articles and reviews. For information address Harper & Row, Publishers, Inc., 10 East 53rd Street, New York, N.Y. 10022.

Library of Congress Cataloging-in-Publication Data

Walker, Barbara G.
  The woman's dictionary of symbols and sacred objects.

  Bibliography: p.
  Includes index.
  1. Symbolism. 2. Women—Folklore. I. Title.
CB475.W35 1988   001.56   88-45158
ISBN 0-06-250992-5
ISBN 0-06-250923-3 (pbk.)

90   91   92   HC   10   9   8   7   6   5

CONTENTS

UTCHAT
from Section 6,
"Sacred Objects"

POPPET
from Section 7,
"Secular-Sacred Objects"

GHOST
Pueblo Indian ghost figure
from Section 10,
"Supernaturals"

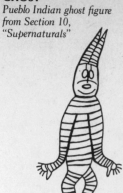

GARUDA
from Section 15,
"Birds"

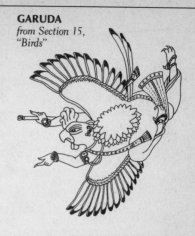

MISTLETOE
from Section 18,
"Plants"

STONE
holed stone
from Section 21,
"Minerals, Stones,
and Shells"

INTRODUCTION

Symbolism is a slippery subject. Any one symbol may have hundreds of interpretations, according to the differing beliefs of people who have interpreted it. Any basic symbol of worldwide distribution—such as the triangle, circle, cross, square, or star—can represent many disparate things in various times or places. Symbols now associated with orthodox religions originally evolved from very different contexts in the prepatriarchal past, like the crescent moon of intensely male-oriented Islam, which descended from the female-oriented worship of the Moon Mother in archaic Arabia.

An example of debased popular interpretation is shown by the swastika. During and after World War II, the swastika was seen as a symbol of totalitarianism and cruelty. Previously, however, the swastika was an ancient Oriental emblem of peace and creativity, related to the sun wheel, with such meanings as "let it be" or "amen." It was even a sacred sign, probably representing rebirth, in Paleolithic times twelve thousand years ago.

Some symbols tap archetypal imagery deep within the mind. Human responses to symbols are artificially learned from the culture, yet also intensely subjective. Consider the way we respond to the purely arbitrary symbols of a written language. The alphabetical marks have no relationship whatever to the sounds they are supposed to represent. Yet, as we read, our minds hear those sounds instantly and accurately. The sounds, moreover, have no relationship whatever to the ideas they are supposed to indicate. Yet we grasp the ideas also, immediately. From printed letters to words to ideas is an enormously complex mental journey that we can make thousands of times a minute as we read a page of a book. Once we have learned to read, we identify alphabetical symbols with such ease and speed that we can even use reading as a form of relaxation. Our minds *rest* by going through this complicated process of sorting, remembering, identifying, and associating symbol systems!

So readily and intensely do human beings respond to symbols that it is hardly a surprise to find symbols deified and divinized in every human culture. People seem prone to attach feelings of awe to their own works, especially when the works bear esthetic significances, such as an orderly symmetry. People also revere external objects that strike their fancy for either esthetic or associative reasons. Whatever is perceived as somehow special in one's experience can become an object of worship. Thus we find human traditions littered with holy trees, holy stones, holy mountains, rivers, animals, and other elements of the natural environment, as well as every kind of personal or collective fetish. Reverence focuses attention on the object as a feedback mechanism arising from the initial focus of attention that generates the reverence in the first place.

Furthermore, it might be said that graphic symbols represent the essential preverbal language. Infants think in images before they learn to think in words. That preverbal language is the most vital of all, remaining throughout life as the language of dreams and unconscious perception. The infant can sense that its very life depends on establishing communication with the mother or other caretakers. Without the ability to sense, project, and respond to imagery, the human being lacks the very essence of humanness.

Since the primary function of the mind is to associate ideas, people naturally associate many things without regard to their real connections— or lack of them—in the external world. Often, the vaguest kind of resemblance will do to connect a picture with a real form. A stick figure can be readily seen as a man. The letter *M* can be two mountains or nurturing breasts of Mother Earth. A plain circle can be the moon, the sun, a wheel, time, the universe, or a cosmic principle of wholeness. The simpler the symbol, the more meanings it can accumulate as it is contemplated and discussed through generations.

Still, there are some related constellations of meanings that adhere to the same symbols again and again, so it becomes possible to say a symbol represents this or that with at least a degree of consistency. Sometimes, historical changes in interpretation may be recovered, so we can know both the archaic meanings of the symbol and the more recent ones—which may even be mutually contradictory, especially in the case of religious symbols.

A typical example of this is the dove, adopted by Christianity as a symbol of peace, purity, the creative Logos, or the Holy Ghost. As the ancient Hindu *paravata* and the divine totem of Mother Aphrodite, the dove used to represent female sexual lust, which was once viewed as the prerequisite to all acts of creation. When the advent of patriarchy forced denial of female sexuality, its symbols were either diabolized, or desexualized and pressed into service with new meanings—sometimes even both at once, so irrational but tenacious is the symbolizing impulse. An example of the latter is the serpent, which came to represent the devil in Christian tradition yet still retained its ancient pagan healing magic, as in the hermetic caduceus still used today to symbolize medicine. Various Gnostic sects during the medieval period even represented Christ in the form of a serpent.

It is hardly to be wondered at, that many symbols are associated with sexuality, since this is always a subject of intense interest whether it is of the positive or the negative sort. Other common symbols obviously express perennial human preoccupations such as health, wealth, fertility, power, control of the environment, or maintenance of the food supply. Ultimately, symbolism boils down to human needs and desires, just as language-making itself arises from every child's need to establish interpersonal communication for the sake of its own welfare.

Herein lies some of the true fascination of symbols. No matter how arbitrary their associations, they always seem meaningful. The longer any given symbol is contemplated, the more meaningful it becomes—for the very process of contemplation brings additional interpretations. Symbols may be studied from both individual and collective viewpoints. One learns the symbol's past implications and also brings one's own imaginative responses into play. Symbolism thus offers a creative learning experience almost as complex as the learning of language itself.

It is especially important for women to learn more about the language of symbols, because many common religious symbols were stolen from ancient woman-centered systems and reinterpreted in the contexts of patriarchy. As women struggle out from under centuries of patriarchal oppression, they find it necessary to reclaim their symbols and reapply them to feminine interests. For example, a triangle may be said to represent the primordial Virgin, Mother, and Crone trinity as readily as the Father, Son, and Holy Ghost; the former interpretation does have chronological precedence to recommend it.

While it is true that symbols are whatever one cares to make of them, it is also true that Western civilization's symbolism has gone in directions that ignore or belittle the female principle. A case in point is that women have been encouraged to worship a cross, which is known to have been a phallic symbol throughout most of its historical career. There are dozens of time-honored female symbols that would be more appropriate for contemplation by women seeking contact with their own inner essence.

One purpose of this book is to supply women with symbols of this kind. Another is to increase awareness of symbols generally. To gain clearer ideas of what certain visual stimuli meant to our ancestors is to learn a little more about our own symbol systems and personal responses to what we see. And that can be a useful kind of learning for anyone.

1

ROUND AND OVAL MOTIFS

The universe begins with roundness; so say the myths. The great circle, the cosmic egg, the bubble, the spiral, the moon, the zero, the wheel of time, the infinite womb: such are the symbols that try to express a human sense of the wholeness of things. *Everything* and *everywhere* are circular in most pictographic or alphabetic systems. Birth is roundness: the pregnant belly, the full breast. Death brings life full circle: back to the beginning again. Vessels are round. The house is round, containing all stages of life. The temple is round, making wholeness visible. The sacred dance is circular.

Prepatriarchal thought the world over is nonlinear and multidirectional. Life's experience is not a progression but a mandala. All things fit into the great round of existence. There is as much awareness of the environment as of the ego. The world is conceived as a sphere in which all parts relate reciprocally to all other parts.

This mindset changed radically when ego-centered, world-condemning patriarchal religions began to predominate in certain areas of the earth. Men's gods tended to be coercive and exclusionary. They tended to be shapers of the environment, rather than the environment itself. The intimacy of the mother-child relationship with the universe was lost in a depersonalized father-child relationship that automatically set up a hierarchy: the superior as opposed to the inferior, a ladder or a pyramid with God at the summit looking down on everything else. At this point, human morality became a question of personal obedience or disobedience to commands from above, rather than a sense of what is right for the good of the whole.

In the world of symbolism, however, the old ideas yet remain and may be rediscovered today, in an age that is beginning to realize the folly of patriarchal thinking carried to extremes. The circle symbolizes a democracy beyond what we consider democratic, a system having no head or tail, no higher or lower. Unlike the cross, which always had masculine/phallic connotations, rounded symbols are without status clues. Up, down, left, and right are parts of an unbroken continuum merging birth and death, light and darkness, heaven and hell in a holistic ideal. Such was the old feminine vision.

The modern world needs a sense of wholeness, of the essential unity of all peoples, creatures, and nature on this earth. We need to restore the idea of the great round, before our linear, "power-over" mindset destroys not only the concept of life all together, but even the fact of life altogether. We have not many places left from which to begin. The ancient symbolism of roundness may be one of them.

AUREOLE
*Buddhist, 2nd–3rd
century A.D.*

BLACK SUN

Aureole (Aura)

The literal meaning of *aureole* is a circlet of gold. As a **crown**, or "glory" upon the head, it was a symbol of divinity. Early Christians confused this with the **halo** (a "ring" of gold) or the nimbus (a "cloud" of gold), or simply the *aura*, which means "golden." Byzantine iconography in particular attached solid-looking gold discs to holy heads in their pictures. These discs were often shown so realistically that if a face appeared in profile, the golden aureole was flattened and foreshortened, like a gold dinner-plate glued to the back of the head. Early Byzantine art provided even Satan with a gold halo.[1]

Association with other forms of the halo linked the aureole (aura) with all emanations of the body viewed as spiritual symbols, and eventually to the idea of the "astral" (starlight) body, believed by mystics to be coexistent with the material body, yet like the soul at times separable from the flesh. Some claimed the ability to see this immaterial body in the form of an aura, or halo of light or color surrounding the living person.

In the Orient, the aureole was often identified with the "thousand-petaled lotus of light" that could spring toward heaven from the head of the most enlightened sage, that is, one who had succeeded in drawing spiritual energy upward from all the rest of the body to the top of the head. Eastern mystics sometimes associated this with the immortal soul that they said was made of the same

ethereal light as the stars, which came down from heaven to inhabit the body of flesh, and might return to the starry heaven after death, as did the star-heroes of antiquity. In Rome it was said that Aura was a spirit of **air**, who could fly up to heaven.

1. Hall, 144.

Black Sun

A plain black **circle** was to symbolize the spirit of the solar or heavenly god during his cyclic passages through the underworld. In this phase, according to Egyptian scriptures, he became "the hidden one" (Amen), or the Lord of Death, Seker, hidden in a secret pyramid of "blackest darkness" at the earth's core.[1] His blackness was as intensely dark as the sun's light was intensely bright. He soon became mythologized as the sun god's dark twin brother, like Ahriman to Ahura Mazda in Persia, or Nergal-Ninib to Anu in Mesopotamia.

The dark brother became an opponent of the bright brother with further development of dualism, which divided the world between forces of light and dark (good and evil). Thus the Black Sun came to symbolize many underworld gods,

including **Saturn, Pluto,** Hades, Python, Apollyon, Zeus Chthonios, Yama, and such fallen-angel figures as Lucifer, Satan, or Beelzebub who became assimilated to the Christian devil.

Yet all the while, the sun continued to rise and decline in the sky hourly, daily, and yearly. Seeing this, many people retained the original idea of the Black Sun as a secret, wiser version of the solar god, who knew the nether world as well as he knew the heavens.

To medieval alchemists, the *Sol Niger* (Black Sun) meant "prime matter," or matter in an untouched primordial state.[2]

1. *Book of the Dead,* 145.   2. Cirlot, 304.

Circle

The circle was always one of the primary feminine signs, as opposed to the line, cross, or phallic shaft representing masculine spirit. Early matrifocal villages had round hearths, round houses, round fences and defensive shapes. The circle was associated with the idea of a protected or consecrated space, the center of the motherland, a ceremonial space where all participants were equal. Worship circles like the Hindu *chakra* (Arabic *halka*) were those in which female influence was prevalent. Pagan sacred **dances** were circular, as are European folk dances to this day. Prehistoric stone

circles, like Stonehenge—known as the Giants' Dance—attest to ancient love of circularity. The concept of equality was still connected with the circle in medieval legends. Arthur's knights of the Round Table were seated in a circle to eliminate the sense of hierarchy among their brotherhood.

The famous cliché, "God is a circle whose circumference is nowhere and whose center is everywhere," was cribbed from a Hindu catechism concerning the deity called the One: "an unbroken circle with no circumference, for it is nowhere and everywhere." The idea of the cosmos as an unbroken circle was repeated in the Gnostic image of the world **serpent** forming a circle with its tail in its mouth. Closed circles continued to be thought protective, especially for workers of magic. A sorcerer's title dating from the first century B.C. was "circle-drawer."[1] The circle invoked by analogy the full face of the moon, the pupil of the All-Seeing Eye, the circle of the visible horizon, and a thousand other natural forms.

1. Trachtenberg, 121.

Cosmic Egg

It used to be a common idea that the primeval universe—or the Great Mother who created it—took the form of an egg. There are myths like that of Leto, who hatched the **sun** and **moon** (Apollo and Artemis) out of an egg; and Hathor, who hatched the "golden egg" of the sun at the beginning of the world. Petronius described a zodiacal table with an egg-shaped Goddess at its hub: "Mother Earth lies in the world's midst rounded like an egg and all blessings are there inside her as in a honeycomb."[1]

The Cosmic Egg of mystical iconography carried all arabic numerals and alphabetical letters combined within an ellipse, to show that everything that can be numbered or named is contained within one form at the beginning. The Cosmic Egg thus becomes a substitute for the **Logos,** and an expression of the Primum Mobile where deities are created by human symbols.

According to the Egyptian Ritual, the whole universe is "the egg conceived in the hour of the Great One."[2]

1 Lindsay, 287. 2. Cirlot, 90.

Diameter

The diameter is a symbol drawn from the flat horizon of sea or desert plain, dividing the world into two halves above and below. The word *diameter* means literally "Goddess Mother" and may refer to ancient creation myths in which the body of the world mother herself (Tiamat, Themis, Temu, Maa) was divided into upper and lower halves. Often, **water** was said to be her primordial substance, so the symbol of the Dia Meter also suggests the division of waters above the earth plane from waters below the earth.

In alchemical symbolism the diameter meant "salt," which is appropriate in view of its connection with the sea.[1]

1. Koch, 66.

Dome

The word *dome* comes from Latin *domus,* a house, via Italian *duomo,* a house of God, that is, a church. Before the domed churches, there were domed pagan temples in Rome. A famous example, still extant, is the Pantheon. Because the original idea of the dome was to symbolize the overarching sky, temple domes were often painted blue on the inside and speckled with stars or with symbols of the planetary deities and other heavenly personages.

Double Wheel

In ancient Oriental tradition the double wheel meant infinity, showing the eternal circles of life on earth, enveloped in the larger circle of cosmic existence. Therefore it was often used as the sign of a universal deity, or of elemental spirits.

Ezekiel's vision of "a wheel in the middle of a wheel" (Ezekiel 1:16), created by the traditional personifications of the elements—man, **lion, ox,** and **eagle**—seen as winged angels, was nothing original with biblical thought but rather a labored reinterpretation of classical symbols. The biblical writer used such symbols because he knew his audience would recognize them as holy. This had been the meaning of the double wheel for as long as anyone could remember.

Elements

Signs of antiquity's four elements appeared in either triangular or circular form, arranged in order of their supposed density or refinement. Heaviest of the four was **earth,** which sinks to the bottom when mingled with **water** in a vessel. Conversely, **air** in water bubbles upward, while **fire** rises upward in air and is therefore the "lightest" element. Sometimes the Greeks postulated a fifth element even lighter and brighter than fire, existing only in the heavens. It was called ether, the star-stuff of which the "astral" (starry) bodies of heavenly beings were made. This "ethereal" fifth element became the mystic *quinta essentia* of medieval alchemy. So attractive was the idea of ether that some people clung to it long after science had demonstrated that there is no such substance (and also had begun to discover the real elements, none of which are the classical four). Even up to the nineteenth century A.D., it was popularly believed that all of outer space was filled with a rarefied gas known as ether.

The basic four elements passed into European tradition via Greek literature, but the Greeks were among the last to hear of them. They had been part of human thinking all over the world for thousands, perhaps hundreds of thousands of years. The real origin of the elements lay somewhere in the Neolithic Age, when people discovered that there are only four possible ways to dispose of their dead (other than cannibalism): burial, cremation, sinking in waters, or exposure to carrion birds of the air. All four of these funerary practices were known to the ancients, who envisioned death as a reversal of birth: a return to the Mother who brought forth all life in the world.

For this reason, some of the oldest images of the primordial Mother Goddess are closely connected with the idea of the

ROUND AND OVAL MOTIFS

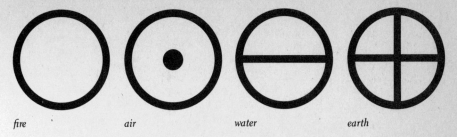

fire   *air*   *water*   *earth*

elements. The four elemental symbols are found in the four hands of India's pre-Vedic Great Mother **Kali,** who invented the sounds of the Sanskrit letters and from these created the primal mantras that brought the universe into being. These sounds were classified as La, earth; Va, water; Ya, air; and Ra, fire. Uniting them all was the Goddess's own spirit, Ma, meaning both "Mother" and "intelligence."[1] In the *Mahanirvana-tantra,* the same Goddess is addressed as Earth, Water, Air, and Fire, as well as Life-in-this-World, Knowledge-Itself, and Supreme Divinity.[2] She mingled the four elements to create life from flesh (earth), **blood** (water), **breath** (air), and fire (vital heat).[3] This theory persisted all the way into medieval European medicine with its insistence on mixtures of the four "elemental humors" of the body.

Stoic philosophers had a similar notion of personified Nature as the Mother Goddess who created life from the four elements. She was the "origin of everything and the guardian of mysteries." She built the walls of the world and made the earth a globe hanging exactly in the center, surrounded by flocks of stars. (This ancient Greek idea of the global earth was supplanted in the Middle Ages by the Judeo-Christian biblical idea of a flat earth.) The Stoic writer Manilius said the Goddess "organized heterogeneous parts—air, earth, fire, floating water— into a unity and ordered them to feed one another so that harmony would

rule all these discordant principles and the world might endure."[4]

Correspondences proliferated as more and more thought centered on the elemental theory throughout the centuries. Medieval thinkers, for example, believed in four sets of elemental spirits: **gnomes** for earth, undines for water, **salamanders** for fire, **sylphs** for air. The four suits of the Tarot deck were element-signs whose mingling (shuffling) was supposed to reflect the creation of events: **wands** (fire), **swords** (air), **cups** (water), and **pentacles** (earth). Male authorities seized the two elements considered higher, or more refined, declaring that fire and air were "male" and superior, while water and earth were "female" and therefore unspiritual, heavy, cold, passive, and muddy. However, occult tradition maintained that "only Earth and Water bring forth a living soul."[5] In India it was said that mantras with largely fiery or airy letter-sounds were "cruel," while mantras with largely watery or earthy letter-sounds were "kind."[6]

The traditional circular symbols for the elements express the customary notion of their ascending degree of rarefaction. A plain empty circle stands for fire, showing that it has no "weight." A dotted circle, which also represents the **sun,** stands for

air. The horizontal line of the sea horizon, called *diameter*, stands for water. The cross in a circle, with its many variations representing the four quarters (see **Four-way Motifs**), signifies the earth. Superimposed on the other three signs, the earth sign covers and embraces them all.

1. d'Alviella, 240.   2. *Mahanirvanatantra*, 262.
3. *Bardo Thodol*, 15–16.   4. Luck, 336.
5. Agrippa, 49.   6. Rawson, A.T., 70.

Globe

Many ancient civilizations saw the earth as a flat table, covered by a "firmament" like a roof, or series of roofs (the nested, domed celestial spheres), floating on the waters of the great abyss, or supported on the back of a huge turtle, **elephant, serpent,** or other creature. The earth was supposed to have four corners, a top, a bottom, and an underworld. After making careful measurements and astronomical observations, however, the Pythagoreans concluded that the earth must be a globe. Plato and Aristotle were proponents of this idea, and some thinkers even arrived at the concept of a global earth floating in space without visible means of support. Lucan's *Pharsalia* spoke of the spherical earth "suspended in empty space."[1]

Though some early Christian authorities accepted Aristotle's view of the earth as a globe, most did not. Eusebius, Basil of Caesarea, and others opposed the study of all scientific realities as vain and futile. Ephraem Syrus, Saint John Chrysostom, and Lactantius said that the study of the heavens was bad and senseless, and that the doctrine of a global earth was proved false from the evidence of both reason and scripture. Not for a long time would the globe become *the* earth symbol.

In the sixth century A.D., the monk Cosmas Indicopleustes settled the question of the earth's shape, to the satisfaction of most churchmen, based entirely on biblical interpretation. The world was like a vast tent, he said, with the heaven upheld by its "pillars"; above it in the solid vault of the "firmament" lived the **angels** who pushed and pulled the heavenly bodies around their courses. The world according to Cosmas remained the orthodox Christian vision for several centuries. In Columbus's time, the redness of the sun at dawn and sunset was considered proof of the reflection of the fires of hell. Even theological reformers like Luther, Melanchthon, and Calvin insisted on the letter of scripture and hence the image of a flat earth.[2]

1. Luck, 281.   2. White 1, 91–97.

Halo

The halo was the same as the **aureole** in effect, being a circle drawn around or behind a head to indicate divinity. The word came from Greek *halos*, "threshing floor," originally a round space where circular harvest **dances** were performed in the Eleusinian Mysteries, at the festival called Haloa.[1] The circular sign of the Haloa came to represent the apotheosis of its god, Dionysus incarnate in a human Triptolemus, sometimes called Iasion or Iasus. So the circle around any head meant a godlike nature. Christian artists "haloized" not only God, Jesus, and Mary, but also **angels, saints**, Old Testament figures, apostles, martyrs, and even popes and kings.

1. Potter & Sargent, 185.

Horseshoe

The horseshoe shape was one of the most sacred in the ancient world, because it was a stylization of the **yoni** and signified entrances and exits in general. Druidic temples, Hindu and Arabic arches testify to the importance of the yoni.[1] The sacred alphabet of the Greeks enclosed all things (letter symbols) between the birth-letter alpha and the horseshoe-shaped omega, the name of which means "Great Om," representing the conclusion of each cycle, the other side of the Goddess, the Kali part of Kali-Maya. The Christian God's description of himself as "the

Alpha and Omega, the beginning and the ending" (Revelation 1:8) was usurped from older titles of the Mother of birth and death.

The omega-shaped horseshoe continued to be hung "for luck" over doorways throughout the Christian era, protecting the **threshold** as it did in pagan times. There was always controversy, however, about whether its opening should point upward or downward. Orthodox piety insisted that the omega should be reversed, so "the luck wouldn't run out." Pagan tradition said the symbolic yoniform doorway should retain its original upward arch. The two ways of hanging the horseshoe actually echoed the magic signs called Dragon's Head and Dragon's Tail, the ascending node and descending node, connected with the path of the moon above and below the ecliptic, which when plotted would result in the wavy line representing the lunar **serpent.**

1. de Lys, 113.

Infinity Sign

Our standard mathematical symbol of infinity came into the Western world by way of "arabic" numerals—whose real place of origin was India, not Arabia. In Indian religion this sign stood for infinity or completeness because it is composed of

a clockwise circle and a counterclockwise circle: that is, a male, solar, right-hand half united with a female, lunar, left-hand half. Like the figure eight that it resembles, the infinity sign used to mean sexual union and the sense of perfection: two becoming one. Since neither circle lies above the other as in the figure eight, the infinity sign implies equality between male and female powers, leading to intimate knowledge of "the infinite."

Like the yang-and-yin symbol of dualism, the infinity sign was adapted to many concepts of twinning or pairing. Some said it was the mark of the twin gods known as Sons of the Mare (Asvins), born of the Goddess Saranyu who took the form of a mare like her Western counterpart, Demeter. The twin gods were famed as magicians, healers, horsemen, and fertility spirits.[1]

1. G. Jobes 1, 146.

Mandala

A mandala is a symbolic diagram, usually round or oval with radial symmetry, but sometimes square, triangular, diamond-shaped, or polygonal. Oriental mandalas, especially in India, can become enormously complex. They are often viewed as mystical maps of the cosmos, or of the realm of deities, and are intended for contemplation as a religious exercise. Other mandalas may be simple, personal expressions of feeling or awareness. The graphic material included in a mandala may be anything at all, from recognizable human, animal, or vegetable forms to highly abstract designs. The circular mandalas frequently refer to the cyclic view of life, nature, fate, time, or all of these combined in the symbol of the **Goddess.**

Mandorla

Mandorla means "almond," which was one of the more cryptic synonyms for this symbol, also known as *vesica piscis,* the Vessel of the Fish, and more simply as the **yoni.** Almonds were female-genital symbols and maternity charms from very ancient times. The virgin birth of the god Attis was conceived by a magic almond. Even the Israelites' tabernacle made use of its fertility *mana* (Exodus 37:20), and Aaron's **rod** produced almonds in token of a general power of fructification (Numbers 17:8).

Although the yonic meaning of this sign was well known in the ancient world, it carried such sacred overtones that Christian artists seized upon it to frame the figures of saints, the Virgin, or Christ. Christian mystics redefined the mandorla as the arcs of two circles, left for female matter, right for male spirit.[1] Even God himself appeared sometimes, incongruously enclosed in this female-genital emblem. A well-known twelfth-century panel in Chartres Cathedral shows "Christ of the Apocalypse" within a mandorla.[2] With an unintentional double entendre, the mandorla was sometimes piously interpreted as a gateway to heaven.

1. Cirlot, 194.   2. Campbell, *M.I.*, 181.

Medicine Wheel

There are about fifty known examples of the Indian medicine wheel in the Rocky Mountain area, some dating as far back as 2500 B.C. The usual number of spokes in a medicine wheel is twenty-eight, the lunar number, with a twenty-ninth signified by the center post. Although the nineteenth-century Plains Indians had forgotten how to tell time and follow the seasons by ancestral medicine wheels—which seem to have served much the same purposes as the megalithic stone

circles of Europe—they nevertheless continued to set up their lodges for the Sun Dance celebration with twenty-eight poles in a ring, and a pivotal twenty-ninth pole supporting the roof beams.[1]

1. Campbell, *W.A.P.*, 222–223.

Orb

The three-dimensional orb was regarded as a model of the earth until the anti-intellectualism of the Dark Ages obscured the earlier discoveries made in the classical period. Still, the holding of an orb in the left (female) **hand** continued to represent a monarch's claim to domination of the whole earth. The orb's counterpart was the phallic **scepter** held in the right (male) hand, so that the monarch in himself represented the sacred marriage between king and country, which was literally enacted long ago by an actual marriage between the king and high priestess embodying the spirit of Mother Earth.

During the Christian era, the orb acquired a crowning cross to suggest the church's dominance of the earth, and to remind kings that they ruled by the grace of God (not by union with a **Goddess**). Nowadays, nearly every royal orb is surmounted by a cross.

Ring

Rings were traditional symbols of the bond between chieftains and their warriors in Anglo-Saxon Britain. Overlords in *Beowulf* are referred to as "givers of rings." Among the Celts, a ring given by a woman to a man represented her sexual availability; putting the **finger** through the ring was a sign of sexual intercourse. Similar "betrothal rings" were once used by Christian monks as a symbol of their marriage to the Virgin Mary, just as wedding rings were used in the marriage of nuns to Christ. Legends tell of young knights who were wedded to Mary by a ceremony of rings upon entering the monastery. In pagan times, the same stories were told of youths who became bridegrooms of **Venus** when entering the service of the Goddess.[1] In the Middle Ages, dukes of Venice continued to celebrate an annual marriage to the same Sea Goddess every year on Ascension Day, by throwing into the sea "a gold ring of great value."[2]

The idea that a wedding ring should be placed on the fourth finger of a woman's left hand began with the Egyptians, who believed in a "love vein" extending directly from that finger to the heart. The ring was a fetter to keep the "sentiments of the heart" from escaping. With similar notions in mind, Jews changed the wedding ring to the index finger of a woman's right hand, because that was the magic finger, which could cast spells or curses by pointing.[3]

Hebraic tradition spoke much about magic rings. Solomon used a magic ring to enslave the **demon** Asmodeus into helping build the famous temple; but the demon tricked Solomon into lending him the ring, then exiled the king and put on the king's shape to rule Jerusalem, while the real Solomon lived as a wretched beggar.[4]

Most Europeans believed in the magic powers of rings; but not all. The sixteenth-century writer Ramesey was an outspoken disbeliever in the powers of magic rings or other amulets. He also doubted the curative properties of "sigils of the planets, saints, images, relics, holy-waters, shrines, avemarys, crucifixes, benedictions," and other charms.[5]

1. Baring-Gould, 224. 2. Scot, 173.
3. de Lys, 287–288. 4. Cavendish, 105.
5. Hazlitt 1, 103.

Rose Window

The rose window of a Christian cathedral typically faced west, the direction of the **Goddess**'s paradise in ancient pagan tradition: that mysterious sunset land that medieval mystics converted into the land of faery, ruled by its divine queen. The Gothic cathedral opposed this primordial female symbol in the west to its male symbol (cross) in the east, that is, in the apse. Christian congregations turned their backs on the great female rose; yet they were bathed in her multicolored light. A rose window was generally dedicated to the Virgin Queen of Heaven, and the whole cathedral was described as her "palace." The rose window was essentially a female-symbolic **mandala,** expressive of the spirit of **Mary** as mystic rose, Wreath of Roses, Mother of the Rosary, or "Queen of the Most Holy Rose-Garden."[1]

Roses, rosaries, and rose-shaped mandalas had represented the ancient Goddess in Oriental countries from time immemorial. Her Rose-Apple Tree in the western paradise had been the source of the fruit of eternal life from India to Ireland in the oldest myths.[2] Worshipers of Aphrodite used to call their ceremonies the Mysteries of the Rose. Even medieval churchmen understood that the rose was a female sexual symbol expressing the mystery of Mary's physical gateway, source of the Redeemer's life.[3] Thus the rose window was a necessary if underemphasized component of the whole ecclesiastical symbolic unit.

1. Wilkins, 93, 106.   2. Tatz & Kent, 37, 84.
3. Wilkins, 113.

Sphere

A generally accepted view of the universe in antiquity was the doctrine of the planetary spheres, conceived as great crystal domes or inverted bowls nested inside one another over the earth, turning independently of one another at various rates, and making the "music of the spheres" with their motions. The theory was evolved to explain the apparently erratic movement of planets against the background of the fixed stars. Reading from the innermost sphere outward, arranging them according to the days of the week, they were the spheres of the moon, Mars, Mercury, Jupiter, Venus, Saturn, and the sun. Outermost was the eighth sphere, the Empyrean, the home of fixed stars and the ultimate God: the highest heaven.

As a corollary to this theory, it was also assumed that there were seven nether spheres descending under the earth: the "seven hells" to which Dumuzi and Inanna (or Tammuz and **Ishtar**) journeyed, whose seven gates were guarded by the seven Anunnaki or Maskim, the nether counterparts of the planetary spirits. According to an Akkadian magic tablet, "They proceed from the ocean depths, from the hidden retreat."[1] From the ancient idea of the seven nether spheres, Dante took his vision of the descending circles of hell.

Early Christians taught that each human soul descends from heaven, picking up one of the seven deadly sins from each planetary sphere along the way: lust from Venus, anger from Mars, and so on. After death, the soul returned to the highest heaven, shedding the same sins one by one while passing the "innkeepers" of the spheres—providing, of course, that the soul was Christianized and therefore properly enlightened.

1. Wedeck, 23.

Spiral

Both single and double spirals were among the most sacred signs of Neolithic Europe. They appeared on megalithic monuments and temples all over the continent and the British Isles. Spiral *oculi*—double twists resembling eyes—appear prominently in places like the threshold stones at New Grange in Ireland and the Al Tarxien temple in Malta. Similar double twists mark the classic Ionic columns. A spiral **labyrinth** penetrated by a (probably phallic) cross is a common symbol from Finland to Cornwall and from Crete to Chartres; it occurs in the Americas as well.[1] Spirals represented the serpent guardians of Sumerian temples.

The spiral was connected with the idea of death and rebirth: entering the mysterious earth **womb,** penetrating to its core, and passing out again by the same route. Sacred **dances** imitated this movement, which is why so many pagan-derived European folk dances use the spiral line of dancers circling into a center and out.[2] Spiral labyrinth designs were also common in cathedral decoration, transposed from the older shrines formerly located on the same sites.

The magical staff called *lituus*, used by Roman augurs (diviners) to mark out sacred areas such as temple sites, usually terminated in a spiral.[3]

1. Hitching, 237. 2. Cirlot, 291.
3. Whittick, 319.

Sun Sign

According to the oldest symbolism, the circle enclosing a dot represented the primal **womb** containing the spark of creation, like the *bindu* within the **Yoni Yantra** of Hindu tradition. Ancient Mesopotamian myths depicted the **sun** as a Goddess, such as Estan among the Hittites, who was later revised into a male divinity, Istanu. Another Sun-goddess name was Arinna, "Queen of Heaven and Earth." She was also Hepat or Hebat, whose consort was the sun god. This name passed into biblical tradition as Hebe, Eveh, or Eve.

In Arabia, Japan, and northern Europe, the sun retained feminine gender. The German language still calls her *die Sonne,* which is feminine. Norse myths say that although the Sun-goddess—named Glory-of-Elves—will disappear at doomsday along with the rest of the world, during the cosmic night she will give birth to a daughter sun, who will illuminate the world to come. Perhaps it was an anticipation of this Sun-goddess of the next universe that placed her symbol on the rock faces of Celtic megalithic monuments, such as New Grange, where she appears as a dotted and rayed sun sign.

It became more usual, however, for the sun to be considered a male deity in contrast to the **moon,** which was almost always female. The Greek brother-

sister pairing of Apollo and Artemis represents this kind of **yang-and-yin** dualism. The biblical God was also assimilated to an older male sun under the name of Azazel or Aziz-El, "the Strong One," who received the Hebrews' scapegoat-sacrifices. This Semitic sun god was Azeus in Boeotia, Azon in Syria, and founder of the city of Aza (or Gaza), where the name of Samson was given to the sacrificed sun-hero.[1] In Arabia they called him Shams-On, the sun bound to the "mill-wheel" of the circling year. In early Gnostic literature, this solar deity or his earthly representative was identified with Cain, who was named a god, the sixth of the Great Aeons, "whom men call the sun."[2]

Many mythical connections between the sun and the male spirit led to a tendency for men to identify themselves with the solar day, the solar calendar, the gods of light and fire, in opposition to the female powers of night, the moon, the abyss, uterine darkness, secrecy, water, and earth. Yet, despite the sun god's glory, he was always swallowed up in the uterine darkness before he could be reborn at the dawn of each day or at the year's turning point (the winter solstice). The sun sign may have shown the sun at noon on high in the middle of heaven's dome, but it was also very much like the male *bindu* as embryonic spark of life beginning to take form within the cosmic womb, which sur-

rounded and supported it. According to Maori myth, the sun god had to descend every night into the **cave** of the deep, where he could bathe in the uterine Waters of Life, in order to arise reborn the next day.[3] Egypt's **Osiris**-Ra, represented by the winged sun disc, also died each day to enter the womb of the Great Mother and to be reborn from her eastern "**gate**" each morning.

By the early Christian era, Roman emperors were routinely identifying themselves with the sun god and all his symbols: cross, **eagle, fire, gold, lion,** and so on. Constantine I, whom conventional history hails as the first Christian emperor, was actually a worshiper of the sun god, whose image he placed on his coins, dedicated to "the invincible sun, my guardian."[4] Contemporaneous Christian Gnostics used the sun sign surrounded by the Gnostic **serpent** as the symbol of the heart-soul of Terrestrial Man.

It has been suggested that this dot-in-a-circle sun sign may have originated with the circular lens for starting fire by focusing sunlight on tinder. In ancient times this was known as "drawing down the sun" or "fire from heaven."[5] Altar fires were often started this way, especially the heavenly fire to consume sacrificial victims, like the sons of Aaron, who were devoured by "fire from the Lord" (Leviticus 10:2).

1. Brown, 65.   2. Robinson, 201.
3. d'Alviella, 175.   4. Seligmann, 76.
5. Huson, 235.

Vesica Piscis

"Vessel of the Fish," *vesica piscis*, was a worldwide ancient synonym for the **yoni**, or vulva. In religious symbolism it stood for the feminine creative force, the Mother-spirit that gave birth to the world and the gods. In prepatriarchal philosophy the general explanation for sexual activity was that spiritual nourishment for males was inherent in the act of "plugging in" to this female power, resulting not only in a moment or two of godlike bliss, but also in an essential contact with the mysterious magic inside a woman's body that could actually produce new life.

The ancients insisted that women's sexual secretions smelled like **fish**, which is why the sign of the yoni came to be called *vesica piscis*. One of the Hindu titles of the Great Goddess was "a virgin named Fishy Smell, whose real name was Truth."[1] Particularly in her Love-goddess aspect, the ancient Mother was associated with fish, seashells, seawater, salt, ships, and fishermen. She often appeared in **mermaid** form with a fish tail, or even two fish tails like the medieval Siren. In her honor, fish were eaten on Friday, which was her official day, named after Freya, her Scandinavian incarnation. (Latins called it the Day of Venus.) Thus it was— and in some areas still is—believed that fish are aphrodisiac food.

The *vesica piscis* passed into medieval Christian art as a frame for holy figures (see **Mandorla**), however incongruous this might have seemed in the light of its older connotations. Renaissance painters often showed the "cloud" that took Jesus up to heaven in the form of a *vesica piscis*, which appeared to be swallowing him headfirst, so that sometimes only his dangling legs remained visible.

1. Campbell, C.M., 13.

Wheel

Wheel symbolism was ubiquitous in ancient religions. The whole universe was envisioned as a vast wheel whose rolling could be seen in the cycles of heavenly bodies and in the progression of seasons. Small wheels, as models of the cosmos, accompanied the dead into their graves. Wheels were used as magical protective emblems on helmets, shields, weapons, and houses. Celtic gods exhibited wheels in their hands or by their sides. Altars and tombstones were decorated with wheels.[1] One of the Celtic names for the **Goddess**, Arianrhod, designated her the Goddess of the Silver Wheel (the stars), whose hub was the Revolving Castle, Caer Sidi, hidden in the underground spirit-land of Annwn. Similarly in India, Mother **Kali** continually ruled the Wheel of Time (*Kala-cakra*), where all the life-breath of the world was fixed "even as the spokes of a wheel are held fast in the hub."[2]

A comparable hub was the ***omphalos*** of Greek myth, ruled by the Goddess

Omphale, to whom Heracles-the-Sun was subject. His mythical twelve labors represented the slow progress of the sun through the twelve zodiacal houses. Priests of Heracles traditionally dressed as women, which led to the development of the late Hellenic myth about the sun hero disguised in female clothing, working among the ladies on Omphale's spinning wheel.

The Etruscans called the Wheel-goddess Vortumna, She Who Turns the Year, and the Romans altered this name to Fortuna, the Goddess whose constantly turning heavenly wheel marked all the seasons and the fates of men. Sometimes she was envisioned as a trinity, the Fortunae, or **Fates**, whom the Greeks also called Nemesis or the Moerae.[3] She ruled the *kyklos geneseon*, the wheel of rebirth and of transformations throughout time. The ancients' belief in reincarnation produced many cyclic images of existence rather than the linear patriarchal insistence that an individual could have only one life, ending in a permanent choice between heaven and hell.

Nevertheless, wheel symbolism carried on into patriarchal Judeo-Christian culture because it was so deeply embedded in symbolic language everywhere. Hebrew scriptures called the angels of the galaxy *gel* or "wheels," whose revolutions meant revelations: a concept not unrelated to the Hindu idea of the universe as a gigantic **chariot** carrying all gods and creatures on its wheels through an eternal round. The *Book of Secrets of Enoch* stated that the sun travels on wheels.[4]

The mighty wheel of the Goddess Fortuna gradually degenerated into the medieval Wheel of Fortune and its Goddess into Lady Luck, who ruled the *roulette* ("little wheel") in **Carnival** games, which so often preserved pagan traditions in a new, trivialized form. Fortune's wheel, which remains popular to this day, sometimes had six spokes, sometimes eight, the latter apparently modeled on the Hindu *dharma* wheel.[5] In Germany the same eight-spoked wheel was the *Achtwan*, a magic **rune** charm. In the time of Dante, the Wheel of Fortune was depicted with eight spokes of opposite conditions of human life, cyclically alternating: poverty-riches, peace-war, humility-glory, and patience-passion.[6] The Wheel of Fortune joined the Tarot trumps, often with climbing and falling figures as the wheel was described by Boethius.[7] The Tarot's Wheel of Fortune card still shows these figures.

1. Green, 42–61. 2. Campbell, C.M., 418–419. 3. Graves, G.M. 1, 126. 4. Barnstone, 497. 5. Lehner, 96. 6. Moakley, 87. 7. Hall, 127–128.

Yang and Yin

This classic Chinese emblem of conjoined male (yang) and female (yin) powers is known throughout the world and interpreted as cyclic alternation of all sorts of dualities: light and dark, summer and winter, good and evil, youth and age, earth and heaven, war and peace, sleep and waking, birth and death, and so

on *ad infinitum*. Since each lobe contains a spot of the opposite color, we are cleverly reminded that every half of a dualistic pair contains something of its opposite within its heart.

The yang-and-yin design itself is cleverly composed of two tangential circles on the same diameter of a larger circle; then the lower half of one and the upper half of the other circle are removed to form the S-curve.

About a thousand years ago, the Chinese viewed this symbol as an expression of the phases of the **moon**, which meant that it was "female" in both light and dark aspects.[1] Throughout the imagery of the ancient world are found similar lunar signs of the Two Ladies or Two Mistresses, like the dual Goddesses of Egypt and Anatolia. The biblical wives of Lamech are assumed to have originated with this kind of imagery, because they are obviously mythical and their names, Adah and Zillah, mean Brilliance and Shadow (Genesis 4:19).

1. Campbell, *Or.M.*, 24.

Yoni

The Sanskrit term *Jagad Yoni* was often delicately translated "womb of the world" by male scholars who did not clearly distinguish between a womb and a vulva. The sign of the yoni was meant to convey the shape of external female **genitalia**, which the ancients clearly recog-

nized as the seat of female sexual power. Tantrics viewed that power as the source of all creative action. Far from describing female sexuality as "passive," in the Western manner, Tantric Hindus regarded female orgasm as the energizing principle of the universe.

In the mythology based on this sexual symbolism, the paradise island Jambu was "shaped like the yoni." It was the location of the holy life-giving Rose-Apple Tree and the "diamond seat" (*vajrasana*), which apparently represented a cosmic clitoris, focus of the **Goddess's** creative spirit.[1]

The sign of the yoni passed into Western symbolism under such titles as **mandorla** (almond) and *vesica piscis* (vessel of the fish). Its original meaning was not entirely forgotten; it was often described as a "gateway."[2] In a particularly curious twist, worshipers of the mythical British saint, George the Dragon-killer, adopted the yoni as their saint's sign. It was reinterpreted as a spearhead.[3]

A similar reinterpretation was used by devotees of the patriarchal god Indra. At first he was marked all over his body with a multitude of yoni emblems to indicate that he took over the Goddess's power of fertility. In his later portraits, the yonis were reworked to resemble eyes, so Indra became known as "the Watcher," or the Thousand-Eyed One, rather like the Greek Argus and the mysterious primordial "Watchers" of Hebrew tradition.[4]

1. Tatz & Kent, 84. 2. Cirlot, 361.
3. Brewster, 209–210. 4. G. Jobes 1, 830.

2

LONG MOTIFS

Freud's indefatigable search for phallic symbolism in every long shape, from cigars to furled umbrellas, reflects a typically patriarchal process of projection, which may be also related to the deep-seated male desire to be taller than others. Apart from obvious phallic connotations, long motifs represent the patriarchal vision in various ways. The up and the down, the ladder between heaven and hell, the ferocious dichotomy between the weapon's point and its hilt fitting the hand: these are emblems of differentiation, one thing from another, We from They. To draw the line means to declare a separation between one end of the line and the other.

The long vertical motif suggests upward aspiration rising above its own foundation in the earth, which now serves only as a support for the upward movement. The soaring lines of a Gothic cathedral demonstrate such verticality. Spires and belltowers may be phallic, as the Egyptian obelisks before them quite deliberately were; but ascetic patriarchy tended to deny this. In a fully male-dominant society, symbolic sexuality went underground and could find its unconscious expression only in dissimulation and complexity. Therefore, although any long motif may be found as phallic as Freud could wish, its constellation of meaning is not always so simple. In ancient times the feminine spirit also found expression sometimes in trees, towers, and weapons. The witch's magic wand was not a phallus but a pointer, a director of magical energy. The world's first tool was a stick.

It is even possible that the intense human response to vertical extension is related to the body image in general. Human beings are the only four-limbed animals that stand fully upright. Would it not be natural then for all other animals, whose bodies lie in the horizontal plane, to perceive more readily a world of horizontals while human creatures are more intensely interested in the vertical?

Arrow

Ever since the invention of the bow—whenever that might have been—arrows have been used as sacred symbols. Arrows carried by the Goddess Artemis represented her control of the hunt and of wild animals. Arrows borne by Eros, the god of carnal love, signified the eye-beams carrying messages of love to pierce the heart of a beloved. An arrow piercing a heart became a traditional sign of sexual union.[1] Consequently the arrow was often viewed as a phallic symbol as well as a weapon of war. Arrows became representative of the war god **Mars** and of his Scandinavian counterpart, Tyr.[2] An arrow also represented the **lightning** bolt of the Balkan storm god, Perkun.[3] On Roman coins, the arrow appeared as an emblem of Mithra,[4] the

Empire's popular Zoroastrian savior god. Arrows also gave omens, as in the Bible (Ezekiel 21:21).

With the development of warlike patriarchal societies, arrows were increasingly monopolized by male gods and their followers, especially military men. Some American Indian tribes revered arrows as symbols of male power. The "sacred medicine arrows" of the Cheyenne represented the dominance of Cheyenne warriors over other tribes and over the animals they hunted. Women were not supposed to look at these sacred arrows, nor even to listen when men spoke of them.[5]

In our own time, perhaps appropriately, the arrow has come to mean a direction or a directive. It says "go that way" in a language that almost everyone can understand. In a sense, it is a curious anachronism that this language is still so universally understood, since arrows are no longer commonly used for their original purpose, hunting or warfare. Thus the arrow has become almost entirely symbolic.

1. Cirlot, 19. 2. Koch, 102. 3. d'Alviella, 45. 4. Whittick, 209. 5. Sanday, 151.

Athame

An athame is the traditional knife or dagger used symbolically by witches; but whether it was widely designated a magic tool per se in past centuries seems doubtful. Apparently the name was taken from *al-dhamme*, the sacred knife used in a ritual scarring ceremony by Moorish-Arab-Andalusian cults of moon worshipers known as the Double-horned Ones. In their coven it was customary for a blacksmith to impersonate *Rabbana*, "Our Lord": the origin of the witches' "Robin."[1] Perhaps this was because blacksmiths forged the athames. Certainly there were many traditions associating smiths and other metalworkers with witchcraft.[2]

A seventeenth-century Byzantine writer mentioned "the Berber sect of the Horned Ones" who met at **crossroads**, and worshiped the Two-Horned Lord.[3] Any outdoor magical meeting would have involved drawing the protective circle or **pentacle** on the ground, and a knife or sword was used for this purpose.[4] Modern witches still so use the athame, in the belief that they follow a time-honored tradition.

1. Shah, 210. 2. Walker, *W.E.M.S.*, 944. 3. Daraul, 169–170. 4. Trachtenberg, 160.

Axis Mundi

Believing that the entire starry universe turned about the north and south poles, the ancients envisioned these poles quite literally, as the ends of an actual pole or axis that passed all the way through the earth. The heavens, the earth, and the underworlds were arranged around this *axis mundi*, "axis of the world," whose still points could be seen or inferred at the celestial poles. Northern Europeans were sure that the *axis mundi* was planted in the earth at the north pole, and in the regions around it the gods dwelt, and the sun never sets (which it doesn't, of course, in summer).

There were many symbolic imitations of the great axis. Altaic shamans used to place an "axis of the world" in the form of a birch trunk in the middle of the yurt, and by it climb to the "other world" as an initiatory rite.[1] Pagan Germans worshiped an "axis of the world" in the form of a huge phallic **pillar** called Irminsul or Hermeseul at Heresburg, the City of Hera. This pagan "idol" was pulled down and destroyed by Charlemagne in A.D. 772.[2]

Many other versions of the *axis mundi* have been postulated: Yggdrasil, the World Ash Tree; the **Tree of Life**; the Cross; a vast golden chain; and in Asia, the Great Serpent Vasuki. It has been seen also as the backbone of the World Goddess.

1. Duerr, 30. 2. Reinach, 144.

Dorje

The Tantric-Buddhist scepter called *dorje* meant the same in northern India as the *vajra*: a jewel, a thunderbolt, and a phallus all at once, derived from the ancient concept of the lightning god as fertilizer of Mother Earth's hidden depths, and of gems, embedded in the rocks, as solidified drops of his divine semen. There is an obvious relationship between this double-ended, six-pronged object and the thunderbolt symbol of Mesopotamian gods (see **Thunderbolt**). The dorje was called "diamond-holder," where the **diamond** was taken as a metaphor for divine spirit sensed through sexual orgasm. This is the real reason that diamonds acquired such undisputed value as symbols of both royal power and the power of love.

The city of Darjeeling takes its name from the dorje-lingam or dorje-phallus, the "jewel" perpetually buried in the feminine

EUCLID'S RECTANGLE

FASCES
*from a
stone relief,
Ephesus,
ca. A.D. 100*

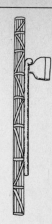

"lotus," according to the ubiquitous Tantric phrase, *om mani padme hum*. A Tantric temple or monastery on the site in ancient times was called Dorjeling, and this name passed on to the modern city.[1]

Examples of the dorje are still seen in India, but few Westerners take the trouble to discover their real meaning.

1. Waddell, 258.

Euclid's Rectangle

Euclid's Rectangle, also called the Golden Section, was long regarded as the perfectly proportioned building plan, especially for any structure of religious significance. Classic Greek temples were based on it, as were many Renaissance buildings. The short and long sides of the rectangle were based on the division of a line into two parts, so that the shorter section is to the longer section as the longer section is to the whole. The proportion is .382 to .618, or approximately 19 to 31.[1]

This rectangle has been called the most rational, secure, and regular of all geometric forms.[2] Because of such reverence for it, Euclid's Rectangle or approximations of it are seen in common objects everywhere: houses, rooms, beds, tables, windows, doors, pictures, books, and many pieces of furniture.

Among Navajo Indians the rectangle is considered a female form, probably because it is the standard form of the house, which symbolizes the woman who owns it.[3]

1. Whittick, 249. 2. Cirlot, 260. 3. G. Jobes 2, 1327.

Fasces

The original Roman fasces were bundles of birch rods bound together with red thongs, accompanied by an arrow or an ax. This was a symbol of authority, implying power to punish the disobedient. When leading Roman magistrates marched in procession through public streets, they were accompanied by attendants called *lictors*, who carried the fasces as a way of displaying their masters' legal powers.[1]

The fasces emblem was adopted by the Italian nationalist movement under Mussolini in the 1930s. Thus, the members of this group became known as *fascisti* or fascists.

1. Whittick, 240.

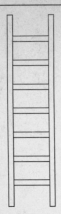

Gnomon

A gnomon is any vertical object—pillar, post, standing stone—the purpose of which is to tell time by the position of its shadow. It is the essential element of a sundial. To Paleolithic and Neolithic peoples, standing stones often served as gnomons for the seasons. For example, the shadow cast by a standing stone at sunrise on the summer and winter solstices would reach the southern and northern limits of the arc, while the shadow cast at the two equinoxes would mark the center. In this way, calendars could be plotted on the ground, and the change of seasons predicted with fair accuracy. Naturally, such gnomons were considered sacred and were supposed to be inhabited by deities. The word *gnomon* means "one who knows."

Ladder

Initiates of the Mithraic Mysteries climbed a sacred ladder of seven rungs, each rung made of a different metal to correspond to the seven planetary **spheres** and their deities.[1] Older religions were rich in "ladders to heaven," copied by an anonymous biblical writer in the vision attributed to Jacob. Egyptian Ladders of Horus or Ladders of Set featured helpful angels who would assist pharaohs in their climb to heaven.[2] Egyptian tombs contained heaven-ascending ladders in the form of amulets.[3] Mohammed and Buddha also climbed to celestial regions by heaven-ascending ladders.[4] To climb to heaven and return by ladder was characteristic of shamanistic initiations in Central Asia, China, and Black Sea regions.

Greek *klimax* meant a ladder to heaven, and also a sexual encounter with the **Goddess** or with one's own female soul (*psyche, shakti*); in either case the result was mystic enlightenment. Thracian kings ascended to the Goddess Hera.

The Christian, seventh-century monkish author of *The Ladder to Paradise* tried to explain the many examples of the heaven-ladder preserved at Mount Athos and elsewhere by glossing them as steps toward the attainment of moral perfection. The author was canonized as Saint John Climacus (John of the Ladder), and his book was translated into English in 1959 under the title of *The Ladder of Divine Ascent.*[5]

1. Cumont, *M.M.*, 145. 2. Gifford, 78.
3. Cirlot, 297. 4. Campbel, *M.I.*, 169.
5. Attwater, 199.

Lingam

Large phallic **pillars** in India represented the lingam of Shiva, in much the same way that the Egyptian **obelisk** represented the penis of Geb. Around each large lingam for a radius of 100 cubits stretched the sacred Kingdom of Shiva, where miracles and remission of sins could occur.[1]

In the temples there were smaller, human-sized linga, or priapic statues of the god, intended to deflower brides before their wedding night. This operation was what biblical terminology called "opening the matrix." Firstborn children were regarded as fathered by the god upon mortal virgins, because of the defloration custom—which was prevalent not only in southeastern Asia but also throughout the Middle East and in Rome. Such divinely begotten "sons of God" were often chosen for lives of religious devotion.[2] The phallus or lingam was usually painted red and anointed with holy oil, to which the Greeks gave the name of *chrism*. Thus the divinely begotten one was given the name of Christos, meaning "anointed."

Of course, oil was necessary to the insertion of a stone phallus into a virgin. Later, the oil itself became a symbol. Kings' heads were anointed with oil, being likened to the "head" of the god-penis, inserted into the flower wreath that represented the virgin matrix. When Roman brides deflowered themselves on the phallus of the priapic god, they placed a wreath of flowers on his head at the same time. Early Christian fathers deplored the custom because it came uncomfortably close to their own version of the god-begotten Christos; but they did understand, as Lactantius said, that its purpose was to make the bride fruitful "by her communion with the divine nature."[3]

1. *Mahanirvanatantra*, 335.   2. Rawson, *E.A.E.*, 29.   3. Knight, 103

Maypole

The Maypole was a pagan symbol for the May King's **phallus,** traditionally set up for the festivities of Beltane (**May Eve;** Walpurgisnacht) that initiated the new season of growth and fertility, and "wearing of the green" in imitation of Mother Earth's new green cloak. The Maypole dance was the origin of the square dancer's Grand Right and Left, as men and women alternately passed in and out of each other's circles, winding the ribbons around the pole.

Springtime display of phallic emblems

appeared from time to time throughout the Christian era. Perhaps Christian dedication to the masculine principle made it inevitable that the festivals of Priapus should continue in some form, whereas the ancient festivals of female sexuality disappeared altogether. In 1282 the parish priest of Inverkeithing conducted a Maypole procession, "carrying in front on a pole a representation of the human organs of reproduction," these "organs" meaning only male organs.[1]

Stukeley wrote in 1724 of a permanent Maypole near Horn Castle, Lincolnshire, "where probably stood an Hermes in Roman times" (see **Herm**). Boys celebrated May Day around the phallic image, carrying peeled white willow **wands** and dancing around a bonfire.[2]

1. Phillips, 169.   2. Hazlitt 2, 402.

Merudanda

Merudanda means the mystic spine in Tantric tradition: the central "axis staff" of the human body, around which the Kundalini **serpent** is supposed to twine upward through the *chakras,* after she has been awakened from her coiled sleeping position in the pelvis and by yogic exercises is drawn up toward the head. Merudanda is an inner, individual echo of the cosmic *axis mundi,* just as the heartbeat is an inner, individual echo of the perpetual world-sustaining dance of Shiva.

The Kundalini energy was supposed to coil around the merudanda in a double **spiral,** one solar (rightward) and the other lunar (leftward). These were known as Pingala and Ida. The resulting design was remarkably like the Hermetic **caduceus** with its twin serpents twining around a central staff—or the double helix of DNA.

Obelisk

The word *obelisk* comes from Greek *obelischos,* "pointed pillar." The old joke that calls the United States' largest modern obelisk "Washington's greatest erection" is not so incongruous after all, because the original Egyptian obelisks were quite seriously conceived as phalli. Specifically, they represented the erect organ of the earth god Geb, as he lay on the ground trying to reach up to unite himself with Nut or Neith, the Goddess of the overarching sky.[1]

The ancients believed that the ideal proportions for an obelisk were eight to

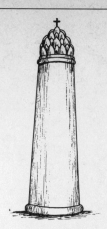

ten times as high as the width at the base, with a pyramidion at the top inclined sixty degrees. Washington's obelisk is 555 feet high and 55 feet square at the base. [2]

1. Huxley, 69.   2. Whittick, 286.

Perron

The perron or "Big Peter" was a medieval version of the phallic **pillars** called petra, Pater, or Peter throughout the ancient Roman empire. Tacitus called them "pillars of Hercules," but the pinecone ornamentation on the top indicates a closer connection with the cults of Dionysus or Bacchus Liber, who was also called Liber Pater, and whose phallic **scepter** or thyrsus was tipped with a pinecone.

Such stone pillars represented the phallic spirit of a god for many thousands of years. The pagan concept of the petra combined "father" and "rock," in the same manner as the biblical description of a paternal God as "the Rock that begat thee" (Deuteronomy 32:18). The name of Peter or "Rock" was allegedly bestowed by Jesus on a disciple named Simon, in order that the latter might father a church in Rome, where—strangely enough—the patriarchal petra had been worshiped on Vatican Hill as a father-rock since Etruscan times. This particular biblical myth was purely fictional, however, having been invented about the third century A.D. and inserted into the Gospel of Matthew to uphold Rome's claim to primacy over the Byzantine see. [1]

In any event, thyrsus-shaped phallic pillars were erected in almost every Romanized town throughout Europe, and many survived into medieval times. They also appeared on coins. Christian authorities had no particular objection to phallic symbols as long as they were not too explicit. Since the perrons were usually found in or near a church built over an ancient shrine or pilgrimage center, most of them were left in place and sketchily Christianized by the addition of a small cross on top. [2]

1. Reinach, 240.   2. d'Alviella, 103–117.

Pillar

Pillars were the phallic emblems of many gods and heroes, such as Shiva who bore the title of Sthanu, "the Pillar," or the Great Lingam. The biblical Absalom was commemorated for his virile spirit by an erect pillar (2 Samuel 18:18). Pillars of stone or wood represented the Saxon god

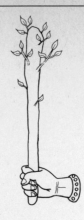

Irmin (**Hermes**), like the famous Irminsul destroyed by Charlemagne.[1] Zeus lived in a sacred pillar at Tarentum. Pillars of **Jupiter** were numerous throughout the Roman empire. Many of these were destroyed by early Christians, but a few survived in Germany, among them the Jupiter column at Mayence.[2] In Japan, the pillar god Nu-boko represented the phallic principle.

The biblical God himself was a pillar-resident in his early days, when he lived in a **stone** of the sort called *beth-el*, dwelling-place of a deity: "This stone, which I have set for a pillar, shall be God's house" (Genesis 28:22). The Egyptian convention of twin phallic pillars at the temple gate was copied by the temple at Jerusalem, where the right pillar was named Jachin, "God makes him firm," and the left pillar was named Boaz, "Eagerness, strength" (1 Kings 7:21). The temple with these suggestive pillars was called Solomon's, but it was really built by King Hiram of Tyre, to whom Solomon paid annual tribute. Centuries later, the Freemasons gave the pillars Jachin and Boaz occult meanings, pretending their order dated all the way back to the Tyrian masons of Solomon's time. In Masonic symbolism the pillars are colored white and black, representing the god of light and the god of darkness, or sun and moon. The twin-pillar symbol also descended into astrology as **Gemini**.

Pillar worship was Christianized in the cult of Simeon Stylites and other saints' tales. The Athenian church of Saint John of the Column was built around an ancient sacred pillar, and a legend was invented to explain the old pagan custom of binding the pillar as a healing charm. Saint John allegedly tied all diseases to the pillar with silk threads, saying "Let any sick come and tie a silk thread to the column and be healed."[3]

1. d'Alviella, 106. 2. Whittick, 221.
3. Hyde, 109.

Rod

In biblical symbolism the rod was variously interpreted as a **scepter** of rulers, a club of chastisement, and an ever-erect **phallus** signifying the king's sexual attachment to the **Goddess** of the land. The rod that blossomed meant a virile king, able to beget general fertility. It also meant patriarchal descent, envisioned

as many "rods" (branches): "And there shall come forth a rod out of the stem of Jesse, and a branch shall grow out of his roots" (Isaiah 11:1).

The overnight miracle of the flowering rod was an easy one to stage, and seemed to convince the simple, as when Moses elected Aaron according to the convenient order of God, who said: "And it shall come to pass, that the man's rod, whom I shall choose, shall blossom" (Numbers 17:5). Next morning, Moses came out of the tabernacle with one flowering rod and said it was the same dead one that Aaron had placed among all the other dead ones the night before. One might think this kind of story would invite doubt by its very nature. Nevertheless, the same story was told all over again about the manner of selecting Joseph to be Mary's husband. When all the candidates laid their rods on the altar, only Joseph's budded and bloomed. Not only that, but the sacred **dove** of the Goddess came down from heaven and perched on it, just as she later appeared at Jesus' baptism.[1]

The story was repeated yet again in the legend of Tannhäuser, whose rod burst into bloom before the pope, proving to the latter that he should have forgiven Tannhäuser his peccadillos with the Goddess

Venus before it was too late.[2] Budding rods also became popular symbols of the Tarot suit called rods, wands, staves, or clubs, which evolved into the modern suit of clubs.

1. Walker, W.E.M.S., 479.   2. Goodrich, 174.

Scepter

In antiquity the scepter of a sacred king was made of **reeds** and was broken at the time of his sacrificial death. Insofar as the scepter symbolized his phallic spirit, its breaking signified castration and the end of his useful virility. The reed scepter of the Phoenician god Mot was ritually broken when he was "forsaken" by his Heavenly Father and was given up to the death ordained for him.[1] In Egypt, the reed scepter was carried by Set, the god of the Hyksos kings, who was annually crucified on a **furka**.[2] In Rome, reed scepters signified the phallic spirit of the castrated and sacrificed deity Attis and were carried in his solemn processions by special *cannophori*, "reed-bearers."[3]

In later centuries, the scepter of a king became sturdier and more permanent, as did the office of kingship itself. The scepter was made of precious metals and jewels, a rod of power in the economic sense, still bearing the old phallic connotation because it was always displayed along with the feminine **orb**.

1. *Larousse*, 76–78.   2. Graves, G.M. 1, 283.
3. Cumont, A.R.G.R., 56.

Spear

Like other pointed weapons such as the lance and **sword**, the spear often bore phallic connotations that probably would be quite comprehensible to the modern patriarchy, which all too often equates manhood with a gun. In the Japanese creation myth, it was the spear of the first god that reached down to stir and fertilize the **womb** of the deep: another version of the **lightning-phallus** fertilizing the Sea Mother. A spear alone could symbolize a god. Greeks told the story of Kaineus the Lapith, who worshiped nothing but his own spear, and was hammered into the ground by the **Centaurs**. The story seems to have been based on setting up a ceremonial spear as a god symbol, in the manner of a **Maypole**.[1]

Assuming a feminine role in relation to the spear, some sacrificial gods were themselves pierced by it and produced fructified or life-giving **blood**. Odin was pierced by a spear as he hung on the World Tree. His son Balder was sent to the underworld by a spear thrust, but would be resurrected in the next world. Jesus was similarly opened by a spear thrust delivered by a Roman centurion who was—amazingly enough—blind. He was Longinus, later canonized as Saint Longinus by a church that apparently saw nothing peculiar about a blind man following the profession of a soldier. At any rate, it was claimed that Longinus's blindness was cured by Jesus' blood falling on his eyes, whereupon he abandoned his martial profession and spent the rest of his life preaching Christianity.[2]

In the legends of the Holy **Grail** it was related that Longinus's spear was set upright in the divine vessel, making a design suspiciously similar to the Oriental **lingam-yoni**.[3] The Christianized Grail stories based this symbolic lingam on the pagans' holy Spear of Lug, which "had such destructive force that its head has always to be immersed in a cauldron so that the town where it was being kept did not go up in flames."[4] Since the **cauldron** was always a womb symbol, and the spear both lightning and a phallus, the sexual implication of this symbolism is clear.

1. Gelling & Davidson, 33.   2. Brewster, 135–136.   3. Baring-Gould, 613–614.
4. Markale, 175.

SWORD
*ceremonial sword
from temple
of Kali, Bengal*

Sword

In ancient Scythia the Sarmatian Alans and Quadi worshiped their swords as gods. The deity of war was an iron sword anointed with human blood.[1] Swords belonged to men in pagan Europe when most other things—fields, houses, furniture, utensils—belonged to women. A sword was buried with its owner, or went with him out to sea in a boat funeral, or was flung into water at his death. Many Viking swords have been recovered from riverbeds.[2] The connection between manhood and the phallic sword is shown in the Norse wedding custom of plunging a sword into the main beam of the house, as "proof of the virility of the bridegroom."[3]

Swords of heroes and sacred kings typically came out of a stone, a tree, or water, having been forged in fairyland or under the earth by magical beings. On the hero's death, the sword returns to its origin. Some famous magical or holy swords include Arthur's Excalibur, Lancelot's Arondight, Saint George's Ascalon, Siegfried's Balmung, Dietrich's Naglering, Roland's Durendal, Oliver's Glorious, Charlemagne's Flamberge, Sigurd's Gram, Beowulf's Hrunting, Ogier's Sauvagine, Fergus's Caladbolg, Paracel-

sus's Azoth, Ali's Zuflagar. Often, the breaking or loss of the sword signaled the loss of royal authority or of heroic mana, and the hero's consequent death.

The Syracusan legend of Damocles shows that the sword meant doom for the sacred king. Hanging over his head, it represented ceremonial beheadings. Later the beheadings were restricted to surrogates or animal victims, or became symbols only. Such a symbol is the knighthood ceremony: the sword touches each shoulder but no longer passes from one shoulder to the other through the neck.

The doom suit of the Tarot deck was the suit of swords, which evolved into the modern suit of spades by derivation from Spanish *espada*, "sword."

1. Goodrich, 217.   2. Davidson, *P.S.*, 112.   3. Gelling & Davidson, 38, 150.

Thyrsus

The thyrsus was the sacred **rod** of Dionysus (Roman Bacchus), a fennel stalk topped by a pine cone. Women devotees, the Maenads, apparently used the thyrsus like a weapon. They are shown in vase paintings aiming the thyrsus at the genitals of their attendant **satyrs**, as if to strike them.[1] The god is usually shown carrying a thyrsus also. It was said that a touch of the thyrsus could turn water into wine: the

standard Dionysian miracle, which was copied into the Gospel myth of the marriage at Cana.[2]

The word *thyrsus* has been connected with Hittite *tuwarsa*, "grape," and Ugaritic *tirsu*, "strong drink."[3] The Romans called the thyrsus *baculus*, because it was the staff of Bacchus. Eventually, the Roman pope inherited the staff of Bacchus, which was still called *baculus*; but according to a Christian legend, he lost it in the process of working a resurrection charm to raise a man from the dead. This legend was supposed to explain why the pope never carries a staff.[4]

1. Keuls, 367. 2. M. Smith, 25, 120.
3. Duerr, 197. 4. Borchardt, 68.

Triple Arrow

Closely related to the **trident-thunderbolt** that represented the pagan god's mating with the Triple Goddess, the triple arrow used to be viewed as a sign of virility. Three arrows bound together seems to have represented male bonding for purposes of hunting or aggression. This symbol possessed much the same connotation as the Roman **fasces** (bundle of rods). Sometimes, it was said to be a general sign of unity.[1]

1. Koch, 96.

Wand

Witches' wands have been envisioned in a great variety of ways: as wooden rods, or bone, or ivory, or amber; a natural shape or one that was artificially worked; crystal-tipped, crooked, beribboned, or set with magic stones; and of any size from a delicate willow switch to something resembling a small club. The wand is simply another version of the magical **rod** of power. Other forms include the royal scepter, marshal's baton, mayor's staff, bishop's crozier, flagstaff, battle standard, dowsing rod, and even the walking stick.[1] It is an archetype, probably dating all the way back to prehistoric people's first use of tools. As any child can attest even today, it "just feels good" to carry a stick in the hand.

Fairies carry wands too, usually tipped with a glowing star instead of the conventional crystal, to show that they are truly magical creatures. The wand is the tool of transformation. Therefore, the wand invokes the power first attributed to the Mother spirit, the Goddess who constantly transformed everything in the universe into something else: she who was called Heart of Transformations, "from whom all becoming arose."[2]

1. Cirlot, 344. 2. *Book of the Dead*, 454.

3

THREE-WAY
MOTIFS

N early all three-way designs have been assimilated by Western tradition to the Christian trinity. Even the Celts' sacred shamrock, which once represented the divine Three Mothers, was laboriously Christianized by a legend to the effect that Saint Patrick used it as a demonstration of the church's triadic God. Of course this never happened; and in view of the fact that Saint Patrick was not heard of until four centuries after his purported lifetime, it is possible that he never happened either. What was true about the shamrock was that it, and all other symbols of trinity, was much older than Christianity, dating back in most cases to a pagan faith of the Goddess, whose three personae were usually known as Virgin, Mother, and Crone.

The triangle represented the three-in-one unity of this Goddess "from the earliest scribblings of primordial man."[1] In Egypt the triangle stood for the female principle, motherhood, and the moon. In Arabia it signified the three lunar Goddesses under the names of Al-Uzza, Manat, and Al-Lat: the earlier, feminine form of Allah. Greece and Rome had many triadic versions of female divinity, with many symbols for them.

As always when older religious images are supplanted or discredited by later forms, the elder symbolism passes into the realm of the occult or of magic. Hence it was said in Christianized Europe that anything repeated three times is magical.[2] Fairy tales and folk traditions produce nearly everything in triplicate, often showing also the same three colors associated with the Virgin-Mother-Crone trinity: white, red, and black.

As a fundamental expression of tripleness, the triangle has assumed many variant forms and has been elaborated into a universal element of design.

1. Hornung, 207.   2. Trachtenberg, 119.

Alpha

Alpha, the birth letter of the Greek alphabet, is also an alternate name for the river Styx, which represented both death and rebirth. Like the sacred **spiral**, the Styx was said to enter the underground **womb** and reemerge after seven turns through the nether **spheres.**

In some of the oldest forms, such as Cretan, Syrian, and Sinaitic scripts, the letter was upside down (to our eyes) and obviously represented a horned bovine head of triangular shape. Even now,

alpha's Hebrew counterpart *aleph* is named the "ox." In various Palestinian, Aramaic, and Attic versions the head was tilted sideways until it finally turned completely over and became our letter A. Probably the original symbol was not an ox but the universal Cow Goddess associated with the birth of all things. The letter A was a name of the Goddess of beginnings in Babylon. In southeastern Asia it was

said that Alpa Akshara, the letter A, is the mother of all wisdom and hence the spiritual birth-giver to all enlightened persons.[1]

1. Waddell, 161.

Double Triangle: Creation

The double triangle symbolized creation in the Tantric tradition, because like the Chinese **yang and yin** it stood for the essential conjunction of male and female principles. The downward-pointing triangle was the **yoni yantra,** signifying the Mother Goddess. The upward-pointing triangle was her son/spouse, the renewable god to whom she gave birth again and again, and who copied her trinitarian form in mirror image.

This reversed triangle, or pyramid, became the symbolic model of feudal society. Power issuing from a single source (God) was seen as percolating downward toward a broad base of peasants, slaves, animals, and all the rest of creation. Lost and forgotten was the upper feminine triangle that might have suggested the opposite view, that all power issues from Mother Earth who supports everything else including the gods.

Nevertheless, European mystics and hermetic practitioners wrote the secret name of God as the **Tetragrammaton** within the downward female triangle, just as the male *bindu* or embryonic spark of life

appeared within the same figure in Oriental religious symbolism.

The double triangle also became a sign of infinity, like the similar figure eight, and as a stylized hourglass it was taken as a symbol of time. Saracen magicians adopted the double triangle and regarded it as a powerful charm.[1]

1. Koch, 4, 83, 94.

Dragon's Eye

The Dragon's Eye used to be a favorite shape for cutting magical **stones,** especially transparent or translucent crystals that might resemble the popular mind's imagining of a dragon's eye. The figure has an illusory quality. Steady gazing at its center can develop the illusion of three dimensions, so that it appears to be a tetrahedron seen from above or from one corner. Certain minerals naturally form crystals of this shape. Whenever such crystals were found, they were usually regarded as foci for magic powers.

The Dragon's Eye also forms a triple triangle, sacred to the ancient **Goddess** in some of her ninefold forms, such as the nine **Muses** or the nine Morgans. This figure and certain of its variations appeared often in medieval books of magic, to invoke the protection of female spirits.

Fate

Three triangles created the emblem of the
Fate Goddesses: the Greek Moerae,
Teutonic Norns, Roman Fortunae, medieval Parcae or **Weird Sisters** (from the
Saxon *wyrd*, meaning "fate"). Three of
anything arranged in triads suggested a total of nine, so in some traditions the
Fate goddesses became nine, like the Nine
Morgans of the Fortunate Isles in Celtic
myth. In Scandinavia, the sign of fate was
called the *valknut*, Knot of the Vala.[1] A Vala
was either a female spirit ruling the fates
of men—a **Valkyrie**—or her representative on earth, a mistress of magic **knots**.

In most archaic traditions, the deciding
of men's fates was a function of the
Goddess. Babylonian myth spoke of the
"mother of destinies" who determined the
fates of men. She was Mammetun,
the same creatress who first formed human
beings out of clay.[2]

Folk worship of the female trinity of
fate persisted all the way up to the
Renaissance and beyond. In the eleventh
century, Burchardus of Worms complained that at each turn of the year, people set out tables of food and drink
with three knives for the pagan triad of
sisters.[3] The Fates appeared in many fairy
tales as "fairy godmothers" who hovered over
the infant's cradle and decided the
course of its future life. Among Hungarian
Gypsies, baptismal ceremonies included the
careful placement of three pieces of
food on the infant's bed as offerings to
sweeten the tempers of the three Goddesses of Fate.[4]

1. Davidson, G.M.V.A., 147. 2. *Epic of
Gilgamesh*, 107. 3. Miles, 181. 4. Trigg, 80.

Furka

The furka or "fork" was the cross on
which the Egyptian god Set was crucified.
He also carried the **reed scepter** in token of
sacred kingship and was wounded in
the side.[1] As the original of the biblical
Seth, the "supplanter" of the **Good Shepherd** (Abel, or Horus-**Osiris**), Set ruled the
alternating halves of the year in Egypt's
predynastic sacred-king cult.[2] The
Christian version of the sacrificial sacred-
king figure also copied a number of
details from the archaic worship of Set.
The **ass** that Jesus rode into Jerusalem, "as
it is written" (John 12:14), was the
totem animal and sometime alter ego of
Set, and probably the same steed ridden by
men who impersonated him at the
time of his seasonal sacrifices, two thousand years earlier. Annual rebirth of the
world was said to be achieved by the
blood of Set, which was spread over
the fields.[3]

Even Christian authorities remembered that Set's holy furka was somehow connected with a crucifixion scene, for they took to calling it the Thieves' Cross.[4] Christian artists occasionally showed the two thieves hung up on furkas, like Set. The figure probably began as a stylized tree, with uplifted branches supposed to receive blessings from heaven and channel them into the earth, like the body of the god himself.

1. Campbell, *M.I.*, 29.   2. Graves, *G.M.* 1, 284.   3. Budge, *G.E.* 2, 59.   4. Koch, 16.

Love Charm

This Norse variant of the Venus mirror is a love charm that resembles a Goddess sign right side up, and a God sign (**trident**) upside down. Such gender ambivalence might be interpreted as an **androgyne,** hence an expression of male/female union. It is also a diagrammatic human figure, recalling the common magical process of establishing power over the feelings of another, by drawing some kind of manikin and calling it his/her portrait. See **Poppet.**

Mannaz

The old runic sign *mannaz* stood for "humanity," which male scholars naturally called "man." But in the original Old Norse, *man* meant "woman," and humanity in the generic sense of woman-created or woman-born people, the gift of the Moon Mother, Mana.[1] (A male human being was not "man" but *wer.*) The same Moon Mother was the ancestress of all people in southern Europe also. Up to the beginning of the Christian era, Romans continued to worship her and her ancient children, the ancestral **ghosts** called *manes.*

The runic sign resembles the **double triangle** of creation that joined male and female principles together in Oriental symbolism; therefore it probably stood for humanity's two sexes considered as a unit. Ancient Scandinavian sacred dances sometimes called for a couple to join hands in the "**handfasting**" gesture, her right to his right and her left to his left. The sign *mannaz* could well be a stylized representation of two people thus joined, therefore standing for the "togetherness" of humanity in general.

1. Steenstrup, 105.

Money Charm

In this money charm design a person with very large arms is shown grasping for largesse that descends from heaven. The lines say almost as plainly as written words, "My need is great." The symbol was originated by Norse pagans and repeated in medieval books of magic, which inevitably concentrated on love and money as being the two preeminent desires of magic practitioners.

Tau Cross

Named for the Greek letter *tau*, or *T*, this three-way version of the cross once stood for a druidic tree god. **Oak** logs were stripped of their branches and fastened together to make a wooden idol that the druids called Thau.[1] Among pagan Germans and Celts the tau cross sometimes meant the divine mallet or double-headed hammer of the rain god. At times, the cross of Christ was represented as a tau. It was also known as the gibbet cross or Saint Anthony's cross, though its connection with Saint Anthony was purely mythical.[2]

An older tradition made the tau cross a symbol of Saint Philip, whose feast day at the beginning of May was a Christianization of a major pagan festival. The same feast was supposed to commemorate the Invention of the Cross, an aptly named legend specifically invented by early Christians to pretend that the empress Helena had discovered Jesus' true cross in a crypt under the temple of Aphrodite in Jerusalem. At that time the true cross was believed to be a tau and not a **Latin cross**.[3] The legend was necessary to explain why so many tons of pieces of the true cross were turning up in churches all over Europe—enough wood to make a full load for a good ship, as Calvin remarked, and more wood than Jesus could have carried to Calvary even if he had been a giant seventy feet tall.

According to Jewish tradition, the tau cross was the mark made by the Israelites on their doorposts at the first Passover, in the land of Egypt.[4] Since the tau is in effect the lower portion of the ankh, this idea was probably copied from the Egyptian habit of marking doorposts with an ankh as a life-preserving good luck charm—perhaps deliberately omitting the upper, oval, "female" portion of the design. See **Ankh**.

1. Elworthy, 103.   2. d'Alviella, 16.
3. Brewster, 226.   4. Hall, 78.

Three-Pointed Star

Actually a triangle with indented sides, the three-pointed star is an unusual star shape. It is found especially in Arabic fretwork and allover pattern designs. The narrow passage of the center may represent an opening intended to repel evil powers by its tendency to close up against them.

Three-Rayed Sun

This three-rayed figure represented the sun suspended in the midst of heaven by three powers, perhaps originally the triple Goddess who was supposed to have given birth to it.[1] According to Tantric tradition, the Goddess concealed herself behind the sun's brightness; it was "the mayik vesture of Her who is clothed with the sun."[2] This image reappeared in the New Testament as "the woman clothed with the sun" (Revelation 12:1).

1. Budge, G.E. 1, 473.
2. *Mahanirvanatantra*, x.

Trefoil

One of the earliest emblems of trinitarian divinity, known as far back as the Indus Valley civilization (ca. 2500–1700 B.C.), the trefoil was sacred in the eyes of many Indo-European peoples. Irish Celts even had a god of the trefoil, Trefuilngid Tre-Eochair, whose spirit produced three basic kinds of beneficial trees. Like Shiva before him, he was called Triple Bearer of the Triple Key. His emblem was eventually assimilated to the legend of Saint Patrick, whose "shamrock" was supposed to have demonstrated the principle of the Christian trinity to the Irish pagans—who, however, must already have been perfectly familiar with the concept, since they had been worshiping the trefoil for centuries.

Triangle

As the four-way designs of squares and crosses usually represented the male principle, so the three-way design of the triangle and its many relatives usually represented the female principle. One reason the ancients so greatly revered the number seven was that the four and the three were united in it. The **Goddess** was the original trinity, for most of her oldest manifestations had three aspects: the classical Virgin, Mother, and Crone. All three were the same individual just as each woman is one even though her life encompasses all three states or *personae*. This triangular Goddess existed even for early Christian Gnostics who worshiped her as the Female Protennoia, who had three names, "although she exists alone, since she is perfect."[1]

In India the Goddess was the original Trimurti, or Trinity, although the three gods Brahma, Vishnu, and Shiva later laid claim to this title. Nevertheless, the Goddess as Parashakti—the Mother of these gods—was represented by a triangle holding the gods as three small seed pods within herself.[2]

Australian aborigines worshiped the Goddess as Kunapipi, meaning "Old Woman" or "Mother," in a triangular dancing area that they viewed as the Mother's genital center.[3] The connection between this concept and that of the triangular **yoni yantra** in ancient India is quite clear, especially since anthropologists believe the aborigines were Dravidian migrants from India some time in the distant past.

The Greek letter *D* (delta) is a triangle. As in India, it was similarly described as "the letter of the vulva," and also as the Holy Door (of birth). It was the first syllable of Demeter's name, the rest being *meter*, "Mother." One of the oldest of Greek Goddesses, in fact pre-Greek, Demeter was also a trinity represented by the female triangle. Although she was the earth, she was three. Her young consort in classical myth, Triptolemus or "Three Plowings," was so named because he had to "seed her fields" three times in order to fertilize the whole Triple Goddess.[4]

It seems likely that the triangle became a common symbol for "woman" largely because it was originally a symbol for "Goddess" and many of the objects associated with her. Cakes for religious festivals were often baked in triangular form. The Jewish tradition of triangular *hamantaschen* for Purim apparently adopted the Egyptian custom of making triangular cakes for public rituals.[5] Even in the twentieth century, Scottish countryfolk baked triangular cakes for **Halloween** (the old Celtic feast of Samhain), calling the woman who baked the cakes "the

Bride." After a reign of one year, she would be displaced by the Caillech, or "Auld Wife"—that is, the incarnation of the Crone.

In Christian Gnostic literature there was a holy trinity of **Marys,** copied from the Moerae or Fates, who stood by the tree of the god's sacrifice as the three Marys stood by Jesus' cross. Gnostic scriptures agree that two of them were "Mary his mother . . . and Magdalene, the one who was called his companion." But the third Mary remained mysterious; she was called his sister in one sentence and the sister of his mother (his aunt) in another sentence.[6] No one really knew who those Marys were, but it was traditional for them to be present.

Certain folkloric sources even remembered that the triangle was a sign of the Goddess as Wise Crone (**Athene**/Minerva), and gave it the title of Creative Intellect.[7]

1. Robinson, 462. 2. Lehner, 35. 3. Eliade, 48–49. 4. Graves, G.M., 93. 5. Budge, D.N., 75. 6. Robinson, 135–136. 7. Koch, 8.

Triceps

A Nordic design of three **earth diamonds** drawn by a continuous line, the triceps is a powerful invocation of earth powers according to the principles of symbol magic. If the broken sides are filled in by a straight line carried all the way through from tip to tip, then the triceps becomes an ordinary triangle bearing a six-pointed star in its center.

Triple Alpha

This sign repeats the birth letter *Alpha* three times, and so constituted a talisman of protection for women in childbirth. The triple alpha was also used for other magic charms. The **Double Triangle,** representing creation, is formed three times in the same figure. This used to be considered a graphic means of invoking the Triple Goddess, whom early Gnostic Christians entitled "Triple-Formed Primal Thought" (Trimorphic Protennoia), "She Who exists before the All," and "Invisible One within the All." In ancient sacred **alphabets,** the first letter was usually a symbol of creation.

Triple Ring

Three rings were supposed to invoke the three **Fates** in several ancient traditions. Rings, as opposed to lines or crosses, were typically female forms; and the overlapping arcs of the three circles create a triple *vesica*. Rings and threes were frequently connected in folklore, fairy tales, and magic charms. English girls used to make a symbolic offering to the three Fate Goddesses by passing crumbs of **bread** three times through a wedding ring, calling upon "Sancta Fata" to be rewarded by a vision of their future husbands.[1] Clergymen, recognizing this as a pagan procedure, tried to soften it by claiming that the girls were calling upon "Saint Faith," a spurious Christian demigoddess with an artificially constructed life story.[2]

Many mystical meanings were assigned to the triple ring: perfection in thought, word, and deed; or love, power, and wisdom. From the Greek triad of body, mind, and shadow (shade; ghost) came the primitive Christian *corpus, anima, spiritus* (body, mind, spirit), based in turn on Oriental and Hebrew precursors represented by the triple ring.[3]

1. Hazlitt 2, 373. 2. Walker, W.E.M.S., 301.
3. G. Jobes 2, 1565.

Tripod

The tripod, meaning "three-foot," was an early Greek form of the **altar** on which offerings were made. For ceremonies held outdoors, it was obviously better than a four-footed table, which will not stand firm anywhere but on a perfectly flat floor. A tripod, however, can stand without instability on any kind of ground. In Athens, the avenue leading to the sanctuary of Dionysus became known as the street of Tripods because it was adorned with so many small altars.[1]

At Delphi and other oracular centers, the tripod was the official seat of the Pythoness and her sister **sybils.** It was believed that three legs signified the connection between the priestess and the triadic spirit of prophecy. Similarly, when the god Odin stole the knowledge of oracular **runes** from the priestesses of Mother Earth, he rode a "three-legged horse."

According to the fourteenth-century Austrian codex of Saint Florian, witches always sat on tripods while conjuring.[2]

1. Whittick, 340.   2. Duerr, 247.

Triquetra

The triquetra is an ancient symbol of the female trinity, being composed of three yonic *vesicas* (see **Vesica Piscis**) interlaced so as to form the continuous "gateless" type of design, always regarded as protective. Sometimes the three *vesicas* were further interlaced with a surrounding **circle.**

Naturally, this symbol was exploited by Christian mystics as a sign of the male trinity, however inappropriate its basic shaping was to such an interpretation. Thus the triquetra came to be called a symbol of "glory," with the understanding that the glory somehow belonged to a paternal god.[1]

1. Hornung, 208.

Triskelion

The triskelion is simply the triple-triangle form of **Fate** (or the Fates) with one side of each of the three triangles removed, so that a swastikalike figure results. It is one of the lively symbols, giving a distinct impression of movement. This is the basic pattern for the **tryfuss,** the three-armed design, and similar variants.

Tryfuss

The "Three-Foot," also called Tri-pes, Tri-Pedes, or the Three Legs of Man, is a variation of the **triskelion** commonly known today as the official seal of the Isle of Man, which perches in the Irish Sea with a foot toward each of its three neighbors, England, Scotland, and Ireland. However, the tryfuss was not originally Manx. It appeared on coins from ancient Lycia about 480 B.C. In the fourth century B.C. it was adopted by Agathocles as the emblem of Sicily, a triangular island then called Trinacria or "Three Capes."

The sign was brought to England by King Henry III (1216–1272), who was for a time also king of Sicily. Alexander III of Scotland adopted it on behalf of the Isle of Man, after driving out the Norwegians in 1266.[1]

The tryfuss is considered by some to be a runic sign of the life force, signifying "the will to create."

1. d'Alviella, ix, 20.

Weird Sisters

Shakespeare's three witches were called Weird Sisters after the Saxon trinity of Wyrd, the Three **Fates**, who were identical with the Norse Norns, Greek Moerae, and Roman Fortunae. Originally there was only one Goddess, Wyrd,

Wurd, Urd, or Urth (Mother Earth), who evolved into the trinity of She-Who-Was, She-Who-Is, and She-Who-Will-Be.[1] Wyrd or Wurd also meant the "word" of the Great Mother, that is, her immutable law. Some old English writings claimed that the Christian God himself was subject to the irresistible power of the Goddess Wyrd. Some Christians attempted to assimilate her to Christianity by renaming her "Providence." Alfred the Great claimed that Wyrd really represents "the work of God."

Perhaps this is why the sign of the Weird Sisters (based on the **Kali Yantra**) was turned around and reused to represent the Christian trinity.[2]

1. Campbell, *C.M.*, 121.   2. Koch, 30.

World Triad

Although the World Triad sign was adopted by western Gnostics as an emblem of cosmic creativity, the threefold nature of reality or **fate**, and the eternally spiraling cycles of time, it was of Oriental provenance. In Japan it was *maga-tama* or *mitsu tomoe*, the world soul or any individual offshoot of it.[1] In Bhutan and Tibet it is still known as the Cosmic **Mandala**, a sign of the Trimurti. Like the twofold **yang and yin** that it resembles, the World Triad symbol was usually understood as a graphic image of eternity.

1. Hornung, 215.

Yoni Yantra

The Sanskrit word *yantra* means a meditation sign. Like a shorthand form of the **mandala**, it is intended to convey spiritual insight to those who sit still and contemplate it. This "yantra of the yoni" was one of the oldest and most meaningful, representing the pubic area of a woman's body and many philosophical concepts centering on this reality: creation, birth, love, motherhood, sexual attraction, fulfillment, cyclic time, kundalini force, the mystery of conception, the Goddess within, the Shakti, and so on.[1]

The *yoni yantra* and a good many of its Oriental significances migrated into the Middle East and then into Europe several thousand years ago. It was always regarded with awe by the more learned mystics. A medieval text, the *Amor Proximi*, described it as "the triangle of life . . . not foreign or external but most intimate in every one, though hidden."[2] One of the Magic Papyri equated it with paradise. The enlightened magician could declare himself Keeper of the Key of the Kingdom, "the three-cornered paradise of the earth."[3]

Among the Gypsies, whose racial and religious roots lay in India, the *yoni yantra* always remained a favorite design for laying out divinatory **Tarot cards**.[4]

1. *Mahanirvanatantra,* 127.   2. Silberer, 170.
3. M. Smith, 114.   4. Trigg, 48–49.

FOUR-WAY MOTIFS

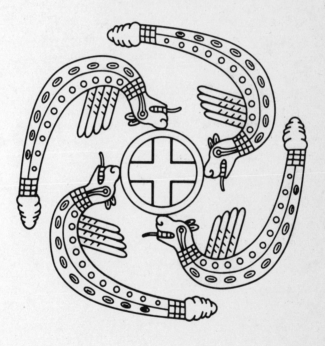

Seven was a prime sacred number to the ancients, because it represented the unity of a feminine three with a masculine four. Division of the universe into quadrants by squares, crosses, and other right-angled designs seems to have been associated with the gradual rise of patriarchal civilizations. The round village was replaced by the city laid out in squares and oriented east-west, north-south. Directional quadrants were linked with the four winds, four elements, four seasons, four angelic guardians, and so on.

It was believed that the earth was flat and had four corners, like a man-made square building. People still speak of the four corners of the earth. Though most realize that this is only a fanciful metaphor, it is not widely considered as incomprehensible as it really is.

Imaginary straight lines drawn to and from the four corners of the earth were forerunners of our parallels of latitude and longitude. Meetings of lines at a central point formed the cross. Crosses represented male gods long before Christianity. Crosses even represented the god's sacrifice, generally assumed to take place at the center of things, where all forces came together: the usual location of the Tree of Life, *axis mundi*, omphalos, source of the four mystic rivers, summit of the world mountain, center of the world body, and other interpretations of the X that "marks the spot."

We are still very familiar with many four-way sequences such as the cardinal points, solstitial and equinoctial time segments, four royal stars (Aldebaran, Antares, Fomalhaut, Regulus), four ages of the world, four horsemen of the apocalypse, and so on.

Celtic Cross

The symbol that we call the Celtic cross was known to the Hindus as the *kiakra*, a sign of sexual union: the cross (**phallus**) within the circle (**yoni**). The Gypsies, whose original home was Hindustan, adopted both elements as sexual symbols. They would mark a cross on a horse's right (male) foreleg, and a circle on the left (female) foreleg, on the theory that the two symbols would attract one another, draw the horse's feet together like a hobble, and keep the animal from running away.[1]

Like all other cross designs, this one too was adopted by Christianity. Nowadays it often appears as a grave marker.

1. Bowness, 41.

CELTIC CROSS

COPTIC CROSS

CROSS CROSSLET

Coptic Cross

The original form of the Coptic cross was simply a sun symbol, showing the heavenly orb in the center of heaven, supported by the four "pillars" that were supposed to uphold the sky in each of the four directions. The four nails were added by Coptic Christians to identify the sacrificed Christ with the heavenly deity, and to suggest that the blood drawn from his wounds by the nails had spread, symbolically, to the four corners of the world.[1]

During the Middle Ages, however, Christian artists began to omit the fourth nail from their crucifixion scenes. The deity's feet were fastened together with a single nail, making a total of three. The Gypsies' story about this was that the fourth nail had been stolen from Jesus' executioners by a Gypsy. In gratitude for this partial relief, Jesus granted all Gypsies the right to steal from non-Gypsies.[2]

Whatever the original number of nails may have been, they proliferated to sufficient numbers to place a nail in every square inch of a human body, when the church discovered how profitable it could be to enshrine relics of the crucifixion. Today there are at least twenty of the Holy Nails still extant.[3]

1. Koch, 20.   2. Groome, xxx.   3. Hall, 82.

Cross Crosslet

Much admired as a prophylactic good luck charm, the cross crosslet combined pagan and Christian graphic themes. Consisting of four **Latin crosses** joined at the foot, it also echoed the popular magic principle of marking a crossline as defense, like a barrier. In effect, the design says, "I can repel attack from any direction."

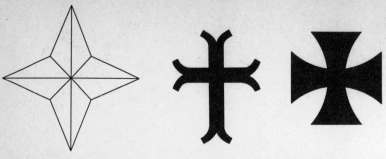

Cross Etoile

The cross etoile or "star cross," a pretty variation on the **Greek cross** of equal arms, frequently appeared on the compass rose as an indicator of the eight major directions. For a long time it was accepted as a sacred symbol invoking the powers of the four corners of the earth.

Cross Fourchée

This "forked" decorative cross was popular in medieval heraldry. It hints at Christian piety, combined with an ineradicable trust in the pagan magic of the forked stick.

In another interpretation, the flaring points of the cross may have represented flames. The burning cross of the Ku Klux Klan descended from an ancient Scottish call to battle, in the form of a cross with tips on fire, sent from village to village in order to muster troops. It was usually supposed that the torches at the tips of the cross would be extinguished with blood.[1]

1. G. Jobes 1, 262.

Cross Patée

The cross patée was one of the most popular forms of the cross in medieval heraldry, perhaps because it created a synthesis between the Christian cross and **Wotan's cross.** It is clearly seen to be shaped within a square. On a banner or surcoat, it is solidly colored and broad enough to be seen at a distance. Another name for this figure is cross formée. In northern Europe it was often shown as the insignia of the god Frey.

Cross Pommée

Cross pommée means "the cross finished with apples." Crosses with circles at the ends of the arms were common on Jewish amulets,[1] and were also found earlier on Assyrian monuments.[2] Such a cross represented the Assyrian god Asshur, who was sometimes shown with four faces of a man, lion, eagle, and bull (or ox): the same totems much later adopted as symbols of the four Christian evangelists.[3] It is said that the ancient god ruled time or the seasons, so the four totems faced the four crucial solar positions throughout the year, the solstices and the equinoxes. Similarly, the evangelists were assigned to four quarters of the zodiacal round.

1. Trachtenberg, 141.   2. d'Alviella, 65.
3. G. Jobes 1, 143.

CROSS POMMÉE **CROSS POTENT** **CROSS SALTIRE**

Cross Potent

The cross potent was one of several cross-symbols of the sky god or sun god in ancient Mesopotamia. To the Assyrians, a cross potent with a small circle at the center was the sigil of the heaven-god Anu.[1] Like the original of the **Coptic cross**, this probably stood for the deity suspended in the midst of a four-way heaven.

In medieval times, the cross potent was sometimes called "the windlass" because of its resemblance to that useful object.[2]

1. d'Alviella, 13. 2. Koch, 79.

Cross Saltire

Cross saltire means literally "tumbling cross," or a cross performing a somersault. It was well known in Vedic India, where it was sometimes equated with the *vajra* (jewel-phallus) of Indra. According to the Vedas, it was "the stone with four points that brings rain," that is, a **thunderbolt** sign, like the hammer of **Thor.**[1]

Fairly late in the Middle Ages, the cross saltire came to be called Saint Andrew's cross, because churchmen concocted a story that Andrew was crucified on an X-shaped cross. Andrew, from the Greek word for "man" (*andros*), had been adopted by the Greek church in its political struggles against Rome during the fourth century, in order to claim that because Andrew was Saint Peter's older brother, his church could take precedence over the church of Rome. Neither legend—Peter's or Andrew's—of churchmaking or martyrdom had any foundation in fact.[2]

An even less probable legend made Saint Andrew the patron of Scotland. It was claimed that a monk carried Andrew's bones on a ship, which was wrecked off the Scottish coast, so the bones came into the possession of the Scottish church. Thus the cross saltire was placed on the Scottish flag (a white X on a blue ground). The X of the Scottish emblem now appears along with the red rectilinear "cross of Saint George" on the British Union Jack.

1. d'Alviella, 99. 2. Attwater, 45; Brewster, 5.

Cross Voided

In this context, "voided" simply means hollow in the middle. The voided cross can be seen as not a cross at all, but four right-angled gamma figures close together; or it may be seen as a **Greek cross** with a central stripe of background color. This was a popular heraldic variation on the cross.

Crux Dissimulata

The figure known as the *crux dissimulata* took its Latin name from an apocryphal story that early Christians had to disguise their sign of the cross with extra arms, to prevent detection by pagan authorities. This story was fiction, of course. Early Christians did not use a cross symbol at all, but rather worshiped an image of Christ as a sacrificial **lamb.** The cross was not considered a typically Christian symbol until the seventh century, and was not fully accepted by the church until the ninth century.[1]

The *crux dissimulata* was really an ancient variation of the **swastika,** well known in pagan iconography and usually representing the four winds, or the anthropomorphized spirits thereof.

1. H. Smith, 188; Whittick, 226.

Earth Diamond

The rhomb or **diamond** was said to be the sign of the Virgin Earth, that is, Mother Earth at the beginning of creation. To early Gnostic Christians, she was not a metaphor but a true spiritual personality, the cocreator of the universe along with another female spirit. Gnostic literature said Adam was not created by God but by "two virgins," the Spirit (**Sophia**) and the Virgin Earth.[1] The latter was also taken as another title of Eve.

Like other **Goddess** symbols, such as the **circle, triangle,** and **yoni,** the earth diamond has been designated "emblematic of the female sexual organ."[2]

Another name for this symbol was the Eye of Fire, especially in Nordic tradition.[3] This would naturally associate the symbol with the Goddess Hel, the underground Earth Mother whose name was later applied to the Christian idea of a vast torture chamber under the earth. Hel was not originally "hellish," however, except perhaps that her fiery eye always saw the truth and mortal faults could not be concealed from her. A golden diamond, sometimes marked by the cross, was the most common sign of the Earth Mother in the Orient, where she was the vast foundation and support of the holy mountain that upheld all the paradises of the gods.

1. Robinson, 143.   2. Cirlot, 261.
3. Lehner, 99.

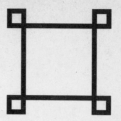

Earth Sign

All over the world, people evolved the idea
that the earth must have four corners,
four quarters, four directions, and a center
point marked by a cross. The basic
earth sign comes from China, where the
"four-square" earth also represented
law and order, given to humanity by the
Earth Mother after originating with
Tao, Mother of All Things, and passing
through heaven.[1] The Earth Mother on her
central holy **mountain** also gave tablets of the
law to ancient Babylonian kings and to
the rulers of Minoan Crete: an idea that
was later copied into the legend of
Moses. A fundamental Oriental idea was
that all the world was created around a
primordial cross.[2]

A similar idea was found among the
Pueblo Indians of North America. They
said the creatress of the world was
Thinking Woman or Spider Woman. She
first spun two **threads** to the cardinal
directions, so they would cross at the center
of the world and create the four horizons.[3]
Then she could proceed to populate
the earth with plants, animals, and people.

In accord with what was believed
the divine prototype, many people divided
a country or city into four quarters
with a governing place, temple, plaza, or
ruler's dwelling in the center. Ireland
used to be called the Island of the Four

Kings, because it was divided into
four subkingdoms with a "high king" ruling at Tara in the center.[4] To this day,
sections of a city are known as "quarters"
whether they are actually quarters or not.

1. Perry, 217.   2. d'Alviella, 14.   3. Stone,
A.M.W. 2, 92.   4. Cirlot, 320.

Earth Square

The magical protection supposed to
inhere in the earth square was based on
ancient ideas of earth's four guardian spirits who stood at the four corners and
held up the sky. In northern Europe, their
names were North, East, South, and
West. Babylonians invoked the corner-gods
in protective prayers as "Shamash
before me, behind me Sin, Nergal at my
right, Ninib at my left." They descended
from Babylonian scriptures into a copycat
Jewish prayer of invocation: "On my
right Michael, at my left Gabriel, before
me Uriel, behind me Raphael."[1]

In Egypt, the corner-gods wore animal
heads like all other Egyptian deities,
following a tradition of earth-guarding animals that could be found everywhere
from China to Rome. Chinese sages assigned the east to the blue dragon,
the south to the red bird, the west to the
white tiger, and the north to the black tortoise.[2] Babylonians also placed a quartet of
animal spirits in the cardinal directions, the
lion of Ishtar, the bull of Marduk, the
eagle-headed dragon of Nergal, and a

manlike figure for Enlil.[3] Christian tradition took over these totems and assigned them to the four evangelists.

As for the Christianized form of the four earth-guarding spirits, they became the same four archangels, mentioned in Revelation 7:1 as angels standing on the four corners of the earth.

1. Trachtenberg, 156.   2. Cirlot, 257.
3. Beltz, 168.

Earth Square, Christianized

A new version of the **earth square** emblem became current during the Middle Ages.[1] Now the "protective" corner devices were rendered acceptable with the simple addition of crosses.

Since the Judeo-Christian Bible-based tradition was that the earth had four corners, as infallibly attested by God himself (Isaiah 11:12; Revelation 7:1), the flat, four-cornered model was adopted by church fathers like Augustine and Lactantius. Christian authorities ignored the pagans' evidence of a global earth. The geographer monk Cosmas unequivocally denounced "the heathen doctrine of the rotundity of the earth" on the ground that people living on the other side of the world would be unable to see Jesus descending from heaven on Judgment Day.[2]

1. Koch, 34.   2. Abelard, 38.

Gammadion

The gammadion is a short-armed **swastika,** taking its name from the fact that it is composed of four Greek gammas. It was one of the most widely distributed sacred signs, an ornament of **Goddess** images in Troy, Cyprus, Rhodes, and Greece. Gammadions appeared on coins of Macedon, Thrace, Crete, Lycia, Corinth, and in several locations in Italy even before the Etruscans. The symbol was popular also in Gaul, central Europe, and Britain. Christians copied it and used it liberally on tombs and catacombs.[1]

Like its relative the swastika, the gammadion probably represented the solstices and equinoxes, or the four directions, four elements, and four divine guardians of the world.

1. d'Alviella, 33–36.

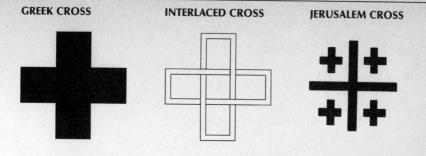

GREEK CROSS   **INTERLACED CROSS**   **JERUSALEM CROSS**

Greek Cross

Up to Carolingian times (eighth to ninth century A.D.), the Greek cross was the usual Christian symbol, not the **Latin cross.**[1] It was known as the *crux imissa quadrata.* It is still commonly used in liturgical texts to indicate where the sign of the cross should be performed or to set off holy names.

Before Christianity, the Greek cross was an emblem of Hecate as the Goddess of Crossroads. Like the infinity sign or the ankh, it also represented union of male and female principles as vertical and horizontal members, respectively. Thus it became a plus sign: one-plus-the-other.[2]

1. Jung, 243. 2. G. Jobes 1, 387.

Interlaced Cross

The interlaced cross is a sign of interdependent dualism, like that expressed by the **yang and yin** of China. Here, the earthly world (horizontal) and the supernatural world (vertical) are shown interpenetrating one another so as to form the basic unit of a mesh. What happens to one must affect the other. It is a graphic demonstration of the fundamental magicoreligious principle "as above, so below," and vice versa.

Jerusalem Cross

Because Judeo-Christian tradition declared Jerusalem the center of the earth, the pagans' ancient earth-center cross was named after it. The four subordinate crosses apparently represented the astrologers' Four Royal Stars, to which the four directions, four **winds,** four **seasons,** four **elements,** four ages, and other quadrate concepts were related. These stars were: (1) Aldebaran, the Eye of the Bull, the alpha star of Taurus, culminating on January 5; (2) Regulus, the Heart of the Lion, the alpha star of Leo, culminating on April 5; (3) Antares, the Heart of the Scorpion, the alpha star of Scorpio, culminating on July 5; and (4) Fomalhaut, the Mouth of the Southern Fish in Pisces, culminating on October 22.

The large cross amid the four smaller star-crosses was supposed to indicate the earth's geographical center where lay the *omphalos,* hub, and site of the Goddess's chief temple. Long before the Christian era, Jerusalem (meaning "House of Peace") was sacred to a combination of male and female deities. The original tutelary Goddess may have been Eve, under the Hittite version of her name, Hiba, "known from other sources as a Hittite Goddess." The name of the first historical king of "Urusalim" was Abdihipa, which means "servant of Hiba."[1] Other early titles of Eve were "Divine Lady of Eden" and "Goddess of the Tree of Life."[2]

1. Beltz, 197. 2. d'Alviella, 153.

Knot of Eternity

Originally a Chinese design, the Knot of
Eternity is an **earth square** variation
supposed to be made of two short loops
and one long loop of rope.[1] It is reminiscent of some of the cabled lattice designs
carved on old Norse pillars and doorposts,
and even today worked into traditional ca-
ble-knit sweaters. It served as a **mandala** for
contemplation, probably with many
numerological analogies drawn from its
nine inner spaces and eight outer
ones, the relative twists of the strands, and
so on. Buddhists claimed that the
Knot of Eternity signified the entrails of
the Enlightened One, which presumably
arranged themselves in this orderly
shape while he sat in meditation.[2]

1. Wilkins, 206.   2. G. Jobes 1, 513.

Latin Cross

Contrary to current popular belief, the
Latin or "Passion" cross was not a
Christian emblem from the beginning. It
was not assimilated into the Christian religion until the seventh century A.D., and
was not fully authorized until the ninth
century.[1] Primitive churches preferred to
represent Christ by the figure of a
lamb, or else a **"Good Shepherd"** carrying a lamb, in the conventional manner of
Hermes and **Osiris.**[2] In several places
the New Testament says that Jesus was
hanged on a tree, not a cross (Acts 5:30;

1 Peter 2:24), and some sects believed this
tree to be literal, not metaphorical.
This would have envisioned Jesus rather
closer to such tree-slain savior figures as
Krishna, Marsyas, Odin, and Dodonian
Zeus.

Some early Christian fathers specifically
repudiated the Latin cross on the ground that
it was a pagan symbol. On a coin of
Gallienus, it appeared as the scepter of
Apollo. On the Damietta stone, it
set off the words "Ptolemy the Savior."[3]
According to the Greeks, this cross
signified "the life to come" in the Egyptian
religion of Sarapis.[4]

Once the Latin cross was accepted by
Christianity, all kinds of pious nonsense
began to accrete around the symbol. It was
claimed, for example, that the very
wood of the **Tree of Life** in the Garden of
Eden had been preserved by Adam
and all the patriarchs after him, in order
to be fashioned into Jesus' cross—
for Jesus was declared the second or reincarnated Adam designed to correct
the fault of the first one.[5] This Tree of Life
legend contributed to the enormous pro-
liferation of tons of wood splinters of the
True Cross that brought huge revenues
into the medieval church when touted as
healing charms. To explain the presence
of all those splinters, the legend called Invention of the Cross was devised, claiming
that the empress Helena had found

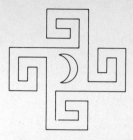

Jesus' cross in a crypt under Jerusalem's temple of Aphrodite and had carried it back to Europe. Of course there was no genuine record of any such event, but the credulous do not demand proof.

The Latin cross is not inappropriate for a church that composed itself entirely of men, for in several early societies the Latin cross was a primary phallic symbol. Its mythological alter ego, the Tree of Life, is still a metaphor for male genitals among the Arabs. Phallic-masculine meanings of the cross are broadly hinted at in the fifth-century Gospel of Nicodemus, which says Jesus descended into hell and redeemed Adam, together with Old Testament patriarchs, prophets, and forefathers, by making the sign of the cross on their foreheads. "He took them and leaped up out of hell."[6] No mention was made of Eve, matriarchs, or foremothers.

It was also claimed that Golgotha, the "Place of the Skull," was the burial place where Adam's skull lay directly under the cross so the **blood** of Jesus could drip on it, thus washing away the original sin (again, there was no mention of Eve). Official theology was always vague about whether Jesus' death had really washed away original sin or not. If not, then there seemed to have been little point in the sacrifice; but if so, then there would have been no need for a church.

1. Whittick, 226. 2. Abelard, 54,
3. d'Alviella, 14–15. 4. Baring-Gould, 355.
5. Mâle, 153. 6. Hall, 100.

Lunar Swastika

This swastika design from Knossos shows fretted arms turning counterclockwise like the arms of the Hindu *sauwastika*, which was also expressive of the moon's retrograde path. The counterclockwise (widdershins) direction was always viewed as female, lunar, mysterious, and sacred. The curled arms of the lunar swastika suggest Cretan **labyrinth** patterns.[1]

1. d'Alviella, 71.

Lunate Cross

A magic sign of protection, the lunate cross seems to defend its center with crescent moon horns directed outward. The sign was used by northern European shamans, for whom the four crescents may have represented four phases of the moon or four positions of the moon in the heavens, depending on the season.

Magic Square

The familiar design of the Magic Square
is the basis of that ageless game, tic-tac-toe,
beloved by nearly all children until
they discover that the first player can always win. Before it became a grade-school
pastime, this nine-lobed figure was
known as the Square of **Saturn,** considered
mysterious and magical because of
the way numbers could be arranged in it
to add up to the same sum across
every row, down every column, and
through both diagonals. The simple Magic
Square in the illustration is based on
the number 5—which appears at the center—and always totals 15. Larger Magic
Squares have more compartments and total higher numbers.

The Magic Square was important in
medieval numerology, was often used as an
amulet, and was thought to conceal
mystic revelations about the natural world.
Certain secret societies in the Middle
Ages referred to it as the Cabala of the
Nine Chambers. Each compartment contained a mystic letter or other symbol.
Read together in a certain way, the signs
conveyed an occult message. Doubtless this
tincture of forbidden magic did much
to ensure the symbol's survival, even
though its old meanings evaporated as it
became a children's game.

Maltese Cross

The island of Malta had one of the
world's oldest **Goddess** temples. The cross
associated with this island was another of
those designs that direct attention to
a center or *omphalos* such as ancient
Goddess temples displayed. One can see
the Maltese cross as a two-dimensional
version of either a flat-topped or a
pointed pyramid, the sides separated from
one another along the corners so as
to spread out the diagram on a flat surface.

Like all other varieties of crosses,
this one too was adopted by Christianity
and declared to have no other meaning than
a variation on the Christian cross.[1]

1. d'Alviella, 265.

Mary

One of the symbols of the Virgin Mary
reveals the reason that four-leaf clovers were
considered "lucky." The four-leaf clover
design in Mary's sign develops from a
Maltese cross, and also includes symbols
of night and day (or dark and full
moons) while it points to the four directions.[1] As a pagan design, which it
used to be, this probably referred to the
four solar turning-points of the year and the
nocturnal "eves" when their celebrations
were held.

Pagan symbols often became "lucky" in
a nonpagan society that refused to
recognize their original sense, just as the

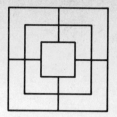

Goddess Fortuna became Lady Luck, and a rabbit's foot became a charm instead of a sacred talisman of the Moon-hare. The basic paganism of Mary as a composite of the ancient **Goddess** images led church fathers to oppose her worship most bitterly in the early centuries, and to declare heretical those who claimed she was truly divine.[2] Anastasius insisted that she must never be called Mother of God, for "it is impossible that God should be born of a woman."[3] Nevertheless, people went right on calling her Mother of God. Eventually, realizing her powerful hold on the masses, churchmen themselves adopted all manner of extravagant praises of the ancient Goddess, newly applied to Mary. She was declared "queen of heaven, empress of hell, lady of all the world."[4] The *Office of the Virgin* even made her the world's primal being, "created from the beginning and before the centuries."[5]

Therefore it was perhaps not so strange that Mary should be symbolized by a sign of the old Goddess who established the four **elements** and the four directions at the same time that she gave birth to all the gods.

1. Lehner, 108.   2. Briffault 3, 183.   3. de Riencourt, 150.   4. Scot, 348.   5. Mâle, 238.

Morris Square

The Morris square, also known as the Mill, is the board used for the modern game of Morris, a simple procedure for placing counters on the lines, reminiscent of tic-tac-toe. As a sacred figure in ancient Celtic paganism, it was called the Triple Enclosure, delineating the center of the world with the four quarters, four cardinal directions, four **elements,** four **winds,** four **rivers** of paradise, and so on emanating from the holy Mill or **Cauldron** at the center.[1] Like many other remnants of pagan religion, it was secularized by Christian opposition and therefore passed into folklore and children's pastimes.

1. Huxley, 169.

Nandyavarta

The Nandyavarta symbol is a Hindu **labyrinth** design based on the **lunar swastika.** If one allows the eye to follow one line inward from its free end at a corner, it leads by a devious route into the center, where there is a choice of three other routes to be taken in the outward direction. The symbolism points to a penetration of "inner mysteries," that is, a revelation to be found in the Holy of Holies in a temple, or in the womb, or in the unconscious mind.[1]

1. d'Alviella, 42.

Pointed Cross

The pointed cross is a rather elegant variation on the **Latin cross.** Its other name is *cross fitchy,* which meant "fixable," as a sharpened spike stuck into the ground. Military symbols and family emblems sometimes appeared on stakes or spikes designed to stand upright at an outdoor position and identify those who occupied a tent or campsite.

Protection Cross

This is a runic figure used by Icelandic magicians. Like the **lunate cross** that it resembles, the protection cross obviously "defends the center" with threatening crescent **horns** or **tridents** directed outward in all four directions. Crosslines on the shafts of the cross are symbolic shorthand for blocking, shielding, or preventing the passage of some entity or power; thus the protection cross makes its center doubly "safe."

Quatrefoil

The supposed good-luck magic of the four-leaf clover descended from pagan reverence for the quatrefoil, one of several **world symbols** similar to those of the Gnostics. In this design the four realms of north, east, south, and west are implied by joined circles, with their four elemental spirits, guardians, peoples, and lands merged into the center. The design is very simply constructed, of circles drawn around each corner of a square and allowed to overlap.

Rattlesnake Swastika

This rattlesnake swastika design from a Mississippian Indian burial mound recalls the reverence in which poisonous snakes used to be held, both as essential elements in the natural scheme of things, and as potentially dangerous spirits possessing the power of life-renewal. Around a solar cross lie four spirit-rattlesnakes, having not only rattles on their tails but also strange doglike faces, mouselike ears, humanlike teeth, and stylized wings. These were connected with the winged or feathered **serpent** deities of Mexico and Central America.[1]

1. Campbell, W.A.P., 216.

RATTLESNAKE SWASTIKA
from Indian burial mound

ROMAN SWASTIKA

ROSE CROSS

Roman Swastika

Like the **cross voided,** the Roman style of
swastika can be seen two ways: as a
long-armed black swastika with extra,
shorter gamma-shaped arms; or as a large
bulky swastika with white stripes at
its centers. Sometimes this figure was
viewed as a kneeling man with arms
upraised in worship.

Rose Cross

In view of the ubiquitous female and
male symbolism of the **rose** and the cross,
respectively, one might well assume
that the cross with a central rose used to be
a bisexual sign, comparable to the
Celtic cross and the **ankh.** It was usual in
Christian iconography to associate
the cross with Christ and the rose with
Mary, but this would not preclude
a concept of their sexual union in the
mystical sense. Pagan saviors nearly always
begot their next incarnations on their
own mother, the **Goddess.** If Christ was
God, then he was also a similar amalgam
of son and spouse in the same entity.

A unique legend grew out of the symbol
of the rose cross, and out of the legend
grew an organization, the Order of the
Rose Cross (Rosicrucians). The order was
first heard of in A.D. 1614, with the
publication of a mysterious document
called *Fama Fraternitatis*, which purported to record the journey of one Christian Rosenkreuz (Rose-Cross) during
the fourteenth century. In Fez, Damascus,
and Egypt, he learned a body of occult
wisdom that he later imparted to seven
other men. All eight scattered to different
countries, vowing that their order would
remain entirely secret for a hundred years.

It was claimed that Rosenkreuz
lived to the age of 106 and died in 1484.
For 120 years his tomb remained hidden.
When it was finally discovered, within it
were found written versions of the
basic teachings of the Rosicrucian order:
that is, the *Fama.* This material was
translated into English in 1652.

Although the figure of Rosenkreuz
seems to have been purely mythical, and
his legend apocryphal to say the least, the
Rosicrucians have continued to practice, off
and on, for the past three centuries in
several European countries and the
United States.

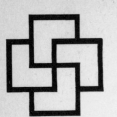

Runic Swastika

The runic version of the swastika appeared on pagan tombstones in Scandinavia.[1] The closed arms may have conveyed the idea of a return to the earth and a recycling, which was the ancients' usual conception of death as a reabsorption into the **womb** of Mother Earth or Mother Sea. The swastika and many crosslike variations were used throughout Teutonic paganism. An elaborate scabbard of the seventh century shows the cross and the swastika side by side as emblems of magical regeneration.[2]

1. d'Alviella, 39. 2. Davidson, G.M.V.A., 83.

Saint Peter's Cross

For almost two thousand years, the Roman church "infallibly" taught that its alleged founder, Saint Peter, was crucified in Rome on a cross that was turned upside down at his own request. Therefore, Saint Peter's emblem became a **Latin cross** upside down. However, even modern Catholic scholars now admit that this crucifixion story is "very uncertain," which is the modern Catholic scholar's expression for any of the church's long-held tenets that turn out to be simply untrue.[1]

The fact is that no one knows where, when, or how Saint Peter died, or even whether he lived at all. The so-called Petrine passage in the Gospel of Matthew, about Peter's acquisition of the symbolic keys, was forged and inserted during the third century A.D. for political reasons.[2] The church never did have any continuous record of popes or "bishops of Rome" from the beginning; most of the early popes were fictions. Even the New Testament accounts of Peter's acts and the epistles bearing his name seem to be apocryphal.[3]

The symbol of the upside-down cross had a curious development in the Middle Ages. Instead of preserving an aura of holiness from the Saint Peter legend, it became known as a sign of unholiness. Churchmen claimed that witches turned the cross upside down to signify contempt for it. Witches also denied Christ, which medieval inquisitors considered so terrible a crime that only burning at the stake would do for its punishment. Yet denial of Christ was exactly what the biblical Saint Peter did also, three times in one night (John 18:17–27). The Gospel story was something of an embarrassment, but was allowed to stand as an example of Christ's power of forgiveness. Unfortunately, the church allegedly founded by the erring Peter did not display the same spirit.

1. Attwater, 274. 2. Reinach, 240.
3. Attwater, 275.

SQUARE

SUNBIRD SWASTIKA
from a Mississippian Indian mound, Oklahoma

SWASTIKA

Solar Swastika

This variation on the swastika depicts the turning of the year with its four solar festivals, the equinoxes and the solstices. The solar swastika is the Gnostic **world symbol** with four of its shafts erased, to convey a more definite feeling of movement. Therefore it was often viewed as an emblem of the inexorable progress of time.

Square

The square or quadrangle was "emblematic of the four corners of the earth. Thus, sunrise, sunset, midday and midnight, the equinoxes and the solstices, and the four cross-quarter days marking the seasons are all bound together in the unity of the symbol."[1] To this day the square is still emblematic of down-to-earth honesty and truth. It has generated many figures of speech: four-square, square deal, square shooter, on the square, and so on, implying trustworthiness. A town square is still supposed to be the public center, like the ancient agoras and central meeting places once considered the heart of the tribal spirit.

In astrology, the sign of the square means a distance of ninety degrees, since all four corners of a square are ninety-degree angles.

1. Brennan, 182.

Sunbird Swastika

The sun swastika formed of four mythological long-beaked birds has been found in Native American burial mounds. In view of the numerous connections between archaic Native American symbols and those of the Orient, it is possible that this solar bird is related to the **Garuda** of southeastern Asia, who flew up like the Promethean eagle to steal the sun's fire for the benefit of humanity.

Swastika

Named from the Sanskrit "so be it," or "amen," the swastika has been a religious emblem of worldwide occurrence since at least 10,000 B.C.[1] It appeared on the oldest coinage in India, on images of Buddha in Japan, and on Greek and Roman figures of the Great Goddess. On artifacts dating from the thirteenth century B.C. onward, the swastika has been found in Asia Minor, Greece, China, Persia, Libya, Scandinavia, Britain, and Iceland. It was still used as a magic sign in Europe up to the beginning of the twentieth century.[2]

A swastika with arms pointing clockwise was generally regarded as a solar emblem. A counterclockwise one (*sauvastika*)

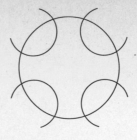

represented the moon, night, and the feminine principle.

The swastika was much used in medieval church decoration and heraldry, where it was known as the *croix gammée*, fylfot, gamma cross, or *croix cramponnée* ("hook cross," German *Hakenkreuz*). It was adopted by Hitler's Third Reich on the supposition that it was a "pure Aryan" sign. This was not true, although a variant eight-armed swastika had long represented German anti-Semitic secret societies like the *Vehmgericht*. A twelve-tailed German swastika appeared in magic books as a victory charm.[3]

1. Campbell, *F.W.G.*, 147. 2. d'Alviella, xi, 33–40. 3. Lehner, 99.

Tetrascele

A tetrascele is a **swastika** with arms softened by curves or by naturalistic figures: human arms or legs, animal heads, wings, serpents, or any similar design. The horse-headed example in the illustration comes from a Gallic coin. It is interpreted as a symbol of the sun **chariot**: "the four fiery steeds which draw the chariot of Helios."[1] The sun disc appears at the center.

1. d'Alviella, 58.

Wishing Well

The wishing well shown in the illustration is a runic charm from Iceland, obviously originating in a lunar context because the four "dippers" into the well are crescent moons. Iceland retained matriarchal symbols and practices longer than any country on the European continent, because of its isolation and its age-old tradition of respect for the priestess or wise-woman. Springs and **wells** of all kinds used to be guarded, served, and honored by groups of sacred women. Making a wish, followed by an offering to the well, was a form of prayer to the resident Water-goddess. People still throw coins into wells or fountains to make a wish, but they have forgotten why.

The moon-shaped dippers recall the medieval opinion that even after Christianity become their official religion, women were supposed not to pray to God for what they wanted, but to pray to their own deity, Mother Moon.[1]

1. de Lys, 458.

Witch Charm

Also known as the Magic Knot, the witch charm had many variations using various proportions of the circle to the four interlaced *vesicas*. Apparently it suggested the four winds under female control, because the *vesica* as a female-genital symbol always implied control of the forces of nature. Connected with the concept of the magic knot was the medieval conviction that witches could control the winds, raise storms, and otherwise influence the weather by making knots with cords, threads, or their own hair. Witches' knots could also function as love charms, "binding" or "loosing" the passions according to the treatment of the interlaced design.

On the same principle that made the sign of the **devil's horns** a prophylactic charm against evil spirits, so also the witch charm became a sign of protection against malefic witchcraft.[1] The theory behind this usage seems to have been one of fighting fire with fire.

1. Koch, 33; Lehner, 99.

Wolf's Cross

This cross was an old Nordic calendrical sign, representing the first month of each New Year, which was known as Wolf Month (in Saxon, Wulf-Monat). As a variation of the **swastika** that implied annual sun cycles, the Wolf's Cross probably announced each new journey of the sun out of its northernmost recession under the guidance of Fenrir, the Wolf of the North. Sometimes the constellation surrounding the north star (Ursa Minor) was envisioned as a dog or wolf. Canines were supposed to have a special relationship with the mystic **gates** of life and death, especially in northern countries.

Under the influence of Christianity, the name of Wolf Month was changed to After-Yule, or Jesu-Monat.

World Symbol

This sign was thought to represent the four elements, which appeared in medieval alchemy as four circles, marked to distinguish them from one another (see **Elements**).[1] By extension the world symbol meant "everything that exists," the entire world order, held together by a mysterious, unseen central force that the Hindus called Maya—the Goddess who created the material universe. In another interpretation of the symbol, the circles might represent the bases of the four colossal **pillars** that were supposed to uphold the heavens, while the pillars could be seen in perspective, converging on the central point called *axis mundi* or the Pole of the World.

1. Koch, 93.

Wotan's Cross

Wotan's cross was another version of the
ubiquitous cross-and-circle, male-
and-female symbols of cosmic union.
Geographically, it stood for the round of
the earth horizon with the four directions
meeting at the center. In celestial
terms, it stood for the sun embraced by
the round of heaven, and so was sometimes called the sun cross.[1]

In cabalistic lore, this sign was described
as the union of the (female) Rose with
the (male) Cross.

1. Koch, 94.

5

MULTIPOINTED
MOTIFS

D esigns with five, six, seven, or more points around a central focus are esthetically interesting. Their radiant symmetry draws the eye toward the center, even when the center is blank. In an archetypal way, the multipointed motif suggests a secret hidden behind appearances—the outward shapes—which can draw everything together from all directions at once. Perhaps this is why multipointed motifs have been so often associated with ideas of the divine.

From flowers to starfish, nature shows us many multipointed shapes. Human artists have long observed and copied such shapes. Islam forbade artists to portray living beings, so Islamic designers perforce developed an entire esthetic of multipointed motifs interlocked in complex patterns, to lead the eye over large areas like walls, floors, domes, screens, carpets, and other surfaces. Medieval Arabic methods of wedding geometry and art have given us some of the world's most visually intriguing objects.

As some of the simple design units in this section show, there is esthetic satisfaction in following a line through its intersections with other lines. If such eye travel eventually returns to the starting place, it seems especially fitting. A cycle is completed. A lesson has been taught without a word spoken. Endless lines in a radial pattern have something hypnotic about them, which may explain why such patterns have been universally credited with the power to repel evil forces, and to invite enlightenment from within.

Cinquefoil

The flowerlike five-petaled cinquefoil imitates many plant forms, in particular such consistently female-symbolic items as the **apple** and the **rose,** which were associated with worship of the Great Goddess in antiquity, and with worship of her ideological descendant Mary in the Christian era. Five was the number officially sacred to Mary. It was also the number of the sacred rose, which used to represent **Venus**-Aphrodite and her temple hierodules, who provided sexual demonstrations of her transcendent love.[1] The cinquefoil therefore stood for sexual secrets. Often used as an element of interior design, it conveyed hidden meanings.

1. Wilkins, 108, 136.

Double Furka

The **furka** was the Y-shaped cross on which Egypt's god Set was crucified, signifying his passage into the underworld for his season of eclipse, until the turning of the year should again resurrect him. Thus the combination of two Y-shaped figures, one upward and one downward, stood for the full cycle of the seasons and the fundamental unity of nature.

This six-pointed figure was also associated with Roman and Greek images of the **Goddess** as a ruler of time, a component of the sign of **Juno,** in her Crone forms as Minerva or Anna Perenna. It is said of the double furka that it "radiates strength," and "though itself motionless, generates motion all around it."[1] In astrology, the double furka is a sextile sign.[2]

1. Koch, 7.   2. Lehner, 56.

Double Square

Since the **square** was often interpreted as the quintessential sign of orderliness, the breaking of its lines by another square, set askew, was sometimes viewed as a sign of disorder, or at least of intrusion.[1] Then

again, the double square was seen as a union of disparate principles, as in the **hexagram, yang and yin,** or **double furka.** In a sense the natural universe itself could be alluded to by an interweaving of order and disorder (ninety-degree and forty-five-degree angles), which ultimately created a harmonious design.

1. Koch, 13.

Eightfold Interlacement

Interlacement patterns were always popular magic charms, because the endless line drew the eye around and around the figure without any break; thus the pattern could become a yantra for meditation or even to induce a trance. Among the magical properties of this design were its twelve small triangles (the zodiacal twelve) and central diamond or square, around which the apexes of four larger triangles interlock with one another. Therefore, the design covers not only eight points but also many references to the mystic threes and fours.

The eightfold interlacement pattern was related to Buddhism's concept of the

Eightfold Path, consisting of right con-duct, right contemplation, right effort, right faith, right occupation, right resolve, right self-awareness, and right speech. Connected with such sets of eight were varying lists of the Eight Precious Things. According to at least one of these lists, they were: a book, coin, mirror, pearl, artemisia leaf, jade gong, musical lozenge and rhinoceros horn.[1]

   1. G. Jobes 1, 495.

Fixed Star

An eight-pointed star, usually black, indicated the fixed stars in ancient astrol-ogy.[1] The term *fixed stars* really means all stars. What the skywatchers of antiquity believed to be wandering—or nonfixed—stars were the other planets of our own solar system, which look like stars to the naked eye, but continually shift their positions against the background of the constellations. This perpetual restless movement made them the objects of much attention, and the planets still hold great significance in astrological lore.

   1. Lehner, 56.

Flower of Aphrodite

The Flower of Aphrodite is composed of six *vesicas* within a shape resembling a cobweb. The design is simply executed by establishing the six points at sixty-degree intervals on a circle, then drawing arcs through the center using each of the six points in turn as the fulcrum. Six was the sexual number especially sacred to the Goddess Aphrodite; Pythago-reans called six the perfect number, or The Mother. Because of its feminine-divine and sexual connotations, Christian authorities called six "the number of sin."[1]

   Some of the old magic of Aphrodite's flower still clung, however, up to the twentieth century, when it was found on the special amulets worn by women in Arabia and northern Africa during pregnancy: an unconscious appeal to the Mother to facilitate motherhood again—or still.[2]

   1. Baring-Gould, 652.   2. Budge, A.T., pl. VIII.

Hexagram

Though now widely accepted as the emblem of Judaism, and given such names as Magen David, Star of David, and Solomon's Seal, the hexagram has been officially Jewish for only about a century.[1] At the time that stories about David and Solomon were being written into the Bible, the hexagram had nothing to do with either of them. It was then revered in India as a symbol of the perpetual sexual union between Kali (the downward-pointing triangle) and Shiva (the upward-pointing triangle) that was supposed to maintain life in the universe.[2]

The hexagram reached Judaism by a devious route, passing through the Tantric influence on medieval Jewish cabalists, who spoke of the desired reunion between God and his spouse, the **Shekina** (a Semitic version of Kali-Shakti). This reunion was symbolized by the Tantric sexual **mandala.** Hence the curious rabbinical tradition that the Ark of the Covenant contained not only the tablets of the law but also "a man and woman in intimate embrace, in the form of a hexagram."[3]

In India the male-female union also meant a union of the elements **fire** and **water,** which were considered, respectively, male and female. So the hexagram also meant fertilization of the primordial female Deep by "fire from heaven," the phallic **lightning.** In alchemy the same symbol meant alcohol (fire-water), based on a belief that alcohol was water somehow infused with heat.[4]

The hexagram appeared also in the New World. At Uxmal in Yucatan it is a symbol of the sun shedding its rays on earth.[5]

1. Trachtenberg, 141. 2. Jung, 240.
3. Silberer, 197. 4. Whittick, 246.
5. d'Alviella, 226.

Magic Hexagram

Medieval magicians always favored interlacement patterns, constructed of a single unbroken line, because of their belief that such patterns were protective, offering no "gates" for evil spirits to enter. Magic ceremonies could hardly take place without some such pattern being first drawn on the ground around the working space, to preserve those within from spiritual dangers.

Though the **pentacle** was perhaps the most popular interlacement pattern for such purposes, the **hexagram** too was widely respected, especially in cabalistic circles. The hexagram, however, consists of two triangles that, though interlaced, are entirely separate from each other. Therefore it is not formed of a single unbroken line. Because some thought that the power of the hexagram

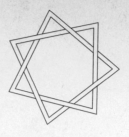

was weakened by this circumstance, a "magic" version was invented, with one line connecting the hexagram's six points in such a way that the line need never be broken.

Microcosmic Man

This was a favorite symbol among medieval wizards, alchemists, and philosophers: man the microcosm, man as the basic magic **pentacle.** It was considered an illustration of the theological principle "as above, so below," and also a graphic demonstration of the idea that man is the measure of all things. In other words, man is the world, the world is man, and his genitals are the center of the universe. There are echoes of this idea throughout every patriarchal society even today.

Microcosmic Man was so familiar in books of "natural science," with his encircling cosmos and pentacle, that Gypsies, witches, and other practitioners adopted the image itself as a magic charm. A Gypsy method of healing was called measuring the pentacle. It consisted of stretching a string to the patient's five extremities as shown on Microcosmic Man's pentacle, then steeping the string in healing waters, or burning it and mixing the ashes in water, to make a potion for the patient to drink.[1]

1. Gifford, 87–88.

Mystic Star

In a magical version of the **Eucharist,** medieval sorcerers used to recite seven divine names seven times over a cup of wine, then drink the wine thus consecrated.[1] This echoed the ancient ritual of invoking seven planetary spirits, who became the Seven Angels of Gnostic Christianity mothered by **Sophia,** according to Irenaeus. Collectively, they also became a sevenfold mystery-god sometimes known as Iao Hebdomai, whose star interlaced seven points. These mystical ideas may be traced back to Akkadian *maskim* or creative spirits: "They are seven! They are seven! In the depths of the ocean, they are seven! In the brilliancy of the heavens, they are seven!"[2]

Seven spirits were supposed to act as guardians to wizards who operated within the inscribed Mystic Star. This seven-pointed design, like the **pentacle,** formed a continuous interlacement. Therefore it was usually regarded as an effective protection against evil influences and rival magicians. Numerous mystic sevens include the seven deadly sins, seven churches of Asia, seven sacraments, seven days of creation, seven ages of man, seven pillars of wisdom, seven liberal arts, seven virtues, seven wonders of the world.

1. Trachtenberg, 123. 2. Wedeck, 23.

Ninefold Goddess

Like the **Star of the Muses,** that of the
Ninefold Goddess recalls many sacred female nonads in mythology and folklore, and
becomes a magic sign by invocation of
them. But while the Star of the Muses
consists of three interlocked triangles, the
sign of the Ninefold Goddess is composed
of a single unbroken line, covering
all sections of the figure in the accepted
tradition of continuous enclosures
representing spiritual protection.

This design is created by drawing every
line from each point to the fourth
next point around the star's circumference.
By contrast, the Star of the Muses is
created by drawing every line from each
point to the third next point. Despite
their appearance of complexity, both
designs are easily executed on a circle divided into forty-degree arcs (9 × 40
= 360). Such designs represent nine-way
world divisions, like the Nine Worlds
of Norse myth: Muspellheim, Asaheim,
Ljosalfaheim, Vanaheim, Manaheim
(Midgard), Jotunheim, Svartalfaheim,
Helhiem, and Niflheim, the worlds of
fire, the gods, the light elves, the sea,
earth dwellers, giants, dark elves, the dead,
and the mists.

Another reason for the sacredness of
nine in Arabic numbers is that the digits
of every multiple of nine add up to
nine again. $2 \times 9 = 18 (1 + 8)$; 3×9

$= 27 (2 + 7)$; $4 \times 9 = 36 (3 + 6)$; $5 \times 9 = 45 (4 + 5)$; $6 \times 9 = 54 (5 + 4)$; $7 \times 9 = 63 (6 + 3)$; $8 \times 9 = 72 (7 + 2)$; $9 \times 9 = 81 (8 + 1)$; $10 \times 9 = 90 (9 + 0)$. The second
decade of multiples add up to twice nine,
the third decade to three nines, and
so on.

Octagram

The central motif of the octagram is two
squares, interlaced—one straight upright,
the other diagonal, so the combination may
be seen as a square and a diamond.
These two figures alone are separate from
one another, as are the two triangles
in the basic hexagram. The desirable con-
tinuous-line, "gateless" design is achieved by
extending all eight sides of the squares
until they meet at the points of an eight-
pointed star. On contemplation it seems
mysterious that a figure with an even
number of termini should be formed of a
continuous line, which may account
for the magical implications so often drawn
from the octagram.[1]

In a religious context, the octagram was
usually said to represent the idea of
regeneration.[2]

1. Hornung, 213. 2. Lehner, 108.

Penelope's Web

Penelope's Web is an interesting pattern of ten small **pentacles** ranged around a central wheel of ten spokes. All the pentacles together are composed of only two lines, as can be seen by following their interlaced paths with the eye. This is a sign of protection like the simple pentacle, made even more suggestively defensive by the ring of twenty outward-facing points, and the lines of connection drawing all sections together in the center, as a unifying cause or concept draws people together for the preservation of all.

The mythological figure of Penelope is especially associated with preservation and protection because it was she, with her consistent refusal to cut the **thread** of life, who preserved the life of her husband Odysseus through his many adventures, even after a death curse had been been laid on him by the Trojan queen and high priestess of Hecate.[1] Penelope, whose name means "Veiled One," was really a title of the Fate-goddess who could determine men's destinies by the treatment of her woven threads. When she cut, the man would die. According to Homer, Penelope unwove her web each night rather than cut the thread that represented Odysseus; and so he escaped all dangers and eventually returned to his home.

1. Graves, G.M. 2, 341.

Pentacle

The most widely revered of all esoteric symbols, the pentacle has received many alternate names: pentalpha, pentagram, Solomon's seal, Star of Bethlehem, Three Kings' star, wizard's star, Star of Logres, devil's sign, witch's cross, goblin's foot, or (in Germany) *Drudenfuss*, the Druid's Foot.[1] From this assortment of names it can be seen that the pentacle is associated with magic, paganism, deviltry, and Christian mysticism all together.

In ancient times, the pentacle meant "life" or "health." It was derived from the apple-core pentacle of the Earth Mother. To this day, Gypsies cut an apple transversely to reveal the pentacle, which they call the Star of Knowledge.[2] The pentacle was sacred to the Celtic death-goddess Morgan and was carried in her honor on a blood-red shield, according to the tale of *Gawain and the Green Knight*. It is still the sign of the **earth** element in the Tarot suit of pentacles, which evolved into the modern suit of diamonds. With one point downward, the pentacle was supposed to represent the head of the Horned God.

The pentacle not only forms a continuous, "gateless" protection sign; it also relates to numerological mysticism. To draw a pentacle, one divides a circle into five arcs of seventy-two degrees each. Seventy-two is the prime magic number, divisible by all other numbers from 1 to 9 except for 5 itself, and the other magic number, 7; it is also divisible by the zo-

diacial number, 12, and multiples of 12 by 2, 3, and 6. So magical was 72 that one of the most durable myths about the origin of the Bible called it the Book of Seventy-Two (Septuagint), claiming that it had been translated from Hebrew to Greek in the third century B.C. by seventy-two scholars simultaneously, and that each version was precisely the same as all seventy-one others. This silly story was an article of Christian faith throughout the Middle Ages.

During the Middle Ages it was also said that witches and pagans used the pentacle to make the sign of the cross. Hence the name, witch's cross. Since the pentacle was thought to be such a powerful protection sign, it is quite possible that people used to cross themselves with a pentacle as much as, or more than, with a four-pointed cross or a Hermetic 4. The self-blessing with a pentacle is done with the right hand, as follows: touch the left breast, the forehead, the right breast, the left shoulder, the right shoulder, and finally the left breast again to complete the last point of the pentacle.

1. Trachtenberg, 141; Huson, 225.   2. Derlon, 157.

Pentacle Flower

The two separate components of this design are (1) a pentacle and (2) a flower-like form of five lobes created by extending the sides of a smaller pentacle past their points and out into a wider space. Each motif is precisely interlaced with itself in the usual over-and-under fashion; in addition, the two are interlaced with each other. Flower and star together indicate earth and heaven.

This and other variations on the pentacle sometimes represented the Goddess's five stations of feminine life: birth, menarche, maternity, menopause, death. When these stations were adapted to the use of both sexes, they were usually listed as birth, initiation (puberty), marriage, rest from labor, and death.[1]

1. G. Jobes 1, 577; 2, 1668.

Ringed Pentacle

A pentacle interlaced with five rings was considered a highly mystical combination: points and circles, male and female, the unity of perpetual combination as in the **Egg and Dart Frieze**. This handsome design also forms an interesting **mandala** of over-and-under weaving that carries the eye through endless meditation.

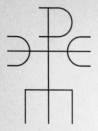

Spell Symbol

The spell symbol is a runic charm once used by northern European magicians to prevent adverse spells cast by a rival magician. It is a bare-bones stick-figure stylization of a human being with defensive power in both hands. The gender may be either male or female. The base of the figure can suggest a skirt or a broad female pelvis, or else the central "leg" might mean a phallus. Perhaps, according to the ancient tradition of bisexuality among wizards, both are intended.

Star

The ancients generally regarded stars as living entities: sometimes heavenly **angels**, sometimes legendary heroes, sometimes the souls of the unborn or the souls of the dead, newly provided with "astral" (starry) bodies made of that mysterious nonexistent star-stuff called ether, the Greeks' fifth **element** that was supposed to be lighter, finer, and more volatile than fire. This ethereal body was the one Gnostics referred to when they spoke of Jesus and other holy persons given "bodies of light" for their lifetimes in heaven.

Some traditions located each person's soul in a star as a matter of routine, or else assigned an external soul to one of the stars in heaven, in addition to the soul that occupied the earthly body. Psychic dangers were attributed to perilous passages in the life cycle "when a man's star is low." Jewish scriptures maintained that "every affair in which a man is engaged here on earth is first indicated up above by the angel of his star"—another instance of the ubiquitous "as above, so below" theory underlying both astrology and eschatology.[1]

Several names of the **Goddess**, as Queen of Heaven and mother of stars, identified her with the morning star: **Astarte**, Astraea, Esther, **Ishtar**, **Venus**, Stella Maris, Diana Lucifera. The same star also came to represent her male counterpart, known to biblical writers as Lucifer ("Light-bringer"), Son of Morning, appearing in Isaiah 14:12 as God's rival. Oddly enough, the same morning star also appears in the Bible as God's son, Jesus (Revelation 22:16).

The standard image of a star was five-pointed, like the **pentacle**. Its natural prototypes were the five-pointed star in the apple core, and five-petaled flowers like the apple blossom and the rose, all of which were originally sacred to the Goddess. Her five-pointed star remained preeminent in the Middle East even after the advent of patriarchal Islam, whose banners adopted it. That star appears even today on the flags of many nations that have been touched by this tradition of pre-Islamic Arabia: Syria, Turkey, Iraq, Yemen, Jordan, Albania, Yugoslavia, Russia, Algeria, Morocco, Tunisia, Libya,

Mauritania, Liberia, Senegal, Ghana, Somalia, Pakistan, and Burma, not to mention the United States and other New World nations who simply accepted as a given the worldwide opinion that five is the proper number of points for a star. Of course, real stars do not have points at all, of any number, though one may imagine points from the twinkling effect imparted by the passage of their light through Earth's atmosphere.

A five-pointed star rising triumphant over a cross was the sign of Saint Genevieve, patroness of Paris.[2] Genevieve was another of the phony **saints** whose life story was invented centuries after her purported lifetime, to account for the presence of her cult and relics. As her name of "generator of life" suggests, she was probably a local manifestation of the pagan Goddess who had to be somehow assimilated into the church because the people would not renounce her.

Perhaps the most controversial star in Judeo-Christian myth is the star of Bethlehem, which was considered essential in order to assimilate Jesus to the prophecy of Numbers 24:17: "There shall come a Star out of Jacob." Among the numerous explanations put forward by recent scholars on behalf of this star, it is called a comet, a nova, a supernova, a meteor or meteorite, and the conjunction of two planets. Nothing occurring in the heavens, however, could possibly point to a particular place on the earth's surface: "Neither a comet nor any other type of heavenly body could possibly guide travelers to a particular building. As for meteorites, or 'shooting stars,' which *do* fall to earth, it all happens so fast that the Magi would not have had enough time to pack their lunch, let alone follow the star to Bethlehem."[3]

The whole myth seems to have been based on the Egyptian "three wise men"—the three stars in the belt of Orion—whose rising announced the coming of Sothis, the Star of Osiris: that is, Sirius, the brightest star in the sky, whose coming heralded the annual flood of the Nile.

1. Trachtenberg, 47, 69.   2. Brewster, 52.
3. Arnheim, 27.

Star of the Muses

Sacred women or female spirits in groups of nine occur everywhere in folklore and myth. There were the Muses of classical Greece, the nine Morgans of the Celtic paradise, the nine Korrigen on their sacred isle, the nine moon maidens who created Scandinavian gods, and so on. Medieval superstition sometimes called them *mares*, or *maers*, who dwelt in wild woodlands and might behave like succubae, settling on top of the bodies of sleeping men, choking off their breath, and taking away their power of speech: hence the night-mare. This was a patriarchal reversal of the original powers

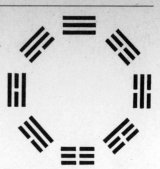

of the Muses, who gave *inspiration* (breathing-in) of the powers of speech and poetry.[1]

The Star of the Muses is a triple trinity, shown as three interlaced triangles. The archaic Muses themselves were at first only three aspects of the Goddess Mnemosyne (Memory), later multiplied again by three. They became the divine **nymphs** guarding the spring of inspiration on Mount Helicon. Classical writers named them Thalia, Clio, Calliope, Terpsichore, Melpomene, Erato, Euterpe, Polyhymnia, and Urania—the last meaning "Celestial One."

Naturally, Christian symbolists appropriated this star of the nine Goddess-forms; so now it is sometimes declared a symbol of the (masculine) Holy Spirit.[2]

1. Trachtenberg, 39. 2. Lehner, 108.

Star of the Seven Sisters

In medieval magic, seven was the most popular number of mystic power after the three.[1] It was often associated with the heavenly Seven Sisters, guardians of the *axis mundi*; they were either the seven bright stars of the pole-encircling Ursa Major, or the Pleiades, whose name is Greek for "a flock of doves." Seven legendary priestesses bearing this name were said to have founded major **oracle-shrines** in the ancient world. In the Middle East, they were the Seven Pillars of Wisdom. In Southeast Asia they were the Krittikas, or Seven Mothers of the

World. Egyptians called them the Seven Hathors, or the "seven beings who make decrees," whom the dead would meet on their journey through the seven **spheres** of the afterlife.[2] Arabians called them the elder Seven Sages, now masculinized but originally female (*imam*, "sage," from *ima*, "mother").[3] In Gnostic lore, the seven pillars were woman-shaped **caryatids** associated with shrines of **Sophia**, mother of wisdom. These too were "seven sisters."

As yet another continuous interlacement design, the Star of the Seven Sisters was popularly used as a defense against outsiders' penetration of one's secrets.

1. Trachtenberg, 119. 2. Budge, E.M., 165.
3. Briffault 1, 377.

Trigrams

These are the eight figures of China's famous *I Ching*, the divinatory "Book of Changes." The trigrams combine the classic four **elements** with four subelements familiar to the human experience: Air/Breath, Water/Sea, Earth/Mountain, and Fire/Thunderbolt (lightning). The original invention of the trigrams was attributed to the culture hero Fu Hsi, who may be dated back to China's matriarchal period because he had no father, only a mother. Like the similar

unfathered Athenian culture hero
Cecrops, he had a **serpent** tail and was
the first man to institute monogamous
marriage.[1] Fu Hsi was mated, however, to
the primal Creatress, China's archaic
Great Mother, Nu Kua, maker of heaven
and earth, the source of his ideas.
Together, with serpent tails entwined, the
Goddess and her spouse created the
skills of civilization and gave them to
humanity.[2]

1. Graves, G.M. 1, 97.   2. Perry, 212.

Twelve-Pointed Interlacement

There are various ways of contemplating
the twelve-pointed interlacement pattern. In
each direction the design can be seen
as three interlocked triangles. If they point
up, there are two above and one below. If they
point down, there are two below and one
above. Thus the trinitarian spirit of
the **Muses**, **Fates**, or **Norns** is invoked by
the six possible ways to view the basic pattern. The open spaces display seven
hexagrams.

Twelve points may be related to the
zodiacal signs, like the original twelve
knights of the Celtic Round Table, who
may have been two seated at each
side of a hexagonal table. Similar arrange-
ments composed the twelve lictors of
Romulus, the Twelve Peers of France, and
the twelve *Namshans* of the Round
Council of the Dalai Lama.[1]

1. Cirlot, 263.

Underworld Sign

In Egyptian hieroglyphics this sign stood
for the Tuat: the underground realm of the
dead.[1] By extension, it also stood for
the nether aspect of the **Goddess**, variously
called Nephthys, Maat, or Hekat the
Crone and Midwife. Five-lobed shapes
generally referred to a female deity. In the
Middle East, she was named Ana.

The same sign became the sigil of her
Christianized form, Saint Anne, patroness of obstetrics.[2] Since Anne was
made the mother of the Virgin Mary—
her earlier pagan combined form having
been Mari-Anna, the Virgin-Crone—she
was credited with the same immaculate
conception as her daughter. That is, she
was supposed to have been born without
the taint of original sin. According to her
legend, though, Saint Anne had three
husbands and innumerable other children
in addition to Mary, most of whom
became various fictitious **saints**. Finding
the doctrine of Anne's immaculate
conception too awkward to uphold theo-
logically, the church eventually reconsi-
dered and rejected it.[3]

1. Budge, E.L., 75.   2. Brewster, 343.
3. Neumann, 57, 59.

Universe

The eight-rayed sun, supported in the center of the dome of heaven, was a popular Gnostic symbol of the universe.[1]
At the core of the design lay the divine **serpent** symbol, the letter S, which was derived from the serpent's recurved body, and whose sibilant sound was an imitation of the serpent's hiss. The serpent was an alter ego of the sun god in many ancient belief systems; he was Python/Apollo, Apep/Ra, Sata/Osiris, Ahriman/Ormazd, and even Ophis/Christ, according to the Ophite-Gnostic Christians. A similar ideogram stood for the heaven-god on cuneiform tablets of Assyria and Babylon.[2]

1. Koch, 22.   2. d'Alviella, 216.

Vehmic Courts

This double **swastika** design represented the medieval Vehmic Courts (*Vehmgericht*) of Austria and Germany, which began as secret civil tribunals for persecuting heretics and Jews, and soon became connected with the Inquisition.[1]
In the nineteenth century, the courts continued as underground societies of summary justice, especially as hotbeds of anti-Semitism. In the twentieth century, the Nazi party took over a variant of the Vehmic symbol and a new version of the old courts' activities.

1. Koch, 95.

6

SACRED OBJECTS

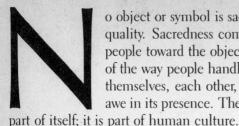o object or symbol is sacred in or of itself, as an inherent quality. Sacredness comes only from the attitude of people toward the object. A thing becomes holy because of the way people handle it or talk about it, teaching themselves, each other, and their children to feel proper awe in its presence. The numinous spirit of the object is not part of itself; it is part of human culture.

Moreover, sacred objects and symbols frequently have no existence whatever outside of human culture. While natural phenomena may sometimes be considered sacred, by far the largest number of holy things are human inventions. The objects discussed in this section are of this manufactured variety. They are, or were, holy only because they were deliberately created for that purpose and for no other.

There is a Chinese saying that the image maker worships no god, because he knows what stuff the gods are made of. And yet there is also a profound human tendency to forget what stuff the gods are made of, in order to invest them with supernatural mana. Once sacralized, an object or symbol seems to take on a life of its own. It becomes usable for magic, divination, meditation, or prayer.

The human impulse to sacralize is everywhere the same. An African tribesman, dancing to propitiate a homemade idol of wood and feathers, is not intrinsically different from a European Catholic fervently clicking a rosary before a plaster statue of the Virgin. Although Catholics may define the former as idolatry and the latter as reverence, words cannot disguise their essential identity. Both persons are sacralizing manufactured objects, by treating them as if they had eyes to see and ears to hear.

For the worshiper to protest that his holy object is "only a symbol" of a more abstract deity is begging the question. Clearly, the object itself is invested with sacred qualities. For example, a patriot feels outrage if an enemy tramples on his country's flag. Obviously this symbolic act does not harm the country. But the flag itself has been sacralized, so that its very cloth seems different from other cloth. Human emotions have been trained to respond to it in a particular way.

An object may be sacralized by only one person (such as a souvenir of a deceased loved one); or it may be sacralized by multitudes (such as the Christian cross). It does not matter how many share in the agreement that any given object shall be holy. The impulse is the same.

Nevertheless, there is always a certain vagueness to the line between sacred and secular. Things may wander back and forth across that line. What began as a secular product of art or nature may become sacralized. Conversely, sacred objects may become secularized in time, when their

religious meanings have been forgotten. The civilized man who worships the plaster Virgin may not take the same reverent attitude toward a Roman statue of Venus, even though the Venus may be greatly superior as a work of art. The people who used to worship Venus in her divine nudity are all dead now, and she has become a secular object. More than that, some of the objects and symbols earnestly worshiped by our ancestors have even become diabolized by centuries of opposition from the prevailing religion, so they are now declared evil rather than holy. This too is a product of human culture. The feeling it produces is a learned response.

The study of sacred objects, past and present, provides insight into the minds that create them and respond to them. Such a study expands the horizons of thought, which may lead to better understanding of the self as well as the rest of humanity.

Aegis

The aegis was the emblem of divine sovereignty among the Greek gods, a goat-skin breastplate dyed red, with oracular **serpents** and the **Gorgon** head. It was usurped by Zeus, but belonged by the longest-established tradition to **Athene,** whose wisdom was embodied in serpents and the serpent-haired Gorgon. The famous Phidian statue of Athene in the Parthenon showed her, not Zeus, wearing the aegis.

Athene was not originally Athenian, but Libyan; and the Medusa head on her aegis was not a gift from the leg-endary Perseus, but a representation of herself as the Libyan Goddess Medusa (Metis), whose snake-haired **mask** was credited with petrifying powers. The aegis was formerly "a magical goat-skin bag containing a serpent and protected by a Gorgon mask."[1] Herodotus said the goat-skin aegis came from the women of Libya.[2]

1. Graves, G.M. 1, 44.   2. Herodotus, 270.

Altar

The pyramidal symbol of an altar dates
from an early representation of the
Holy Mountain, towering into the sky to
achieve close contact with heaven.
Horns were ubiquitous on ancient altars.
They may have been expressive of
the deity's horned head, or the assimilation
of horned animals for sacrificial purposes,
or the traditional idea that sacred persons as
well as sacred structures wore horns in
token of their holiness. The Bible
speaks of altars bearing horns, and of
Moses coming down from the holy mountain with a horned head, according
to the original Hebrew, which translators
usually render "radiant."[1]

Some scholars believe that the altar was
originally a tomb, where offerings
were made to the deified ancestor. The
Christian custom of burying **saints'** relics
under the altar was an outgrowth of
this primitive practice. However, the biblical vision "under the altar the souls
of them that were slain for the word of
God" (Revelation 6:9) came from the pagan belief that the newly dead were
gathered on the borders of the sky, under
the constellation called the Altar.[2]

1. Elworthy, 185.   2. Rose, 289.

Anchor Cross

As a variant of the Egyptian **ankh,** the
anchor cross was adopted by the Christian
community about the fourth or fifth
century A.D. It was associated with other
maritime symbols such as the **fish**
and the ship, as well as with the clergy
self-described as "fishers of men." The
anchor cross was carved on Christian
tombs in the catacombs, but whether it was
a symbol of faith at that time or a
token of seafaring is unknown. Sometimes
it was claimed that the anchor cross
was a magic charm able to prevent any
ship from sinking in a storm.

Ankh

In Egyptian hieroglyphics, the word *ankh*
meant both "life" and "hand mirror."[1] Akin
to the Mirror of Hathor and the Mirror
of Venus, the ankh was originally
a female symbol derived from primitive
Libyan and Phoenician images of
the **Goddess:** a narrow triangle, surmounted by crossbar-arms and an oval
head.[2] It became known in Egypt
as a sign of sexual union and the immortality of gods, granted by the Goddess's
divine **blood.** In token of this, the yonic
loop portion of the design was usually
painted red, while the phallic cross re-

mained white.[3] Egyptian deities of all kinds were shown carrying the ankh as a symbol of the gift of eternal life, promised to their royal or priestly servants.[4]

The ankh was also known as the Key of the Nile, because it represented the mystic union of **Isis** and **Osiris** that was supposed to initiate the annual Nile flood, upon which the life of Egypt depended.

1. Brier, 145.   2. d'Alviella, 186–190.
3. Jung, 55.   4. Budge, A.T., 128.

Ansated Cross

Derived from the Egyptian **ankh,** the ansated cross combined the Tau with an earth symbol. Sometimes it was viewed as a human figure. Like every other kind of cross, it was assimilated to Christianity early in the medieval period.

Apex

The apex was a conical miter worn by the Pontifex Maximus, Rome's high priest, at all times whenever he was outdoors. It symbolized his spiritual power descending from heaven upon his head.[1] Many other gods and godlike beings wore the

apex. Mithra always appeared with a pointed cap on. The Norse god Frey wore a conical cap like the Roman priest's.[2] In Egypt, the god of Heliopolis was said to have arisen out of the primordial water-womb as a conical pointed *benben* stone or pyramidion, prefiguring the pointed tops of the obelisks and the tall, pointed diadem of the pharaohs. Even as late as the nineteenth century A.D., Egyptian **carnival** kings were sacrificed in effigy wearing the tall pointed "fool's cap" in the role of a clown, one of the usual trivialized forms of ancient god-kings.[3]

Medieval European legend gave the pointed cap not only to fools and clowns, but also to those revisions of pagan spirits, the **elves,** pixies, **gnomes,** and **fairies.** During the Inquisition's reign of terror, the paganism of the pointed cap was underlined by its use on the heads of convicted heretics en route to the stake. During the nineteenth century, this erstwhile badge of (1) divine kingship, (2) priesthood, (3) paganism, and (4) heresy attained the final stage of trivialization and became an adjunct of the schoolroom: the "dunce cap" placed as a badge of shame on the heads of children who had failed to learn their lessons.

1. Rose, 209.   2. Davidson, *P.S.*, 134.
3. Campbell, *Or.M.*, 73.

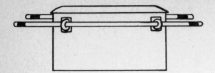

Ark

The word *ark* comes from Latin *arca*, a chest or box, especially one in which secret religious objects were concealed and transported. The Greeks called such a box *cista*, a chest. The biblical references to the ark of the covenant are translated from two different Hebrew words, *tebah* and *aron:* the latter meaning a wooden chest or coffin, the former meaning a box or a flat-roofed building of rectangular shape, twice as long as the height or width; it could also mean a floating box or boat, like the vessel of the infant Moses on the Nile, for which the same word was used.

The idea of the ark of the covenant was copied from the Egyptian, Akkadian, and Chaldean ark-shrines, which held sacred fetishes, usually of a sexual nature, and were borne by poles passed through rings at their sides. Therefore God directed that "Thou shalt put the staves into the rings by the sides of the ark, that the ark may be borne with them" (Exodus 25:14). Another holy object, the *kapporeth* or mercy seat, was associated with the ark but not part of it (Exodus 31:7, 35:12). This seat seems to have been a golden plate flanked by two cherubim, perhaps placed on the lid of the ark for the purpose of rendering judgments.

The ark's contents have been the subject of many different guesses. Some say it contained two idols, male and female; or the brazen **serpent** Nehushtan; or the stone tablets of the law; or symbols of Yahweh and his consort Mari-Anath. At any rate, it was considered so full of *mana* that God struck dead anyone who touched it (2 Samuel 6:7), and even killed 50,070 of his worshipers for looking in it (1 Samuel 6:19). Yet God decided that it should be abandoned and forgotten in the time of Jeremiah: "Neither shall it come to mind: neither shall they remember it; neither shall it be magnified any more" (Jeremiah 3:16). One could assume from this that the ark's symbolism was uncomfortably female, or partly so.

Indeed the Sanskrit *argha* was a female symbol, the pregnant moon-boat that carried the seeds of all life from one universe to the next through the Great Flood of **chaos** between world destruction and world re-creation.[1] The other meaning of the ark, as a floating vessel, was lifted from Babylonian scriptures. Noah was made the tenth descendant of Adam because the Babylonian flood hero was the tenth king.[2] According to the Chaldean scriptures, the god warned the

CADUCEUS
Sumerian,
ca. 2000 B.C.

flood hero to build such a vessel because "by a deluge I will destroy substance and life. Cause thou to go up into the vessel the substance of all that has life."[3]

Even pious scholars have boggled at the myth of Noah's ark because of its sheer absurdity. Excluding species that can live in fresh or salt water, the ark would have had to house 7,000 species of worms, 80,000 species of mollusks, 30,000 species of crustaceans, 50,000 species of arachnids, 900,000 species of insects, 2,500 species of amphibians, 6,000 species of reptiles, 8,600 species of birds, and 3,500 species of mammals, plus food for one and all. The only vessel truly capable of holding all this is Spaceship Earth.

As a footnote to the story of Noah's ark, Gnostic scriptures declared that Eve's daughter Norea burned up the first ark that Noah made, by blowing it with her hot **breath.** So Noah had to start again from scratch.[4] A curious story, hinting that Norea was the elemental **fire** spirit or perhaps a volcano Goddess like Pele in Hawaii.

1. Jobes & Jobes, 121.   2. Frazer, *F.O.T.*, 62–65.   3. Lethaby, 239.   4. Barnstone, 78.

Caduceus

In Mesopotamia, intertwined snakes represented the healing god Ningishzida, one of the lovers of the Goddess **Ishtar.** This god's symbol was "a staff round which a double-sexed, two-headed serpent called Sachan was coiled."[1] Biblical writers renamed the healing **serpent** Nehushtan, worshiping it as an early form of the God of Moses (Numbers 21:9; 2 Kings 18:4). Greeks adopted a similar double-snake symbol for their medicinal god Asclepius.[2] The same healing emblem was found in ancient India, and also in the Americas among Aztec and North American Indians.[3]

Classical Greek writers claimed that **Hermes** inherited the caduceus in his character of Conductor of Souls (Psychopompus); it was said that his magic staff had enough healing power to raise even the dead from Hades and bring them back to the light of day. Early versions of the Hermetic caduceus topped the staff with a solar disc, bearing **horns** in the shape of snake's heads, like the present sigil of Hermes-Mercury.[4] Some devised the story that the caduceus was first invented by the two-sexed sage Teiresias of Thebes, who stuck a cane between two copulating snakes and discovered that their orderly arrangement around this staff provided mystic clues to cosmic

geometry.[5] The symbol was, however, much older than the legend of Teiresias.

This ancient symbol is preserved even today as a universal emblem of the medical profession.

1. La Barre, 82.   2. Zimmer, 74.
3. Campbell, M.I., 282–295.   4. d'Alviella, 228, 231.   5. G. Jobes 2, 1576.

Calvary Cross

This cross was named after Mount Calvary, supposedly the site of Jesus' crucifixion, the mount being represented by the three steps. Long before Christianity, however, similar crosses on steps were dedicated to the god **Hermes,** in his mystery-religion aspect as the **Logos** of Father Zeus. Sometimes the head of the cross was rounded, in the manner of the Egyptian **ankh.**[1]

1. d'Alviella, 194.

Caryatid

A temple **pillar** carved in the shape of a woman, as shown on the Acropolis at Athens, was called *caryatid* after Artemis Caryatis, said to have been modeled on priestesses of the Moon Goddess at Caryae in Laconia.[1] The name referred to a nut tree and was connected with the

myth of the **nymph** Phyllis who was metamorphosed into an almond tree— almonds being a classical female-genital symbol (see **Mandorla**).

In effect, women were the original "pillars of the church" and were often referred to as pillars of wisdom, like the seven pillars of **Sophia** in Proverbs 9:1. Heads of the caryatids literally held up the temple roof. In the manner of the replicated pharaoh images in Egypt, or the crowds of identical Buddhas in Asian temples, the woman-pillars could have been portraits of the same Goddess.

1. Graves, W.G., 372.

Cathedral

Gothic cathedrals were generally known as "Palaces of the Queen of Heaven" or "Our Ladies" because they were dedicated almost exclusively to the Virgin Mary, replacing earlier images of the Great Goddess and in many cases built on the same sites as the Goddess's former shrines. One of Mary's other names was Ecclesia, "The Church," meaning not only the organization but the physical building, in contrast with the phallic-masculine campanile or steeple. Temples and their attendant **pillars** were viewed as female and male, respectively, as far back as early Egypt. In ancient Memphis, the whole temple structure was called by the Goddess's title, Mistress of Life.[1]

As the official name of any church, Ecclesia originally referred to a female political assembly or a parliament of women, first organized during the annual Skira festival in Athens.[2] This meaning was soon forgotten under Christianity, which denied women's spiritual authority altogether; but the men reigning in their all-male church never ceased calling it "she" or Mary-Ecclesia or Bride of Christ. They also "symbolified" every part of their pseudofemale cathedral. The three doors stood for faith, hope, and charity. The central rosette was the Lake of Life, where heaven and earth meet. The four piers that subdivide the facade were the four rivers of paradise. The church's platform represented paradise itself, and hell (personified by **gargoyles**) lay beneath. Church walls were said to signify redemption; the flying buttresses, moral strength; the roof, giving; the pillars, dogmas of the faith; the ribs of the vaults, pathways of salvation; the spires, God's pointing finger; and so on.[3] If the eastern apse represented the male solar spirit, the western facade with its "rose" was female and lunar, usually the location of Mary's emblems (see **Rose Window**).

Cathedrals were built at the holy places of many pagan deities, beginning in the earliest Christian centuries when temples of **Isis, Juno,** Diana, or Minerva were simply usurped and renamed in honor of Mary. Hundreds of the local deities of pagan polytheistic tribes were adopted in the new guise of **saints,** so that the same shrines could be turned to Christian use. Churches were built over famous tombs of pagan heroes, or else some unidentified bones were buried within them and hagiographical myths were created to canonize the remains. "A cathedral without a well-known saint was missing an important source of revenue; and for this reason efforts were made to secure from Rome the canonization of people buried within the fabric; but Rome had to be cajoled, and paid."[4]

The women, after whose assemblies the churches were named and whose Goddess the churches revised, were forbidden to participate in church councils and in some cases even forbidden to enter the church itself. Throughout the Middle Ages women were barred from church buildings if they were menstruating, and for forty days after giving birth. Men claimed these primeval female Mysteries would pollute the sacred precincts—magically, of course. As late as 1886 the Revised Statutes of the Catholic church forbade any woman living apart from her

husband to enter the church, though Bishop Healy of Portland, Maine, approved a ruling that she might enter the church in extremely cold weather, provided she take a back seat.[5]

1. Frankfort, 31.   2. Keuls, 357.   3. Cirlot, 17.   4. Johnson, 226.   5. Gage, 517.

Chrism

Christian artists made the little vessel of chrism the constant symbol of Mary Magdalene, identifying her with Martha's sister Mary who anointed or "christ-ened" Christ with her precious unguent.[1] There was much more to this image than meets the eye. Jesus became a Christ or "Anointed One" through the very process of being anointed by this woman. What she applied was either an oil that she poured over his head (Matthew 26:7) or an ointment that she smeared on his feet (John 12:3). In either case, it was an *anointment*, immediately preceding the triumphal procession in the role of *Christos*; and as Jesus himself said, it was done for his imminent burial (Matthew 26:12; John 12:7). The act was identical with the anointing of a sacred king prior to his immolation. It was the official act of a priestess.

Mary Magdalene and her women further officiated, in the style of priestesses of the traditional sacred drama, by announcing the resurrection of the sacred king to his male followers, who were not allowed to attend in person the vigil by the tomb. The men were even ignorant of the written tradition: "They knew not the scripture, that he must rise again from the dead" (John 20:9). Mary alone was the first to observe and report the alleged miracle. In just such a manner, pagan priestesses had been announcing the resurrection of savior gods like Orpheus, Dionysus, Attis, and Osiris every year for centuries.

Mary Magdalene was described as a harlot; but in those times, harlots and priestesses were often one and the same. A sacred harlot in the Gilgamesh epic was connected with a hero-victim in a similar way: "The harlot who anointed you with fragrant ointment laments for you now."[2] The ceremony of anointment was formerly a woman's office, because it represented a baptismal "birth" into the kingship. In India, kings used to be anointed with the sacred blood of the Goddess Sarasvati, symbolized by the waters of her river, in the rite of *abhishek-aniya*, which was an imitation of birth. Even after male priests took over the ceremony, it was said that the officiating priest caused the king to be born.[3]

Under Christianity, priests soon took

over all the rituals that had been conducted by women, declaring that women had no right to lead any religious ceremony whatever. One of the earliest schisms in the church arose from the protests of women against being baptized naked by male priests, and "anointed with oil" by male hands. Christian women demanded to be baptized by others of their own sex. However, the priests opposed them "strenuously."[4]

1. Malvern, 28, 176. 2. *Epic of Gilgamesh*, 95. 3. Perry, 129. 4. Gage, 215–216.

Colors, Sacred

The original three sacred colors were white, red, and black, signifying the trinity of the **Goddess** as Virgin, Mother, and Crone. In India these colors were known as the *gunas* or "strands," the interweaving threads of living nature, representing the Goddess Prakriti, a title of Kali as the totality of natural forces. The strands of *sattva* (white), *rajas* (red), and *tamas* (black) ran through every life as ordained by **Fate** (*karma*), or the Three Fates, which were yet another manifestation of the same female trinity.

This color symbolism was equally prevalent in Western civilization. Ovid, Theocritus, Horace, and others spoke of the sacred life-threads that were white, red, and black.[1] The same succession of colors appears often in folklore and fairy tales, suggesting an ancient pagan tradition. The Tartar prince Tamerlane conducted his battles by the three-color principle. On the first day of besieging a town he set up a white tent for the Virgin of Mercy, meaning that he would spare the inhabitants' lives if they surrendered. On the second day the tent was red, meaning that only the leaders would be slain. On the third day the tent was black, the color of the Destroying Crone, meaning that all leniency was gone.[2]

Christianity also adopted the three sacred colors, just because they were too familiar to be forgotten. Veils of white, red, and black were laid on Christian altars for three days of Christmas matins.[3] A nineteenth-century *Handbook of Christian Symbolism* actually had the temerity to declare, of these ancient Goddess-symbolic colors, that white is "the first of the canonical colors," representing purity, innocence, virginity, faith, life, and light; red is the color of "suffering and martyrdom for the faith, and the supreme sacrifice of Christ"; and black is "also a canonical color," emblem of death and mourning, to be used in the church on Good Friday.[4]

1. Wedeck, 66. 2. Kunz, 32. 3. Miles, 93. 4. Kunz, 274.

Cornucopia

Cornucopia means Horn of Plenty. It was originally the horn of the Great Mother in her **cow** or **goat** incarnation, as Io, Ceres, Hera, Hathor, and other versions of the sacred cow, or as Amaltheia, the nurse of God (Zeus) in her totemic form as a she-goat. All good things poured forth from the hollow horn, which became a symbolic prayer to the Goddess for ongoing fertility of the earth and an abundance of its fruits. Cornucopiae were liberally used as items of decoration to invoke the blessing of the all-giving Mother on houses, temples, and storehouses. The cornucopia is still a popular decorative motif, although its sacred meanings have been forgotten.

Eastern Cross

The cross shown in the illustration above became identified with the Eastern or Byzantine churches (Russian and Greek Orthodox). Just why the lower crosspiece was placed on a slant remains something of a mystery, though several *ex post facto* explanations have been offered.

Grail, Holy

Although the paganism of the Grail romances was concealed under a thin coating of Christian reinterpretation, scholars now have little doubt that there was no authentic tradition of the lost Last Supper chalice that Christians called the Holy Grail. The vessel was entirely pagan and feminine, another transformation of the Celts' **Cauldron** of Regeneration, the female body-symbolic bowl of life-giving **blood**, often appearing in conjunction with a male symbol just as the Grail appeared in conjunction with the Holy Lance. According to Weston, the lance and cup are known to be "sex symbols of immemorial antiquity and world-wide diffusion, and Lance, or Spear, representing the Male, the Cup, or Vase, the Female, reproductive energy."[1]

The Grail shows its paganism and feminine orientation at every turn in the romances. Its sacred procession appeared in a fairy queen's castle, not in a church. The holy vessel was always carried by a maiden, not a priest.[2] "Behind its almost exaggeratedly Christian exterior, the Quest for the Grail is really just a vast pagan epic, its ancient text showing through the Cistercian ornamentations. Every detail, every anecdote in this inspired work is a mere travesty of the

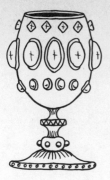

Celtic quest for the submerged woman represented by the Grail."[3]

Even the Christianized stories gave the Grail some rather suspicious origins. It was created from a jewel that fell from Satan's crown as he descended into the underworld. This jewel was variously identified as the Phoenix stone, Lapis Exilis, Lapis Judaicus, or Theolithus (God stone). Its magic could renew one's youth, or provide inexhaustible supplies of food.[4] Wolfram von Eschenbach said that "by virtue of this stone the phoenix perishes and becomes ashes from which life is reborn. Through this stone, the phoenix changes its feathers to reappear in all it former brilliance. There is no man so ill that, once before this stone, he will not be certain of avoiding death for a whole week after the day he saw it. Whoever sees it stops growing old. After the day on which it has appeared to them, all men and women resume the appearance they had at the height of their strength; and were they to stay in its presence for two hundred years they would not change except that their hair would turn white, for it gives such vigor to man that his skin and bones immediately return to their youthfulness. The stone has the name Grail."[5]

Material such as this indicates that the Grail was envisioned as being carved out of a **stone.** Certain churchmen picked

up on this tradition and created appropriate objects for the edification (and pious offerings) of the faithful. The famous Sacro Catino, a green vessel preserved at Genoa, was said to be the Holy Grail carved out of a single enormous emerald. It was revered for many centuries, until further investigation revealed that it was made of green glass, whereupon it ceased to be the Grail.[6] Chrétien de Troyes envisioned the Grail as a vessel of metal, studded with gems: "of the purest gold, and set with precious stones, the richest and most varied to be found in the earth or the sea. No gem could be compared to that of the Grail."[7]

All Europe was feverishly interested in the stories of the Grail cycle for several centuries, until the feminine connotations of the holy vessel began to show through in various ways. Almost overnight, the stories stopped coming. In fifteenth-century Brunswick there was an important popular festival called The Grail, held every seven years. It was outlawed in 1481.[8]

1. Weston, 71. 2. Darrah, 47. 3. Markale, 110. 4. Spence, 246. 5. Markale, 181. 6. Kunz, 258. 7. Markale, 175. 8. Jung & von Franz, 121.

Herm

The classic Greek herm was a phallic **pillar** dedicated to the god of magic and of crossroads, **Hermes,** whose head appeared at the top. Herms were usually plain shafts without projections except for the realistic phallus in front; some, however, had short crossbeams, probably drawn from identification between Hermes and the Egyptian god Thoth, his counterpart in the south, whose image was the **ankh** or Key of Life.

Herms guarded nearly all the important **crossroads** of Greece and the Roman empire, where they were named for the Roman Hermes, Mercury. Hermes and Hecate were worshiped together as lord and lady of crossroads, which were magical places because they always symbolized choices. Sometimes the herms were called *Lares compitales,* the cross-road spirits, to whom offerings were made and for whom there were special festivals called Compitalia.[1] In the Christian era, the numerous herms at crossroads throughout Europe were replaced by stone crosses.

A mysterious incident occurred in 415 B.C.—at the height of a very patriarchal period—in Athens, where public thoroughfares were protected by hundreds of herms. The night before the Athenians were to launch an expedition against Sicily was what came to be known as the night of the Mutilation or Castration of the Herms. In the morning, almost all the city's herms were found with their penises knocked off. The culprits were never discovered, but it is believed they were militant Athenian women, using this threatening magical gesture to protest against the war.[2]

1. Hyde, 137.   2. Keuls, 391–392.

Host

The small round wafer of flour paste that Christians called the host (from Latin *hostia,* "victim") replaced the abundant feasts of pagan times, when the "host" of god-spirit was a whole bull, stag, goat, or other animal whose meat was shared among the worshipers. Although the animal so used was consecrated to the service of the god it represented, the pagans did not insist that what they ate was the god's literal flesh. Porphyry said the Christians' symbolic cannibalism was "absurd beyond all absurdity, and bestial beyond every sort of bestiality, that a man should taste human flesh and drink the blood of men of his own genus and species, and by so doing should have eternal life." Nevertheless, this symbolism

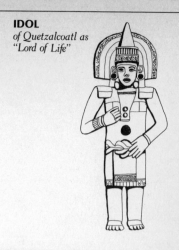

IDOL
of Quetzalcoatl as
"Lord of Life"

was common enough in mystical circles. According to the Magic Papyri, a divine magician "gives his own body and blood to a recipient who, by eating it, will be united with him in love."[1]

The doctrine of transubstantiation—insistence that the flour paste was literally transformed into the actual flesh of Jesus—was a historical stumbling block for the Catholic church and one of the main theological causes of the Protestant Reformation. Nevertheless, it was officially reaffirmed yet again by a papal encyclical of 1965. In the light of this doctrine, it is odd that the church seemed unable to understand what was called a "great heresy and abominable sin" among Mexican Indians, the "creation by the Aztec priests of dough images of their god which were distributed and eaten."[2] The dough man was "killed" with a flint-tipped dart, then divided into small pieces and given to all the people. The ceremony was called *torqualo,* meaning "God is eaten."[3]

1. M. Smith, 66, 123.   2. Arens, 67.
3. Elworthy, 111.

Idol

By strict definition, an idol is any religious object made to imitate a shape that a deity is, or was, supposed to wear; or any manufactured object in which the deity's spirit is supposed to dwell. People have always worshiped idols and still do, even in sects like Catholicism that profess to oppose idolatry. Statues of Christian saints, Jesus, or the Virgin are no less idols than statues of a heathen deity, because they are addressed and worshiped in the same way.

The Lapps had wooden idols containing spirits that they called *seidi,* recalling the Sanskrit *siddhi,* magical spirit.[1] Africans still believe that the spirit of a dead ancestor can occupy an effigy; so praying to the effigy is direct communication with the ancestor.[2] Christians, like the pagans before them, believed the same thing about their holy images. Thomas Aquinas said the image of Christ must be treated with the same respect as the god himself. "The instant we ascribe to an image . . . real power to act, we make of it an inspired being in itself, and all the sophistry in the world as to its being a means of faith, or a symbol, or causing a higher power to act on the suppliant, is rubbish."[3]

1. Davidson, *P.S.,* 79.   2. de Lys, 431.
3. Leland, 237.

INCENSE
in censer

Incense

Incense has always been an important
religious symbol, because it makes smoke,
and fire or smoke rising up toward
heaven was supposed to be a major route
whereby the deities received offerings
made to them on earth. Meat cooking on
the **altar** was also "a sweet savor, an
offering made by fire unto the Lord" (Exodus 29:18), but the very fact that
ancient altars and their environs were also
places of slaughter surely gave them
smells that were not so sweet. Burning incense helped to cover those smells too.

The major producer of incense
in biblical times was southern Arabia, under its wealthy matriarchal queens of
Sheba. Certain Middle Eastern tribes were
particularly associated with the incense
caravans. The biblical "sons of Keturah,"
Zimran, Jokshan, Medan, and Midian, were
not real individuals but the names of
incense-trading groups (1 Chronicles
1:32). Keturah was made Abraham's concubine only to connect a founding
father of the Hebrews with the lucrative
incense business. Keturah was not
a real person either; her name means simply "incense."[1]

1. Teubal, 95.

Isiac Table

The mysterious artifact known as the Isiac
Table was often mentioned by mystics
and magicians, who claimed that its symbolic decorations revealed great religious
secrets of ancient Egypt. Originally
an offering to the Goddess **Isis** in the form
of a portable **altar,** the Table was acquired by
Cardinal Bembo from the sack of Rome
in 1525, then passed into the possession of
the Duke of Mantua in 1630. So runs
the tradition. The Isiac Table was
learnedly discussed (with illustrations) in
a book by W. Wynn Westcott, *The
History and Occult Significance of the
Tabula Bembina sive Mensa Isiaca*; but the
present whereabouts of the sacred Table are
unknown.

Jewel in the Lotus

Om mani padme hum, "the jewel in the
lotus," was the verbal equivalent of
the sacred **lingam-yoni** of India, representing not only male and female genitals
in conjunction but also combinations of fire
and water, light and darkness, creation
and destruction, maleness enclosed within
femaleness as child in mother, man
in woman, corpse in tomb. It was an all-
purpose mystical phrase.

The jewel was also called *vajra,*

meaning a phallus, a gem, or a lightning
bolt, all of which stood for the male
principle. The **lotus** was the primary
Asiatic symbol of the cosmic **yoni,** from
which all life arose in the beginning.[1] In
China the same image was known
as the diamond body born of the golden
flower. Western mystics also had a
version of it, the **Dewdrop** in the Rose,
which was inevitably likened to the
relationship of Christ and Mary.[2]

1. Cirlot, 324.　2. Wilkins, 113.

Labrys

The labrys or double-bladed ax stood for
the Amazons and their **Goddess** under
several of her classical names: Artemis,
Gaea, Rhea, Demeter. Perhaps originally a
battle ax, it became a ceremonial
scepter in Crete and at the Goddess's oldest
Greek shrine, Delphi. Her priests
adopted the name of *labryadae,* "ax-bear-
ers." The labrys became an attribute
of Cretan kings in their **labyrinth** (House
of the Double Ax) and was probably
used in ritual slaughter of the sacred **bulls.**

The labrys also appeared in India,
carried by the hand of Shiva.[1] Egypt's god
Ptah was also represented by an ax.

So was a Mayan deity known as God of
the Ax. Tantric Buddhists explained that the
gods use axes as weapons against unbe-
lievers. In Brittany, stone axes were built
into chimneys, in the belief that they would
avert the lightning that the pagan gods
used to control.[2] The theory behind this
custom seems to have been that the
lightning gods would be mollified by
seeing that their ancient symbols were still
used.

In modern times the labrys has been
remembered for its Amazon associations,
and has therefore been adopted by
lesbian women as their amuletic symbol.

1. d'Alviella, 178.　2. G. Jobes 1, 163.

Labyrinth

Often scratched or carved on Stone Age
monuments and grave sites, the labyrinthine design apparently represented
the soul's journey into the center of the
uterine underworld and its return toward
rebirth. A labyrinth was not the same as a
maze. A labyrinth had only one path,
winding but branchless, heading inevitably toward the goal. Designs of this
type were common on ancient coins, tiles,
floor patterns, and especially tombs
and sacred **caves.**

Labyrinth means "House of the Double
Ax," from *labrys,* the sacred ax of

Crete. The word was originally applied to the Minoan palace at Knossos, home of the fabled **Minotaur** ("Moon-bull"), who guarded the central underground chamber as his Asian counterpart, bull-masked Yama, guarded his underworld. The journey into this central chamber seems to have been a death-rebirth ritual, although the classical myth of Theseus makes it a hero's ordeal.

The pagan tradition of walking the labyrinth as an initiatory procedure passed down through the centuries in children's games like "Troy Town."[1] Christian authorities also took it over and created many labyrinthine floor patterns in churches and cathedrals. Ritual walking of the pattern was said to represent a pilgrimage to the Holy Land and back again.[2] And yet, paradoxically, the labyrinth was also a symbol of hell, because Virgil's *Aeneid* said it marked the gate of the **Sybil**'s temple at Cumae.[3] This temple was always considered to be one of the entrances to the underworld, in both pagan and Christian traditions.

1. Lethaby, 155. 2. Cirlot, 167. 3. Hall, 300.

Mem-Aleph

The Hebrew letters *mem*, meaning "water," and *aleph*, "the beginning," constituted one more version of the world's primary mother-syllable, MA, which stood for divine maternity, cosmic birth, nurture, and the female wisdom principle in most of the world's languages.[1] MA was the name of the Great Goddess of Comana; MA was the amulet representing Isis's fountains of nourishing fluid; MA was the Primal Deep, the world womb; MA was the death-rebirth syllable of the Persians; MA was the spirit of Intelligence, which in Hindu belief first bound together all the elements to make coherent forms.[2] Ma-ma, Mah, Maa, Mata, Mana, and many other variations are found everywhere in names and titles of the Goddess of creation.

Since this syllable was already widely understood as a charm of great power, the Hebrews adopted it too and wrote it on protective amulets appealing to the Mother spirit. Archaic Israelite seals dating from the ninth century B.C. have been found with this symbolic invocation of the Goddess.[3]

1. Potter & Sargent, 229. 2. d'Alviella, 240.
3. Albright, 198.

Menat

The menat was the Egyptian version of the **lingam-yoni,** representing male and female vessels in conjunction. "The might of the male and female organs of generation, mystically considered, was supposed to be united therein."[1] When laid on a mummy as an amulet, the menat was believed to restore the power of reproduction in the afterlife. It was also displayed and carried by gods, kings, priests, and priestesses as a charm of powerful magic.

The archaic Egyptian zodiac placed the menat in the heavens as a very large constellation, extending across half the sky from Arcturus in Boötes to Antares in Scorpio.[2] Astrologically, it was supposed to promote fertility and joyful relations with the opposite sex.

1. Budge, *E.M.*, 60.   2. Jobes & Jobes, 108.

Menorah

The earliest known representation of a menorah appears on the Arch of Titus, erected in Rome in A.D. 82 to commemorate the fall of Jerusalem, and the public display of its temple furniture in the emperor's triumphal procession.[1] The Bible gives very detailed directions for manufacturing a golden menorah for the temple: "Six branches shall come out of the sides of it; three branches of the candlestick out of the one side, and three branches of the candlestick out of the other side: three bowls made like unto almonds, with a knop and a flower in one branch; and three bowls made like almonds in the other branch, with a knop and a flower: so in the six branches that come out of the candlestick. . . . And thou shalt make the seven lamps thereof: and they shall light the lamps thereof, that they may give light over against it" (Exodus 25:32, 33, 37). The seven lights probably were intended to represent the "days" of creation, since they were usually lighted one at a time on seven successive days. But, oddly enough, the golden flowers, knops, and almonds were recognized female symbols throughout the Middle East from prebiblical times.

Later occult traditions associated the menorah with Hebrew archangels of the seven celestial spheres, which were originally female spirits like the Seven Hathors. They were listed as: Michael (Sun, likeness of God); Gabriel (Moon, strength); Madimiel (Mars, blood,

redness); Raphael (Mercury, healing); Zadkiel (Jupiter, justice); Haniel (Venus, splendor); and Cassiel (Saturn, the keeper of secrets). The totality stood for the Shek:..a, the female presence of God.[2]

1. Whittick, 273.   2. G. Jobes 1, 284; 2, 1090.

Mezuzah

The mezuzah is a small metal case affixed to the doorpost of a Jewish home, attesting even today to the ancient belief in the power of written words to repel evil influences. The texts placed within the mezuzah are Deuteronomy 6:4–9 and 11:13–21. The biblical injunction that established the custom in Jewish tradition was Deuteronomy 6:9: "And thou shalt write them upon the posts of thy house, and on thy gates." Rabbi Meir of Rothenburg officially pronounced that no **demon** can have power over a house to which the mezuzah is properly fastened.[1]

Originally, the custom was copied from the Egyptians, who used to place little rounded tablets bearing magical hieroglyphics, the so-called Pillars of Horus, on house walls and doorways to repel evil spirits.[2]

1. Trachtenberg, 107.   2. Budge, *D.N.*, 247.

Mural Crown

The ancients placed mural crowns on the heads of Goddesses like Rhea or Cybele when they were viewed as special protectresses of the city walls (*murae*). Cities were always regarded as female—which is why they are still called "she"—and womb-symbolic for their inhabitants. A city was often described as "a woman who shelters her inhabitants as if they were her children."[1] Even in the patriarchal Bible, cities retain their female character. The name of a city is often identical with the name of the tribal Goddess.

A terracotta medallion from Vienne, in France, shows the Goddess of Fate as Tutela, patron deity of the city. She is enthroned in a garland of **laurel** and wears a mural crown.[2]

Because the mural crown represented city walls, the commander of a besieging army sometimes awarded a symbolic mural crown to the first soldier to scale the wall of a beleaguered city.[3] Similarly, conquering kings or generals might assume the mural crown of victory over a city.

1. Cirlot, 47.   2. Lindsay, 379.   3. G. Jobes 1, 389.

Om

The *Upanishads* referred to Om as "the supreme syllable, the mother of all sound," and sound was Great Goddess's tool of creation. She invented the Sanskrit alphabetical letters, which were *matrika*, "mothers." Om was the *mantra-matrika*, the Mother of Mantras; that is, the first of all the creative spells spoken by the Goddess to bring the world into being.[1] When the Goddess created all things by speaking their names in her magic language, "as from a mother comes birth, so from *matrika*, or sound, the world proceeds."[2]

The meaning of Om was something like "pregnant belly," certainly a prerequisite for symbolic maternal creation, comparable to the Deep of biblical and Middle Eastern creation myths, which bore the name of the Mother (*tehom*) even in Hebrew. The Arabic cognate of the word, Umm, meant mother, matrix, source, principle, or prototype—all concepts derived from the primal **womb.**[3]

Oriental teachings surrounding the Om as "creative Word" were the true roots of the Christian doctrine of the **Logos,** the Word of God that was supposed to have made the world, and to have become incarnate in Jesus. Before it was Christian, this doctrine was Greek (Hermes was the Logos of Zeus), and before that, it was common property of Mesopotamian gods like Marduk and Enlil, who claimed to create by the power of their words.[4] It was also the doctrine of *hekau*, Words of Power, in Egypt, where it was under the jurisdiction of the Crone-goddess Hekit (Hecate). Priests of the male gods seized eagerly upon the idea of creating by a word, because it avoided the difficult problem of assigning creativity to a nonbirth-giving entity. Thus the Logos became a prominent part of nearly every patriarchal religion.

1. Wilkins, 201.   2. *Mahanirvanatantra*, cvii.
3. Shah, 175.   4. *Epic of Gilgamesh*, 24.

Omphalos

For many centuries, scholars have accepted the designation *omphalos*, meaning "navel" (Latin *umbilicus*), for the sacred baetyl stone in the temple of Delphi—that oracular center of ancient Greece, once viewed as the midpoint of the cosmos, whose name really meant "womb." The temple itself is usually styled the property of the Hellenic god Apollo, for we are seldom reminded that

Apollo stole this **oracle** from the primal Goddess under her various titles of Delphyne, Phoebe, and Themis, mother of all Themistes ("oracles").

The *omphalos* at Delphi has been looked at, walked around, sketched, photographed, and discussed for all those centuries; yet no one seems to have pointed out that it really bears no resemblance to a navel. A few scholars have hesitantly suggested that it might have been intended for a heap of ashes on what was once considered the world's central hearthstone. But what it actually resembles is the tip of a penis, which might have suggested itself readily enough to antiquarians familiar with the worldwide habit of installing carved phalli in the ancient gods' temples. The phallus was supposed to embody a god's essential spirit, directly perceptible to his male worshipers by means of the same organ.

However, the representation of a truncated or partial penis would have been alien to patriarchal iconography. This is not a phallus but an *om*-phallos, that is, a small phallus of the belly (*om*) or of the womb. The legend tells us that it was originally a female symbol.

Here we are led inevitably to the clitoris, a word of Greek derivation meaning "divine, Goddess-like," indicating an organ that women worshiped for exactly the same reasons that men worshiped the phallus.

Indeed this mysterious baetyl, and many others like it, might be related to traditions of Goddess worship through symbolic representations of the most "Goddess-like" portion of female anatomy. The famous aniconic stones embodying such primordial deities as Artemis or Themis and Cybele, "Great Mother of the Gods," seem to have been similar conic or pyramidal erections once taken literally as the geographical/genital center of Mother Earth.

This interpretation of the *omphalos* is further supported by its frequent appearance on ancient coins and bas-reliefs flanked by two **doves**.[1] Despite its later Christianized transformation into a symbol of the Holy Ghost, the dove formerly represented the specifically sexual aspect of the Goddess. It was the bird sacred to Aphrodite and often associated with female genitalia. Without much strain of the imagination, one can see the *omphalos* between two doves as a clitoris between "feathery" labiae, as a female Mystery once expounded to maidens upon their initiation into the secrets of the Goddess's temple. Since early Goddess worshipers would have been no less inclined to revere female sexual symbols than the later patriarchs were inclined to worship phalli, it seems reasonable to assign such obvious implications to the *omphalos*.

It is also reasonable to suppose that these implications were carefully hidden when the male god usurped the temple. Suppression and concealment of female sexuality is always a primary goal of patriarchy. Christian Europe even officially denied the existence of a clitoris and forgot the words for it, which is why the ancient Greek term is still in use. The church taught that women should not feel sexual pleasure, so the female organ of sexual pleasure became unmentionable.[2] Even Freud was to insist on denying its true function. But with eyes cleared of such patriarchal blinders we might be able to look at the ancient *omphalos* of the great womb-temples in a different way.

1. d'Alviella, 92.   2. Simons, 141.

Oracle

The oracles were the ancient world's combination of counseling center, holy place, fortune-teller, opinion shaper, school for prophets, dispenser of medical and political advice, and point of contact between the human and the divine.

Needless to say, control of the oracles was essential to control of public policies. Therefore, with the advent of patriarchy, gods promptly took over the oracles formerly dedicated to worship of the Goddess.[1]

Perhaps the best-known example is the famous oracle at Delphi, whose very name meant "womb" (of the earth).[2] It was originally dedicated to Gaea, Mother Earth, "oldest of divinities," to whose name even the later Olympian gods rendered homage. It was taken over by Apollo, who killed the high priestess Delphyne—incarnation of the Mother's spirit—to enter the shrine over her dead body.[3] His priests claimed that Apollo had also killed the oracular underground **serpent** Python, who used to speak through the Pythoness (priestess); but the underground serpent continued to give oracles throughout the classical period so he, or it, or she could not have been altogether dead. In fact, the prophetic utterances were delivered by women only, by immemorial tradition, all the way up to the time when the shrine was finally destroyed by the Christian emperor Arcadius.

1. Briffault 3, 153–154.   2. Graves, G.M. 2, 388.   3. Stone, A.M.W. 2, 171.

Palladium

No one knows exactly what the famous Palladium was, although all writers agree that it was a symbol of exceptional holiness, connected with the archaic shrines of Athens, Troy, and Rome. The welfare of the entire state seemed to depend on careful preservation of the Palladium, which was brought from the sack of Troy by founding father Aeneas and installed in the Roman temple of **Vesta,** to be tended by the Vestal Virgins in later centuries. The Greeks claimed that it was an image of **Athene,** or else a sacred stone (baetyl) representing her, that fell from heaven. Alternatively, it was a relic of either a warrior maiden or a male giant named Pallas, whose name Athene took after killing her/him. The name *Pallas* meant either "maiden" or "youth."[1]

The most likely possibility is that the Palladium was some form of a *lingam-yoni*, signifying the eternal union of male and female deities that used to be considered essential to a country's well-being. Perhaps the female portion of the fetish was lost or destroyed, for according to Roman tradition the Palladium of Vesta's temple was the **scepter** of King Priam of Troy, "in the likeness of a male

sex organ." A Roman legend said a certain consul named Caecilius Metellus was blinded when he entered the temple and looked at the Palladium, perforce, to save it from a fire. Blinding was a customary consequence of gazing unprepared upon a holy thing; but the name *caecilius*, "little blind one," also referred to a penis.[2]

1. Graves, G.M. 2, 403.   2. Dumézil, A.R.R. 1, 323–325.

Papal Cross

The three arms of the papal cross may have been intended to represent the trinity, but sometimes it was associated with the old pagan idea of the **Ladder** to Heaven. A trip up this ladder, and back down again, was once considered essential for every spiritual leader with pretensions to firsthand authority.

Patriarchal Cross

This is the Father-and-Son cross, sometimes in the form of a crucifix with the INRI scroll stretched across the top. The Eastern churches made use of it, as a representation of each local Patriarch.

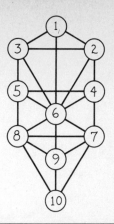

Phylacteries

A Greek text gives directions for preparing a *phylacterion* or "amulet of undertaking": it is to be a **lodestone,** cut in the shape of a heart and engraved with an image of the Goddess Hecate.[1] The *tefillin* or phylacteries worn by Jewish men on the forehead and left arm developed from such ancient amulets and were originally designed to drive away **demons.**[2] Attesting to the ancient belief in the prophylactic power of the Word, they contained scriptural passages on small pieces of parchment within leather pouches. They were classified with other kinds of amulets, including the **mezuzah.**

Because Jews forbade image making, biblical texts were cited to support the wearing of phylacteries: "And thou shalt bind [the words] for a sign upon thine hand, and they shall be as frontlets between thine eyes" (Deuteronomy 6:8; Exodus 11:9, 16). The thong of the arm band was to be wrapped seven times around the arm and held in the hand. With the formerly engraved images replaced by words, the stricture against image making seemed to be upheld.

1. Kunz, 40.   2. Trachtenberg, 145.

Sephiroth

The Sephiroth are the ten qualities of the Mystical Tree, set forth as a major doctrine of the cabalistic *Book of Splendor* (*Sefer ha-Zohar*), which was first published about A.D. 1280 although its legend claimed a much earlier origin. The Mystical Tree stood for the "World of Union" showing the process of life flowing from divinity into the whole creation, and back again.

As numbered on the Tree, the Sephiroth are: (1) Kether or Keter Elyon, the Supreme Crown; (2) Hokhma or Chokmah, Wisdom, the Beginning; (3) Bina or Binah, Intelligence, Understanding, the Supernal Mother of the cosmic womb; (4) Hesed or Chesed, Love, Mercy; (5) Geburah or Gevura, Power, Severity; (6) Rahamin, Compassion, or Tiphareth (Tiferet), Beauty; (7) Nezah or Netzach, Endurance, Victory; (8) Hod, Splendor, Majesty; (9) Yesod, the Foundation; and (10) Malkuth or Malkut, the Kingdom, Earth, identified with God's spouse, the **Shekina.** Sometimes, the Shekina was described as the mother of the whole Sephiroth. Cabalists called all ten collectively the *Merkabah* or "chariot" of God, whereby he could descend from heaven into men's souls.

Some secret traditions added an eleventh Sephira, Daath, the Abyss,

representing Knowledge—specifically, the kind of knowledge forbidden by God, which was the cause of Adam's fall, yet was deemed essential to the mystery of salvation. Daath was hidden in the (female-symbolic) **triangle** of the first three Sephiroth and was often personified as a Goddess, like a dark twin sister of the Shekina; she mothered the element Nephesh, "Soul of the Earthly World," and the ancestral shades of ghosts, the *nephilim*. Her Greek counterpart was Nephele, the dark twin sister of Hera. Her Norse counterpart was Nifl, Queen of the Dead.

Sheila-Na-Gig

Female figures prominently displaying the **yoni** as a *vesica piscis* were once common ornaments of Irish churches built before the sixteenth century. As a rule the sheila-na-gig was carved into the keystone of a window or doorway arch. Undoubtedly it was a protective sign left over from pre-Christian **Goddess** worship. Figures of the same type were found throughout Europe as cathedral decorations, on the capitals of columns, at the ends of ceiling beams, and so forth. Squatting Goddess figures almost identical to the sheila-na-gig guarded the doors of

temples in India, where all who entered would touch the gaping yoni as an act of self-blessing.[1]

Many sheila-na-gig figures also showed the same fleshless rib cage that distinguished similar Indian figures of the Goddess Kali in her "corpse" aspect: she whose name was suggestively like the Irish Caillech or Crone, also a creatress and devourer of the world. The yoni she so prominently displayed represented principles of both birth and dissolution.

Irish churchmen got rid of as many sheila-na-gig figures as possible, though some still remain in or near their original places. Others have found resting places (or hiding places) in the Dublin Museum.[2]

1. Rawson, *E.A.E.*, 30. 2. Knight, 132–139.

Shepherd's Cross

The Shepherd's Cross, Crook, or Crozier was originally dedicated to **Osiris** as the "Good Shepherd" of souls in the afterworld. Egyptian funerary art showed the crook and flail—guardianship and plentiful harvest—in the hands of Osiris's mummy as well as those of pharaohs and other dignitaries. Assyro-Babylonian god-kings bore similar

emblems and were addressed as "Shepherd of the People."

The symbol was inherited by the Greek **Hermes** as another version of the Shepherd of Souls, then by the Christian deity in turn, and finally by Christian bishops as a scepter of office. A common theme for the fancier, elaborately carved croziers of bishops was a coiled **dragon** or **serpent** head, giving rebirth from its jaws to the divine **Lamb**.

Shibboleth

Shibboleth is the Hebrew word for the sacred ear of **grain** exhibited at temples of **Astarte** (biblical Ashtoreth) throughout the Holy Land, and hence identified with paganism. Exhibition of the shibboleth was the culmination of the Goddess's fertility rites. Upon initiation to the highest degree of the Eleusinian Mysteries also, "there was exhibited as the great, the admirable, the most perfect object of mystic contemplation, an ear of corn that had been reaped in silence."[1] This corn ear ("corn" meaning wheat or barley), together with the **dolphin**, represented Demeter as Mistress of Earth and Sea, multiplier of loaves and fishes,

whose annual miracle was plagiarized by Gospel writers. Both of her attributes were later adopted by the Freemasons, with their own version of the holy shibboleth: "An ear of corn near a fall of water."[2]

1. d'Alviella, 2.   2. Elworthy, 105.

Sistrum

The sistrum was a sacred rattle, used in the worship of the Egyptian Great Goddess (**Isis,** Nephthys, or Hathor). The sound of its clattering wires was said to dispel evil spirits, the same kind of magic later attributed to church **bells** in medieval Europe. It was decorated with various designs, sometimes a head of the Goddess, sometimes a small **phallus** representing her consort.

Egyptian paintings show the sistrum not only in the hand of the Goddess herself, but also in the hands of her priestesses and other high-ranking women.[2] Plutarch relates its many mystical meanings. The curved top stood for the orbit of the moon, presided over by a figure of the Goddess in her cat form (Bast). The four rattles represented the four **elements** whereby she created the universe. Their sound indicated mingling of the elements in the process of creation.[2]

1. Budge, G.E. 1, 422.   2. Knight, 96.

Sri Yantra

In Hinduism and Buddhism, a yantra is any graphic design intended for meditation, to teach spiritual doctrines by way of the design's composition. Like a **mandala**, the yantra is used to focus the mind.

Most revered of all yantras is the Sri ("Great") Yantra, composed of interlocking triangles based on a single *yoni yantra* (down-pointing triangle), symbol of female creativity. From it, or her, all male and female life forms develop, shown by upward- and downward-pointing triangles spreading like concentric ripples in water. Hindu scriptures say, "The downward-pointing triangle is a female symbol corresponding to the yoni; it is called 'Shakti.' The upward-pointing triangle is the male, the lingam."[1]

Usually, the whole design is surrounded by first eight, then sixteen petals of the cosmic **lotus**, and a border depicting the four directions, elements, faces of the holy mountain, rivers of paradise, and so on. The ultimate center is not shown because the viewer must supply it mentally. The Sri Yantra is called "form in expansion," a mystical representation of the creative process.[2]

1. Zimmer, 147. 2. Cirlot, 39, 194.

Tattvas

The *tattvas* represent one of several Hindu systems for classifying the **elements**. Water is a silver crescent moon, *Apas*. Air is a blue circle, *Vayu*. Fire is a red triangle, *Tejas*. Earth is a yellow diamond or square, *Prithivi*. The fifth element, spirit (corresponding to the Greek *ether*), is a black or indigo egg called *Akasa*, the Void. According to another system, the colors of water and air are transposed, while the red and yellow of fire and earth remain the same. The names of the *tattvas* are also the names of deities, who might be invoked individually when some boon is craved.

It will be noted that these sacred colors are precisely what we have all learned to call the primary colors, because from the elemental red, yellow, blue, white, and black, all other colors can be obtained by mixing—just as the elements were believed to be mixed in order to create a world in all its hues.

THRONE
Egyptian hieroglyphic

TJET

TOMB
Mycenaean tholos, entrance

Throne

Thrones have always been sacred objects, dedicated to the use of selected persons who usually embodied a divinity. This diagrammatic throne symbol meant support, exaltation, and security in Egyptian hieroglyphics.[1] It also appeared on the head of the Goddess **Isis** (or Maat), to indicate that she was the pharaoh's throne—in other words, his magisterium depended on his being seated in her lap. Pharaohs were often shown so, sitting on the lap of the Goddess and protected by her long wings.

The symbol *mu'at* meant "foundation of the throne" and was also a variant of the Goddess's name meaning Truth, Justice, Judgment.[2] Biblical scribes copied an Egyptian address to a king as connected with his Goddess, when they said: "Justice and judgment are the foundation of thy throne" (Psalm 89:14).

1. Cirlot, 323.   2. Gaster, 769.

Tjet

The *tjet* was one of Egypt's most sacred amulets, thought to be an archaic form of the **ankh,** and apparently resembling a small standing angel. However, it was not an angel. "The Coptic makes it clear that this amulet was intended to represent the *vulva* or *matrix* of Isis." It was "supposed to bring to the wearer, living or dead, the virtue of the blood of Isis,"[1] that is, menstrual **blood,** the divine stuff of life emanating from the Goddess's genitalia. The amulet was commonly made of something red: red jasper, red agate, or carnelian; red porphyry, red wood, or red glass.

1. Budge, A.T., 137.

Tomb

As a construction sacred to the dead, having no other purpose, the tomb was a feminine and maternal symbol in antiquity, when death was usually linked with the idea of rebirth.[1] The word *tomb* descended from Latin *tumulus,* which also meant a pregnant belly or a swelling "tummy."[2] Mycenaean *tholos* or beehive tombs, like Celtic burial mounds, provided imitations of Mother Earth's pregnant belly from which the dead could be reborn, through a short "vaginal" passage, often with a triangular door. Roman tombs were called *columbaria*, "dovecotes," dedicated to the Goddess Venus Columba, whose symbol the Holy Dove was later taken over by Christianity and renamed the Holy Ghost, just as tombs in general were Christianized.

The more prestigious and sacred kinds of tombs, within the walls of the church, were reserved only for a male elite according to the Council of Rouen, 1581. Rich men could buy their way into such blessed resting places because their acquisition of "honors and success in the world" was said to have proved that they were "instruments of the Holy Spirit." The privilege of church burial was not extended to women, not even to the most pious of nuns except in rare cases of what was called "necessity."[3]

1. Cirlot, 326.   2. Potter & Sargent, 28.
3. Aries, 47.

itself was often used as a magical healing amulet. It was said that women's labor pains or children's diseases were eased if the Torah was brought from the synagogue and laid on the sufferer. However, continuing belief in the "uncleanness" of women extended to the handling of the Torah. Rabbinical ruling said that a man must not kiss the sacred scroll right after kissing his wife or child, for fear of spiritual pollution.[1]

Such ideas were part and parcel of Judeo-Christian belief from the beginning of our era. According to the *Book of Thomas the Contender*, Jesus also spoke of the uncleanness of women in no uncertain terms: "Woe to you who love intimacy with womankind and polluted intercourse with it!"[2]

1. Trachtenberg, 105.   2. Barnstone, 586.

Torah

The sacred **scroll** of a Jewish synagogue is the *Sefer Torah*, Book of the Law, composed of the Pentateuch (first five books of the Old Testament). The scroll

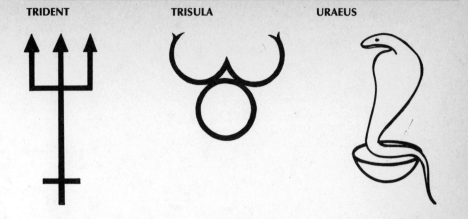

Trident

The devil's pitchfork is the end product of long association between various pagan gods and the trident. Long ago it seems to have been a triple *phallus*, symbolizing a god's sexual union with a Triple Goddess. In India, Shiva was the "trident-bearer" as spouse of Triple Kali. His trident signified the *vajra* (phallus-lightning-jewel). In the possession of Chaldean gods, the trident was usually identified with lightning.[1] (See **Thunderbolt; Lightning.**)

The lightning bolt that fell from heaven to fertilize the Abyss eventually became attached to the abyssal gods, like Poseidon and **Neptune** in Greco-Roman mythology. Thus the trident became one of the alchemical signs for water.[2] Being linked with the deep places of the earth, and also with the deity who fell from heaven as lightning—the biblical Lucifer—the trident inevitably became an attribute of the Christian devil. He is seldom seen today without it.

1. d'Alviella, 98, 256.   2. Cirlot, 217.

Trisula

The mysterious *trisula* is a sign of great importance in India. Worshipers of Shiva say it is their god's **trident.** Worshipers of Buddha say it is their deity's monogram, or a symbol of the Law (*dharma*). Worshipers of Vishnu say it is their god's footprint. Others call it the Flame in the Lotus, or the Trident on the Wheel, or the sun surmounted by moons. Its name means "three points." It has been shown to have a relationship to the sign of **Mercury** (**Hermes**) extant in the West.[1]

1. d'Alviella, 237–245.

Uraeus

The uraeus was the Egyptian cobra symbol of the **Goddess** as Creator. The symbol was worn on the foreheads of deities and rulers in the position of the "third eye" of insight. It stood for royal spirit, healing, and wisdom.

The uraeus was a hieroglyphic sign for "Goddess," derived from one of Egypt's oldest deities, the Serpent Mother variously called Uatchet, Uachit, or Ua Zit. To the Greeks, she was Buto, after her sacred city Per Uto. Together with the Vulture

Goddess Nekhbet, she represented cycles of birth and death, beginning and ending. These archaic Goddesses were known as the Two Mistresses, by whose authority all pharaohs ruled and the cycles of nature were constantly renewed.[1]

The Cobra Goddess eventually merged with Maat as the All-Seeing Eye, and with **Isis** as the Mother of the sun.

1. Budge, G.E. 1, 24; Stone, W.G.W., 92.

Urim and Thummim

Urim and *thummim* are Hebrew words for the divinatory objects used by Old Testament high priests. These objects seem to have been small stones, or possibly knucklebones, like the divinatory dice used in Greek temples, which were said to have been invented by Hermes. Dice were commonly used for divination for millennia in Asia. Similarly, the urim and thummim gave prophecies and advice.

Many people today have at least heard of the official Mormon interpretation of the urim and thummim, stemming from the bucolic ignorance of Joseph Smith, founder of the sect; therefore this interpretation should be explained at some length. Smith did not know what the words meant, but he applied them to a purely imaginary "large pair of spectacles," which he claimed had some inherent magic that enabled him to translate at sight the mysterious language of his equally imaginary golden plates, the alleged origin of the *Book of Mormon*. This language Smith called "reformed Egyptian," a language that never existed, "according to every leading Egyptologist and philologist ever consulted on the problem."

The golden plates that Smith said he dug out of the ground were never seen. The only three "witnesses" to their existence were Martin Harris, David Whitmer, and Oliver Cowdery, whose names are given in the front of the *Book of Mormon*; but all three later defected from the faith and were called "thieves and counterfeiters" by their former brethren. Harris denied that he ever saw the plates with his physical eyes. Instead, he said, he had seen them with "the eye of faith."

This same Harris took some papers on which Smith had pretended to copy the characters that he was translating with his urim and thummim spectacles and visited Professor Charles Anthon at Columbia University. Harris claimed in writing that "Professor Anthon stated that the translation was correct, more so than any he had before seen translated from the Egyptian. I then showed him those which were not yet translated, and he said that they were Egyptian, Chaldaic, Assyriac, and Arabic; and he said they were true characters."

Professor Anthon's account of the matter was very different. In a letter to E. E. Howe in 1834, Anthon disclaimed any connection with "reformed hieroglyphics" or "the Mormonite inscription." He said the paper he was shown contained a "singular scrawl," consisting of odd crooked Greek and Hebrew and Roman letters, upside down or sideways, with a crude circle "evidently copied after the Mexican Calendar given by Humboldt, but copied in such a way as not to betray the source." The professor asked Harris where the plates were and was told that Joseph Smith kept them in a trunk along with "the large pair of spectacles." Anthon advised Harris to get the aid of a magistrate and have the trunk opened, for he was certain that Harris was being conned and robbed—he had sold his farm to give Smith money. Harris replied that if he did that, "the curse of God" would fall on him. Anthon offered to accept any such curse himself, "provided I could only extricate him from the grasp of the rogues." Finally, Professor Anthon asked Howe to "publish this letter immediately, should you find my name mentioned again by these wretched fanatics."[1]

When the mysterious gold plates conveniently disappeared again, being taken away by the same angel who announced them, the magic spectacles urim and thummim went with them; so of course no one ever saw them at all.

1. Martin, 172, 181–182, 187.

Ur-Text

Next to the **Philosopher's Stone,** the Ur-Text was one of the greatest of medieval alchemical symbols, literally believed in. It was another development of the Neoplatonic theory of the **Logos** (Creative Word), which in turn derived from the Hindu theory of Kali's creation of the magical Sanskrit language and of her subsequent creation of all other things by pronouncing their names in that language. The alchemists believed that the Ur-Text was a magical scripture in which God, or Thoth, or Hermes Trismegistus had written the names of everything in the creative language, so a magician who knew that language could change any substance into any other, such as lead into gold and similar feats. The Ur-Text, they said, had been lost to the world when it was hidden in a secret place like the legendary, similar Book of Thoth. Yet several alchemical treatises claimed to have found it and transcribed some of its miraculous language for the understanding of the initiated.

Ushnisha

Ushnisha meant the "flame of invisible light" that sat upon the head of a Buddhist holy man, indicating divine intelligence. The idea was not restricted to Buddhism; it became widely copied. Even the Christian scriptures provided each of the apostles with an *ushnisha:* "And there appeared unto them cloven tongues like as of fire, and it sat upon each of them" (Acts 2:3).

Utchat

Egypt's sacred **eye** symbol, the *utchat,* was at various times the eye of Maat, of Horus, of Thoth, and of Ra. Probably the male gods came later chronologically, since Maat was the original All-Seeing Eye and Mother of Truth, her name based on the verb "to see."[1] Eye amulets were enormously popular among the Egyptians. "Throughout the Dynastic Period the Two Eyes, *Udjatti,* were painted or cut upon coffins and sarcophagi and other articles of funerary equipment and they were painted on the bows of boats."[2] The Two Eyes were usually interpreted as the eye of the moon (Thoth) and the eye of the sun (Ra), and were believed to be prophylactic against all manner of evils.[3]

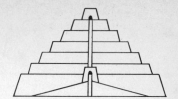

To this day, boatmen all around the shores of the Mediterranean believe that eyes similar to the *utchat* must be painted on their boats, lest the boat should lose its way.

1. Budge, E.L., 55,   2. Ibid., A.T., 360.   3. Ibid., G.E. 2, 413.

Winged Sun Disc

The winged sun disc has been called the Egyptian symbol par excellence.[1] There were many variations. As a rule the sun disc was carried on the **hawk** wings of Horus, surmounted by the spreading horns of the **ram** god Amon. It was also flanked by two **uraeus** snakes (cobras) with opened hoods, sometimes wearing **crowns** on their heads.

The pharaoh Akhnaten (or Ikhnaton) tried to eliminate all other deities and institute worship of the sun disc alone, personified, naturally, by himself. He failed. Polytheistic Egypt buried his memory, erased his name from stelae, and called him a criminal. His dead body disappeared and was never found.

Nevertheless, the sun disc became a primary symbol of the chief heaven god under many of the names by which he was known in Egypt: Sarapis, Ra, Horapollo, Jupiter, Zeus Meilichios, even Mithra or Jehovah. Of all these it was said at sunrise, "He is risen." He was called Sun of Righteousness with healing in his wings—titles later adopted for the Christian deity.

On many Egyptian tombs and temples the sun disc was carved over doorways. The symbol may have formed the basis of the Greek myth of Ixion the sun hero, who was sent "spinning through space bound to a winged wheel."[2]

1. d'Alviella, 205.   2. Whittick, 349.

Ziggurat

The ziggurat was the Mesopotamian version of the Mountain of Heaven, resembling the pyramids of Egypt and Central America in that its summit was a meeting place between deities and mortals. At the peak of the ziggurat the **Goddess** came down to mate with the king, or the God to mate with the queen. Sumerian towns were crowned by ziggurats as early as 3500 B.C.[1] In Babylon, the ziggurat was the core of the city, Bab-ilani, "Gate of the Gods," or as the Bible calls it, Bab-El, the "tower" that purported to touch the sky. It was re-constructed by Nebuchadnezzar and officially named Temple of the Seven Spheres of the World, or Etemenanki, House of the Seven Directions of Heaven and Earth.[2] Its seven stages were supposed to represent the seven heavenly **spheres.** According to a tablet in the Louvre, which gave Roman names to the Babylonian deities, the seven stages were colored black for Saturn, orange for Jupiter, red for Mars, gold for the sun, yellow for Venus, blue for Mercury, and silver for the moon.[3] It is believed that the seven nether spheres were also represented, in the form of successively deeper pits dug underneath the structure.

A similar idea of the ascending heavens formed the pagoda in China. The word *pagoda* is a Portuguese corruption of Persian *butkadah*, a temple.[4] The series of umbrellalike roofs on a pagoda—usually nine—symbolized the various heavens rising one above another.[5]

1. Whittick, 352. 2. Lethaby, 129. 3. Cirlot, 316.   4. Whittick, 290. 5. Lethaby, 50.

7

SECULAR-SACRED OBJECTS

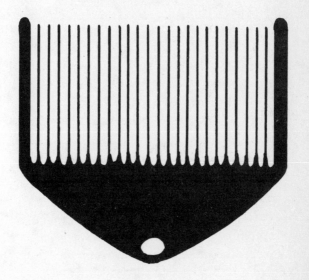

Objects listed here are ordinary for the most part, yet known to have been treated as sacred by some groups of people at some times. Many are household items somehow associated with ancient religious symbolism and used long ago in the way that has been called "living in a sacred manner." This manner was characteristic of woman-identified cultures in the past. Each daily act performed with attention and respect sacralized the objects of daily use, so that living itself could become a ceremony.

A simple experiment can show the reader what it is like to create a secular-sacred object. Set aside, in a special place, any ordinary thing that you particularly like: a family heirloom; a souvenir of a happy experience; a piece of jewelry or china that you think especially appealing; an example of your own artwork; a natural object like a stick, stone, or crystal; a book; a deck of Tarot cards. Touch the object only with special care, at special times. Make some reverent gesture each time you pass by it: nod, or turn your palm to it, or speak. Make a daily offering to it: a fresh flower, a crumb of food, a coin. Think of it as lucky or propitious. Soon the object takes on an air of sacredness. One becomes reluctant to treat it rudely. A habit is established. Before long, a few moments of meditation in the presence of the object will usually produce insightful thoughts from one's own mental depths.

Children often sacralize toys in this way. It seems a natural human act. In prepatriarchal times, when the earth itself was Mother and the ultimate personification of divinity, relations between people and their environment were generally sacralized. Men never felled a tree without first praying for its forgiveness. Seed was planted, the harvest gathered, food prepared, dwellings built with appropriate ceremonies all along the way. Clay pots were used in mindfulness of their Mother-womb symbolism. Everything was endowed with a spirit that must be treated with care and respect.

Later civilization eroded such attitudes toward daily living, though there are a few exceptions still—the Jewish Passover meal, the traditional family observances of Christmas, the Japanese tea ceremony, or birthday parties. Religious institutions have now seized the important personal ceremonies related to birth, marriage, and death, removing them from private control. Old ceremonies that used to be part of pagan worship have been trivialized as Carnival games, Maypole dances, well dressings, Halloween tricks, Easter egg hunts, midsummer bonfires, harvest-homes, Oktoberfests, New Year's Eve parties, and children's games. Still, we should remember how ancient mother-priestesses sacralized the acts of daily living. Among the writings of early missionaries are found many specific condemnations of European women's ritual acts, simply because women considered them sacred, and accompanied them with prayers or invocations of their Goddess.

To study old traditions of secular objects applied to sacred use is to recall a different symbolism and different life-style, which many people now seek in the modern world. It seems necessary today as never before to enhance our day-to-day experience with a new sense of significance. This is particularly true for women, who have always engaged in ritualistic behavior in their homes even though a patriarchal society refuses to honor what they do. It helps to know that once upon a time, women's work was perhaps never finished, but as it was being done it was a series of sacred acts with sacred materials.

Alphabet

A Goddess, not a God, was usually credited with the invention of alphabetical letters. All letters were originally sacred symbols—the literal meaning of *hieroglyph*. In Egypt the art of writing was the gift of the Goddess **Isis,** Maat, Menos, or Seshat; in Rome, that of the Goddess Carmenta or the Fata Scribunda (writer-Fate); in Scandinavia, that of the **Norns** as *Schreiberinnen,* "writing-women"; in Babylon, that of the Gulses or **Fates.**

Written letters were symbols of **Logos** power, that is, the power to create the world by means of words.[1] That is why the fifty letters of the Sanskrit alphabet appeared on the necklace of skulls worn by Kali Ma, perhaps the oldest Goddess of Creation. These letters were *matrika,* "the mothers," which brought all things into being when Kali formed them into words.[2] The Logos doctrine is still extant in Christian theology, though the original idea of creation by the Word has been made more abstract to conceal its primitive naivete. In the third century A.D., Jewish mystics spoke of the biblical smith Bezaleel as an expert on alphabetical wizardry: he "knew how to combine the letters by which heaven and earth were created."[3]

A number of symbol systems have been devised for alphabetical letters. Here is one for the English alphabet in its present

ATHANOR
from an alchemical engraving

form: A, the cone, mountain, pyramid, First Cause or birth; B, mother's breasts; C, the moon; D, day, diamond, brilliance; E, the sun; F, fire of life, G, creative power; H, Gemini, dualism, the threshold; I, number one, selfhood, the *axis mundi*; J, tree and root; K, connections; L, power arising from the earth; M, undulating mountains; N, a serpentine path; O, perfection, completion; P, the staff; Q, the sun tethered to earth (rising or setting); R, support; S, the serpent; T, the double ax, hammer, or cross indicating conflict or sacrifice; U, the chain; V, convergence, a receptacle; W, water waves; X, the cross of light, union of two worlds; Y, the three-way crossroads , meaning choices and decisions; and Z, the lightning (destroyer.)[4]

1. Walker, W.E.M.S., 545.
2. *Mahanirvanatantra*, cvii.
3. Trachtenberg, 82.   4. Cirlot, 176.

Ashes

Ashes have symbolized atonement for sins, ever since Vedic sages decided that the fire god Agni gave his **seed** to the world in the form of ashes, and that bathing one's body in ashes would remove all traces of past transgressions. The Romans also bathed in ashes at their New Year festivals of atonement, in the month of March, which was when the year officially began. The Christian church adopted the same date and converted it into Ash Wednesday. The carnival celebrations on the preceding "Fat Tuesday" (French *mardi gras*) derive from the Roman pagans' custom of merrymaking just before the day of bathing in ashes, on the theory that any sins committed then would be forgiven twenty-four hours later by way of the atonement rituals.[1]

1. Walker, W.E.M.S., 67.

Athanor

The alchemist's furnace called *áthanor* was a mystic vessel of creation variously regarded as the **womb** of matter, the *vas spirituale*, the Vessel of Hermes, or the dwelling place of the Anima Mundi. Like all mystic vessels, it served as a metaphoric uterus as well as a piece of laboratory equipment. The regenerative process that was supposed to take place within the athanor was written *Solve et Coagula*: dissolve the present, reconstitute the future.[1]

The vessel's other name, furnace, came from the Roman Goddess of the oven, Fornax, patroness of bakers.[2]

1. Cirlot, 6, 235.   2. Jobes & Jobes, 178.

SECULAR-SACRED OBJECTS

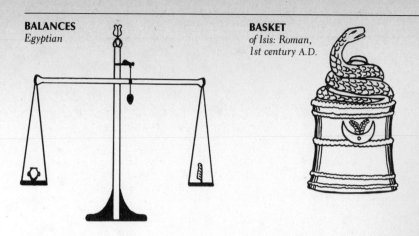

BALANCES
Egyptian

BASKET
of Isis: Roman,
1st century A.D.

Balances

Daniel's prophecy to Belshazzar, "Thou art weighed in the balances, and art found wanting" (Daniel 5:27), was drawn from Egyptian scriptures that placed the balances in the underworld, ready to weigh all hearts against the **feather** of Maat (Mother of Truth). Wall paintings and papyri showed the balances manipulated by Anubis, or by Maat herself, with the feather in one pan and the hieroglyphic symbol for a heart in the other. The balances were so important in ancient religious ideas that they became part of the zodiacal symbols in the heavens (**Libra,** the Scales) and were still supposed to weigh the hearts of the recently deceased upon their arrival in the celestial realms. Libra was the instrument, and sometimes the title, of the female figure of Justice, also called Astraea, the Starry One. In a Greek vase painting, **Hermes** was shown weighing the souls of Achilles and Memnon in balances before the throne of Zeus.[1] In Christian iconography the archangel Michael took over the caduceus and winged hat of Hermes along with his job

of weighing souls. Michael was often shown in the role of the pagan god and of the older Goddess Maat weighing everyone in the balances before the throne of God.[2]

1. Whittick, 305. 2. Hall, 188, 208.

Basket

A basket of **rushes** was the legendary boatcradle not only of Moses on the Nile, but also of Sargon on the Euphrates, Romulus and Remus on the Tiber, the holy child of the Goddess Cunti on the Ganges, and various other god-begotten heroes. The child whom Apollo fathered on the virgin Creusa was also left in a woven basket.[1]

Basket-making was a female craft, so baskets were often sacred to the **Goddess** as agriculturist and harvest spirit. Baskets were carried by Moon-goddesses like Diana and Hecate, of whom Porphyry wrote: "The basket which she bears when she has mounted high is the symbol of the cultivation of the crops which she made to grow up according to the increase of her light."[2] As both Lady of the Moon and Mother of the Crops, **Isis** was worshiped with baskets of **grain** offerings, guarded by her sacred **serpent,**

as shown by carvings in her Roman temple early in the Christian era.[3]

On Greek coins, a basket covered with **ivy** stood for the Dionysian Mysteries. Like that of most other containers, the symbolism of the basket referred to the maternal body.[4] Today, it is sometimes a metaphor for "scrotum."

1. Rank, 18.   2. Briffault 2, 605.
3. Campbell, *M.I.*, 339.   4. Cirlot, 22.

Bell

Bells have always been associated with mystical happenings and communication with spirits. **Goddess** images in the shape of bells are known from very ancient times. In the Christian era, bells signified the arrival of holy spirit and also delineated times of worship. Magical powers were attributed to church bells especially because of their position, hanging in the steeple "between heaven and earth"; the traditional situation of passage between the worlds. During processions and thunderstorms the church bells were rung in order that, as Durandus solemnly said in the thirteenth century, the **demons** "may be terrified and flee away."[1]

Saint Agatha was made the patron of bell founders because of a misunderstanding of some of her early icons. According to her apocryphal myth, Aga-

tha's martyrdom consisted of having her breasts sliced off. She was shown carrying them on a *patera* (offering dish). Some of her devotees mistook the crudely painted breasts for a pair of bells, and so assumed that she had power over bell manufacture.[2]

Ritual uses of bells in Europe were influenced by Oriental traditions. The Buddhist sacred bell (*ghanta*) was rung for the same reasons later given by Christian churches. Children of both East and West used to wear bells to repel evil spirits or avert the evil eye. Priests of Yahweh were directed to adorn themselves with bells (Exodus 8:33–34), although laws were made to forbid their wives and daughters, and all other women, from doing the same (Isaiah 3:16–18). The bell's spiritual implications made it an article of value. Before the winners of races and contests were rewarded with "loving cups," the usual prizes were bells—that is, vessels of symbolic mana inverted.[3]

1. Frazer, *F.O.T.*, 418.   2. Attwater, 34.   3. G. Jobes 1, 198.

Boat

Much ancient literature suggests that the boat, like other vessels, was often chosen to represent "the cradle rediscovered and the mother's womb."[1] Norsemen used the same word for boat, cradle, and coffin, sending their dead into the sea-womb by boat to be reborn.[2] Even those who lived inland buried the dead in boat-shaped coffins and made offerings to the Water-goddess in boat-shaped containers.[3] The crescent moon was viewed as a boat carrying souls to heaven; it was also the maternal symbol of fertility, the *argha* (Ark), "Container of the Germ of all life."[4] Babylonians called the moon "Boat of Light."

In Egypt, the sun god's diurnal death and rebirth placed him in a boat that represented Mother **Isis,** whose temples featured boats carved in stone, placed at the door. One of Isis's lunar boats is still preserved in front of the Roman church of Santa Maria della Navicella, Our Lady of the Boat, on the site of an ancient Isian shrine.[5] Isis had another folkloric incarnation expressing Christian abhorrence of her cult, as the fairy-tale Witch in the Stone Boat.

1. Cirlot, 29.   2. Turville-Petre, 276.
3. Green, 148.   4. Avalon, 423.   5. Wilkins, 146.

Book

A book symbolized intellectual freedom. The written word has always been numinous, conveying a sense of awe especially to the illiterate, who admired alphabetical symbols even if they could not read them. "It is written" was another way of saying "It is so." In a way, reading can create a magical reality that exists in the imagination, to be sure, but can be vivid enough to block out the natural world while the reading lasts. Books are the primary conveyances of all abstract ideas.

Civilized priesthoods always understood how dependent were their deities on the written word for their very lives, as those lives could be perceived by the laity. Therefore, it was always important for religious authorities to control literature, and to gain the legal right to destroy books that contradicted their own teachings. Few people were so assiduous in this endeavor as Christians. In the third to sixth centuries, whole libraries were burned, schools and universities destroyed, and citizens' books confiscated throughout the Roman world, on the pretext of defending the church against paganism. Under the early Christian emperors, people were framed by ecclesi-

astical investigators who planted "magical writings" in their houses, then legally confiscated all possessions. Saint Augustine condemned secular books as unnecessary, along with "the vain and curious desire of investigation, known as knowledge and science."[1] When in Renaissance times the papacy took note of ancient books still sequestered in monastery libraries, mercenary captains in paid papal armies were authorized to sack the libraries and remove their treasures to Rome.[2]

Whereas literacy is often a prerequisite for intellectual freedom, it may also become another form of bondage to mental rigidity. In Judeo-Christian tradition, the primary object of book worship is the Bible. Extreme fundamentalism professes to find justification for every one of its doctrines in the Bible alone. This is always possible, as any collection of writings as extensive and diverse as the biblical collection may be used and/or interpreted to justify anything. A good example of book worship is found in the Baptist fundamentalism of Walter Martin, who thinks that every Christian sect not conforming to his own brand of Bible exegesis is "blasphemy and the product of untutored and darkened souls," and considers biblical quotations the only valid means of refuting them. Martin even pretends to find "clear" Old Testament verification for his favorite doctrine of the

trinity, an obviously impossible task; yet he defines Unitarians as "wicked" on account of their rejection of this doctrine: a rejection that demonstrates "irrevocably their love of darkness, rather than light, because their deeds are evil."[3] Martin's example shows how even educated people may be led to absurd lengths of intolerance by their extravagant devotion to the printed page.

1. Seligmann, 70, 81.   2. J. H. Smith, 248.
3. Martin, 62, 505–506.

Bowl

Sacred bowls were used at all ancient sacrificial ceremonies to catch the **blood** of the victim. As a rule, the blood was distributed to the worshipers to enhance their identification with the sacrificed deity. The Greek word for such a bowl was *amnion*, which also meant the container of blood in the **womb**.[1] The uterine-symbolic meaning of the bowl extended to many different kinds of vessels for the containment of fluids. In Egypt, a water bowl often represented the divine female principle.[2] In Babylonian scriptures, the whole earth or the whole cosmos was represented as the Goddess's mixing-bowl. Some cosmological views of

the seven heavenly spheres maintained that they were nested, inverted bowls. Similarly, to the American Indians an inverted bowl represented heaven.

1. Keuls, 131.   2. G. Jobes 1, 238.

Broomstick

A popular name for medieval witches was "broom amazons."[1] The broom had been associated with female magic and the social contributions of the wise-woman ever since ancient Rome, where sacred midwives used special broomsticks to sweep the **threshold** of the house after childbirth, to repel evil influences from mothers and their babes. The broom was also associated with the ceremony of marriage as conducted by priestesses. Among Gypsies, whose marriages continued to be performed by wise-women, jumping over the broomstick was an essential part of the rite.[2]

So closely connected were the wise-women and their brooms that medieval authorities naturally supposed the broom to serve as a magical steed able to carry a witch to her sabbats. Hence the image of the broom-riding heretical women: "So witches some enchanted wand bestride / And think they through the airy regions ride."[3] Many superstitions

attached themselves to this basic idea. Because witches were thought unable to cross running water, it was considered the worst of bad luck to move a broom across water.[4] The rationale here seems to have been fear of the witch's curse, should her magical tool be removed from her in such a way that she couldn't follow.

1. Duerr, 174.   2. Trigg, 86–87.   3. Hazlitt 2, 655.   4. de Lys, 467.

Candle

Burning candles have always been intimately associated with religious ceremonies, to disseminate sweet odors from scented wax, as well as a soft but dramatic light. The lighting of a candle was a highly symbolic gesture, often linked with a theoretical preservation of the soul, which was viewed as a small light in the darkness of death (or, of the womb). In Christianity, the paschal candle took on the same phallic significance as the ancient **lightning** god whose descent fertilized the **womb** of the abyss. The candle was plunged into the baptismal font, which was termed the Immaculate Womb of Mary, whose waters were thereby fertilized with the "sacred fire."[1] Pagan traditions, however, maintained a feminine interpretation of the candle's light,

formerly honored as a symbol of **Juno** Lucina, Mother of the Light, who governed the sun, moon, and stars, and also gave newborn creatures the "light" of their vision. Her festival of lights at the winter solstice became the Christian feast of "Saint Lucy," still celebrated in Sweden with a Lussibruden or Lucy Bride, that is, a maiden wearing a **crown** of candles.[2] Some folk dances feature young girls jumping over a candle, evidently bearing the same erstwhile sexual significance as jumping over a broomstick.

The Yule candle was especially important as a household omen. It was traditionally oversized and set to burn through the night from Christmas Eve to the dawn of Christmas Day. If the candle went out before the rising of the sun, it was a bad luck sign for the coming year.[3] A few days displaced from the original solstice festival, this custom arose from ceremonial rekindling and encouraging of the new sun.

1. Walker, *W.E.M.S.*, 539.   2. Miles, 221–222.   3. G. Jobes 2, 1712.

Capstan

The nautical capstan—or sometimes, a windlass—became sacralized in Christian hagiolatry when associated with Saint Elmo, a transformation of the old pagan god of sea fire. His spirit was seen in the electrical discharge from masts and spars of ships during storms; it is still known as Saint Elmo's fire. The saint, however, was a fiction. Known as Ermo in Spain, or Erasmus in some versions of the canon, he was said to have been a bishop of Formiae in Campania, where he was martyred in A.D. 303 in a strange manner: by having his entrails wound on a capstan or a windlass. Therefore the capstan became his symbol.[1] His cult was not heard of until the sixth century, however, and was obviously a spurious device invented to make Formiae a pilgrimage center.[2]

1. Hall, 115.   2. Attwater, 117.

Cauldron

The cauldron was the prime female symbol of the pre-Christian world, which is why Christians universally associated it with witchcraft. The Egyptian hieroglyph of the great female Deep (**womb**) that gave birth to the universe and the gods was a design of three cauldrons.[1] Similarly in India, the life-giving female trinity of wombs from which Indra drank the magic *soma* (moon-blood) was represented by "three mighty bowls," or cauldrons.[2] The same three cauldrons stood for the female power of cosmic creation in Norse mythology. Odin, like Indra, acquired his wisdom, insight, and magic power of the creative Word by drinking "the wisest blood in the world" from the three cauldrons Odrerir, Són, and Bodn, which lay in the belly of Mother Earth. It was also necessary for him to give himself up to self-sacrifice, visiting the nether world of death before he could be anointed with the precious birth-fluid Odrerir, after which he knew female magic and could become fruitful and fertile.[3]

Among the Celts, the Three Matriarchs kept the magic Cauldron of Regeneration at the bottom of a lake (or alternatively, of the sea), until it was brought up by Bran the Blessed to resuscitate men slain in battle.[4] This Celtic god moved on into the **Grail** cycle of myths, as Bron the Fisher King, and his cauldron became confused with the Christian version of the life-giving, blood-filled vessel.

There can be no doubt that the cauldron represented the womb of the Great Goddess, who was often a trinity. It is certain also that men used to believe their reincarnation and rebirth depended upon entering such a uterine vessel to be reconstituted by its magic. Celtic cauldrons of regeneration came from the Land Beneath the Waves because the Sea Goddess was held to be the universal birth-giver.[5] The god Cernunnos was dismembered and boiled in a cauldron in order to rise again from the dead.[6] Boiling cauldrons gave rebirth and/or magic power to Taliesin, Minos, Aeson, Pelops, the emperor Elagabalus, and even Saint John the Evangelist, according to a Christian legend that remained an accepted church tradition all the way up to the year 1960, when it was finally admitted to have been a falsehood.[7] Siberian shamans say they cannot practice until after experiencing visions in which they are dismembered and boiled in magic cauldrons by ancestral spirits. Sometimes the latter are identified as the Three Mothers of Fate, who were the Moerae of pagan Greece, the Norns of Scandinavia, and the triple Goddess Wyrd of the Saxons, later transmuted into Shakespeare's three **Weird Sisters** around their cauldron.

Cauldrons continued to be worshiped as symbols of the universal womb even into Christian times, as long as pagans met together to carry on their religion. The Salic Law specifically condemned people who "carried the cauldron" to such meetings.[8]

1. *Book of the Dead*, 114. 2. Campbell, Or.M., 182. 3. Turville-Petre, 42. 4. Rees & Rees, 47. 5. Davidson, G.M.V.A., 129–130. 6. Jung & von Franz, 373. 7. Brewster, 230; Attwater, 190. 8. Baroja, 59.

Chariot

According to the *Eddas*, the chariot of the sun was drawn by the horse Arwaker (Early Waker) and driven by the Goddess Sol, or Sul, or Sulis: the same whom the Celts honored as Lady of the Sun. Her vehicle was comparable to—and probably derived from—the Sun Chariot that esoteric Buddhism called the Great Vehicle, or the Chariot of Fire. Deities, fairies, and supernatural heroes frequently traveled by fire-chariot, especially en route to celestial regions, like the prophet Elijah (2 Kings 2:11). Jewish tradition gave God himself a chariot like that of the pagan sun deity. It was called Merkaba, the holy chariot.[1] Medea, the Great Goddess of the Parthian Medes, recalled the original female charioteer in her winged chariot drawn by fiery serpents (lightning?); for before she became a Greek antiheroine she was the all-wise, immortal, celestial ruler of sun, moon, and stars.[2]

One of the Indian temples of Vishnu was planned to resemble a gigantic chariot, symbolic of the world with all its freight of creatures, carrying the god above all under his title of Jagganath, "Lord of the World." At the annual Puri festival, God and Goddess were transported on a real chariot of immense size, which became the "Juggernaut" drived from a corruption of *Jagganath*.

The sun chariot on the isle of Rhodes was annually destroyed as a sacrifice to the deity in heaven, being thrown into the sea as the sun god himself was engulfed in the abyss at each sunset.[3] The Greek legend of Phaethon, son of the sun god, was drawn from this source. Phaethon aspired to his Heavenly Father's position, but was unable to control the solar horses, and nearly burned up the world. His Heavenly Father killed him and threw him into the sea as a sacrifice to himself.[4] Associating the soul with the solar spirit on his way to destruction, Babylonian scriptures called the road to the land of death either "the road of no-return" or "the way of the chariot."[5]

Taking the idea of chariot-riding to death or to heaven as an allegory, Plato's *Phaedrus* envisions the human body as the soul's chariot. The soul is a winged charioteer, whose wings fall away in coming to earth to be born in a terrestrial body.[6] The reverse journey was that of apotheosis, which was taken quite literally as riding back to heaven in the fiery chariot of the sun, according to the biblical story of Elijah. Rising to heaven, Elijah let his mantle fall on his apprentice prophet, Elisha: the origin of the popular metaphor of inheriting the mantle.[7]

CHARIOT
Trump number 7 from the Barbara Walker Tarot Deck

Carl Jung found archetypal symbolism in images of the chariot as the body carrying the mind. The charioteer is the inner self; the horses represent life-force, or id; the reins are intelligence or will.[8] Similar associations have been suggested for the **Tarot card** of the Chariot, the seventh trump. This is interpreted as the card of earthly existence and material success, a godlike charioteer under a heavenly blue star-canopy, his chariot wheels likened to the days and nights of the turning world. In Tarot designs, however, he has no reins and therefore cannot control the forces of the terrestrial environment.

1. Patai, 134.   2. Graves, G.M. 2, 253; Herodotus, 390.   3. Cirlot, 145.   4. Walker, W.E.M.S., 793.   5. *Epic of Gilgamesh*, 27. 6. Lindsay, 125.   7. Hall, 112.   8. Cirlot, 41.

Clothing

When men began to take over the spiritual authority formerly vested in women, they frequently put on women's clothing, and/or made themselves pseudo-women by other means. Priests dressed as women in the Lydian cult of Heracles, among the Germanic tribes of northern Europe, in religious festivals of Argos, in Crete, and in Rome.[1] The priests of Attis, called *galli*, were self-castrated

transvestites.[2] Patagonian sorcerers, priests of the Sea Dyaks, Kodyak wizards, and many other priesthoods dressed and behaved as women. Sacrificial priests of Madagascar wore female dress and were "glorified" by the title of Grandmother.[3]

Transvestism continued to be prominent in the pagan survivals of medieval Europe. The philosopher Moses Maimonides, and many magical texts after him, insisted that men wishing to invoke the aid of the Goddess **Venus** must wear female clothing. The inquisitor Bodin believed that cross-dressing in the witch cults actually turned men into women and women into men.[4] Among the Lapps, when a man sacrificed to the Goddess he wore a woman's bonnet with a flower crown, and a white kerchief over his shoulders, on the theory that the Goddess looking down from heaven would mistake him for a woman.[5]

There is an overwhelming amount of this sort of evidence to suggest that priestesses everywhere predated priests, and that the latter had to insinuate themselves into holy office by imitating the women insofar as possible.

1. Walker, W.E.M.S., 1014.   2. Vermaseren, 126.   3. Crawley 1, 250–251.   4. Scot, 71. 5. Dumézil, M.F., 116.

COFFIN
Egyptian; lid with Goddess

COMB

CORD

Coffin

A coffin, like a coffer, was conceived in antiquity as another version of the symbolic **womb**, from which the dead might rise in rebirth. Pre-Hellenic Greeks used to bury the dead in large clay pots (*pithoi*) that were likened to the womb of the Goddess. In Egypt, the mummy was provided with a sarcophagus—a Greek word, meaning "eater of flesh"— with the Goddess herself painted on the inside of the lid, where the dead person could see her and respond to her kindly ministrations. As always, the hope of rebirth was intimately and inextricably involved with the divine Mother.

Comb

The comb was an eminently female symbol associated particularly with water spirits: **mermaids, sirens,** nereids, and the **Goddess** herself under such names as Venus Salacia, Aphrodite Marina, Thetis, and Thalassa. Goddess images recur often in folktales and ballads about the sea **fairy** discovered while combing her **hair.** In effect, she was making magic. Female hair-combing was anciently associated with control of the weather.

Witches were said to raise storms by combing out their hair, which was likened to falling water. Perhaps the original comb was a fishbone, since it was linked with the marine Goddess and her "fishy smell." The Greek word for a comb, *kteis*, also meant a vulva.

The comb became a symbol of Saint Anne, mother of the Virgin Mary, when Christianity evolved her from the pagan composite Virgin-Mother Goddess of the sea, Mari-Anna.[1]

In fairy tales, the comb represented maternal protection in the same way that the hair of Isis represented the thicket of reeds that shielded her child from danger. Usually it was a magic comb that could be tossed behind the hero fleeing from a pursuing ogre or giant. The comb would grow instantly into a thick, tangled forest that would impede or halt the pursuer.[2]

1. Brewster, 342. 2. G. Jobes 1, 361.

Cord

Mythic connections of the cord are with the umbilicus. The return to the **womb** before baptismal rebirth, symbolically reenacted in all mystery religions, was in a sense finding one's way back along the cord. Ariadne's thread leading Theseus

through the Labyrinth (into the darkness and out again) represented the rebirth journey. Cords led initiates through artificial underworld journeys in the darkness of caves or underground temples, the "purgatories" of Celtic paganism.[1]

In Babylon, cords were used as healing amulets, because of the rebirth or renewal connected with this symbolic umbilicus. Scriptures said that "cords of light-colored wool" bound on the patient's right side would surely cure "jaundice of the eye."[2]

In the Egyptian underworld, magical cords with or without **knots** signified the binding force of matriarchal law. Certain angels carried "cords of law" that meant obedience to the Mother, Maat. The god Ra said, "Their law is the cord in Amentet."[3]

Witches also used knotted cords to tie up the weather or anything else they wished to "bind" magically, and to lay out mystical figures on the ground, magic circles of protection, ritual interlacements, and such. It was often said, and is sometimes repeated even today, that every witch should possess her own sacred cord.

1. Walker, W.E.M.S., 828. 2. Kunz, 35. 3. Budge, G.E. 1, 188.

Corn Dolly

The corn dolly was made not of corncobs but of **grain** stalks—wheat, barley, oats, or rye, collectively called "corn" in Europe. The corn dolly was a traditional harvest figure made of the last sheaves of grain or, in some areas, the first sheaves of each year's crop. She was dressed in appropriate clothing and treated in various ways as an embodiment of the harvest. Some folk left her in the field. Some brought her to the harvest dance and set her up in the center. Some placed her on a funeral pyre heaped with flowers and set fire to it. Some drenched her with water as a fertility charm. Some married her to a corn-man in a mock ceremony. Some hung her up in the farmhouse, until the next year's harvest. Some preserved her until Yule, when she was fed to the cattle "to make them thrive all the year round."[1]

The corn dolly had many names. Among them were: Corn-mother, Harvest-mother, Great Mother, Grandmother, Mother of the Grain, Mother-sheaf, Old Woman, Old Wife, the Caillech, the Hag, the Queen, the Bride, the Maiden, the Ceres, and the Demeter.

1. Frazer, G.B., 463–477.

Cradle

The cradle of the infant god was an important symbol in all mystery religions of the early Christian era. Prominent in the cult of Dionysus was the *liknon* or winnowing basket used as his cradle. A special cradle bearer, *liknophoros*, carried it in processions.[1] There is little doubt that this sacred symbol prefigured the "manger" of Jesus. Usener declared that the Christmas celebration of mass over a manger was instituted by one of the legendary early popes, Liberius, who seems to have been nothing but a name derived from Dionysus Liber.[2]

The Roman word for a real child's cradle was *cunabula*, related to similar words for the protective maternal body, such as *cunicle*, a hole; *cunctipotent*, all-powerful; *cunnus*, Cunti the Great Goddess of the Vedas, and of course their English derivative, *cunt*. The title of Rome's Queen of Heaven as protectress of infants in the cradle was Cunina.[3]

1. Guthrie, 161. 2. Miles, 107. 3. Dames, 110–114.

Crossroads

Witches were said to hold sabbats at crossroads, for the reason that in the ancient world crossroads were sacred to the Goddess Hecate, the Lady of the Underworld in pagan belief, the Queen of Witches in Christian belief. Her images and those of **Hermes** and Diana stood at crossroads throughout the Roman empire, until they were replaced by crosses during the Christian era. The Roman word for crossroads was *compita*, and the *Lares compitales* or crossroad spirits were regularly honored at roadside shrines during festivals called Compitalia.[1]

Christians continued to honor the chthonian deities at crossroads until they were persecuted for doing so, when the elder deities were newly defined as **devils.** In the tenth century A.D. it was ordered that any woman must be sentenced to a three-year fast if she was found guilty of dedicating her child at a crossroads to the Earth Mother.[2]

1. Hyde, 137.
2. Hitching, 210.

Crown

As a symbol of royal authority, the crown
evolved from the double diadem of
Egyptian pharaohs, the tiaras of Middle
Eastern god-kings, and the holy wreath
of flowers or leaves that Goddesses—from
India to northern Europe—used
to place on the heads of their chosen
consorts, to indicate acceptance of the
sacred marriage. Decoration of the head
has always accompanied some form of
apotheosis. Early Christians referred
to martyrdom as "the crown" because
they were taught that all martyrs would
be given special thrones in heaven
and would sit at the right hand of God,
wearing crowns of precious metals
and gems.

In Greco-Roman culture it was customary for the gracious host to provide
each guest with a crown: usually a garland of olive, laurel, or other decorative
leaves. This was a symbolic expression of
the rule of hospitality, that every guest should
be treated like royalty.

The oldest extant royal crown belonged
to Queen Theodelinda of Lombardy
(d. A.D. 627). The famous Lombard "iron
crown" has been dated from the ninth
century.

In the symbolism of the cabala, Kether
the Crown stood for a form of God
that was never separated from his female
aspect, the Shekina, and therefore
represented androgynous Wisdom just as
Hermes gained his crown of wisdom
through his union with Aphrodite as Hermaphroditus. Kether was another symbolic survival of the once universal idea of
the god's sacred marriage, whereby
he acquired divine powers directly from
their original source, the Goddess.[1]

1. G. Jobes 1, 389; 2, 920.

Cup

Symbolism of the cup is complex,
beginning with matriarchal images of the
womb vessel and passing on to its
patriarchal replacement, another kind of
blood-filled chalice of resurrection. The
cup remained, the blood was masculinized. The womb's life-giving moon-blood
was reinterpreted as the blood of a male,
who naturally had to die to produce it,
because men never could learn the female
trick of bleeding without injury—
though it wasn't for lack of trying. In
dying, the male victim became a "savior"
whose blood was supposed to give
rebirth just as mother-blood used to do.

This basic story was laid down long
before Christianity came along to repeat it
yet again. All sorts of male victims,
human and animal, had been tried. For

untold centuries their blood had been offered to both gods and human communicants. It was decided that blood so valuable must be food for gods as well as spiritual nourishment for humans.
Thus the act of sacrifice was demanded by the Heavenly Father who also partook of the victim's blood and was propitiated thereby. The biblical God demanded all blood shed by animal butchery, hence the "kosher killing" that drained the carcass of its blood, which was taboo and set aside for God; "For the life of the flesh is in the blood . . . it is the blood that maketh an atonement for the soul" (Leviticus 17:11). The ritual gesture of feeding the god his portion of sacrificial blood was raising the blood-filled cup toward heaven, the gesture still practiced at Christian altars as "elevating the host."

Eventually the god's cup of blood became transmuted into a cup of **wine** because human sacrifice became distasteful and animal sacrifice expensive. Wine was the blood of the earth, or of Dionysus-Bacchus the sacrificial wine god, or of Adonis (the Jewish Adonai), or of Osiris. The ritual gesture of elevating the cup became common at every pouring of wine, because the jealous gods must be offered their portion, lest they be angered and vengeful.

This superstitious god-propitiating gesture was the common ancestor of both the Christian raising of the communion cup, and the secular cup-raising in a salutation or toast. "Salutation" means literally a wish for good health, the usual wish of the raised cup, which was intended to show that the god had received his due portion and was satisfied, so he would not send the scourge of sickness. Cup-raising also became a standard way of calling upon deities to witness an oath, to hold the parties responsible for their word. When two drank together from the cup first offered to heaven, they became as one blood in the sight of God.

This idea was soon incorporated into the pagan marriage ceremony. The aim was to make bride and groom one blood in the eyes of the gods, so they would be prevented from harming one another by the oldest kinship laws on earth, the laws of (uterine) blood relationship. The couple either drank a few drops of each other's blood as in the Gypsy marriage ceremony, or drank from the same wine cup in symbolic assumption of kinship, officially declaring by this that their common blood came from the same "womb."

In Switzerland, the gesture of a couple drinking together was considered a legally binding marriage ceremony in and of itself, up to the eighteenth century. The church forbade such marriages in 1541, demanding that weddings take place

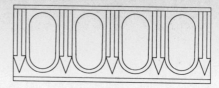

under its own auspices; but the pagan practice continued nevertheless.[1]

The custom of smashing the cup after particularly important vows had been shared from it—still a custom of Jewish weddings—said in effect that the oath so taken could never be changed or reversed, because the vessel that held it was no more.

To medieval pagans, witches, and alchemical mystics, the cup was a universal symbol of the mother element, **water**—especially the waters of the sea womb that was supposed to have given birth to the earth and all that lived on it. In the **Tarot,** the suit of cups stood for the same water element and was replaced in later card packs by the equally maternal symbol of the heart. In Celtic tradition the magic cup from the sea meant Truth. It would break in three pieces if three lies were spoken over it.

Magical ideas continued to attach themselves to cups, especially those that were considered holy, such as a chalice from a church. Clergymen themselves promoted the chalice as an instrument of magical healing and other miraculous events. A curate of Rye in 1538 declared that three drinks from a Christian chalice would surely cure any child of the whooping cough.[2] Princes had special cups designed for them, made of the richest materials they could afford, some elabo-

rately carved and encrusted with jewels. Votive cups were created especially for occasions like coronations, royal weddings, and victory feasts. To this day, the "loving cup" is the standard emblem of victory in races and other sports.

1. Crawley 2, 124–125.   2. Thomas, 50.

Egg and Dart Frieze

The classic Greek version of the architectural decoration known as the Egg and Dart Frieze was popularized by the nineteenth-century Neoclassic movement, and now appears as both interior and exterior trim on many buildings. Its original meaning was an endless line or circle of men (darts) and women (eggs) alternating, as in the Tantric magic circle (*chakra*), where each man was accompanied by his Shakti, the female embodiment of power.[1] This arrangement is still traditional in folk dances and in witchcraft where blessings, initiatory information, and so on must pass from male to female and from female to male. In Rome, the design was known as the Frieze of Venus and Mars. The odd numbers (eggs) were said to represent immortality because odd numbers invoked the life-giving power of women.[2]

The ancient sexual connotations of the Egg and Dart Frieze are even more

clearly portrayed in the Egyptian version, which alternated downward-pointing phallic symbols with narrow oval slits each topped by a diamond-chaped "clitoris." This decoration appeared particularly along the roof of the fifth pylon among the Gates of the Other World. Without recognizing its specifically genital meaning in so many words, Egyptologists interpret this frieze as "heat," "strength of youth," or "fecundity."[3]

1. *Mahanirvanatantra*, cxxi.   2. Wedeck, 66.
3. *Book of the Dead*, 273.

Feather

Feathers had a very sacred significance in Egypt, where it was believed that each soul would be weighed in the **balances** after death against the Plume of Maat, the Mother whose name meant "Truth," to find out whether the deceased was heavy with sins. To be "light as a feather" was to be exonerated from the burden of guilt. Maat's feather was used in hieroglyphics as a symbol of truth.[1]

Feathers were also symbols of the **air** element, and, naturally, of birds—which were usually regarded as reincarnated souls. One of each Egyptian's seven souls was actually depicted as a bird, the *ba,* which could put on feathers and fly in and

out of the tomb. Feather plumes were used in Juno's Roman temples and other Goddess shrines.

The ancient magic of the feather continued in European folklore. Manx sailors rarely went to sea without carrying a protective feather from one of the wrens ceremonially slain on New Year's Day throughout the Isle of Man, which used to be sacred to the Moon-goddess, Mana. The Goddess's sacred bird became known as "Jenny Wren" (see **Wren**).

1. Budge, *E.L.*, 68.

Flail and Crook

The winnowing flail and shepherd's crook were primary symbols of **Osiris** as both the harvester and the wheat of the Osirian eucharistic meal, and the **Good Shepherd** of the flocks of souls. His body was likened to the grain, sprouts of which were actually raised on effigies of the god and made into communion cakes. Each of the faithful who ate him thus became "an Osiris" and could aspire to godlike eternal life.

Other gods, pharaohs, priests, and similar dignitaries were often shown in mummy forms like that of Osiris, bearing the same badges of office and promises of immortality.

Furrow

The rather obvious female-genital symbolism of the furrow appears in many myths and mythological names, such as the name of Rama's wife Sita, meaning "Furrow." An archaic Etruscan myth spoke of a great hero named Tages, a son of Mother Earth, "born from the Furrow."[1] Male gods were sometimes mated with Mother Earth figures to leave evidence of their mating in the form of "flints" in the Furrow. An Egyptian resurrection ritual mentioned "finding of a scepter of flint in the furrow of Maat."[2] A significant Roman religious ceremony involved finding "the flints of Jupiter" in the furrow that represented his consort.

The sacredness of the furrow led to its use in establishing boundary lines and borders of the home nation. Romulus was supposed to have created the site of Rome by plowing a furrow around it. Norsemen said the Goddess Freya separated the island of Zealand from Sweden by plowing a furrow around it.[3] Some may have likened her to the queen of boundaries and constellations in heaven, the zodiacal sign of the Virgin, whose name along with that of her principal star Spica meant "Furrow."[4]

1. Dumézil, A.R.R., 636. 2. Budge, G.E. 1, 420. 3. Davidson, G.M.V.A., 113.
4. Lindsay, 81.

Gate

Janua coeli, "Gate of Heaven," was the name given to sanctuary screens in Christian churches. This was also a Gnostic title of the pagans' Virgin Goddess Brimo, who was worshiped at Eleusis with her holy child, "the blessed Aeon of Aeons." The same title was inherited by the virgin Mary.[1] Much allegorizing was employed to conceal the fact that the gate was another emblem of female genitals, the gate through which life emerged at birth, and into which at least a part of a man might pass to a sexual "paradise," as well as to the symbolic death of phallic spirit. Yet in biblical exegesis, God's remarks concerning the east gate of the temple of Ezekiel's vision were taken as a prophecy of the coming of Jesus. The gate symbolized his mother's virginity: "This gate shall be shut, it shall not be opened, and no man shall enter in by it; because the Lord, the God of Israel, hath entered in by it, therefore it shall be shut" (Ezekiel 44:2). This passage was cited by early church fathers endeavoring to prove that Mary never produced any further children conceived in the usual way, even though the scriptures mentioned Jesus' brothers

and sisters; and the passage also served as a metaphor of virginity in general.[2]

Enodia was a title of Artemis or Hecate, viewed as the guardian of both **crossroads** and gates—especially the gate of birth, since the Goddess under either name was represented as a divine midwife and frequently invoked for assistance in childbirth. Sophocles said Enodia was also a title of Persephone, the underworld Goddess as "Destroyer," who ruled the gates of death.[3]

Ludgate Hill in London was named for Lud's Gate, an entrance to the underworld, according to worshipers of the sacrificial god Lud or Lug, once patron deity of London (Roman *Lugdunum*). A great stone called Crom Cruaich, the Bloody Crescent, stood at the gate to commemorate the sacrifice of Lud, and his passage through the deadly gate. This may have been the same gate that Geoffrey of Monmouth mentioned in connection with a mythical sacred king, Belinus, that is, the god Bel, another version of Lud. It was said that Belinus constructed in London a marvelous gate, "which the citizens do still in these days call Billingsgate."[4] Nowadays, Belinus's Gate or "billingsgate" has become a

British colloquialism for cursing, possibly because the formal curse that sent each sacrificial god to the underworld was always associated with the gate.

1. Campbell, *P.C.M.*, 46.   2. Hall, 118; Walker, *W.E.M.S.*, 609.   3. Gimbutas, 198. 4. MacKenzie, 165.

Hearth

In Latin, the family hearth was designated by the word *focus*.[1] It was the center of clan and tribal life, sacred to the ancient Goddess **Vesta** (Greek Hestia), presided over by the ruling matriarch and illuminated by the fires of the living family spirit. The hearth pit was often supposed to provide access to the spirits of ancestors now dwelling in the underworld.[2] With the growth of the Roman empire, the central heart of the entire city as a political and social unit was located in the *focus* of Vesta's temple, where sacred women tended the hearth fire that must never be allowed to go out.

Modern Greeks still remember their ancestors' homage to Hestia of the Hearth, symbolically at least. At Christmas in Ionia, wine and oil are poured through the center of a large ring-shaped cake onto the hearth fire. "Such a hearth cermony goes back to the old domestic custom of making offerings

HELMET
*of Athene, from a Greek
amphora*

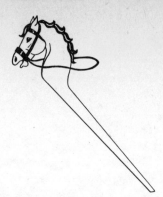

to Hestia . . . whose symbol was the
hearth-fire, the religious center of the
family."[3]

1. Funk, 353. 2. Duerr, 124. 3. Hyde, 133.

Helmet

Elaborate shapes and decoration of
ancient helmets indicate that they were
much more than mere head protectors.
Like **crowns,** helmets could be used as
badges of rank or even of divine status.
The Goddess **Athene,** for example, nearly
always wore a helmet with a prominent crest,
perhaps symbolizing her wisdom.

The English word for a helmet descended from the Goddess Hel, queen of
the underworld, who could provide magical headgear for her favored ones on earth.
Such a magical helmet was the Hel-
kappe, also known as Tarnkappe or Tarn-
helm, the Cap of Darkness. A person
wearing this magic helm would be as invisible as a ghost of the dead. He or she
could pass unseen into the underworld,
or the rose garden of paradise—that is,
Hel's secret land—and yet return to the
world of the living, none the worse for the
experience. Needless to say, this wonderful
talisman was much sought after during the
Middle Ages and became the focal point
of many songs, ballads, and stories.

Hobbyhorse

Like many other pagan symbols, the
hobbyhorse survived longest in the area
of children's games. It became the horse-
headed stick that children put between their
legs for make-believe riding. This apparently innocent toy was named after
Hobbe, or Hobbin, or Old Hob, a variant
of Robin and another name for the
devil in colloquial English. To ride the
hobbyhorse was to "raise Hob," or
to raise the devil, symbolizing the ancient
pagan shaman who rode the horse of
the other world as a sign of mystic enlightenment or apotheosis (see **Horse**).

Renaissance festivals featured hobbyhorses ridden by jesters, whose title came
from Spanish *chistu*, Arabic *chisti*,
a school of mystics founded in Afghanistan
during the thirteenth century. They
called themselves God's Fools, and sometimes feigned idiocy to escape persecution. Traveling westward as itinerant
apostles, they attracted crowds in public
places with music and droll antics,
and told Sufi mystical stories. Arab min-
strels and Basques adopted their horse-
headed canes, which were called
zamalzain (*Zamil el-zain*, the "gala limping horse").[1] The limping gait was

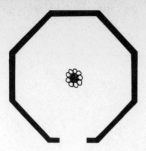

like the child's imitation of a horse's canter, leading to another variation of the object itself as *hobblehorse*.

1. Shah, 223.

Hogan

The octagonal dwelling called *hogan* by the Navaho Indians has always been a symbol of the entire cosmos. The eight sides face the four quarters and the alternate points. The doorway always faces the rising sun in the east. The central fire pit is the heart of the house, as the people's own land was considered the heart of the universe. The smoke rising through the central smoke hole in the roof communicates with heaven.[1]

1. Campbell, *W.A.P.*, 248–249.

Horns

The ancients' reverence for horns and horned deities may have arisen originally from associating them with the horns of the **moon.** Keroessa, "Horned One," was an archaic title of Mother Hera or Io as the divine Moon-cow.[1] Scholars have suggested that the name of Cronus (Kronos) also meant "horned," from Assyro-Babylonian *garnu*, Hebrew and Phoenician *geren*, *Qarnuim*, or *Kerenos*,

the name of a horned god resembling Apollos Karnaios, who was a variant of Cronus.[2] Cernunnos, the Celtic Horned God, was a similar deity. When Christianity declared all of them **devils,** collectively, the composite devil figure inherited horns from all.

Hollowed-out animal horns often served as drinking vessels, helmet ornaments, and musical instruments in northern Europe. In pagan belief, the Last Trump of doomsday would be blown by the god Heimdall on his "ringing horn" called Gjallarhorn. Horn-blowing is still a celebratory ritual (as at our New Year) because the sound was formerly believed to drive away evil spirits, like the sound of church **bells.** Jews still retain the ancient custom of blowing the sacred horn (*shofar*) at the conclusion of Yom Kippur, to clear away evil influences.[3]

Both horns and hair on male heads were common symbols of sexual energy, associated with the old bull-, ram-, stag-, and goat-gods as well as with their Christianized forms, the excessively virile devils.[4] Medieval authorities continued to believe in the fertility magic of horns, claiming that rams' horns buried in the ground would grow up as stalks of asparagus.[5]

1. Elworthy, 183.   2. Brown, 115–116.
3. Trachtenberg, 154.   4. Rawson, *E.A.E.*, 25.   5. Agrippa, 111.

JAR
design, Lagash, ca.
2200 B.C.

Jar

A jar spouting streams of water was a fertility symbol in Egypt and the Middle East from the beginning of civilization. The Goddess **Isis** wore on her neck a jar-shaped amulet representing her own **fountains** of living water, "the emblem of Ma," or Mother as the primordial Deep. According to Apuleius, water in a jar also represented **Osiris**.[1] It was Nile water, lifted up in the ritual of the god's resurrection, exactly as the chalice is elevated at Christian altars today.[2]

In India, any deity could be incarnated in a jar of water, which was called the holy seat (*pitha*) of the deity for the duration of the worship.[3] In Greece the cognate word was *pithos*, a jar. Merging of the Goddess with her consort was often described as a mingling of waters from two jars. When Demeter Cabiria took the young god Cabirius as her consort in the Cabirian Mysteries of Phrygia, both deities were represented by water jars.

The Gospel story of a mysterious man bearing a jar of water to lead Jesus into Jerusalem (Luke 22:10) was based on the Babylonian precedent, wherein the savior god Nebo, or Nabu, was led to the place of his immolation and resurrection by a "jar-bearer." As in the worship of Osiris, Cabirius, and other fertility

gods, the jar temporarily symbolized the deity himself.

Jar ceremonies were prominent in the three-day Anthesteria, a spring rebirth festival of Dionysus. The first day was Jar Opening (Pithoegia), when the new wine from the previous vintage was tasted. The second day was Pitcher Feast (Choes), when the wife of the chief archon was formally impregnated by the god. The third day was the Feast of Pots (Chytroi), when spirits of the dead were propitiated and supposedly, like the vine god himself, resurrected from the underworld.[4] Association of the jar with the springtime Savior was already old, long before Christianity assimilated it.

1. Elworthy, 125, 301. 2. Frankfort, 31.
3. Zimmer, 34. 4. G. Jobes 1, 102.

Key

The key was a mystical symbol of knowledge about the afterlife, long before Christian popes laid claim to the "keys of the kingdom." The Egyptian **ankh** was viewed as a key of the Nile, both the earthly river and its heavenly reflection in the star-fields of the blessed (the **Milky Way**). Like the pagan *petra* who became Peter, key-holding deities could grant or refuse admission through the heavenly gates. The Book of Enoch mentioned "key-holders," gatekeepers (Latin *janitors*) of the celestial mansions.[1] The Goddess Persephone was the original holder of the key to Hades.[2]

A key often meant the unlocking of occult mysteries, the door of the Inner Shrine representing enlightenment. Such keys were verbal formulae, like "Open, Sesame," the Egyptians' *hekau* or "words of power." According to the Osirian Mysteries, the holy words were keys to heaven and must be concealed from noninitiates, as "a great mystery."[3] Similarly, Sophocles spoke of a golden key on the tongue of the ministering hierophant in the Eleusinian Mysteries.

Such verbal "keys" were also claimed by the papacy, by virtue of the famous Petrine passage (Matthew 16:19) where Jesus was supposed to have delivered the keys to Peter. Unfortunately for the Petrine magisterium, the passage was a fraud, deliberately inserted into the Gospel three centuries after its purported date, in order to assist the Roman see in its political struggles against the Eastern church.

According to the medieval symbolism of the **Tarot**, it is not the Pope but the Papess who holds the all-important keys. She is still equated with Persephone as guardian of the underworld gate (the veiled opening at her back), where the Greeks located both sinners and blessed ones after death.

Keys had so many occult connotations that medieval magicians made great use of real keys as magic tools whenever any sort of opening, releasing, or letting go was wanted. Iron keys were buried with the dead in Ionia, to unlock the gates of the underworld. Germans kept a key in a baby's cradle so the fairies would not be able to seize and kidnap the child. It was customary to place a key to a church, or other sacred building, under the head of a dying person to facilitate passage of the soul. An old Serbian birth control charm consisted of separating a lock and key from each other, and walking between them—a symbolic separation of female and male elements. Certain magic words were to be spoken meanwhile. Since the charm must have failed with considerable consistency, the failures were probably attributed to incorrect pronunciation of the magic words.[4]

Jewish midwives used to place the key to a synagogue in the hand of a woman in childbed, on the theory that this sacred key would "unlock" the infant and facilitate delivery. This magic was ecumenical. If there was no synagogue in the neighborhood, they borrowed the key of the nearest church.[5]

1. *Forgotten Books*, 96. 2. Vermaseren, 80.
3. Budge, E.M., 116. 4. G. Jobes 2, 921. 5. Trachtenberg, 169, 175.

Knife

Like the witch's **athame,** knives in general
were associated with magic or divination.
Knives served women as both tools
and weapons. The carrying of a knife at
the belt was characteristic of Celtic
women, until Christian legal reforms in
Ireland forbade women to carry weapons of
any kind. Nevertheless, the traditional
knife at the belt remained an integral part
of the costume of a bride, all the
way up to the seventeenth century.[1]

European folklore abounds in magic
knives and magical stories about knives.
A surefire poison detector was a knife
with a handle made of that highly unusual
substance, "snake horn." It was said
that "If there is any poison present the
handle will quiver, for the snake is full of
venom, and like attracts like." Popes
Clement V and John XXII both owned
knives whose handles were "made
of serpents' horns."[2] Perhaps the blades
were made of hens' teeth.

1. Hazlitt 1, 75. 2. Trachtenberg, 184.

Knot

The female arts of weaving, knitting, and
knotting were once considered magically
able to control winds and weather,
birth, death, and fate. As a rule, men regarded knots with awe, and used them as
graphic symbols in the manner of a
mandala: the eye following the windings
of the knot would traverse a mystic
path. Hence, the elaborate knotwork expressing the course of fate, in Norse and
Islamic monuments.

Rome's high priest, the Flamen Dialis,
was forbidden to wear any knot or
closed **ring** on his person, for fear of "tying
up" his virile spirit, to the detriment of
the empire.[1] For similar reasons, Roman
women were forbidden to knot or twist a
thread on their spindles when passing a field
of grain, lest they should "bind" the
crop.[2] Female knot magic was greatly
feared throughout the Middle Ages by
men, who believed their sexual function-
ing could be immobilized by such
magic, which was known as ligature
(German *Nestelknüpfen*). Witches were
also supposed to close up throats,
mouths, eyes, or other body parts by knot
magic.[3] Jews forbade the tying of knots on
the sabbath—the traditional day of
marital relations—except for those knots
that might be untied with one hand.[4]

LAMP
Roman terracotta, from
Syracuse

Moslems believed that Jewish witches were especially learned in the lore of knots, and that they had once nearly killed Moham-med with "a cord of knots."[5] Knot magic was widespread among Gypsy women, who always untied knots and braids in clothing or hair during childbirth so as not to "tie up" the delivery.[6]

For all the fear of knot magic, however, some of its original benevolence was remembered. Some claimed that diseases could be cured by tying weaver's thread into seven or nine knots, pronouncing the name of a widow at each knot.[7]

1. Cirlot, 109.   2. Spence, 339.
3. Trachtenberg, 127.   4. Barrett, 147–148.
5. Budge, A.T., 62–67.   6. Trigg, 58.
7. Agrippa, 157.

Lamp

Aladdin's magic lamp had plenty of counterparts in folklore and occultism. A lamp was an almost universal symbol of enlightenment, as it is to this day. "Light in the darkness" was also a charm of creation or birth, under the rule of Juno Lucina or Diana Lucifera, bringers of "light" to the newborn. The old idea was copied by the biblical God's *Fiat lux.*

A popular magic-lamp story concerned the tomb of Cicero's daughter Tullia. When her tomb was unsealed, it was found to contain not only Tullia's body but also a miraculous lamp that had been burning continuously for centuries: an early version of the tale of the Eternal Flame. A similar perpetual lamp was sup-posed to illuminate the sealed tomb of Christian Rosenkreuz, alleged founder of Rosicrucianism.

Many ancient terracotta lamps were given distinctly female-genital shapes. The orifice for the wick was placed in the position of the clitoris, cited as the focus of sexual "fire." The enlightenment associated with such lamps may have been linked with mystical knowledge that the ancients attributed to sexual experi-ences with priestesses of the **Goddess.**

Lyre

Pre-Hellenic Mother Goddesses often appeared holding lyres, both as a symbol of the altar **horns,** and as a reminder that the musical sounds they invented were said to have initiated the birth of the universe.[1] According to Scipio the Elder, the seven-stringed lyre was directly connected with the heavens: "The spheres . . . produce seven distinct tones; the septenary number is the nucleus of all that exists. And men, who know how to imitate this celestial harmony with the lyre, have traced their way back to the sublime realm."[2]

One of the men most frequently credited with this ability was the highly popular savior Orpheus, whose cult was a serious rival of early Christianity and a model for many of its sacraments.[3] Orpheus descended into the underworld and returned, like Jesus, bearing the revelations whereby his followers could achieve resurrection.[4] The classic myth of Orpheus's descent in search of his bride Eurydice was a red herring, designed to conceal the fact that Eurydice was only another name of the underground Goddess, Persephone, to whom Orphics prayed for a happy afterlife. The Orphic Mysteries taught that the Goddess would make each enlightened one "god instead of mortal."[5]

The **head** of Orpheus was supposed to reside in a sacred **cave** and produce oracular speeches and songs, like the head of Osiris at Abydos. The lyre that served as his instrument of transcendence was placed in the stars, as the constellation Lyra, which contains the brightest star of the summer sky, Vega. That the lyre first produced the seven-toned "music of the spheres" became embedded in European tradition and contributed to the formation of the present musical scale.

1. Cirlot, 286. 2. Seligmann, 245. 3. Angus, 154, 202. 4. *Bardo Thodol*, lxvi. 5. Angus, 110, 154.

Mansion

Jesus' assertion that his Father's house had many "mansions" (John 14:2) was a conventional expression borrowed from Egyptian scriptures, which described many mansions in the afterworld.[1] In like manner, the Asgard divinities of northern Europe had "mansions" in their holy places.[2] The original meaning of these mansions was "houses of the moon," that is, the zodiacal constellations through which the Moon Goddess passed on her monthly round.

1. Budge, E.M., 165. 2. Branston, 120.

Mask

The classic theatrical masks of Tragedy and Comedy were taken from Greco-Roman models featured in the ancient sacred drama, where actors and members of the chorus were not expected to display emotions on their own faces. Instead, they held up bronze masks with very broad versions of the appropriate expression for each character. Japanese *nō* plays have a similar convention today, using either masks or heavy traditional makeup.

The Greek *theatron*, "theater," meant a place for dramas to be watched by the deities; therefore the expressive mask was supposed to make matters plain to the dwellers on Olympus as much as to the human audience. Sacred dramas were ritualistic imitations of what the gods had done, or were expected to do.

Masks were common attributes of deities from the most primitive times, when people wearing masks literally impersonated their divinities. Egyptian art shows clearly that the gods appeared as human beings with elaborate masks that covered the entire head. The Teutonic word for mask, *grim*, was also a common component of the deities' names, showing

that the divine personality was literally believed to reside in the mask. To prevent manifestation of pagan deities, the medieval church forbade the wearing of masks, but the practice continued anyway at such pagan survivals as **Halloween** and **Carnival.**

The Persian sect called *Maskhara*, "Revelers," used **henbane** to produce their visions, and wore animal masks, or else blackened their faces with a dark substance called *mascara*.[1] In 1518, this sect was mentioned by Johannes de Tabia as a cult of witches calling themselves Mascarae.[2] Today, mascara is still a dark substance to be placed around the perimeter of the eyes in the manner of a domino.

1. Shah, 208.   2. Daraul, 170.

Mirror

Because of the once universal belief that one's reflection is a vital part of one's soul, mirrors and other reflective surfaces were long regarded as soul-catchers or doorways to the other world of spirits. Egyptians used the same word for "mirror" and "life." Celtic women were buried with their personal mirrors, which were supposed to be their soul-carriers.[1] In India, the Great Goddess was called

the Mirror of the Abyss, in which the Great God (Shiva Mahadeva) constantly reflects himself.[2] Buddhists said that all existence is like a reflection in a mirror, anticipating the New Testament writer by some five hundred years in the claim that life on earth is like seeing "through a glass, darkly" (1 Corinthians 13:12). Later, the truth is to be revealed "face to face."[3]

Beginning with the myths of Dionysus, whose soul was caught in a mirror by the Titans, and of Narcissus, whose soul was trapped in his water reflection, Europe abounded with fairy tales about magic mirrors and their dangers. Witches were said to be adept at scrying with magic mirrors. The rather muddled theory behind this form of divination seemed to be that if all existence was but a reflection of a hidden truth, then looking through the "doorway" of the mirror would reverse the process and reveal reality instead.

Medieval scribes sometimes claimed that the spiritual power inherent in a mirror could strengthen the eyes tired by excessive study. They set mirrors before them when writing, to gaze into occasionally, "so that their sight may not be dimmed."[4]

1. Green, 125. 2. Avalon, 231. 3. *Bardo Thodol*, 227. 4. Trachtenberg, 195.

Money

Perhaps the primary symbol of power in patriarchal society today, *money* is a linguistic derivation from Roman worship of the Great Mother under her name of Juno Moneta: Juno the Admonisher. Since Juno's temple housed the Roman mint, the coins produced there were considered blessed by her and so became valuable "monetas."[1]

The Sanskrit word *artha* also connects money with both Mother Earth and *materi*al wealth. Names for the Goddess Earth, such as Ertha, Hretha, Urda, Urth and similar variants in northern Europe, came from the same root. The Goddess was the giver of all the earth's riches: land, food, even the precious metals and gems dug out of her bowels. So the Gypsies were following an extremely ancient tradition when they gave the name of "earth" to all forms of money.[2]

1. *Larousse*, 204. 2. Leland, 99.

Name

Of all the symbols invented by incessantly symbolizing humanity, names are probably the most significant. The essence of human society and communication is language, which is name-giving. Naming things is the very process of creation in many archaic myths. Naming people often meant bestowing life or soul upon them. Egyptians postulated a name-soul (*ren*) bestowed by every mother on her newborn child, along with a **baptism** of her **milk**. Ancient India recognized only named children as fully living members of the clan: an infant who died before receiving its name was not mourned because it was considered soul-less. The Burmese still believe that a midwife must pronounce the child's name the instant it is born; otherwise an evil spirit will give it a bad-luck name and it will die.[1]

The privilege of naming children was one of the first privileges coveted by patriarchal groups because it was so important in maintaining the matrilineal succession of the earlier matriarchal clans. Mothers gave life and also souls represented by the names they handed down to their descendants. Chinese family names are still made with a sign meaning "woman," dating from the time when people knew their mothers but not their fathers.[2] "Irish and Welsh divine and heroic groups are named after the mother, not the father . . . in the older strata of Celtic tradition it is common for heroes to be matronymous, the father's name being omitted." Despite the lists of "be-gats," Old Testament newborns were given names only by their mothers.[3] Like the similar Brahman patriarchal custom of paternity recitation, the biblical "begats" were obviously deliberate attempts to reverse the old system of matrist nomenclature.

The Great Goddess, often considered the source of all names, possessed multiple names because every clan traced its origin (and the origin of its soul-name) back to her in one way or another. Egyptians prayed to Isis of the Myriad Names. India worshiped Thousand-Named Kali.[4] The multiplicity of gods' names was copied from this earlier tradition, but many lists still retain incongruously female names. Of the famous "ninety-nine secret names" of Allah, a majority are female or reflect female characteristics.[5] It is the same with the "secret names of God," usually set at a more modest seventy-two; but different lists, of course, differ.

It was always important for priests and magicians to know the secret soul-names of their deities, because they imagined that control of the deities' names meant control of the deities' actions. Such is ever the case with human beings, the language-makers who constantly confuse their own words with that which the words represent. Magicians of the early medieval period claimed to derive all their powers from knowledge of the holy names. A magician's formula ran, "Whatever I say must happen . . . for I am the son of the living God . . . I have been united with thy sacred form. I have been empowered by thy sacred name."[6] Yet many magical formulae of the period were preserved from an earlier matrilineal system, when the names of fathers were not used. Magical Papyri refer to people by their maternal names only, as "X, whose mother is Z."[7]

Christian liturgies, prayers, invocations, blessings, baptisms, and all other procedures were largely based on name magic. "In the name of the Father, Son, and Holy Ghost" was the all-purpose formula that accomplished everything. The writing of names on tombstones was another derivation from ancient beliefs that reading a speaking the name of the dead would help preserve the **ghost** in the other world. The formula "God rest him," accompanying the name of a dead man, was based on the fear that the speaking of his name would bring his ghost

out of the grave to haunt the speaker. It was a custom of Roman pagans, borrowed by later Christians.[8] The multiple "secret names of God" also remained popular throughout the Middle Ages. The church itself sold amulets printed with "many secret names of God," guaranteed to preserve the bearer from "any evil death."[9]

1. Frazer, *F.O.T.*, 435.   2. de Riencourt, 170.
3. Briffault 1, 372, 418.   4. Boulding, 252.
5. Phillips, 152.   6. M. Smith, 103.
7. Luck, 18.   8. Halliday, 47.   9. Scot, 188.

Palace

The word *palace* descended from the Goddess **Vesta** under her alternate name of Diva Palatua, Lady of the Palatine temple.[1] Not only was a sacred palace the residence of a deity on earth; the paradises of the gods' other worlds were also envisioned as palaces. The Asgard of Norse myths centered on a golden palace, Gladsheim (Joyous Home), where the gods dwelt.[2] Arthurian legend adopted the place and made it over into Lancelot's palace of Joyous Gard. Cathedrals were "palaces of the Queen of Heaven"; and her pagan counterpart the Queen of Fairies also lived in a paradise-palace.

1. Briffault 3, 18.   2. Branston, 86.

Pit

The peculiar story of Joseph's sojourn in a pit (Genesis 37:24) seems to have been derived from an ancient custom of initiation, featuring a symbolic descent into the **womb** of the earth and a rebirth into a new condition of enlightenment. Joseph afterward became a soothsayer or interpreter of dreams; and his "coat of many colors" might be likened to the many-colored robes worn by Assyrian soothsayers.

Nearly every ancient temple included a pit in the inner chamber, the *mundus* or "womb" of initiatory rebirths. The Greek term for this pit was *abaton*, which the Jews altered to "Abaddon," another name for the pit Sheol.[1] The Spirit of the Pit mentioned in the book of Revelation (9:11) was Apollyon, who was simply Apollo-Python, the underground aspect of the sun god, variously perceived as **Black Sun, serpent, Ouroboros, Saturn,** or a solar hero as Lord of Death previous to his resurrection.

After the manner of ancient temples, old European churches also used to be furnished with a pit in the nave, the Holy Ghost Hole, usually covered by a wooden lid. To make the sacred drama clear to illiterate folk, each Ascension Day a statue of Jesus was solemnly drawn upward out of the pit.[2]

1. Bromberg, 11.   2. Duerr, 362.

Poppet

A witch's poppet was not the sort of puppet or doll that a child might play with. It was meant to represent a real person, so it was very much a magical symbol. Anything done to the poppet was supposed to happen to the person also. It was usually claimed that poppet magic was effective only when the figure contained hair, spittle, fingernail parings, blood, semen, earth from a footprint, or some other relic of the real person, or was dressed in a rag taken from his or her garment. The principle was always "a part for the whole," the foremost principle of sympathetic magic.

One charm for causing the death of an enemy involved making the poppet out of mud taken from two banks of a river, and shooting it with a miniature bow and arrow made of reeds. Another charm for attracting love involved a wax poppet "with the sex organs clearly delineated," to be consecrated, buried, and dug up again to receive the needle of passion in its heart.[1]

Poppet magic was probably one of the

oldest female procedures, dating back to Middle Eastern motherhood charms, consisting of clay baby figures anointed with menstrual blood to bring them to life. This was the same kind of life-giving "bloody clay" called *adamah*, the female Adam. It is so easy for human beings—and not children only—to see human-shaped dolls as living creatures, that we need hardly wonder at the universality of the poppet and its supposed influence on real human life.

Poppets also served as surrogate sacrifices. English and Welsh harvest festivals sometimes involved the "killing" of the cornbaby or Kernababy, a poppet made from the sheaves of the previous harvest. As in all sacrifices, the idea was to give back to the Mother part of her gift of nourishment. The poppet was burned or "drowned" at the Kern Supper (harvest feast).[2]

1. Trachtenberg, 124–125. 2. G. Jobes 2, 919.

Pot

One of the Sumero-Babylonian titles of the **Goddess** was the Potter, also called Aruru the Great, who first created human beings out of clay. Also known as Ninhursag, Mami, Mama, or Mammitu (Mother), she made the people, "male and female created she them," according

to the prebiblical scriptures. Early societies viewed pottery and other workings of clay as belonging to women, because clay (**earth**) was woman's element. The Maya called their oldest form of pottery Mamom, "the Grandmother."[1] Pottery was "a feminine invention; the original potter was a woman. . . . Only under the influence of advanced culture does it become a man's occupation."[2] The biblical God's creation of Adam out of clay was stolen from ancient scriptures of the Potter-Goddess, whose creative substance was *adamah*, "bloody-clay."

Clay pots therefore occur everywhere in mythology as metaphoric human beings, souls, or divine persons. Celtic clay pots crudely incised with human faces represented either the souls of the dead or the deities to whom the dead were consigned.[3] In pagan Scandinavia, upturned pots were soul symbols. Many of them have been found in passage graves in East Jutland.[4] In India, a black pot was the symbol of the Goddess Kali. Farmers hung it in their fields to avert the evil eye from their crops.[5] The Hindu hero Drona was born from a pot.

A sacred pot known as the *kernos* at Eleusis signified the **womb** from which the dying god Adonis would be reborn.

Sacred "gardens of Adonis" (sprouting kernels of grain) were planted at Easter time each year by the women of Italy all the way up to the twentieth century.[6]

1. von Hagen, 27.   2. Briffault 1, 466.
3. Green, 222.   4. Davidson, *P.S.*, 34.
5. Gifford, 80.   6. Frazer, *G.B.*, 396–402.

Purple

Most people are aware that purple is the traditional color of royalty and may be envisioned as a darkish shade intermediate between blue and red. Most people are not aware that the "royal purple" of Roman emperors and other ancient dignitaries was not the color that now bears the name. It was a dark wine-red, often likened to the color of menstrual **blood**. Originally it stood for the sacred blood bond of tribal unity. Its Latin name was *purpureus*, meaning "very, very holy."[1] Even in Shakespeare's time, blood was still called "purple."

Strict rules regulated the number and width of purple bands that Roman aristocrats were allowed to wear on their togas, depending on relative rank. Only the royal families wore all-purple garments. The dye was the so-called Tyrian purple, taken from Mediterranean sea snails of the family Muricidae. It was said that the garments of Roman patricians were "colored by blood." The differing Gospel accounts of Jesus' robe as purple (Mark 15:17) or scarlet (Matthew 27:28) really meant the same royal-blood-color, established thousands of years earlier by ideas of feminine moon-blood that held the secret of future life.

1. Graves, *W.G.*, 395.

Razor

Razors have always symbolized the cutting edge, the universal standard of sharpness. In the oldest Indo-European traditions, razors epitomized the keenness of female judgment. India's "Seven Mothers of the World," or Seven Sisters embodied in the Pleiades, were known as the Krittikas, which means "razors."[1] From this term descended the Greek *kritikos*, "judge." The Seven Mothers (or Sisters) judged and approved candidates for the office of sacrificial god, a solar hero destined to be slain, wounded in the side with a **spear**, and resurrected. The "cutters" they used may have been the moon sickles signifying castration of the sacred king, in order that his life spirit might be reborn.

1. Walker, *W.E.M.S.*, 803.

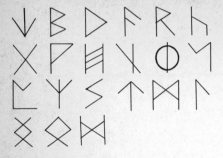

Runes

Among the pagans of northern Europe, women were the traditional custodians of rune magic. Like many other **alphabets**, the runic letters were first credited to the invention of the **Goddess**. Mother Idun, keeper of the Norse gods' magic apples of immortality, allowed her consort Bragi to learn the magic of letters when she engraved the runes on his tongue, thus making him the first great poet. The god Odin—possibly a late masculinized form of Idun herself—had to acquire knowledge of the runes by self-sacrifice, hanging himself on the World Tree for nine days and nights, and giving up the sight of one eye.

Celtic and Teutonic tribes had several variant runic alphabets, one of which is illustrated here, a series of twenty-one letters. From left to right, top line to bottom line, they are: (1) *Feoh*, cattle; (2) *Beorc*, birch; (3) *Porn* or Thorn; (4) *Os*, god; (5) *Rad*, a journey or ride; (6) *Ken*, torch; (7) *Gyfu*, gift, offering; (8) *Wyn*, glory; (9) Haegl, hail or snow; (10) *Nyd*, need; (11) *Ger*, spear; (12) *Eoh*, yew; (13) *Pear*, of uncertain meaning; (14) *Eolh*, defense; (15) *Sigel*, sun; (16) *Tyr*, the war god; (17) *Mannaz*, humanity; (18) *Lagu*, water; (19) *Ing*, the Danes; (20) *Odal*, Land; (21) *Dueg*, day.

Rune number eleven in this system is probably not authentic, since it contains a circle as part of its design. True runes never used curved lines or circles. They were always formed of straight lines and sharp angles because they were made to be cut in pieces of wood, sometimes in the form of chips that were thrown like dice for divination. This was called "casting the runes." It was a special practice of female diviners and therefore inevitably became associated with witchcraft in the minds of medieval male authorities. Soon, all runic alphabets were forbidden, and women who were formerly the custodians of literacy were deprived of the very letters with which they had once written.

Naturally, the letters did not altogether disappear. They continued to be used for casting spells and such witchlike pursuits, and for divination.

SCARECROW   **SCROLL**   **SCYTHE**

Scarecrow

It is well known that scarecrows don't scare crows, or any other birds. But the custom of setting up the effigy of a man on a wooden cross, as a magical protection for fields, has been practiced from remote antiquity.[1] The original scarecrow seems to have been an actual sacrifice in prehistoric times. Later, the sacrificial god-man was dismembered, like **Osiris,** and pieces of his flesh or blood were distributed to all the fields of the land to encourage the crops.

Sacrifice of a god-man for the sake of fertility, usually in the spring, was a common event long before Christianity came along to claim that its own sacrificed god-man was unique. Even within Christianity, the springtime sacrifice of Jesus was emulated by other heroes, such as Andrew, Philip, or Peter. The latter's alleged inverted crucifixion used to symbolize the *petra* (phallic spirit) passing down into the Earth, to fertilize her. In modern Finland, the sacrificial spirit supposed to protect the fields is still known as Pellon Pekko, "Little Peter of the Field."[2]

1. de Lys, 42. 2. Dumézil, M.F., 133.

Scroll

the scroll was the original form of the book and is still used as a general symbol of learning, study, enlightenment, communication, and sacred texts, like the elaborately decorated scrolls used in Jewish synagogues. In mysticism, the scroll represents Time. The present is the written portion that can be seen. The past and the future are the writings hidden in the rolls at either end; the part that has already been unrolled and read, and the part that has yet to be unrolled.

Scythe

Curved blades were traditionally sacred to the female principle, allegedly derived from the lunar crescent. The curved blade of the reaper's scythe was not only a harvest instrument, but also a symbol of death, cutting down all forms of life in their due season. Named for the Scythian Goddess whom the Greeks called Gaea, Artemis, or Rhea Cronia, the Crone, Mother Time, the scythe became a symbol of her death aspect as she devoured her children (that is, took back all the life-forms that she birthed). Later, this Scythian weapon became an attribute of the spouse who was given to her by Greek mythology,

Cronus, Father Time, who similarly
devoured his children. To the Romans he
was Saturn, the underworld god of
death.[1] In the medieval mystery play, he
became the Grim Reaper, wearing
a **skeleton** suit and **mask** (*grim*) and
wielding his scythe that cut down the just
and the unjust alike.

In Britain, the lunar scythe represented
the Harvest Home festival, or Feast
of Ingathering, which was finally Christianized under the name of the Feast of Our
Lady of Mercy.[2] Father Time, Chronos-
Cronus, now appears on New Year's Eve as
the old Aeon, to be replaced by a new
infant spirit of the year to come.

1. Cirlot, 268. 2. Brewster, 424.

Shield

A warrior's shield became the principal
bearer of heraldic designs because
the latter evolved from magical totemic
themes. Every warrior felt the need for
protective magic concentrated particularly
in the shield, upon which his life
could literally depend.

The warrior figure shown here was
rather crudely drawn on a terracotta panel
from Phrygia. Though somewhat lop-
sided, the cross is obvious on the shield as
a reminiscence of the protective magic
connected with this sign since the Stone

Age. There are also defensive triangular
"teeth" pointing outward to fend off
enemy attacks.

Also notable as a sign of personal
protection is the wheel on the warrior's
thigh, perhaps an appeal to the spirit of
swiftness, should it become necessary to
run away from the battle.

The best-known classical Roman story
about shields is that of the maiden
Tarpeia, who was killed and buried under
the shields of many warriors, as a
punishment for having betrayed the Capitoline garrison to enemy Sabines.
This was another of the patriarchal writers'
revisions of earlier Etruscan matriarchal
religion. The famous Tarpeian Rock, supposedly named for the maiden's death site,
was originally a shrine of the Goddess under
the same name. Her statue received
thank-offerings of warriors' shields and
jewelry after military victory; and her
rock—one of Rome's most sacred places—
received annual libations in her name
throughout the classical period. See **Stone**.

Shoe

Many sources identify shoes with female
sexuality.[1] Shoe fetishism was notable in the
religions of Egypt and Greece, where
an archaic fertility rite consisted of insert-
ing phallic objects into a woman's

shoe.[2] Throwing shoes after a newly married couple was another form of the wish for good sexual relations and many children. The old woman who lived in a shoe, in the nursery rhyme, seems to have had "so many children that she didn't know what to do" because her life was centered in her sexual organs. Among Anglo-Saxon tribes it was customary to give a bride's shoes to her bridegroom, in token of his right of sexual access to her. This may be likened to the Irish pagan practice of throwing a woman's shoe over the head of a new tribal chief, symbolizing his physical marriage to the Goddess of the land.[3] A similar sacred marriage ceremony was the Hindu *svayamara*, where the female-genital symbol thrown over the hero's head was not a shoe but a wreath of flowers. Extreme smallness of the shoe, emphasized in the fairy tale of Cinderella, apparently represented the state of virginity. During centuries of Chinese bound-foot fetishism, male poets evinced highly erotic responses to the tiny shoes made for women's stunted, mutilated feet. In somewhat the same vein, European women squeezed their feet into tight, sharp-toed, high-heeled, crippling shoes in the belief that this made them sexually attractive.

Teutonic traditions provided the dead with special shoes, the *Todtenschuh,* strapped to the feet of corpses for the arduous journey to the after-world. These "death shoes" were the same as the Norse *Helsko* (Hel-shoes) put on the dead for their trip to the land of Hel.[4]

1. Cirlot, 282. 2. Graves, G.M. 1, 94; W.G., 357. 3. Joyce 1, 47. 4. G. Jobes 2, 1440–1441.

Tarot Cards

Tarot cards have always served both sacred and secular purposes. As the forerunners of ordinary card decks, Tarot decks were used for games as well as for divination, meditation, and spiritual enlightenment. The series of pictures on Tarot cards have been linked with initiatory procedures and the serial display of deities in ancient temple processions and sacred rituals.[1]

The Tarot deck differs from the modern bridge deck principally in its possession of a fifth suit, the suit of trump cards called Major Arcana (Greater Secrets). The other four suits, or Minor Arcana (Lesser Secrets), are associated with the four archaic **elements**—earth, water, air, fire. The principle of cartomancy, or card divination, rests on the theory that shuffling the deck is like mingling the elements in the real world of events, so the one may foreshadow the other in a miniature, manipulatable version.

There are fifty-six cards in the Minor Arcana, twenty-one numbered cards in the Major Arcana, and one more card, whose number is zero: the Fool. He still survives as the Joker, but all other cards of the trump suit have been suppressed, so that one of the regular suits must now be designated "trumps" for trick-taking games. These numbers, twenty-one and fifty-six, had highly complex mystical connotations in both Oriental and Occidental traditions. They were also related to divination by dice. The number of all possible combinations with two dice is twenty-one; the number of all possible combinations with three dice is fifty-six. A typical medieval magic incantation opened with an invocation of fifty-six angelic names, followed by another list of twenty-one angelic names.[2]

It was usually the clergy who objected long enough and loud enough to the figured cards of the trump suit to have them eliminated from the deck altogether. Churchmen believed, perhaps correctly, that the figures represented pagan or at least non-Christian spirits and theological principles, and that these pictures were used to teach heretical ideas to the illiterate population of Europe—which meant 98 percent of all Europeans in the medieval period.

Because the cards were popular, there was a short-lived attempt to relate the Major Arcana to various episodes in the story of Christ's passion, as if they depicted stations of the cross.[3] This did not catch on. Older connotations of the cards were too well known, and preserved especially by Gypsies, to whom the cards were not only divinatory tools but also a picture Bible of their pagan faith. Gypsy meant "Egyptian," and so occultists began to identify the Tarot with Egypt's famous mythical Book of Thoth, a text of magical secrets that was enclosed in a gold box, within a silver box, within a box of ivory and ebony, within a bronze box, within an iron box that lay under the Nile.[4] Several people claimed to have brought this mysterious book to light in the form of cards.

It might be said that the Tarot did point the way to alternative religious beliefs, especially emphasizing the nearly forgotten feminine principle. The culminating card of the Major Arcana—the World, or Universe—represented the Naked Goddess surrounded by symbols of the elements. The trump cards' final revelation resembled the revelation of the Universal Shakti of Tantric sages. Many other powerful female images occur throughout the Tarot, and in India the

A. Ace of Cups

B. Ace of Wands

C. Ace of Pentacles

D. Ace of Swords

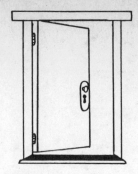

Goddess herself appears with symbols of the Tarot suits: cup, wand, ring (or pentacle), and sword. These stand for the elements that she eternally mixes.

1. Walker, S.T. 2. Trachtenberg, 98. 3. Jobes & Jobes, 79. 4. G. Jobes 1, 236.

Thread

Thread was the usual symbol of fate among people who worshiped the Triple Goddess as **Fate,** or the Fates (Greek Moerae, Norse Norns, Roman Fortunae, and so on). Fate was one of the titles of the pre-Hellenic Aphrodite, model for the Moerae who spun, measured, and cut the thread of every life. In classical literature the trinity bore the names of Clotho, spinner; Lachesis, measurer; and Atropos, cutter. Most religious traditions call the Fates "weavers." In Anglo-Saxon poetry, every man's fate is "woven." Latin *destino* means that which is woven. Greek peasants still speak of the Moerae as fate-weavers; when a man dies, they say his thread is cut.[1]

Perhaps the most famous thread in mythology was that of Ariadne, whose name means "Very Holy One" and was a title of the Cretan Great Goddess, erstwhile ruler of the Aegean world. She was also Áphrodite. The Hellenes mythologized her as a Minoan maiden whose "clue" (thread) led Theseus

through the **labyrinth.**[2] This imagery depicted a womb journey and a return or rebirth.

For many centuries, men feared the magical effects of women's arts of thread. On certain saints' days, women were forbidden to sew. Superstitious folks would not mend a garment while its wearer still wore it, lest the breaking of the thread should bring evil upon the body that had the garment on. European women used to create a counter charm by holding a bit of thread in the mouth while such mending was done.[3]

1. Hyde, 198. 2. Gimbutas, 149.
3. Trachtenberg, 190.

Threshold

The custom of carrying a bride over the threshold of her new home has deep roots in magic and superstition. Like the "crack between the worlds" encountered at New Year's and other important season changes, the threshold was a place of transition between inside and outside, the place where spirits were thought to gather, therefore a dangerous place for a stranger to pass. Often it was literally a grave. Watchdogs used to be buried under the

threshold, to become ghost dogs who could guard the house even more effectively. In northern India, dead infants were buried under the threshold, so that their spirits might enter a woman as she passed in or out, and thus be born again.[1]

1. Frazer, *F.O.T.*, 320.

Torch

The torch was used in Mithraic shrines to represent the rising and setting sun in the hands of the Heavenly Twins. One twin held the torch upward, the other held it downward. Consequently, the downward-pointing torch also came to represent the solar god entering his dark underground phase, becoming the **Black Sun** or the demonic **Saturn.**

Like any other light source, the torch was often viewed as protection against the powers of darkness. In the Hebrides, when clergymen refused to baptize a newborn baby right away, people used to carry a torch three times a day around the infant's cradle to repel evil spirits.[1] After baptism, the church's magic was supposed to replace the torch.

Holding high the torch or passing on the torch are metaphors for enlighten-

ment. That is why the torch and book of Lady Liberty in Upper New York Bay were chosen to show that America's United States would provide education for all citizens.

The Goddess of Enlightenment in ancient Arabia was Atthar, known as the Torch of the Gods. Greeks identified her with Artemis, Athene, Aphrodite, and Cybele. Syrians identified her with Astarte and Anath. Persians identified her with Anahita, who also had a torch for her symbol. Among her many titles were Golden Mother, One Born to the Gold, or The Glory.[2]

1. Elworthy, 65. 2. G. Jobes 1, 90.

Valentine

The Roman Lupercalia in the ides of February was the original Valentine's Day, sacred to the sexual frenzy (*febris*) of the Goddess **Juno.** Men and women chose partners for erotic games by means of love notes or "billets" with partners' names on them. This February custom was denounced by fathers of the Christian church as lewd and heathenish, but it went on anyway.[1] Then the clergy tried substituting pious sermons on the billets, but that soon went out of favor. Christian Gnostics called Valentinians retained the

VASE
Roman sepulchral

sexual license of the festival but described its
central sacrament as copulation of
"angels in a nuptial chamber."[2] They
claimed to be reenacting the marriage of
"Sophia and the Redeemer." The liturgy
said: "Let the seed of light descend
into thy bridal chamber, receive the bridegroom . . . open thine arms to embrace
him. Behold, grace has descended
upon thee."[3]

After suppression of the Gnostics, the
orthodox church invented a Saint Valentine, who was given several conflicting
biographies by different writers; but
through it all, he remained the patron of
lovers in unconscious reminiscence
of the festival's original intentions.
Throughout history it remained a ceremony "never omitted among the vulgar, to
draw lots, which they term Valentines,
on the eve before Valentine Day," to establish the relationships of sweethearts.[4]
The custom of drawing lots on Valentine's
Eve to determine one's marriage partner was
still common in eighteenth-century
England, where clergyman Henry Bourne,
author of *Antiquitates Vulgares*, pronounced it "altogether diabolical."[5]

1. Brewster, 104.   2. Angus, 116.
3. Seligmann, 65.   4. Hazlitt 2, 608.
5. Pegg, 10.

Vase

Forerunner of the funerary urn in Old
Europe was the large earthenware vase
representing the Earth Mother's **womb** of
rebirth. When cremation was the chosen
funerary rite, reducing the body to
ashes, small vases were created to contain
these remains and still serve as womb
symbols. The uterine shape of the vase so
often bore the connotation of rebirth,
that even when corpses were no longer
stuffed into actual earthenware vases like
the funerary *pithoi* of early Greece,
a vaselike shape persisted in various re-
ceptacles for dead bodies. "The sarcophagus seems to take the shape of the
uterus in many societies."[1]

In pre-Hellenic Greece, a title of
Mother Rhea as the Womb of Matter was
Pandora, the All-Giver. Her symbol
was a great vase, originally signifying the
source of all things, like the great
cauldron of the Mother Goddess in northern Europe. Hesiod's antifeminist fable
converted Rhea Pandora's womb-vase into
the source of all human ills and evils.[2]
Centuries later, Erasmus mistook *pithos*

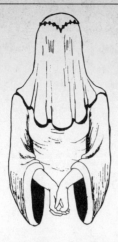

(vase) for *pyxis* (box), and mistranslated Hesiod into the now-conventional story of Pandora's Box.[3]

The vase retained its uterine symbolism in alchemy, where the Womb of Matter was called *vas spirituale*. A vase containing the Water of Life remains the symbol of the Chinese Great Mother Goddess Kwan-Yin.

1. Duerr, 176. 2. Graves, G.M. 1, 148.
3. *Larousse*, 93.

Veil

Revelation comes from Latin *revelatio*, meaning "to draw back the veil."[1] The veil was worn by the **Goddess**, particularly in her Crone aspect, which represented future fate. Her Celtic name of Caillech meant a Veiled One.[2] The ancients believed that a peek behind the veil often meant a view of one's own death, which is why the Goddess's hidden face was dreaded and thought deadly, like the face of Athene-Gorgo, or Medusa. According to the Goddess's inscription on the temple at Sais, "No man has ever lifted the veil that covers me."[3] Much as people earnestly desired a look into the future, they also feared what it might reveal.

Sometimes the Goddess was supplied with seven veils, which represented the seven planetary **spheres** concealing the true face of celestial divinity. Such was the original symbolism of the seven veils of dancing Salome, actually a priestess enacting the sacred mystery of Ishtar's seven veils.[4] Isis also had the same sevenfold covering.[5] As the White Goddess, Ino-Leucothea, she was said to have rescued Odysseus from drowning by means of her divine veil.[6] In this act she was identified with Odysseus's spouse Penelope, a fate-weaver, whose name also meant a Veiled One and whose reluctance to cut the **thread** of his life preserved Odysseus through many near-fatal adventures.

Veils were formerly worn by widows in expression of their Crone character. Then it was said the veil was to protect the woman from attack from the ghost world, whence her spouse had gone. Then brides were veiled, because at a transitory stage in life they were thought especially vulnerable to evil influences. Nuns and Islamic women were veiled to conceal their sexuality.

The most famous veil in Christian tradition was "discovered" in Saint Peter's

basilica about the eighth century A.D. and widely advertised as bearing Christ's "true image," *vera iconica*. From a corruption of this Latin term, churchmen developed the myth of Saint Veronica, who used her veil to wipe Christ's face as he was toiling along to Calvary, so that the veil magically took on his "true image."[7] This hoax was a highly profitable one, because Veronica's veil became immensely famous. Its fraudulence has not yet been completely admitted, although some clergy oppose the inclusion of Veronica's veil in the Stations of the Cross.[8] A similar hoax is the veil of the mythical Saint Agatha, still preserved in the Duomo at Florence, and thought capable of putting out fires and deflecting lava from volcanic eruptions.[9]

1. Funk, 282. 2. Joyce 1, 316. 3. *Larousse*, 37. 4. Cirlot, 359–360. 5. Angus, 251. 6. Graves, G.M. 2, 363. 7. Brewster, 65. 8. Attwater, 335. 9. Hall, 9.

Vitriol

The illustration shows the common alchemical symbol of vitriol, which meant sulfuric acid. Alchemists used the word as a secret acronym of occult signifi-

cance: *Visita Interiora Terrae Rectificando Invenies Occultem Lapidem:* "Visit the interior of the earth; by purification you will find the hidden stone." The reference was usually taken to mean the **Philosopher's Stone.**

Web

The orb type of spiderweb awed the ancients just as it still awes naturalists today. Considering the orb-spinning spider an incarnation of the Goddess of spinning, weaving, and other **thread** arts, the Greeks named her Arachne after a famous priestess of **Athene**. The story of the spinning contest between Athene and Arachne was a scurrilous attempt by patriarchal writers to make the Goddess seem jealous of mortal skills: hardly likely, since she was considered the giver and teacher of those skills to women. She also created the Web of Fate, which the Stoics pictured as inevitably catching souls just as the spider's web catches flies.

Women of Europe continued to

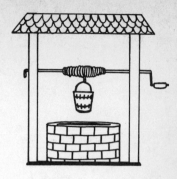

worship the Goddess as patroness of their spinning and weaving activities, even when Christian authorities inveighed against her. Hence, an early Christian writer said one of the sins that would send women to hell was "calling upon Minerva (the Latin name of Athene)" when they began to spin.[1]

The Native American legends of the creatrix Spider Woman or Spinning Woman cast light on earlier concepts of the Goddess as weaver of the web of fate. She wove the universe every day and unraveled her web every night. The world will end when her web is finished.[2] This suggests the pre-Hellenic Penelope, not the loyal wife of absent Odysseus but the great weaver of every man's fate including his. Her "many suitors" originally meant that all men try to woo the Goddess of Fate—even in her modern incarnation as Lady Luck.

1. J. H. Smith, 240. 2. G. Jobes 2, 1671.

Well

Well-dressings and well-worshipings were among those pagan customs that most annoyed Christian clergymen throughout the Middle Ages, because they were known to be celebrating the female principle in an overtly sexual way. The church denounced many of the formerly holy wells with the term *cunnus diaboli*: "devilish cunt." Martin of Braga said that female devils called **nymphs** lived in wells.[1]

People used to visit sacred wells to pray to the nymphs for their hearts' desire; from this habit descended the popular "wishing well," and the custom of throwing coins into wells as an offering to the resident deity. Wells throughout the British Isles were formerly sacred to the underground Goddess Hel, and her Celtic counterparts Morgan and Brigit; which is why there are now so many place names like Hellywell, Hollywell, Holywell, Helen's Well, Morgan's wells, Brigit's wells, or Bridewell.[2]

In Greece, before a wedding people bathe in the local *hagiasma* (sacred well) to gain the power of fertility.[3] A related European superstition said that on Christmas Eve the water in every well or spring would turn to blood (or its sacramental equivalent, wine); but no one wanted to see this miracle because all witnesses were fated to die within a year.[4] Here we have both the symbolic manifestation of menstrual blood magic and its accompanying taboo.

The pagan custom of well-dressing, with games and feasts, survived into the modern era and was usually assigned to Ascension Day, forty days after Easter.[5] One might assume that this was the same day on which the Underworld Goddess gave new birth to the pagan hero. Eventually the church adopted the festivals that it couldn't eradicate, and monks actually sold love potions at the formerly sacred Well of Branwen, once dedicated to the Celtic Goddess.[6]

1. J. H. Smith, 240.   2. Phillips, 112.
3. Halliday, 37.   4. Miles, 234.   5. Brewster, 233–234.   6. G. Jobes 1, 244.

8

RITUALS

To behave in a predetermined way toward sacralized objects or symbols is to behave ritualistically. A ritual rarely has a specific symbol, because it is a symbol in itself, as the act or series of acts. Rituals can be performed by one person alone, by one or more persons watched by others, by a whole group together, or by any combination of these. A complex ritual may include all three types.

A basic characteristic of ritual is that it cannot be understood except within its own cultural context. Hieratic gestures, speeches, costumes, or poses convey little meaning to the uninformed observer, unless they are very graphic pantomimes. Participants in a ritual must know in advance what it is all about.

For example, one never exposed to Christianity would not be able to guess, from the raising of the communion cup, what that cup is supposed to mean to Christians. The gesture alone gives no clue; it is meaningless. Similarly, white observers of an Indian rain dance would not know the meaning of the dance unless they were told. People expect their neighbors and their deities to know what the ritual is for; but outsiders only see actions that are without discernible purpose, however impressive or dramatic they may be.

Thus it can be said that the essential ingredient of ritual is the mental attitude of participants. Why should a married state depend on words spoken by a clergyman? Why should the dead be "saved" by certain gestures made over them, otherwise not saved? Why should making the sign of the cross constitute a protection? Such behaviors seem purposeless but have meaning in the context of the culture.

Therefore, ritual is symbol indeed, just as alphabetical letters are symbols. Written words are incomprehensible to one who has not been taught to read. Rituals, too, have to have their meaning explained. The group of rituals collected here have some unusual and interesting explanations.

Most of the religious rituals now in use come from outside the Judeo-Christian context and were adopted syncretically. Many had already been "traditional" for thousands of years at the time of the Roman empire. Kneeling and prostration of the body were once the means of closer contact with Mother Earth. So was the custom of going barefoot in sacred places, as Yahweh ordered Moses to do (Exodus 3:5). Rome distinguished four "holy solemnities": sacrifice, communion banquets, public festivals, and games (*ludi*), including sacred dramas and masked processions. Blood-sprinklings, lustration, and censing were common purifying rituals.[1] Many ritual tools now considered Christian were of pagan origin, including

lustral or baptismal waters, candles, incense, floral offerings, priestly vest-
ments, chants, bread-and-wine sacraments, reliquaries, bells, images,
banners, seasonal decorations like holly and ivy, and the altar itself.

There is a need to recognize ritual meanings outside of what our culture
finds currently familiar. "So little has been done to extend the analysis
across modern and primitive cultures that there is still no common vocabu-
lary. Sacraments are one thing, magic another; taboos one thing, sin
another. The first thing is to break through the spiky, verbal hedges that
arbitrarily insulate one set of human experiences (ours) from another
set (theirs)."[2] The sacramental and the magical are in effect one, although
the followers of "accepted" rituals try to make us forget this.

Ritual might be defined as any repetitive individual or group action, or
series of actions, having no practical purpose except the creation of a
certain frame of mind in the participant(s). This leaves out the supernatural
explanation, which always means a belief that superhuman beings are
constrained or persuaded by the ritual to act in certain ways, or else that
nature can be directly controlled by it. This explanation is really an
expression of impotence, for "The control offered by magical rites is necessarily illusory, for charms cannot make crops grow or wounds heal."[3]
Nevertheless, human beings have always lived less in the world of objective
nature than in their own minds, and so they will probably always invent
rituals and love them.

1. Spence, 338.   2. Douglas, 8.   3. Thomas, 647.

Agape

Agape or "love feast" was a rite of primitive Christianity, adapted from pagan sexual worship. Another name for the *agape* was *synesaktism*, that is, the imitation of Shaktism, which meant the Tantric kind of love feast involving sexual exchange of male and female fluids and a sense of transcendent unity drawn therefrom. Early church fathers of the more orthodox strain described this kind of worship and inveighed against it.[1] Some time before the seventh century, the *agape* was declared a heresy and was suppressed.[2]

1. Walker, *W.E.M.S.*, 640. 2. Sadock, Kaplan, & Freedman, 23.

Anathema

"Let him (or her) be anathema" was the ritual curse that the Christian church placed on those who were excommunicated or consigned to the **devil**. The biblical foundation for the curse was 1 Corinthians 16:22, "If any man love not the Lord Jesus Christ, let him be Anathema Maranatha." Like other magical invocations and liturgical Greek or Latin, the phrase was rarely explained; it was just adopted.

Originally, the Greek word *anathema* bore the double meaning of "accursed" and "sacred"—like *taboo* or *sacer*, it meant something set aside for a religious purpose, especially some thing, person, or animal devoted to sacrificial immolation as an offering to a deity.[1] It seems to have referred to sacrificial victims of the Canaanite death-goddess Anatha, or Anath-Ma, or Mari-Anath, who annually sacrificed the "lamb of expiation," a dual deity named Mot in his dying phase and Aleyin or Baal in his resurrected phase. Therefore, the "curse" of Anatha was a death curse even though the object of the curse was a holy sacrifice.

The anathema of the medieval church carried much weight when people believed that it would automatically doom them to an eternity of suffering in hell. However, when the Reformation brought doubts on this point, even pious heads of state dismissed it. Pope Pius V invoked anathema in 1570 against Queen Elizabeth I of England: "Out of the plenitude of our Apostolic power we declare the aforesaid Elizabeth to be heretic and an abetter of heretics, and we declare her . . . to have incurred the sentence of excommunication and to be cut off from the unity of the Body of Christ. Furthermore we declare her to be deprived of her pretended claim to the aforesaid kingdom and of all lordship,

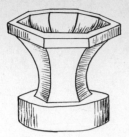

dignity and privilege whatsoever."[2] Elizabeth paid no attention to these ecclesiastical thunderings; neither did the majority of her subjects.

1. Robertson, 36. 2. Dunham, 113.

Baptism

Baptism rituals were originally centered on motherhood and the maternal prerogative of name-giving. Mothers pronounced their infants' names while squirting them with **milk** from their breasts. In pagan Europe, even inanimate objects were baptized with milk when given their names. There was an ecclesiastical ballad stating that the Christ child was specifically *not* baptized in this ancient matrist manner.[1] Baptism for adults was always a matter of symbolically reentering the **womb,** to pass through its waters and attain a new birth, often with a new ceremonial name as well. The Egyptians did a great deal of baptismal dipping, sprinkling, anointing, and washing with holy water sacralized by protective or healing charms pronounced over it; these ideas were copied by early Christians.[2]

When the church adopted infant baptism, the ritual was promptly taken out of the hands of mothers and placed in the hands of priests, who claimed that all children were demonic "children of darkness" as a result of passing through the female body and inheriting original sin; and this demonism could only be exorcised by the church's baptism.[3] Far from being blessed by motherhood, pregnant women were told that they carried in their bodies "the enemy of God, the object of his hatred and malediction, and the shrine of the demon."[4] It was universally taught by churchmen that children who died unbaptized would suffer forever in hell. The Greek church copied the soul-bestowing ritual of Brahman fathers, by blowing three times in the infant's face to "cast out the devil."[5] Still, there were certain pagan traditions that denied the Christian condemnation of unbaptized children. One ballad of pagan provenance said that unbaptized children would go to heaven "just by our Savior's knee," and live among lovely red roses.[6] Others said such children would be cared for in the afterworld by the Goddess herself, Frau Holda (Hel) or Perchta.[7]

Austrian peasants continued to trust the magic of the witch-midwife over the magic of ecclesiastical baptism. Even while a priest conducted the baptismal ceremony, the wise-woman was expected to hold the traditional "threads of life," braiding red and white **cords** in her hands while she pointedly omitted the black cord of death.[8] Thus she secretly played the role of ancient priestesses who not only acted as midwives, but also invoked the female trinity for protection of infants through their knot and cord magic. (See Colors.) Indeed the very title of "those who had performed the bathing ceremony," *baptes*, was originally a title of priests of the Goddess under one of her Thracian names, Cottyto, one more version of the Hag or Crone.[9]

Water used for baptism in a church was sold to parishioners, throughout the Christian era, for numerous magical purposes. It was sprinkled on ailing cattle and chickens. It was sprayed on houses to protect them from storm damage. It was used as a fertility charm and a protection for infants' cradles. It was drunk as a cure for all kinds of sickness. The church allowed crudely superstitious uses of its holy water, "provided they were performed out of genuine Christian faith," which meant in effect a belief that the charm would work. Skepticism was rare enough. So great was the faith of common people in the efficacy of holy water that it was even used to project curses on enemies, reversing the salvation that the water was supposed to ensure.[10]

1. Wimberly, 373.   2. Brier, 264.   3. Gifford, 51.   4. Warner, 57.   5. Spence, 152. 6. Wimberly, 409.   7 Miles, 242.   8. Duerr, 196.   9. G. Jobes 1, 179.   10. Thomas, 30.

Blessing

Old English *bletsain*, older *bleodswean*, "blessing," meant to sanctify by application of **blood**. **Altars** used to be "blessed" or sanctified by the blood of animals or of war captives.[1] Altars still are "blessed" or sanctified by sprinkling with salt, which was a universal magical substitute for blood because they taste alike, and both were identified with the Mother's primal sea.

Sprinkling the blood of sacred victims on the gathered people was once the accepted way of blessing them. Followers of Cybele or Mithra bathed in the blood of sacrificed **bulls** in order to be reborn into a new life of piety. Early Christians insisted that they were bathed in the blood of the **Lamb** (Jesus). Mandaean Christian sects revered John the Baptist as the true savior, rather than Jesus; so their claim was that John's holy blood had "bedewed" the mothers and children of Jerusalem as a charm of fructification and protection.[2] Indeed, a ritual pronouncement of such a blessing was repeated in the Gospels, in connection with the sacrificial Jesus: "His blood be on us, and on our children" (Matthew 27:25). This was one of the most unfortunate phrases in Bible tradition, because it was reinterpreted by European Christians throughout history to signify that the Jews voluntarily assumed blood guilt for Jesus' death on behalf of all their descendants, who continued to suffer persecution as "Christ-killers" despite the fact that the killing was assumed to have been ordained by God.

Nowadays, the "blessing" gesture practiced in churches is not a real sprinkling of anything; yet the hand waves in the air as if some kind of sprinkling were being done.

1. Pepper & Wilcock, 217.   2. Reinach, 77.

Candlemas

The old name of the festival of Candlemas was Imbolg. This meant "the surrounding belly" or "around the belly" in Old Irish, indicating the Earth Mother's **womb** as the land or the soil. It featured circumambulatory rituals for the benefit of the crops, and the lighting of fires.[1] By the pagan Celtic calendar, Imbolg in early February was the beginning of spring. It was Christianized as Saint Brigit's Day, after Brigit herself had been converted from a Celtic Great Goddess to a phony Christian **saint**.[2]

Candlemas was also sacred to several other versions of the Great Goddess. In Rome it belonged to Juno Februata as virgin mother of Mars. Christian writers noted that the pagans burned candles in her honor. Pope Sergius renamed it the Festival of the Purification of the Virgin, "to undo this foul use and custom" of Goddess worship, and "turn it onto God's worship and our Lady's."[3] Nevertheless, Candlemas remained a special day of women and the Love Goddess rather than of Mary.[4] The latter's "purification" was what Christian authorities called **"churching,"** based on the premise that every mother had to be purified in the church forty days after giving birth, including the mother of Christ. Some authorities objected to this explanation of Candlemas, on the ground that while all other women were rendered ritually impure by motherhood, Mary would have been exempt from this "pollution." Nevertheless, the church finally declared even Mary in need of its cleansing ministrations.

1. Berger, 71.   2. Joyce 2, 388.   3. Hazlitt 1, 85–86.   4. de Lys, 127.

Carnival

Now an intrinsic part of the Lenten ritual in most European countries, the Carnival is derived in a roundabout way from one of the oldest Goddess figures known to the Romans: Carna, mother of all flesh (*carnes*). She was annually propitiated with foodstuffs, to encourage her continued protection of human flesh, especially hearts, livers, and other vital organs. In classical times she presided over the viscera, although her influence was wider when she was the Goddess of all nourishment, and of the miraculous inner transformation of dead meat into living human bodies.[1]

The annual festival of Carnival became a farewell to flesh (*carne vale*) in Christian countries. The old rites of Carna were placed at the beginning of the Lenten fast and marked by an orgy of feasting before the onset of the lean time. Many pagan rituals, dramas, games, processional figures, symbolic decorations, and amusements were associated with Carnival: **masks,** mummers, sword dancers, the Wheel of Fortune (or **Fate**), love charms, mock kings, animal sacrifices. A Portuguese Carnival play was reported in 1932, in which the ancient rite of mock birth was enacted by men after the manner of pre-Christian priesthoods. One of their number was dressed as the mother-to-be, who pantomimed labor, and then was delivered of a celluloid baby doll.[2]

1. Dumézil, A.R.R. 2, 386–387.   2. Pegg, 109.

Churching

The custom of churching denied postparturient women admittance into any church for a forty-day period following childbirth, on the theory that giving birth made them spiritually impure. The forty-day period was known as *quarantine*, meaning "forty." After this period expired, a woman could be churched with a ritual designed to remove the impurity of her motherhood. Between birth and the churching ceremony, both the woman and her new baby were officially designated non-Christian heathen.[1] Women were encouraged to believe that "grass will hardly ever grow where they tread before they are churched." It was even said that a woman who died before churching, of childbed fever or some other birthing trauma, would be refused Christian burial.[2] The same rule applied to an unbaptized infant.

The biblical text that gave rise to this custom actually ordered the forty-day quarantine only for a woman who gave birth to a boy (Leviticus 12). If her baby was a girl, a mother was isolated for a period of eighty days, because the patriarchal priesthood considered girls twice as impure as boys. At the end of this time, the mother had to make a sin offering to the priest, in atonement for her "crime." In other words, it was sinful to bring forth a child, but only half as sinful to bring forth a male child as to bring forth a female one. Needless to say, such antifemale ideas were greatly enhanced by the church's doctrine of original sin transmitted to all generations via the flesh of women.

The gentler pagan forerunner of the churching ceremony was conducted by the mother herself, and consisted of a presentation of her child to Mother Earth, usually at a **crossroad**. A tenth-century Penitential firmly forbade women to perform this ceremony any more, "for this is great paganism."[3]

1. Wimberly, 372.   2. Thomas, 39.
3. Hitching, 210.

Circumcision

The antiquity of circumcision is attested by the fact that flint knives were generally used, and by pictorial evidence dating to 2300 B.C. The custom must have antedated the Bronze Age, and thus in all probability the age of recognition of paternity. Circumcision and other forms of penile mutilation began as obvious imitations of female menarche, being performed on boys at the age when girls first "bled," and even being described among some peoples as "man's menstruation."[1] Among the Masai, newly circumcised boys are still dressed as women. Similarly in ancient Egypt, boys were dressed in girls' clothes for their circumcision rituals.[2]

Circumcision probably began as a less drastic reminder of earlier castrations, which used to be considered essential for men to assume religious authority among the priestesses of the Goddess. Suffering castration, putting on women's clothes, and behaving as women characterized many early priesthoods, such as those of Cybele, Omphale, and the Mantes of Thebes. Eventually the modified form, a symbolic offering of genital blood to the deity, was imposed on the male population even by masculine gods, as a coming-of-age ceremony.

DANCE
*as performed
by Shiva*

However, religious castration was still to be found even in Jewish and Christian tradition. The Midrashic version of the story of Noah says that Ham did not merely uncover his father's nakedness; but like the Cronus-Uranus story that served as a model, Ham castrated his father.[3] Sacred kings were often castrated by their successors, and this was considered an offering pleasing to the god. The *Acts of John* seems to recommend castration to Christian converts, saying "Cleanse your heart and purge your belly, and cut off that which is below it."[4] Jesus said that any man who could "receive it" should make himself a eunuch "for the kingdom of heaven's sake" (Matthew 19:12). Church fathers such as Tertullian and Origen declared that the kingdom of heaven is thrown open to eunuchs.[5] Religious castration was so common among early Christians that the emperor Domitian pronounced it illegal, which is one reason that Domitian was vehemently accused of persecuting Christians—when the Christians were writing the histories.[6]

Even where ceremonial castration was discontinued, however, its symbolic imitation often found favor with male gods. The Jews copied it from Egypt, making it a sign of their covenant with Yahweh. Transference of the ceremony from puberty to infancy was attributed to Moses, whose Midianite wife Zipporah did not like having it done to her infant. After cutting off the child's foreskin, she flung it at Moses, calling him a bloody husband (Exodus 4:25). But the story makes it clear that the foreskin was viewed as a redemption offering to Yahweh in place of the whole child, for Yahweh demanded the lives of firstborns unless they were properly redeemed (Exodus 13:15). The male puberty ceremony was kept, among the Jews, even though it became a bloodless one, and it evolved into the bar mitzvah. Later priestly editors provided their circumcision ritual with a mythic precedent, by writing it into the story of Abraham (Genesis 17:10), since they did not want to admit (or perhaps had already forgotten) that the ritual was originally Egyptian.

1. Walker, *W.E.M.S.*, 144. 2. Crawley 1, 319.
3. Cavendish, 104. 4. Barnstone, 417.
5. Briffault 3, 372. 6. Boulding, 365.

Dance

Dancing used to be an important component of all religious rituals. Repetitive, rhythmical movement was thought essential to build up to the moment of ecstatic union with the deity, just as rhythmic sexual movements build up to orgasm;

in many ways the two were interconnected. One purpose of ceremonial dance was the same as that of ceremonial sex: to imitate the process of cosmic creation, to renew the world by influencing divine powers to conceive, gestate, and bring forth yet again.

Ancient worshipers of the **Goddess** attributed the initial creation of the universe to her magic dance over the Waters of **Chaos**, or Great Deep (Hebrew *tehom*). With rhythmic movements she organized the as-yet-unformed elements, making orderly patterns that the Greeks called *diakosmos*, the Goddess's Ordering. She is still found even in the Bible, as the spirit that "moved" (danced) on the face of the Deep before God came along to *talk* the universe into being.

The Goddess did not speak. She, who danced the world to birth, came from remote ages when the male role in reproduction was unknown, and only women were credited with the creative power. Many primitive people thought women could churn or curdle the magical moon-**blood** in their wombs, by means of their rhythmic movements, causing the blood to coagulate and form a fetus. Hence, the dances of primitive women used—and still use—many pelvis and belly motions as baby-making charms.

The rhythm of the primal female dance was the same one continuously heard by every fetus *in utero*, the basic heartbeat rhythm underlying nearly all human music, which automatically seems the most satisfactory accompaniment to dance. Tantric tradition called this rhythm the Nada, the Sound of Power or Heartbeat of the Absolute, made manifest in the human heartbeat, perceptible to the yogi when he "plunges deep into himself."[1]

Oriental mystics said the true self, which is identical to the eternally dancing deity, resides in the Cave of the Heart (Chidambaram). The concept is like that of the ancient Egyptian *ab*, the "heart-soul," most important of one's seven souls according to Egyptian belief. The *ab* was the soul given by divine living blood from the heart of one's mother, descending before birth into her womb. The same *ab* was the soul that would be weighed in the **balances** after death by the Mother of Truth, the Goddess Maat. In hieroglyphics, the *ab* was shown by a little dancing figure. As a verb, the same word meant "to dance."[2]

Egypt thus first produced the doctrine of the vitalizing blood of the Sacred Heart, though it was the mother-blood that first created the "blood bonds" of clan and family, passing down through the generations in the female line. Women celebrated the idea through dance, linking hands or arms to signify the linking of their hearts in a group heart-soul. Such dances were originally supposed to have power to conceive children.

India's four-armed Goddess Maya-Kali was another version of the dancing Creatress in the female heart of the cosmos. Carrying emblems of the four elements in her four hands, she was shown dancing on the body of her consort Shiva, who lay in his "dead" phase as Shava the Corpse, like the "dead" phase of Egypt's god Osiris when he became the Still-Heart.[3] Later, men began to worship Shiva in his own right as a world-sustaining deity whose dance expressed the rhythms of ongoing existence. However, even the now-familiar figure of Dancing Shiva was enclosed within a symbol of his Goddess in the form of a fiery horseshoe-shaped **yoni**.

The illustration on page 174 shows a typical Dancing Shiva. Every portion of the design holds symbolic meaning. One left hand holds the flame of spiritual light that burns away the veils of illusion; the other points with the "elephant" or "teaching" gesture toward the raised left foot that signifies "release." One right hand shows the "fear-dispelling" pose; the other holds the drum that makes eternity's rhythms. Underfoot, instead of Shiva himself in the inert part of his cycle, lies the dwarf Forgetfulness, who takes away the memory of past lives, as did the mystic fountain Lethe ("Forgetfulness") in Orphic legend.[4]

Gods and Goddesses who revealed doctrine through dance were not confined to the Orient or to paganism. In the Gnostic gospel *Acts of John*, even Jesus danced and said to his disciples, "To the Universe belongs the dancer. He who does not dance does not know what happens. Now if you follow my dance, see yourself in Me."[5] Early Christian churches carried on liturgical dancing in imitation of all their pagan contemporaries; but a new wave of asceticism about the sixth or seventh century outlawed ecclesiastical dancing on the ground that it was too sensual and too much enjoyed by women.

Subsequently, religious dance was confined to surreptitious remnants of the "old faith," and to their semi-Christianized festivals and carnivals, where it became incorporated into mystery plays and folk traditions that defied the hostility of the clergy. One of the things medieval inquisitors always said about witches and devil-worshipers was that they danced.

1. Zimmer, 205.   2. Budge, E.L., 44.   3. *Book of the Dead*, 410.   4. Campbell, *M.I.*, 359.
5. Pagels, 74.

Eucharist

"In the beginning," says the *Satapatha Brahmana*, "the sacrifice most acceptable to the gods was man"; then in later ages "for the man a horse was substituted, then an ox, then a sheep, then a goat, until at length it was found that the gods were most pleased with offerings of rice and barley."[1] Some of the Hindu deities are still offered blood, however; and the Christian God is still offered the flesh and blood of his own son, symbolically at least. The Catholic doctrine of transubstantiation is still an article of faith, insisting beyond all reasonable knowledge of chemical or physical reality that the bread and wine of the Eucharist are literally human flesh and blood.

Bread and **wine** were substituted for the flesh and blood of numerous ancient savior gods, such as **Osiris**, Adonis, and Dionysus. There was no doctrine of transubstantiation, however, to insist that the flesh and blood were real. Cicero said it was a common figure of speech to call the wine Bacchus; "but do you imagine," he asked, "that any one is so insane as to believe that the thing he feeds upon is a god?" This belief was demanded of Christians throughout the Middle Ages, although, as Duerr maintains, it was "nothing but an act of sacrificing one's reason."[2] A large part of the Protestant Reformation focused on rejection of the Eucharist as crude magic. Yet Douglas correctly points out that "Fundamentalists, who are not magical in their attitude to the Eucharist, become magical in their attitude to the Bible."[3] Whenever a line is drawn between ritual and magic, it is only a matter of the semantic preferences of different groups.

1. Robertson, 27.   2. Duerr, 306.   3. Douglas, 19.

Exorcism

The Roman ritual of exorcism is surely one of the silliest survivals of medieval superstition and credulity still extant, though the church has wisely relegated it to a dusty back shelf and rarely permits its use. Still, it is officially held that **demons** possess people, and that certain priests must be assigned the function of exorcist. According to the ritual, the exorcist is adjoined not to believe in "superstition," yet in the same sentence is incongruously directed to discover any "magical spell, sorcerer's symbol," or "occult documents" that might have caused the possession.

Interestingly, one of the alleged signs of demonic possession is the same sign that Saint Paul took as a sign of divine possession: speaking in tongues. "When the subject speaks unknown languages" or understands unknown languages, demonic possession is indicated.

The exorcist's first concern is for his own safety. At the invocation, God is ordered not to remember the sins of the exorcist or his assistants, and the possessed "should be tied down, if there is any danger of violence." The demon is commanded to "do no damage" to anyone. However, since demons are defined throughout as disobedient, recalcitrant, and perverse, one wonders what can be the use of such commands. The demon is also said to answer questions falsely; yet the exorcist must ask it all sorts of questions about its name and antecedents, the numbers and names of its companions if any, its reasons for possessing the victim, "and other questions of the same kind." In other words, the "possessed" person is encouraged to be highly creative in inventing responses.

During the course of many long and tiresome addresses to the demon(s), to God, to angels and archangels, to saints, and in fact to almost everyone except the subject himself, the invasive spirit is commanded to surrender, to go away, to leave, to give in, to desist, to take flight, to get out (twice), to retire (twice), to go out (four times), to depart (six times), to give way (seven times), to be uprooted and expelled, and to be put to flight *now*. Yet all these dismissals are interspersed with rhetorical questions showing that the creature is not dismissed: Why do you stay? Why do you resist? Why dare refuse? All the foregoing commands are bolstered up by the Mysteries of the Incarnation; the Suffering, Death, Resurrection, and Ascension of Our Lord Jesus Christ; the sending of the Holy Spirit; the Last Judgment; the name of the Judge of the Living and the Dead; Our Creator; God the Father; God the Son; God the Holy Spirit; the faith of the Holy Apostles; the blood of Martyrs; the purity of the Confessors; the pious and holy intercession of all the Saints; the Word made Flesh; and the strength of the mysteries of the Christian faith, not to mention assorted Cherubim and Seraphim, Powers and Virtues and Dominations of Heaven, and much more. One would think that all this heavy armament would be effective. In fact the demon is told that "it is impossible for you to will to resist," and "it is impossible for you to refuse to obey." And yet, one little demon can hold out quite well against all these superpowers, it seems. The creature hangs on, and must be told again and again to depart. Exorcism seems at best a creaky vehicle for God's intercession.

The ritual is kept up until the exorcist sees "signs of liberation," which, however, are not described. The directions only include a warning that demons often produce a false appearance of liberation, as if "the subject of Exorcism is not possessed at all." How this is to be distinguished from the real thing is never made clear. Apparently, the ritual of exorcism is virtually interminable, going on until everybody is tired of it and/or the victim-hysteric-performer runs out of ideas for outrageous things to say or do. Then, he or she is either pronounced cured, or relegated to psychiatric ministrations that probably should have been applied in the first place.

Fasting

Fasting has been a common religious ritual ever since people discovered—probably involuntarily, in periods of famine—that hunger produces hallucinations. Hallucinations, like dreams, have always been regarded as forms of communication with the supernatural. Among some American Indian tribes it was routine for young men to fast until they began to see visions, which were supposed to show them their personal spirit guides. Medieval **saints** too were much given to fasting, which undoubtedly accounted for the angelic and/or demonic visitors they so often encountered.

Fasting was highly recommended as an important ritual in both Christian and Jewish traditions. Rabbinical sources claimed that "God forgives all the sins of everyone who fasts on three consecutive days and nights, four times a year."[1] It was a small price to pay for complete exoneration from guilt. Muslims universally observed their fast of Ramadan for similar reasons. Christians likewise kept the fast of Lent, which was of pre-Christian origin. The women of Rome used to observe a period of chastity and fasting throughout the Kalends of March after their Matronalia, or Feast of the Mothers, which was celebrated in the sacred **grove** between the Aventine and Palatine hills, and was forbidden to men.[2] This springtime fast was copied by the Christian church and renamed Lent, from the Anglo-Saxon *Lenet-monath*, the month of "lengthening" (of the days).

Ritual fasting could be used to curse as well as to bless, because the very act was supposed to bestow magic powers. Fasting in order to cause harm to an enemy was known as the black fast. A woman named Mabel Brigge was executed in 1538 for carrying out a black fast against Henry VIII and the Duke of Norfolk. The bishop of Durham officially forbade black fasting in 1577.[3]

1. Trachtenberg, 157.   2. *Larousse*, 204.
3. Thomas, 512–513.

Halloween

Our Halloween rituals are relics of the
pagan All Hallows Eve, the original night-
time festival according to the lunar
calendar, preceding the solar-calendar
daytime version that was Christianized as
"All Saints." The festival used to be
the Feast of the Dead (Celtic Samhain, or
Vigil of Saman). It was perhaps the
most important of the cross-quarter days,
when the "crack between the worlds" could
open up and let the spirits pass through.
Therefore the ghosts of dead ancestors could
revisit the earth, join their descendants
at the feast, and give necromantic
interviews and omens. In Ireland, all the
sidh or fairy hills (grave mounds) were said
to open up for the occasion. Folks
insisted that it was impossible to keep the
fairies underground on Halloween.
Since these "fairies" were simply pagan
spirits, the church naturally insisted that
demons were abroad on Halloween,
summoned by witches, which was the
usual term for the ancient pagan
priestesses whose business it was to com-
municate with the dead.[1]

Halloween trick-or-treat customs
descended from a belief that the family
dead would bring gifts or goodies to the
children during their temporary return from
the other world. Gifts, food, and sweets
were always the standard method of attracting children's attention to religious
holidays, as is still shown by our own
Christmas and Easter customs. Thus, "the
dead relations have become the good
fairies of the little ones."[2] Black cats, owls,
bats, and broomsticks were the **familiar**
spirits and tools commonly associated with
witches, who retained a dominant
position in the Feast of the Dead despite
the church's attempt to assimilate
it in honor of its own canon of saints.

1. Joyce 1, 265.   2. Miles, 192.

Handfasting

Handfasting was the old pagan ritual of
marriage in the British Isles; it remained
legal in Scotland all the way up to
1939, even after Lord Harwicke's Act of
1753 declared marriages in England valid
only when performed by a clergyman.
Previous to that act, common-law marriages had been quite acceptably validated
by the couple themselves simply joining
their hands in the presence of witnesses.
After Lord Harwicke's Act, the Scottish
border town of Gretna Green became a
mecca for eloping couples who fled there to
handfast themselves in legal wedlock.

The handfasting gesture seems to have
been derived from one of the ancient

Indo-European images of male-female conjunction, the infinity sign, whose twin circles represented sun (male) and moon (female) cycles, one right-handed and the other left-handed as when the figure 8 is drawn with one clockwise and one counterclockwise circle. The right side of either sex was always considered the solar or male side, while the left side was lunar or female. Marriage, then, consisted of uniting the two right hands like an ordinary handshake, and then the two left hands, so that the partners' arms formed the graphic cycles of "infinity" or completeness.

It is interesting to note that patriarchal society retained only the right-hand handshake in token of agreement, friendliness, or greeting. The use of "female" left hands was dropped, except for one purpose: to formalize the Morganatic marriage, which was known as "marriage of the left hand," by joining left hands only. This type of marriage was invented by the German nobility to allow men of rank to live openly with their lower-class concubines, having legally secured the "marriage" against any rights or claims on the part of the wife or children to inheritance, property, or family name. Its only real purpose was to place "the shield of protection around man in illicit relations."[1]

Two-handed handfasting still consti-tuted a fully legal marriage in Europe, however, whether the blessing of the church was sought or not. Clergymen, of course, recommended that newlyweds attend church as soon as possible after the signing of the contract and the handfasting; but marriage had been for so many centuries ignored by the church, left under the jurisdiction of common law rather than canon law, that ecclesiastical rules on marriage were difficult to enforce.[2] In Switzerland from the sixteenth to eighteenth centuries, a couple could marry each other legally just by publicly drinking together.[3] The now-popular secular gesture of drinking through one another's linked elbows was once another way of forming the infinity sign of sexual union.

Like many other relics of paganism, the handfasting gesture was retained in children's games and traditional folk dances. Continental versions of the swing-your-partner movement call for a couple to join their hands in this same manner and whirl around each other.

1. Gage, 375.   2. Walker, W.E.M.S., 585–597.   3. Crawley 2, 124–128.

Hieros Gamos

Hieros gamos is Greek for "sacred marriage." It was the essential ceremony of king-making throughout the ancient world, because no king could be allowed to rule unless he was an accepted spouse of the **Goddess** (who represented the earth) through her mortal incarnation, the queen.[1] Among the Celts of Ireland and Wales, kings married the territorial Goddess.[2] "Headmen, who made up the council or assembly of elders of a tribe, served as the governing body for a Divine Woman or Queen, who personified the Great Mother and presided over a matrilineal society. The early king of such cultures ruled, not in his own right, but in his capacity as consort of the Divine Woman."[3] In Africa, installation of a Bahima tribal chief was a ritual union with Imama, the Goddess.[4]

Kings seldom held office for life. They were frequently replaced, on the theory that the Goddess needed constant revitalization in the form of new lovers: hence the many husbands of such pagan queen figures as Mab, Theodelinda, Hermutrude, and others. "Sacred queens used to have two husbands, a fact that emerges from an inscription by Urukagina of Lagash . . . after the passage of a year the sacred king was sacrificed and a new one chosen in his stead, to preserve the matrilinear succession."[5] Kings began to hang on to their godlike position on earth only after developing the idea that a substitute victim could be sacrificed in their stead, and the *hieros gamos* with the queen could be made more permanent.

The position of the wife retained sacramental importance up to and even after the beginning of the Christian era in Europe, and almost to the present day in the Orient. In the third century B.C., the Parthian dynasty of Iran was overthrown by a Persian, Ardashir, founder of the Sassanian empire, whose success was attributed to the fact that he had "the royal glory with him" in the person of the last shah's favorite wife, a personification of the Goddess. Jan Coen, the first governor-general of the East India Company, was widely believed to have been fathered by Sakender the Merchant, an incarnation of the divine Alexander the Great, upon the princess of Pajajaran, an incarnation of the Goddess Durga. Through descent from the legendary hero and the "Goddess who embodies kingship," Coen was declared heir to the Indies.[6]

Sacred marriage usually meant apotheosis for the bridegroom. The Greek writer Tzetzes said that all kings were once called Zeuses. Agamemnon of Mycenae

was named Zeus in Laconia. New light might be shed on Agamemnon's death by Macrobius's remark that the "consecrated men" called Zeuses "were put to death as a sacrifice to the gods. . . . They are said to have been slain or metamorphosed by Zeus."[7] That is, the Heavenly Father was made flesh, then killed by his own command, just as in the more familiar story of Jesus as sacred King of the Jews and Bridegroom of Zion.

The idea that marriage to the queen was a necessary prerequisite for male sovereignty grew naturally from the time when women owned lands and home places, and men acquired stewardship of property only through marriage. Even among nomadic desert dwellers, the tents belonged to the women. Pre-Islamic Arabian women signified acceptance of their husbands by positioning the tent. If a wife turned the tent so the door faced west, her husband was cast off and forbidden to enter.[8] In the biblical story of Noah lying "uncovered within his tent," the original wording says "within *her* tent," because the tent was owned by Noah's wife.[9]

The *huppah* or "tent" still appears as a Jewish wedding canopy because the ceremony used to mean formal permission for a man to enter his wife's tent. The Egyptian equivalent was the *senti*, a canopy under which the marriage and

coronation of a pharaoh were celebrated simultaneously. In ancient Israel also, kings were married and crowned at the same time, having been chosen by the royal women, who performed the ceremony. Solomon was crowned by his mother on the same day as his wedding (Song of Solomon 3:11). The marriage of Abraham, too, could only have been a *hieros gamos*, because the name of his wife Sarah means "the Queen."

1. Walker, *W.E.M.S.*, 501–508. 2. Green, 73. 3. Perry, 10. 4. Frankfort, 125. 5. Beltz, 10–11. 6. Cavendish, 77, 127. 7. Perry, 159–161. 8. de Riencourt, 187. 9. Cavendish, 104.

Hocus Pocus

The term *hocus pocus* arose from the habit of magical charlatans of peppering their nonsense chants with scraps of ecclesiastical Latin; it was a corruption of *hoc est corpus meum*, "this is my body," from the communion service. Such chants were usually accompanied by hieratic gestures and solemn poses, designed to impress. Thus, *hocus pocus* became a generic term for ritualistic behavior without any particular underlying symbolism: a ritual undertaken for its own sake, to awe

KISS
*God and Shakti, Puri
temple, Orissa, 12th century*

but not to enlighten the observer. Wizards of all types inevitably discovered that the average person responded just as strongly to this use of ritual as to any other kind.

Incantation

An incantation means literally a "singing-in" or an en-chant-ment. Chanting or singing was the usual manner of casting spells and calling spirits up from the underworld or down from heaven, as practiced by the Roman priestesses called *carmentes*, the singers of *carmen* (holy songs). They had their own Goddess, Carmenta, said to be the mother of the **alphabet** and thus of spoken or written charms. The word *charm* was another derivative of *carmen*, through Anglo-Saxon *cyrm*, a hymn.[1]

Trachtenberg says "the spirit world recognized a different principle than did the human," because "all incantations are in the name of the mother," not of the father.[2] Mandaean Christians, Greeks, and Arabs based incantations on the name of the mother, a holdover from various matriarchal traditions. Therefore, incantations and enchantments were always associated with women as former holders of the "words of power."

1. Potter & Sargent, 49.   2. Trachtenberg, 115.

Kiss

Kissing seems to have begun in southeastern Asia, where the Sanskrit term was *cusati*, "he sucks," derived from mothers' habit of premasticating food and feeding it to their babies mouth-to-mouth. Adult kissing evolved with the Tantric theory that men required female juices in order to retain their vitality. The Chinese version, Tao, called women's **saliva** "a great medicine," along with the other two divine yin juices, breast **milk** and menstrual **blood**.[1] The curative power of female saliva was cited on an Assyrian clay tablet: diseases of the eye could be cured by the saliva and milk of a temple harlot. Both Mohammed and Jesus copied this female magic by curing the blind with saliva (Mark 8:23). European pagan heroes sometimes did the same, so that the church fathers had to claim that this was a special talent of Antichrist. Pagan Romans believed blindness could be cured by the saliva of a mother of sons—a belief still prevalent among Italian peasants in the nineteenth century.[2]

Early Christians practiced the "kiss of peace" between men, yet they still had recourse to female symbolism. They claimed that men could impregnate one another (spiritually) by kissing: "For it is by a kiss that the perfect conceive and give birth . . . we receive conception from the grace that is in each other."[3]

1. Rawson, E.A.E., 234.   2. Gifford, 63, 120.
3. Robinson, 135.

Lammas

Lammas means "Feast of Bread" (Saxon *Hlaf-mass*). It constituted the Christian name of the pagan Lugnasad, the Celtic "Games of Lug."[1] Lug was the **grain** god sacrificed and resurrected to honor the Harvest Mother at the beginning of August, the month of harvest (named for Rome's Juno Augusta). One of the "games" celebrated at Tailteann was the special temporary marriage, supposed to last only a year and a day—the usual period of the ancient lunar calendar—after which the married couple could separate and go their own ways.[2]

In Ireland, special "Lammas towers" were built, and Lammas dancers circled around a female effigy representing the Harvest Mother. Because August was particularly sacred to the Goddess who gave life, the Scots considered it a propitious month to be born. Augusta gave gifted children. For a Scot to say someone was born in August was not a reference to a real birthday, but rather a compliment to a "well-skilled person."[3] When the church adopted Lammas, it was assigned to commemoration of the imprisonment of Saint Peter.[4]

1. Joyce 2, 439.   2. Pepper & Wilcock, 273.
3. Dames, 164–165.   4. G. Jobes 2, 968.

May Eve

May Eve was known as Beltain or Beltane to the Celts, Walpurgisnacht to the Teutons, and Floralia to the Romans. The presiding deity was the Goddess Flora, or Walpurga, or Maya—also known as Maj, May, Maia, and The Maiden.[1] The festival celebrated her virgin or "flower" aspect, harbinger of the fruit to come. It was a time of "wearing of the green," in honor of Earth's new green garment, as well as a time of sexual license, symbolizing nature's fertilization: a honey-moon when marriage bonds were temporarily forgotten and sexual freedom prevailed in rural districts all the way up to the sixteenth century.[2] The Maypole, still known in the East as the god's phallus, was planted in Earth's womb and celebrated with dance and song.[3] In northern Europe there were traditional "May ridings," featuring the King and Queen of May who represented Frey and Freya. Couples paired off and followed them into the woods for orgiastic encouragement of the new growth season.[4]

Because of the seemingly ineradicable sexual license of the May rituals, and their well-remembered pagan connotations, churchmen viewed May Eve as a major sabbat of witches.

1. Walker, *W.E.M.S.*, 624.   2. Briffault 3, 198.
3. Avalon, 517.   4. Gelling & Davidson, 163.

Midsummer

The festival of the summer solstice remained a major pagan holiday, despite efforts of the clergy to rededicate it as the birthday of John the Baptist. The only practical result was that Saint John's Day became associated with wild **dances,** horseplay, and general rowdiness. In pagan times, the solstices and equinoxes were important festivals keyed to the progress of the growing season. Midsummer was the vital, somewhat scary time when the sun reached its turning point and began its slow decline toward another winter. Therefore, Midsummer was always a festival of fire, when bonfires burned all night to encourage the solar deity to return again in due course.[1]

1. Frazer, *G.B.*, 399, 720–721, 761.

Mothering Sunday

English folk honored their mothers on the fourth Sunday in Lent, centuries before the now official American Mother's Day was founded by a Philadelphia woman in 1906. Mothering Sunday was mentioned as a popular tradition in 1644.[1] Mothers were offered gifts of simnel-cakes (from *simila,* "fine flour"), and asked to bless their children. The ceremonial visit to the mother was known as "going-a-mothering."[2]

1. Pegg, 29.   2. Brewster, 144.

New Year

The Carnival principle always attended the turning of the year in ancient Rome: that is, gluttony, drunkenness, and other sins were permitted on the theory that the next day brought the turning of a new leaf. Sinful offenses of the past year would be forgiven after the slaying of the mock king in atonement for them. The Roman New Year used to occur in the ides of March, during a season that later entered Christian tradition as the pre-Lent **Carnival.** Others, however, celebrated the turning of the year around the winter solstice (the northern Yule).

Churchmen never liked the pagan survivals associated with such holidays.

Puritan writer Philip Stubbes condemned turn-of-the-year revels in the sixteenth century. He described the choosing of the mock king to be Lord of Misrule, together with his anointing and investment as a supreme potentate; the gaudy costumes, the **hobbyhorses, dragons,** "and other Monsters," appearing in public streets along with "bawdy Pipers and thundering Drummers." For feasting all day and performing "the Devil's dance," Stubbes said the people were "devils incarnate," terrestrial furies, and hellhounds.[1]

Much milder New Year customs still provoked disapproval in the nineteenth century, when New Year's Eve was called the Hagmenai, an evening of visiting. Guests and hosts would remain together until midnight, then mutually kiss and wish each other a Happy New Year. A contemporary clergyman wrote that this custom indicated the presence of the devil in the house.[2]

The devil attending our own New Year celebrations, often turning them into orgies of highway death, has been described with better accuracy as the Demon Rum.

1. Pegg, 86–87. 2. Hazlitt 1, 296.

Ordeal

The ritual of ordeal was a crude method of resolving disputes, or establishing the guilt or innocence of a person accused of a crime. It was much practiced in pre-Christian Europe, and occurs to this day in parts of Africa, the South Pacific, and southeastern Asia. The ordeal consists of a dangerous act, such as swallowing poison, handling fire, walking on red-hot coals, or some other such feat of luck or endurance. If the subject survives, or perhaps even seems unharmed, it is established that the gods have favored his cause.

Trial by ordeal was conducted under the auspices of the Christian church all the way up to the thirteenth century. The clergy took over the pagan custom and derived a large segment of ecclesiastical revenues from administration of ordeals, which were held in or near the church building, where vessels and other implements of the ordeal were kept. The Fourth Lateran Council of 1215 finally discontinued priestly participation in ordeal trials, which caused the custom to lapse altogether, because by that time people had come to consider priestly participation essential and the judgment delivered by the Christian God.[1]

1. Brasch, 174.

 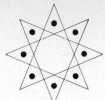  

A. *seven-point interlacement*   B. *eight-point interlacement*   C. *nine-point interlacement*   D. *ten-point interlacement*

Ritual Interlacement Patterns

Ritual interlacement patterns were used in pre-Christian tribal religious ceremonies, such as weaving-spells, invocations, and magic circles, by druids, shamans, witches, wizards, pagan healers, and seers; and in medieval times by ordinary folk at seasonal festivals, **Maypole** dances, and even in children's games. The basic idea of such an interlacement is that the pattern line must be continuous, endlessly tracing the figure without stops or breaks. This endless, "gateless" line was thought to form a barrier against evil influences, providing magical protection for persons or things inside, and knitting them together in symbolic communion.

One of the simplest examples of a ritual interlacement pattern is the ever-popular **pentacle,** said to have been inscribed on the floor or ground wherever sorcerers required protection from any demonic forces that their magic might call up. Other figures, with more than the pentacle's five points, could also be formed of similarly continuous lines, to make star shapes around any objects in a circle: pillars, posts, pegs, standing stones, candles, censers, images, upright swords, rocks, shells, flasks, barrels, or people standing or seated.

Eight diagrams here show the construction of an interlacement pattern around any group of from seven to fourteen objects or persons, which are represented by black spots within the kite-shaped extremities. For simplicity's sake, the reader may imagine that these black spots are people facing the center of the circle, passing a continuous cord around themselves to form each design, and perhaps pinning the cord to the ground at each star-point behind their backs.

The seven-, nine-, eleven-, and thirteen-point diagrams (the last, a "coven star" for the traditional thirteen witches) show that any odd number of units will make an unbroken interlacement when the line passes behind one and in front of the next, all the way around. Twice around the full circle in this manner brings the line back to its starting point.

Eight-, ten-, and fourteen-point diagrams show the line continuous when passed behind one and in front of the next two, all the way around. In these cases, three full circuits are needed to bring the line back to its starting point.

The twelve-point diagram is different. The line cannot pass behind one and in front of the next, because the figure would end at the sixth point and have to be restarted. Neither can the line pass

E. *eleven-point interlacement*

F. *twelve-point interlacement*

G. *thirteen-point interlacement*

H. *fourteen-point interlacement*

hind one and in front of two; then the figure would end at the fourth point. Nor can the line pass behind one and in front of three; then the figure would end at the third point. The only way to obtain a continuous twelve-point inter-lacement is to pass the line behind one and in front of four, as shown. Five times around the circle will complete the figure.

For modern ritual groups there are many creative ways of using interlacement patterns. Outdoors, a pattern can be laid out on the ground with ribbon, cord, chalk, or an incised furrow. It can mark a pathway for circumambulation or dance, accompanied by chanting or singing, or the pathway can simply sur-round a circle of posts or people. Indoors, the figure can be marked on a floor or carpet with string pinned or weighted at the points; or string may be passed around the bodies of participants to weave them together as a symbolic unit. Such figures can also be made of the participants' arms, weaving over-and-under around the circle and holding scarves or ropes to lengthen their reach. In dancing, the whole circle can turn like a wheel. A cord used for the interlacement can be cut afterward into separate portions, one "point" for each participant to keep as a souvenir.

Rosary

Although the church liked to pretend that the rosary was invented by Saint Dom-inic, actually it was an ancient Oriental ritual tool for constant multiple repeti-tions of prayers and mantras. An early form of the rosary belonged to the Goddess Kali as her *japamala*, "rose-chaplet." Rosaries were used in Arabia and Egypt from the beginning of the Christian era if not before. Their purpose was to build up equity in the afterworld by re-citation of magical preservative formulae on behalf of deities and souls, "regularly and continually millions of times."[1]

In fact, the Gospels' Jesus apparently forbade the use of rosaries, prayer wheels, and other aids to repetition. He said, "When ye pray, use not vain repetitions, as the heathen do: for they think that they shall be heard for their much speak-ing" (Matthew 6:7).

Having begun with Goddess worship, the rosary was more closely associated with the female principle. So, when Christians adopted it, they applied it primarily to the cult of **Mary**. The Litany of Loreto calls Mary "Queen of the Most Holy Rosary." She was identified with the rosary in her own titles of Rose-garland, Rose Garden, Mystic Rose, and Wreath of Roses.[2]

Christian rosaries usually contained beads in multiples of five and ten, the traditional numbers of the Goddess. Muslim rosaries held ninety-nine beads, for Allah's ninety-nine secret names; or sometimes thirty-three beads divided into three groups of eleven.[3]

1. *Book of the Dead*, 567. 2. Wilkins, 42, 106.
3. Budge, A.T., 437.

Sabbath

Sabbath observances were much older than the biblical deity whose seventh-day rest was supposed to have established them. Seven-day weeks extend back to the lunar calendar, which is why they no longer fit the months of our solar calendar. Lunar sabbaths were kept every seventh day by Babylonians and Assyrians, who thought it was bad luck to do anything during the changes of the moon. The seventh-day worship was attributed to the Goddess Durga in India. Her rites of protection for a new mother and her infant ended after six days; the seventh was a day of rest.[1]

Several Middle Eastern gods copied the idea before it was inherited by the biblical Yahweh. Baal, Marduk, Ptah, and Ahura Mazda all rested on the seventh day.

As applied to the celebrations of witches, "sabbath" seems to have been a misnomer arising from confusion with the Jewish sabbath, which was Saturday, the day of Saturn rather than the day of the Sun. Sometimes it was spelled Sabbat. Some believe this pagan "sabbath" was based on the Moorish *zabat*, "an occasion of power." Alternatively, it could have been derived from the Sabazia, nocturnal festivals of Dionysus under his Phrygian name of Sabazius.[2] The so-called witches' sabbath was not, however, a "black" or perverse parody of the Christian mass. Evidence for this theory came only from the torture chambers of the Inquisition and was invented by the inquisitors themselves, to be confirmed by their victims under torture.

1. Walker, W.E.M.S., 258. 2. *Larousse*, 160.

Tingeltangel

This colorful German word meant a sexual orgy: hinting at bodies "tangled" together for the sake of a "tingle." A variant of the term was extant among witches in Scotland, according to records of witch trials there. One of the women executed for witchcraft sang "a merry song" entitled *Tinkletum Tankletum*. It is quite possible, however,

that this was nothing but a nonsense chorus, and the singing of the song did not mean the accused witches were engaged in an orgy; on the contrary, their reported behavior sounded rather sedate.

Vigil

The Christian custom of "keeping vigil" overnight in a church descended from the pagan custom of doing the same thing in a temple; it used to be called incubation. Sometimes the participant in the rite was supposed to sleep and thus receive prophetic dreams. At other times, it was assumed that wakefulness would be maintained all night, which would bring mysterious visions or omens of future events.

Christian communities of the sixteenth century believed in the visionary efficacy of all-night vigils at certain crucial times of the year, when women sat up on the church porch to receive visions of persons who would die within the ensuing twelve months. **Midsummer** Eve, with all its leftover **Goddess** connotations, was considered particularly prophetic. John Aubrey wrote that the women "tell strange stories of it." In 1608 the archdeacon of Nottingham condemned a woman "for watching upon St. Mark's Eve

at night last in the church porch to presage by devilish demonstration the death of some neighbors within the year."[1]

1. Thomas, 240.

Yab-Yum

Yab-yum, meaning "Father-Mother," was the Tantric term for sacred coital postures in which a god or man was fully united with his Goddess or Shakti. Though Brahman and other patriarchal groups (such as Muslims and Roman Catholics) insisted that the male-superior sexual position was the only permissible one, the yab-yum position placed the partners face to face, either sitting or standing. In the latter case, the Shakti always had her left leg lying over her consort's right thigh.

This is so often illustrated in Hindu art that it may well be assumed to represent the *Maharutti* or "Great Rite" of Tantric worship. Yab-yum meant either that the sexes were equal in power, or that the power of the female was somewhat favored, since no male entity could function without being united with her.

9

DEITIES' SIGNS

W hat is a deity? Everyone defines *God* or *Goddess* in a different way. Coming from a patriarchal tradition, modern theologians naturally talk more about God than about Goddess. One of their required attributes of deity seems to be masculinity. Other attributes might include: omnipotence, omniscience, righteousness, benevolence, generosity, fairness, attentiveness, affection—or might they? God is also said to be vengeful, destructive, warlike, unforgiving, limited in foresight, and powerless to prevent evil. Does God have a sense of humor? Does God play dice with the universe? Does God rejoice in suffering? Did God really withhold forgiveness for some primordial crime, until mollified by the suffering of his "beloved" son, who was somehow also himself, as many Christians incomprehensibly insist?

Theologians profess to know God's attributes while simultaneously proclaiming that God is unknowable. Theologians put words in God's mouth (if God can be said to have a mouth), to tell others what God wants them to do. Theologians make God in their own image, according to what each thinks a deity ought to be. Thus God is a composite picture of men's *oughts*. Women's *oughts* may have been embodied in the Goddess, but for a long time women have been forbidden to talk about Her.

Aside from the multiple human definitions of deity, where is there any external, objective, empirically ascertainable foundation, any irreducible minimum that may be perceived and labeled *deity*, as a tree or a rock may be perceived? Some have argued that because the universe is, then a creator-of-the-universe must be, or at least must have been. But this does not necessarily follow. An uncreated, eternal universe may be postulated just as easily as an uncreated, eternal deity. Moreover, such qualities do not indicate any particular need for worship, praise, ceremonies, hymns, prayers, or any other trappings of religion. There has never been *any* statement about God that is empirically ascertainable.

The point here is that, whatever a deity may be in (undiscoverable) fact, every deity is pure symbol.

That means the usual relationship of symbol to object is reversed. Most symbols represent something external; they are shorthand forms of communication about the object's perceived qualities. In the case of deities, however, "perceived qualities" proceed from the communication and not from the object itself. Gods are whatever human beings say they are. Thus we create symbols of symbols, and learn to respond to them as if they were realities.

The symbols in this section are only a few of the graphic designs known to have been related to specific deities. Any or all of their attributes could be interchangeable, depending on how people discussed them in the

past—or even in the present. Any of these symbols could be reworked and held to "represent" a God or Goddess who exists now. For each of us, deity is whatever qualities we choose to attach to the symbol. The more mental associations we create, the more complex the deity becomes. But whatever treatment we give it, we cannot escape knowing that in the final analysis, for human beings, God is symbolism and symbolism is God—or Goddess.

Alpha-and-Omega Cross

This cross was a late Christian symbol, based on the New Testament deity who claimed to be "Alpha and Omega, the beginning and the ending . . . which is, and which was, and which is yet to come" (Revelation 1:8). The cross was hung with the Greek letters *alpha* and *omega* to illustrate this passage.

Unfortunately, the passage was neither original nor Christian. It was taken from the much older temple of the Goddess at Sais in Egypt, where her words were carved in stone: "I am all that has been, that is, and that will be."[1] **Alpha** and omega, the first and last letters of the alphabet, were frequently applied to the Goddess who united birth and death.

1. *Larousse*, 37.

Androgyne

Several secret traditions of the early Christian era clung to the ancient Asian concept of the combined male/female deity, the Primal Androgyne, said to resemble a man and woman embracing, or else a two-sexed being, Ardhanarisvara, with a left female half and a right male half.[1] In India this being was sometimes interpreted as a combination of Shiva and Shakti, or "the Lord Who Is Half Woman." Hermes and Aphrodite were similarly united as a deity called Hermaphroditus. The diamond shape of the androgyne symbol apparently combined the two triangles, seen in somewhat different format as the male/female **hexagram**.

Jewish mystical tradition viewed the original Jehovah as an androgyne, his/her name compounded of Jah (*jod*) and the pre-Hebraic name of Eve, Havah or

Hawah, rendered *he-vau-he* in Hebrew letters. The four letters together made the sacred **tetragrammaton**, YHWH, the secret name of God.

Again, Jewish Gnostics declared that Eve was once androgynously combined with Adam, not as a pseudochild "born" from his side, but as a complete half. "When Eve was still in Adam death did not exist. When she was separated from him death came into being. If he again becomes complete and attains his former self, death will be no more."[2] A second Adam would appear, entitled The Hermaphrodite.[3] The true revelation of a two-sexed deity, the Father-Mother spirit, was claimed by certain Jewish or Christian Gnostics who said this realization was the only way to the sacrament of "release" (*apolytrosis*). Some sects of Ophites or Naassenes called this androgynous spirit "the heavenly horn of the moon."[4]

Others declared that the true divine revelation could only come from an androgynous Christ, who was hermaphroditically united in heaven with the Goddess **Sophia**, "Mother of All."[5]

1. Cirlot, 189.   2. Robinson, 141.
3. Barnstone, 71.   4. Jung & von Franz, 136.
5. Malvern, 53.

Anguipede

Literally "Snake-foot," the anguipede was derived from the snake-footed or snake-tailed wind gods of Greece. He was also a common form of the Jewish Jehovah as shown on sacred medallions of the second and first centuries B.C.[1] He usually carried a shield and a "whip of Helios," identifying himself with the sun charioteer whom the Bible called Elias. Jesus called upon this personage as his God, in his last words upon the cross—at least, as these words were reported by two of the evangelists (Matthew 27:46–49; Mark 15:34–35).

The head of the anguipede was sometimes that of a man, sometimes that of a **lion**, sometimes that of a **cock**. His name was written below, Yahweh or Jehovah, on Gnostic coins and gems. Sometimes he was given a different title, Abraxas or Abrasax, who was also called Our Father and Lord of Hosts.[2]

1. Campbell, *M.I.*, 294.   2. Budge, *A.T.*, 209.

Asherah

The word that the Bible, with evident distaste, translates "grove" was not really a grove at all, but an *Asherah*: the stylized multibranched tree symbolizing the

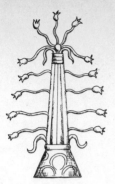

Great Goddess of Canaan. Closely related to Syrian **Astarte** and Babylonian **Ishtar**, Asherah was the original mate of the Semitic father-god El. Sometimes called Elath, "the Goddess," she was the mother and queen of all the Semitic pantheon. She reigned over Tyre, Sidon, and many other cities. The port of Elath on the Gulf of Aqaba was named for her. On the Ugaritic tablets (fourteenth century B.C.) she was identified with Astarte-Anath.[1]

Asherah's Canaanite titles included "Lady Who Traverses the Sea" and "She Who Gives Birth to the Gods."[2] Her tree symbol was alternately "tree of knowledge" or "**tree of life.**" In northern Babylonia she was known as the Goddess of the Tree of Life, or the Divine Lady of Eden.[3] The fruit of her tree represented all food, including spiritual nourishment.

Biblical writers were implacably opposed to any manifestation of the Goddess, as shown by their periodic descriptions of God's hostility toward kings who worshiped the "groves" and of reforming priests who destroyed Asherah's symbols. Jewish patriarchs continued to claim in the *Sefer Hasidim* that certain food-bearing trees harbored terrible she-demons, sometimes known as the daughters of Lilith.[4]

1. Patai, 32–34. 2. Albright, 121.
3. d'Alviella, 153. 4. Trachtenberg, 34.

Astarte-Tanit

Astarte was the biblical Ashtoreth, Goddess of Byblos—the linguistic origin of all "bibles." She was also known as Ashtart, Athtar, Attar-Samayin, Ishara, Ishtar, Asherah, Attart, Athra, and the Greek Aphrodite Aethra, "the Heavenly" or "the Holy One."[1] She was the Star, the Moon, the Heavenly Virgin, Queen of the Stars, and the Queen of Heaven to whom the Israelites burned incense, offered wine, and baked cakes in defiance of Jeremiah's God (Jeremiah 44:16–19). Sidonian kings always titled themselves high priests of Astarte. Pilgrims from far places visited her great shrines at Byblos and Aphaca.

She was assimilated to Isis/Neith in North Africa, and so was sometimes represented by the **ankh**. Another of her signs was a modified ankh, a lunar disc surmounted by **horns**, standing above the pyramid. The triangular base with full-moon head and arms represented her as the Carthaginian Queen of Heaven, **Tanit**. The same sign was still used as a tattoo mark in Tunis in the nineteenth century A.D. and was recognized by a French investigator as "the symbol of the Punic trinity."[2]

1. Albright, 143, 210, 228. 2. d'Alviella, 202.

Athene

Sulfur used to be sacred to Athene as a
Goddess of healing and purification, when
people believed that burning brimstone
(**sulfur**) would drive away the spirits of disease. The element was named after
her under the title of Brimo, virgin mother
of the Holy Child Brimus. Alchemists
therefore used the sign of Athene for sulfur,
which they were always trying to combine
with mercury in a "marriage of Athene and
Hermes," believing this process could
make gold. It never did.

Athene was much older than the city of
Athens that finally adopted her as its
patron. Her origin was not even Greek.
She was the Libyan Triple Goddess, var-
iously named Neith, Metis, Medusa, An-
ath, or Ath-enna; Egyptians said Athene was
a title of **Isis** and it meant "I have come
from myself."[1] Athene's display of the
Gorgon head on her **aegis** referred to her
own Destroyer aspect. Her Crone self,
Medusa-Metis, was twice mythologized as
Perseus's petrifying monster and as
Athene's mother, who was swallowed by
Zeus in order that he might give birth to
Athene from his own head. This male birth
imitation was often cited to show that
Athene recognized no mother and gave all
her loyalty to her heavenly father; but
its real meaning was that Athene was his

Sophia, his wisdom, the guiding female
spirit within his head.

The name of Athene's major temple,
the Parthenon, means "Virgin-house."
Athene was "virgin" in the old sense: independent of male attachments, a
spouse to none, a free agent. Yet, according to archaic traditions, she had lovers: Pan
and Hephaestus, for example.[2] Her sign
represents female self-determination, freedom, and great skill in the civilized
arts, of which she was supposed to have
been humanity's primary teacher.

1. Budge, G.E. 1, 459.   2. Graves, G.M. 1,
149.

Ceres

Ceres was a Roman title of the Great
Goddess as Mother of the Harvest and
ruler of all **grains**, which are still called
"cereals" after her major early-summer
festival, the Cerealia. Up to the nineteenth century in parts of the British isles,
it was said that "farmers go round
their corn with burning torches, in memory of the Cerealia."[1] Probably related to the
Greek Kore and the female spirits of
fate called Keres, Mother Ceres was not
only the fertile earth but also another
form of **Juno** as Queen of Heaven.
Her priestesses may have founded the
Roman legal system back in the age of

"mother-right." Their Goddess was
also entitled Ceres Legifera, "Ceres the
Lawgiver."[2]

The sign of Ceres was the lunar
crescent and inverted, or underworld-en-
tering, cross (see **Saint Peter's Cross**). The
combination probably represented the
sickle for cutting grain, as well as the hint
of lunar seasonality and the planting
of the (male) seed in the earth's womb.
The rites of Ceres were originally Greek,
probably based on traditions from
the great temples of Demeter.[3]

1. Hazlitt 1, 101.   2. Bachofen, 192.
3. *Larousse*, 211.

Cernunnos

The figure of Cernunnos from the
Gundestrup Cauldron (second century
A.D.) is probably the best-known representation of the Celtic Horned God. His
very name is really the title, "Horned
One." Holding a torc and a **serpent**, wearing an antlered cap, he sits in a yoga
pose with his right heel against his genitals. Nearly all seated statues of Hindu
deities show the same conventional pose.
The torc and serpent are also genital
symbols, female and male respectively.
Cernunnos is the spirit of the sacrificed
stag-god, a nature deity to whom
sacrifices were dedicated in order to main-

tain the wild creatures and the cycles
of nature with his holy **blood**.

There has been considerable speculation
about Cernunnos's costume, which
appears to be a form-fitting suit of ribbed
knitted fabric, with knee-length pants. It is
one of the pieces of evidence cited for
the antiquity of the art of knitting among
Celtic peoples.

Chrismon

The usual interpretation of this Chrismon
or *signum dei* (sign of God) was that
it stood for the initial letters of the Latin
phrase *Iesus Hominum Salvator:* "Jesus,
Savior of Man." Another interpretation favors the initial letters of the phrase *in
hoc signo,* "in this sign," referring to the
apocryphal legend of Constantine's
vision (see **Labarum**), with the **Latin cross**
added over the H.[1] Still another interpretation identifies the letters as Greek
rather than Latin, iota, eta, sigma, once
an identification of Bacchus as the
sun god.[2]

In reality this "monogram of Christ" is
of comparatively recent provenance,
and its original allusion seems to have
been forgotten.

Another version of the Chrismon was

written simply IS (Iesus Salvator).
Later, the two letters I and S were superimposed. The resulting combination
evolved—with singularly appropriate
irony—into the modern dollar sign.[3]

1. Koch, 23.   2. Walker, *W.E.M.S.*, 522.
3. G. Jobes 1, 841.

Dagon

The Philistine god Dagon received a bad
press in the Bible, because he was
Yahweh's chief rival at the time and also a
more popular deity. One writer claimed that
the mere presence of Yahweh's **ark** in
Dagon's temple, as a spoil of war, destroyed
Dagon's image and caused the temple to be
deserted forever (1 Samuel 5:1–5). This
seems to have been mere wishful thinking, because a century or so later
the cult of Dagon was still lively, and the
Philistine god received the head of Saul as
another spoil of war (1 Chronicles 10:10).

Actually, the fish-tailed god Dagon
was just another form of the Babylonian Ea
or Oannes, king of the sea, who in
turn was the basis for the legend of Jonah.
An icon of the fish-tailed god, or of
his human-headed spirit arising from the
mouth of a fish, was later reinterpreted as
Jonah emerging from his whale. Dagon or
Oannes also represented the sun going down

into the sea and "reborn" from the
waters, the latter personified as his mother-
spouse, Atargatis or Derceto.[1] It was
this mystic birth that gave rise to the derivative legend of Jonah's incubation and
rebirth from the "womb" of the whale, as it
was called in earlier biblical translations.[2]

One of the names of this Mesopotamian deity actually suggested that he was
identified with the biblical Yahweh
at some period in his history. The name
was given as Yah-Daganu, meaning
literally "Yahweh is Dagon."[3]

1. Baring-Gould, 494–497.   2. Potter &
Sargent, 180.   3. G. Jobes 2, 1697.

Djed

The curious Egyptian idol known as the
Djed column was set up annually
at the festival of **Osiris**'s death and rebirth.
It represented the lowest vertebrae of
the god's spine, his sacrum, which even
now takes its modern English name
from the Latin for "sacred bone."

Why this should have been an especially
sacred part of the body is something
of a mystery. Perhaps Tantrism offers a
clue, in regarding the general area deep
within the pelvis as the seat of kundalini
energy, which may have been viewed as the

origin of the god's renewed life. Mythology is not lacking in notions about certain holy bones, from which the entire body may be reconstructed.

The Djed column not only depicted the sacrum; it was also provided with the **crown**, sun disc, **feathers** of Maat, **horns** of Hathor and Amon, and the magical **eyes** of sun and moon.

Eye Goddess

Many figurines of the early Sumerian Eye Goddess (3500–3000 B.C.) have been found in Syria and around the Mediterranean.[1] Like Maat in Egypt, she represented the spirit of truth and law. Hers were the All-Seeing Eyes from which no crime could be hidden. She later merged with the Goddess Mari, who was also depicted with huge staring eyes although her form was more human. Eventually the Eye Goddess developed into the mysterious wise creatress Mari-Ishtar, or Mari-Anna, once worshiped as the consort of Yahweh in Jerusalem.

The Goddess's staring eyes aroused uncomfortable feelings in men, who came to look upon her as a spirit of the evil eye.

1. Campbell, *M.I.*, 476.

Eye of Horus

The old Egyptian symbol known as the Eye of Horus is rather incongruously perched on the Great Seal of the United States, and on every U.S. dollar bill. The reason seems to be that designers of the Great Seal were strongly influenced by Freemasonry, which had adopted a number of Egyptian religious symbols, this among them.

The eye within a pyramid originally represented the god enclosed, during his "dead" period, awaiting rebirth. He was entombed in the underworld, thus becoming Seker, the Hidden One, Lord of Death: **Osiris** as the mummy, the **Black Sun**, the Still-Heart. Nevertheless, his soul remained alive and watchful, as indicated by the open eye.[1] Parallels from southeastern Asia might be found in the *bindu* or life-spark within the triangle of the Goddess-womb, and in the open "third eye" of Hindu gods while their other two eyes were closed in their periods of deathlike sleep.

1. *Book of the Dead*, 145.

stone head from Cyprus,
6th century B.C.

Goddess

Recent research has established the
primacy of the Goddess figure in human
thought, as a direct outgrowth of the
primacy of the mother in every individual
experience, and also because biological
fatherhood was unknown until fairly late in
the development of civilizations. Though
male scholars still use the term *gods*
for the supreme creative deities of prehistory and myth, it has been shown
that the creative power in all the oldest
traditions was female.

Egyptians said the primeval sea **womb**
was the Goddess Nun or Naunet,
who gave birth to the sun and all the gods.
In Sumeria she was Nammu who
created the sky and the earth (An and Ki).
In Babylon she was Tiamat, "the Deep" who
gave birth to all the deities, including
the municipal god Marduk who later became her matricidal killer. In Greece she
was the primal Goddess Gaea who gave
birth (without benefit of consort) to the sky
Uranus, and later made him her spouse.
Assyria told of the wise Goddess Mami (or
Nin-ti) who made human beings out
of the **clay** that was part of her womb, animating them with her **blood** as women's
uterine blood was supposed to create and
animate their own children.

"The 'old gods' of late Sumerian
tradition were without exception Goddesses. Antum, Ninlil, Damkina, Ishtar
and Baba, the sacred queens of the
five ancient cities, Uruk, Ur, Eridu, Larsa
and Lagash, were older than their
husbands, Anu, Enlil, Enki, Utu and
Nergal. Their spouses were all of lower
rank."[1] Avalon remarks that "in the beginning the Goddess everywhere antedated, or
at least was predominant over, the
God. It has been affirmed that in all
countries from the Euphrates to the Ad-
riatic, the Chief Divinity was at first in
woman form."[2]

With the advent of patriarchal societies,
many of the names and symbols of
the Great Goddess were suppressed and
finally forgotten. The new father-gods
usurped her world-creating functions, her
attributes, even the very words and
phrases of her ancient scriptures. The Bible contains many plagiarized excerpts from
earlier hymns and prayers to **Ishtar**
and other Goddess figures, with the name
of Yahweh substituted for that of the
female deity. In biblical Hebrew, the word
for "Goddess" does not exist.[3]

As God has been made by men's
words, so the Goddess has been unmade
by them. The process still goes on.
*Webster's Third New International Dic-
tionary* defines capital-G *God* in a great
variety of ways, in which it seems

the editors just can't say enough in his favor. Definitions include: "the holy, infinite, and eternal spiritual reality presented in the Bible as the creator, sustainer, judge, righteous sovereign, and redeemer of the universe who acts with power in history in carrying out his purpose . . . the eternal, invisible, arbitrarily omnipotent Lord of the worlds and final judge of all men [sic] . . . the unchangeably perfect Being that is the first and final cause of the universe . . . the supreme or ultimate reality . . . the Being supreme in power, wisdom, and goodness that men [sic] worship and to whom they pray." And as an ultimate offense, *Webster's* further defines God as "the one ultimate infinite reality that is pure existence, consciousness, and bliss"—a phrase lifted directly from the Yoginihrdaya Tantra where it was a description of the Goddess, She Who is "the radiant illuminatrix in all beings."[4]

By contrast with these effusions, small-g *goddess* is defined briefly as a divinity of the female sex, then as "a woman who is the object of adoration . . . something personified as a woman that is honored as a goddess." Only three citations are given, all of them belittling and one even grossly erroneous. They are: (1) "like the lover whose imagination makes a *goddess* of some commonplace young

woman"; (2) "that characteristic middle-class *goddess*, the English Common Law"; and (3) "the Hindu assassins used hashish as devotees of the *goddess* Thuggee." No Goddess was ever named Thuggee. The Hindu Thuggee cultists worshiped the Goddess Kali. Moreover, the *hashishim* or "hashish-takers" from whom the word *assassins* came, were not Hindus but Saracens; so the reference is wrong as well as an obvious attempt to emphasize only evil connotations of Goddess worship.

Today a few well-meaning reformers sporadically try to restore a semifemale component to the basic idea of God, which has been so immovably and implacably masculine throughout the distressing period of his acting "with power in history," as the dictionary puts it. Some try to call him "God the mother" or present him as either bisexual or sexless. Every symbol for what Western civilization now calls God has been so heavily weighted with masculinity, however, that no such equivocations can make much difference. Nelle Morton suggests that even retention of the word *God* can only serve "to keep women shortsighted and the Goddess suppressed."[5]

Whatever else deities may be, they are certainly symbols par excellence; and what

*Pelasgian statuette, Hermes
the sheep-bearer*

they symbolize is the idealized human being. Men stole women's greatest symbol and left them spiritually impoverished while they went on to inflate their own male deity to positively blimpish dimensions. It may take more than words to redress that wrong.

1. Beltz, 10. 2. Avalon, 409. 3. Teubal, 99.
4. Avalon, 27. 5. Morton, 142, 144.

Good Shepherd

Christians' adoption of the title "Good Shepherd" for their particular version of the savior god was a deliberate theft from some of that god's oldest images. Nearly all pagan saviors assumed the Good Shepherd role, caring for souls in the "green pastures" of the afterlife, as if souls were their sheep. Babylon's Tammuz (Sumerian Dumuzi) was called shepherd of the stars, when the latter were thought to be visible souls of the blessed. **Osiris** also bore the shepherd's crook, which became a sign of divinity in Egypt, and was called the Good Shepherd. The Greco-Roman **Hermes** (**Mercury**) appeared as a Good Shepherd carrying a sheep on his shoulders: this image, antedating the foundations of either Greek or Roman civilization, was found in the earliest pre-

Hellenic Aegean cultures.[1] His title of Kriophoros (sheep-bearer) was preempted by early Christians who simply renamed all the pagan god's statues "Christ."[2]

1. *Larousse*, 88. 2. d'Alviella, 94.

Hermes

The sign of Hermes was the original "sign of the cross" that Christians traced on their heads and breasts, that is, the numeral 4, which was Hermes' sacred number. He was known as the Fourfold God. He also had many other names and titles. He was the Roman **Mercury**, the Egyptian Thoth, and the early-medieval Hermes Trismegistus, "thrice-great Hermes," legendary founder of astrology, alchemy, and other occult sciences. Sufis claimed Hermes as an adept of their craft.[1] He was amalgamated with Anubis as "Hermanubis" because, like the jackal god, he was a guide in the underworld and a conductor of souls (**Psychopomp**). He was amalgamated with Aphrodite herself, as "Hermaphroditus," whereby he learned his great wisdom and magical powers. He became her Wise Serpent, later revered by the Gnostics as **Ouroboros** or Ophis, a king of heaven and revealer of mysteries. As a phallic god he was worshiped at Hermeseul (Irminsul) in Germany, in the form of a huge "Column

of the World." The Church of Saint Peter now stands on the same spot.[2]

Early Christians viewed Hermes as a Christlike figure. From Hermetic worship they borrowed the *logos spermatikos* or "seminal word" that the pagan god incarnated, and they applied it to their own savior.[3] According to Lactantius, Hermes was a divine prophet, nearly the equal of Christ. Hermes knew "almost the whole verity."[4] Like Buddha, he was called the Enlightened One.

Hermes' sacred number sign arose from the moon boat, emblem of his virgin mother Maia (whose Asian form was Maya, virgin mother of Buddha the Enlightened One). The same figure 4 is found in the Chinese concept of the Primal Arrangement, attributed to the all-purpose Chinese culture hero Fu Hsi. It was brought to him by a dragon horse from the Yellow River (Ho), thus was called Ho-t'u. This Primal Arrangement was a series of nine numbers, represented by groups of dots, tracing the figure 4.

1. Shah, 196.   2. Borchardt, 122, 216.
3. Cirlot, 198.   4. Seligmann, 88.

Hermetic Cross

This version of the Christian cross was adapted from the sign of **Hermes**. Some said it was a "hermaphroditic" sign of male and female principles together: the male god (cross) arising from the female (crescent moon). Since the **moon** was a common symbol for all forms of the Virgin Mother including even her Christianized, mortalized one, the Hermetic cross was often interpreted as an emblem of Christ born of the Virgin.[1]

1. Koch, 32.

Hokmah/Holy Ghost

Hokmah or Hokhma is the Hebrew version of the Great Goddess as "Wisdom," possibly from Egyptian Heq-Maat, Mother of the creative words of power whereby the universe was formed. Authors of the *Targum of Jerusalem* insisted that the first word of Genesis, *bereshith*, usually translated "in the beginning," actually referred to this "Lady Wisdom" who was the designer of everything. Like her Gnostic, Greco-Roman counterparts, **Sophia**-Sapientia or Metis, Hokmah was expressly described as the wife of Jehovah in the writings of Philo of Alexandria.[1] Not only that, but like the Shakti of any Oriental god, she was the

original source of all his creative energy and ideas. It was stated in The Wisdom of Solomon that Hokmah's orders were always obeyed; she was the cause of everything that happens; and it was she who always decides what God shall do.[2] The obvious supremacy of the female principle in this "wisdom literature" was the reason for its being removed from the biblical texts and placed in the Apocrypha.

The triumphant **dove** having been the most common symbol of the Goddess's spirit brooding over the waters of creation, this became a representation of Hokmah-Sophia-Sapientia just as it also represented Aphrodite and Venus. Early in the Christian era, it was understood that God's inner spirit or soul was female and embodied in the image of the dove. From her he received his *i-deas*, "goddesses-within," and the souls even of gods were considered feminine (*anima, psyche, pneuma, alma*, and similar words for "soul" were always feminine). Later, the Holy Ghost was masculinized, God's Wisdom was no longer personified as a Goddess, and editors of the scriptures did their best to remove all hints of the earlier meanings of Hokmah.

1. Patai, 139. 2. Stone, A.M.W. 1, 126.

Ishtar

So common in the Mesopotamian area were the clay figurines of Ishtar/Inanna/Ashtart in her characteristic **breast**-offering pose, that this has come to be known among archeologists as "the Ishtar pose." She was addressed as "Mother of the fruitful breast," and much more as well: Queen of Heaven, Lady of Victory, Light of the World, Star, Mountain-shaker, Leader of Hosts, Creator of People, Guide of Humanity, Shepherdess of the Lands, Mother of Deities, Supreme One, River of Life, Exalted, Glorious, Judgment-giving, and many similar titles that were often appropriated by biblical writers for their own God.[1]

Ishtar was worshiped in Jerusalem, where her priestesses annually staged the time-honored drama of the death and resurrection of her son-lover Tammuz, whose Sumerian name was Dumuzi, and whose Syrian name was Adonis (Ezekiel 8:14). The breast-offering pose suggested her function as the Goddess of all nourishment; therefore the early patriarchal cultists feared to offend her and placed her alongside their Yahweh in the temple. Jeremiah 44:19 describes her as Queen of Heaven and shows the people's reluctance to abandon her for a new, untried male god. Eventually, however, Christian writers

belittled her holy sexual character by calling her the Whore of Babylon, Mother of Harlots (Revelation 17:5), and similar epithets drawn from among her own titles.

1. Walker, *W.E.M.S.*, 450–453; Stone, *A.M.W.* 1, 105–111.

Isis-Hathor

Isis and Hathor were two of the major names of the Great Goddess in Egypt. Hathor was called the mother of every other deity, who "brought forth in primeval time herself, never having been created."[1] She was Queen of Heaven, and her name was part of every royal name in the earliest dynasties. Isis, also, was "the Oldest of the Old," who existed from the beginning, "the Goddess from whom all becoming arose."[2] Both were said to have given birth to the sun, Hathor as the Nile Goose (mother of the Golden Egg), and Isis as the womb of Horus—which was the real meaning of the title Hat-Hor.

As a pair, Isis and Hathor sometimes represented the Bright Mother and the Dark Mother, according to the birth-death-rebirth cyclic system of matriarchal religions. In the later dynasties, the Dark Mother was often Nephthys, the twin underworld sister of Isis. It was Isis-Nephthys who guaranteed the immortality of pharaohs, promising to resurrect them as

Osiris was resurrected by motherly magic.

The usual emblem of the composite Goddess was the sun disc lying between the horns of the Moon-cow: the male spirit enclosed and protected, soon to be reborn. The disc was sometimes a full circle, sometimes a flattened oval representing either the World Egg, or the oblate shape of the sun as it rises or sets. The Goddess was addressed as "Great Cow who gives birth to the sun." He, Horus-Osiris-Ra-Helios, later took the form of the Golden Calf that the Israelites brought from Egypt and worshiped under the tutelage of Aaron (Exodus 32:2–4).

The cult of Isis became enormously popular throughout the Roman empire. Roman writers called her the "eternal savior of the race of men."[3] The image of her, suckling her child Horus under the sacred tree of Hathor at Dendera, became the archetypal model for similar images of the Virgin Mary.[4] The glorification of Mary descended directly from the scriptures, scenes, and hymns once dedicated to Isis as mother of the divine child. "Isis was the typical Hellenistic Divine Mother, and her cult was widely celebrated. The transfer of parts of mythologems from Isis worship to Mary the mother of Jesus undoubtedly took place in the middle third of the first century A.D."[5]

One of the Gnostic Christian sects, the Carpocratians, maintained that Jesus received all his ideas from the temple of Isis in Egypt, where he studied for six years.[6]

1. Budge, G.E. 1, 92–93.   2. Stone, W.G.W., 219.   3. Angus, 139.   4. Budge, G.E. 2, 220.   5. Beltz, 227.   6. Spence, 94.

Janus

Two-faced Janus was the Roman god of gateways—the *janitor*, "gatekeeper"—looking both ways across a threshold.[1] In the imperial period he was identified with **Jupiter** under the name of Jupiter Bifrons, "Two-Faced Jupiter," a name that turned up again in Christian literature fifteen centuries later as one of the devil's names.[2] Previous to the imperial period, Janus figures guarded property lines among neighboring tribes, each of which had its separate *ianus*.[3] Even earlier, one of the two faces was female: the Jana who was assimilated to **Juno**. This pair, typical of the ancient **androgyne**, may even have originated with the two-faced Goddess herself, addressed at her festival of the year's turn in January as "She who looks backward and forward," Postvorta and Antevorta. She was the Mother of Time, ruling the Celestial Hinge at the back of the North Wind, around which the universe revolved at the transitional "gate" of midwinter.[4] There were many other mythic parallels with this Mother of Time with her two aspects, often visualized as the Two Ladies. A medieval Neapolitan word for a witch was not the usual Italian *strega* but *janara*, after the archaic female spirit of January.[5]

Having accepted the all-male Janus as the New Year god, however, medieval writers continued to refer to him as the archetypal duality. According to the author of *Gawain and the Green Knight* (which was about the midwinter sacrificial encounter of two year-gods), January was still the month of Janus.[6] The two-faced god was even canonized as a mythical Christian **saint**, Januarius, when his old shrine at Naples was taken over by the church. A bottle of dried blood of the imaginary Januarius was preserved there, and like other dried-blood relics made to turn liquid periodically, especially when "placed by the head of a martyr." Pope Pius II attested to the authenticity of this miraculous method of distinguishing genuine relics—which, however, seemed to be quite unknown before the fourteenth century.[7]

1. Dumézil, A.R.R. 1, 328.   2. Scot, 323.   3. Whittick, 206.   4. Graves, W.G., 184.   5. Elworthy, 353.   6. Williamson, 178.   7. Brewster, 415; Attwater, 184.

Juno

Juno was the Roman Queen of Heaven and Mother of the Gods, the composite, nearly monotheistic deity of women. Her numerous titles indicate that she took care of almost everything. She was Juno Fortuna, Fate; Juno Regina, the Queen; Juno Lucina, the Light; Juno Moneta, Admonisher; Juno Sospita, Preserver; Juno Martialis, the Warrior; Juno Populonia, Mother of the People; Juno Pronuba, Arranger of Marriages; Juno Domiduca, leader of brides; Juno Nuxia, perfumer of the marriage chamber; Juno Cinxia, dresser or undresser of brides; Juno Rumina, giver of mothers' milk; Juno Ossipago, strengthener of bones; and so on. In sickness and in health, in wedlock and without, Juno watched over her daughters on earth.[1]

In addition, every woman was a *juno*. That was the name of her soul, as *genius* ("begetting father") was the name of a man's soul. The terms obviously dated back to ancestor worship, when the ancestral founders of clans were supposed to bequeath their spirits to their offspring.[2] Juno Curiitis was the primeval mother of all the clans (*curiae*). On their own birthdays, Roman women used to make offerings to their *junos*.[3] Patriarchal society naturally retained the word *genius* for the idealized male soul, but forgot the corresponding word *juno*.

Juno's star-shaped emblem identified her as Star of the Sea, a title inherited by the Virgin Mary, along with Queen of Heaven, Lily, Rose, and Blessed Virgin. Though ostensibly mated to **Jupiter**, Juno renewed her virginity each year, and miraculously conceived her holy child **Mars** without any male assistance. Like other versions of the original **Goddess**, she was both a chaste virgin and—in other phases—a deity of sexual lust, as Juno Caprotina, whose fertility rites were held to fructify the fig trees.[4]

1. *Larousse*, 203.   2. Rose, 193; Reinach, 102. 3. Huson, 146.   4. Rose, 217.

Jupiter

Jupiter's sign is applied to both the planet and the god, who was Rome's rain and thunder deity, evolving into a Father-of-Gods. Like his Greek counterpart, Zeus, Jupiter was believed to fertilize his consort, the **Goddess**, by raining on her or entering her as **lightning**. Yet he was not a simplistic rain god but a highly complex deity who passed through many stages of development.

Jupiter, Zeus Pater, and the Babylonian god Zu the Storm Bird all stemmed from Aryan Dyaus Pitar, "Father Heaven."

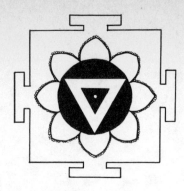

Jupiter first appeared as "the Youth,"
Jove (*juventus*), to replace the Virgin
member of the formerly all-female Capitoline Triad, consisting of Juventas,
Juno, and Minerva—the Greek Hebe,
Hera, and Hecate.[1] The young Jove was
regarded as interchangeable with the Father, just as son and father became
interchangeable in later Christian theology. Eventually, the Capitoline Triad consisted of Juno, Minerva, and Jupiter.[2]

Like Juno, whose consort he became,
Jupiter had innumerable titles, ranging from
Jupiter Pluvius (Jupiter-Who-Rains) to
Jupiter Opulentia (Jupiter-joined-to-the-
Goddess-Ops). His name was given to the
planet Jupiter because of the ancient
astrologers' conviction that the heavens
consisted of seven ascending **spheres**, each
the residence of a different planet.
The sphere of Jupiter was occupied by the
planet Jupiter. Therefore, astrologers
through the ages have assigned to the
planet Jupiter various characteristics associated with the "Jovian" image: leadership, lordly manner, jollity, expansiveness,
generosity, and the like. What the
sign of Jupiter originally meant is not
known; but it looks very much like a
turned-around version of the sign of **Ceres**,
which was another name for Juno,
Queen of Heaven.

1. Dumézil, A.R.R. 1, 201.   2. Rose, 116.

Kali Yantra

The meditation sign of India's Great
Goddess Kali incorporates both female-
sexual and maternal symbolism. The
background is the four-sided emblem of the
world, with its four directions, four
winds, four primal rivers, and so on.
Within that, the eight-petaled **lotus** represents the Goddess in her loving, nurturing
aspect. A black orb shows that she is
also the Destroyer, Mother Night, who absorbs everything eventually into her
dark womb of nonbeing or **chaos** between
universes. Then a downward-pointing triangle, the *yoni yantra*, is inhabited
by the pearly spark of new life called
bindu, promising a new creation and a
new birth of living worlds from the
eternal female principle.

King of Kings

Our common sign for a medical prescrip-
tion came from a Latin shorthand
invocation of **Jupiter** as king of heaven or
king of kings (*Iupiter Rex*), who was
thought able to cure all diseases. Therefore, the sign R-*x* became a healing
charm in itself. Some authorities maintained, however, that the true healing king
of kings was not Jupiter but his dark

underground counterpart **Saturn**—perhaps on the theory that healing must come not from above but from within, as the earth's "healing waters" came from deep springs. Often it was believed that the prescriptive charm R-x, or any other medical invocation, should be written on paper that was then swallowed by the patient.[1] Crude healing magic as simplistic as this is not unknown even today, in our supposedly enlightened age.

1. Waddell, 401.

Labarum

Shown sometimes with its encircling ring and sometimes without, the labarum was once touted as the monogram of Christ, which the emperor Constantine saw in the sky before the battle of the Milvian Bridge: an event that supposedly converted him to Christianity on the spot. Actually, the labarum was already a sacred sign to Constantine's troops, not because it was Christian but because it was the sigil of their favorite deity, Mithra.

A late development of the Egyptian **ankh**, the Mithraic labarum perhaps denoted the wheel of the universe with the rising sun enthroned at the beginning point of the year.[1] It was the "sign of the cross" that was marked on the foreheads of Mithraic initiates.

Later development of the Christianized myth insisted that Constantine's labarum appeared in the sky, despite the evidence of Lactantius who said the emperor saw it in a dream, not outdoors, and that it was not a cross but "the letter X with a perpendicular line though it, turned over at the top."[2] Some early Christians claimed that it incorporated the Greek letters *chi* and *rho*, for *Christos*. Some said, however, that the labarum was derived from the ancient Cretan symbol of the double ax.[3] In any event, it was not originally Christian; and Constantine was not converted to Christianity at the Milvian Bridge or anywhere else, until he finally accepted baptism on his deathbed.

1. d'Alviella, 180.   2. J. H. Smith, 48.
3. Whittick, 211.

Logos

Christian theologians liked to pretend that the Logos doctrine began with their own scripture: "In the beginning was the Word, and the Word was with God, and the Word was God" (John 1:1). Thus Jesus was declared a symbol made flesh, of the creative Word (*logos*) whereby God brought things miraculously into being by speaking their names. In fact, though, the Logos doctrine was one of the most derivative of all Christian concepts. Before

Jesus, the god **Hermes** was declared an embodiment of the Logos of his heavenly father Zeus, the *logos spermatikos*, creative word. This made Hermes the Light of the Life of Man, and also a female-imitative "fruitful Womb of All," according to a third-century Hermetic text, *The Perfect Word*.[1] He was identified with the Egyptian Thoth, another manifestation of the creative Word. Thoth was the spouse of the Goddess Maat, "whose Word is Truth," another way of saying that whatever she spoke became reality. Thoth took over the Goddess's powers and spoke the Word of creation, according to his priests. He also became a "fruitful Womb" that gave birth to the first gods.[2] It was written in Egyptian hieroglyphics: "The Word creates all things. . . . Nothing *is* before it has been uttered in a clear voice."[3] In spite of Thoth, however, it was still the Goddess Maat who enabled the pharaoh to maintain the right order of creation by her word, the *hu* or "Creative Utterance."[4]

Gods had to demonstrate their command of the Logos before they could claim creative spirit. The Babylonian god Marduk could rule among the gods only after he showed his ability to destroy and re-create by the power of his Word. Just as Christ was called the Logos of Jehovah, so many centuries earlier Enlil of Nippur was called the Logos of Anu the heavenly father. "The spirit of the Word is Enlil," said the *Epic of Gilgamesh*.[5]

The real reason behind all this scramble of gods to adopt Logos power was that it was one of the few methods of creation by the primordial Mother that male deities could conceivably use, without female aid. Priesthoods talked of male gods giving birth, or even of men—like Adam—giving birth to women; but everyone knew this kind of talk made no sense. So the priests eventually seized upon the creative Word, which originally belonged to the Goddess also, because it is from mothers and not from fathers that young children usually learn their language.

India's Goddess Vac, "Voice," was a manifestation of Kali as Mother of Creation. She reigned at the summit of the Cosmic Tree or Mountain of the Gods.[6] She spoke the first word Om to bring forth the universe: the *mantramatrika*, "mother of mantras." She invented the **alphabet** whose letters were called *matrika*, "mothers." Her scriptures said: "She is contained in all that lies between the first and the last letters of the alphabet, which contains the original root forms from which the names of everything in the world are compounded."[7] (See **Om**.)

Having preempted the ancient Goddess's

power of the Creative Word, patriarchal religions made it the primary process of world-making gods, and a power present in their earthly incarnations from birth. A naive example of this thinking is found in the boyhood of Jesus as recounted in the *Book of James*. Because he had the power of the Logos, "all of his words became facts"; so when his schoolmates made fun of him, he simply spoke their names with a curse, and they promptly fell down dead.[8]

1. Angus, 243.   2. *Larousse*, 27–28.
3. Seligmann, 39.   4. Frankfort, 61.
5. *Epic of Gilgamesh*, 24.   6. d'Alviella, 162.
7. Rawson, A.T., 198.   8. Warner, 13.

Mars

The sign of Mars is now standard, not only for our neighboring planet, but also for "male" in botany and zoology, as a counterpart to the **Venus** sign which means "female." Mars became associated with Venus in classical mythology, as one of her lovers, possibly because the pair stood for a yang-and-yin type of alternation of opposites: love and hate. The Greek version of Mars was Ares, god of strife and discord. The Scandinavian version was Tiw, a warlike god displaced by Odin. The Assyrian version was Nergal, "Shedder of Blood," a god linked with misfortune and disaster, a Lord of Death.

Mars was not originally a god of war, however. His earliest Etruscan image was that of a sacrificed fertility god, Maris, worshiped at an ancient shrine in northern Latium.[1] Like most fertility saviors he was mated to the Goddess, Marica, upon whom he begot the divine king Latinus, legendary ancestor of all Latin tribes. Mars was incarnate in the sacrificial goat called Faunus, who was the flayed satyr-hero Marsyas in Greek myth. It was his flaying that earned him the name of the Red God.[2]

Probably because military exercises were held on the Roman Campus Martius, "Field of Mars" where the ancient sacrifices had once taken place, Mars became the patron of Roman legions, and then a god of battle as soldiers carried his emblems with them on their campaigns. They called him Marspiter ("Father Mars"). His sacred day was *dies martis*, Tuesday, named in English after Tiw whom the Romans called the northern Mars.

Classical writers insisted that Mars was virgin-born (the usual requirement for heroes) from the Queen of Heaven herself, **Juno**. To conceive Mars, she rejected her spouse Jupiter and magically fertilized herself with her own sacred **lily**.

1. Whittick, 247. *Larousse*, 207.

Mercury

Mercury was the Roman name for the god **Hermes** (Egyptian Thoth), apparently derived from Latin *merx* or *mercator*, a merchant.[1] As a god of commerce as well as magic, illusion, and trickery, Hermes-Mercury was often seen as the joker in the deck of the gods, a sharp dealer, very clever but not altogether trustworthy. In both Greece and Rome he was the patron of mercantile endeavors, metals, smithcraft, and the arts of "natural science" that became medieval alchemy. He gave his name to the only metallic element that is liquid at ordinary temperatures, and is also called quicksilver ("living silver"), difficult to pick up or to pin down, like the "mercurial" personality of the god himself.

As his sign suggests, the complexity of Mercury's character may have been based on his intimate association with the **Goddess**. Both the planet Mercury and the metal mercury are shown by what is essentially the sigil of Venus, with horns added at the top: a distinct resemblance to the Horned God who was her consort. Alchemists seemed to recall something of this. They identified Mercury with the female Anima Mundi, who was sometimes called Anima Mercury, and sometimes Rebis, the bisexual Duality.[2] Sometimes Mercury's sign meant all the hermetic arts in general.

Mercury's sign also means Wednesday, which was *dies mercurii* to the Romans. In English it is Woden's day, because Mercury was identified with Woden in northern Europe and with nearly every other major god among the barbarian tribes, as far as the Romans were concerned.[3] Like Hermes, he was also a god of the dead. His sign was found in catacombs and other subterranean places of worship.[4]

1. Huson, 124. 2. Cirlot, 198. 3. Green, 85. 4. Silberer, 189.

Neptune

Neptune was the Latin name of the Greek sea god Poseidon. Like most male deities of the earth's deep places or abysses, he carried the **trident**. In the case of this oceanic deity, the trident was interpreted as a fish spear.

The same trident now represents the planet Neptune, which was discovered in 1846 after extensive investigation of

666

its action on the orbit of Uranus. The late discovery of the outer planets, Uranus, Neptune, and Pluto, caused consternation in astrological circles because previously unsuspected "planetary influences" would have to be considered. As a rule, Neptune came to be regarded as highly mysterious, mystical, and occult, perhaps chiefly because of the resemblance of its trident symbol to one of the conventional signs of the devil.

Number of the Beast

Six hundred threescore and six (666) is called the number of the beast in Revelation 13:18, where it is a numerological conundrum. It is also "the number of a man." Christian authorities long assumed that the man must be Antichrist, so this "beast" was identified throughout the centuries with many whom the church disliked for one reason or another: Attila the Hun, Genghis Khan, Saladin, Frederick the Great, Napoleon, Hitler—always playing number games with the letters of each name to add up to 666.

As a result of constant association with the powers of evil, 666 came to be regarded as the devilish number par excellence. Aleister Crowley thought himself a very devilish fellow, delighted in his self-imposed title of The Great Beast, and put the number 666 on his personal sigil. Even today, 666 evokes a superstitious response from people who hardly understand its origin.

The other mention of 666 in the Bible makes it the mystic number of Solomon's golden talents (1 Kings 10:14), apparently coming to him by way of his alliance with the Queen of Sheba. The "beast" was once a hermaphroditic beast with two backs—that is, sexual union—in the religion of Triple Aphrodite, to whom the number six was sacred. The sexual connotations of six made church fathers declare it "the number of sin."[1] Tripled, then, it was a whole trinity of sin. Nevertheless, a mystic labyrinth in Chartres Cathedral, with Aphrodite's six-lobed symbol in its center, was planned with a path exactly 666 feet long.[2]

1. Baring-Gould, 652. 2. Pepper & Wilcock, 159.

Osiris

The sign of Osiris identifies the Egyptian god as Savior of the World. His "body" is the **ankh** or Cross of Life. His arms make the *ka*-symbol of the soul, upholding the sun disc that came to represent Osiris-Ra, both heavenly father and dying-and-resurrecting son. Osiris was one of the earliest of the dying gods whose worshipers ate his body in the form of **bread,** confident that this sacrament would make them divinities in the afterlife by partaking of the divine essence. He was the Egyptian form of "the god-man who suffered, and died, and rose again, and reigned eternally in heaven."[1]

The cult of Osiris was one of the Holy Mysteries highly popular in Rome about the beginning of the Christian era. Many of its details were copied by the Christian church, except for one vital point: the agent of Osiris's resurrection was not the heavenly father, but the Goddess Isis, who was also the Savior's mother, sister, wife, preserver, and Holy Spirit, all in one. The Osirian trinity was a complicatedly incestuous combination of father, son, and mother-spouse—as was the original

Christian trinity also, until **Mary** was mortalized and **Sophia** masculinized— and in Egypt, the Goddess was the most powerful of the three. (See **Isis-Hathor.**)

1. Budge, G.E. 2, 126.

Pluto

The planet Pluto was unknown to the ancients, because it cannot be seen from earth with the naked eye. Therefore it was rather arbitrarily named Pluto in 1930 by its discoverer, C. W. Tombaugh, after the classical Greek version of the dark god of Hades. A tailed-P symbol was invented for it. Astrologers now had to fit Pluto into their system, even though no astrologer knew of its existence until a mere half century ago.

The dark god Pluto was himself a Hellenic revision of a former Great Mother's title, meaning "riches" or "abundance." There was a female Pluto among the pre-Hellenic elder deities whom the Greeks despised and discredited in their myths.[1] This Pluto seems to have been combined with Demeter in a triple form, as Kore (Virgin), Pluto (Mother), and Persephone (Crone, i.e., "Destroyer").

1. Graves, G.M. 2, 25.

Purusha

According to the Brhadaranyaka Upan-
ishad, "In the beginning only the
Purusha existed. He was as wide as a man
and a woman embracing, and divided in two,
from which came the husband and the
wife."[1] *Purusha* means "man" or "person." The images of this creature show
"him" to have been another version of the
Primal **Androgyne,** male and female
in the same body, the right side male and
the left side female according to the
classic, worldwide gender division. Other
stories said Purusha as a male being
would have to be intimately joined to the
female nature spirit Prakriti before
he became a viable life-form. Similarly,
all Hindu gods, including the allegedly
supreme Brahma, were helpless unless
bonded to their female halves, their Shak-
tis, who represented the Great Goddess as
Bhavani, "Existence."[2] "Brahma, the
great immaterial Whole, is a passive, con-
templative male figure who is powerless
without his wife Shakti, who is energy in
motion."[3]

Whereas Indian art often shows the
original concept of the androgynous deity,
the image faded from Western civilization
even though myths referred to it. There were,
for example, the two-sexed people of the
Golden Age that Zeus severed down the
middle to punish them. And there

were Adam and Eve, modeled on the Persian androgynous pair Mashya and
Mashyoi, created male and female both
together in at least one of the two or
three different creation stories in Genesis.
Rabbinical traditions sometimes contradicted the story of Eve's pseudobirth by
saying that God, like Zeus before him,
parted the male and female halves
of the first human being out of jealousy
for their constant sexual bliss.[4]

In more patriarchal times, Purusha was
revised away from the original androgynous form, and represented as a giant
outline filled in with hundreds of little
men: that is, the male-female "person"
became a collective "man."

1. Markale, 155.   2. Walker, W.E.M.S., 587.
3. Markale, 99.   4. Walker, W.E.M.S., 33.

Saturn

Another variant of the cross-and-curve
seen in the signs of **Jupiter** and **Ceres,** the
sign of Saturn depicted the dark underground god who was the Heavenly
Father's alter ego, just as Pluto was the
alter ego of Zeus, Ahriman the alter ego of
Ahura Mazda, or Satan the alter ego
of God. To Babylonian astrologers, Saturn
was the same as their **Black Sun,** the
solar god entombed. At Harran, Saturn

was worshiped by people in black clothing, burning special candles made with incense and opium. They addressed the deity as "Lord Saturn the cold, the dry, the dark, the harmful . . . crafty sire who knowest all wiles, who art deceitful, sage, understanding, who causest prosperity or ruin."[1]

In Rome, the sacrifice of Saturn took place at the year's end festival of Saturnalia, at first in the form of a human victim, later in an effigy that became transformed into the mock killing of King Carnival, "a vestige of the ancient Saturnalia, when the man who had acted as king of the revels was actually put to death." Human victims were still immolated in early Christian times.[2] The killing of King Saturn actually represented the passage of the solar god or heavenly king into the underworld at the end of the year, to be followed by his joyous resurrection as the heavenly king reborn.

The day of Saturn was Saturday, the last day of the week, said Agrippa von Nettesheim, which "hath correspondence with the last end of life, and is ruled by Saturn which carries the sickle of death."[3] The reason for this image of Saturn as death-bringer was his identity with the Greek Titan-god Chronos, Kronos, or Cronus, who became "Father Time"

with his death-dealing sickle, by virtue of his alliance with the older goddess Rhea Kronia who was Mother Time. Personifying both time and the earth, like Kali the Destroyer before her, Rhea naturally devoured all that she brought to birth. Thus the cult of Chronos or Cronus depicted him as the devourer of his own children, and Saturn too became a child-eater. The only child who escaped this paternal cannibalism was Zeus, who later defeated his father and drove him out of heaven. The same Oedipal rivalry figured in Persian and Jewish legends of the War in Heaven, although with a different outcome.

As might be expected of a chthonian god, Saturn was associated with darkness, heaviness, density, and melancholy. A "saturnine" personality was said to be ruled by the **earth** element. Saturn's metal was lead. His planet, also, came to be regarded as a beclouded influence, even though the Saturnalia was a day of great festivity and cheer. Eventually, of course, it was declared a day of sin and so became even more closely associated with deviltry.

1. Cumont, A.R.G.R., 28, 90. 2. Moakley, 55.
3. Agrippa, 147.

Shekina

The Shekina was to the Hebrew God what Kali-Shakti was to Shiva: his female soul, his mind, his energy, his creativity, and his essential spouse. Rabbinic literature said the splendor of the Shekina feeds the angels; she can castigate God for his vengefulness. She was "a great heavenly reality whose shining countenance shoved the theoretical doctrine of the Oneness of God into the background." According to Gikatilla, she was Sarah in the days of Abraham, Rebekah in the days of Isaac, Rachel in the days of Jacob. She was also Matronit (Mother), Malkuth (Kingship), Discarded Cornerstone, Pearl, Moon, Earth, Night, Garden, Well, Sea, and Supernal Woman.[1]

The Shekina was often defined as God's "Glory," which, like "Holy Spirit," was another way of concealing the original Goddess relationship that gave Yahweh his powers. Sometimes her name was simply omitted from scriptures, and another word substituted in its place. The Targum of Onkilos, an Aramaic version dating from about A.D. 130, gave "Shekina" where later authors substituted "name" in Deuteronomy 12:5: "God shall choose that his Shekina may dwell there, unto the house of his Shekina shall you seek."[2]

Some Talmudic literature said the Israelites carried two caskets in the wilderness, one containing Joseph's corpse, the other containing the Shekina in the form of two stone tablets. Israel's sins caused the Shekina to leave the tabernacle, but some rabbis insisted that she returned when the second temple was built. Her presence was indicated by the ringing of **bells,** just like the presence of the Catholic host.[3]

To Jewish Gnostics, the Shekina occupied the same position as **Sophia-**Sapientia or Mari-Anna or Myrrha of the Sea to Christian Gnostics: that is, she was a thinning remnant of the formerly all-powerful image of God's spouse. For Christians, the Holy Spirit was masculinized. For Jews, the Shekina was almost completely forgotten, until certain cabalistic sects resurrected her in the thirteenth century.

1. Patai, 147–149, 161, 177–178.
2. Mollenkott, 38.   3. Patai, 141–145.

Sige

Sige, "Silence," was a mysterious hooded female figure with her finger blocking her lips. Some said she represented the secret name of Rome, which could not be spoken aloud; or else she represented the taboo against speaking it. To the

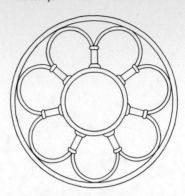

Gnostics, however, Sige was the primordial female power of creation, who gave birth to **Sophia;** for out of Silence came the first creative word. This formerly female cosmogony infuenced the Neoplatonic doctrine of the **Logos,** by which God was supposed to have brought the world into being by his speech.

Another name for this Roman Goddess of silence was Angerona. Her cult, rituals, and spiritual meanings were so carefully hidden that virtually nothing is known about them to this day.[1]

1. *Larousse*, 214.

Sin

If Moses climbed Mount Sinai to meet the resident god, then the god he met would have been the moon god Sin, who had been enthroned on that mountain since the rise of Sumeria, and gave his name to it. In fact, Sin gave his name to the whole Sinai peninsula, formerly "the Land of Sinim" (Isaiah 49:12), or the land of the lunar mountain. The original Yahweh was only another form of this "primitive lunar deity of Arabia."[1] Sin became part of the Babylonian trinity along with Shamash the sun and **Ishtar** the star.[1]

The symbol of Sin shows a mountain crowned by the moon's horns, with a shaft reaching to the underworld: the whole somewhat resembling a stylized tree. Sometimes, the moon-crowned tree was also an emblem of the **Goddess,** whose son-consort Sin was, in the usual fashion of Mesopotamian divinities.

1. Briffault 3, 106.   2. Campbell, *M.I.*, 88.

Sophia

The sevenfold **mandala** represented Sophia in a twelfth-century manuscript from Landsberg, the *Hortus deliciarum* (Garden of Delights). Within the seven arches appeared seven female figures labeled as the seven branches of learning: Arithmetic, Geometry, Astronomy, Grammar, Rhetoric, Dialectic, and Music. Sophia herself appeared in the central circle as Wisdom, or Philo-Sophia, or Universal Mind.

Sophia's seven **pillars** were the ancient Seven Pillars of Wisdom inherited from some of the oldest manifestations of the Middle Eastern **Goddess.** The temple of Aphrodite-**Astarte** on Cyprus

had seven pillars. A Moabite temple at Bab ed-Dra was built with seven menhirs in the third millennium B.C.[1] The Bible mentions the Goddess of Wisdom who has "hewn out her seven pillars" (Psalm 9:1).

Gnostic literature said Sophia created Adam from seven consistencies: his flesh from earth (clay), his blood from dew, his eyes from the sun, his bones from stone, his mind from cloud, his hair from grass, and his soul from the wind that was her own breath. Sophia Zoe ("Wisdom of Life") was the mother of Eve and produced Adam later. Eve at first had no husband.[2]

The Holy Ghost was a Gnostic creation, and its (her) original name was Sophia. Valentinian Gnostics said, "The world was born of Sophia's smile."[3] An early Gnostic work, *The Everlasting Gospel*, quoted Jesus: "My mother the Holy Ghost took me by the hair of my head up into a mountain."[4] In the *Pistis Sophia*, Jesus said he found the soul of "the prophet Elias" in heaven and gave it to Sophia the Virgin of Light. She put it into the womb of Elizabeth so it could be reborn as John the Baptist. Later church fathers, rejecting the doctrine of reincarnation, insisted that John was not technically a reincarnated Elias but that he acted with Elias's "spirit and power," whatever that was supposed to mean.[5]

1. Gaster, 804. 2. Robinson, 171–172. 3. Neumann, 56. 4. Gage, 47. 5. Evans-Wentz, 361–362.

Sun Goddess

Although it seems traditional to associate the sun with the masculine principle, the archaic image of the sun as a **Goddess** was once widely diffused. The Great Mother of southern Arabia, Atthar or Al-Ilat, was the sun, also known as Torch of the Gods.[1] The Goddess Sun was known in North America and Siberia. The ancient Germans called her Sunna, Sol, or Glory-of-Elves. To the Celts she was Sul or Sulis, from *suil*, the sun's eye. At doomsday, said the *Eddas*, she would give birth to a daughter sun who would illuminate the new world to come.[2] In England she was worshiped at Silbury Hill (Sulisbury or Solbury) and at Bath, where the Romans identified her with Minerva and built altars to Sul Minerva.[3]

Japanese royalty traced their descent to the Sun Goddess Amaterasu. The

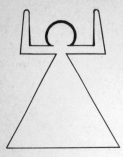

sun was considered the "clothing" of the Great Goddess, according to the *Mahanirvanatantra*: a tradition that certainly influenced the biblical image of the "woman clothed with the sun"(Revelation 12:1), who was, inevitably, identified with **Mary.**[4] Buddhists also called the Sun Goddess Mari, or Marici, "Sun of Happiness."[5]

1. *Larousse*, 323. 2. Branston, 152, 288.
3. Dames, 154. 4. *Mahanirvanatantra*, xl.
5. Waddell, 218.

Tanit-Astarte

A stylized female figure with upraised arms (see illustration) was one of several symbols for **Astarte,** Goddess of Syria, Phoenicia, and western Mediterranean colonies like Carthage, where she was usually called **Tanit,** or sometimes Astroarche, Queen of the Stars.[1] Her body is a modification of the **triangle,** or the aniconic cone that represented so many ancient Goddesses. Her symbol was also sometimes seen as a **lotus,** the flower of life, "symbolical representations of the universal matrix."[2] Moreover, it resembled the Egyptian hieroglyph *ka,* meaning a

spirit-soul, or a woman's invocatory gesture drawing down the essence of the Queen of Heaven into herself.[3]

The son-spouse of Tanit-Astarte in Carthage was Baal-Hammon, a solar god known as "Lord of the Brazier," the same as Egypt's Amon and Susa's Haman. His sacrificial victims "passed through the fire to eternal life," in the biblical phrase, meaning they were burned.[4] Virgil wrote of Aeneas narrowly escaping such a fate by fleeing from the Carthaginian queen. Actually, the worship of Tanit did emigrate to Rome where she became known as Libera, the Goddess of Libya, in whose honor the Liberalia was celebrated each year during the ides of March.

In the fifth century A.D., the Carthaginian temple of the Goddess was converted into a Christian church. It was discovered, however, that nominal Christians were still making their devotions to the old Queen of Heaven in the church; so Bishop Aurelian ordered the structure destroyed.[5]

1. Lindsay, 327. 2. d'Alviella, 189.
3. *Larousse*, 84; Budge, *E.L.*, 57. 4. Albright, 233. 5. J. H. Smith, 229.

יהוה

Tetragrammaton

Tetragrammaton means "four-letter word," referring to the four Hebrew letters *yod, he, vau, he* (YHWH) usually called "the Ineffable Name of God." The Ineffable Name was so secret and holy that it could not be pronounced, except once a year, only by the high priest.[1] Like certain other deity names it was accorded great magical powers, was frequently written on amulets and charms, and was regarded as a direct embodiment of the spirit of Yahweh himself.

And yet, the most secret element of the tetragrammaton was its root, the radical HWH, which means "being" or "life" or "woman," just as a Sanskrit title of the Goddess, Bhavani, signified "existence."[2] Translated into Latin letters, this was EVE, another suggestion of the Gnostic concept of Eve as the mother of Jehovah (Yahweh), as well as the "Mother of All Living" for the world in general (Genesis 3:20).

In fact there were two versions of the tetragrammaton: the usual "male" YHWH and a "female" EHYH that often appeared on Samaritan amulets. On the parchments that were used in **phylacteries,** these two versions were frequently intertwined.[3]

Medieval Christians lost track of the real meanings of the tetragrammaton,

understanding only that it was commonly written in magic books. Therefore they assumed that it was the name of a powerful **demon.** In the seventeenth century, Tetragrammaton was described as a mighty devil whose business it was to protect witches from their persecutors.[5]

1. Trachtenberg, 90. 2. Waddell, 117.
3. Budge, A.T., 261. 4. Hazlitt 2, 656.

Thor

The emblem of Thor, the Norse god of thunder, is his magic hammer, named Mjölnir or Mullicrusher. The **lightning** was said to be caused by sparks struck from this hammer's blow, and the thunder was its sound. Some scholars derive Thor's hammer from the double ax or **labrys** borne by Cretan and Hittite thunder gods.[1]

Small replicas of Thor's hammer, elaborately decorated, as shown, were often used as amulets, protective pendants, or tools of magic. Smiths, who were also wielders of hammers and commonly associated with pagan witchcraft, were thought to be special favorites of Thor.

The hammer was not the exclusive property of Thor or any other male god. It

was also associated with several versions of the Goddess. For example, a hammer represented the Greek Fate-goddess Ananke, who used it to forge the chains of destiny that indissolubly bound both men and gods.[2]

1. Branston, 122.   2. G. Jobes, 1, 91.

Tyr

Tyr was the Scandinavian name of Tuesday's god, who was Tiw to the Saxons, Ziu in southern Germany, Tiuz or Tiwaz in the north. These names were related to the Indo-Germanic word for a god, *dieus,* related also to the Greek Zeus. Tyr was also an alternate name for Odin.[1] Tyr or Tiw preceded Odin as a supreme sky god, and was later displaced by the Heavenly Father of the Aesir, just as his Roman counterpart **Mars** was displaced by **Jupiter.** Both Mars and Tyr survived to become war gods, and both were assigned to Tuesday (Latin *dies martis,* the day of Mars). Both were represented by a **spear** point attached to a "female" disc, although

the sign of Tyr sometimes appeared without the disc, so that only the spear or arrow remained.

1. Davidson, G.M.V.A., 57.

Uranus

This sign of Uranus is a comparatively recent invention, used by astrologers to denote the planet Uranus after its discovery in 1781 by Sir William Herschel. Having been previously unknown, the planet had no sign. An alternative sign for the planet was a variant of the sign of **Mars,** with its arrow pointing straight up instead of aslant.

The new planet was named after the Greek god Uranus, meaning "Heaven": a linguistic descendant of the Vedic heaven-god Varuna. According to Hesiod, Uranus was the oldest of gods and the father of the primordial Titans who were born of his consort Gaea, "Mother Earth." Uranus was attacked and castrated by his son Cronus, who threw the severed genitals into the womb of the sea, which then gave birth to Aphrodite

(**Venus**). This was the classical story of divine Oedipal rivalry. It was built on earlier myths that made Aphrodite herself the original Queen of Heaven. One of her oldest titles was Urania, "the Heavenly."

Venus

The "mirror of Venus" symbol is similar to the Egyptian **ankh**, sign of life, love, and sexuality; these were also the connotations of the Goddess Venus, Rome's version of Aphrodite. Her sign is now the botanical and zoological emblem of femaleness generally, as well as the astronomical emblem of her planet Venus, the morning and evening star as seen from earth. It also denoted the day sacred to her, Friday (Latin *dies veneris*), in pagan tradition the day of eating **fish**— which was thought to be an aphrodisiac food—in anticipation of sexual rites honoring the Goddess. The practice was copied by Christians, who changed its meaning.

"Veneration" used to mean the worship of Venus because the Romans regarded her as one of the most sacred of all deities. The Latin word for "grace," *venia*, meant

the Goddess's favor. Julius Caesar worshiped Venus Genetrix (Venus the Ancestress). He built a marble and gold temple in her honor and had his own statue placed near hers in the guise of her consort.[1]

The symbol of Venus meant "copper" in alchemy, because copper was sacred to the Goddess ever since her major shrine was located on Cyprus, the Isle of Copper, a mining and copper-working center. She was often called Cyprian Aphrodite or Cyprian Venus, the Goddess of Copper.

Early in the Middle Ages, Venus became the reigning Fairy Queen of numerous holy **mountains** called Venusbergs, where some of her many ancient shrines had been located. Christians execrated these sites, and also other sites of the Goddess's temples, which were condemned as "schools of wickedness." A sixth-century writer insisted that women's sinful observation of "the day of Venus at weddings" would be punished by hellfire.[2] Nevertheless, the church was forced to absorb the Goddess in some way, because her worship proved ineradicable. As a rule she was converted into a mythical

Saint Venerina or Venere. "Towns and shrines dedicated to Venus were renamed in honor of 'St. Venus.'"[3] At the same time, traces of Venus worship survived in magical charms, particularly those connected with sex. Her "mirror" symbol figured in procedures like the following love charm: the egg of a black hen must be buried at a crossroad after sunset and left for three days; then it must be dug up by night and sold; the money must then buy a mirror, to be buried in the same spot, "in the name of the Lady Venus." After sleeping on the spot for three nights, the magician may dig up the mirror. Any woman who looked in it would fall in love with him.[4]

Another curious remnant of Venus's worship was the feast day that the church renamed Holy Innocents Day, purportedly recalling King Herod's slaughter of the innocents. The official sign of the day was a row of four Venus mirrors.[5] Perhaps some pious monastic innocent had assumed that these could represent small children.

1. Dumézil, A.R.R. 1, 94; 2, 546. 2. J. H. Smith, 241. 3. Fisher, 383. 4. Trachtenberg, 43. 5. Brewster, 42.

Vesta-Hestia

Vesta was the Roman name of the Greek Goddess Hestia, "first of all divinities to be invoked." Her name began and ended all prayers and rituals of sacrifice, said Cicero, because she is "guardian of the innermost things."[1] According to Pythagoras, the fire of her hearth/altar was the center of the earth.[2] Thus the **altar** of Vesta in Rome, tended by the Vestal Virgins, was also a center-of-the-earth symbol. In Greece a similar altar was the Prytaneum or public hearth, ruled by the same Goddess, who was "of all deities the most venerated."[3] Vesta or Hestia was left over from the matriarchal age, when the hearth of the clan mother was the first fire altar, and her housewifely functions of fire-keeping, food preparation, and creating the sacred center of clan life were considered the holiest of human activities. In strong contrast to this is the modern attitude toward housewifely keeping of the home and fireside, which is widely viewed as nonwork,

*silver plaque from Luristan,
8th century B.C.*

unworthy of payment, and certainly secular rather than honorably sacred.

The sign of Vesta (or Hestia) was an altar table with twin flames rising from it, like serpents ascending to heaven. The shape of the altar was that of the Greek letter *pi*, which bore great significance in the number magic of the Pythagorean sect, as every modern schoolchild knows.

The Vestal Virgins were the most sacred women in Rome because of their association with the eternal fire that was the empire's heart. Vesta's altar flames were never allowed to go out, for that would bring down the empire. The priestesses were at first *virgines* in the old sense, not necessarily chaste, but living independent of men. Later, they became nunlike celibates except that they were "married" to the spirit of Rome, probably in the form of the phallic **Palladium,** in the same sense that Christian nuns were "married" to Christ. Their title was Amata, "Beloved."[4] In the fourth century A.D., Christians extinguished the Vestal fire and withdrew the Virgins' political and religious privileges, causing outrage among educated Roman pagans who still believed in the old faith. The Virgins were highly sacred women, even though patriarchal Rome had forgotten (or deliberately obscured) their original character of orgiastic priestesses and virgin mothers impregnated by gods at their solstitial ceremonies prior to the sixth century B.C.[5] As soon as the Christian church acquired enough political power, it erased the Goddess Vesta and her holy priestesses. "Their Christian enemies feared them as mysterious and magical: they did not understand them and did not want to do so; they wanted only to see them destroyed."[6]

1. Dumézil, A.R.R. 1, 322.   2. Lethaby, 81–82.   3. *Larousse,* 136.   4. Graves, W.G., 395.   5. G. Jobes 2, 1018.   6. J. H. Smith, 149.

Zurvan

According to a silver plaque from Luristan, dating from the eighth century B.C., the figure shown in the illustration was the Primal **Androgyne** called Zurvan, who was both male and female in one body. Zurvan gave birth from his/her womb to both God and the Devil simultaneously: a doctrine that reflected the ancient belief in the twin deities of good and evil (Ahura Mazda and Ahriman), leading to Persian dualism and eventually to the Christian universe divided between heavenly and chthonian deities of approximately equal power. It was written that the figure of Zurvan Akaran, "Boundless Time," was "so incomprehensible to man that we can but honor it in awed silence."[1]

1. Seligmann, 14.

10

SUPERNATURALS

The human mind seems to contain a rich population of never-never beings: ghosts, ghouls, giants, monsters and mermaids, demons and dragons, fairies and fates, impossible animals, improbable anthropomorphs. Many have come down through the centuries as part of our symbolic heritage, graphic expressions of primitive fears or wishes, re-visioned in every generation. Even today the process of creature-making goes on, projected into new worlds of future and fantasy: robots, androids, Martians, King Kong, Godzilla, Pod People, every conceivable composite mingled in beings from outer space. We have always been good at seeing what is not there, by combining multiple distorted fragments of what is. Now it is even easier, with monsters by the ton inhabiting films, television, magazines, and the oddly misnamed "comic" books.

Still, supernatural beings out of historical and religious tradition are something more than bright-colored plastic bogeys for children. They are also symbols, drawn from archetypal material in the collective mind. The division between deities and all other kinds of supernatural entities is a mere hairline, often crossed—both ways. Gods, human beings, sacred animals, good and evil spirits all have a disconcerting habit of blending unpredictably into one another, because the composite mind does not consistently distinguish among them. Gods can behave like devils and vice versa. Human beings or animals can be possessed by either. Departed souls can be ghosts, vampires, zombies, angels, stars, shadows, familiar spirits, or ancestral genii.

We must remember too that, unlike today's artificial monsters, the supernaturals of the past were usually believed to be real. Therefore, they had more impact on the minds that made them than our modern fantasies, which even children can see through without too much trouble. It is not at all a frivolous endeavor to study these supernaturals and consider the question, What did they really mean?

Akeru

Akeru gods were the supernatural **lions** who guarded the **gates** of sunset and sunrise, according to Egyptian mythology. Between them ran the dark passage of the underworld, through which the sun must pass each night. The Akeru gods were shown as a two-faced sphinx, a sort of animal **Janus,** supporting between its heads the sun disc on the horizon. Sometimes they were distinguished as Xerefu and Akeru, or else as Sef and Tuau, the Lions of Yesterday and Today. Although the lions were provided with separate bodies back to back in the art of later dynasties, their archaic two-headed pushme–pullyou form was regarded as a primary symbol of Time (like Janus-Jana in Rome).[1] Mysteriously, the same two-headed sphinx form became hitched to the Chariot, on the seventh trump of traditional **Tarot card** designs dating from the thirteenth or fourteenth century.

1. Budge, G.E. 2, 98, 360.

Alborak

Alborak was the magical milk-white winged **horse** with a woman's head and a **peacock's** tail, ridden to heaven by Mohammed on his famous night journey, by which he achieved his vision and his spiritual authority. This myth attributes the authority of even the founder of one of the world's most patriarchal religions to a female spirit, comparable to the Pegasus horse born of the blood of Medusa, or "Female Wisdom." The peacock tail was an ancient attribute of the Great Goddess in Rome, and obviously in eastern lands also, since the peacock was an Asian bird. It was long held by Eastern mystics generally that only a female spirit—shakti, fravashi, peri, psyche, anima, alma mater, and so on—could show a man the way to divine knowledge.

There may have been a roundabout connection between Alborak and the leader of the Teutonic elves or **kobolds,** whose German name was Alberich. The kobolds were ancestral wizards, left over from memories of paganism. Their name originally was *kaballoi,* "horse riders."[1]

1. de Givry, 315.

Angel

Angels were originally female: the "dis-
pensers of bliss" who were every man's
notion of the perfect reward in heaven,
"ever desirable, ever willing mistresses of
those blessed souls who are reborn
into Indra's heavenly world."[1] And not only
Indra's, but many others. Persian warriors
fought bravely in the unshakable faith that
if they died in battle, they would go
to the sensual heaven of the *houris* and
spend eternity in dalliance with these
beautiful female angels. The medieval
concept of fairyland as a place of endless
sexual delights owed much to this
archaic view of the pagan paradise.

Angels were masculinized, however, in
the patriarchal tradition with its ascetic
rejection of women and sexuality.
Biblical angels were not only male, they
were even as subject as mortal men to the
"wicked" temptations of mortal women.
According to the Testaments of the
Twelve Patriarchs, the fallen angels were
those who had been seduced by earthly
women. The Book of Enoch also
mentions the women who "led astray the
angels of heaven."[2]

Yet one wonders how this might be
managed, if all angels resembled the two
who allegedly presented a Christian

scripture to the learned church father
Hippolytus in the second century A.D.:
they were each 96 miles high, with feet 14
miles long.[3] Even the seduction of
King Kong by a human actress the size of
his finger would seem unremarkable
by comparison.

The association of mortal female
sexuality with angels apparently arose from
the fact that the angels or "cherubim"
(Akkadian *karibu*, Hebrew *kerubh*, Sheban
karribim) were priestesses who wore
artificial **wings** in token of their affiliation
with the heavenly spirits. The Jerusalem
temple also connected male and female
"cherubic" spirits within the Holy
of Holies, realistically as a priest and
priestess who were "mingled and united,"
as Josephus said, and symbolically as
the two angelic beings guarding the **Ark**.
A Midrashic passage of the second
century A.D. called them "the head of
everything that was in the Temple,
for the Shekina rested on them and on the
Ark." In the third century it was written that
the two cherubim demonstrated "the
love of male and female." Josephus pru-
dently declined to say what Titus's
soldiers found in the Jerusalem temple,
but we know the cherubim somehow represented sexual union because the
Roman soldiers displayed them in the
street and mocked them for their
lewdness.[4]

The Egyptian form of the cherub symbolized the Heavenly Goddess—Nut, Hathor, or the Celestial Cow—having a body covered with eyes to represent the stars, and wings to represent the air.[5] As she was often called a sevenfold deity ("the Seven Hathors"), she passed into Gnostic tradition as the seven planetary spirits called Cosmocrators or Builders. The Zend-Avesta also spoke of seven chief angels, the Amesha Spenta or Amshaspends, the Benign Immortals.[6] The Christian church eventually adopted the seven as archangels, heads of the Celestial Host led by Michael, officially styled the Seven Angels of the Presence.

Christian angelology had a gradual development. It was given a great boost by the spurious writings attributed to Dionysius the Areopagite, who never really existed, but whose book (written about the sixth century A.D.) purported to be the work of the first bishop of Athens, who learned all about the heavenly hierarchy through a personal visit from the spirit of Saint Paul. Pseudo-Dionysius described nine orders of angels: Seraphim, Cherubim, Thrones, Dominions, Virtues, Powers, Principalities, Archangels, and ordinary angels. For centuries the church accepted this as a factual view of the divine ranks, and even modeled the earthly orders upon it.

Despite their compulsion to name and classify angels, religious establishments were firmly opposed to allowing unofficial invocation of them. In Carlovingian times the church took action against one Bishop Adalbert for invoking the angels Uriel, Raguel, Tubuel, Inias, Tubuas, Sabaoc, and Simiel. The difficulty was that invocation of angels by their names was the common mode of magic charms, presented in dozens of magic books. It was universally thought that any spirit invoked by name, angel or demon, would be forced to comply with the magician's request. Eleazar of Worms was one who boasted of intimate conversations with angels and learned of the *Sefer Raziel*, a mystical book supposedly given to Adam by the angel Raziel.[7]

To command the assistance of angels, however, remained a basic idea of spiritual power. Jesus himself announced that he could summon seventy-two thousand guardian angels (twelve legions) whenever he cared to (Matthew 26:53). This was the common claim of most magicians of the time. The Magic Papyri contain many spells to secure just such help and protection of angels.[8] From the annals of magic arose the concept of the guardian angel, amalgamated with the personal

daemon envisioned by the Greeks as a familiar spirit, or part of one's self. Like gods and demons, angels have gone through many phases, ranging from intimate portions of a man or woman to immaterial, celestial entities like lesser deities. Indeed the gods, the demons, the ghosts, the star-souls, the familiar spirits, and the angels were all of a piece with the human mind's propensity to people the nonhuman world with humanlike creatures.

1. Zimmer, 163.   2. Tennant, 183–184.
3. Abelard, 37.   4. Patai, 104, 115, 120, 122–123.   5. Cirlot, 43.   6. *Larousse*, 317.
7. Trachtenberg, 76, 89.   8. M. Smith, 109.

Anima Mundi

The Anima Mundi (Soul of the World) was invariably female, even in the medieval period when her image was restricted to crude drawings in magical and alchemical books, while the male God was being painted by the likes of Michelangelo and Leonardo da Vinci. Yet Plato had said that the Anima Mundi was diffused throughout all nature, and the Stoics maintained that she was the only vital force in the universe.[1]

Occultists understood the Anima Mundi as a development of the Goddess Isis, among others, as depicted in the works of Plutarch. She was shown as the Naked Goddess with her usual **halo** of stars, one foot on land and the other in water to show her dominion over earth and sea. Her left breast was a moon, which figure was repeated on her pubis. Her right breast was a star or sun pouring forth blessings on the world.[2]

1. Spence, 26.   2. Seligmann, 44.

Banshee

From Gaelic *bean-sidhe*, "woman of the fairy-mounds," the Banshee was another form of the Goddess-voice, for she was heard, but rarely seen.[1] The creative aspect of the Voice was variously known as Vac, Echo, Bath Kol, Samjna, or the **Logos** of **Sophia**: that is, the creative Word, able to bring forth all existence by the magic of speech, as Kali brought forth the universe by speaking the names of all things in her sacred language of Sanskrit. Being ever cyclical, the Goddess had a destructive Word as well. The blessing of life would always be counterbalanced by the curse of death: the **anathema,** the malediction, the bane-

saying of the Banshee. Irish folklore said
the voice of the Banshee was sometimes a
terrifying shriek or ghastly wail that
would cause any hearer to drop dead at
once; or, at other times, it was a soft,
comforting voice addressed to those whom
the Goddess loved, "a welcome rather
than a warning" of the coming passage
into the realm of death.[2]

1. Goodrich, 177.   2. Pepper & Wilcock, 275.

Basilisk

The basilisk, from Greek "little king
serpent," was sometimes also known as a
cockatrice. It was supposed to combine
elements of bird and snake. Some
said the fabulous basilisk was hatched from
a hen's egg brooded by a serpent, or
perhaps a serpent's egg brooded by a hen.
Some said the creature wore a three-
pointed crown on its head, or that it had a
three-pointed tail.[1] But the outstanding
characteristic of the basilisk was its
poisonous gaze. Like the **Gorgon** Medusa,
the basilisk was able to kill whatever
it looked at, or, alternatively, breathed on.
Thus it was an animal embodiment
of the evil eye.

Also like the Gorgon, the basilisk was
associated with menstrual **blood.** It
was often claimed that a basilisk would
grow from the buried **hair** of a menstruat-

ing woman. Or again, its ancestors
were the very same snakes that grew on
the Gorgon's head, which was the
ancient symbol of warning about menstrual mysteries.[2] According to popular
belief, the basilisk could be killed only by
the same method used by Perseus
against the Gorgon: that is, one must back
up to the creature, holding a mirror
so that the basilisk might see its own poisonous reflection and drop dead.[3]

Old-fashioned cannons were sometimes
decorated with snakelike forms, and
were referred to as basilisks. The name has
been given also to an ordinary animal, a
lizard of the iguana family.

1. Cirlot, 22.   2. Silberer, 139.   3. G. Jobes 1,
184.

Baubo

In the Eleusinian Mysteries, celebrated at
one of the oldest temples in Greece,
Baubo was a female clown who managed
to draw laughter from the Goddess
Demeter in the midst of her grief, when
she was hiding away and withholding the
gift of fertility from the world. Along with
limping Iambe, the female spirit of
lewd verse in the "limping" iambic meter,

Baubo induced the Great Mother to forget her anger long enough to take a little nourishment.

Hellenic writers described Baubo as an old nurse, that is, a Crone figure corresponding in the usual trinitarian fashion to the Virgin Iambe and the Mother Demeter. However, statues of Baubo consisted of the lower half of a woman's body with a face on a large (perhaps pregnant) belly, the rest concealed by a fantastic wig/costume.[1]

Apparently Baubo symbolized the lascivious jokes made by women during Demeter's fertility rites. Such jokes used to be considered essential to the efficacy of the ceremonies. The resemblance between a face and the front of a female torso seems to have been a perennial favorite thousands of years before Magritte painted his well-known *Le Viol*, which expresses the same theme.

It is interesting to find a Baubo figure also in ancient Japanese mythology. She was the Alarming Female, Ame-no-uzume-no-mikoto, who created a face on the front of her body to draw laughter from the Heaven-Shining-Great-August-Goddess Amaterasu, when she was hiding her light in a cave. The Alarming Female induced Amaterasu to emerge, bringing sunlight to the world again.[2]

In both mythological traditions, the "alarming" idea seems to be that the world's welfare depends on the relief of female sadness or fear and the restoration of female sexuality, merriment, and joy.

1. Huxley, 156.   2. Chamberlain, 64–68.

Behemoth

Behemoth was the Hebrew name of the **elephant** god Ganesha, or a derivative of him (whose Hindu name meant "Lord of Hosts"), once worshiped by Israelites at the Nilotic shrine city of Elephantine. The book of Job calls him "chief of the ways of God" (Job 40:19), but he was much diabolized by later Christian interpreters and eventually became one of hell's leading **demons.** Various biblical scholars argued about whether Behemoth was an elephant or a hippopotamus, because the Old Testament description is murky, to say the least. However, most of his "portraits" were modeled on Indian pictures of Ganesha with his man-shaped body and elephant head. Behemoth the demon usually had a huge belly with a protruding navel, conforming to God's word that "his strength is in his loins, and his force is in the navel of his belly" (Job 40:16).

CENTAUR
from an Attic amphora,
7th century B.C.

CHIMERA
Etruscan bronze

Centaur

The image of the centaur seems to have expressed to the early Greeks the awe in which horse-riding tribes were held by those who had not yet learned to domesticate horses. That the riders of Central Asia and the Black Sea "Amazons" elicited such awe is shown by the centaurs' other name, Magnetes, meaning "great ones." Hellenic myth made the centaurs wild, shaggy, archaic people always battling with the Lapiths, men who used weapons of chipped stone. Yet the centaurs were also accounted great wizards, shape-shifters, and fountainheads of occult lore. The centaur Cheiron of Magnesia was the teacher of the Trojan War's greatest heroes: Achilles, Heracles, Jason, and many others. Cheiron was the son of a god, "renowned for his skill in hunting, medicine, music, gymnastics and divination."[1] After he was killed at the hands of Heracles (thus becoming confused with the other centaur Nessus), Cheiron was made the Bowman of the Greek zodiac.

1. Graves, W.G., 256.

Chimera

The monster called Chimera in classical mythology was a demonized leftover from earlier matriarchal imagery. Her name means "she-goat." In the myth of Daphnis she was a divine **nymph,** but in that of the hero Bellerophon she appeared as a fire-breathing amalgam of **goat, lion,** and **serpent.** She was shown with a snake tail, lion body, and a second head like that of a goat or antelope.

This monstrous guise actually depicted the three totems of the ancient tripartite year, which was replaced by the Hellenic calendar. Conflict between the two systems was mythologized as Bellerophon's killing of the Chimera by pushing a lump of lead down her throat to be melted by her fiery breath.[1] In rather similar style, the Babylonian patriarchal hero Marduk killed the monster Tiamat, who was originally the mother of all gods including himself.

The primordial maternity of Chimera was made clear in some of her portraits, which showed the swollen teats of a nursing lioness along her belly.[2] She evidently represented the Goddess who had given the original version of the calendar to her priestesses, while the matricidal hero represented a newer priesthood bent on seizing her ancient powers.

1. Graves, G.M. 1, 66, 253–254.
2. Lehner, 135.

Cupid

The plump little infant "cupids" or *putti* so popular in Renaissance art were a far cry from the original Latin *cupido* meaning "lust, greedy desire"—from which we derive *cupidity*. This was a Latin name for the Greek Eros, who also represented lustful desire: that is, the *erotic* spirit behind all sexual union and hence behind the impulse of life itself. This was once a holy concept, until ascetic patriarchy declared it a devilish one. Another name for Cupid was Amor, "Love." His arrows were supposed to prick the heart with passionate affection. He usually accompanied his mother **Venus** (Greek Aphrodite). The Renaissance painters liked to multiply him into a host of chubby little **angels** surrounding almost any female figure, especially a naked one, or any representation of sexual union, such as a wedding.

Thanks to a confusion of these cupid figures with baby angels, they were also called "cherubs." This word acquired quite a different meaning from the biblical cherubims (*sic*), which were fearsome spirits placed with flaming swords to guard the entrance to the Garden of Eden and keep people away from the **tree** of life (Genesis 3:24). These descended from the Hebrew *kerubh*, Sheban *karribim*, former guardians of the shrine of the Moon-goddess at Marib. They also guarded Yahweh's **ark** (1 Kings 8:7). These "cherubs" became one of the two major types of angels, the others being seraphim, who were originally the six-winged fiery flying **serpents** of Chaldean myth, representing the **lightning** (Isaiah 6:2). Their Hebrew name meant "fiery ones."

Christian asceticism is symbolized in an Italian icon by Cupid blinded and prostrate at the feet of a female Chastity, who breaks his bow and holds a whip to beat her own flesh into submission. Her girdle reads *Castigo corpus meum* (I punish my body).[1]

1. G. Jobes 1, 316.

Cyclops

Cyclops means "wheel-eyed" in Greek. According to Homer, the Cyclopes were **giants** with only one eye in the middle of their faces. One of them, the savage man-eating Polyphemus, was outsmarted and blinded by Odysseus, who managed to escape from the Cyclops's cave by hiding himself and his crew under the bellies of a flock of sheep. It is supposed that the Greek concept of the Cyclops was related to giant Hindu images of Shiva or some other god with his "third eye of insight" prominently displayed in the center of the forehead.

A Sicilian legend said the Cyclops Polyphemus fell in love with Aphrodite-of-the-Sea, under her name of Galatea, "Milk-white Goddess." She, however, scorned Polyphemus and instead chose the handsome youth Acis, whereupon the jealous Cyclops killed Acis by hurling a great boulder at him.[1] This is a variant on the Homeric story of Polyphemus hurling huge boulders after Odysseus's ship: apparently a common explanation for large offshore rocks along almost any coast. Cyclopes were said to be clever at fitting great stones without mortar; hence "cyclopean" masonry.

1. Hall, 134.

Dakini

A dakini was a Tantric priestess, especially a woman connected with funerary rites, and also one of the many Goddesses of the afterworld, emanations of Kali. Like Aphrodite's Horae or the sacred harlots of Ishtar, the dakini seems to have been an apotheosized form of an earthly Goddess-woman. The title means "Skywalker." Dakinis presided over secret rituals held in cremation grounds and other places of the dead, where ordinary folk feared to go.[1] This may have some bearing on the European tradition of funerary priestesses called *vilas* (wilis) or *valas*, who held meetings in cemeteries; the idea also entered into the "witch" tradition. Intimately connected with the Tantric initiation was the famous Red Dakini. An inner realization of her spirit was considered essential to the enlightenment of the yogi.[2] As a death Goddess, she would be encountered in the afterworld.

1. Rawson, *E.A.E.*, 152. 2. Rawson, *A.T.*, 165.

DEMON
from a German woodcut

Ego sum Papa.

Demon

A sixteenth-century German woodcut shows the pope revealed as a demon under his robe and tiara, while he says "I am the Pope" (*Ego sum Papa*). Obviously a piece of Lutheran propaganda, the picture also reveals the perpetual human tendency to characterize other human beings with different ideologies as incarnate devils.

The very word *demon* came from patriarchal diabolization of earlier peoples who believed their souls were given to them by their mothers. The Greeks' *daemon* or indwelling spirit—the part that could go to heaven after death—was an *umeteros daemon* or mother-given soul, as Epictetus said. English translators rendered this simply "your Daemon."[1] The very idea that one's soul could emanate from a mother was abhorrent to Western patriarchy, whose official opinion was that souls are transmitted only through paternal "seed" (semen) to be grown in passive maternal "soil." Some hint of the older idea of mother-given souls may have surfaced in medieval depictions of male demons with grotesquely female breasts, large pregnant bellies, and other hints of feminine nature. Words for "soul"—*anima, psyche, umbra, alma, Seele, âme*—consistently retained the feminine gender even when allegedly transmitted from male gods through fathers only. The earlier view that human souls came from the Moon Goddess through mothers appeared only in such medieval beliefs as the persistence of "demons" inhabiting shadows cast by the moon.[2]

In any event, the indwelling *daemon* of antiquity became the possessing demon of the fear-haunted Middle Ages, universally accepted as reality, and credited with the ability to cause every possible disaster. As late as the eighteenth century, priests were seriously asserting that at least one-third of all illnesses were caused by demonic possession. A Swiss priest named Gassner claimed to have personally cured some ten thousand diseases by **exorcism**.[3] Authorities generally accepted the computation made from the Talmud, that the world population of demons was exactly 7,405,926.[4] Even in the nineteenth century, Rawlinson, the learned translator of Herodotus, could solemnly declare his conviction that the Delphic **oracle** was a demon.[5] Since Delphi was literally the "womb" of Greece and one of its oldest matriarchal shrines, originally sacred to Mother Earth, this provided another example of diabolization of the female principle. According to the missionary Martin of Braga in the sixth century, all the woods, rivers, and springs of Europe

DEVIL
*from a
15th-century
manuscript*

were still inhabited by pagan female spirits, who were demons one and all.[6]

Demons were masculinized, of course, but even then they retained a close connection with women. They became demon lovers (*incubi*), symbolizing men's fears of sexual inadequacy, since the demons were said to give women much more pleasure than their husbands did. There were also demon possessors, who seemed to afflict women far more often than men. This is hardly surprising in view of the extreme suppression of European women and the few opportunities they had to express their rage against the establishment. Demonic possession was an excellent attention-getter and an unbeatable opportunity to curse the oppressors.[7]

1. Glover, 59.   2. Trachtenberg, 34.
3. Evans-Wentz, 271.   4. Wedeck, 94.
5. Halliday, 119.   6. J. H. Smith, 238–241.
7. Walker, *W.E.M.S.*, 807–814.

Devil

It has been truly said, "The Devil is the curse of those who have abandoned the Goddess."[1] Even his name was derived ultimately from the Sanskrit *devi*, meaning "Goddess," through Persian *daeva* and Latin *diva*, *divus*, or *deus*. Patriarchal Europe always confused woman with devil, her **genitalia** with "the mouth of hell," her very motherhood with the vehicle of original sin: and male artists often painted or sculpted the Christian devil with female breasts.

The devil was deliberately constructed by the Christian church for good reasons having to do with another kind of confusion that equated him with God. The God of Isaiah, who claimed to be the creator of evil (Isaiah 45:7), was no more acceptable to Christian theology than the cyclic Goddess who gave both birth and death, and so encompassed all blessing and misfortune at once. Christian apologists insisted on a God who was all-good, all-pure, uninvolved with ordinary matter, and incapable of evil. So, out of bits and pieces of the old pagan deities, they created a devil to account for the world's obvious evils, pretending that their all-good God had actually created him (an insoluble paradox, to this day). Instead of facing up to death, illness, natural disasters, and other vicissitudes of fate, they could blame such things on the devil and woman— even though some were still called "acts of God." For example, early Christian theologians held that there was no such thing as death in the world until God created it as punishment for the sin of Eve.

The fact of Christian theology is that the entire scheme of salvation was utterly dependent on belief in the devil. Not only did the devil relieve God of responsibility for the world's evil; he also provided the "need" for a Savior through the myth of temptation and Fall. He gave the church its greatest weapon, the fear of damnation, by which to control the recalcitrant populations of an entire continent. The idea of the devil could never be abandoned, lest the whole power structure of the church should crumble away.[2]

The devil took charge of the eternal torture of sinners, on God's orders, an unfortunate notion that seemed to place God in the position of a Hitler commanding his concentration-camp overseer. Still, this notion could not be forsworn. A devil who blatantly disobeyed God, and refused to torture sinners, would have been no use at all to the ecclesiastical establishment. In effect, the devil was God's alter ego, his shadow self, as prefigured by the Persian twin deities, dark Ahriman and bright Ahura Mazda. In the Middle Ages there were still many remnants of the Gnostic idea that the creator, Jehovah, was the evil deity himself, having constructed the world of matter to trap souls and bring them to destruction.

During the centuries of the witch hunts, the devil assumed preeminence as the witches' god, supposedly carrying out his plan to take over the world with an army of his worshipers, mostly women. How this was to be done, against the will of "all-powerful" God, the church never explained; it simply used the devil as an excuse to slaughter millions of women in five centuries of persecution, such as the world had never seen before. On this bloodshed, modern patriarchal society was built.[3]

The devil had many names. Some were drawn from Yahweh's biblical rivals, others from classical pantheons or popular titles for ancient deities: Satan, Beelzebub, Belial, Apollyon, Hades, Pluto, Lord of Flies, Great Serpent, Great Beast, Old Nick, Old Scratch, Dragon, or Lucifer the "Light-bringer." A fifteenth-century woodcut shows a typical devil image with a monk's robe, curiously mismatched wings, and the four-horned crown of Osiris. "When there are any mighty winds and thunders with terrible lightnings," a clergyman wrote, "the Devil is abroad." In classic circular reasoning, the clergy proved the existence of the devil from that of God, and vice versa. Roger Hutchinson said if there is a God,

"verily there is a Devil also; and if there be a Devil, there is no surer argument, no stronger proof, no plainer evidence, that there is a God."[4]

1. Sjöö & Mor, 233. 2. de Givry, 49. 3. Sjöö & Mor, 298–314. 4. Thomas, 472, 476.

Dragon

The illustration shows a wingless dragon from a Babylonian bas-relief: a long catlike body with scales, lion forelegs, bird hind legs, snakelike head and tail, a crown of horns. Such composite animals were usually symbols of the seasons. In alchemy, the wingless dragon represented earth or "fixed" **elements**; the winged dragon represented volatile ones.[1]

Chinese Taoist symbolism revered the dragon as a spirit of "the Way," bringing eternal changes. It was shown coiling among clouds, revealing only parts of itself. Often the dragon was the guardian of the Flaming Pearl (spiritual perfection). White dragons represented the moon.

The European dragon was often synonymous with the **Ouroboros** or Earth Serpent. In Brittany he was "the dragon of the Bretons." Each May Day, it was said, he uttered a terrible scream that could be heard underneath every hearth

fire, demanding burial of a tub of mead as an offering to him.[2]

The official emblem of Wales is still the red dragon, derived from the Great Red Serpent that once represented the old Welsh god Dewi, who later metamorphosed into Wales's mythical patron saint David. The Christian myth of this fictional **saint** was composed in A.D. 1090, five centuries after his alleged lifetime. His earlier incarnation, the red dragon, was placed on the royal arms of England by Henry VII, who was of Welsh descent. This dragon, which served as a dexter supporter, was later removed by James I.[3]

Christians usually equated the subterranean dragon with the devil. In fact the devil's nickname "Old Harry" was taken from the Persian dragon-god Ahriman (Arimanius), the dark twin brother of the supreme god of light.[4] Like angelic Lucifer, Ahriman had fought his brother god and had been sent down to the underworld to rule over the demons. Thus dragons became traditional guardians of buried treasure.

1. Cirlot, 83. 2. Duerr, 207. 3. Whittick, 236. 4. G. Jobes 1, 54.

Dryad

Dryad is the Greek version of a female "druid," that is, a tree **nymph**, the soul or the human incarnation of the **oak** tree. It was believed that a dryad lived in or near her special tree and would never die until the tree itself died. Some said dryads could take on human or arboreal shapes at will, which explains the many classical myths about maidens who turned into trees. According to Hindu mythology, tree nymphs were necessary to the growth and fruiting of all trees, which would not flourish unless touched at the root by these female spirits.[1]

Dryads or oak nymphs dwelt in the Holy Land up to the twentieth century under the name of Benat Ya'kob: Daughters of Jacob. They lived in sacred oak **groves** whose trees—and even fallen branches— were never touched, even in a land where wood is scarce. Offerings were made to these oak nymphs at small shrines, many of which were nominally rededicated to some mythical Moslem saint.[2]

Another term for a dryad was *hamadryad*—a confusing usage, because the same word is applied in zoology to a type of cobra, and also to a baboon.

1. Zimmer, 69.   2. Frazer, *F.O.T.*, 329.

Dybbuk

Also rendered *dibbuk*, this is a Hebrew term for a possessing spirit or **demon** able to enter the body of a live human being. A dybbuk was often envisioned as the wandering soul of a dead person. The concept was only a short step from the Stone Age belief in reincarnation through mothers: that is, the soul of a dead person would enter the body of a woman— preferably but not always a woman of the same family or tribe—in order to be born again as a new child. All ideas of spirit possession may have originated with the imaginary conversations between women and the "spirits" they carried in their wombs. Certainly the idea of an alien entity occupying a human body must have been based on the experience of pregnancy.

Elf

Innumerable cautionary folktales proved that it paid to be kind to elves. Properly propitiated with gifts of food or clothing, elves might come in the night to do all the housework, sew boots for the shoemaker, cut cloth for the tailor, or make the porridge for the cook. They would watch over children or domestic animals. Sometimes they would bring the heart's desire. On the

other hand, elves not properly propitiated could be mischievous and destructive. These tales obviously arose from ancient customs of offering gifts to the dead. It was well known that "elf" used to be another name for an ancestral **ghost**, especially a pagan spirit from pre-Christian times.[1]

There were many kinds of elves, just as there were many kinds of pagan spirits: elves of the woodland, of the mountain, of the household. Norse elves were sometimes ugly, sometimes beautiful. They lived in Alfheimr, "Elf-Land," which became synonymous with Fairyland. Like the ancient Goddess of the north, they created the sun.[2] Icelandic elves were clearly identified with pagan deities or ancestral ghosts—which amounted to the same thing, under the old system of ancestor worship. The Kormaks Saga said they would cure sickness if the patient offered a feast of bull's flesh and blood to the elves inside a pagan burial mound; then "you will be healed."[3]

Sometimes the elves took human beings away with them, either for a short period or permanently as in the case of a "changeling" (elf-child) left in place of a human baby. Elves joined Odin in the legendary Wild Hunt, based on the image of ghosts riding through storm clouds. It was said in the Palatinate that a man could participate in the Wild Hunt, or could be seduced by an elvish woman; but then he became *elwetritsch*, elvish, eldritch.[4] This happened to Thomas Rhymer, Tannhäuser, Ogier the Dane, and many other medieval heroes.

1. Wimberly, 127. 2. Turville-Petre, 231.
3. Davidson, G.M.V.A., 156.
4. Duerr, 43.

Fairy

The fairy-tale image of the fairy as a tiny female sprite with butterfly wings and antennae seems to have been drawn from the classic Greek *Psyche*, which means "soul" and also "butterfly." Like **elves,** the fairies were originally the souls of the pagan dead, in particular those matriarchal spirits who lived in the pre-Christian realm of the **Goddess.** Sometimes the fairies were called Goddesses themselves. In several folk ballads the Fairy Queen is addressed as "Queen of Heaven."[1] Welsh fairies were known as "the Mothers" or "the Mothers' Blessing."[2] Breton peasants called the fairies Godmothers, or Good Ladies, or **Fates,** from which comes *fay (la fée)*, from the Latin *fata*. They claimed that, like Medusa or Circe, a fairy could transform a man into an animal or turn him to stone.[3]

Most medieval sources reveal, however, that the fairies were perceived as real women, of ordinary size, with supernatural knowledge and powers.[4] Their Queen was their Goddess, under such names as Titania (Gaea, ancient mother of the Titans), Diana, **Venus, Sybil,** Abundia ("Abundance"), and Hecate. Sometimes all fairies were designated "Moon-goddesses." In other words, they were women who still followed the ancient religion. The "fairy godmothers" of folktales were the female guardian spirits of deified ancestresses who were supposed to watch over children in the olden time. Even Christian sources depicted fairies as real people, almost synonymous with witches, and Fairyland as a real place. It was also known as the earthly paradise or the western paradise. Some said it existed as an island far across the sea toward the sunset, like Avalon or the Fortunate Isles. Others said it was an alternate location somewhere between heaven and hell: the third of Thomas Rhymer's three mystic pathways led to it. Some believed that Fairyland was inside the "fairy mounds" or burial chambers of ancient people. Fairyland was the same as the ghost world, the Hesperides, the Elysian Fields, the Isles of the Blest, and other pagan visions of the destination of the dead during the reign of the Great Mother.

Fairy lore was so ubiquitous and so confusing that orthodox writers hardly knew what to make of it. Churchmen condemned the practice of leaving out food or drink for the fairies, because they "naturally resented the propitiation of other deities." After they denied the possibility that fairies might be ghosts of the dead, then "Fairies could only be good or evil spirits," and the latter was thought most likely. The fairies made convenient scapegoats. Sick animals or people were often described as "fairy-taken" or "elf-shot." Parents could disown retarded children on the ground that they were fairy changelings. Quack doctors covered their ignorance of childhood diseases in the same way.[5]

As an example of the "logical" explanations for fairies' shape-shifting ability, Kirk's *Secret Commonwealth* remarks that their bodies are so "pliable through the subtlety of the spirits that agitate them, that they can make them appear or disappear at pleasure. Some have bodies so spungious, thin, and delicate, that they are fed only by sucking into some fine spiritous liquors, that pierce like pure air and oil."[6] So much for logic.

1. Wimberly, 407. 2. Rees & Rees, 41.
3. Evans-Wentz, 199, 203. 4. Wimberly, 170.
5. Thomas, 607, 610, 612. 6. Evans-Wentz, 279.

Familiar

The idea of a witch's familiar spirit, or **demon,** or **imp,** embodied in some kind of animal, arose from the ancient concept of the personal *daemon* in animal form. Sometimes this was imagined as a guardian or tutelary spirit, like the totem animals of the American Indians. Sometimes it was viewed as an animal incarnation of a part of one's own soul, like the *ba* of the Egyptians. Just as a loved person could be considered a kindred soul, so a beloved pet might also seem soul-connected.

All these ideas of connection between human and animal were more or less diabolized under the Christian system, which regarded animals as soulless or demonic, or at the very least devoid of any feelings that needed consideration. Men, jealous of women's propensity to make pets of animals and treat them with love, soon found ways to condemn women for sensual, affectionate relationships with their dogs or cats. A woman seen fondling or talking to her pet fell under suspicion of witchcraft. Even a woman who spoke to any animal, as one might say "Hello there" to a squirrel or a bird, could be considered a witch. During the centuries of persecution, women were often burned for keeping cats, or nurturing lambs, or talking to frogs, or raising colts, or even for having mice in the house or toads in the garden.[1]

Black animals were especially suspected of harboring demons, since black was the color of underworld beings in general. That is why the popular image of a witch is attended by a black cat, even today. Witch-finders insisted that their victims suckled familiar demons through a supernumerary teat located somewhere on their bodies, and this was identified with the "devil's mark." An important aspect of witch-finding was stripping the accused woman and searching minutely for this mark, or pricking her all over with sharp instruments, which the male investigators seemed to enjoy. Needless to say, no one ever succeeded in distinguishing "familiars" from ordinary animals.

1. Walker, *W.E.M.S.*, 222.

Fata Morgana

Fata Morgana is the Latin name for Morgan le Fay, the Arthurian version of the old Celtic Death-goddess, Morrigan or Mara. The term *fata morgana* is now applied to a certain kind of mirage, often seen in the Strait of Messina, said to

FAUN
playing panpipes

represent Morgan's secret palace beneath the waves. It was Morgan who ruled the Fortunate Isles of the honored dead, and who carried away the corpse of King Arthur to this western paradise, even though Christianized versions of the story insisted that King Arthur was buried in a church.

"Morgan the Fate" was once considered literally the **fate** of every man, the female death spirit that he feared to meet, although every man born of woman carried this "fate" within himself as the necessary biological limitation of his life. It was, of course, this very concept of the inevitability of biological death that patriarchal religions opposed. Therefore, all symbols of the Death-goddess were especially hated and avoided, or else extensively reworked, in Christian literature.

The term *fata morgana* has been applied to a variety of illusory phenomena in addition to the mirage. "Saint Elmo's fire" seen on ships at sea, and the glowing will-o-the-wisp (marsh gas) seen over swamps, have been known by the same name. Such mysterious night lights received many other names too: *ignis fatuus*, Jack-o-lantern, walking fire, corpse candle, Fair Maid of Ireland, friar's lantern, and spunkie.[1]

1. G. Jobes 1, 821.

Faun

A faun was the Latin version of a **satyr,** that is, a woodland deity or spirit pictured as half man, half goat, with horns, pointed ears, and a goat tail. Fauns inhabited the wild forests and were apparently conceived as emanations of the god Faunus, consort of Fauna, who was also Diana of the Animals and Bona Dea, the Good Goddess.[1] As Diana of Ephesus, she ruled over all woodland creatures and was shown with many breasts all over her torso to indicate that she nourished all forms of life.

Fauns were naturally identified as **devils** during the Middle Ages. Having been originally conceived as lusty creatures, they were confused with the "incubus devils" always seeking sexual intercourse with women, according to the handbooks of the Inquisition. Christian authorities were just as firmly convinced as the ancients were that such creatures really did live in the wild places; they just didn't like them as well as the ancients had.

1. *Larousse*, 208.

FURIES

GARGOYLE
Notre Dame, Paris

Furies

The three Furies represented one of Greece's oldest images of matriarchal law: the triple **Goddess** as punisher of transgressors. The Furies were also known as Erinnyes (Angry Ones) after Demeter Erinys, the Avenger; or Eumenides (Kindly Ones) in an effort to flatter and pacify them; or Solemn Ones, to whom altars were dedicated for propitiatory sacrifices. Individually, they were Tisiphone (Retaliation-Destruction), Megaera (Grudge), and Alecto (Unnameable). They were older than all the gods.[1] As relics of the matriarchal age, they recognized no principle of paternity but punished only those who sinned against kinfolk in the maternal line.

The Furies pursued Orestes for having committed matricide, the one unforgivable crime under the old law. It was believed that the blood of a slain mother called down the Furies' wrath upon the criminal, automatically. Orestes bit off one of his fingers in an attempt to absolve himself of blood guilt—a custom that is still common in some parts of the world—and left it at the so-called Finger Tomb, surmounted by a finger of stone.[2]

Sophocles called the Furies "Daughters of Earth and Shadow." Aeschylus called them "Children of Eternal Night." Either epithet made them offspring of the female spirit of primal darkness at the creation and linked them to the primordial concept of the Mother's Curse whereby the Goddess inevitably ended each life that she brought forth. Some said the Furies were monsters with Gorgon-like snake hair, black dog faces, and bat wings. Others said they were stern but beautiful women carrying scourges and swords. Psychologically, they were images of the Scolding Mother and projections of the young child's death fears and pangs of conscience.

1. Graves, G.M. 1, 122. 2. Ibid., G.M. 2, 67.

Gargoyle

Gargoyles were not strictly mythical but were invented late in the Middle Ages, during the great age of **cathedral** building. Gothic cathedrals were liberally covered with gargoyles to provide churchgoers with **demon** figures to populate their nightmares and fears of hell. Gargoyles were also used as extensions of the ancient

belief that holy buildings should have ugly, threatening stone guardians to keep away evil influences. It was believed that man-made demons could frighten away real demons. Some churches were so heavily ornamented with gargoyles that an objective observer might think the churches were built in honor of the pandemonic residents of hell instead of the angelic population of heaven.

Genie

Among the oldest forms of the genie were the winged **angels** with **masks** of bull or eagle, shown on Assyrian and Babylonian tablets in the act of fecundating sacred trees, such as the Goddess **Asherah** as **Tree of Life.** Similar genie forms appeared on early Christian tombs in the guise of guardian angels.[1]

The word *genie* came from Arabic *djinni*, meaning "begetter," that is, an ancestral spirit in the male line. Romans converted the word into *genius*, which meant the same thing, corresponding to the female ancestral spirit known as *juno*. Of course all reference to the *juno* eventually disappeared from patriarchal society, while the term *genius* remained and became a tutelary spirit of inspiration.

1. Whittick, 200.

Ghost

No matter where the spirits of the dead are supposed to go, in any prevailing religious system, there yet remains the ineradicable belief that they continue to hang around the places where they lived, or where their bodies were put; and that those still living usually have reason to be afraid of them. It seems that no amount of theological insistence on heavens or hells or purgatories has appreciably modified popular belief in ghosts. Many people still talk to the ghosts of the dead, in the kind of ritual that used to be called necromancy and is now called spiritualism.

The old religions accepted the presence of ghosts throughout the environment, which dissolved and absorbed the dead in one way or another, so that living nature was just an altered form of the living spirits of deceased ancestors. Ghosts were invited to participate in festivals and other important occasions among their descendants; hence the "death's-head at the feast," a relic of the preserved ancestral **skull** actually placed at the meal among living members of the family. For this reason "ghost" and "guest" derive from the same word, Germanic *Geist.* The two English words were pronounced exactly alike in northern England.[1]

In ancient Greece, a popular synonym for "ghost" was "hero," that is, one dedicated to the Great Goddess, Hera, erstwhile queen of souls.[2] A similar European belief relegated all ghosts to the realm of the Goddess Hel, Queen of the Ghost World, who also sent them back to earth to be reborn as new children. Under the name of Frau Holda, she kindly took the souls of children who died unbaptized (whereas Christian authorities relegated them to eternal suffering in hell), and they became *heimchen* or little-ones-going-home (to Mother).[3]

Christians usually believed that ghosts "walked" the earth whenever they had failed to be buried under the auspices of the church. Therefore, all pagan spirits could become ghosts and meet the living, especially at **Halloween,** the pagans' Feast of the Dead.

1. Hazlitt 1, 27. 2. Halliday, 47. 3. Miles, 242.

Ghoul

The word *ghoul* descends from Arabic *ghul* or *ghala*, perhaps related to names of the Tantric Death-goddess Kali Ma, who also appeared throughout Europe in such guises as the Celtic Caillech and the Finnish Kalma, She-Who-Eats-the-Dead.[1] Indian sacred art showed her devouring the entrails of her dead consort Shiva, in a very ghoullike pose, reminiscent of many other Goddesses of antiquity whose Death-goddess aspect was always some form of corpse-devourer. Such female spirits were usually mythologized as fearsome haunters of graveyards, whose rites were forbidden to the eyes of men.

Of course she was much more than the simple horror-bogey now described by "ghoul." Her image reached back to a primitive stratum of human thought, long before patriarchy or its recognition of fatherhood, to a time when it was believed that only mothers could give birth and rebirth. In many areas then, women really did cannibalize the dead, with the benevolent purpose of becoming pregnant with their spirits and so giving them another birth. Even when cannibalism was replaced by symbolic imitations, such as rituals of sacrifice and communion, still the Death-goddess was represented by corpse-eating creatures like vultures, crows,

*Cerne Abbas giant;
from Dorset,
England*

dogs, and swine, all of which were sacred transformations of herself.

Kali the Devourer naturally signified the earth, which gives birth to all things, and swallows them again. "She devours all existence," her worshipers said; "She chews all things existing with Her fierce teeth."[2] Her yogis insisted that she was their loving Mother who gave them birth and loved them, yet a man's "image of Her is incomplete if he does not know Her as his tearer and devourer."[3] This rather subtle philosophical point was illustrated by gruesome pictures of the Mother-as-Ghoul, eating her dead lover. The real reason for her ghoulishness was that she would become the Virgin Mother Maya and give birth to him again, and again, forever.

1. *Larousse*, 306.   2. *Mahanirvanatantra*, 295–296.   3. Rawson, A.T., 112.

Giant

Myths of every nation preserve the archetypal idea of a primordial race of giants, ruling the world before the present gods. The idea is obviously an outgrowth of the universal human experience of living in a "giants' world" during the dream time of early childhood. The giants also were associated with the rule of the Mother **Goddess**. According to Norse myth, the later gods Frey, Njord, and Odin acquired their divine powers by marrying the wise-women of the elder giant race.[1] These elders were called *risi*, derived from Sanskrit *rishi*, a sage. They came to their end by being drowned in the **blood** of their own kind: a myth that could indicate bloody slaughter of the elder races by Indo-Europeans, or could simply refer to the ancient belief that death meant immersion in female moon-blood, the magic substance that formed new, reborn bodies.[2] In India, the primordial giants were sometimes called Daityas, and their guru was **Venus,** the planet usually associated with feminine magic.

Even the Bible speaks of the archaic time when there were "giants in the earth" (Genesis 6:4). They were called *nephilim,* children of Nephesh, the ancient, pre-Jahvistic "Soul of the World." That this "Soul" was considered female may be indicated by the Greek parallel of the Goddess Nephele, the shadow side of Hera, ruling over the land of the shades—that is, ancestral ghosts—and therefore identifiable as another name for Hecate or Persephone. It was often repeated and believed, as Philo said, that Adam and other early biblical figures were giants.[3] Patriarchal writers, however, naturally ignored the tradition revealed in Tantric scriptures: the ancient races grew to enormous size and lived to enormous ages because their lives were "centered in the blood" of the Goddess whose blood first formed and birthed the universe.[4]

England still has a portrait of one of the archaic giants, 180 feet tall, cut in the chalk of a Dorset hillside. He is the ithyphallic Cerne Abbas giant, said to represent either the Saxon god Heill—whose name meant "virility"—or the Celtic Cernunnos, after whom the nearby town was named, and whose shrine was taken over by Christian monks for the local abbey. The enclosure for **Maypole** ceremonies was placed above this giant's head. Since the Maypole rituals anciently commemorated the god's sexual union with his Goddess, the position of both the giant and the Beltane shrine in close association clearly points to preservation of the old religion. Giant images still figure in folk ceremonies throughout European **carnivals,** processions, and holy days. As late as 1770, the **Midsummer** Festival at Douai included a huge effigy known as Le Grand Gayant (the Great Giant).[5]

According to one of the oldest strata of classical Greek myth, the elder giants were known as the Titans. They were children of Mother Earth by Father Heaven, but their mother encouraged them to attack their father, in a parallel to the Judeo-Christian and Persian stories of the revolt of the angels. The Titan Cronus castrated and killed Father Heaven (**Uranus**), throwing his genitals into the sea. Drops of his blood that fell on Mother Earth begot the three **Furies** and also the ash-tree **nymphs.**[6]

This classic designation of the elder gods as Titans was remembered in the time of the Renaissance, when it was widely believed that the Fairy Queen's name was Titania, which would have been a title of Mother Earth as the source of all Titans. **Fairies,** however, shrank in size over the centuries until they were not only *not* larger than human, but ever smaller and smaller than human.

1. Gelling & Davidson, 162.   2. Turville-Petre, 24, 231.   3. Tennant, 134.   4. *Mahanirvanatantra*, xlvii–xlviii.   5. Gelling & Davidson, 158.   6. Graves, G.M. 1, 37–39.

SUPERNATURALS   **253**

Gnome

Gnomes were the spirits associated with
the **earth** element, as were **sylphs** with the
air, undines with the water, and **salamanders** with the fire. Their name may
be likened to the Greek *gnome*, to know
(*gnosis*, knowledge), for all creatures
dwelling in the bowels of the earth were
supposed to understand the Mother's hidden secrets. Gnomes were supposed
to live in mines, caves, pits, and similar
deep places; and to have miraculous
knowledge of rocks, stones, minerals,
gems, mining techniques, and the magic
palaces at the roots of mountains.

Gnomes are prevalent in Germanic
folklore. At one time they served as guardian spirits of miners, smiths, and
metalworkers. In some areas it is still
believed that gnomes inhabit old mine
shafts and the unexplored passages of caves
and can kill those who trespass on
their territory by burying them under
rockfalls.

Golem

In Hebrew, a golem meant literally
shapeless matter, like mud, **clay**, or clotted
blood, brought to life as a living-dead
sort of monster by invocation of divine
secret names. Several Jewish magicians,
such as Elijah of Chelm, were credited with
having created a golem, thus becoming
forerunners of Dr. Frankenstein.[1]

Behind the concept of the golem, far
back, one might find the original
creation story that held that in conditions of primal **chaos**, all potential
life appeared in the form of shapeless
matter as the uterine blood of Mother
Tiamat, or Maa, or Anna-Nin the "nether
upsurge." Her vast sea of blood was
neither liquid nor solid, neither hot nor
cold; all **elements** existed in it as potential
but not actual order. Many myths
said her words brought order out of chaos,
creating each form as she spoke its
name. This idea is still clear in legends of
Kali Ma and her creative **Logos**, framed from
the sacred language of Sanskrit, giving
form to the primitive Ocean of Blood.
Male gods like Yahweh borrowed the idea
of bringing forth a living universe by
speech alone. Then finally, mystics and
magicians imagined that they might do the

same, if they could obtain some "primal matter" and say the right words over it. However, the man-made golem even when alive would be soulless, because it was believed that only God would know how to make a soul.

1. Trachtenberg, 85.

Gorgon

The Gorgon head (*Gorgoneum*), with its protruding tongue, snake hair, and huge fangs, appeared often in antiquity as a painted or carved warning to men. Her basic meaning was: Female Mysteries; keep away! She threatened to turn intruders to stone, like her mythical Crone form Medusa, eldest of the trinity of Gorgons. As an emblem of feminine wisdom, the Gorgon head appeared on the **aegis** of **Athene** and represented Athene's Crone form, Metis or "Wisdom," whom the Greeks mythologized as Athene's mother. But Metis was only a Greek version of Medusa, and Gorgo (Gorgon) remained a title of Athene's elder, destroying aspect. The Gorgon head was not brought from Libya by Theseus as the myth claimed. It was an attribute

of Athene from the beginning, when she was herself the Libyan royal Goddess, inventor of the **alphabet** and other civilized arts, guardian of female secrets of birth and death, and especially of the forbidden (to men) mystery of wise lunar **blood.**[1]

Blood figured prominently in the myth of Medusa. Even as she died, her blood gave birth to the lunar horse of godlike aspiration, Pegasus. Her **serpent** hairs symbolized menstrual secrets: the mystic combination of woman and serpent that men feared and diabolized in nearly all mythologies. Even in the Middle Ages, men were still insisting that the hair of a menstruating woman, buried in the ground by moonlight, would turn into a snake.[2] Some even claimed, in accord with the ancient connotations of the Gorgon, that the sight of menstrual blood could turn a man to stone.

1. Boulding, 193.　2. Cirlot, 273.

Graces

The conventional image of the three naked Graces (Charites), the center one with her back to the observer, occurs again and again throughout Greek and Roman art, and similar figures are even found carved on Hindu temples. It was apparently one of the most popular pictures of the Triple Goddess, all three of her aspects seen as beautiful, joined together as one, like all divine trinities.

Classic names of the Graces were Aglaia (Brilliant), Thalia (Flowering), and Euphrosyne (Heart's Joy). They had older names, Pasithea, Cale, and Euphrosyne, which were really nothing but a title of Aphrodite whose attendants they were: *Pasithea Cale Euphrosyne*, "The Goddess of Joy who is Beautiful to All."[1] Aphrodite, too, was once a trinity. Pausanias said her Charites or Graces were worshiped at Orchomenos in the form of three very ancient standing stones that were said to have fallen from heaven.[2] Homer mentioned only two Graces, Pasithea and Cale, who seem to have personified the **seasons,** which the Athenians knew as two Goddesses Thallo and Carpho (Sprouting and Withering). Two Graces were worshiped in Athens under the names of Auxo and Hegemone (Increase and Mastery).[3]

In any event, the Charites were very old. The *charis* or "grace" they bestowed was the gift of the Goddess: beauty, kindness, love, tenderness, pleasure, creativity, artistry, and sensuality. The sense of this word was much changed when it was incorporated into the New Testament as *caritas*, the quality greater than faith or hope (1 Corinthians 13). It is translated sometimes "love" and sometimes "charity," the latter based on the early Christian belief that one could buy one's way into heaven by giving charity to the poor. The sensual and joyful implications of the Goddess's "grace" were quite lost.

1. Graves, G.M. 2, 14.   2. Dumézil, A.R.R. 1, 166.   3. Graves, G.M. 1, 55.

Green Man

The Green Man was a traditional decoration in many old churches, where he was usually a carved face on a **pillar,** swathed in a covering of carved leaves, or seeming to be enclosed in the trunk and branches of a tree. Among his other names were Green George, Jack-in-the-Green, Leaf Man, and May King, after the symbolic tree spirits whose roles were played in springtime folk festivals by men dressed in leaves.[1] It is likely that Green Man pillars were erected origi-

GRIFFIN

GROTESQUE
Freiburg Cathedral, Germany

HAG

nally on the sites of sacred trees. The common occurrence of Green George ceremonies on Easter Monday indicates that he was an alternate version of the tree-sacrificed savior, a continuation of the pagan practice in conjunction with the Christian one.

1. Frazer, G.B., 146–149.

Griffin

As one of mythology's numerous composite animals, the griffin descended from the famous composites of Babylon and Persia: winged, eagle-headed, goat-bearded, lion-bodied spirits like the ancient cherubim. As symbols of the **seasons,** they became guardians of the sun, of the Golden Apples, of the jewels of the stars and other celestial phenomena. This may explain why griffins are so often found in legend as guardians of treasure.[1]

1. Whittick, 251.

Grotesque

A grotesque was literally "a creature from the grotto," referring to the sacred **caves** where pre-Christian Europeans worshiped their deities. The caves apparently contained composite animal gods and statues of nature spirits, some of which were moved into the early churches to encourage attendance. Missionaries were instructed to adopt the people's holy images and incorporate them into the fabric of the church, so that the pagan prayers and pilgrimages would seem to be directed to the Christian deity. It became a custom to provide nearly every church with grotesques, even after the spirit of paganism had declined and the meanings of the original grotesque figures had been forgotten.

Hag

The popular cartoon image of the hag as an ugly old witch loses sight of her original meaning. A hag (*hagia*) used to be a "holy woman" or wise-woman: the female shaman of pre-Christian Europe, or the tribal matriarch who knew the wise ways of nature, healing, divination, civilized arts, and traditions of the **Goddess.** The mother of Hel, queen of the dead, was known as Angurboda, the Hag of the

Iron Wood. The Celtic chooser of kings was the Hag of Scone, whose spirit was embodied in the famous Stone of Scone, which still rests under the coronation throne in Westminster Abbey. Christian tradition insists that she was turned to stone by a missionary's curse.[1]

Like all female elders, hags have been generally cursed with pejorative meanings in patriarchal society. But there are still indications of their former spiritual authority. In sixteenth-century English literature, "hag" is a synonym for "fairy."[2] The New Year festival used to be a "Hag's Moon" (*Hagmena*), although clergymen insisted that the ceremony meant the devil was in the house.[3] Like the word *crone*, hag once connoted an elder woman with the spirit of the Goddess within her, just as after menopause her "wise blood" remained within her body and brought her great wisdom.

1. Wimberly, 36.   2. Scot, 550.   3. Hazlitt 1, 296.

Harpy

The carrion-eating harpies of Greek myth—whose name meant "pluckers"—probably evolved from Cretan funerary priestesses who plucked harps in their ceremonies and wore costumes of vulture feathers in honor of the Vulture Mother. Her name in Egypt was Mut or Nekhbet; even **Isis** had a vulture incarnation as the bearer of the dead. The image of the harpy vulture with a woman's head and breasts comes from an old stratum of culture, when women controlled the methods of giving the dead to the birds of the air (see **Vulture**).

Hellenic myth claimed that two harpies were vanquished by the Argonauts in eastern Thrace and driven back to their Cretan cave.[1] They were portrayed as foul creatures, indicating a patriarchal priesthood taking over funeral rites and denigrating the priestesses. However, the harpies like the **furies** remained fearsome symbols of the Death-goddess whom men were afraid of offending. In medieval heraldry, the harpy appeared as an emblem of victory, without evil connotations other than those of intimidating, triumphant power.[2]

1. Graves, G.M. 2, 230.   2. Cirlot, 133.

Hippocampus

The hippocampus was the original "sea horse," its name meaning a horselike sea monster. As there were **mermaids** and mermen, according to popular superstition, the hippocampus was their mer-horse. The idea probably arose from classical references to the white horses of the sea god. Poetic vision saw their streaming manes in the spray blown back from wave crests. It was believed—often literally—that the **chariot** of **Neptune** was drawn by hippocampi.[1]

1. Hall, 221.

Hobgoblin

The word *goblin* means a spirit, probably derived from the same root as *kobold,* a spirit of caves or mountains. A hobgoblin, however, was a spirit of the **hearth** (hob), a domestic **ghost** or ancestral guardian of the family fireside, like the old Roman *lares* and *penates*. Because of the primitive practice of burying family dead under the **threshold** or under the central firepit, their ghosts were long supposed to inhabit and protect the house—even when later customs made burial places elsewhere. Under Christian rule, all such pagan ancestors were at least partly diabolized, and hobgoblins like all other goblins were reinterpreted as minor **demons.**

Hydra

Today the hydra is known to grammar-school science students as a little polyp with waving ciliae, commonly seen under the microscope in a drop of pond water. In Greek myth, however, the hydra was a water monster born of the **serpent** woman Echidne, and eventually killed by Heracles as one of his Twelve Labors.[1] Its heads were all poisonous serpents, and for each one that the hero cut off, two more heads grew in its place—which is why we now call "hydra-headed" any problem that seems to raise more problems with any attempted solution.

The Greek image of the hydra seems to have been based on the squid or octopus; but the mythical creature symbolized fresh water and was even found inland, dwelling under a plane tree. Some said its many heads represented an association of water priestesses, or else the many mouths of the river Amymone. The number of heads varied. Some said seven, others nine, others fifty or a hundred.

1. Graves, G.M. 2, 108.

Imp

Usually viewed as a citizen of hell, the imp was derived from a word meaning "bud, sprout, or offspring": hence, a junior **demon.** The concept arose from pagan beliefs about dead ancestors dwelling as **ghosts** in the underworld. The little imps would have been those who died in childhood. They were solidly black, like shadows, because of the ancient identification between souls and shadows. The dead were *shades*, or Nibelungen (shadow people), and soulless creatures were supposed to cast no shadow.

Since pagan ghosts and gods alike were defined as **devils** by Christian authorities, the definition of an imp was extended to any hellish entity, and even to ordinary living animals when they were perceived as witches' **familiars.** In transcripts of witch trials, a woman's dog, cat, or other pet is often referred to as her imp.

Another Christian idea was that disobedient children were possessed by demonic spirits, their baptismal exorcism having presumably failed for some unaccountable reason, or because they were changelings (**fairy** children substituted for the real

ones). Thus, a naughty child was often called an imp of hell, or just an imp. Nowadays the term has lost most of its diabolic connotations. That which is "impish" is generally thought rather cute.

Incubus

Temples of the ancient world usually included a **womb** chamber where people in search of enlightenment or healing could "incubate" (sleep overnight) in anticipation of a spiritual rebirth or a vision. Presiding priests were incubi, attendants of the womb chamber, whom Christian theology converted into **demons** who seduced women. Male insecurity and sex fear evolved many stories about the lusty incubus, so expert a lover that after his attentions no woman could ever again be satisfied with a mere man.[1]

Religious authorities wasted much of their time speculating on whether incubi could beget children. The consensus was that an incubus could take a female form as a succubus (or succuba) and copulate with a sleeping man, causing erotic dreams and nocturnal emissions to fertilize herself.[2] Some said the succubus, who was also known as a Night-Hag,

KACHINA
Nataska, from the Hopi

KOBOLD

LAMIA

could transform herself back into an incubus and impregnate a mortal woman with semen thus obtained from a man.[3] For many centuries all manner of erotic night fantasies and fears were universally attributed to the sexual habits of incubi and succubae.

1. Walker, *W.E.M.S.*, 431–433.
2. Trachtenberg, 51. 3. Scot, 512.

Kachina

Kachinas are the polytheistic population of spirits revered by Hopi and other Pueblo Indian tribes. Many kachinas are nature spirits, governing the rain, the sun, the crops, the animals, and so on. Some are spirits of law or tribal rules of behavior. Kachinas have become well known and popular among non-Indian people because of the interesting kachina dolls created and sold by the Indians, according to fixed ancestral designs.

Kobold

Kobolds were seldom seen. German miners used to say they saw only the eyes of the kobolds, shining in dark holes in mines and other underground places. They were not entirely distinguishable from **gnomes** and dwarves. Some said the kobolds were ruled by Alberich, who was the English fairy king Oberon, spouse of Titania—which leads to the pre-Hellenic Titans or earth **giants,** many of whose myths dated back to the horse-riding Amazon tribes. Again, the word *kobold* may have descended from Greek *kaballoi,* horse-riders.

The mineral cobalt was named after the kobolds, because of the difficulty of smelting cobalt-bearing ores. Miners claimed that the mineral was bewitched by the kobolds.

Lamia

The conventional image of a lamia was a **serpent** with a woman's head and breasts. The original Lamia was the Serpent Goddess of Libya, whom the Greeks called Medusa and the Egyptians called Neith.[1] She was also worshiped at Der in Babylon as a serpent-bodied woman, and

perhaps bore a more than passing resemblance to the kundalini serpent.

Hellenic Greeks humanized her into a mortal virgin impregnated by their own god Zeus, to whom she bore several children. However, she was also a Gorgon-faced devourer of children, after the manner of the ancient **Goddess** who took back what she brought forth. Later Christian tradition spoke of "lamias" as snakelike she-devils or witches able to transform themselves into snakes. Martin of Braga wrote that lamias were female devils who lived in rivers and forests.[2] Centuries later, John Keats created a fanciful poem about the serpent woman and entitled it *Lamia*.

1. Graves, W.G., 246. 2. J. H. Smith, 240.

Leviathan

Leviathan was the Hebrew name of the great **serpent** god called Lotan or Lawtan in northern Canaan, Ladon in Greece, and Sata or Apep in Egypt. Ladon was the guardian of the holy fruit of the **Tree of Life** in Hera's garden, and his appearance in the Garden of Eden seems to have been copied from a similar image. Leviathan or "the Wriggly One" was a title of the brazen serpent Nehushtan whose worship was established by Moses, but later discredited (2 Kings 18:4). The Levite priests first took their name from Leviathan the Hebrew serpent god. Gnostic Jews of the first century A.D. worshiped him under the name of Ophion (Serpent), claiming that he was the real king of heaven and that Yahweh had usurped his kingdom.[1]

Since he was a rival deity, Leviathan was diabolized by the Christian followers of this same Yahweh, and converted into a prominent resident of hell. At the same time, Leviathan the sea serpent (like Oceanus) was identified with the whale, which is still sometimes poetically named Leviathan.

1. Graves, W.G., 367.

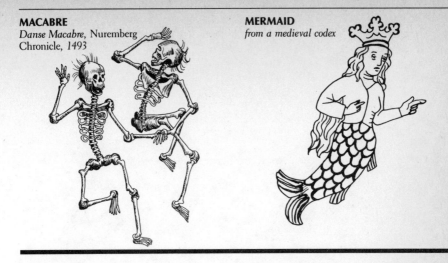

Macabre

Macabre was the French version of the
death figure that played an essential role in
medieval mystery plays, usually as an
actor costumed in a **skeleton** suit, carrying
a **scythe** and/or an hourglass. The
danse macabre (German *Totentanz*) was a
high point of these plays, reminding
the audience that the horrors and morbid-
ities of death are but a step away, and
that one should see to the state of one's
immortal soul.

The illustration from a fifteenth-
century tract shows that the artists of the
time had little notion of skeletal anatomy,
owing to the church's prohibition of
the use of cadavers to study the actual
construction of the human body. Yet they
did the best they could with what
little they knew, and often produced lively,
striking pictures.

Macabre figures of the European
mystery play demonstrate the Oriental influences of the early Renaissance.
Centuries before, skeleton-suited priests
performed similar dances in India
and Tibet. Death dances of the Buddhist
citapati featured male and female
pairs with corpses under their feet and
skull-topped wands in their hands.[1]

1. G. Jobes 1, 344.

Mermaid

The mermaid descended from very old
traditions connecting **Goddess** figures with
the sea as a universal **womb.** Fish-
tailed Aphrodite and the similar mermaid
Goddess Tirgata (Atargatis) of Syria
were identified with another fish-tailed
figure, the Goddess Derceto of Palestine,
whose name meant Whale of Der.[1] Mermaids and mermen were also prefigured
in India by the Nagas who were human
above the waist and water-serpents below.
They lived in springs and rivers, guarding
treasures in their underwater palaces.[2] A
popular African mermaid Goddess
was Yemaya, whose hair was said to be
long green strands of seaweed and
whose jewels were shells.

Medieval books of alchemy described
the mermaid as the Siren of the Philosophers, crowned and lactating the milk of
enlightenment. She was usually shown
naked, but several texts provided her, as
shown in the illustration, with a modest
little jacket—possibly a later addition. As
late as the nineteenth century, British law
claimed that all mermaids found within the
home waters would be the property of
the Crown.[3]

Perhaps the best-known legendary
mermaid was Melusine, who married
Raymond of Poitou and built her own

Yama, the Oriental minotaur

castle at Lusignan. One day a week she spent lying in her bath in strict privacy, because her fish tail would appear then. She was discovered and exiled. But the stories say she returned with every full moon to watch over her children. When her wailing voice is heard over Lusignan, it means the death of a king.[4]

1. Baring-Gould, 497.   2. Tatz & Kent, 79.
3. Walker, *W.E.M.S.*, 652.   4. Baring-Gould, 478.

Minotaur

The **bull**-masked underworld king, ancient Crete's **labyrinth**-dwelling Minotaur, still appears in Hindu and Buddhist art as bull-masked Yama, ruler of the labyrinthine ways underground. In Crete he combined *tauros* the sacred bull with Minos the king, actually a series of kings, whose name means "one dedicated to the moon." Like the similar sacrificial bull god Apis in Egypt, he was both a sacrificed animal and a man wearing the royal bull mask.

This led to his portrayal in classical mythology as a man-bull monster, born of an unnatural liaison between the Cretan queen Pasiphaë and the sacrificial bull. The real meaning of the myth was "a ritual marriage under an oak between the Moon-priestess wearing cow's horns, and the Minos-king, wearing a bull's mask."[1]

The story of Theseus entering the labyrinth and killing the Minotaur apparently represented warfare between Athens and Crete. It was also claimed that Theseus killed "the bull from the sea," the banner of the Cretan ships, bearing the image of the royal lunar bull that was the Minoan totem.

1. Graves, G.M. 1, 297.

Muse

It was common for troubadours and romantic poets to speak of their individual Muses, often embodied in mortal women: wives or lovers, who awakened the male poet's creative energies. The theory was that woman inspires and man creates. It was a sexist theory that in effect denied women the true inner spirit of artistic creativity. But in her original form, the Muse was a Goddess whose fires might illuminate the mind of either sex. Still, like the Hindu Goddess as Shakti, she taught the way of the left hand to those upon whom she poured her gifts. We still say a creative person is "gifted."

The oldest tradition of the Muses shows that they were symbolic of the Triple Goddess as a triad. The first of them was Mnemosyne, "Memory," the most essential gift because no poet could repeat his verses without her.[1] Like the three **Graces,** the original three Muses provided a better than average ability in some field of artistic endeavor. Later they were multiplied to nine (see **Star of the Muses**). A great temple of the Muses in Alexandria was called the Museum. Unlike a modern museum, it was chiefly a school of the arts. It was destroyed early in the Christian era.[2] The Muses still give their name to "music" and "amusement," as well as the verb "to muse," which means to search the inner mind for inspiration.

1. Graves, *W.G.*, 377.
2. Walker, *W.E.M.S.*, 701.

Nixie

In Germanic legend, a nixie was a water spirit, often fish-tailed, like a **mermaid.** She bore many similarities to the Greek nereids, which were female spirits of rivers, springs, pools, lakes, and oceans, as well as demoted or discredited Goddesses of nature generally. The nereids were known to Christian authorities as "she-devils," and their leader was said to be a serpent-tailed **lamia.**[1] Another name for a nereid or a nixie was undine: a water-elemental, first offspring of the primal Mother as water, which Thales of Miletus called the first of all substances, like the amniotic fluid of the universe.[2]

The Orphic name for the primal Goddess hovering over the dark watery abyss at creation was Nyx: that is, Mother Night. She was what the Bible would later call the Spirit (of God) moving on the face of the Deep, after having changed her gender.[3] Her daughters may well have been the nixies, whose Germanic mother was named Nött: that is, Mother Night.[4]

1. Hyde, 146.   2. Campbell, *P.M.*, 64.
3. Gimbutas, 102.   4. Branston, 145, 152.

Norns

The Norns of Scandinavia were among the oldest and most mysterious manifestations of the Triple Goddess. Like the Greek Moerae and the Saxon **Weird Sisters,** they represented the past, present, and future: "Become, Becoming, and Shall Be."[1] They lived in the magic womb-cave at the root of the World Tree, determining the

NYMPH
from a Greek bas-relief

fate of every creature. They were identified with the three phases of the moon, waxing, full, and waning. They ruled over the heavenly father (Odin) and every other god, setting limits to their lives and establishing the cosmic order that would bring each god to his end at doomsday.[2]

Obviously based on the great Indo-European Goddess as Creator, Preserver, and Destroyer—like Kali—the Norns also governed the mystic fountain of life, Urdarbrunnr or the Well of Urd. Urd was the first of the Norns, her name cognate with that of Mother Earth and also with the Saxon Weird or Wyrd, "Fate": Urd, Urth, Wurd, Werd, Wyrd. The second Norn was Verthandi, the third Skuld, or as the Saxons called her, Skadi, Goddess of death. All of Scandinavia was named after her; so was Scotland, after the Latinized form of her name, Scotia.[3]

Like other female triads, the Norns were left over from the original feminine form of the Holy Trinity. Though patriarchal traditions assimilated them as "fairies" or "witches," they retained an aura of fearsome power throughout a thousand years of Christianization.

1. Campbell, *C.M.*, 121. 2. Branston, 208–209.   3. Graves, *G.M.* 1, 72.

Nymph

The ancient Greek temples called *nymphaeae* were located at sacred springs, and staffed by "colleges" of unmarried priestesses. Greek *nymphe*, Latin *nympha* meant a nubile young woman, originally one considered independent of men because of her unmarried state, like the older meaning of *virgin*. Later it came to mean a bride, through the mystic marriages of the nymphs as "brides of God" when they attended temples of Zeus, Hermes, or Priapus.[1] In Roman times, the *nymphaeae* were temples specifically dedicated to wedding ceremonies.[2]

During the Middle Ages, "nymphs" became synonymous with **fairies,** witches, or nature spirits like tree nymphs, river nymphs, mountain nymphs, and so on. Their sexual connotations were preserved in legends of their orgiastic seasons under the influence of the moon: hence the term *nymphomania*.

1. Cirlot, 227. 2. Whittick, 246.

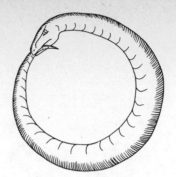

Ogre

The word *ogre* descended from a title of
the Aryan god Odin as Lord of Death:
Yggr, meaning "Terrible One."[1] An ogre
was often depicted as one-eyed, like
a **Cyclops,** because Odin was known as
the One-Eyed God, having given up one of
his eyes to acquire the female secrets
of magic and **rune** spells. Since Odin was
diabolized along with all other pagan
gods, especially in his more fearsome aspects, the popular concept of an ogre was an
ugly, demonic being of great strength
and destructive power: a manlike monster.

1. Branston, 114.

Ouroboros

Ouroboros was a Gnostic name for the
great World Serpent, who was supposed to
encircle the earth—back when most
people thought the earth was a flat disc—
or else to embrace the mystic World
Egg. Among many other names for this
serpent were Taaut of the Middle East,
Thoth or Sata of Egypt, **Hermes** or Zeus
Meilichios of Greece, Vasuki of India, and
Ophion of the Ophite Christians, who
identified him with Christ. To Jewish
Gnostics he was Nahash or Nehushtan,
the serpent god whose worship was
established by Moses and dismantled by

Hezekiah (Numbers 21:8; 2 Kings
18:4). This deity was an earlier Goddess
Nehushtah, and possibly a parallel
of one of the Hindu names for the world-
creating serpent, Nahusha.[1] See **Serpent.**

A number of traditions indicate
that the original serpent protecting the
World Egg was female, a mother-serpent,
like Ananta the Infinite in India, or
Mehen the Enveloper (Ua Zit, Buto,
Uraeus) in Egypt. The male serpent became the guardian of the Egg only
after patriarchy was well established. His
swallowing of his own tail (to make
an endless round) was probably based on
the primitive notion that the female
serpent swallows the male in order to fertilize herself: a notion that was reported by
Pliny and solemnly believed throughout
Christian Europe.[2] Sometimes, Ouroboros was androgynous or a pair of mated
serpents swallowing each other's tails.

This serpent image once commanded
great devotion as a symbol of the entire life
of nature. He, she, or it often bore
the caption *Hen to pan:* "The One, the
All."[3] Ouroboros was also equated
with Okeanos (Oceanus), the water-serpent
personifying the outer sea, surrounding all
the land mass of the earth. Norsemen
called this being the Midgard-Worm.[4] To

PERI
*from a 16-century
Persian miniature*

POOKA

the Japanese he was Koshi the dragon of the sea, who penetrated Russian folklore as Koshchei the Deathless, great serpent encircling the underworld.[5] There were obvious parallels with the Christian "Great Serpent" Satan. Some folk still speak of the great earth dragon whose subterranean movements cause earthquakes.

1. Walker, *W.E.M.S.*, 905. 2. Briffault 2, 667. 3. Cirlot, 235. 4. Branston, 96. 5. Lethaby, 168.

Peri

A peri is the Persian-Arabic version of a **fairy**: that is, a spirit, usually female, left over from prepatriarchal (pre-Islamic) ages. It was claimed that the peris were the same as *djinn* or fallen **angels**; or again, that they were female spirit guides like the *shakti* of India. To the Sufis, each man's peri was his *pir* or "lady-love," a teacher of sexual mysticism like a Tantric yogini. Sometimes a peri was considered identical with a houri: a heavenly **nymph** who would provide sexual bliss for the dead hero or sage.

As with all such concepts, the fairy companion was also viewed as the female portion of a man's own soul, the *anima* or *psyche*. This notion descended from one of the oldest matriarchal beliefs, evolved long before the recognition of fatherhood: the belief that the female principle was the true life-giving, thinking, feeling, and living spirit, instilled into each child by his or her mother through all generations—in much the same way that the European church later envisioned the transmission of original sin. In Armenia, the peri was openly recognized as a man's female, emotional soul. To express affection he would say, "My peri loves you dearly."[1]

A peri could also be a kind of **Muse**, that is, an inner source of inspiration or the inspiration provided externally by the relationship with a loved one.

1. Kunz, 207.

Pooka

The pooka of Irish legend was a magic spirit-animal, usually a **horse**; but a pooka could appear in humanlike form also. To see a pooka was an omen of death. Therefore, the horse form probably descended from the spirit-horses of Celtic religion, whose function was to carry dead heroes to paradise, like the winged horses of the Greeks.

The pooka was a cognate of Old English *puca*, a fairy creature, which also produced *spook* and *Puck*.[1] Such ancestral fairy beliefs are still preserved in a number of Irish place names, such as Puckstown, Puck Fair, and Pooka's Ford.[2] The pooka is still sighted occasionally, in remote and lonely places, particularly swamps and bogs.

In Scotland, the creature was usually called a kelpie. This was a water spirit embodied sometimes in a seal, sometimes in a white horse whose mane was like the foaming crests of the waves. The white horse was an important Indo-European symbol of the Second Coming of the universal god or savior-hero, born of the sea (*maria*). Hindus named him the Kalki Avatara, or final incarnation of Buddha, who was in turn one of the avatars of Vishnu. On his last appearance at the end of the world, he would either ride or become a white horse (*kalkin*).[3]

1. Potter & Sargent, 295. 2. Pepper & Wilcock, 279–280. 3. G. Jobes 2, 904, 916.

Psychopomp

In Greek, a psychopomp meant any "conductor" or "leader" or "carrier" of souls to, in, or through the afterworld. The term was applied to **Hermes**, Charon, Persephone, Orpheus, the death **dogs**, the winged **horses**, the **harpies**, and other carrion-eating creatures such as **vultures.** **Angels, Valkyries,** and savior figures were also psychopomps, like the "Good Shepherd" **Osiris** who led souls to his "green pastures." Yama, Lord of the Dead in India, was a psychopomp; so was his Persian cognate, Yima the Splendid. Christians conceived various **saints** as psychopomps, not to mention Christ himself, whose primary function was to carry the faithful to heaven. This was the whole meaning of salvation, as understood by the laity.

Probably the concept of the psychopomp is as old as human recognition of the inevitability of death and the human desire to avoid frankly facing it. Thus the Egyptian worshiper of Osiris said that, because of steadfast faith in the savior, "I shall not decay, and I shall not rot, I shall not putrefy, I shall not turn into worms, and I shall not see corruption . . . I shall live, I shall live; I shall flourish, I shall flourish, I shall flourish; I shall wake up in peace."[1]

1. *Book of the Dead*, 463–464.

Revenant

Literally, "one who returns," a revenant was envisioned as a person having come back from death to some sort of earthly existence, whether as a **ghost**, a **vampire**, or a walking corpse like the West Indian zombie. Even though Christianity taught that the souls of the dead were removed from the earth, superstitions abounded throughout Christian society and even Christian theology about dead bodies that could be reanimated by some magical or diabolical means. Graveyards were avoided always, out of the almost universal fear of dead spirits that might be moving about as if living. Probably a large contributing factor to the belief in revenants was the appearance of the dead in dreams; for the dreamers were prone to believe in the reality of their nocturnal visions.

As a symbol, a revenant embodied both the fear of death and certain relics of the ancient belief in reincarnation, through which most of the world's people managed to convince themselves that the dead could come back, one way or another. However, after having been permanently altered by the fact of death, they were often considered inimical to the living, envious, or bloodthirsty, as in the case of vampires. Pagan religions sometimes defused the fear by impersonating the returned dead, as is still done—playfully—by our **Halloween** ghosts.

Saint

The canon of saints was the Christian technique for preserving the pagan polytheism that people wanted, while pretending to worship only one God. In fact, a good many of the same pagan deities were brought into the church, refurbished as phony saints so that popular devotion to them would bring profit to the church instead of diverting it elsewhere. The great age of saint-making began about the ninth century, when hagiographers busily attached fictional life stories and martyrdoms to former heathen heroes, and ransacked old cemeteries in their highly lucrative treasure hunt for purported relics. "They invented names for skeletons, and actions for names."[1]

Among the canonized pagans were Diana, Artemis, Castor and Pollux, Helios, Bacchus, Dionysus, Nereus, Aphrodite, Mercury, Silvanus, and even Buddha.[2] Multiple images of the Great Goddess Cybele at Acrae were canonized en masse as the Santoni, "saints."[3] The martyrs of the famous Roman "persecutions" under such emperors as Nero and Diocletian, seven centuries earlier, were largely invented at this time, since there were no records of any such specific martyrdoms. Names were picked at random from ancient tombstones, and the martyr-tales were written to order. In reality, it was the early Christian church that did much more persecuting and made many more martyrs than Rome had ever done, because religious tolerance was the usual Roman policy.[4]

The saints proved eminently useful as fund-raisers. Their holy relics were in great demand as healing charms, and this medicinal use always required monetary contributions. Fourteenth-century lunatics were supposed to be cured by drinking wine into which a saint's bones had been dipped. A single hair of a saint, dipped in water, made a widely prescribed purgative. A recommended cure for tumors was oil from the lamp burning before the tomb of Saint Gall.[5] Churches all over Europe advertised the miraculous cures effected by their own local saints' fingerbones, teeth, shreds of garment, hairs, skulls, and other charnel bits and pieces, most of them enshrined in gold and silver reliquaries encrusted with gems, created by the finest artisans in Europe, and worth fortunes. Many did not even bother to use human remains. The famous healing bones of Saint Rosalia were found to be the bones of a goat, and the Eleven Thousand Virgins of Saint Ursula left bones that were mostly those of pigs.

The medieval church paid more attention to the legends and cults of saints than to Christ, perhaps because the saints brought in more money as well as catering to the people's natural inclination toward polytheism.[6] Some of the most famous saints still worshiped today are some of the least historical. The patron saints of England, Scotland, Ireland, and Wales were all fictional. The patron saint of France, Saint Denis, was only a transformation of the god Dionysus in his Orphic cult of the oracular head, which explains the nonsensical legend that Saint Denis, having been beheaded on Montmartre (Martyr's Mount), then tucked his severed head under his arm and walked to the present site of his abbey.[7] Some time ago there was an attempt to identify Saint Denis with the

supposedly real first-century bishop Dionysius the Areopagite; but the attempt was abandoned after scholars made it clear that Dionysius the Areopagite was a fiction too, and that his purported writings were sixth-century forgeries.[8]

1. Campbell, *Oc.M.*, 392.   2. Walker, *W.E.M.S.*, 880.   3. Vermaseren, 68. 4. J. H. Smith, 40, 131; Angus, 277. 5. Abelard, 56.   6. Mâle, 176.   7. Hall, 98. 8. Walker, *W.E.M.S.*, 236.

Satyr

A satyr, like a **faun,** was an embodiment of the horned god of wild nature, whom the Greeks called Pan. He came to represent the spirit of sexual desire in particular, which is why Christian authorities, who equated sex with sin, found it easy to view the satyrs as **demons.** The Greeks identified the Egyptian god Amen-Ra with the satyr deity Pan, showing that the latter was once a powerful king of heaven at least in some areas, rather than the minor woodland spirit that the Hellenes made of him. Amen-Ra's holy city of Chemmis was given the Greek name of Panopolis, "city of Pan," origin of *panoply,* which meant elaborate

religious ornamentation. The Greek writers said this city was inhabited by "Pans and satyrs."[1]

The Roman satyr head in the illustration shows the horizontally twisting ram's horns characteristic of the Egyptian god.

1. Budge, *G.E.* 2, 22.

Sea Serpent

The sea serpent was a favorite wonder-tale among sailors of every nation, probably dating back to ancient images of the world-encircling ocean as a vast serpent (see **Ouroboros**). Sightings were frequent. Sailors saw whales at a distance, or porpoises leaping one after another, their curved backs suggesting the conventional image of the sea serpent with its back emerging from the water in successive waves. Large snakelike sea animals such as the moray eel may have contributed to the legend also. As a symbol, the sea serpent represented the unknown and mysterious abysses far from the sight of land. The "swallowing monster," thought able to engulf whole ships, was the sea itself. Certain images of the great water dragon persist even today; the Loch Ness monster is a prime example.

Siren

The double-tailed siren was a cross between a **mermaid** and a **sheila-na-gig.** For centuries she was a popular form of decoration for churches. Many of Europe's cathedrals have sirens carved on pillars, arches, cornices, choir stalls, and other surfaces.

One reason for the siren's popularity was her mystical meaning in medieval secret societies, such as the Freemasons. Alchemical books called her the Siren of the Philosophers, another version of Fish-tailed Aphrodite Marina, the Sea Goddess as revealer of the mysteries of nature. Her suggestive pose, like that of the sheila-na-gig, referred to female sexual mysteries in particular.

The medieval siren should not be confused with the Sirens that Homer thought so dangerous to Greek ships. These were not mermaids, but the women of Cyrene in Libya, a city established by an Amazon queen of the same name, who was said to be so strong that she could wrestle with lions.[1] The myth probably arose from icons of the Libyan Goddess riding a lion or sitting in her lion-drawn chariot.

One of the earliest pagan images of the siren was found carved on a stone from Gotland in the Baltic, about A.D. 600. Seated, face-on, the naked Goddess Freya-Nerthus spread her legs wide apart like a sheila-na-gig; but they were legs, not fish tails. In each hand she held up a huge **serpent,** making her own body like the central shaft of the healing **caduceus.**[2] It seems clear that in later copies the feet of the Goddess became merged with the tails of her serpents, so that the whole figure took on the Gothic outlines of the siren.

1. Huson, 177.   2. Sjöö & Mor, 321.

Soul

The term *immortal soul* means essentially the same as a **ghost:** that is, some sentient part of a human being that continues to exist after the human being dies. The term *soul* without any qualification, however, is a true symbol, in that it stands for the totality of an individual's thoughts, feelings, memories, attitudes, affections, hopes, fears—the whole personality, immortal or not. Though seldom pictured, the idea itself is the symbol.

The ancients envisioned composite souls with various parts located in the blood, or the heart, or the liver, or the secret name, or even in external things such as the shadow and the reflection. The last-named belief gave rise to the superstitious conviction that soulless creatures like **vampires** are shadowless and cast no image in a mirror. The matriarchal age almost universally supposed that the important animating spirit lay in the **blood,** from which substance, under the influence of the moon, the person took shape while still in the womb. The mother's child-forming menstrual blood was believed to emanate directly from her heart, which is why the heart or "heart's blood" became synonymous with the soul.[1] Mothers were the givers of souls. An archaic king of Rome, Erulus or Herulus, received three souls from his mother and so was compelled to die three times.[2]

Patriarchal religions naturally sought to reverse this idea in favor of fathers. They seized on one kind of soul, the kind supposed to reside in the **breath,** which fathers or paternal gods might conceivably bestow by speaking or breathing on the new being. Although Gnostic literature said it was the breath of the Goddess **Sophia** Zoe, mother of Eve, who gave Adam his soul, biblical writers insisted that a male God "breathed" soul into Adam.[3] Although most of the words for "soul" remained feminine—such as

psyche, pneuma, anima, alma—yet the theologians of the male-dominated church eventually succeeded in establishing the idea that only a father gives "soul" to a child, and that the essence of soul is in male semen. On occasion, churchmen even denied any soul to women. In A.D. 660, the third canon of the Council of Nantes ruled that women have no souls, immortal or otherwise. At the end of the sixteenth century, clergymen declared that the Indian women of the newly discovered American continents were soulless creatures, halfway between animal and human. According to the Greek church up to the time of Peter the Great, the census of the empire's "souls" counted men only.[4] Even when it was conceded that women had souls, they were sometimes not included in the scheme of salvation. Guillaume Postel presaged modern psychologists in postulating a male and a female soul, the animus and anima; then he went on to say that the male part was redeemed by Christ, while the female part is still unredeemed and awaits a female savior.[5]

Communication with the souls of the dead was another sore point to patriarchal theology, because ancient priestesses and their ideological descendants the witches had claims to this. The Bible seemed to prohibit necromantic interviews, in recounting the incident of Saul's

SPHINX
Greco-Egyptian

visit to the female spirit medium at Endor (1 Samuel 28). Yet a number of high-ranking churchmen were recorded as having conducted necromantic conversations with the dead. It seemed that this was acceptable if it was performed under the auspices of the church and not by women. In 1675, the monk Albert de Saint Jacques published a book, *Light to the Living by the Experience of the Dead*, describing interviews with souls necromantically summoned from purgatory, and their remarks about the afterlife.[6]

1. Walker, W.E.M.S., 375. 2. Dumézil, A.R.R. 1, 244. 3. Robinson, 171–172. 4. Gage, 56–57. 5. Seligmann, 223. 6. Spence, 345.

Sphinx

It is rarely pointed out that the classical tragedy of King Oedipus was brought about by the curse of the **Goddess** in her Sphinx form, a derivation of Egyptian Hathor as the lioness-destroyer. Trying to overturn the matriarchy in Thebes and preserve himself as a permanent king, Oedipus threw the sacred statue of the Sphinx off a cliff and broke it. He defied the Goddess by guessing her famous riddle. The Sphinx had her revenge. Some said Oedipus was not only blinded but also slain in the Goddess's sacred grove by her avenging **Furies**.[1]

The Sphinx was not only Egyptian, but also a Greek image of female divinity in pre-Hellenic times. The nonrecognition of fatherhood that led to Oedipus's allegedly incestuous marriage was really an ancient custom, when every king was called a son of the preceding king even though they had no real relationship, but were simply successors chosen by the queen. The name of Oedipus's mythical father, Laius, meant nothing more than "king."

Greek versions of the Sphinx often wore wings to suggest divinity.

1. Graves, G.M. 2, 10, 15, 396.

Sybil

Among the most powerful women in Rome were the oracular priestesses of Cumae, known as sybils (or sibyls). Like the comparable name of the Goddess Cybele, this meant "cavern-dweller." The cult of Cybele was brought to Rome upon the specific orders of the Cumaean sybil. The **cave** she occupied, and its nearby lake, were considered entrances to the underworld, whence the priestess could summon up spirits of the dead for consultation.[1]

The Roman writer Varro (second century B.C.) described Eleven Great Sybils and their attributes. Sibylla Persica carried a lantern and had a **serpent** under her feet. Sibylla Libyea held a lighted **torch.** Sibylla Erythreia held a white **rose** and a naked **sword.** Sibylla Cimmeria carried a cross. Sibylla Cumana was represented by an ancient stone manger. Sibylla Delphica wore a **crown** of thorns. Sibylla Cania bore a **reed** and a **candle.** Sibylla Phrygia prophesied resurrection and carried a banner. Sibylla Tibertina dressed in animal skins and carried a bundle of **rods.** Sibylla Helles-pontina carried a flowering branch. Sibylla Europa carried a sword.[2]

Because some of the sybils' attributes could be assimilated to Christianity, early Christians preserved the Sybilline Books and extensively rewrote them to prove that the sybils were foretelling the advent of Christ. Eventually the sybils like all other magical women were diabolized, but still believed in. In the fifteenth century A.D., a priest named Don Anthon Fumato, "whose senses had been confused by the action of the moon," entered the sybils' cave on the Monte della Sibilla, and saw beautiful women beckoning lasciviously.[3] In the same period, magic books were recommending conjurations of the sybils: "I conjure thee, Sibylia, O blessed virgin of fairies, to appear . . . and to give me good counsel at all times, and to come by treasures hidden in the earth, and all other things that is to do me pleasure, and to fulfil my will."[4]

1. Graves, W.G., 273.   2. Brewster, 415–417.   3. Duerr, 28.   4. Scot, 340.

TRITON
from a 16th-century
engraving

Sylph

A sylph was originally conceived as one of the four types of elemental spirits, made of or representing **air.** The others were: **gnomes,** earth; undines, water; and **salamanders,** fire. Air spirits were essentially the same as breath-souls, or **ghosts.** They used to be the ancestors that left their bodies with the final breath, and thereafter dwelt invisibly in the air or in the sky, as part of the atmosphere.

Due to the once universal doctrine of reincarnation, people believed to be re-born spirits of such ancestors in new bodies could also be called sylphs. Apparently the female shamans of European tribes sometimes considered themselves reborn air spirits, for they were called sylphs—as were the ethereal nature deities who spoke to them out of the wind. Sylphs became almost synonymous with witches in some areas. An edict of Charlemagne, later re-newed by Louis the Pious, forbade sylphs to "appear"—meaning, perhaps, to gather together—and threatened them with heavy legal penalties.[1]

1. Spence, 165.

Triton

Tritons were envisioned as fish-tailed river or sea gods able to raise the moaning storm winds by blowing their conch-shell trumpets. They seem to have descended from one Triton, one of the three children of "the Triple Moon-goddess as ruler of the sea" under her Homeric title of Amphi-trite, "the All-Encircling Triad." The name of Triton means "being in her third day," and was originally a female name, associated with the new moon. Later, Tri-ton was masculinized. A sea god Triton was propitiated by Jason of the Argonauts and consented to pull their ship by its keel into the Mediterranean Sea.[1]

European mapmakers often regarded tritons as the male counterparts and spouses of nereids (or **mermaids**), and drew them all around the oceanic portions of their maps, to suggest that such creatures might actually be sighted by a ship upon the high seas.

1. Graves, G.M. 1, 61; 2, 246.

Troll

The troll was a Scandinavian image of a mountain spirit, with a body made of rock, the same stuff as the crags and **caves** where trolls were said to live. Some trolls habitually squatted under bridges and seized people who tried to cross at the wrong times.

The idea evidently grew out of the natural human propensity to see faces and humanlike figures in jumbled rocks, in dark caves, on cliff faces and outcroppings. Like trees, the rocks lent themselves to anthropomorphism. The demonic, threatening nature of the troll would have been based on the real dangers of mountainous, rocky places, where human visitors seem to be discouraged by the very nature of the terrain.

In the islands of northern Scotland, the troll became transformed into the *trow*, a supernatural being who might dwell under hills or in the sea. To see such a creature was to be stricken with abject, unreasoning terror like the *"pan-*ic" supposedly engendered by the cry of the god Pan.[1]

1. G. Jobes 2, 1600.

Unicorn

The heraldic unicorn underwent centuries of development, apparently beginning with Babylonian and Egyptian animal symbols of the **seasons** depicted in profile. When the bull of spring was shown rearing up against the lion of summer, the bull's two horns merged into one horn. Similarly, an Egyptian papyrus sketch shows the contention of the seasons as a game of draughts played between a lion and a goat (or gazelle), the latter's horns drawn as one horn emerging from the forehead. The lion and the unicorn still contend in profile on the British coat of arms, where they are said to represent the sun and the moon, respectively. The unicorn, though horse-faced and horse-bodied, still retains a goatlike beard and sometimes cloven hooves as well.[1]

The **horse** was often artificially horned as a magical strength charm among equestrian tribes in central Asia. Horse skulls have been found in Siberian burial sites, wearing artificial leather horns.[2] Such practices could account for the confusion between the zodiacal horned animal and the horselike unicorn. This unicorn

was understood as a phallic symbol, always yearning to place his "horn" in a maiden's lap. Medieval legend said he would be immobilized by his love for a virgin, so hunters could easily catch him. Again, despite the erotic overtones of the legend, Christian sacred art often identified the unicorn with Christ and showed him within the magical **enclosed garden** (womb) of the divine Virgin.[3]

The only real animal found to have a single central horn on its face was the rhinoceros. Therefore, this unfortunate beast became identified with the virile unicorn of myth, and its "phallic" horn was long considered a magical cure for impotence. This belief is still widespread in Asia, which is why the rhinoceros has been hunted almost to extinction to indulge a crude and erroneous superstition.[4]

1. Brown, 146. 2. Davidson, *P.S.*, 57.
3. Williamson, 163. 4. Woods, 176.

Valkyrie

Norse skalds (poets) called the Valkyries "battle-maids." They were sometimes represented as death **angels** who delighted in warfare, or as corpse-eating carrion crows who flew to battlefields in order to feast on the dead. Valkyries wore **raven feathers** and were known as "man-eating women" in Old Saxon, while the blood of dead warriors was described in skaldic verse as "the raven's drink."[1]

Valkyries were shape-shifters who could also turn themselves into **swans, hawks,** or **mares.** A mare-woman in Swedish was a *volva,* related to several old words for funerary priestesses: *vala, vila, wila,* or *wili.* All could be related to the Sanskrit *vilasa,* a heavenly **nymph** who took care of the dead.[2] Valkyries took care of fallen heroes who had died bravely in battle, according to the warlike cults of Odin, Thor, and the Aesir. It was believed, perhaps literally, that Valkyries would come on their cloud-horses and carry dead warriors to Valhalla.

The title of a Valkyrie meant "chooser of the slain." According to the *Grimnismal* there were thirteen Valkyries, the number of annual lunations and of witches in a coven. Other sources said there were nine Valkyries, as there were nine **Muses** and nine sea-maidens who brought forth heroes.[3] They were powerful female symbols even in a male-dominated society based on war and loot. Many heroes, such as Siegfried, had Valkyrie lovers bestowed on them by the poets.

1. Turville-Petre, 58. 2. Avalon, 199.
3. Branston, 191.

Vampire

Modern concepts of the vampire have been so deeply influenced by Bram Stoker's *Dracula* and its multitude of literary and cinematic offspring that few people are informed about any earlier ideas on the subject. The idea that the dead require **blood,** to restore them to a semblance of life, is as old as Homer and probably older. It began with the primitive view of lunar (menstrual) blood as the very stuff of life, the substance of every living body, and the medium of reincarnation for the souls waiting to be born again. Greeks thought the shades in the underworld, being bloodless, were always hungry for blood. That is why Odysseus was able to call up the **ghosts** of his dead comrades by necromantically pouring out offerings of blood for them. The gods likewise lived on blood and were invoked by blood offerings.

This classic idea that the dead always craved blood, and could live indefinitely if they could get enough of it, was sufficient in itself to account for vampire stories. In addition, vampires were generally identified with cannibals during the early Middle Ages. Man-eating vampires seem to have been regarded as mostly female,

according to the Salic law that levied a fine of 8,000 deniers on a she-vampire found guilty of devouring a man.[1]

Throughout most of the Christian era, vampires were thought as real as all the other accepted supernaturals: **demons, angels,** ghosts, **fairies,** and so on. Rousseau pointed out that the reality of vampires was supported by exactly the same kind of evidence usually adduced for the reality of God: "official reports, testimonials of persons of standing, of surgeons, of clergymen, of judges; the judicial evidence is all-embracing."[2] In the Balkans, where vampire legends were particularly rife, certain magicians specialized in capturing vampires in bottles. The classical technique of piercing the suspected vampire in his/her tomb with a wooden stake was still practiced in the twentieth century by Balkan priests.[3]

1. Spence, 164. 2. Seligmann, 302. 3. Hyde, 182–184.

Werewolf

Werewolf superstitions arose from the belief that most ancient deities, and their followers, could put on the nature of certain animals by wearing their skins or **masks.** Such "shape-shifting" customs gave rise to bull gods, cow goddesses, goat

WYVERN

gods, horse gods, boar gods, and ram gods, not to mention all the numerous deities of Egypt who could become crocodiles, beetles, hawks, hippopotami, jackals, and birds, as well as the monkey, elephant, tiger, and cobra deities of India. Wolves were revered as **psychopomps** or carriers of the dead, the same as dogs and vultures. Worshipers of wolf deities wore wolf skins and regarded themselves as honorary wolves. Such "werewolves" were sacred to Zeus Lycaios (Wolfish Zeus) at the temple on the summit of Mount Lycaion in Arcadia. Zeus's devotees lived nine years as wolves in the forest, then resumed human form if they had not eaten human flesh. It was said of Zeus's wolf temple that people lost their shadows by entering its doors—a later characteristic of werewolves. Up to the seventeenth century A.D., Latvian peasants "became werewolves" by similar means on Midsummer, Pentecost, and Lucia's Night to save their crops from "sorcerers" who would carry barley, rye, and oats away to hell.[1]

Certain Irish tribes claimed that their ancestors were wolves, and prayed to wolves as their tribal totems for help and healing. One Irish clan was said to become werewolves automatically every seventh year. This "becoming" seems to have been a ritual transformation,

as German folklore said a person might become a werewolf by putting on a wolf skin.[2]

Diabolization of werewolf legends was assured by the fact that wolf clans worshiped the Goddess as the Great She-Wolf, Lupa or Feronia, "Mother of Wolves," other names for Diana of the Wild Animals, later declared queen of witches.[3]

1. Duerr, 34, 63. 2. Wedeck, 173, 179.
3. Walker, W.E.M.S., 1068–1072.

Wyvern

The wyvern (or wivern) was a composite of a composite: a **basilisk,** with its bird legs and serpent tail, topped off by the head of a dragon. Medieval artists had an astonishing affinity for impossible combinations of disparate animal parts, and human parts also (as in the work of Hieronymus Bosch). Such creations may be taken as symbols of social or psychological fragmentation, a deep sense of discontinuity or of unnatural discrepancies: a redesigning of reality characteristic of the symbolizing human mind's eye.

ZODIAC

Signs of the zodiac have ancient origins, to be found in Egyptian hieroglyphs and in symbol systems of Babylon and Persia. The constellations were identified with various symbolic figures at an early date, probably in Sumeria, where the study was evolved by priestesses of the Moon-goddess. Even the later Roman historians like Pliny said the study of the heavens was a traditional occupation of women, who are thus enabled to determine the seasons, draw up calendars, predict eclipses, and perform divinations.

Ancient Chaldean astrologers defined themselves as moon worshipers, calling the zodiac the Houses of the Moon. Unlike modern astrologers, they paid no attention to the position of the sun against the background of the constellations, but rather took their observations from the position of the moon. After all, the moon's progress in relation to the stars could be clearly seen, whereas that of the sun was invisible because the sun's light obscured all the stars behind it. In the beginning, therefore, all astrological systems were based on the Moon's course through her various "houses."

The animal shapes or artifacts envisioned in the zodiacal constellations were popularly supposed to impart the qualities of the same creatures to human beings born under the various signs. Thus, a person born when the moon was in the House of the Bull (Taurus) was expected to be bull-like: strong, stubborn, earthy, lusty; and a person born when the moon was in the House of the Crab (Cancer) would be crablike: tenacious, sharp, water-loving, quick-moving, and so on. To a large extent, the broad outlines of these animalistic qualities are still to be found in today's astrological interpretations of character, although centuries of elaboration and modification have invested them with subtleties and complexities.

With the advent of male priesthoods and sun worship to replace the older, female-dominated religion of the moon, the main astrological pointer became the sun, even though extra, difficult calculations were required to place the solar orb against the constellations that could not be seen by day. In effect, the new astrologers had to figure the sun's position by what they could observe of the heavens six months previously, when the sun occupied the other half of the sky. This is the system that is still followed today.

Unfortunately for those who wish to interpret character by astrological signs, the zodiacal system is now skewed almost one full month out of place by the precession that has occurred over the past three thousand years or so. A person whose modern horoscope assigns him a particular sign was not really born under that sign, according to the actual position of the stars, but under the sign ahead of it (see chart).

DATES	ASTROLOGICAL DESIGNATION	SUN'S ACTUAL POSITION	SUN'S DATES
Dec. 22–Jan. 20	Capricorn	Sagittarius	Dec. 16–Jan. 18
Jan. 21–Feb. 19	Aquarius	Capricorn	Jan. 19–Feb. 18
Feb. 20–Mar. 20	Pisces	Aquarius	Feb. 19–Mar. 18
Mar. 21–Apr. 20	Aries	Pisces	Mar. 19–Apr. 15
Apr. 21–May 20	Taurus	Aries	Apr. 16–May 15
May 21–June 20	Gemini	Taurus	May 16–June 15
June 21–July 22	Cancer	Gemini	June 16–July 15
July 23–Aug. 22	Leo	Cancer	July 16–Aug. 15
Aug. 23–Sep. 22	Virgo	Leo	Aug. 16–Sep. 15
Sep. 23–Oct. 22	Libra	Virgo	Sep. 16–Oct. 15
Oct. 23–Nov. 22	Scorpio	Libra	Oct. 16–Nov. 15
Nov. 23–Dec. 21	Sagittarius	Scorpio	Nov. 16–Dec. 15

As the chart indicates, there is still some overlapping, but by and large the sun has moved out of the traditional zodiacal houses and into the preceding ones. Therefore, modern horoscopes are not based on the aspects of the heavens at all, but on an artificial system that is internally self-consistent without regard to external reality.

Neither is there any truth to the claim, often put forward by modern astrologers, that the zodiacal constellations assumed their present forms in human eyes several thousand years ago and have remained consistent ever since. On the contrary, like every other religious or occult concept, the zodiac has evolved gradually through many transformations and revisions, and has presented entirely different pictures to different peoples throughout the centuries. A brief survey of some of its popular names will indicate how much variety was seen in it.

In ancient Akkad, the zodiac was known as *Innum* or *Pidnu-sha-shame*, the Furrow of Heaven, plowed by the heavenly bull (the god El) as he slowly traveled through the path of the year. To the Chaldeans, it was *Hadronitho Demalusche*, the Circle of the Signs. Arabs called it *Al Falak*, the Expanse of Sky; or *Al Mintakah al Buruj*, the Girdle of Signs, which medieval Europeans corrupted to Almantica seu Nitac. The Hindu zodiac was *Rsai Chakra*, the eternal wheel. The Chinese zodiac was the Yellow Road, or *Tsieki*, that which announces changes in the weather; or simply *Kung*, Signs. Egyptians sometimes called it the Nile in the Sky, equated with the Milky Way, which was the river of milk flowing from the breasts of the Heavenly Mother (Hathor, Neith, or Nut).

Patriarchal Persians of the Zoroastrian period called the zodiacal signs Akhtars, meaning the twelve generals of the sun god Ahura Mazda.

Like the archangels of Judeo-Christian tradition, these "generals" fought the Awakhtars, who were the rebellious angels led by the dark god Ahriman.

Hebrews called the zodiac *Galgal Hammazaloth*, the Circle of Signs; or sometimes, copying the Greek poets, they named it *Opus Phrygionarum*, "Phrygian work," which originally referred to the gold embroidery done by Phrygian craftswomen. Greeks also gave the zodiac its present name, meaning "circle of animals" in their language. The Romans had many names for it, gathered from various parts of their empire: *Balteus stellatus*, the Starry Belt; *Circulus Signifer*, the Sign-bearing Circle; *Orbis Signiferus* or *Orbita Solis*, Orbit of the Sun; *Media Via Solis*, the Sun's Middle Way; *Signiportant*, the "portentious" signs. In Low Latin it was called *Sigillarius* or Little Images; *Limbus Textilis*, the Woven Girdle; or *Fascia*, the Band. In Italian, it became *Rubecchio*, the Mill Wheel.

Wheel symbolism was also prominent in the Celtic view of the heavens, which became the Silver Wheel of Arianrhod, sometimes viewed as a mill wheel or as a mysterious paddle-wheeled boat carrying blessed souls to their home among the stars. An Anglo-Saxon name was *Twelf Tacna*, the Twelve Signs. Old England knew the zodiac as the Bestiary, Cercle of Bestes, Eyrish Bestes, or Journey of the Beasts; it was also the Girdle of the Sky, the Houses of the Sun, the Solar Walk, or the Monthly Abodes of Apollo. There even remained a trace of the old Teutonic *Manavegr*, "Moon's Way," recalling the original image of the zodiac as the path of the Moon Goddess (Mana, universal mother of "man"), for the British after Christianization still insisted on calling it Our Ladye's Way.

Medieval monks tried to Christianize the zodiac as they Christianized everything else, by renaming it the *Corona seu Circulus Sanctorum Apostolorum*: the Crown of the Circle of the Holy Apostles. They placed the figure of John the Baptist at the position of Aquarius, to finish off the circle. This revised version never took, however. In Germany, the Holy Apostles were ignored and the zodiac continued to be called *Thierkreis*, the Circle of Little Animals.

Today, of course, not all the signs are animals. Only the Fish, Ram, Bull, Crab, Lion, Scorpion, and possibly the fish-tailed sea-goat (Capricorn) actually qualify as inmates of the celestial "zoo." We no longer know what the other animals were. The present zodiac appears to be an amalgam of some ancient theriomorphic system with an anthropomorphic one, in which the heavenly houses were assigned to divine godlike or goddesslike guardians. Aquarius may have been based on the holy midwife Akka, the Water-Drawer and eponymous mother of Akkad. Libra was probably one of the many versions of the Goddess Maat, who was Libera in Carthage, judge and weigher of souls in her balances. Virgo was always the Queen of Heaven, Sagittarius any one of many celestial hunter-gods, while nearly every mythology had its own version of the divine Twins (Gemini) born of the great river (Nile, Tiber, Euphrates).

Chinese calendars used to be entirely lunar. They were known as Hsiu, "Houses." Each house was occupied by one of the Moon Goddess's warrior-hero consorts, so she rested with a different lover each night of the month in one of her twenty-eight celestial mansions.[1]

Astrology survives in our own culture because Christianity embraced it with one hand, while condemning it as a devilish art with the other. Church fathers like Augustine, Jerome, Eusebius, Chrysostom, Lactantius, and Ambrose all anathematized astrology, and the great Council of Toledo prohibited it for all time.[2] Nevertheless, six centuries later the consistory and the dates of popes' coronations were determined by the zodiac; aristocratic prelates employed their own personal astrologers; and signs of the zodiac appeared all over church furnishings, tiles, doorways, manuscripts, and baptismal fonts.[3] The traditional Twelve Days of Christmas were celebrated by taking astrological omens each day for the corresponding months of the coming year. This was the same custom followed in China and India during twelve sacred midwinter days.[4]

Protestant theologians of the fifteenth to eighteenth centuries never quite knew what to make of astrology. Some condemned it, and others studied it assiduously. The Puritan Philip Stubbes was sure that the study of the stars would undercut religion. When people heard that "the sun, the moon, the stars, the signs and planets, do give both good things and evil, blessing and cursing, good success and evil success, yea, life and death, at their pleasure . . . and that they rule, govern and dispose all things whatsoever, yea, both the bodies and souls of man," then everyone would "fall from God and worship the creatures that give such blessings. . . . Why should not planets and stars be adored and worshiped as gods, if they could work these effects?"[5]

The real fear of course was that the pagan deities might return, since their names and attributes were still preserved in the symbolism of the planets and many of the constellations. Indeed, there were cults of "Junonians" and "Saturnians" in seventeenth-century London, and certain countrypeople were reported as believing that the sun was Christ and the moon was the Holy Ghost. Moon charms were rife as always, incongruously combined with Christian prayers. Any bad luck was attributed to planetary influences, even well into the eighteenth century, when London Bills of Mortality listed frequent deaths caused by "planet"—meaning the victim was "taken under an ill planet" or "planet-struck," the term for sudden, unexpected illness.[6]

Farmers' almanacs, books of hours, tapestries, church carvings, and many other sources equated the signs of the zodiac with the seasons of the year and the Labors of the Months. For example: Aquarius presided over felling of trees; Pisces over grafting of fruit trees; Aries over pruning of vines; Taurus over training of vines and planting of flowers; Gemini over scything grass; Cancer over haymaking; Leo over cutting and threshing grain; Virgo over harvesting; Libra over treading the grapes; Scorpio over casking the wine; Sagittarius over gathering wood and picking olives; Capricorn over baking and butchery of pigs. [7]

The custom of celebrating birthdays was zodiacal magic in effect, even though in some areas the church succeeded in converting birthdays into "saint's days," insisting that children be named after the saints on whose days their births occurred. Sometimes the saint's days were reduced to "name days," when worship of the saint was largely forgotten.

Like all forms of divination, astrology was supposed to be useful chiefly in predicting disasters so they could be avoided or averted. Here, of course, one runs into the notorious paradox of prophecy. If the predicted disaster is successfully avoided, then the prophecy is proved false. On the other hand, if the prophecy is true and the disaster cannot be avoided, then there is little point in knowing it beforehand.

1. Jobes & Jobes, 37.   2. Agrippa, 22.   3. Whittick, 353.   4. Cirlot, 335.   5. Thomas, 383.
6. Ibid., 384, 633.   7. Hall, 314–315.

Aquarius

To the Greeks the constellation of Aquarius was Hydrokhoos, the Water Pot. The Persians called it Dul, the Water Pot. In Sanskrit it was Khumba, the Pot. But the Babylonians named it Gula, the Goddess; and the Romans followed them by naming it **Juno.** The traditional sign, however, signifies waves of water.

Aquarius was said to be ruled by the planet **Saturn,** until the discovery of the next planet, **Uranus,** in the eighteenth century. After that, Aquarius was said to be under Uranian influence. Uranus was the god castrated and deposed by Saturn (Cronus). Uranus or "Heavenly" was the original Heavenly Father and the husband of Mother Earth.

Aquarius pours out the waters of the world; therefore Aquarians are said to be like water, hard to pin down, erratic, subject to fits of unrest, and often shallow. Yet they are also called thoughtful, mystical, serene, and artistic. Aquarians are associated with freedom, inventiveness, collective reform movements, and causes that are opposed to prejudice or narrow-mindedness in any form. No doubt this is why the various trends toward liberation in the twentieth century are taken to indicate an Aquarian Age.

Aries

To the Greeks, the sign of Aries was Krios, the Ram. To the Persians, it was Varak, the Lamb. In India it was Mesha or Aja, the Ram or the Goat. Babylonians had two choices: it was Zappu, the Hair, or Hunga, the Worker. Romans knew it as Minerva.

Because of a possibly linguistic confusion between Aries the ram and Ares, the Greek war god whose Roman counterpart was **Mars,** the zodiacal ram is traditionally associated with the warlike planet Mars and with somewhat martial characteristics, such as quick temper, aggression, determination, impetuosity, courage, high levels of activity, and sometimes rashness. Aries is also associated with the element of fire and related ideas of warmth, enthusiasm, vital powers, and sanguine spirit. Domestic strife and varying fortunes are often attributed to Aries people.

Cancer

The Cancer sign has been widely interpreted as a crab: Greek Karkinos, Persian Kalakang, Sanskrit Karkata, Babylonian Al-Lul are all *crab*. The Egyptian Zodiac of Dendera shows the crab as a scarab beetle, sign of the god Khepera.[1] Cancer is viewed as a water sign influenced by the moon. Cancerian people sometimes call themselves Moon Children, to avoid association with the dread disease, anciently called "the crab" because of its claw-like agonizing tenacity. Moon Children may be a more euphonious name, but it defeats the purpose of connection with the stars, removing the constellation of Cancer from the picture altogether. Of course, the moon is not a zodiacal sign.

The constellation of Cancer was vitally important to Egyptians, Persians, Hindus, Chinese, Babylonians, and other ancient civilizations, even those of South America. All were convinced that the world would end when the planets move into line with each other in the constellation of the Crab.[2] Romans maintained that the Crab was placed in the heavens by the Goddess Juno, thus would signal the end of the world by her decree.[3] The creation of the present earth was also supposed to have coincided with another past alignment of the planets in Cancer.

Such association with both creation and destruction might explain why Cancer characteristics have been viewed as paradoxical. Cancer people are said to be practical, yet vividly imaginative; presumptuous, yet discreet; timid, yet bold; brilliant, yet dull; home-centered and undistinguished, yet at times evincing the greatest genius. Perhaps the only quality of Cancer that all astrologers can agree on is that of crablike tenacity.

1. Budge, G.E. 2, 316. 2. Campbell, M.I., 149. 3. G. Jobes 1, 283.

Capricorn

Nearly all the ancients agreed on the
interpretation of Capricorn as a goat-
horned or goat-headed sea monster. Babylonians called him Suhurmas, the
Goat-fish. Persians called him Vahik, the
Sea Goat. Greeks called him Aigokeros, the
Goat-horned One. In Sanskrit he was
Mahara, the Sea Monster. The Romans,
however, saw the Goddess **Vesta** in
this constellation.

Capricorn was said to be ruled by
Saturn; therefore Capricorn people were
"saturnine," heavy and melancholy
in disposition, impassive, serious, persistent, and sometimes subject to depression.
Outward patience and conscientiousness
may conceal ruthless ambition. Capri-
corns are supposed to partake of goat
nature in the sense of lecherous desires
and may be inconstant in their affections.
Despite its connection with the sea, the
Capricorn goat was associated with the
element of earth, which was supposed to
impart qualities of coldness and dryness.

Cosimo de' Medici, the sixteenth-
century Grand Duke of Tuscany, took the
sign of Capricorn the sea-goat for his
personal *impresa,* after winning a battle
under its influence.[1]

1. Hall, 140.

Gemini

The Egyptian symbol of Gemini was not
a pair of male twins, but a woman
and a man with joined hands.[1] In Sanskrit, they were called Mithuna or
Maithuna, the Lovers. Romans viewed
them as the god Apollo coupled with his
twin sister Diana (Artemis). Babylonians
named them Mastabagalgal, Twins
of indefinite gender. Persians and Greeks
called them Dopatkar and Didumoi, Twins.

Male twins like Castor and Pollux,
the Dioscuri, may have been patriarchal
revisions of earlier androgynous pairs. In
older myths, the God and Goddess
were twins as well as spouses and even
mother-child dyads. Mother, sister,
and bride of the god were all embodied in
the same Triple Goddess.

Astrological designations of the heavenly Twins usually connect them with
Romulus and Remus, alleged founders of
Rome, and twin foster-sons of the famous
Sabine She-Wolf. Originally, there was
some doubt about their gender also.
Some said the real founder of Rome
and of the Romulian gens was a woman
named Rhome. She was either a Greek,
or a fugitive from fallen Troy. The Syracusan historian Callias (ca. A.D. 300)
supposed that she was the wife of
the legendary Sabine king Latinus. In the
second century B.C. she was called
the Amazonian daughter of Mars. Alternatively, others said she was the wife of
Aeneas, the *other* founder of Rome

according to a different legend. Just as pre-Roman matriarchs were apotheosized as Goddesses, so the male Romulus was apotheosized as the god Quirinus, having appeared in a roadway vision to his followers exactly as Jesus appeared in the Pauline legend, which bears a suggestive resemblance to the older Romulus myth.[2]

It seems clear that Rome developed out of the Sabine matriarchate, which produced the Romulian clan. Later stories held that the followers of the male Romulus were forced to steal Sabine wives in order to have the *sanguis ac genus,* the holy **blood** of the race, which was embodied and transmitted only by women.[3] Each of the early Roman clans was named after its founding mother, in the Sabine style. These tribal matriarchs seem to have been assimilated to the spinning Fortunae (Fate-goddesses) because their only duty was to spin.[4]

An androgynous view of the astrological Twins makes much more sense than supposing them to be two males, because they have always been interpreted as a union of opposites, much like the **yang-and-yin** symbol. Gemini people are said to be dualistic in their interests and tastes, as if inhabited by two contradictory personalities. Therefore, restlessness, cleverness, and inventiveness are Gemini qualities, along with impatience and a tendency to become easily bored. Gemini is influenced by Mercury, it is said, and so becomes "mercurial" in its union of opposites. Gemini governs arts and sciences, covering many different kinds of knowledge.

1. Budge, G.E. 2, 315.   2. Grant, 98, 113, 115, 117.   3. Dumézil, A.R.R. 1, 68.   4. Gage, 464.

Leo

On the Zodiac of Dendera, the symbol of Leo was similar to the **Tarot card** called "Strength": a woman taming a lion. The woman held the lion's tail and waved a flail at him as if driving him forward.[1] To the Babylonians, the constellation was Urgula, the Lioness. This was evidently the origin of the Roman name for the star Regulus, the Lion's Heart, which is the brightest star in the constellation of Leo, a classical symbol of midsummer. Though the Romans associated the constellation with **Jupiter,** the Greeks, Persians, and Hindus called it respectively Leon, Ser, and Simha, "Lion."

As the sign of high summer, Leo was always linked with the sun and said to have a "hot nature." It was said that the hairs of the lion's mane "stand out eminent like sunbeams."[2] A long mane of hair was an attribute of the biblical hero Samson, who descended from the Arabic Shams-on, a name of the sun. The

honeycomb, growing in the corpse of Samson's lion (Judges 14:8), indicates a solar myth copied from that of the lion-slaying sun hero Heracles. The zodiacal lion encounters the sun in the season of honey.

Because the lion was called king of beasts, the zodiacal lion was assigned a "kingly" nature supposedly passed on to Leo people: bold, brave, generous, somewhat autocratic, gifted with leadership, loving money and pleasure. Leo also had some of the royal faults such as tendencies to pomposity, overindulgence, and egotism. On balance, however, the qualities of Leo are noble and also partake of the fire element as befits a creature long associated with the sun.

1. Budge, G.E. 2, 312–315. 2. Williamson, 113.

Libra

The Sanskrit name for the sign of Libra was Tula, the Balance. Persians called it Tarazuk, the Balance. Babylonians called it Zibanitu, the Scales. Greeks called it Zugos, the Yoke. The traditional sign of Libra does look more like the kind of yoke worn over the neck of an ox than like the balances that the ancient world used for weighing. Nevertheless, it has always been understood as a scale, similar to the scale of Maat that weighed hearts in the Egyptian afterlife.

The Roman zodiac placed Vulcan in the position of Libra, perhaps because he was the god of weights and measures. The sign was ruled by his official spouse, **Venus.** This Goddess was related not only to Maat in Egypt, but also to her Carthaginian counterpart Tanit, who was also known as the heavenly judge and held the title of Astroarche, Queen of the Stars, and Astraea, the Lady of Justice. (See **Tanit.**) Another Roman name for her was Libera, assimilated as the consort of Dionysus/Bacchus Liber, worshiped together with him at the annual festival of the Liberalia. Part of Tanit's symbol produces the modern symbol of Libra, the very name of which is a short form of her Punic-Roman title Libera.

Traces of the Goddess's influence may be seen in the traditional qualities of Librans: artistic instincts, love of pleasure and beauty, generally good-natured charm. Librans are also said to be jealous, impatient, subject to up-and-down mood swings—as anyone would be who resembled a seesaw balance— and sometimes overenthusiastic in rashly embracing new fads. Libra may also imply lack of initiative: perhaps because it is an inanimate object rather than a sentient being.

Pisces

Greek, Persian, and Sanskrit names for
the constellation of Pisces all meant "Fish":
Ikhthues, Mahik, Mina. Babylonians
called it The Two Tails, and sometimes
divided the constellation into two parts: the
Southern Fish was Simmah, the Swallow;
the Northern Fish was Anunitum,
the Goddess.

Fish were traditionally sacred to the
Moon-goddess, and the sign of Pisces represents two crescent moons: one waxing, one
waning. In its earliest form, this sign
meant the waxing and waning of each life
in cycles defined by the moon. Since
the moon was also considered the world
source of water, the two crescents easily
suggested two fish. The constellation of
Pisces now contains "the first point of Aries" reached by the sun about March
22, which still marks the beginning of the
astronomical year.

Pisces used to be ruled by **Jupiter,** but
astrologers transferred its allegiance
to "**Neptune** the Mystic" after the discovery of this planet and its official naming after
the Latin sea god. Still, the generally
feminine implications of water, fish, the
sea, and the moon give Pisces personalities many of the qualities that were
usually viewed as feminine: domesticity,
sensitivity, receptivity, imaginativeness, love
of home, as well as the supposed feminine
faults like dreaminess, unreality, laziness,
and intellectual dishonesty. Pisces
people are said to be friendly and dependable on behalf of those whom they
love, and often to display strongly spiritual
tendencies.

Sagittarius

In India the constellation of Sagittarius
was Dhanus, the Bow. In Persia it
was Nimasp, the Centaur, who was presumably drawing his bow. In Greece it was
Toxotes, the Archer. Rome associated
the sign with Diana, Goddess of the Bow,
who used to rule the horse-riding
Amazonian "centauresses" of the Black
Sea area, where one of the world's
oldest matriarchal shrines was established
at Themiscyra. The Goddess's warriors used
to call themselves her hunting dogs
(*alani*) and each of her male consorts, in
turn, the Lord of the Hunt.

Like the divine hunter, the people
astrologically connected with the starry
archer Sagittarius are said to aim high, to
achieve, and to take pride in their
achievements, sometimes to the point of
unseemly vanity. Sagittarians are supposed to be clever and quick, full of energy, independent, and sometimes
combative. They love the arts and sciences. In the Middle Ages, such love was

believed to include the so-called black arts, because Sagittarius was associated with the "archer wizards" anathematized by the Inquisition. These seem to have been rustic hunters who still worshiped Diana in the depths of the forest and practiced a kind of Dianic Zen as the source of their skill. Part of their initiatory magic was to send three shots in succession at a roadside crucifix.[1] Churchmen complained that many crucifixes were damaged by this habit.

1. Walker, W.E.M.S., 190.

Scorpio

As one of the few constellations that really resembles the creature whose name it bears, Scorpio was named "Scorpion stars" even in the New World. Sanskrit Vrischika meant Scorpion, as did the constellation's Babylonian, Greek, and Persian names: Gir-Tab, Skorpion, Gazdum. The red star Antares, called the Scorpion's Heart, was one of the significant year-markers. Like the red planet **Mars,** it was sacred to Mars in the Roman pantheon.

As a sign of the season of decline and death, Scorpio bore some rather grim connotations, made even grimmer by the poisonous nature of the animal. Strife and war, cruelty and lewdness—all under the aegis of Mars—were long associated with Scorpio. The passion and death of the savior **Osiris** took place, according to Egyptian scriptures, "when the sun was in Scorpio."[1] The heavenly scorpion presided over the Celtic festival of Samhain (**Halloween**), the Feast of the Dead, when ancestral ghosts haunted the atmosphere.

Since it would be neither polite nor politic to load all Scorpio people with the sign's more dismal interpretations, astrologers have been at pains to establish some positive qualities for Scorpio. The animal's bad reputation implies malice, aggression, and a quarrelsome nature; but the positive qualities include boldness, courage, loyalty, and determination. Scorpio is said to be indolent, but when aroused can be swift, efficient, and effective.

1. Budge, G.E. 2, 188.

Taurus

Greek, Persian, Sanskrit, and Babylonian
astrologers agreed that the star group
known as Taurus was a bull: Tauros, Tora,
Vrisha, Gudanna. The alpha star of
Taurus, Aldebaran, was known as the
Bull's Heart. It was traditionally ruled by
the planet **Venus** and the element of
earth.

The qualities of Taurus were always
eminently bull-like: slow, strong, a lover of
routine and order, productive, dependable,
usually obedient to authority but uncon-
trollably violent when enraged. The
influence of Venus was supposed to provide an amiable disposition, sensual
pleasures, broad friendships, and sometimes excessive materialism. Taurus is said
to be quietly supportive under normal
conditions.

In addition to Aldebaran, Taurus
contains the Pleiades or "Seven Sisters,"
which had profound meanings in the
ancient religion of Venus-Aphrodite as the
Goddess of Wisdom, whose "pearly gates"
they tended, and whose "seven pillars"
represented them in the temple.

Virgo

The Egyptian symbol of Virgo was a
woman holding a stalk of wheat (European
"corn"), which meant she was the
virgin form of the Grain Goddess.[1] Romans identified her with **Ceres**, Mother of
the Corn. Babylonians made her month
sacred to **Ishtar** and called her sign
Ab-Sin, the Furrow. Virgo's alpha star,
Spica, was called the Goddess's Ear of
Corn.[2] She was Sanskrit Kanya, Persian
Khusak, Greek Parthenos, all meaning
Virgin or Maiden.

Some early representations of Virgo
made her a winged angel. She was often
identified with Egypt's Goddess Maat, the
Libyan Goddess of Truth, Astraea (Starry
One), whom the Romans regarded
as an incarnation of justice. Her **balances**
also entered into the zodiac in the
form of **Libra**.[3] She was viewed in many
areas as the great judge of the world, who
assessed the souls arriving in heaven
and assigned them places according to
their merits.

Gypsies believed that the cathedrals of
France were laid out so as to form
the stars of the constellation Virgo across
the face of the land, because all these cathedrals were dedicated to the Virgin. Gypsy
tradition said the famous Black Virgin
in the crypt under Chartres Cathedral was

really Sara-Kali, the virgin mother of the Gypsy race, assimilated to the Virgin in heaven.[4]

The sign of Virgo was ruled by **Mercury** and hence devoted to agriculture and the arts, communication, and handicrafts. Virgo's qualities included tact, intuition, skill, and musical ability. Having a "feminine" sign, Virgoans whether male or female were associated with "feminine" attributes such as fastidious neatness, affectionate nature, difficulties in love affairs, and overemphasis on the trivial. But these were qualities wished on women by patriarchal experts who probably wanted to forget the former associations between Virgo and the original Great Goddess.

1. Budge, G.E. 2, 315.   2. Lindsay, 81.   3. Ibid., 277.   4. Derlon, 210.

12

BODY PARTS

A common symbolic technique is taking the part for the whole. Since human beings are endlessly aware of and attentive to their own bodies, it is only natural that parts of the human body should become popular symbols. Hands, feet, heads, eyes, and genitalia are everywhere found in sacred pictures, pictographs, and hieroglyphs. Today's graffiti, consisting of crude sketches of human reproductive organs, are not really new. They may be the oldest of all art forms. "Obscene" scrawls on the walls of modern subway tunnels can be readily compared to similar scrawls on the walls of Neolithic caves, though their intent obviously differs.

Body parts are often taken as deity symbols, like the Eye of Horus, Feet of Vishnu, or Phallus of Priapus. Our ancestors liked to imagine also that each part of the body had a special deity to watch over it and protect it from harm. There was little propensity to despise or mortify the body, until patriarchal asceticism became widespread.

In Europe, a highly sophisticated body-centered art, which produced the exquisite Greek and Roman statues, was replaced by the body-hating crudities of the Dark Ages, when artistic skill in depicting the human body was lost. The classic sense of harmonious proportion gave way to stiff, awkward figures concealed in unconvincing robes, more like the labored efforts of children than the creations of trained artists. When nudity was despised, the body could no longer be studied.

Nevertheless, body-part symbolism did not disappear. It is still perfectly comprehensible. Indeed, why not? We all know our bodies and their parts. We can relate personally to pictographic reminders of them. Body symbolism is one of the signposts leading to Sir Richard Francis Burton's conclusion after studying all the great religions, that man has never worshiped anything but himself.

Men have always been particularly prone not only to anthropomorphize the universe, but even to universalize the human form as if it were the only significant one. "Man is the measure of all things," said Protagoras. To Albertus Magnus, man was not only the *imago dei*, "image of God," but also the *imago mundi*, "image of the universe." Origen claimed that the human form is a miniature world with sun, moon, and stars. Nicholas of Cusa said all the heavens are in the likeness of man, and Pico della Mirandola insisted that man contains all things because man is the center of all things. Cornelius Agrippa von Nettesheim believed that man's body is a complete image of the entire world, and Robert Fludd liked to view man as the center and replica of the whole divine order. In other words, the hubris of men knows no bounds. Despite its inefficiency by comparison with most animal bodies, the human male body has been viewed by our patriarchal society as the very model of the cosmos.

As for the human female body, which creates this wonder, man: she has never ceased to seem a strange amalgam of heaven and hell, alien yet familiar, intimate yet mysterious—expressly forbidden to partake of the "image of God," yet somehow the most attractive image known to collective man. In spite of all his hubris, man's body symbolism inevitably concentrates on the female body that brings him forth and takes him back: both of these events universalized through all the myths of creation and doom.

Blood

The Bible views blood as the primary symbol of the life force (Genesis 9:4; Leviticus 17:11), because all the ancients were convinced that living people were literally made of their mothers' uterine blood, retained and coagulated into the form of a baby. In the most primitive myths, this was the way the Mother Goddess herself created the world, by clotting it out of her Primal Deep or cosmic womb. Certain African tribes still maintain that lineage is synonymous with blood, and only women can transmit tribal blood kinship to descendants. Ashanti women say, "I alone can transmit the blood. . . . If my sex die in the clan then that very clan becomes extinct, for be there one, or a thousand male members left, not one can transmit the blood."[1]

Similarly in ancient India, the spirit of the clan dwelt in menstrual blood, which was known as the kula flower. Each girl "bore the flower" at her first menstruation,[2] the flower preceding the "fruit" of the womb. The Bible too refers to menstrual blood as "flowers" (Leviticus 15:24). In Fiji, a newly circumcised boy is called kula and compared to the kula girl at her first menstruation.[3] Such notions may shed light on the Semitic custom of **circumcision** as an imitation of menarche, especially as it used to be performed at puberty. Medieval Christians sometimes claimed that Jewish men could menstruate as well as Jewish women, a belief that may have evolved from the early view of circumcision as a "male menstruation."[4]

Shades of the ancient Goddess still hover about the very name of Adam, which means "man made of blood," or "clay animated by blood." Adam's long life of nearly a thousand years was rooted in the Vedic tradition, which said that people living closer in time to the primal outpouring of the Great Mother's blood would naturally have very long lives and greater vitality than their descendants, because the lives of the former were "centered in the blood."[5] Greeks and Romans also believed that human life is made of a "coagulum" of menstrual blood. According to Plutarch, the vital principle that nourishes the human body and causes it to grow is that feminine essence that descends from the **moon**.[6]

Blood also remained the primary symbol of kinship and bonding among the Gypsies, whose traditions were rooted in ancient India. Gypsy wedding couples ate bread with a drop of each other's blood, to become one flesh in the ceremonial sense.[7] Sometimes a Gypsy wedding employed the age-old blood-kinship rite of mingling blood directly, from cuts in the two parties' arms or hands.[8]

Over the centuries, male-dominated societies made earnest efforts to assimilate the feminine magic of blood to male gods or savior figures, whose blood might be considered more lively than that of ordinary men. In Scandinavia, the male hero who represented the "wise blood" of the Moon Mother was Kvasir, known as the wisest of men. He was slain by the gods and his blood was preserved in uter-ine **cauldrons** under the earth. A name for this wise blood was *mjodr*, apparently derived from "mother." The Hindu divinity corresponding to Kvasir was named Mada (again, the mother syllable), whose sacrificial slaying brought universal blessings.[9]

Apart from the concept of Christ's similarly life-giving blood, Western society developed other male efforts to take over female blood symbolism and bring it somehow under male control. The alchemists' word *menstruum* became synonymous with *alkahest*, the universal solvent, which was supposed to dissolve all other substances in itself. The idea can be traced to creation myths of universal dissolution of all elements in the Mother's uterine sea of blood, in the conditions of primal **chaos,** before the world was curdled into solid matter. Yet real female moon-blood was still considered a mystic medicine. Medieval doctors claimed that young girls' menstrual blood would cure leprosy or act as an aphrodisiac.[10] In harmony with Tantric traditions emanating from India, various Gnostic sects taught that men could become spiritually powerful by ingesting menstrual blood.[11] Numerous menstrual taboos throughout the world point to an age-old combination of fear and awe in male attitudes toward the "blood of life." Sometimes, as in surviving hints

BONE

of the fairy religion, female moon-blood carried a man to the primal paradise of Fairyland. Like the ancient Goddess who kept the gods alive with infusions of her "supernatural red wine," so the fairy queen Mab gave a red drink to her chosen heroes: a drink that bore her own name and transmitted her sovereign spirit.[12] Yet Christian authorities also claimed that nothing is so unclean as a menstruating woman. In the thirteenth century, the Synod of Wurzburg ruled that no one should come near her.[13] As late as the seventeenth century, menstruating women were still forbidden to enter a church.[14] One of the ideas that underlay the five-hundred-year witch persecutions in Europe was the idea that postmenopausal women were filled with occult knowledge because they no longer sent forth their wise blood, but retained it in their veins and so became magical persons.[15]

1. Sanday, 30–31.   2. *Mahanirvanatantra*, 88.
3. Crawley 1, 79.   4. Montagu, 243; Trachtenberg, 8.   5. *Mahanirvanatantra*, xlviii.
6. Cumont, A.R.G.R., 107.   7. Bowness, 25.   8. Trigg, 88.   9. Dumézil, M.F., 100, 104.   10. Montagu, 113.   11. Walker, W.E.M.S., 640–641.   12. Rees & Rees, 75.
13. Briffault 2, 396.   14. Walker, W.E.M.S., 643.   15. Gifford, 26.

Bone

Medieval Europeans worshiped many bones, which they were told once belonged to living **saints**. This was seldom true. Many alleged martyrs' bones were not even of human origin. Nevertheless, the bones of goats and pigs seemed to effect miraculous cures as well as any other relics. Maximus of Turin told why people wanted saints' bones in their local churches: such bones kept away the creatures of hell, and so "we escape punishment."[1] Churchmen also declared that lunacy and many physical disorders could be cured by a drink of wine or water into which a saint's bones had been dipped.[2]

According to one story, Saint Ambrose was informed in a dream where he should dig to discover the bones of Saints Gervasius and Protasius. As soon as the bones were dug up, they proved their authenticity by restoring sight to a blind man. Similar cures were often attributed to the bones of the Three Wise Men, allegedly fetched from India to Cologne Cathedral, where they remain to this day. Cologne rejoiced in the title of City of the Three Kings.[3]

In biblical times, intact bones were considered essential to reconstruction of the body in the next life. Therefore

God ordered that no bone of the paschal **lamb** be broken (Exodus 12:46; Numbers 9:12), so that the animal could live again and its butchers would escape blood guilt. Scriptures of this sort became prophecies after the fact, when Jesus was identified with the paschal lamb. The psalmist said, "He keepeth all his bones; not one of them is broken: (Psalm 34:20), and so John 19:36 insisted that Jesus' bones were left intact "that the scripture should be fulfilled," although why Romans should be concerned to act in accordance with Hebrew scriptures remains a mystery to this day. The real reason for the prohibition is revealed by a myth of the Scandinavian god **Thor** who damaged the thigh bone of a sacrificial goat, and when the goat was resurrected in its new life, it was no longer a perfect animal because it limped.[4]

It was a popular belief throughout the world that an animal slaughtered for food could be resurrected from its bones, as long as the skeleton was complete. The Plains Indians of North America used to arrange the bones of their devoured buffalo in natural order on the prairie, in the fond conviction that the bones would be re-clothed with flesh and the animal would come to life again before the next hunting season.[5]

Ancient Semites taught that the sacrum ("sacred bone") at the base of the spine contained a mystical seed of each person's future resurrected body. At the Last Judgment, one's new body would be built around this seed bone, called *luz* or *luez*, which was indestructible. Even if all other bones were destroyed, this magical one would form a new, perfect body. The teaching was derived from the Egyptian concept of the sacrum as the seat of Osiris's resurrection and the source of "seed" (semen) that carried the magic of new life. See **Djed.**

Bones have always been invested with various kinds of magical powers. In Australia and the South Pacific, human bones are favored for the cursing ceremony, called "pointing the bone," believed to bring certain destruction to the pointee. In medieval Europe, hangmen sold the bones of executed criminals to a public eagerly convinced of their efficacy as magic charms. Pliny said an ulcer could be arrested if a circle were traced around it with a human bone. Many centuries later, this and many other medical treatments were still calling for human bones or bone powder.

1. Aries, 33.   2. Abelard, 56.   3. Cavendish, 209.   4. Silberer, 82.   5. G. Jobes 1, 220.

Breast

The symbol of a breast is the Egyptian hieroglyph *mena*, meaning "breast" and also "moon."[1] This symbol reflects Egyptian belief that from the breasts of the Moon Goddess flowed the **Milky Way** and all other stars, as well as the life-giving waters of the universe. An odd circumstance is that Egyptologists persist in describing the founder of the first dynasty as a male pharaoh, although "his" name was Mena, an eminently female designation, probably of the incarnate Moon Goddess.

Many ancient traditions speak of the Goddess as a nursing mother to the world, like the famous statue of Artemis at Ephesus, whose breast-covered torso suggested overflowing nourishment for all creatures. In nearly every known language, "Ma-Ma" means "mother's breasts."[2] Enlightenment and even immortality were said to be available to those who discovered how to drink the Goddess's milk. A Tantric aphorism said, "Deathless are those who have fed at the breast of the Mother of the Universe."[3] Egyptian pharaohs were promised that they would become immortal infants, nursing forever at the Goddess's breast. In Rome, the process of enlightenment under an *alma mater* ("soul-mother"; priestess-teacher) was considered a kind of second infancy. The word *alumnus* used to mean a nursling or a suckling child.[4]

Among the Berbers, mother's milk created mystic connections with the home place and the clan spirit, dating back to the matriarchal identification of motherhood with property ownership. If a fugitive succeeded in entering the family tent of strangers, seizing the mother and sucking at her breast, he automatically became an honorary member of the family and could command their protection.[5]

So powerful was the imagery of the nursing mother as Goddess-like creator and nurturer that the adherents of male gods went out of their way to try to adapt this imagery to fatherhood by hook or crook. Patriarchal Jews claimed for Yahweh the title of El Shaddai, meaning a milk-giving breast or a nursing mother. Numbers 11:12 speaks of God as a nursing father carrying the "sucking child" in his bosom. Even more incongruous were some of the writings of later Christian fathers, like Saint Ambrose who talked of "the Father's womb" and "the nourishing breasts of Christ." *Solomon's Ode* said: "The Holy Ghost opened the Father's raiment and mingled the milk from the Father's two breasts."

Perhaps most inconsistent of all, it was **Mary** the real nursing mother who was made to say, "He who is milked is the Father, and the Holy Spirit milked him, because his breasts were full, and it was necessary for him that his milk should be sufficiently released."[6]

An old title of the milk-giving Goddess, Agatha, "Kindly One," was falsely reworked into a Christian saint whose breasts were allegedly cut off because she refused to marry the king of Sicily. (In fact, ancient kings of Sicily were named Agathocles[7] to indicate their union with the Goddess.) Early Christian icons showed the spurious Saint Agatha carrying her amputated breasts on a platter. These were later misinterpreted as bells, so she became the patron of bell founders.[8] The legend of her amputated breasts persisted in the canon, however, and grew into such a widespread cult of mammary relics that the original Agatha could only have had more breasts than Ephesian Artemis. At least six of Agatha's breasts are still preserved in various churches.[9]

1. Budge, E.L., 57.   2. Potter & Sargent, 229.
3. Avalon, 466.   4. French, 166.   5. Duerr,
197.   6. Barnstone, 279; Warner, 195.
7. d'Alviella, 20.   8. Attwater, 34.   9. Hall, 9.

Breath

Breath has been nearly synonymous with "soul" or "spirit" for an enormously long time. The concept dates back to a matriarchal theory that woman not only forms her child out of her own uterine **blood,** but also *anima*tes (provides a mother-soul for) her child's *materi*al (mother-given) body with her own breath. Behind this ancient theory may be seen the habit of gently blowing into the mouth of a newborn to initiate breathing, rather than ungently striking the infant, as in the classical male-medical method. The latter might have been indirectly related to the contention of male theologians that every newborn child was a festering mass of original sin, deserving to start life with a punishment, atonement, and **exorcism** of the evil spirit in the guise of baptism.

After the patriarchal takeover of symbols, breath was claimed by fathers and male gods to represent *their* contribution of essential spirit to the new organism. Brahman fathers pretended to give their newborn children souls by breathing into their faces. Biblical scribes pretended that God "mothered" Adam by breathing "the breath of life" into his nostrils (Genesis 2:7). God also handily brought the dry bones of the dead back to life by the magic application of his breath (Ezekiel 37:5). Adopting the

Oriental concept of the Oversoul (*atman*) as the breath of the world (*atmos*), Hellenic Greeks said the air was Zeus himself, permeating all things by way of their continuous breathing.

However, even in Greece, certain concepts of the *female* universal air-soul lingered on. One of the mystic Greek names of the Gnostic Goddess was Pneuma, "Breath." The **Muse,** who was always female, brought the inspiration or "in-breathing" that gave seers and poets the power of understanding and creativity.

To expire in death means literally to breathe out, that is, to return the air-soul to the *atmos*-sphere. Souls of the dead thus took on an airy form and became gaseous **ghosts,** often supposed to be perceptible in the movement of winds and clouds. Some unsophisticated people still imagine to this day that the final breath carries the soul forth from the body, so that the air is full of spirits and the living are always in the midst of their ancestors' ghosts. The familiar custom of placing a **mirror** before the face of a dying person arose not to check on the cessation of breathing—which could be more easily checked by other means—but rather to magically catch the fugitive soul, for mirrors were always supposed to be soul-traps. Sometimes in folklore, the realm of the dead was known as the Hall of Mirrors.

In another widespread tradition, it was thought that a woman as **dakini,** shakti, vila, or priestess should inhale the last breath of the dying person, to ensure his/her reconception and eventual rebirth. This was the original meaning of what male theologians later diabolized as the demoness's kiss of death. It was then feared as a death-bringing ritual, rather than the favor and comfort of the Goddess. However, she remained in song and story as many versions of Mother Death—such as the Morrigan or Morgan Le Fay—whose voice was heard in the wind and who collected souls in her magic mirror.

Caul

People "born with the caul" were always considered highly magical, with great spiritual powers and the gift of second sight. "The caul" meant a portion of the amniotic membrane, which sometimes covers the head of an infant as it is born. When this occurred, superstitious mothers or midwives would carefully preserve the caul, believing that its possession would bring great good luck.[1]

1. Thomas, 625.

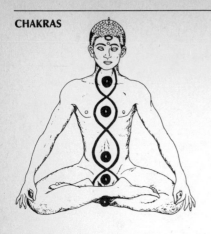

Chakras

In contemporary esoteric studies, the term *chakras* has been more talked about than understood. It is a very ancient Tantric belief that each human body contains seven of these mystic "lotus centers," located at various levels along the spinal cord. The symbolism is profoundly female. The **lotus** has been a female emblem in the East for thousands of years. Moreover, the sign of almost every *chakra* contains a **yoni yantra** (female-genital triangle); and the envisioned ascent through the *chakras* is made by the Kundalini serpent, invariably female even if she inhabits a man's body.

By meditation and proper breathing (*pranayama*), the adept seeks to awaken his Kundalini and to begin drawing her upward through his "lotus centers." Energy for this enterprise is supposedly passed through two intertwined channels flanking the spine, the lunar (*ida*) and solar (*pingala*) channels, which form a double helix around the *chakras*.

It is said that Kundalini sleeps coiled around a **lingam** (phallus) inside a *yoni yantra* at the level of the first *chakra*, *Muladhara*, "Root Support," on the perineal region or pelvic floor. The sign for this *chakra* has four red petals and a yellow square (earth symbol). Once awak-

ened, Kundalini may rise to the second *chakra*, *Svadhisthana*, "Her Special Abode," the genital area. Representing water, this sign has six red petals, a sea monster, and a god with his Shakti. This is the level of sexual desires.

Next comes the navel *chakra*, *Manipura*, "City of the Shining Jewel," whose name recalls the custom of Hindu temple dancers to wear jewels in their navels. The sign of this *chakra* has ten dark blue petals, a red *yoni yantra*, and the figure of a ram representing Agni the fire god; also, Shiva and Kali-Lakini as rulers of sacrificial rites.

Some traditions then interpose an unnumbered, uninscribed Lesser Lotus at the solar plexus, whose sign shows a Wish-Fulfilling Tree on a jeweled altar. This extra *chakra* is usually passed over, however, in favor of the next one on the heart level, *Anahata*, meaning a sound "not made by striking," the sound *Om*, thought to encompass universal creative energy. The sign of Anahata has twelve red petals and a smoke-colored **hexagram**: India's immemorial symbol of male and female sexuality conjoined. The center shows a gold lingam inside the *yoni yantra*.

These four lower *chakras* correspond to the material elements, earth, water, fire, and air (or breath)—the two "female" elements first. The next three *chakras* are supposed to carry Kundalini into non-material realms, giving the adept a new comprehension of spiritual things consonant with Kundalini's increased altitude.

At the level of the larynx comes *Vishuddha*, "Purification," ruled by the hermaphroditic figure of Ardhanarisvara: Shiva and his Kali-Shakti united in a single body. Thus, male and female powers merge at the level of speech (the creative **Logos**). This *chakra* is called the Gateway of the Great Liberation. Its sign has sixteen purple petals and a white *yoni yantra* containing the full moon.

The sixth *chakra* is Ajna, "Command," the creative Logos activated. It is located between the brows, in the place of the "third eye" of insight. Its sign has two white petals, a figure of the Goddess holding a book, drum, skull, and rosary, and the white *yoni yantra* of the previous *chakra* now containing a lingam. When Kundalini attains this level, the yogi is said to be divided from the ultimate vision of the Absolute only by something like a thin pane of glass.

The seventh and last *chakra* is the so-called Thousand-Petaled Lotus of Light (*Sahasrara*) springing from the crown of the head into infinity. In the center of this splendid blossom is "the ultimate yoni-triangle, within which, well concealed and very difficult to approach, is the great shining void in secret served by all gods."[1] In other words, the pinnacle of the *chakras* is the inner female spirit triumphant, the inner female serpent glorified, the transcendent Goddess whose final recognition is the cause of the adept's continuing state of bliss.

The *chakras* are often mentioned without any frank reference to the obviously female orientation of their symbolism. Like many another prepatriarchal system, this one too has been claimed by various male gods whose priests chose not to see it as a revelation of the Goddess within.

In another sense, the word *chakra* defined the Tantric circle of worship, composed of men and women alternately, each man with his *shakti* sitting to his left, and the leading priest and priestess together in the center. Eating, drinking, and sensual pleasures figured in the sacred *chakrapuja* (worship), the aim of which, it was said, was to make each participant feel as close to the Goddess as to his or her own mother.[2] The circular form was intended to eliminate all distinctions of caste, because worship of the Goddess had always been democratic rather than hierarchical.[3]

1. Campbell, *M.I.*, 381. 2. Avalon, 166.
3. *Mahanirvanatantra*, cxxi.

DEVIL'S HORNS

ENTRAILS
*Humbaba, Assyrian
spirit of entrails*

EYE
from a Roman mosaic, Tunis

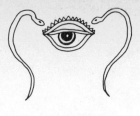

Devil's Horns

To make the devil's horns, as a hand gesture, is one of the oldest prophylactic signs supposed to avert the evil eye and placate harmful powers. In some parts of Europe it is still considered more efficacious than making the sign of the cross. In antiquity it must have represented an appeal to the Horned God; then in the Middle Ages, an appeal to the devil, who was often considered more influential in the earthly realm than God.[1] The hand in the devil's horns position does bear a striking resemblance to the head of a horned animal. Perhaps even more pertinent to the diabolization of the gesture, however, is the fact that it was once intimately associated with the Goddess. In India it is still the sacred *mudra* (hand gesture) of Jagadamba, which is a title of the Goddess meaning "Mother of the World."[2]

1. Briffault 2, 563–564.   2. Rawson, A.T., 50.

Entrails

Entrails were probably the original model of the **labyrinth** with its symbolic twisting journey, and reexit standing for rebirth "from the bowels," as the biblical phrase goes. At that time, people didn't understand that the uterus is never connected with the intestines. Birth is described in the Bible as separation from the bowels. The ancient belief that an infant is nourished *in utero* by its mother's bowels evolved into the image of "bowels of mercy," source of compassion, tenderness, and mother-love.[1]

Mesopotamian diviners sought enlightenment by probing the entrails of sacrificial animals, entering what was known as "the Palace of the Intestines." In Assyria there was even an Entrail God, the spirit of divination by the bowels. His name was Humbaba. His face was made entirely of twisting intestines.

1. G. Jobes 1, 238.

Eye

Human beings react strongly to representations of the eye. One reason that has been cited is the vital importance of eye contact between mother and infant immediately after birth, as an aid to establishing the bond that will ensure the infant's survival. So many ancient traditions identify the birth-giving Goddess with the All-Seeing Eye that there might well be an archetypal connection. In Egypt the universal mother-word Maa was both the name of the Goddess and a hieroglyphic eye. The name of the Gaelic Sun-goddess Sulis was related to *suil*, an eye.

prints of God's feet,
Rajasthan, India

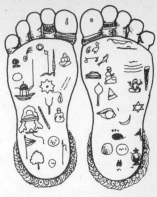

The same word meant a hole, like the "eye" in a strap, or a whirlwind. *Suileath* meant "wise, all-seeing, farsighted," describing the Goddess whose eye saw everywhere.[1] Romans identified this wise Goddess with their own Minerva, the all-seeing Crone aspect of the Capitoline Triad. Altars were set up in Roman Britain to "Sul Minerva."[2] According to the Hindu *Lalita Sahasranamam*, the Great Goddess created and destroyed universes just by opening or closing her eyes.[3]

Because the eye of the Goddess was often the eye of judgment, patriarchal societies feared it and tended to describe it as the evil eye. Anat or Anath, the Crone aspect of **Astarte**/Hathor, became an old witch woman called Aynat, the Evil Eye of the Earth, in Christianized Abyssinia, where it was claimed that Jesus destroyed her.[4] The evil eye was generally the left or "female" one.[5] Medieval Europe greatly feared the powers of the evil eye attributed to witches, but men and even clergy could have it too. Pope Pius IX was so notorious for possessing the evil eye that women, when kneeling for his blessing, would hide their hands in the folds of their skirts to make a countersign to avert the evil.[6]

1. Stewart, 80.   2. Dames, 154.   3. Avalon, 396.   4. Gifford, 57.   5. Elworthy, 138.   6. Trachtenberg, 54.

Feet

All over India the "footprints of Buddha" are still worshiped at holy shrines; but some of these Buddhist feet were originally worshiped as the Feet of Vishnu. Even earlier, some may have been the red, **henna**-dyed feet of the **Goddess.** In antiquity, stones dedicated to **Isis** and **Venus** were marked with footprints, meaning "I have been here." The custom was copied later on Christian tombs, where the footprint bore the legend *In Deo.*[1]

Egyptians, Babylonians, and other ancient peoples considered it essential to step on sacred ground with bare feet, so as to absorb the holy influences from Mother Earth, or from the floor of the temple built over her shrine. That is why God commanded Moses to take off his shoes, "for the place whereon thou standest is holy ground" (Exodus 3:5). As it became customary to go bareheaded in the presence of a king, so in antiquity it was customary to go barefooted in the presence of a deity. During the first century A.D., Roman witches (priestesses) invariably performed their rites with unbound hair and bare feet, so as to contact the chthonian spirit of the Mother.[2]

So vital a part of the person was the footprint that believers in witchcraft

almost always assumed that anyone could be injured through deliberate defacement of the footprint. Sores or lameness were often attributed to malevolent acts of sorcerers who placed sharp stones, nails, or knife stabs in one's footprint.

A curious modern form of the ancient mark of divinity, "footprints in stone," is the popular deification of Hollywood stars by leaving their footprints in cement.

1. d'Alviella, 62–63.   2. Wedeck, 152.

Finger

Our common symbol for silence, placing the finger on the lips, dates back to a Greek misunderstanding of an Egyptian god. To the Egyptians, the newborn sun of each day was the child Horus, shown at dawn as a small toddler sucking on his finger. The Greeks took this as an image of secrecy concerning his Mysteries, enjoining silence. They called the child Horus Harpocrates, God of Silence, and invoked him by the finger-to-mouth gesture.[1]

In Greek mythology the fingers were the Dactyls, spirits born from the fingerprints of the Goddess Rhea while she gave birth to Zeus. Five male Dactyls sprang from the prints of her right hand, and five female Dactyls from the prints of her left hand.[2] These finger spirits became associated with major deities according to the later rules of palmistry, but the question of which deities go with which fingers has been somewhat inconsistent. According to some systems, the index, middle, ring, and little fingers were assigned to Apollo, Jupiter, Venus, and Mercury, respectively. Others preferred to call them Jupiter, Saturn, Apollo, and Mercury: another instance of Goddess-erasure. However, the Venus/Apollo finger is still connected with the mythic "love vein" and wears the wedding ring.[3]

The Jupiter/Saturn finger also still symbolizes a **phallus**, as it did in Roman times when male prostitutes used it to signal potential customers, and in medieval times when the church labeled it *digitus infamis* or *obscenus*, the obscene finger.

The index finger was the magical, feminine-symbolic one used in cursing one's enemy. Thus it is still considered rude to point this finger at someone, or to threaten by shaking it. As the middle finger was "father," the index finger was "mother." To cross the one over the other was a prophylactic sign of sexual intercourse, still used as a charm to ward off punishment for lying. In Egypt, these two parental fingers formed a protective amulet of the Two Fingers.[4]

1. d'Alviella, 85.   2. Graves, G.M. 1, 185.
3. de Lys, 287–288.   4. Budge, E.M., 55.

Fingernails

It has been an almost universal custom to dispose of fingernail cuttings with great care, because most people have believed that harmful magic can be worked against them by anything that was once part of their bodies: hair, skin, excrement, spittle, blood, and so on. In China, very long fingernails were admired as a mark of aristocracy; one who did no manual labor could grow them, but peasants' nails were necessarily short. Sometimes false fingernails were applied to signal the right degree of lordly inactivity. The reddening of women's nails was an old Oriental custom, still preserved today. Instead of nail polish, the ancients used **henna.** In the Middle Ages, the use of henna to redden the nails was considered a sign of witchcraft.[1]

Nails of the dead were usually cut short for funerals. In Northern Europe it was believed that the doomsday ship Naglfar was being constructed of corpses' fingernails. When the ship was completed, the end of the world would come. Therefore the dead were closely manicured, to keep from adding too much new material to the fatal ship.[2]

1. Walker, W.E.M.S., 391. 2. Branston, 278.

Foreskin

Circumcision, the removal of the foreskin, was one of the most common forms of penile mutilation practiced in imitation of female bleeding at menarche. After the introduction of patriarchal gods, the custom continued with different rationales, such as a god's demand for a redemptive symbolic sacrifice, the part for the whole. Instead of claiming a child's life, the biblical God, for example, learned to be satisfied with either a sacrificial animal (Genesis 22:13) or the child's foreskin (Genesis 17:10). Offering of the foreskin became the "sign of the covenant" between God and the Jews, although God never quite carried out his side of the bargain to the letter.

One of the early rationales for circumcision was related to primitive Jewish worship of the phallic serpent **Leviathan** (or Nehushtan). The shedding of the foreskin was likened to the serpent's trick of shedding its skin, to become immortal. There was a notion that shedding the foreskin helped to preserve the life force that men spent in sexual union. The alleged purity of the circumcised was based on fear of the "little death" of ejaculation, and the idea that a symbolic sacrifice of the part would help preserve the whole.[1] Later rationales insisted that the circumcised penis was cleaner or

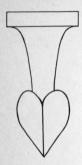

healthier, or both, though recent evidence has cast doubt on this.

The foreskin of Jesus turned up in many different places during the medieval frenzy of relic worship and invariably proved a great fertility charm whether it was the real thing or one of the numerous imitations. The church of Antwerp seems to have been the first to announce its possession of Jesus' foreskin, but the same relic soon appeared at Aix-la-Chapelle, Coulombs, Rome, Paris, Bruges, Bologna, Besancon, Nancy, and many other locations. At least thirteen Holy Prepuces still survive today, hinting that Jesus must have had some extreme physical peculiarities.[2] In the fifteenth century, Pope Eugenius IV established forty days' indulgence for any pilgrim who visited the foreskin and a plenary indulgence for priests; but he didn't say which foreskin was the right one.[3]

1. La Barre, 80. 2. Budge, A.T., 26.
3. McLoughlin, 246.

Genitalia

Scholars bred in the puritanical traditions of Western civilization had serious trouble interpreting the attitudes of earlier cultures that worshiped genital organs because the sensations localized in them were considered divine: a part of the gods' paradise miraculously embedded in human flesh. After centuries of training in Judeo-Christian doctrines of sin and sexual guilt, even intelligent Westerners tended to be puzzled or disgusted by the profusion of genital symbols in archaic religions.

Nevertheless, this ubiquitous sexual imagery could not be ignored. A typical example is the Egyptian "Amulet of the Sam," or *sma*, obviously a **lingam-yoni** design, which Egyptologists delicately call a sign of "union."[1] To the Egyptians it was a sign of knowledge, in the biblical sense that "knowing" equals sexual intercourse, and one "knows" divine power by feeling it. Another Egyptian hieroglyph for knowing was *seshemu*, meaning sexual intercourse.[2] To invite knowledge of the Goddess, according to Herodotus, priestesses of Bast would draw up their skirts and display their genitals as a holy rite.[3]

Ordinary words in many languages still attest to old pagan ideas of wisdom and religious revelation involved in sexual "knowing." Root words for knowledge and wisdom in Indo-European languages—*kennen* and *konnen* in German, *ken* in Gaelic, *gnosco* and *gnosis* in Latin and Greek—came from a common source with *genital, genetic, genus,* and *engender.* English words like *cunning, kenning,* and *ken* (knowledge) descended from

a spectrum of words related to *cunt*, which in turn was the Great Goddess Cunti: Latin *cunnus*, a vulva; Middle English *cunte*, Old Norse *kunta*, Basque *kuna*; cundy, a culvert; cunicle, a hole or passage; the Roman Goddess Cunina who protected the cradle (*cunabula*); the British Goddess's sacred river at Silbury, Cunnit or Cunnt, now called Kennet.[4]

Many places in pagan Europe were sacralized by a fancied resemblance to the genitalia of Mother Earth and her phallic consort. Cave-temples, springs, groves, hills, and many artificial constructions were deliberately viewed as sexual areas. Churchmen condemned all such places with the blanket term *cunnus diaboli*, "devilish cunt." As late as the sixteenth century, Pope Pius II said witches were holding their meetings on a sacred hill called Mons Veneris (the Mount of Venus).[5]

Words referring to the genital organs or their functions are the usual coin of profanity in all European languages. The real reason for this is not usually made clear. Not only did Christianity inculcate the idea that genitalia represented deviltry, but there was also something of the pagan reverence left, in the hidden notion that a curse would have to be reinforced by invoking a supernatural power. Therefore the allegedly supernatural power of sexuality came to be used against enemies as magic reinforcement of ill wishes. So the profanity of Spain includes *carajo* (penis), *cojones* (balls), and *coño* (cunt); in Italy there is *cazzo* (penis) and *conno* (cunt); in France, *foutre* (fuck), *couillons* (balls), and *con* (cunt); and Germans curse with the word *Potz* (penis).[6] The latter term passed into English as *pox*, originally applied only to venereal diseases.

1. Budge, *E.M.*, 61; Lehner, 82. 2. Budge, *E.L.*, 58. 3. Ibid., *G.E.* 1, 448. 4. Dames, 110–114. 5. Wedeck, 160. 6. Wright, 118.

Hair

Women's hair carried heavy symbolic and spiritual significance in Oriental religions. Tantric sages proclaimed that the binding or unbinding of women's hair could control cosmic powers of creation and destruction.[1] The hair of the Goddess **Isis** carried magical powers of protection, resurrection, and reincarnation; she gave rebirth to **Osiris**-Horus by "shaking out her hair over him."[2] Long, thick hair on male gods and heroes, like Shiva or Apollo-Heracles, indicated virility and vital power. One foundation of the myth of the sun hero lay in his sacrifice to the Moon Goddess who cut off his hair, a castration of his vital force. The biblical symbol of this Goddess was Delilah, "She Who

Makes Weak," and the shorn Samson was her sun hero, named after an Arabic title of the sun, Shams-On.[3]

Judeo-Christian patriarchy was generally hostile toward hair because of its pagan sexual connotations. Celibate priesthoods often adopted the tonsure or shaven head because it symbolized genital mutilation: castration or circumcision. Saint Paul, whose epistles contain veiled recommendations for emasculation, said "If a man have long hair, it is a shame unto him" (1 Corinthians 11:14). Paul also insisted that women's hair must be concealed under head coverings when they attend religious services, "because of the angels" (1 Corinthians 11:10), meaning the spirits that were supposed to be attracted or controlled by unbound female hair. Medieval churchmen commanded women to wear head coverings to church, and even demanded complete shaving of the heads of religious women, such as nuns. In eighth-century Bavaria, the law listed "lewd loosing of the hair" as a crime on a par with adultery.[4] The Inquisition took it for granted that witches could raise storms, just by loosing their hair.

British churches used to order men to cut their hair on the day before Good Friday, so they would be "honest" (i.e., Christian) for the Easter holidays. Therefore, this haircutting day came to be known as Shear Thursday.[5] The Anglican church also directed that a woman at her **churching** after childbirth must be "decently appareled," which was interpreted by the chancellor of Norwich in 1661 to mean that she must be covered by a veil. One woman protested and took her case to court. The judges asked the opinion of the archbishop of Canterbury and a panel of bishops, who ruled that the "ancient usage" of the Church of England was to veil women. The case was thrown out. Churchmen continued to regard women's head covering as an essential symbol of female suppression. A New Jersey Presbyterian, the Reverend Dr. Craven, said in the 1870s that "Under every clime, from the peasant woman of Naples with a handkerchief over her hair, to the women before me with bonnets, every one wears something on her head in token of subordination."[6] It is curious to see how contradictory was the rule applied to the two sexes. For men, removing the hat was a token of subordination, whereas to remain covered in the presence of a person of authority was an indication of equality.

1. Rawson, A.T., 67.   2. Budge, G.E. 1, 443.
3. Beltz, 150.   4. Duerr, 59.   5. Hazlitt 2, 541.   6. Gage, 60–61, 480.

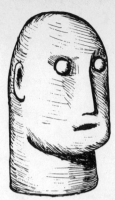

Hand

The so-called "hand of blessing" adopted by Christian clergymen was originally the *Mano Pantea*, "Hand of the All-Goddess," of which many carved examples have been found on the sites of ancient Roman towns. With the thumb and first two **fingers** raised in the familiar "blessing" gesture, the *Mano Pantea* was often encrusted with magical symbols, animals, and signs of the zodiac.[1]

Of the three raised digits, the index and middle fingers stood for the Goddess and God, respectively. The magic mother finger—which points, and casts spells—and the phallic father finger were also part of the Egyptian Amulet of the Two Fingers, which invoked the protection of parental spirits.[2] The thumb stood for the child (Horus). Moslems adopted the Mano Pantea as "Hand of Fatima."[3]

Christian authorities claimed that witches transferred the "hand of blessing" to the left, though this was perhaps the pagan custom from the beginning. Christian Europe also demonstrated great fear of the witches' so-called Hand of Glory, said to be the severed hand of an executed criminal, steeped in beeswax and made into a **candle** with a flame at the tip of each finger. Such an article would have been difficult to manufacture, to say the least, so it was probably just one more of the witch-hunters' macabre fantasies.

1. Gifford, 92. 2. Budge, *E.M.* 55. 3. G. Jobes 1, 718.

Head

Ancient Indo-Europeans quite correctly assumed that the real seat of human personality or "soul" is in the head. Therefore they worshiped heads, which were sometimes detached from the bodies of dead heroes or deified ancestors and preserved as **oracles.** The *Ynglinga Saga* tells how the god Odin himself depended on the mummified head of a much older deity, Mimir, to whisper to him the secrets that constituted his magical wisdom. Mimir was once a "being of supreme power," who was "classed with the Norns as originally one over whom Odin held no sway and to whom even Allfather had to appear as a petitioner."[1]

Mummified heads were speaking oracles in numerous Celtic tales. Bran, Lomna, Finn macCumaill, Sir Gawain and the Green Knight were all heroes of the oracular head cult. Similarly the head of **Osiris** was supposed to give oracles at the ancient shrine of Abydos; the head of Orpheus gave forth sacred poems and prophecies in a Dionysian temple; and the biblical *teraphim* were said to be the mummified heads of deified ancestors. Celts often made fetishes not only of real heads, but also of heads carved from stone or wood for the same purposes.[2]

Beheading, real or symbolic, became a ritual of deification or sacred initiation. Men were dedicated to the Goddess Artemis at Brauron by a cut on the neck, remnant of earlier beheadings.[3] The ceremony of knighthood—touching with a **sword** first one shoulder, then the other—was another remnant of earlier beheadings that made heroes or gods out of ordinary men.

One of the old Celtic gods of the oracular head metamorphosed into a Christian saint named Alban, originally Albion, "White Moon," an archaic name for Britain. The Christianized story said that Saint Alban was beheaded in the third century A.D., but this story was written three hundred years later by the monk Gildas, a great inventor of mythical sainthoods, all of them replete with marvels and miracles.[4] Saint Alban was depicted with a **fountain** springing from between his feet, a common pagan symbol of esoteric knowledge.[5] The archaic Norse deity Mimir was also the spirit of a fountain, which bore the same name, source of Odin's magic drink of enlightenment. In Irish folklore the oracular spirit took the form of the *dulachan*, a ghost carrying its own head, riding horseback (a Celtic symbol of apotheosis). This Irish spirit was the probable origin of Sleepy Hollow's famous headless horseman. It, in turn, resembled the Hindu *dhundh*, which rode with its head fastened to its saddle.[6]

Headhunters of Central and South America also regarded their cephalic trophies as sacred objects or soul-houses. Heads of ancestors were kept in oratories and offered their share of the feast each holy day. As among the ancient Hebrews and Celts, the mummified head was respectfully treated as a magical oracular object.[7] The general idea was still extant in England during the fourteenth century A.D., when a Southwark sorcerer was found in possession of a corpse's head, which he used for divination.[8] The Hindu Goddess Kali wore a garland of skulls or severed heads identified with alphabetical letters and with her sacred rosary (*japamala*).[9]

1. Branston, 151.   2. Green, 216.   3. Graves, G.M. 2, 79.   4. Attwater, 37.   5. Brewster, 293.   6. G. Jobes 1, 476.   7. von Hagen, 109–110.   8. Walker, *W.E.M.S.*, 1084.   9. G. Jobes 2, 1400.

HEART
*sacred heart: Saint
Margaret's version, 1685*

Heart

The Catholic church claimed that its
symbol of the Sacred Heart began with a
vision of Saint Margaret Marie Alacoque
late in the seventeenth century, depicted by
her as a heart surrounded by the **crown** of
thorns. The symbol was, however, a
great deal older than that. It appeared in
an alchemical text published before
Saint Margaret Marie was born. It appeared in a number of stained-glass windows and cloister decorations several
centuries earlier.[1] And the symbol of the
heart as a stand-in for the soul was
a commonplace of Christian iconography.
The tympanum of Bourges Cathedral
showed the vessel of the soul weighed in
the **balances** after death, bearing a
striking resemblance to the ancient Egyptian *ab* or "heart-soul" that was to
be weighed in the balances by the Goddess
Maat, Mother of Truth.[2]

The *ab* was that one of the Egyptian's
seven souls that was supposed to come directly from the mother's heart, in the
form of holy lunar **blood** that descended
into her womb to take the shape of
her child. The hieroglyphic sign for this
eminently matriarchal idea was a dancing
figure, representing the inner dance

of life perceived in the heartbeat.[3] As long
as the dance continued, life went on.
Osiris in his death phase was called Still-
Heart because he no longer danced.

The idea of a heartbeat-dance at the
core of all living things was vividly
presented in Oriental symbolism by the
perpetual Dance of Shiva (see **Dance**),
taking place in the "center of the
universe," which is also the human
heart.[4]

1. Walker, *W.E.M.S.*, 377.   2. Watts, 213.
3. Budge, *E.L.*, 44.   4. Ross, 32.

Hymen

A Greek name meaning "veil" or "membrane," referring to the maidenhead,
Hymen was also a Goddess who personified marriage. The rending of the
veil in a first sexual intercourse is still
symbolically enacted by the bride who lifts
her veil to receive her bridegroom's
kiss. Sometimes, Hymen represented the
veil of the temple, another term for
the womb, which was the "temple" of the
female body.

The word *hymn* also descended from
Hymen, for the original *hymnos* was a

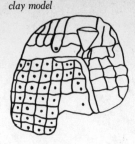

wedding song, probably in celebration of the physical beauties of the bride after the manner of the erotic wedding songs of the Middle East. One example was preserved in the Bible's Song of Solomon. When hymns were taken over by patriarchal religion, their archetypal connection with the "hymeneal rites" was largely forgotten. In fact, modern Christianity has no official wedding hymns whatever; all wedding music is secular.

Lingam-Yoni

The lingam-yoni was a carved symbol of male and female **genitalia** in conjunction, the lingam in the yoni. This was the typical Tantric altarstone, reminding worshipers that sexual love is the source of human life, that all existence depends on union of male and female principles, and that the Goddess and God were perpetually joined in order to keep the universe in motion.

Westerners usually called the lingam-yoni obscene, since it was not the habit of Western religion to view sexuality as a divine motivating power.

Liver

Because of its rich supply of **blood** and its dark lunar-blood color—the sacred color according to ancient Mesopotamian opinion—the liver was often viewed as an organ particularly favored by the deities and capable of revealing divinatory secrets if properly consulted. Still extant are models of livers from Babylon, Assyria, and Phoenicia, done in clay, stone, or metal, carefully marked to show apprentice diviners the meanings of various areas. The Bible mentions the king of Babylon standing at the **crossroad** to take omens by consulting images and looking "in the liver" (Ezekiel 21:21).

Diviners who specialized in interpreting the internal organs of sacrificed animals were known in Rome as *haruspices*, gazers-into-the-belly.

Tribes of central Africa still believe that the liver is the seat of the soul. They say a man eats the liver of an animal in order to enlarge his own soul.[1]

1. G. Jobes 2, 1082.

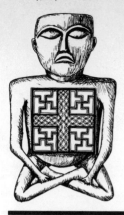

Lotus Position

The universality of the entranced sage in lotus position is demonstrated by an illustration taken, not from a Buddhist *bodhisattva* as might be expected, but from an artifact created in Norway before A.D. 800.[1] A curious decorative breast-plate shows the right-hand and left-hand **swastikas** characteristic of Indo-European iconography on an **earth square** with its typical cross.

The common Aryan roots of India and Scandinavia are made clear by the matching gestures, names, symbols, and customs persisting into the medieval period. The Celtic Horned God was also found sitting in lotus position like a Hindu sage. He appeared in this way on a Gallo-Roman altar at Rheims.[2]

1. Campbell, *M.I.*, 336. 2. Campbell, *Or.M.*, 307.

Mouth

Patriarchal Moslems insisted that women's mouths be covered by **veils,** because of the archetypal fear that equated women's mouths with the *vagina dentata* (toothed vagina) and saw sexual symbolism in the mouth and vice versa. Mouth/vulva symbolism occurs throughout the world. Copulation has often been described as female eating. In some languages, they are the same word; pregnancy is the same word as "full-fed" or "satiated."[1] Babylonian writings said it was the man who "puts forth" or "is taken," while a woman's nether mouth devours or possesses him. About pregnancy it was asked, Who grows fat without having eaten? Male "seed" was regarded as a kind of food. It was pointed out that food does not own the mouth; the mouth owns the food. In some societies, women were forbidden to eat anything where they could be seen by men. A Hawaiian myth about Hina, the Mother of God, tells how her son tried to return to her **womb** in order to be born again, and her mouth bit him in two.[2]

Fear of sex, of course, underlay all the mouth prohibitions. Names of the Greek Lamiae or Empusae meant both devouring gullets and lustful **vaginas.**[3] These became the nocturnal she-demons or

NAVEL
decorated navel of a Persian dancer

succubae of the Middle Ages, feared especially by ascetic men who imagined themselves being sexually eaten in their dreams. Perhaps the most widespread medieval mouth image was the Hell-mouth, a "yawning" **yoni.** Some authorities even declared openly that women's genitals are gates of hell, ready to swallow men.

1. Walker, W.E.M.S., 1035. 2. Briffault 2, 657–658. 3. Graves, G.M. 1, 206.

Navel

As the prenatal point of contact between mother and child, and the link through which every child's life was initially received, the navel was accorded much spiritual significance in ancient times. Many center-of-the-earth shrines were viewed as the cosmic navel, a source of life force for the world. The sacred *omphalos* at Delphi and other, similar stones came to be called navel stones. Calypso's isle of Ogygia was termed the Navel of the Sea.[1]

The original meaning of the navel was often lost or even reversed by patriarchal reinterpretation. An example is offered by the worshipers of the god Vishnu, shown as a root of the World **Lotus,** which grew on a stem from his navel. But the lotus in India formerly represented the Goddess, one of whose titles was Padma, "Lotus." Therefore "the long stem from navel to lotus should properly connote an umbilical cord through which the flow of energy would be running from the goddess to the god, mother to child, not the other way."[2] An umbilical cord often serves as a life-amulet.[3]

According to the Bible, the navel of Solomon's earth-symbolic bride was like the central wellspring of the country: "a round goblet, which wanteth not liquor" and her belly was the omphalic mount surrounded by the Western version of the female lotus: "thy belly is like an heap of wheat set about with lilies" (Song of Solomon 7:2). Deep female navels were admired by the Arabs. Belly dancers still set jewels in their navels, or call attention to the area with tattoos or paint.

1. Duerr, 19. 2. Campbell, Oc.M., 157. 3. G. Jobes 2, 1158.

BODY PARTS

Palm

The **hand** with an **eye** in the palm was shown in the Oriental fear-dispelling gesture by certain Tibetan bodhisattvas, and also, half a world away, in the symbols of Native American mound builders. The entire field of palmistry is summed up in this symbol implying that insight is to be found in the palm of the hand. In fact, the ever-popular search for divinatory clues in the natural lines of the palm may have been initiated by this worldwide symbol, taken as a mystic revelation.

The Oriental "eye of mercy" in the palm of the hand has also been likened to the pierced hands of several crucified saviors, including the Christian one.[1]

1. Campbell, *W.A.P.*, 213.

Phallus

Phallic symbols are objects of either overt or covert worship in all patriarchal societies, which invariably seek to inflate the male role in reproduction to something grander than the female role. But many myths and customs point to a derivative element in such worship, with feminine significance antedating the masculine one. For instance, the Latin *fascinum* or phallus also meant a kind of magic, originally attributed to women who seemed able to control this part of a man's body by looks or gestures. Such magic became the medieval interpretation of a witch's fearful ability to "fascinate." *Penis* is thought to have come from Latin *penus*, meaning a storehouse sacred to the household gods called Penates, or else the inner sanctuary of the temple of **Venus**, also used as a metaphor for the **vagina**. *Penitus* meant something deep inside, so the word came to be applied to the "penetrating" male member.

Early Gnostic Christians worshiped the phallus as earnestly as their pagan neighbors, calling it the **Tree of Life**. An Ophite initiatory formula said, "I have been anointed with white chrism from the Tree of Life." This meant semen. Saint Augustine, who was a Manichean Gnostic for a decade, mentioned the Gnostic habit of eating the Christian **Eucharist** sprayed with human semen.[1] Christian phallus worship went on undiminished into the Middle Ages and beyond.[2] An ecclesiastical tract in the eighth century, *Judicia Sacerdotalia de Criminibus*, ordered bread-and-water penance for anyone who performed incantations on the *fascinum*. But the incantations apparently continued unabated, because the same order was repeated in the ninth, twelfth, thirteenth, and fourteenth centuries. In the district of La Rochelle, Palm Sunday came to be known as the festival of *Pinnes*, a popular vulgarism for "penis." Phalli made of **bread** were carried in procession along with the **palm** branches.[3]

An interesting example of modern phallic symbolism is Aleister Crowley's sign for himself as "To Mega Therion," the Great Beast. Above the biblical number of this creature (see **Number of the Beast**), Crowley placed a head-on view of a phallus, superimposed on the seven-pointed Star of Babylon. The phallic design also stood for the (masculine) sun clasped by the (feminine) crescent moon, or the woman Babylon in conjunction with "the prince-priest the Beast," as Crowley described himself: "the chosen priest and apostle of infinite space." The whole sign, he said, was "yet another form of the Tetragrammaton, the Phallus, showing Sol and Luna, with the number 666 duly inscribed."[4] The sign appears twice in Crowley's deck of **Tarot cards,** on the Prince of Wands, a "male" suit, and on the Ace of Disks, a "female" suit.

1. Barnstone, 672.   2. Walker, *W.E.M.S.*, 795–797.   3. Wright, 29–30, 87–88. 4. Crowley, 211.

Placenta

Ancient Egyptians worshiped the placenta that was "born" along with each pharaoh. It was considered the infant's spiritual twin. The royal placenta bore the name of the moon god, Khonsu, especially when the king himself bore the name of the sun.[1] Primitive people generally considered the placenta an unformed twin of the baby, and made special preparations for disposing of it. Sometimes the placenta was buried under the house in which it was "born," so that the women of the house would receive its spirit and give birth to more children.

The Shilluk of the upper Nile remembered the ancient Egyptian custom, and always preserved the placentae of their kings, so the king and his unformed twin could be buried together in the same grave.[2] Otherwise, the twin might wander the world in search of the fraternal corpse. There is some indication that the concept of the *Doppelganger* or mystic double arose from superstitions concerning the placental twin. Sometimes it could take on human form; then one might unexpectedly meet one's double during earthly life.

1. Frankfort, 71.   2. Montagu, 271.

Saliva

The miracles of both Jesus and Mohammed, curing the blind with saliva, were nothing new. Long before Jesus' time, a clay tablet from Nineveh stated that blindness could be cured by a mixture of saliva and **milk** from one of the holy harlots in the temple. Italian folk healers of the nineteenth century A.D. still recommended a similar remedy for blindness, especially the mingled saliva and milk of the mother of a premature infant.[1] In Tantrism and Chinese Taoism, the saliva of women was called a wonderful medicine, one of the three magic yin juices along with milk and menstrual **blood.**[2] Throughout the centuries, many people continued to believe that saliva could cure blindness. Medieval magicians also claimed that the magic of saliva could repel **demons,** especially if the saliva came from a man who was fasting.[3] The common custom of spitting into a stream while crossing it was supposed to stop any pursuing evil spirit. Spitting over one's shoulder could offset bad luck; spitting through a ring could bring prophetic visions; spitting in a baby's face would render it safe from harmful spells; and so on through many superstitious practices.

Pliny records that boxers spat on their hands as a magic charm to make their blows more forceful. It is still common for men to spit on their hands before starting a manual task. Most people suppose that the ritual is to ensure a better grip. However, damp hands do not always hold as well as dry ones, as anyone knows who has tried to grip something when the hands are sweaty. The gesture's real purpose seems to be an ancient magic.

1. Gifford, 63. 2. Rawson, E.A.E., 234.
3. Trachtenberg, 120, 203.

Skeleton

Nearly all people used to believe, and many still do believe, that information about the spirit world may be obtained from the dead. Therefore, to die and be returned to the earth was often a prerequisite for mystics and magicians. Central Asian shamans insisted on being torn apart by spirits and reduced to a skeleton in their trance state. Siberian and Eskimo shamans still say they must come into their profession through a realistic vision of themselves as fleshless skeletons.[1]

Full skeletons were rare among **saints'** relics, but at least one was worshiped as the Holy Saint Josaphat of India, canonized by Pope Sixtus V in 1590, and again

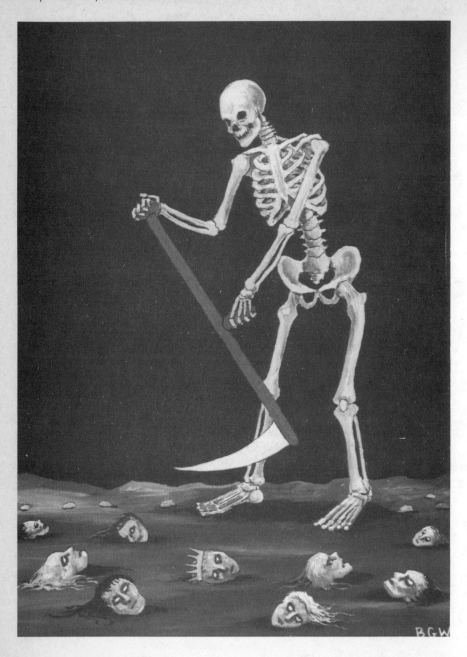

"infallibly" confirmed by Pope Pius IX in 1873. The skeleton was presented as a miracle-working item to the king of Portugal by the Doge of Venice, and later venerated at Antwerp. Despite the evidence of his holy skeleton, however, the Blessed Josaphat never existed. He was only a corruption of Buddha's title Bodisat.[2]

Europe generally regarded the skeleton as a symbol of death, like the **Carnival** figure of **Macabre**. The thirteenth card of the Tarot trumps showed a skeleton, and was intended to represent Death. Some Tarot decks declined to give the card a name, on the theory that to speak or write the name of Death was to invoke it; so the card bore only the "unlucky" lunar number, thirteen.

1. Duerr, 68.   2. Abelard, 78.

Skull

The importance of the head among ancestor worshipers or hero cults often led to preservation of the deceased deity's human **head** in mummified form or as a skull. Savior gods such as **Osiris** and Orpheus had their skulls preserved at Abydos and Lesbos, respectively, to give **oracles** and advice. The name of Golgotha, "Place of a Skull," in the Christian crucifixion story is thought to indicate an-

other tradition of oracular skulls telling the secrets of the afterlife.

Myths sometimes represent the **dome** of the heavens as the skull of a primordial dead god, like the Norse Ymir, and the *axis mundi* (Column of the World) as his spine. Ymir's celestial skull was upheld by four dwarves, Austri, Vestri, Nordri, and Sudri (East, West, North, and South).[1] Norsemen also preserved the skulls of slain enemies and made them into drinking **cups**: hence the Nordic drinking-toast word *skoll* (skull).

In alchemy, the skull stood for the process of putrefaction. Therefore it was drawn along with an X of bones on containers of poison, as a sign of warning. In Christian mysticism, contemplation of a skull was recommended—especially by the Jesuits—as a spiritual exercise, to enforce awareness of death through awareness of the *memento mori*. Paintings of saints, cardinals, and other notables with one hand resting on a skull were supposed to convey the idea of piety. Another convention of artistic symbolism was a skull crowned with Dionysian **ivy** to represent the hope of eternal life.[2] Christian iconography made the skull a symbol of Mary Magdalene. Drinking water from the skull of a suicide was said to cure epilepsy.[3]

1. Branston, 60.   2. Hall, 284, 291.   3. G. Jobes 2, 1465.

Thigh

The Latin name of the thigh bone, *femur,* means "that which engenders." Several myths suggest that the thigh was once thought to serve as an auxiliary **womb.** The heavenly father Zeus gave birth to his son Dionysus from his thigh. In Islamic tradition, the divine Fatima gave birth to her sons from her thigh and so preserved her virginity forever.

The Bible shows that the thigh served as a euphemism for testicles, which were used to bind promises and oaths by masculinity-worshiping Semites. Arab men still seal oaths by touching one another's testicles. Such a magical "testament" invokes future generations—the sons still in the testicles—to hold a man to his promise. Hence the Latin *testis* meant "a little witness."[1] The thigh was substituted in the story that Abraham's servant swore by putting his hand "under the thigh of his master" (Genesis 24:9). Once the euphemistic thigh could be accepted as a possible repository of future life, it became credible that male gods might achieve the maternal miracle of birth by using their fruitful thighs.

1. Potter & Sargent, 298.

Thumb

Hindu scriptures present the idea that each person's soul is a little manikin the size of the thumb, dwelling inside the **heart** and doing the ceaseless dance that may be felt as the heartbeat. At the same time, the human soul is an emanation of Dancing Shiva whose dance beats in the heart of the living universe. This thumb-soul is "the lord of time, past and future."[1] The idea passed into European folklore as the wandering thumb-sized spirit Hop-o-my-Thumb, together with his consort, the **fairy** Thumbelina.

In the symbolism of the hand, the thumb is the Child, extended together with the index (Mother) and middle (Father) fingers in the "hand of blessing" that Christians copied from paganism (see **Hand**). The yogi's mystic gesture places the index finger and the thumb together, while the other three fingers extend and make the sign for a triad. This was once an expression of the unity of mother and child under the protection of the Triple Goddess, connoting security, love, blessings, and other fortunate qualities. This may be why the yogi's mystic gesture was adopted as our ordinary "OK" sign.

1. *Upanishads,* 21.

Tongue

In Asiatic countries, the extended tongue was a sign of potency and life force, because the tongue between the lips imitated the sacred **lingam-yoni**: male genital within female genital. Indeed the vulva is still called *labiae*, "lips," and Latin *lingus*, "tongue," is related to lingam. Because of the life-giving and generally fortunate connotations of the protruding tongue among Oriental deities, sticking out the tongue is still a polite sign of greeting in northern India and Tibet. In Western tradition, however, it is a gesture of insult, a "showing the phallus" equivalent to the extended middle finger.

It was because of the tongue's sexual connotation that medieval devils were usually pictured with protruding tongues, and that the more ascetic Buddhist cults reinterpreted tongues as a symbol of untruthfulness. The fairy tale about Pinocchio's extendable nose was predated by the Hindu story that liars would eventually find themselves in the Great Howling Hell where their tongues would grow to enormous lengths. [1]

Despite the dislike of ascetics in general for the protruding tongue, Gothic **gargoyles** showed their tongues all over churches and cathedrals. According to the old theory, a display of **genitalia** created a prophylactic protection for a sacred building (see **Sheila-na-gig**). This theory filtered down into Gothic sculpture when the tongue was regarded as a comparable equivalent.

Biblical terminology used *tongue* as a synonym for language, in the famous "speaking in tongues" incident (Acts 2). It was claimed that the apostles, under the influence of the holy spirit, could speak every language known to their polyglot audience, and "every man heard them speak in his own language" (Acts 2:6). It is clear that the story was copied from Buddhist tradition, which said that when the Enlightened One addressed gods, demons, men, and animals, each heard the message in his own language. [2] The connection is made even clearer by the assertion, in the same New Testament chapter, that the apostles were visited by "cloven tongues like as of fire" (Acts 2:3), which sat upon their heads, exactly like the Buddhist **ushnisha,** symbolizing knowledge of all languages.

"Speaking in tongues" in the biblical sense later became confused with glossolalia, the phenomenon of compulsive babbling when in a state of religious ecstasy. Believers have always tried to claim that glossolalia is really understandable speech in a language that happens to be unknown to those present, including the speaker. No such claim has ever been proved. Nor, for that matter, has any instance of "speaking in tongues" in the biblical sense ever been shown to be other than a primitive fantasy.

In West Africa the tongue of a tribal chieftain used to be considered a seat of his royal power. When a king died, he was decapitated, and the head was presented to his successor, who was required to eat a small piece of the tongue.[3] Whether the tongue was equated with phallic spirit or with a presumed power of inspired utterance, it clearly embodied some quality thought to be essential to a leader.

1. Tatz & Kent, 69. 2. Waddell, 159. 3. G. Jobes 1, 61.

Vagina

As the **gate** of life and the "devourer" of men, figuratively speaking, the vagina has been given elaborate and euphemistic symbolism. The many substitutes for it in symbol and myth show how men have concentrated on its attributes with a mixture of awe, fear, and desire. Medieval Christianity made the vagina a metaphor for the gate of hell and revived the ancient fear-inducing image of the *vagina dentata* (toothed vagina) that could bite off a man's penis. On the other hand, men have always desired, and sometimes even tried to appropriate for themselves, the life-transmitting and pleasure-providing functions of the vagina.

Vagina symbolism is plain in the sacred trumpets of the male-dominated Mundurucu people of South America. The trumpets belong to the men, and women are forbidden to see them; but the men say they were stolen from women in the first place. Ancestral spirits live in the trumpets. An almost identical symbolism is attached to the molino trumpets of the African Mbuti, which were also "stolen from women" and taken over by men. "Just as the real cavities of women contain the regenerative potential of the people and the clans . . . by taking the trumpets, men symbolically seize ownership and control of female generative capacities."[1]

According to the *Epic of Gilgamesh*, the plant of eternal life grew in "the deep," another term for the **womb** of the world. It was accessible only by a narrow passage (*ratu*) that translators sometimes call a water pipe, or a **well**, or a **fountain:** images that conceal the real nature of the passage, a vaginal gateway to the inner mystery of life.[2] Euphemism is more the rule than the exception in vagina symbols, showing that men generally feel uneasy or threatened by their meaning. Many stories about the vagina imply danger to men. A sixteenth-century Arabian manuscript declared that any man who looks into a woman's vagina will go blind and cited the case of a sultan of Damascus to whom this very thing had happened.[3] The story could have arisen from an ancient, widespread title of the penis as "little blind one."

1. Sanday, 39, 188. 2. de Santillana & von Dechend, 420. 3. Gifford, 143.

Voice

Old Eastern traditions made the female voice an important symbol of creation: the source of the original creative Word, which the Greeks and after them the Christians termed the divine **Logos.** Arising presumably from the fact that every child learns speech from its mother as a rule, thus creating the world in the mind, the Goddess of the Voice first created everything in the universe by speaking its name in her primordial language, which Vedic sages naturally identified as Sanskrit. To them, she was Vac, literally the sound of the Voice. They likened her to the **wind,** blowing from heaven and bringing the essence of soul to all things. Vac created the gods by speaking their names, and she also revealed the holy mantras whereby the gods could be controlled. Vac was the First, the Queen, the Greatest of All Deities.[1]

Early Hebrew mythology had a copy of Vac in the female deity Bath Kol, "Daughter of the Voice." In biblical times she was known as the divine afflatus, source of the prophets' inspiration: a personified Voice of God mysteriously female. Sometimes she was called "the last echo of the Voice," meaning that there was not much left to be heard of the creative Logos. The Greek Goddess Echo was a similar conception, though reduced to a mere water **nymph** in the classical Narcissus story.

In Gnostic literature, the female Logos said, "I am the Mother of the Voice, speaking in many ways, completing the All. It is in me that knowledge dwells, the knowledge of things everlasting. It is I who speak within every creature . . . I am the Womb that gives shape to the All by giving birth to the Light that shines in splendor. I am the Aeon to come. I am the fulfilment of the All, that is, Meirothea, the glory of the Mother. I cast a Sound of the Voice into the ears of those who know me."[2]

1. Briffault 1, 7.   2. Robinson, 466–467.

Womb

The holiest symbols of Paleolithic and Neolithic humanity were symbols of the womb, source of life, primary fountainhead of every creative process. The Sanskrit word for a temple meant "womb."[1] The Sumerian word for the underworld, the sacred **cave**, and the womb was *matu*, from the universal root word for "mother." To the Pygmies of Africa, the same word meant the great cavern that stood for the "Mother of God." To Simon Magus, Paradise was defined as "the Mother's Womb."

The most revered **oracle** shrine in Greece was named Delphi, meaning "womb." It was originally dedicated to the Great Goddess under such names as Themis, Gaea, and Phoebe. The legendary first priestess, Delphyne, was murdered by Apollo when he took over the shrine. A similar Druidic shrine still stands in Pembrokeshire, the Pentre Evan Cromlech, called the finest in Britain. Once entirely enclosed, it formed a dark chamber where initiates were placed for a number of days before ritual rebirth from "Cerridwen's Womb."[2]

Initiatory, baptismal, and consecration ceremonies the world over show men setting up womb imitations to represent rebirth into a new condition of life. They seem to be unable to imagine any other way of symbolizing this, even when participants are entirely male. A symbolic womb was the Hindu priest's cloak, called "womb of knighthood," from which a king was brought forth in his coronation ceremony.[3] The pre-Christian womb shrine of Glastonbury was formerly called Caer Wydyr. Its sacred **well**, running red with iron oxides, was thought to be the **blood** flow from the Goddess's life-giving womb. Christian legend appropriated the Glastonbury temple and called it the home—for a while—of the Holy **Grail.**

In Shakespeare's time, even an old word for a womb, *cod,* had been masculinized and newly defined as a scrotum: hence *codpiece,* the trouser flap worn by men, the Renaissance version of a fly front.

Another Greek word for the womb, *hysteria,* gave its name to an annual festival of Aphrodite and also to an imaginary cause of feminine illness, dating back to Greek medical ignorance but enthusiastically credited by doctors throughout the Christian era. It was believed that the womb sometimes detached itself from its moorings and wandered about inside a woman's body, causing troubles in the lungs, heart, kidneys, and brain. Up to the eighteenth century, churchmen still believed in the uterine causes of hysteria and recommended **exorcism** and conjuration as the only cures.

The original name of Israel meant "the tribe of Sarah." Her name was formerly Sara'i, The Queen, a name of the Great Goddess in Nabataean inscriptions. Priests changed her name to Sarah in the sixth century B.C.[4] The old Hebrew term for a tribe was the same as the word for "mother"; and a tribal subdivision was *batn* or "belly." The word for a kin group meant "womb," a relic of the original Hebraic matriarchy.[5] Sarah's tomb was said to be occupied by the matriarchal Queen and her descendants in the female line, together with her husband and the spouses of her matrilineal progeny. Ancestors of the Jews were only those accepted by the matriarchs Sarah, Rebekah, Leah, and Rachel as members of their descent group. Not all of Abraham's offspring were considered Israelites, but only those stemming from Sarah.[6]

These and many similar bits of evidence point to the womb symbol as one of the most significant in terms of kinship groups, spiritual ideas, and human culture in general. If there had never been such powerful bonding of uterine blood relatives in the distant past, the cooperative efforts required by civilization could hardly have made a start. Though patriarchal society has succeeded in preempting almost completely the meanings and significances of the womb, yet there is an essential element missing, and its lack is felt, if not understood, by all the modern world.

1. Campbell, C.M., 168. 2. Evans-Wentz, 157. 3. Perry, 129. 4. Beltz, 80. 5. French, 55. 6. Teubal, 94–95.

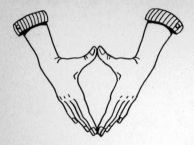

Yoni Sign

Sometimes used today as a gesture of greeting or benediction among feminists, the yoni sign was an occult secret for a long time. Like the meaning of the **cowrie** shell, its meaning was deliberately obscured in a culture that viewed any reference to female genitals as un-thinkably obscene no matter how abstract or esoteric it might be. The yoni sign survived, however, and now represents a symbolic invocation of female power.

13

NATURE

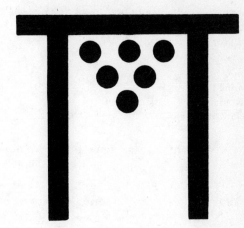

Human beings live with Nature in a state of somewhat uneasy dependence, subject to her whims, like small children of a moody, mercurial mother. Nature is life itself, but she is disturbingly unpredictable. It is hardly surprising that human eyes have so constantly followed Nature's movements in a nervous blend of hope and fear, always trying to foresee what she will do next. People have always longed to know whether the crop will flourish, when the volcano will erupt, how to bring rain in a dry spell, how to avert sickness, where to find riches, when to perform which ceremonies, and so on.

Neither is it surprising that man has expended so much effort on trying to "conquer" and control Mother Nature, just as the child tries to control the mother to its own advantage. Man's accomplishments in this area have a way of backfiring on him. Just when he thinks Nature is subdued, she turns and presents a new problem created by his own lack of foresight in solving the old one.

If man has trouble living with Nature, he certainly cannot live without her. Man is the child who never grows up; Nature is the mother on whom he depends forever. That is why human beings have personified Nature as an eternal mother. One might even say that the feelings any person has about Nature are significantly shaped by the feelings elicited by his or her own mother.

Human beings always try to translate what they want to control into symbols, so as to manipulate the symbols and then believe—rightly or wrongly—that this means manipulating reality. Therefore, symbols have been invented for almost all aspects of Nature that are perceptible to ordinary human senses. To some extent, the power of these symbols resides in our own perception of our complete dependence on the natural qualities and conditions of our own planet.

Air

The elemental symbol of air was also used sometimes as a symbol of the **sun** or of heaven generally. Sometimes it was assumed to represent the eye of God. In ancient India and Persia, the air element was personified by the god Vayu, and in Mesopotamia by Enlil. Many myths around the world speak of a primordial air god who made earth habitable for living creatures, by pushing Father Heaven away from Mother Earth and holding them apart, so human beings and other animals could have room to breathe. Thus the air god became the earliest form of a savior for humanity.

In antiquity it was often assumed that air was the essence of soul, or that souls (**ghosts**) were of the same invisible substance as the air, so their presence could be felt, like wind, but not seen. The Greeks and others postulated a World Soul in the form of air (*atmos*, from Sanskrit

atmen, "breath"). Diogenes of Apollonia said air is both soul and mind, giving life to all creatures through their breath, and "that which has intelligence is what men call air . . . it has power over all things," and so is defined as God. The Heavenly Father Zeus was also named Air, who lived "in all cities, in every home, in every one of you. There is no place where is not Air. And he who is present everywhere, because he is everywhere of necessity knows everything."[1]

It used to be thought that the soul literally departs from the body with the last breath, and thus enters the surrounding air, to be merged with the Oversoul just as a drop of water is merged with the elemental waters upon entering the sea. This was what the Hindus called becoming one with the Infinite.

1. Guthrie, 136, 142.

Cave

Caves were the great natural **womb** symbols and Mother Earth images worshiped by primitive peoples. According to Porphyry, before there were temples, all religious rites were conducted in caves.[1] In Sikkim the gods and earth spirits were established in the Four Great Caves, oriented to the cardinal points.[2] The Hindu Mother of Caverns was one of the oldest emanations of Kali, a *matrikadevi* (Mother Goddess) named Kurukulla.[3] Her

Phrygian descendant Cybele, the Great Mother of the Gods brought to Rome in the second century B.C., was entitled "Cavern-dweller" and worshiped in natural or artificial caves. Her sacred subterranean chambers were the womb-shrines where her emasculated priests deposited their genitals.[4] They believed that members of their brotherhood would never die, but would become bridegrooms of the Goddess in these underground "marriage bowers."

Like Cybele, the Great Goddess called La Dama (The Lady) was worshiped by Basque witches in a cave of the Amboto mountains.[5] A cave sacred to the Triple Goddess in the guise of "three fairy sisters" was revered up to the eighteenth century A.D. in Denbighshire, by folk who claimed to see the sisters' footprints around the magic spring. Another sacred cave and spring in Scotland near Dunskey was still used for healing magic in 1791, when people came to bathe in the uterine waters "at the change of the moon."[6]

According to Hebrew tradition, Abraham was born in a magical cave but was left motherless, so God made milk flow from his little finger to sustain him. After ten days he was able to walk out of the cave.[7] Such a birth story could well have been drawn from prebiblical customs of regeneration and rebirth, because sacred caves were the places of choice for magical incubations. Legend says Abraham's father was Azar, the vizier of King Nimrod; but the Bible gives the name of Abraham's father as Terah, a cognate of Terra, "Mother Earth," whose womb was usually a cave.[8]

Like Abraham, the Persian savior Mithra was born of the earth in the form of a rock, the *petra genetrix*, in a magic cave. The place of Jesus' birth, too, was originally a cave. In the Middle East, many gods were born in womb-caves surrounded by divine animals—that is, the idols of the animal spirits, who traditionally guarded the birthplace of gods. In folk lore and fairy tales also, Paradise or the land of magic wish-fulfillment was found in a cave, like the cave of Aladdin.

1. Robertson, 111.   2. Waddell, 256–257.
3. *Larousse*, 359.   4. Vermaseren, 111.
5. Pepper & Wilcock, 150.   6. Hazlitt 2, 420, 580.   7. Campbell, *H.T.F.*, 324–325.
8. Cavendish, 115.

Chaos

The classical concept of chaos defined what the world was before creation: all the **elements** mixed in a homogenized mass, neither fluid nor solid, neither hot nor cold, nothing differentiated from anything else, a universe of no-form. This was the stage of the Great Goddess, Tantric sages said, when she was the primordial Ocean of Blood, the Generative Womb of All, the Deep, in her condition of "dark formlessness" when she possessed all things in potential only.[1] "When there was neither the creation, nor the sun, the moon, the planets, and the earth,

and when darkness was enveloped in Darkness, then the Mother, the Formless One, Maha-Kali, the Great Power, was one with Maha-Kala, the Absolute."[2] Egyptians called the Great Mother in this condition Temu, the Deep, or Maa; she produced the first elements of existence, which were Water, Darkness, Night, and Eternity.[3] Temu became the Babylonian Goddess Tiamat and the Hebrew *tehom*, the Deep, mentioned in Genesis as the original condition of the universe when it was without form, and void, and dark (Genesis 1:2). But the Spirit that originally floated over the dark waters of chaos was female.

The god Marduk, a Babylonian prototype of Yahweh, divided the "waters which were under the firmament from the waters which were above the firmament" by splitting his mother Tiamat in two parts, opening her watery body by means of winds (air), killing her, and creating the world out of her parts. Patriarchal translations of the myth tend to describe Tiamat as the "dragon of chaos" slain by the heroic Marduk, ignoring the fact that she gave birth to him and all the other gods. However, the Chaos Mother never really died, because most myths said she would come back to reclaim the world and all its gods at doomsday. She would swallow them up, return them to her matrix of formlessness, and eventually re-create the universe.

1. Avalon, 517.   2. de Riencourt, 165.
3. Budge, *D.N.*, 211.

Clay

Clay was a common symbolic synonym for flesh. The biblical God who made people out of clay was copying the magic of much older Mesopotamian Goddesses like Aramaiti, "Mother of the People Made of Clay," or Ninhursag, who created human beings from her own clay and **blood,** or Aruru, the Goddess called "Potter" and "The Great," who infused her clay man with the **breath** of heaven and so brought him to life.[1] Another title of the Goddess was Mami or "Mother." Assyrians said she made the first seven pairs of male and female human beings: "The creatress of destiny, in pairs she completed them; the forms of the people Mami forms." Sumerians called her Nammu, who told a god to make human beings out of clay. "The Earth Mother will have fixed the image of the gods upon it. And what it will be is Man."[2] Flesh manufactured by a deity out of clay went through many cycles of myth before it reached the Judeo-Christian Bible.

The feminine origin of Adam's name was *adamah,* meaning "bloody clay," though male scholars preferred to call it "red earth." The concept seems to date back to primitive women's birth magic: the making of clay manikins and anointing them with menstrual blood—the sacred "blood of life"—in order to conceive real children. Women were still making clay manikins to represent people, and trying to affect the actual people by sympathetic magic through such manikins, in the Middle Ages when such pursuits were redefined as witchcraft. Clay was always a "feminine" material, sacred to women because it was their substance earth. Pottery was a woman's art because of this time-honored association of ideas.[3]

1. *Epic of Gilgamesh,* 121. 2. Campbell, *Or.M.,* 109. 3. Walker, *W.E.M.S.,* 815–816.

Cloud

In Chinese art, images of clouds represent feminine sexuality, while maleness is symbolized by the **rain.** Just as the rain gods of Western antiquity sent down their semen from heaven, so did the heavenly father of China. The female earth essence was manifested in the clouds. "The meeting of clouds and rain is the universal Chinese literary image for sexual intercourse."[1]

In this sense a phallic god might be said to have his head in the clouds. Western art also formed clouds around the heads of **saints** and heroes. This variety of **halo** was known as a *nimbus* or "cloud." A Chinese symbol of achievement of ambition (apotheosis) was a boy flying his kite toward a cloud. Red clouds, formerly emblematic of the womb's dangerous lunar blood, came to signify danger.[2]

1. Rawson, *E.A.E.,* 230. 2. G. Jobes 1, 350.

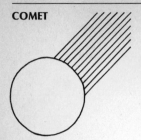

Comet

The word *comet*, from Greek, means "spirit of hair." Comets were viewed as hairy stars, whose unusual appearance and irregular courses made them objects of awe and dread. The sighting of a comet was always supposed to herald dire events on earth. Many believed that the appearance of a major comet, such as Halley's, presaged an imminent dooms-day. Human nature being what it is, one may be sure that even if no major disasters followed a comet's visit, plenty of dire happenings would be found in retrospect to have been announced by the comet.

Some people still confuse comets with meteors or "shooting stars." The latter, of course, move fast and disappear almost instantly; whereas a comet seems to stand still in the sky, although it moves very gradually around the sun. Meteors were wished on, because they were viewed as momentary cracks in the firmament, through which a god or goddess might peek long enough to grant the wish.[1] Alternatively, meteors were thought to be flying dragons, or human souls coming down from heaven to be born in earthly bodies.

1. G. Jobes 2, 1104.

Dewdrop

Dew is usually symbolized by a falling drop, even though dew does not fall, like rain, but rather condenses on surfaces; so it may be said to grow upward, not fall downward. However, dew was formerly equated with the fertilizing rain sent down to the earth by heaven-gods, and like rain it became a common metaphor for semen.

Writers of the Bible understood this metaphor well. The wedding song of the royal bridegroom mentioned his "head" (of the penis) filled with dew, or "drops of the night" (Song of Solomon 5:2). The psalmist said the people would follow only a virile king, full of the "dew" of youth (Psalm 110:3). Dew was recognized as divine semen also by Meister Eckhart: "As in the morning the rose opens, receiving the dew from heaven and the sun, so Mary's soul did open and receive Christ the heavenly dew." The conventional phrase "dewdrop in the rose" meant much the same as **"jewel in the lotus"** or its Chinese version, "diamond in the golden flower."[1] All were poetic symbols of sexuality and fertility.

1. Wilkins, 113.

Earth

Urd, Erda, Ertha, Hretha, Eortha,
Nerthus, Erce, Urth, Artha, Edda, Heor-
tha: a few of the names of Earth in
Indo-European dialects, in addition to
such forms as Terra, Gaea, Rhea, Ops,
Hel, Hera, Demeter, Europa, and many
others. Earth has been the universal
Goddess Mother at the fountainhead of all
mythologies. Herodotus pointed out
that all known names of the earth were
female.[1] There has never been a "father
Earth." As the Gypsies put it, "the
earth is our mother . . . the secret of life
comes from the ground."[2] The Ashanti say
the earth is the mother of all, Asase
Ya; "We got everything from Asase Ya,
food, water; we rest upon her when we
die."[3] Apache Indians said all creatures
were born from the earth in the beginning, "just like a child being born from its
mother. The place of emergence is
the womb of the earth."[4] Classical writers
said the earth produces all things, and
takes them back into herself. "Thus the
Earth Goddess encompasses the mystery
of every woman; the Goddess is the
beginning and end of all life on earth."[5]

The usual sign of earth, a cross
in a circle, also served for other purposes
and other deities, such as Wotan or
the solar spirit. However, the Pueblo legend
of Spider Woman mentions the crosswise
division of earth into four quarters
as the Goddess's first act of creation. Spider
Woman, also known as Thinking Woman,
was the primordial being. To begin

making the world, she first spun a **thread**
from east to west, then another from
north to south, so the point of the crossing
would determine the center of the earth.[6]

Reverence for the earth as a living
mother was characteristic of prepatriarchal
societies, which seemed to understand more
clearly the importance of preserving
their environment than later, male-dominated civilizations did. Tacitus related how
the Germanic tribes locked away their
weapons and put an end to all warfare
during the sacred season of honoring the
Earth Goddess.

Earth remained a Goddess for the
medieval witches, who continued her
worship against the strictures of the
church. Officials of the Inquisition believed that if captured witches were allowed to touch the earth, or if a
sympathetic spectator threw a clod of
earth to them, they could become invisible
and escape.[7]

For Western civilization, then, the
Goddess Earth became mere matter (*mater*), "without any psychic significance for
us," Jung says. "How different was
the former image of matter—the Great
Mother—that could encompass and express the profound emotional meaning of
Mother Earth."[8]

American Indians, who retained the
idea of the Earth Goddess, were distressed
at the way white men treated their
land. "They kill the trees, they treat the

trees unjustly, and the trees cry. They tear out the entrails of the earth, they hurt the earth, and the earth cries. They poison the water of our clear rivers, the fish die, and the fish and rivers cry, the earth cries, the herbs of the meadows cry—indeed, the Whites make all of nature cry."[9]

1. Herodotus, 226. 2. Derlon, 135.
3. Sanday, 32. 4. Campbell, *P.M.*, 240.
5. Vermaseren, 10. 6. Stone, A.M.W. 2, 92.
7. Duerr, 168. 8. Jung, 95. 9. Duerr, 111.

Echo

The **nymph** Echo of the Narcissus myth may be traced to the obscure Greek Goddess Acco, intimately connected with childbirth. Hers was an old name for the Daughter of the Voice, the Hebraic *Bath Kol*, Sanskrit *Vac*.[1] See **Voice**. The classical story said Echo pined away for love of the flower-god Narcissus, until nothing was left of her but her voice, which answered the calls of travelers. But this was a late mythic explanation for what was obviously a magical place with an audible echo.

Echoes always seemed magical and mysterious. They were usually thought to be spirit voices. As late as the nineteenth century, the voice of the Sybil of Cumae was still believed to speak through an echo, in a grotto under the Church of Saint John, which was built over her grave beside a spring that was formerly sacred to her.[2]

1. Leland, 220. 2. Duerr, 208.

Fire

A plain upward-pointing **triangle**, or one side of a pyramid, often appeared as the symbol of fire, alternating with the plain **circle** and other shapes, flamelike or otherwise. The triangle may have represented a volcanic cone, recalling fire mountains. The Greek word *pyramid* meant a spirit, thought, symbol, or idea of fire. In India, fire was a masculine principle represented by the upward triangle (see **Hexagram**) and usually personified by the god Agni, the "eater" of sacrifices that were consumed by fire on the **altar**. Agni was the consort of Destroying Kali under another of her names, Ambika, meaning "Little Mother."

Ashes were called the seed of Agni. The god and/or his followers believed in rebirth from ashes. Another meaning of the triangular pyramid shape was the conelike heap of ashes on the altar or **hearth,** banking the fire that remained underneath in the form of hot coals. Upward aspiration, in imitation of the flame's restless leap toward heaven, is another popular meaning of the fire pyramid.

Fire gods were usually born in wood, like a number of Greek heroes born from tree-maidens who were impregnated by Zeus (lightning) or Apollo (sun). Sometimes a pair of fire sticks were designated the parents of the god. At birth the fire

god is small and weak, a mere spark. Later he becomes strong and terrible. One of his titles, Light of the World, was taken over by the Christian deity.[1]

1. G. Jobes 1, 49.

Fountain

Any upwelling of **water** from the earth used to be called a fountain; but the term had specific mystical connotations as the central feature of the old matriarchal-uterine paradise. Like the primordial "nether upsurge" of **blood/water** from the **womb** of Mother Earth at creation, this fountain or *fons vitae* was the source of the life force. It was the object of mystical heroes' quests, with many half-concealed hints from Tantric tradition to the cults of courtly love that the fount of life lay in women's bodies and was really menstrual blood. Thus the Fountain of Eternal Youth in the fairy paradise was said to well up and overflow once every lunar month.[1] In biblical terms, a young virgin is "a fountain sealed" (Song of Solomon 4:12). Levitical law insisted that a man must never lie with a menstruating woman, because "he hath discovered her fountain, and she hath uncovered the fountain of her blood" (Leviticus 20:18).

According to Roman mythology, the Fountain of Youth was the young Goddess Juventas, who literally became the fountain.[2] In pre-Roman times she had been the virgin aspect of **Juno,** until she was replaced in the Capitoline Triad by the male youth Jove, whose name meant "the Youth," later identified with **Jupiter.**

The Celtic fairyland-paradise was a country of eternal youth with a wonderful fountain at its center, dispensing the waters of life. The fountain was also identified with the **Cauldron** of Regeneration. Several stories told of heroes reaching the fountain by entering a dragon-mouth—a mythic metaphor for the dangerous *vagina dentata* or menstrual taboo.[3]

The Fount of Life, or Fountain of Youth, has been the subject of male desires and fantasies from prehistoric times and has always found expression in terms of female symbolism.

1. Baring-Gould, 256. 2. Hall, 194.
3. Walker, *W.E.M.S.*, 771.

Island

Because the sun, moon, and stars all went westward to die out, and to be regenerated so they could rise again, most ancient peoples believed in the paradise island of the honored dead in the far west, beyond the rim of **ocean.** The western paradise island had many names: Elysium, Hesperides, Isles of the Blest, Fortunate Isles, Fairyland, or Avalon, the Celts' "Apple Isle" that supported the **Tree of Life.** Geoffrey of Monmouth wrote: "The Isle of Apples was also called Fortunate Isle, because all the vegetation grew there naturally with no need of cultivation . . . nine sisters ruled over it . . . and one of them surpassed all the others in beauty and power. Her name was Morgan and she taught how plants could be used to cure illness. She knew the art of changing her outward form and could fly through the air." The *Gesta Regum Britanniae* said it was an island in the midst of the ocean, where people were always young, and there was no sickness, crime, war, or uncomfortable weather. "A royal virgin, fairer than the fairest, governed that island."[1] Celtic island paradises were always ruled by women.

Russians called the fairy island Bujan, where the cosmic tree is guarded by the Virgin of the Dawn, and the sun rests every evening.[2] Finnish mythology said it was a land of peace, without soldiers or warfare. The magic **cauldron** or mill called Sampo, producer of everything on earth, was located on or beneath the island.[3] Norse stories identified the western paradise with the Faroe Islands, which accordingly took their name from *Faeroisland* (Fairyland).

In Hinduism the maternal paradise was the Isle of Gems, where the Great Mother sat enthroned in a jeweled palace.[4] It was shaped like a **yoni,** with the diamond Seat in its center (like a clitoris), and the whole image was likened to the body of a Goddess or *shakti.* It was also known as Jambu Island, the land of the life-giving Rose-Apple Tree.[5] Many similar female-symbolic apple-producing paradises turned up in Western mythol-

ogy. A Danish story told of a hero who entered a dragon's **mouth** and found the bridge to the magic island.[6] The dragon's mouth became the Christian symbol of hellmouth, which was generally recognized as another name for the **vagina.**

The island's Cauldron of Regeneration was sought, in Celtic lore, by the god Bran or Maelduin, who went on a voyage to the western land of immortality, known as the Land of Women. He was later restyled by the Irish church into a mythical Saint Brendan, abbot of Clonfert. A spurious life of the saint was produced in the tenth century, five hundred years after his purported lifetime. There he was said to have voyaged westward in search of a magic Land of Promise.[7] Where the earlier heroes went in search of the Land of Women, Saint Brendan went in search of paradise, "showing that the Land of Women is the Celtic conception of heaven."[8] Such was the perception of sexuality as a regenerative, divine force to be channeled through women—until ascetic patriarchy relegated all such ideas to the realm of heresy and witchcraft. It is interesting to note that the semipagan ballads of the folksingers named Fairyland as neither heaven nor hell in the Christian sense, but a different place altogether.[9]

1. Markale, 79–80. 2. d'Alviella, 168. 3. de Santillana & von Dechend, 102–111. 4. Cirlot, 152. 5. Tatz & Kent, 84. 6. Baring-Gould, 263. 7. Evans-Wentz, 354. 8. Markale, 52. 9. Walker, *W.E.M.S.*, 994.

Lightning

Our conventional zigzag symbol of lightning descends from the phallic **scepters** of ancient sky gods, whose bright spirits were supposed to come down from heaven in this way to fertilize Mother Earth, or the **womb** of the abyss, or sometimes even mortal women. Lightning from the Heavenly Father fertilized the Mother-stone (*petra genetrix*) that gave birth to the Persian savior Mithra.[1] The great Yellow Emperor of China was similarly conceived in the womb of a royal concubine by a flash of lightning.[2] Classical myth says Semele, the mother of Dionysus, was unfortunately burned up by an excess of lightning from her god-lover, Zeus; but Semele was really just another mortalized form of the Goddess.[3]

Like other phallic symbols, the lightning bolt was often viewed as a weapon. After all, lightning is destructive. The Greek name for lightning, Keraunos, meant a destroyer and was personified as a god. Lucifer, whose name means "light-bringer," was not only the Morning Star of biblical tradition but also a lightning god who threw his bolts at church towers. Lightning became the "Golden Lance," Lanceor, an archaic name for Lancelot in the **Grail** cycle of myths. It was also the sword Excalibur, which Geoffrey of Monmouth called Caliburn, from the Welsh Caledvwich, Irish Caladbolg: old names for the lightning.[4]

According to Tantric tradition, lightning was the "blazing lingam" that the Great Goddess quenched in her cosmic **yoni,** the Deep.[5] This love-death was the means by which the god could claim to produce the **blood** that created living things: blood that combined the salty fluid of her sea with the redness and warmth of his fire. It was one of the earlier theories of male begetting.

1. de Riencourt, 135. 2. Perry, 214.
3. Graves, G.M. 1, 58. 4. Darrah, 116,
5. Rawson, E.A.E., 57.

Milky Way

The "river of stars" created by our edge-on view into the central portion of our galaxy was seen as a river of sparkling, life-giving Goddess **milk** by ancient civilizations. Egyptians saw it as the outflow from the udder of the heavenly **cow,** Hathor or **Isis** in her bovine form, with her legs planted at the four corners of the earth. The same moon cow was Io or Europa or Hera in various Greek myths. The word *galaxy* itself came from Greek *gala,* "mother's milk." The Four Rivers of Paradise were often identified with four streams of milk from the four teats of the moon cow; in Norse mythology she existed before every other creature and gave nourishment to the world.[1] The Rivers of Paradise were copied into the Bible as streams emanating from Eden to the four directions; but the stream Hiddekel (Genesis 2:14) was copied from

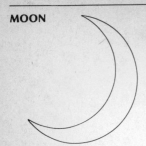

the Akkadian name of the Milky Way, Hiddagal, meaning "River of the Divine Lady." In Arabia it was known as Umm al Sama, "Mother of the Sky."[2]

The Milky Way was also known as the Moon Way, Scandinavian Manavegr, and in Celtic lands as the Track of the White Cow.[3] In the nursery rhyme, the famous White Cow became the animal who jumped over the moon, leaving a trail of her star-milk across the sky.

1. Branston, 57.   2. Jobes & Jobes, 103.
3. Turville-Petre, 76; Graves, W.G., 175.

Moon

Perhaps no other natural object has been more widely revered, from such extremely ancient periods, than the moon. As a rule the new or crescent moon was its recognized symbol, because the full moon would have been a simple **circle,** which carried other connotations, frequently solar.

Because of its apparent connection with women's cycles of "lunar **blood,**" which was supposed to give life to every human being in the **womb,** the moon became the prime symbol of the Mother Goddess everywhere. The Greek name of Europa, eponymous mother of continental Europe, means "full moon" and was a former title of Hera or Io as the white Moon-cow, and of other versions of the Goddess as well, such as Demeter and **Astarte.**[1] Albion, the old name of Britain, meant

"white moon" and referred to the Goddess until the monk Gildas converted her into a fictitious male Saint Alban. A primal deity of Persia was Al-Mah, the moon, whose name became the Hebraic *almah,* "nubile woman": the word that Christians insisted on translating "virgin" when it was applied to the mother of Jesus. Another derivative was the Latin *alma mater,* living mother-soul of the world.

Romans revered the primal Moon Mother as either Luna or Mana (Mania), whose worship Christians condemned as "madness" (lunacy). She was the mother of the archaic ancestral spirits called *manes,* annually propitiated at the Manalia festival. The same Goddess Mana ruled archaic Scandinavia, Arabia, and central Asia. Mana came from Sanskrit *manas,* "mind," an attribute of Ma the primordial Mother; it was also related to Latin *mens,* meaning both "mind" and "moon" as well as a mysterious quality of spiritual power (*nu-men*).

According to Moses Maimonides, moon worship was the religion of Adam; and the Bible contains many traces of pre-Jahvistic reverence for the moon.[2] Old Testament kings wore "ornaments like the moon" and so did their riding animals (Judges 8:21). Prophets denounced Hebrew women for wearing lunar amulets (Isaiah 3:18). Agla, one of the "secret names of God" much used in

Hebrew magic, is usually translated "light" but it meant specifically moonlight; Aglaia was an ancient name of the Moon Goddess. A Talmudic tradition said that Yahweh himself had to make a sin offering for offending the moon.[3] The Moon Goddess showed little respect for Yahweh or any of his cohorts, according to the *Apocalypse of Baruch*: when Adam and Eve wept over their sin, then everything else wept with them, "the heaven and the sun and the stars, and creation was stirred even to the throne of God; the angels and the powers were moved for the transgression of Adam," all except the moon, who laughed.[4]

Saint Augustine condemned women for their "impudent and filthy" dances in honor of the new moon.[5] And yet, lunar timing was so important to the Savior tradition that Christians insisted that the full moon shone on Jesus' crucifixion— even though there was supposed to have been a solar eclipse also, which can only happen during the dark of the moon. Lunar traditions continued to be associated with women throughout the Middle Ages. Folklore and ballads show that women were encouraged to pray for special favors not to God but to their own deity, the Moon Mother, by whom they also swore their oaths.[6] Just as Jeremiah's opponents doggedly continued to bake cakes for the Queen of Heaven (the moon) despite the prophet's fulminations against her (Jeremiah 44:19), so the women of Christian Europe continued to bake moon cakes, which the French called *croissants* or "crescents" for their lunar holidays. Modern birthday cakes descended from the Greek custom of honoring the monthly birthday of Artemis the Moon with lighted full-moon cakes.[7] Witches continued to invoke the Goddess by "drawing down the moon." In some areas, crops could not be sown nor weddings celebrated except at appropriate times of the moon. Everything having to do with the management of domestic animals seemed to depend on the moon. And, of course, no sorcerer or witch undertook magical operations without first checking the proper phase of the moon.[8]

So important was the Moon Goddess in pre-Islamic Arabia that her emblem came to represent the entire country, and still does so, as the lunar crescent on Islamic flags. As Manat, the old Moon-mother of Mecca, she once ruled the fates of all her sons, who also called her Al-Lat, the Goddess. Now she has been masculinized into "Allah," who forbids women to enter the shrines that were once founded by priestesses of the Moon. In Central Asia, her heavenly orb was described as the **mirror** that reflects everything in the world.[9] It is still said that the moon's reflection on water is the prime remedy for nervous hysteria.

1. Graves, G.M. 1, 196.   2. Briffault 3, 78.
3. French, 50.   4. Tennant, 203.   5. Hazlitt 2, 417.   6. de Lys, 458; Wimberly, 363.   7. Brasch, 23.   8. Hazlitt, 143, 418.   9. Jobes & Jobes, 32.

Mountain

The letter *M* seems to have been based on symbols of the twin peaks of the holy **mountain,** which were often seen as **breasts** of the Great Mother. The *Epic of Gilgamesh* describes such a holy mountain, Mashu, whose "paps" reach down to the underworld; she gives birth to the sun and she is as high as the walls of heaven.[1] A similar Mountain Mother, Ninhursag, gave birth to the world in Sumerian myth; she was also a Cow-goddess, milk-giver to the kings, who qualified for the throne by becoming her nurslings.[2] The oldest deity in Greece was the Divine Mountain Mother, Gaea Olympia, the first owner of Mount Olympus before its takeover by her upstart grandson Zeus. She was called Universal Mother, Oldest of Deities, and Deep-Breasted One. She controlled several mountain shrines including the Delphic **oracle,** which was later usurped by Apollo.[3] One of the oldest deities in India was Chomo-Lung-Ma, "Goddess Mother of the Universe," whose mountain shrine is now known to Westerners by a man's name, Everest. Still feminine, however, is the Himalayan peak Annapurna, meaning "Great Breast Full of Nourishment." Double peaks in County Kerry, Ireland, are still called the Paps of the Goddess Anu, or Danu, ancestral mother of one of the early colonies.[4]

The idea of universal breast **milk** flowing down from mountain peaks was common to both East and West. The Japanese symbol of mountains is an M-design with two breastlike peaks.[5] The four rivers of paradise were often equated with streams of the Mother's milk, as in Iranian myths of High Haraiti, the birth-giving mountain at the center of the earth, also "the fountain of all waters."[6] White snowcaps, melting into glacial streams made white with rock dust, probably put the idea into the heads of all peoples living within sight of high mountains.

Often the Goddess as creator of the world began her activities with mountain-making. A Welsh title of the Crone or Caillech was "Hag of the Dribble," because she let **stones** dribble from her apron to form the earth's mountain ranges.[7] However, the "dribble" may have been originally her milk or her uterine **blood,** both of which were once considered the creative fluid whose curdling or clotting made all land masses.

Magic mountains throughout Europe remained sacred to the Goddess and so acquired the reputation of witch shrines. Germany had several Venusbergs. Other peaks in Italy and Britain remained matriarchal pilgrimage centers. Many pagan heroes awaited rebirth from holy mountain **wombs.** Merlin and Thomas Rhymer were said to sleep under the Eildon hills. Epimenides, one of the Seven Sages of Greece, slept in Rhea's holy **cave**

on Mount Dicte. Boabdil el Chico, the last Arabian king of Granada, rested under the mountain near the Alhambra. Frederick Barbarossa slept under the Kyffhäuserberg. Charlemagne slept in the Odenburg (Odin's Mountain) in Hesse, or according to another legend, in the Untersberg near Salzburg.[8]

The pagan Earth Mother was thinly disguised as a fictitious saint in western France, where she was worshiped at a holy mount by the river Sevre. She was described as "drawing from her apron the fertile seed" and throwing it into the **furrow** with her blessings. Miraculous growths of grain were attributed to her influence.[9] The Mother still shelters the pagan dead as the holy mountain Helgafell in Iceland and upholds the pagan gods as the Teutonic Himinbjorg or "Heaven-Mountain."

1. *Epic of Gilgamesh*, 98. 2. Walker, W.E.M.S., 728. 3. Stone, A.M.W. 2, 165–169. 4. Graves, W.G., 409. 5. Hornung, 208. 6. Lethaby, 74–75. 7. Spence, 199. 8. Baring-Gould, 106–108. 9. Berger, 61.

Night

According to Hesiod, Mother Night gave birth to all the gods.[1] She stood for the darkness of the **womb** in which all things are generated, for the blackness of the abyss, and for infinite space, source of stars and other heavenly bodies. She preceded creation. The Orphic creation myth said that even the heavenly father stood in awe of primal black-winged Night, who first laid the silver egg of the cosmos in the womb of Darkness. From this egg (sometimes equated with the **moon**) hatched the double-sexed deity Eros who gave motion to the universe. Night was a Triple Goddess, her other two personae being Order and Justice.[2] In Egypt, she was Nut or Nuit.

In terms of psychological archetypes, Mother Night represents the unconscious, from which all images arise.

1. Cirlot, 218. 2. Graves, G.M. 1, 30.

Ocean

The ancients used to believe that the World Ocean took the form of a vast **serpent** whose body was water, encircling the land masses of Eurasia and Africa around the known world's outer limits. The Greek Oceanus (Okeanos) was the sea god created in the beginning by the Goddess Eurynome, to represent the water-planet **Venus**. Oceanus and Ophion the Great World Serpent were the same earth-girdling deity, whose former name meant "of the swift queen."[1] In other words, Oceanus was the serpent figure universally associated with the primal Goddess. As a water serpent holding his tail in his mouth, he could be identified with

many deities of the outermost ocean: the Gnostic **Ouroboros,** the Phoenician Taaut, the Egyptian Thoth or Tuat, the Hebrew **Leviathan.**

1. Graves, G.M. 1, 27, 30; 2, 402.

Planet

Once the mysterious rings of the planet **Saturn** were discovered, they provided a standard symbol for planets in general, even though most planets in our solar system are ringless and could be represented only by **circles** or **globes.** Symbolically, however, this would confuse "planet" with "sun" or "moon" or any of numerous other things that circles can stand for.

Alchemists and mystics linked the supposed planetary deities with the seven days of the week and seven elemental metals: Sunday, Helios, gold; Monday (Moon day), Luna, silver; Tuesday (Tiw's or Mars's day), Mars, iron; Wednesday (Woden's or Mercury's day), Mercury, mercury; Thursday (Thor's or Jupiter's day), Jupiter, tin; Friday (Freya's or Venus's day), Venus, copper; Saturday (Saturn's day), Saturn, lead. Cabalists made sets of seven **mirrors** out of the appropriate metals, to consult the planetary powers on appropriate days of the week.[1]

Mystery religions, including early Christianity, taught that each soul came down from heaven through seven successive planetary **spheres** to be born on earth, in its passage picking up passions and faults from each planet (lust from

Venus, anger from Mars, and so on). After death, on the way back to heaven, the soul could shed these "seven deadly sins" one by one while passing again through the planetary spheres.[2]

We owe our musical scale to the planetary spheres also. The Greek Muses were supposed to have established it, based on the seven harmonizing notes given off by the turning spheres, each note correlated with a sung vowel sound. Evidently based on the Oriental *Om*, these harmonics—known as the Music of the Spheres—were credited with the power to keep the universe in existence.

The Greek word *planet* means "wanderer," because planets seem to wander inconsistently through the sky against the background of the fixed stars.

1. Jobes & Jobes, 90.   2. Lindsay, 124.

Rain

The Navajo symbol for rain is neatly self-explanatory; it shows clouds piling up, and water descending in waves. Rain was usually associated with the male principle, as in the case of Jupiter Pluvius whose watery "semen" fertilized Mother Earth. Sometimes this was confused with the god's urine, as in the case of Zeus's "golden rain" that fertilized Danae, one of the names of the Goddess Earth. In Iraq up to the present century, when rain

was needed, it was customary to dress a female dummy as the Bride of God and place her in the fields, to induce God to "make water" on her.[1] Rain charms the world over consist of showing the god what is wanted, by pouring water, splashing, wetting things or people, squirting water through tubes, or throwing something into a stream.[2] The medieval church taught that witches could produce rain by slapping wet rags on stones to make the drops fly, or by pouring water into a hole.

Some Native Americans regard rain as a form of their ancestors, whose spirits have gone into water or air.[3]

1. Briffault 3, 210. 2. Frazer, G.B., 80–81.
3. G. Jobes 2, 1319.

Rainbow

Aborigines of Arnhem Land and Kimberley in Australia said the Rainbow Serpent Mother made the world and gave birth to all its people.[1] A similar Rainbow Goddess seems to have been widely distributed throughout Africa. Under her Yoruban name of Oya, she first created the elements of the universe. Brought to the western hemisphere along with African slaves, she became the Rainbow Goddess Olla of Cuba and Puerto Rico, Yansa of Brazil, Maman Brigette or Damballah of Haitian voodoo.

Iris was the Greek name of the Rainbow Goddess, who was more important in archaic religion than in classical Olympian legends. She probably began as a form of Kali-Maya, pre-Vedic mistress of the "rainbow veils" of perceptible reality. It was sometimes thought that all things were based on the rainbow because close inspection of skin, hair, plant materials, or stones in strong sunlight would reveal millions of tiny rainbows. Gems and **crystals** were much admired and regarded as Goddess essence largely on account of their rainbow iridescence. Kali-Maya became the Greek Maia, who was the virgin mother of the god **Hermes** just as Maya was the virgin mother of the god Buddha; but her name was synonymous with "midwife" and she was often viewed as the Crone, Hag, or Grandmother aspect of the Triple Goddess.[2]

The rainbow in the sky was usually seen as a bridge uniting heaven and earth. Oriental sages saw it as a union between male and female principles. Chinese called it the *tai ch'i* or Great Ultimate, literally the Great Ridgepole, uniting **yang and yin.**[3] In Norse mythology it was the heavenly bridge Bifrost, also known as Brisingamen, the jeweled necklace of Freya. It was also the necklace of **Ishtar** in Babylon, although sometimes seen as her seven different-colored veils, which figured in the dance of her priestess Salome in the Bible. Egyptians called these the Seven Stoles of **Isis.**[4] The seven colors of the rainbow were equated with

many other magical and mystical sevens, usually connected with Goddess worship but sometimes taken over by male deities.

A blatant example of such a takeover is the biblical story of God's use of the rainbow as a promise to Noah that there would be no more world-destroying floods. The earlier Babylonian story, from which the biblical flood myth was derived, laid quite a different interpretation on the rainbow. The Goddess Ishtar was angry at the god who caused the flood, because he had killed so many of her people. She set her rainbow in heaven to block him from feeding on the offerings placed on earth's **altars,** just like a mother sending a naughty child to bed without his supper.[5]

1. Campbell, W.A.P., 140. 2. Eliade, 114. 3. Watts, 97. 4. Angus, 251. 5. Walker, W.E.M.S., 315.

River

Sarasvati, "Flowing One," was a Vedic name for the River Goddess whose waters deified Hindu kings. She was also a Queen of Heaven who invented all the civilized arts. Another of her names was Ganga—Mother Ganges. Shiva's hymn of praise to her said that she consumes all sins so effectively that even breezes "charged with her vapor" can erase the sins accumulated through millions of previous lifetimes. Those who die beside the river Ganges are released from every postmortem punishment and go at once

to the House of God (Shiva), and even become identical with him.[1] In view of this, one can hardly wonder at the hordes of people who even today travel many long miles to bathe in the Ganges.

Similar powers were once attributed to the river Jordan, which the Bible says could remake one's flesh into that of a little child (2 Kings 5:14). This was an attempt to interpret the Jordan as a death-and-rebirth river like the Greeks' famous Styx, whose very name meant that it was fearful, magical, and taboo. It was imagined as a river of Goddess **blood,** emanating from Earth's **womb,** and its other name was **Alpha,** the letter of birth.[2] Gods swore their most binding oaths on the name of the Styx. Thetis, the Goddess mother of Achilles, dipped her son in the Styx to make him invulnerable—all except the heel by which she held him, which remained dry and so constituted his weak spot. Styx water was also said to be deadly poison (as was menstrual blood also) and a classic symbol of death. Charon ferried dead souls across it to the underworld. Greeks still put money in the mouth of a corpse to pay the ferryman of the Styx.[3]

Other rivers of the underworld or the earth's surface were personified by gods, water-spirits, **nymphs,** naiads, and serpentlike creatures expressing the river's meandering way. Nearly all rivers

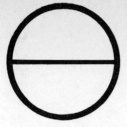

had their attendant deities. The river Boyne in Ireland was once the primal Goddess Boann, wife of the father-god called Dagda, who acquired his power through his connection with her.[4] Baptism in rivers derived its magical efficacy from a symbolic return to the birth fluid of such a Goddess, signifying a "born again" condition after the immersion.

Heraclitus viewed a river as a symbol not only of birth, death, and rebirth, but of time itself, flowing ever onward without reversal. He said, "You cannot step twice into the same river, for fresh waters are ever flowing in upon you."[5] This was offered as a metaphor for the stream of time, which flows in one direction only.

1. Zimmer, 110.   2. Walker, W.E.M.S., 959–960.   3. Hazlitt 2, 338.   4. Green, 149. 5. Cirlot, 94, 347.

Sea

Temu was an Egyptian name for the maternal Deep, or uterine abyss, from which the universe was born. It was cognate with Chaldean Thamte, Babylonian Tiamat, Greek Themis, and Hebrew *tehom*, "the Deep." Other names for Mother Sea include Thetis, Pelagia, Thalassa, Amphitrite, Aphrodite Marina, and her variations Mari, Mara, Marga, and Mary of the blue robe and pearl necklace. The Greek sea god Poseidon was originally a female Posidaeja in Minoan civilization, which recognized no male symbol of the sea.[1]

Mother Sea was a universal emblem of birth and rebirth, with many imitations of her waters such as the baptismal "sea" in Solomon's temple (1 Kings 7:23), copied from similar "seas" (large basins) in the temples of Babylon and Egypt.[2] According to Orphic literature, the earliest Mother Sea was the Goddess Rhea who became Demeter after she had borne Zeus. She separated solid from liquid elements in the primal abyss, creating **earth** and sea, as well as the ambrosia and nectar that were the solid and liquid foods of the gods.[3] Thus, Demeter was always known as Mistress of Earth and Sea. Her sign forms the "dia-meter," meaning "Goddess Mother": the sea horizon.

The Babylonian idea of a creative sexual union between a heaven god, Apsu, and the female sea, Tiamat, also appeared in the biblical creation story. "The original text makes it clear that the creative act is a sexual union." Elohim (God) impregnates the waters with *ruach*, a Hebrew word meaning spirit, wind, or the verb "to hover"; it also means sexual intercourse, in the sense of moving back and forth.[4] The same word is "to brood" in Syriac, an innocuous choice now used in the English Bible.

A good many pagan heroes were born from the maternal sea, which was symbolized by the **Cauldron** of Regeneration and was referred to in Scandinavia as

Spring   Summer   Autumn   Winter

"the Mother's womb."[5] Scyld, ancestor of Beowulf, was deposited on a beach by sea waves as a newborn infant; so was Rig-Heimdall; so was Merlin. Little Gwion was swallowed by Cerridwen, Goddess of the Cauldron, and given rebirth when she sent him forth again "from the sea in a bag of skin," meaning that he would be a spiritually gifted person because he was born with the **caul.**[6] Even in Christianized Europe the sea remained pagan. Icelanders said that even if Christ ruled their island, still the old god **Thor** ruled the sea. Similarly, Scottish fishermen practiced pagan rituals when out in their boats, deeming it bad luck to name a minister or to refer to Sunday until their return to land.[7] Scandinavians thanked their old pagan deities for a good catch of fish.[8]

The African Sea Goddess had many names, such as Agwe in Dahomey and Oshun among the Yoruba. There is doubt as to whether the latter was a native word or a corruption of English "ocean." In the New World, the Goddess became known as Ochun, Oxum, or Erzulie. In Haiti she was sometimes called La Balianne, Yemanja, or Yemaya. Like her counterpart Aphrodite-**Venus,** she was also associated with the moon, love, birth, beauty, sexual fire mingling with the waters. Ghana knew her as Mami Wata, which may also be suspected of an English origin (Mama Water). In any

event, the universality of the Sea Goddess can be no more doubted than the global presence of sea waters themselves.

1. French, 140.   2. Lethaby, 219.   3. de Santillana & von Dechend, 259.   4. Beltz, 35.   5. Walker, *W.E.M.S.*, 934.   6. Cavendish, 200.   7. Spence, 354.   8. Dumézil, *M.F.*, 220.

Seasons

The four designs in the illustration represent seasons from the viewpoint of the vegetation. Spring shows young sprouts beginning to rise from the **earth,** in a pattern resembling a solar head. Summer, like uplifted arms, represents full-blown plants receiving the light of the **sun** and flourishing; it also resembles the **cup** that summer harvest fills with **wine** or juice, running over at the rim. Autumn's cup is reversed. The juice runs out, the cup turns down, the reversed cross represents the savior (**seed**) returning into the earth for a period of dark sleep before the resurrection. Winter depicts the seeds dormant underground, covered by a snow blanket, awaiting a new season of sun and sprouting.[1]

In ancient Greece, the signs of the seasons were four women. Spring wore a **crown** of flowers and stood by a flowering shrub. Summer wore a crown of **grain** ears and carried a sickle and a sheaf. Autumn bore a **basket** of fruit and bunches of **grapes.** Winter stood bareheaded beside a leafless tree.[2]

Buddhist tradition also recognized four

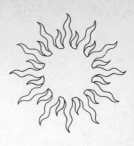

Goddess figures as emblems of the seasons: Vasantadevi, spring; Grismadevi, summer; Saraddevi, autumn; and Hemantadevi, winter. Sometimes these were pictured with human female bodies and animal heads.[3]

1. Koch, 57.   2. Cirlot, 269.   3. G. Jobes 1, 258.

Shadow

The ancients agreed that one's shadow was a more or less detachable part of one's **soul.** The seven souls of an Egyptian included the *khaibut* or shadow. Greeks and Romans said the "shade" (*umbra*) was the part of the soul that went to dwell in the underworld after death, deprived of strength, **voice,** and **blood**—which is why Homer supposed the **ghosts** of the dead to be so hungry for the blood that Odysseus poured out to summon them. A living person's loss of a shadow, however, was equated with loss of the soul. The biblical death curse "their shadow is departed from them" (Numbers 14:9) was intended to make enemies into helpless, soulless zombies.

The idea that soulless creatures like **werewolves** cast no shadows was related to the worship of Zeus Lycaeus (Wolfish Zeus) at his sanctuary in Arcadia. Human bodies lost their shadows in that temple, according to Pausanias, probably to suggest that it was the center of the earth. Similar claims were made by Christians for the temple in Jerusalem, where human bodies cast no shadow at noon because Jerusalem was the center of the earth and the sun hovered directly overhead.[1]

Zeus in his wolf form became an ideological ancestor of werewolves, so of course the latter's soullessness was symbolized by loss of the shadow. Jews continued to fear the "noonday devil" who was supposed to steal one's shadow at noon, or at least to make it so small and weak that one might be attacked by **demons.**[2] Throughout the Middle Ages, both Jewish and Christian lore included many stories about persons who lost their shadows or else gave them away to the devil, as did Peter Schlemihl, whose name thus became synonymous with a fool.[3]

1. d'Alviella, 64.   2. Budge, A.T., 219.
3. Walker, W.E.M.S., 928.

Sun

The popular European tradition usually made the sun male and the **moon** female, chiefly to assert that "his" light was stronger, and that "she" shone only by reflected glory, symbol of the position of women in patriarchal society. However, Oriental and pre-Christian systems frequently made the sun a **Goddess.** The royal families of Japan traced their descent from the Sun Goddess Amaterasu. Before Islam, the Arabs worshiped the

sun as a Goddess named Atthar.[1] According to Tantric scriptures, the sun was nothing more than a garment of light for the Great Goddess.[2] This concept reappeared, oddly, in the Book of Revelation as the "woman clothed with the sun" (Revelation 12:1). Some mystics carried contemplation of the Goddess's garment to such extremes that they made themselves "blinded by the light"— staring at the sun until their eyesight failed —thus achieving sainthood on the theory that having looked at the ultimate brilliance, they could have nothing greater to see.

Vikings also worshiped the sun as a Goddess, Glory-of-Elves, or Sol. The Germans called her Sunna.[3] Among the Celts she was known as Sol or Sul or Sulis. Her rites were celebrated especially on hilltops overlooking springs, like the springs at Bath, which used to be called Aquae Sulis. The Romans set up altars to her under the name of Sul Minerva.[4] Various priestesses dedicated to her entered Celtic mythology as sun women, like Iseult, Grainne, and Deirdre. The Scythian Diana was also a solar deity.[5]

Many of the old pagan festivals involving bonfires, **torches, candles,** and other lights were originally dedicated to the Goddess-as-sun, or to the Goddess as controller of the sun and its cycles.

1. *Larousse*, 323, 408.   2. *Mahanirvanatantra*, xl.   3. Branston, 152.   4. Dames, 154. 5. Markale, 240.

Thunderbolt

In the shape of the thunderbolt **scepter** carried by Assyrian kings, one can see elements of the Oriental **dorje** and the **trident** of lightning wielded by Zeus, Jupiter, Shiva, Keraunos, Pyerun, Perkun, Thunor (Thor) and other storm gods, many of whom had onomatopoeic names sounding like verbal imitations of thunder. The Celtic deity Taranis or Taranus was named from *taran*, the sound of thunder.[1]

The royal scepter tipped with a jewel had phallic significance, related to the worldwide belief that gems hidden in the earth were drops of god-semen, congealed after fructifying the earth's **womb.** The Latin thunderbolt was *Gemma Cerauniae*, the Jewel of Keraunos. Shiva's phallus was the same "jewel" in the genital lotus of his Goddess. Trident-shaped scepters suggested his union with the Triple Goddess.

The image of the phallus as "One-Eyed God" also overlapped with the lore of the thunderbolt. Among the one-eyed Cyclopes was Brontes, whose name means Thunder.[2] The thunderbolt deity was frequently assumed to have lost his life upon entering the earth. His act of self-sacrifice gave life to earthly creatures. Hence the Hebrew phrase, *abreq ad habra*, "hurl your thunderbolt even unto death." The phrase was corrupted into a classic magical invocation: abracadabra.[3]

1. Green, 66.
2. Graves, G.M. 2, 384.
3. Cirlot, 2.

Volcano

Like any other impressive or fearful aspect of nature, volcanoes have been objects of worship for human beings from the earliest Stone Age. In the islands of the Pacific, many of which are of volcanic origin, the Great Mother herself was located in volcanic cones where she regenerated the dead in her **cauldrons** of eternal fire. Malekulans believed that the dead live on in the fire of volcanos, never burning, but conscious only of "bliss." Japan's ancestral Fire Goddess, Fuji, ruled the cauldron of the volcano Fujiyama, a holy place of pilgrimage to this day.[1] The similar Fire Goddess Pele of Hawaii also kept the souls of the dead in volcanic afterworlds, as did her northern European counterpart Hel, Goddess of the fiery underworld that became the Christian hell, although it was not a place of punishment originally. The Germans said that Mother Hel was a fire mountain, and the emperor Theodoric became immortal by entering her womb by way of a volcano. The pagan traditions were diabolized; some medieval authorities declared that all volcanoes were entrances to hell.[2]

Yet the original Yahweh seems to have begun as a volcano god also. Mount Sinai, where Moses encountered him, was the seat of a Midianite god who had formerly dwelt in the volcano Jebel-Al-Aqra, in the Midianites' earlier homeland.[3] He was also identified with the local moon god, **Sin,** after whom the mountain was named. The appearance of Yahweh as "a pillar of cloud by day, and a pillar of fire by night" (Exodus 13:21–22) certainly suggests a volcanic spirit.

The word *volcano* comes from the Latin volcano god Vulcan, or Vulcanus, derived from the older Cretan deity Velchanos. He was said to be a great smith and metalworker, whose forges in Latium lay under Mount Vesuvius or Mount Etna. He manufactured **thunderbolts** and other weapons for the gods. His Greek counterpart was Hephaestus, the lame smith who married Aphrodite, defended his mother Hera against Zeus, shared a temple with **Athene,** was associated with the Amazons, was helped by "golden women" in his Lemnian workshop, and was thrown down from heaven on account of his rebellion, just as "light-bringing" Lucifer was thrown down by God.[4] In general, there seems to be ample reason to regard the volcano deities as prepatriarchal and more Goddess-oriented than otherwise.

1. Campbell, *P.M.*, 336, 450. 2. Borchardt, 242. 3. Walker, *W.E.M.S.*, 133. 4. Graves, *G.M.* 1, 87.

Waste Land

The Waste Land theme appeared in European poetry and symbolism just after the centuries of the crusades and the opening of trade routes to the Middle East. In those centuries, European travelers saw some of the world's most barren deserts and heard the explanations of some of the Sufi mystics and others who opposed orthodox Islam. The earth had become barren, they said, because the new religion neglected the old worship of the Mother, and the land lay under her curse of sterility.

The idea took root in the rural, agricultural paganism still prevalent beneath the surface of European feudal society. Fear of bringing on a Western version of Arabia Deserta may be found behind the myths of the **Grail** cycle and the Arthurian legends. According to these stories, the Waste Land was caused by brutal men who violated the priestesses of the **wells** and springs, and stole their golden **cups.** "As a result the land became barren; the trees and flowers withered and the waters dried up."[1]

New Christian laws were depriving women of their property rights, so that "orphaned maidens" and disinherited widows gathered together in "castles of damsels," awaiting the coming of the Desired Knight or chivalrous savior who would restore correct reverence for mother-right and for Mother Earth.[2] This was both an economic and a spiritual hope, never realized except in poetic fiction of the Grail cycle, which abruptly ceased when the Grail became wholly assimilated as a Christian symbol.

The imagery of the Waste Land has been described as a landscape of spiritual death, where myths are rigidly patterned by dogma instead of evolving from the real needs and feelings of the people. "And this blight of the soul extends today from the cathedral close to the university campus."[3] Even though the earth may retain her fertility and the waters may continue to flow, something vital is lost when patriarchy becomes dominant and domineering.

1. Darrah, 70.   2. Jung & von Franz, 229.
3. Campbell, C.M., 373.

Water

"Water of Life" was once identified with the cosmic **womb,** "the Deep" of many different creation myths. To Thales of Miletus, water was the *arché,* the First Cause at the beginning of all things.[1] Zosimus said, "Without divine water, nothing exists." Porphyry said the souls of the dead are drawn to water, because it is the essence of rebirth.[2]

Water sources were very important in Celtic religion. In some areas the local Goddess of springs was named Coventina, "She of the Covens," appearing in

the typically Celtic trinitarian form of three persons in one. Especially revered in Britain were the waters of the Goddess Sulis at Bath, and the spring and **grove** of the Goddess Arnemetia at Buxton, which used to be named Aquae Arnemetia, "Waters of the Goddess of the holy grove."[3]

Water flowing in two—or sometimes four—streams from the Goddess at the time of creation was a common version of the Rivers of Paradise symbol. The Goddess was shown holding either her own **breasts,** or a **jar** with two streams. The old idea that water could absorb spirits led to the medieval custom of pouring water from all the jars and pitchers after a death in the house.[4] There was an odd parallel to the sequence of the **Tarot cards'** "Greater Secrets" (trumps), where the card of Death is followed by a water-pouring angel; another card, the Star, shows the Naked Goddess pouring water from her two jars onto the earth and sea.

Hindu compendia like the *Tantrasara* declared that **baptism** in water was more effective than any mantra or prayer for protection against enemies, catastrophes, and evil spirits.[5] Water baptism was such a commonplace magical rite that Christians copied it from the pagans and have used it ever since. Another widely copied tale was that of the holy man who could demonstrate power over water by walking on its surface without sinking. Buddha and other Oriental sages maintained that a holy man highly

skilled in yoga would be able to walk on water.[6] The Greek hero Iphiclus could not only walk on water; he could also run over a field of grain without bending the stalks. The god Poseidon claimed such power over the sea that he could even make his horses gallop over the surface of the waves without sinking.[7] So many magicians made the water-walking claim that the satiric poet Lucian put it into the mouth of his mock wizard.[8] The story of Jesus' water-walking was based on precedents like these.

1. Campbell, *Oc.M.*, 181.   2. Cirlot, 85, 347. 3. Green, 80, 153, 165.   4. Trachtenberg, 177.   5. Avalon, 208–209.   6. *Bardo Thodol*, 158.   7. Halliday, 90.   8. M. Smith, 120.

Wind

Because wind was a "male" element, air, in the Indo-European pantheon, many gods were identified with winds. The Vedic Lord of Winds, Vata, evolved into Voten, Wuotan, Woden, and Odin.[1] Under the name of Holy Within, he was adopted by the Christian church as the mythical Saint Swithin. His shrine was located at Win(d)chester, the Latin Venta Castrum or Place of the Winds, and his symbol was the Cross of Wotan.[2] Like Jupiter Pluvius, he was supposed to govern storm winds and **rain.**

The Greeks recognized four wind gods corresponding to the four directions. Medieval symbolists multiplied them to twelve, and pictured them on a wind-rose (corresponding to a compass rose) under the names of Eurus, Solanus, Notus, Auster, Africus, Euroauster, Zephyrus, Stannus, Ireieus, Boreas, Aquilo, and Volturnus.[3] Boreas, the north wind, entered the **Grail** myths as Sir Bors, having been an early god of Britain—known to the Greeks as the land of Hyperboreans: Dwellers at the Back of the North Wind. According to the legend, Bors was a temple child, the son of God, raised by the Lady of the Lake, to be a companion to Galahad during his fatal year of sacred kingship at Sarras. Sir Bors "bedded with a priestess," fathered a hero, then was castrated and pelted with old **shoes,** a traditional marriage symbol arising from pre-Christian customs.[4]

Lucifer inherited most of the old gods' control of the winds, and so became known as Prince of the Power of the Air, given to raising storms. Legends repeated in the Koran claimed that the same demonic power over winds had been possessed by King Solomon, especially when he rode through the air on his flying **throne.**[5]

1. Branston, 109.   2. Brewster, 330.   3. Cirlot, 335.   4. Darrah, 123.   5. Spence, 372.

14

ANIMALS

There is abundant evidence throughout the world that primitive human beings regarded animals as highly spiritual creatures, even deities. The human-bodied, animal-headed gods and goddesses of Egypt were obviously priests and priestesses costumed as animal spirits, wearing elaborate headdresses and masks that probably convinced the common folk that what they saw was an actual deity. In the same manner, native sacred dancers in many areas today enact the roles of mystic animals, wearing costumes and masks and imitating the animals' movements. Amalgamation of human and animal forms even persisted into Christian iconography, for example in the exuberant profusion of monstrosities that were supposed to inhabit hell: the old half-animal gods turned demon and became men with horns, tails, and the legs of goats.

One of the commonest expressions of primitive religion is totemism, the identification of a whole tribe of people with some animal ancestor, deified but still considered spiritually immanent in every member of the tribe. Totemism dates back to the period when men knew nothing of biological fatherhood. It was thought that clan mothers, by eating, touching, or looking at a certain animal, could become impregnated by the animal spirit and transmit that spirit to all their descendants. "When a woman first felt herself to be pregnant the object, whether animal or plant, which occupied her thoughts or fancy at the time was believed by her to have implanted itself into her, and would be born through her in human form."[1] In this way animals came to be viewed as tribal fathers. The Arunta tribe, for example, declared every newborn a reincarnation of the spirit-animal totem ancestor. They maintained that human sexual intercourse does not beget a child. It only "prepares" the mother to receive the sacred animal spirit.[2]

Sometimes totem animals were avoided as food; sometimes they were eaten as holy communion, on ceremonial occasions. Early Israelites avoided pork, because the pig formerly had religious significance as a theriomorphized god, as it did also in Egypt, Syria, Asia Minor, and India. The totem animal always embodied the deity, and thus was declared taboo (Latin *sacer*, meaning both "holy" and "unclean") until such times as it could be ritually slaughtered and its flesh offered to all of its "children" together. The animal deity was often a substitute for the sacred king or savior god cannibalistically eaten, giving his life to redeem his people. This basic idea, of which a version still exists today in modern society, underlies all of the ancient world's ceremonial butcherings: the *taurobolium*, the horse sacrifices, the offerings of goats and rams to deities whose heads wore the same horns, the biblical substitution of lambs and kids for the expected sacrifice of firstborn children, the *agnus dei*. Human and animal worlds

ASS
statuette from Ur

intersect everywhere. At all points of intersection, human beings have both worshiped and destroyed their nonhuman friends (or enemies), and at all times have made symbols of them.

Heavenly animals still dwell in the zodiac ("circle of animals") and elsewhere in the sky: Aquila the eagle, Draco the dragon, Lepus the hare, Serpens the snake, Delphinus the dolphin, Corvus the crow, Hydra the sea serpent, Cygnus the swan, Cetus the whale, Monoceros the unicorn, Columba the dove, Ursa Major and Minor the bears, and Canis Major and Minor the dogs. The Moslems placed ten famous animals in heaven among the stars: Abraham's ram, Balaam's ass, Balkis's lapwing, Jonah's whale, Mohammed's Alborak, Moses's ox, Noah's dove, Saleh's camel, Solomon's ant, and the dog of the Seven Sleepers.[3] Juno's peacock is there too, and the winged horse of the Muses. In fact there seem to be more animals in the celestial regions than heroic-human or deity forms. Surely this is significant.

1. Whittick, 150.   2. Crawley 2, 222.   3. G. Jobes 1, 98.

Ass

North Africa and the Fertile Crescent countries bear abundant mythological and iconographic evidence of totemic worship of the wild ass (onager) and its domesticated cousins. One of Egypt's earliest deities was the ass-headed god Set (biblical Seth), an alter ego of Horus and a crucified sacred king.[1] Palestine was named for the same deity under his Roman title of Pales, who was sometimes said to be both male and female and was identified with **Vesta** as a guardian of flocks and herds.[2] Palestine's God was once given the same form as Pales or Set, a man's body with an ass's head. The Hebrew version of the Messiah, Iao, was said to be Set under another name.[3] Worship of the ass in Palestine is hinted by such biblical stories as that of Balaam (Baal) and his oracular she-ass, and of the official entrance into Jerusalem of Jesus as sacred king, riding a young ass "as it is written" (John 12:14).

Chinese bat spirit,
Han Dynasty

Apart from the ass-headed and ass-haunched figures on the Tarot's Wheel of Fortune, and the old children's game of Pin the Tail on the Donkey (Ass), there is some evidence that worship of the ass persisted into medieval times, half in jest as most pagan customs were preserved. European cathedrals used to celebrate a midwinter Feast of the Ass, when a mother with her infant was costumed as the Madonna and brought into the sanctuary seated on an ass, while the accompanying litany included "hee-haws."[4] The Christmas play also continued the Saturnalian custom of mock-beheading the ass-eared Christmas Fool, who rose again from the dead.

1. Campbell, *M.I.*, 29.   2. *Larousse*, 209.   3. M. Smith, 72.   4. Huson, 115.

Bat

In China the bat means good fortune and great happiness.[1] In Europe, however, bats were often identified with **demons,** which Christian art provided with bat wings. A fresco in the Campo Santo in Pisa, about 1350, showed the Death Goddess as a long-haired woman with a **scythe,** flying over the world on bat wings. She was described as "old shadow of earth, ancient shade of hell."[2]

Bats were the same "demons" who were once pagan ancestors. Some Europeans still repeat the old belief that human souls take the forms of bats when they leave the body during sleep, which is why bats are not seen by day, when people are awake. The association with souls led naturally to a belief that the pagan dead might also become bats, flying about in search of a means of rebirth, or of the blood that was universally supposed to mean the "life" of all creatures (Genesis 9:4). However, the only bats that actually feed on the blood of other mammals are found not in Europe but in South and Central America. Most bats eat only insects or plant products. They do not bite human beings, except perhaps in self-defense; but the teeth of most species are too small to break human skin.

Another popular fallacy is the notion that bats entangle themselves in women's hair. In fact bats expertly avoid all obstructions. Their sonar is so efficient that any bat can avoid a wire as thin as a single hair, even in total darkness. The hair-tangling myth stemmed from the ancient notion that women's hair attracts demons: the same notion that caused Saint Paul to order women to cover their heads in church. See **Hair.**

BEAR
totem of the Goddess Artio,
Berne

Along with snakes and **spiders,** bats have been unjustly maligned by Western symbol-based prejudices. Actually, bats are helpful animals that provide a valuable service in controlling populations of insect pests.

1. Cirlot, 22.   2. Aries, 112.

Bear

The constellation commonly known as the Big Dipper is officially named Ursa Major, the Great She-Bear. Long ago it was the celestial animal incarnation of the Goddess Artemis Calliste, the Beautiful She-Bear, guardian of the pole star or *axis mundi.* Her constellation as seen from northern latitudes never sets below the horizon and is a determinant of the seasons. The bear's tail (pointer stars) lines up due east at nightfall at the beginning of spring, south at the beginning of summer, west at the beginning of autumn, and north at the beginning of winter. Across the Eurasian continent from Greece to China, this constellation was regarded as the **throne** of the Queen of Heaven. Its component seven bright stars were sometimes known as the Seven Sisters.

Though Artemis was a shape-shifter

with many animal forms, the she-bear seems to have been one of her most widely distributed incarnations. She became Artio, the sacred she-bear of Berne, worshiped by the Helvetians in ancient times and still the totemic emblem of that city.[1] In the north, she was the Goddess of the "bear sark," or bearskin shirt, which was supposed to give warriors bear-like strength and courage, thus turning them into *berserkers*, as fearless, tempestuous, and invincible in battle as the she-bear defending her cubs. Two such "cubs" were the little child priestesses dressed as she-bears in the festival of Brauronian Artemis in Attica, perhaps designed to appeal to the Goddess's maternal feelings on behalf of her people.[2] The Trojans also worshiped the Goddess in bear form, declaring that she nourished the infant Paris in the wilderness, before he was discovered and adopted by Trojan shepherds.[3]

In Crete, the two little bear-cub girls grew up to become the twin Ursae, nurses of the infant Zeus when his mother Rhea (another version of Artemis) hid him in the Dictean **cave.** These Ursae were ritually associated with children and the bear-mother cult "frequently in a Semitic connection" also.[4] They were the originals of the two she-bears summoned by Elisha's curse "in the name of the Lord" to tear up forty-two children who had been so ill-mannered as to make

fun of Elisha's bald head (2 Kings 2:24)—
the whole biblical story having been
falsely deduced from an icon of the Ursae
among children.

Where the ancient Cretans worshiped
Artemis as the divine she-bear, the
virgin **Mary** is now addressed as Panagia
Arkoudiotissa, Goddess of the Bear.[5]
Another Christianized form of the Goddess was the mythical Saint Ursula,
based on her pagan Saxon name, Ursel
("She-Bear"), with her "eleven thousand
virgins" who once represented the
stars attending the Queen of Heaven, and
who entered the Christianized story
as an improbable horde of Princess Ursula's handmaidens, slain by the Huns
in the fifth century A.D. This fable was
actually cobbled together by hagiographical clergymen about five centuries
after the alleged event, somewhere between
the ninth and twelfth centuries, and
all sorts of forgeries and manufactured
evidence were composed to substantiate it
for the benefit of Cologne Cathedral.[6]

Remnants of Germanic bear worship
still occur in connection with folk
festivals and seasonal holidays. One of the
notable figures is the man dressed in
a bearskin as the Fastnacht (Shrovetide)
Bear in German villages. No longer a
sacred personage, however, the bear-man

has little to do but dance with all
the village maidens and beg from house
to house for money to buy beer.[7]

1. *Larousse*, 226. 2. Graves, G.M. 1, 86.
3. Rank, 23. 4. Brown, 64, 68. 5. Gimbutas,
200; Duerr, 21. 6. Attwater, 333–334.
7. G. Jobes 1, 549.

Bitch

The female **dog** became a word of insult
in Western civilization because of
her ancient association with **Goddess** religion. Often the Goddess herself was
called the Great Bitch, or her priestesses
described themselves as her hunting
bitches: especially the priestesses of Ar-
temis/Diana, whose original people were
the Alani, "hunting dogs." The nurse of
King Cyrus the Great was a representative
of the Goddess, as kings' nurses had
to be at the time. Her name was Cyno,
meaning "bitch" in Greek, or Spako,
meaning "bitch" in the Median language.[1]

The word *lupae*, "wolf bitches,"
used to be applied to harlot-priestesses in
Rome; and Herodotus described the
wolflike "howlings in the temple" performed by priestesses of **Athene**.[2] The divine queen of Troy escaped death by
transforming herself into "one of those
fearful black bitches that follow Hecate."[3]
Similar Goddess-following, promiscuous

huntresses seem to have kept a foothold in British forest lands, as the Arthurian legends indicate.[4] The English word *bawd*, which came to mean a loose woman, formerly meant nothing more than a hunting dog.[5]

"Son of a bitch" became an insult because it used to be the equivalent of son of a whore, or perhaps even worse, a son of the Goddess—that is, a **devil** by Christian definition.

1. Rank, 29.   2. Herodotus, 270.   3. Graves, G.M. 2, 341.   4. Walker, W.E.M.S., 244. 5. Potter & Sargent, 208.

Boar

Indo-Europeans worshiped the boar as one of the earliest sacrificial god-surrogates. He was identified with Vishnu-the-boar and his three sacrificed boar sons. He was identified with Frey and embodied in Swedish priest-kings who wore boar **masks** as husbands of Freya.[1] He was sacred to the Celtic Goddess Arduinna, patroness of the forests of the Ardennes. He was sacrificed as the Yule pig with an apple in his mouth, and his **blood** begot gods both east and west, in the primitive times when men still believed that only blood could generate offspring because that seemed to be how

women did it.[2] Warriors of northern Europe crested their **helmets** and their **swords** with the boar's image.[3] Greeks sacrificed boars to sanctify oaths by their holy blood. Heracles traded vows with the sons of Neleus over a butchered boar at the Boar's Grave in Messenia. Athletes at the Olympian Games swore on the pieces of a butchered boar not to engage in foul play.[4] Dying gods like Attis, Adonis, and Tammuz were either sacrificed in boar form or dispatched by priests clad in boarskin.[5] The biblical taboo on the eating of pork was based on nothing more than the fact that the wild boar was a sacred totem of the Hebrews seven or eight thousand years ago.[6]

Such a long and complex history amply explains the constant recurrence of the magic boar in folklore and fairy tales, even though the majority of modern folk will never see a wild boar except, perhaps, in a zoo. England still has a number of "Boar's Head" inns and taverns, suggesting that in pre-Christian times the **heads** of sacrificed animals were preserved as oracular fetishes just like the heads of deified ancestral heroes.

1. Gelling & Davidson, 162.
2. Turville-Petre, 147–148.
3. Davidson, G.M.V.A., 98–99.
4. Frazer, F.O.T., 155.   5. Graves, G.M. 1, 72.   6. Reinach, 19–20.

Bull

The Spanish bullfight is one of the last vestiges of ancient sacred games surrounding the formal sacrifice of bulls, who were identified with the greatest gods and the kings embodying them on earth. El, "the Bull" in Phoenicia, was once the supreme Semitic deity.[1] The spirit of El seems to have inhabited King Nebuchadnezzar when he grazed on grass (Daniel 4:33). Israelites used to worship the *shedim*, idols in the form of bulls, probably derived from the Assyrian name of the bull god, Shedu.[2] Bull-leapers of Crete first established some of the classic moves of the bullfight, in times when the kings ceremonially entitled Minos were considered incarnate, for the annual festival, in the *tauros* (bull) and wore bull-head **masks** in the character of the **Minotaur.**

The Roman *taurobolium* or bull-sacrifice was common to the worship of Attis and Mithra, the former associated with the Goddess under her Phrygian name of Cybele, the latter with the same Goddess under her Persian name of Anahita.[3] Just as Christians were "washed in the blood of the Lamb," initiates were "washed in the blood of the Bull," literally, standing under a grating to bathe in the **blood** as the animal's throat was cut. This **baptism** caused the worshiper to be "born again for eternity."[4] The

Mithraic *taurobolium* was supposed to recall the usual totemic premise that all life could arise from a spillage of male blood. Worshipers of Mithra believed that a primal sacrifice of the "Sole-Created Bull" produced the blood that gave birth to all things: another patriarchal effort to eliminate the female principle. However, the classic figure of Mithra sacrificing the original bull seems to have been copied from an earlier figure of the Goddess Kali, the Destroyer, sacrificing a bull as shown in the Ellora caves.[5]

White sacrificial bulls embodied not only Kali's consort Shiva (as "the white bull Nandi"), but also the Druidic oak god, killed at the moment when the sacred **mistletoe** was cut from the tree.[6] A central shrine of this cult in Britain was Bury Saint Edmunds, where the "burial" seems to have been the heads of the annually sacrificed bulls, and the taurine god himself was incongruously canonized as Saint Edmund. The monastery records show that the "martyr" was incarnate every year in a white bull, his virile powers adored by women who "visit the tomb of the glorious martyr St. Edmund to make oblation to the same white bull."[7]

The Presbytery of Dingwall recorded pagan-style bull sacrifices even as late as

the seventeenth century on the holy day of Diana in August, together with adoration of **wells** and holed **stones,** and other local shrines listed as "ruinous chapels" or "superstitious monuments."[8]

> 1. *Larousse,* 74. 2. Beltz, 215. 3. Weston, 138. 4. Angus, 94–95. 5. Ross, 40. 6. Green, 179. 7. Briffault 3, 190. 8. Spence, 355.

Calf

The Egyptian hieroglyphic symbol for a calf was a rather charming little animal in a frisky pose, with its tail up.[1] The calf was actually a deity in Egypt, worshiped as a symbol of Horus, offspring of **Isis** in the form of the Golden Cow. A golden calf called Heru-Nub, "the Horus of Gold," was worshiped at Lycopolis.[2] The Israelites in the wilderness still kept the habit of worshiping the Horus calf. They could not be without him, but contributed all their gold, from which Aaron made them a Horus calf and set up an altar before it (Exodus 32).

When the Goddess was frequently shown in a **cow** incarnation, her son/lover god would naturally take on the aspect of a calf as well as a **bull.** At Catal Huyuk about 6000 B.C., there were images of the Goddess as a woman giving birth to a bull calf.

> 1. Budge, *E.L.,* 60. 2. Budge, *G.E.* 1, 426.

Cat

Cats were sacred to the Egyptians, who named them after their own feline speech, *Mau.*[1] The divine Mother of all cats was the Goddess Bast, whose sacred city of Bubastis was famous for its joyous and elaborate festivals.[2] The Greeks identified Bast with Artemis, whose Roman name was Diana, the name that became widely known in the Middle Ages as Queen of Witches. Therefore the cat was identified with witchcraft and (even worse) with Goddess worship, which accounts for its frequent appearance as a witch's **familiar** and an emblem of **Halloween.** The Goddess Freya rode in a chariot drawn by cats, recalling ancient images of the Mother of the Gods, Cybele, in her chariot drawn by two **lions;** and Freya too was suspected of evil magic by patriarchal thinkers.[3]

Superstitious belief in the cat's magic powers has survived into the present day. Some people even go so far as to turn and retreat if they see a black cat crossing their path. The cat's magic was not always malevolent or "bad luck." Albertus Magnus, the teacher of Saint Thomas Aquinas, insisted that a man could become invisible by wearing on his **thumb** the ear of a black cat, boiled in the **milk** of a black **cow.**[4] Apparently the recipe was never tested; or if it was,

COW

Cow Goddess of Egypt, Nut or Hathor

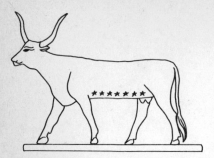

the negative results were ignored. Some people still believe that a cat can smother an infant in the crib, because crib death used to be blamed on vampire-cats sucking babies' breath.

1. Budge, G.E. 2, 61.   2. Larousse, 37.
3. Turville-Petre, 107.   4. Abelard, 56.

Cow

The cow was one of the most common totemic images of the Great Goddess. The animal herself served as wetnurse to the human race. Cattle were first domesticated in order that people might feed themselves and their children on cow's **milk**. Thus, the Goddess in India has always been the sacred cow, "fountain of milk and curds," which meant not only food but also the waters and land masses of the earth itself. The universe was curdled from the primordial Sea of Milk from the Goddess-as-Cow, according to one creation myth. The same story was told in Scandinavia where the Cow of Creation was Audumla, whose name means "Creator of the Earth."[1] From her udder flowed the four primordial rivers (four streams of milk) that nourished the oldest race of beings.[2] In fact, the ubiquitous image of the four rivers of paradise, which appear shortly after the creation even in the Bible (Genesis 2:10–14), seems

to have been based on the observation that a cow's udder has four teats.

The name of the biblical matriarch Leah also means "wild cow," a title of the Mesopotamian Goddess.[3] In Egypt, **Isis-Hathor** was the divine *kau* (cow) whose udder produced the **Milky Way** and all the stars, "the great Cow which gave birth to Ra, the great goddess, the mother of all the gods . . . the Cow, the great lady . . . who existed when nothing else had being, and who created that which exists."[4] She personified the night sky, being named also Nut or Neith, and the stars appeared along her belly.

In Greece, the white Cow-goddess was called Io, the Moon, who wore the three sacred **colors** of the female trinity, white, red, and black.[5] Patriarchal Hellenes invented the story of her rivalry with "cow-eyed" Hera, who was actually another version of herself. The legend of the gadfly sent by Hera to sting Io, and send her galloping over all continents throughout the world, was invented to explain the universality of cow worship. Another legend said Io was watched by hundred-eyed Argus Panoptes ("All-Eyes"), meaning that she was the white moon-cow, focus of the many-eyed gaze of the starry sky. Sometimes the stars were said to be her children, or the child

souls that she produced along with her milk.[6] Another of her Greek names was Europa, mother of the continent of Europe. Her name means "full moon," and she was wedded to the father of gods in the form of a white **bull**.

1. Stone, A.M.W. 2, 140.　2. Branston, 57.
3. Teubal, 99.　4. Budge, G.E. 1, 451, 457, 463.
5. Graves, G.M. 1, 191.　6. Jobes & Jobes, 210.

Coyote

American Indians had great respect for the coyote, representing this highly intelligent animal as a sort of trickster god, very like the figure of Reynard, the trickster **fox**, in European legend. Thus the coyote appears in Indian symbolism as an animal magician, shape-shifter, miracle worker, and often as a totemic ancestor. Because of their nocturnal solo or group "singing," audible for many miles, coyotes were also associated with the moon. Like **wolves**, they have been accused of predations on domestic animals such as sheep, but with little foundation. Coyotes usually prey on small creatures like mice. In common with all other canines, however, they will eat carrion—including the carcasses of sheep or cattle dead of other causes.

According to some Indian traditions, the coyote was the "Opener of the Way"

like Anubis the Egyptian jackal god. He assisted in the creation of the human race, by scratching open the hide of Mother Earth to release the first people from her womb.[1]

1. G. Jobes 1, 377.

Crocodile

Crocodiles were especially worshiped in Egypt, where thousands of carefully mummified crocodiles have been found. Sebek, the primary crocodile god, was sometimes called a reptilian incarnation of Set or Typhon, agent of the death of **Osiris** before his resurrection. But like most other Egyptian gods, Sebek was identified with Ra, who was also another form of Osiris himself.[1]

The illustration shows the crocodile god with the symbols of many other deities. He holds the **ankh** and the royal staff of office, an attribute of Set in the Hyksos period when he ruled the other gods.[2] His elaborate headdress includes the sun disc of Ra, the **ram horns** of Amon, the plumes of Maat, and the **uraei** of the primal serpent Goddess. The crocodile represented Reason, because it can see clearly even when its eyes seem to be veiled by the nictitating membrane.

1. Budge, G.E. 2, 355.　2. Graves, G.M. 1, 283–284.

DEER
Mississippian Indian mask,
8th century A.D.

DOG
mosaic portrait from Pompeii

Deer

Of all the wild animals hunted by human beings, deer may have been the most highly prized: not only for their flesh, but also for their useful **horns** and hides. Deer were always considered magical creatures. The extrusion of horn from their heads was a symbol of powerful life force.[1] Horned deer were the animal prototypes of the Horned God. Medieval wizards expressly preferred parchment made of deer skin for the writing of their letter amulets.[2] Buddha's mission began in a deer park.

Durham Cathedral was founded on the site of an ancient deer shrine. Its name was originally Duirholm, the Meadow of the Deer. It was a pagan pilgrimage center for at least four centuries before its Christianization and the building of its church.[3]

Sacred deer used to be solemnly sacrificed to the Goddess as surrogates for her Horned God and sacramentally eaten. Feasts of venison used to imply the eating of the son of **Venus,** as in the myth of her stag king Actaeon (see **Stag**). American Indians also relished deer meat and made their best clothing from deerskin.

1. Walker, *W.E.M.S.*, 410. 2. Trachtenberg, 144. 3. Brewster, 396.

Dog

It seems that women were the first to domesticate the dog, because dogs were companions of the **Goddess** in many cultures, long before gods or men appeared with canine companions. In Babylon, the dog was the symbol of the Fate Goddess under her name of Gula, "The Great Doctoress," who could cure or cause sickness as she wished.[1] Dogs accompanied Hecate in Greece and the corresponding Queen of the Afterworld in Persia. Dogs were the usual attendants of the Celtic Mother Goddesses. When a god accompanied the Mother, he often took the form of a dog. The Celtic healer god Nodens took on his zoomorphic aspect as a dog.[2] Sirius, the Dog Star, was identified by the Greeks with the Great God Pan, whom Pindar called "the shape-shifting dog of the Great Goddess."[3] In northern Europe, the heavenly moon dogs who carried away the dead were the children of the Goddess Angurboda, "the Hag of the Iron Wood," who also mothered Hel.[4] These were directly related to the Hounds of Annwn and the great black hounds with "eyes like saucers" leading the Wild Hunt of Odin and his ghostly company.[5] Because of their constant association with many ancient versions of the Death Goddess, dogs have been everywhere credited with the ability to see **ghosts** and other spirits who may be invisible to human eyes.[6]

The ancients were also very impressed with canine keenness of another sense, the sense of smell. Pairs of dogs were stationed at the **gates** of death (as on the **Tarot card** of the Moon) to detect the "odor of sanctity" and decide whether the soul could be admitted to the company of the gods. Three-headed Cerberus guarded the door of Hecate's underworld. Anubis the Jackal guarded the Egyptian underworld to sniff each newcomer with his critical nose.[7] One reason the Egyptians were so concerned about packing mummies with sweet-smelling spices and eliminating the scent of decay was that they wanted to be acceptable in olfactory terms. They reasoned that a dog would know more about that than any human, or even any god. The "odor of sanctity" idea passed over into Christian doctrine, which maintained that the corpses of **saints** never stank, but always smelled as sweet as flowers.

With the decline of Goddess worship in the Middle East, the dog tended to be diabolized along with the Goddess's other traditional companions. Like "son of a bitch," the term "dog" became an insulting one. Although Moslems still consider "dog" a mortal insult, there are indications that this prejudice is based on the dog's former sacredness. Berbers still consider the killer of a dog ritually unclean for the rest of his life, the same as if he had murdered a human being.[8]

The frequency with which dogs were cited as **familiars** of witches indicates not only that women never ceased to love their canine pets, but also that the church continued to associate dogs with female-oriented paganism. Ironically, the dog was adopted as a mascot by some of the witches' most enthusiastic persecutors, due to a pun on their name. The Dominicans were known as *Domini canes*, "dogs of God," and represented by a black-and-white dog holding a burning **torch** in its mouth, indicating the order's readiness to put witches and heretics to the fire.[9]

1. *Larousse*, 63.   2. Green, 82, 88.   3. de Santillana & von Dechend, 286.   4. Graves, W.G., 409.   5. Branston, 108.   6. Halliday, 59.   7. *Book of the Dead*, 569.   8. Frazer, F.O.T., 35.   9. Hall, 106.

Dolphin

The name of the dolphin comes from
Greek *delphinos*, which also meant
"womb." It was a totem of Demeter in her
role as Mistress of the Sea, while the
serpent represented her as Mistress of the
Earth. The famous statue called The Boy on
the Dolphin was once a religious image,
depicting the young sun god born
out of the sea, raised up on the back of a
dolphin. At the time, most people
believed that a whale or dolphin was a
large fish; the fact of sea-dwelling
mammals was not known.

According to the classical myth, the
dolphin was placed among the stars as the
constellation Delphinus, because it
played a matchmaking role in winning the
hand of the Sea Goddess Amphitrite
for Poseidon.[1] However, this was a late invention, intended to elevate Poseidon
at the expense of Amphitrite, who was just
another title of the Great Goddess
ruling the sea. "The marriage involved
the interference by male priests with female control of the fishing industry."[2]
Amphitrite was demoted from goddesshood

to being a mere nereid. In Greek art,
nereids were often shown riding over the
waters on dolphins.

Shown on funeral urns, dolphins
represented the soul passing to another
world.[3]

1. Whittick, 231.   2. Graves, G.M. 1, 59,
61.   3. G. Jobes 1, 459–460.

Elephant

One of Yahweh's biblical titles, Lord of
Hosts, was derived from the elephant god
Ganesha, whose name meant exactly the
same.[1] An early version of Yahweh
and his spouse were worshiped as Bull
and Cow Elephant by Jewish mercenaries
of the fifth century B.C. at Elephantine on
the Nile.[2] The Indian elephant god
Ganesha impregnated the Virgin Goddess
Maya, who subsequently gave birth
to Buddha. The same Virgin Goddess
passed into China as Moye, mother of the
primal culture hero Fu-Hi or Fu-Hsi; the
white elephant god impregnated her
by surrounding her with a magic **rainbow**
as she walked near a **river**.[3] In the
West, the Virgin Goddess impregnated by
the Lord of Hosts became the Greeks'
Maia, mother of **Hermes** the Enlightened
One, and of course her more familiar
Christian counterpart as well (see **Mary**).

Elephants were considered symbols of powerful sexual energy in ancient India. Shiva sometimes took the form of an elephant or became the father of an elephant-headed Divine Child. Similarly, Krishna could metamorphose into an elephant in conjunction with his highly sexed consort Radha, whose name means "She-Elephant." The famous "white elephant" (usually painted) of Hindu sacred ritual represented "the dormant sexual energy of the living power."[4] The elephant-headed Ganesha was Christianized as the elephant-headed **demon** Behemoth, still representing sexual energy. Despite such diabolization, medieval traditions continued to regard elephant ivory as a powerful magic. A war horn made of such ivory was mentioned in the *Chanson de Roland*, where it was called an "oliphant." Similar "horns of ivory" figured largely in other medieval romances about knightly battles.[5]

1. Campbell, *Or.M.*, 307.   2. Graves, *W.G.*, 405; Walker, *W.E.M.S.*, 277.
3. Brasch, 139.   4. Zimmer, 108.
5. Cavendish, 218.

Ermine

Ermine is the name given to the weasel-like stoat in winter, when its fur turns white except for a black tail tip. It was the stoat's misfortune that its beautiful white winter coat was much coveted by humans, who thought they had more right to it than its original owner. Even more unfortunately for the animal, ermine fur became a Christian symbol of purity, often shown as clothing for female **saints.** There was a belief that, like the adamantine virgins of *The Golden Legend*, the ermine would simply die if its spotless whiteness became soiled.[1] The furs were so expensive that only the very wealthy could wear them; so ermine became a status symbol for the aristocratic class.

1. Hall, 115.

Ewe

Along with the **ram** gods of the ancient world, their Goddess was sometimes incarnated in the form of a ewe, for the sake of the sacred marriage prior to the ram sacrifice. Her Hebrew name in this form was Rachel, which means "Ewe." According to the Bible, the scheduled sacrifice of Isaac to Yahweh was replaced by the sacrifice of a ram, which

thus "became" Isaac or vice versa. This same Isaac later fathered Jacob, who, having wrestled with "a man who was God" (Genesis 32:30), was renamed Israel. Jacob's marriage to Rachel may well have been based on the ritual marriage of the ram-god-man to the Holy Ewe, for she first appeared on the biblical stage leading flocks of sheep (Genesis 29). Israelites generally counted their wealth in terms of sheep in early biblical times, so the Holy Ewe would have been important to them as a symbol of increase and well-being of their flocks.

The Romanized name of the Holy Ewe was Agna, later Christianized as Saint Agnes, who never existed in human form although she was worshiped as the oldest saint in the canon after the evangelists and apostles.[1]

1. Walker, W.E.M.S., 13.

Fish

Early Christians claimed that their fish symbol was based on the idea that *ichthys* (Greek "fish") was an acronym for "Jesus Christ, Son of God." This rationale was invented after the fact, however; Christians simply copied this pagan symbol along with many others. Ichthys was the name of a son of the ancient Sea-goddess Atargatis, also known as Tirgata, Aphrodite, Derceto, Salacia, Pelagia, or Delphine, whose name meant both "womb" and "dolphin"; all appeared in **mermaid** form.[1] In a way, however, Jesus could be called the same Ichthys as the son of Sea-mother Mari, whose blue robe, pearl necklace, and much-varied name referred to the world's oceans: Maria, Marina, Marian, Mariamne, Myrrhine, Myrrha, Mari-Yamm, Mari-El, and Stella Maris, the Star of the Sea.[2]

The Great Goddess of Ephesus appeared with a fish amulet over her genitals. From the traditions associated with the *vesica piscis,* another version of the fish sign, it is clear that the fish was a female-genital symbol and that its assimilation to Christianity was ill-advised. In Egypt, the fish that swallowed the penis of **Osiris** was sometimes taken as a symbol of the vulva of **Isis,** who was yet another incarnation of the primordial female Deep.[3] Again, the fish sign was constructed of two crescent moons, the conventional representation of the Goddess as the source of all the earth's waters. Fish have always been viewed as "aphrodisiac" food because of their ancient association with the Aphrodite type of Goddess and her sexual implications.

1. Cirlot, 102. 2. Graves, W.G., 438; Walker, W.E.M.S., 584. 3. Budge, G.E. 1, 382.

Fox

In ancient Lydia the totem form of Dionysus or of his human surrogate Orpheus was
a fox. In this animal form the god was
called Bassareus. His priestesses, who wore
fox skins as a badge of their office, were
called Bassarids.[1] A similar fox god
was half-secularized in medieval myths
of the universal trickster Renaud or
Reynard the Fox, who seemed to be an
ordinary animal except that his miraculous exploits were godlike, and he often
talked in a human voice.

Poor Reynard was much hunted for his
(or her) pelt, but in many areas the
fox hunt became a curiously ritualistic
affair, like the bullfight in Spain. It
was regarded as a sport, but such details
as the special costumes, ceremonial
meals, and solemn "blooding" of the fox's
killer point to older and more meaningful
symbolism.

1. *Larousse*, 160.

Frog

Frogs were sacred to the Egyptian midwife
of the gods, the Crone-Goddess Hekit,
prototype of the Greeks' Hekate (Hecate).
The frog probably represented the human
fetus, which it roughly resembles.
Because little frogs, appearing with the
first signs of the annual Nile flood, were
heralds of life-giving fertility in Egypt,
people placed frog amulets on mummies,
to help them find rebirth. Mother Hekit's
"Amulet of the Frog" bore the words, "I Am
the Resurrection."[1]

The Frog Prince of medieval fairy tales
pointed to some remembrance of the
frog's benevolent regenerative powers, although (or perhaps because) frogs
were often cited as the **familiars** of witches.
It was said that a beryl engraved with
the image of a frog would make friends out
of former enemies.[2] Magic books claimed
that a frog's tongue placed under a
man's pillow would force him to speak all
his secrets in his sleep.[3] Because of
their association with water, frogs often
figured prominently in **rain** charms.

1. Budge, *E.M.*, 63.   2. Desautels,
23.   3. Agrippa, 76.

Goat

Probably few other domestic animals have suffered so much sacrificial killing as the goat, not only because people used to relish goat's flesh for the sacred feast, but also because the animal's **horns** were viewed as evidence of godlike *mana*, its skin was useful, and its size manageable. Larger animals like **bulls** and **horses** were sacrificed less often, on somewhat more elaborate public occasions.

In Israel the sins of the tribes were ceremonially loaded onto the head of the scapegoat who represented the god Azazel, "Messenger of the Lord," who took them away each Day of Atonement. The prefix *scape* meant "the Azazel-goat" in the original language.[1] The Horned God Azazel was actually a divine redeemer who took human sins upon himself and atoned for them by his exile and/or death.[2] His Palestinian name was Baal Gad, the Goat Lord, eponymous ancestor of the tribe of Gad.[3]

Sacrifices of goats identified with men and/or gods were common in archaic Greece, giving rise to myths like that of the slain and flayed **satyr** Marsyas, another form of Pan. The oldest Athenian religious festival was the Apaturia, "Feast of Common Relationship," featuring the chthonian Dionysus in a black goatskin,

bearing the title of Melanaigis, which means "black goatskin."[4] In Rome, the sacrificial god of the Mamuralia in the Ides of March was a man dressed in goatskin, led through the streets, and formally flogged as a symbol of earlier atonement sacrifices. The goat-people mythologized as satyrs and **fauns** were originally men identified with the sacred goats, on whose images the medieval goat-horned, goat-hoofed **devils** were modeled. When people continued to worship their goat gods, churchmen denounced them for devil worship. Scandinavians were admonished all the way up to the seventeenth century for the pagan "goat games" associated with religious holidays, yet their symbols persisted. To this day, Scandinavians make the Yule Goat out of straw to serve as a year-end sacrifice.[5] Folk dance patterns have absorbed the ancient *caper*, which meant literally a goat dance, from the Latin word for goat. The same source gave us *capriccio*, caprice, capricious, and Capricorn.[6] There is also the Isle of Capri, once dedicated to the Goat Lord.

1. Whittick, 306.   2. Seligmann, 28.
3. Graves, W.G., 230.   4. Bachofen, 53; Guthrie, 169.   5. *Larousse*, 271.   6. Funk, 253.

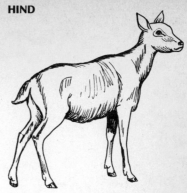

Hare

The Easter Bunny began with the pagan festival of the springtime Goddess Eostre, when it was said that the Goddess's totem, the Moon-hare, would lay eggs for good children to eat.[1] The Easter Bunny still brings eggs to children, though they are now made of chocolate and sugar instead of more nourishing ingredients. Eostre's hare was the shape that Celts imaged on the surface of the full moon, derived from old Indo-European sources. In Sanskrit, the moon was *cacin*, "that which is marked with the Hare."[2] Queen Boadicea's banners displayed the Moon-hare as a sacred sign. Both hares and cats were designated the **familiars** of witches in Scotland, where the word *malkin* or *mawkin* was applied to both.[3]

The hare was a subject of much controversy among fundamentalists and Bible critics of the nineteenth century, when it was noticed that among the Bible's numerous errors was the assertion that the hare is a cud-chewing animal (Leviticus 11:6). The ancients may have assumed this from the hare's habit of rapidly twitching its nose, which may have been mistaken for chewing. At any rate, this and other false statements were cited to refute the doctrine of biblical inerrancy, which the more hidebound religious authorities still maintain. Pope Leo XIII's encyclical *Providentissimus Deus* forbade any admission of erroneous biblical statements. The church's *Dogmatic Constitution* of 1965 again proclaimed God the author of the Bible and all biblical statements "accurate, true, and without errors."[4] In defiance of the church's ruling, however, hares persist in not chewing cuds.

1. de Lys, 117.   2. Baring-Gould, 204.
3. Potter & Sargent, 71.   4. Abelard, 9.

Hind

Hind is another word for a doe, specifically a doe of the red **deer** family, which also provided images of the stag **horns** worn by the Horned Gods of northern Europe. As the divine consort of such a god, the Goddess naturally appeared in the form of a hind. The Celtic woodland Goddess Flidhais habitually took this form; so did the pagan Diana of early medieval romances, incarnate in the White Hind who led men into mystic adventures. In Norse myth, she took her favorite heroes to Hinderfjall, "Hind-Mountain," another name for Valhalla. The Germanic hero Sigurd died in the forest like a hunted

stag, recapitulating the myth of Actaeon, the stag-god of Aphrodite. As an infant he was nurtured by the Goddess in the shape of a hind. She was also the **Valkyrie** who took him to the afterworld.[1] Many old folk songs speak of the dying knight carried away by a magic hind. Saint Giles, a Christianized form of a once-pagan hero, was nourished by a magic hind in a **cave** in the forest of Languedoc.[2]

Hind was also a royal title of pre-Islamic queens in Arabia. The last of these, having the title "Hind of Hinds," was betrayed by her husband into the hands of Mohammedan armies.[3]

1. Turville-Petre, 199. 2. Brewster, 391.
3. Beard, 293–294.

Hippopotamus

Dwellers on the Nile were well acquainted with the hippopotamus and regarded it as a Goddess form in the water, as the **cow** was a Goddess form on land. The divine Hippopotamus Mother was named Taueret or Ta-urt. She was especially associated with the **ankh** or Key of Life and the sign *sa*, meaning life-giving uterine **blood**.[1] She also wore the **horns** and sun disc of **Isis-Hathor**.

Hippopotamus is a Greek word meaning "river horse." The Greeks had no hippopotami in their country, so they were not altogether sure of the animal's shape or habits.

1. d'Alviella, 197.

Horse

With or without wings, the horse used to be a common symbol of the soul journey: a trip to the moon, or to the Other-world, or to the land of the dead where the visitor might learn the great secrets of life, death, and magic, and return to earth with godlike wisdom. According to Islamic tradition, Mohammed rode the wonder horse Alborak, under the guidance of the angel Gabriel, on his famous Night Journey from Mecca to both Jerusalem and heaven. Bellerophon rode the moon-horse Pegasus, who was born of Medusa's **blood,** in an attempt to win immortality. It was claimed that Solomon had a thousand winged horses, and sacrificed nine hundred of them to God.[1] The horse was a special, impressive sacrifice because of its intrinsic value. Only the rich could afford to slay horses in the prime of their working life.

Rome had an annual sacrificial ceremony in which the October Horse was solemnly slain as a surrogate for the ruler. It was also known as the Cut Horse (*equus curtius*) because its tail was cut off and rushed to the temple of **Vesta** to drip blood on the Goddess's altar.[2] Apparently the tail was a substitute for the amputated penis, which was cut from the sacrificed stallion in India and laid between the thighs of the Goddess-embodying queen to "lay seed" on behalf of the fertility of the land and people.[3]

Because the horse was an animal of transition to the other world, it was often regarded as an omen of death. English and German folklore says a dream of a white horse means death.[4] Odin's gray horse Sleipnir was a symbol of death and of the gallows tree.[5] Ghostly gray cloud-horses were the steeds of Odin's "wild hunt," supposedly made up of the souls of the dead, galloping over the treetops. An old pagan tradition said that the dead have their feet on backward. In memory of this, it is still customary in a military funeral to lead a riderless horse with the dead man's boots fixed backward in the stirrups. This used to be the steed who would take the deceased to the underworld. Formerly, the horse was killed and buried in the same grave.[6] The gray horse is still a death symbol in Wales.

The horse was also a symbol of apotheosis. White horses were the choice of Goddess impersonators such as the May Queen, who used to represent Freya at the annual May Riding, while her consort on a black horse represented Frey.[7] The naked lady on the white horse continued to appear each year in traditional processions like that of Coventry, where she was called Godiva, meaning "Goddess."[8] Her ride was considered essential to the welfare of the crops for the season. Her festival was suppressed by Puritans, who may have invented the apocryphal story of Lady Godiva and Peeping Tom; but after the Puritan Commonwealth the annual rite was reinstated, and continued up to 1826.[9] Legendary British "kings" Hengist and Horsa, whose names mean Stallion and Mare, may have been connected with the Riding ceremony.

1. Spence, 372–373. 2. Dumézil, A.R.R. 1, 218–223. 3. Briffault 3, 188. 4. Cirlot, 145.
5. Turville-Petre, 48. 6. de Lys, 261.
7. Gelling & Davidson, 163. 8. Knight, 170.
9. Gifford, 142.

JACKAL
mask of Anubis

LAMB
*paschal lamb from a British
regimental badge*

Jackal

Because of its carrion-eating proclivities,
the jackal used to be revered as a
companion of the Goddess as receiver of
the dead. Like **wolves** and other canines, the
jackal became a guardian of her underworld gates and a **psychopomp** who tended
souls after death. The name of Shiva
meant a jackal, as he was viewed as consort
of Kali the Destroyer.[1] Similarly, Egypt's
jackal god Anubis was the consort of
Nephthys, the underworld aspect of the
Great Goddess (sometimes mythologized as
Isis's dark twin sister). Anubis became
the god of mummification, the keeper of
souls, the spiritual father of sacrificial priests
envisioned in the underworld as jackal-
headed men.[2] His holy city was Canopis,
which means Eye of the Dog, home
of the "canopic jar" used for the **entrails** of
the mummy. In Roman processions
sacred to Isis and **Osiris**, it was the priest
wearing the Anubis mask who preceded the
image of the Goddess in her sacred-
cow form. This priest solemnly impersonated the god "condescending to walk
on human feet . . . rearing terrifically
high his dog's head and neck—that

messenger between heaven and hell."[3] Because he was the guide of souls, Christ was
identified with the jackal god by early
Christian Gnostics.[4]

1. *Mahanirvanatantra*, 113.   2. *Book of the
Dead*, 140.   3. Budge, G.E. 2, 266.   4. G.
Jobes 1, 858.

Lamb

Christian injunctions to be "washed in
the blood of the Lamb" used to mean literal sprinkling with the **blood** of a
firstborn lamb sacrificed to Yahweh in
place of the firstborn son, which the Old
Testament God formerly demanded
(Exodus 13:2, 13). In a reverse substitution, Jesus became the sacrificial Lamb of
God (*agnus dei*) according to the Roman
church. Up to the seventh century
the official image of Jesus was not a crucified man but a lamb, or a **Good
Shepherd** carrying a lamb. The Council
of Constantinople adopted the cross
figure only in A.D. 625, and it was not
immediately obeyed.[1] Seventy years
later the Council of Trullo decreed that
"the representation of Christ, who
takes away the sin of the world, be hence-
forth set up and painted in place of
the ancient Lamb."[2]

The lamb was associated with resurrection long before Christianity. Horace wrote of witches necromantically raising up souls of the dead by sacrificing a black lamb.[3] Black animals were preferred for dealings with the underworld.

A mythical saint based on the lamb sacrifice was Saint Agnes ("Ewe Lamb"), shown in sacred art together with her totem animal. Agnes was enormously popular in the Christian pantheon, her bright reputation in no way dimmed by discovery of the trifling fact that she never existed.[4]

The medieval papacy sold wax cakes called Agnus Dei, stamped with a picture of the Lamb and its flag, carrying the papal blessing, and advertised as surefire protection against death in childbed, drowning, fires, destructive thunderstorms, and other "acts of God."[5] By these highly profitable fetishes, God was invoked as a defense against his own doings; but no one seemed very much bothered by the incongruity.

1. Abelard, 54.   2. Benson, 96.   3. Frazer, F.O.T., 301.   4. Walker, W.E.M.S., 13. 5. Thomas, 31.

Lion

Symbolism usually connected the lion with the **sun.** The lion's tawny color suggested sunlight. The male lion's mane was identified with the long hair-rays of such solar figures as Apollo Chrysocomes ("He of the Golden Locks"), Heracles, and Samson—who was really the Arabic sun god, Shams-On. The lion head, surrounded by a mane of rays, was a solar emblem in Mithraic sun worship. One order of Mithraic initiation was called Lion. The Lion Throne, Simhasana, is still sacred in Buddhism.

Lion symbolism also figured in worship of the **Goddess.** Hathor as the Sphinx was a lion, or lion-headed. She was sometimes called Mehit: the biblical Mehitabel. Cybele, the Great Goddess, rode a **chariot** drawn by a brace of lions. Old images of the naked Goddess often rode a lion. This image was perpetuated in Latin America by the Madonna Leona, or Maria Lionza.[1] An old name for Cornwall was Lyonesse, the country of the she-lion.

Singapore means "city of the lion." Legend says the city was founded by Sri Tri Buana, first of the Malay kings, who claimed descent from Raja Iskander (Alexander the Great). The city was placed where he saw a lion with a white breast, red body, and black head: the classic **colors** of the Triple Goddess, called *gunas* in Hinduism.[2]

Lion images were credited with healing magic by medieval medical texts. It was claimed that a lion carved on jasper would cure fevers and dispel the effects of poison. Carved on **garnet,** the lion could cure all diseases and protect a person from all dangers during travel.[3] Naturally, this would have made the lion symbol popular, if inevitably disappointing.

A story about lions that patriarchal churchmen liked, and often repeated, made the male lion the ultimate life-giver to "his" cubs, rather than their mother lioness. It was claimed by the bestiaries that all lion cubs were born dead, and lay perfectly inert for three days, until Father Lion came to breathe on them, and thus bring them to life.[4]

Another favorite legend of the church concerned St. Jerome's encounter with a lion crippled by a large thorn in its paw. Jerome removed the thorn, and the grateful beast became his devoted companion. The story was trumped up, of course; it was copied from the popular fable of Androcles and the lion, taken from Apion's *Aegyptiaca* (first century A.D.) and retold in the *Noctes Atticae* of the Roman writer Aulus Gellius (ca. A.D. 150); the story also appeared in Aelian's *De natura animalium.*[5] The name of Androcles, which means "famous man" in Greek although the hero was usually depicted as a slave, indicates an even earlier source for all versions of the story.

The conquest of the lion having been the major symbol of strength ever since the myths of Heracles and his Hebraic counterpart Samson, it reappeared on the traditional **Tarot card** of Strength, in the form of a *woman* rather than a man forcing open the lion's jaws.

An archaic connection between the lion and the female principle was particularly offensive to patriarchal scholars, and so is still generally concealed. This was the traditional marriage between the Judeo-Christian Jehovah and the Lion Goddess in Palestine during the fifth century B.C., when they were worshiped together as a divine couple. Local names for the Goddess were Anatha Baetyl, Anat-Bethel, or Ashima Baetyle.[6] Her character seems to have been similar to that of Cybele.

1. Duerr, 162. 2. Cavendish, 79–80. 3. Desautels, 23. 4. Hall, 193. 5. Ibid., 169. 6. G. Jobes 1, 92.

ANIMALS

Mare

Iron Age Britain worshiped the Goddess Epona as the White Mare, who is now called the White Horse as she appears in the famous 370-foot chalk-cut image in an Uffington hillside.[1] She was similar to the Greek/Cretan Leukippe, "White Mare," who was the daytime aspect of Mare-headed Demeter. Her Destroyer aspect was called Melanippe, "Black Mare," otherwise known as Demeter the Avenger (Erinys) in the form of a Night-mare, punisher of sinners. The same title was applied to the Queen of the Amazons, who also appears in Greek myth as Antiope or Hippolyta, "Charging Mare." Epona's name came from Gallic *epo*, in turn from Indo-European *ekwo*, which also gave the Latin *equus*.[2]

Scandinavian witches were said to turn themselves into mares, after the manner of the ancient priestesses who may have worn equine **masks** like Leukippe's mare-headed priestesses. Such witches were called *volvas*.[3] The cult of the divine mare persisted in Ireland up to the twelfth century, when Giraldus Cambrensis described the coronation of a king of Ulster,

involving the king's sexual union with a white mare, which was afterward sacrificed and sacramentally eaten.[4] Pagan religious feasts often used horsemeat, which was otherwise taboo or devoted to the Goddess. Modern prejudice against the eating of horsemeat seems to have developed from Christian condemnation of the old rites.[5]

1. *Larousse,* 225. 2. Markale, 89. 3. Lederer, 195; Turville-Petre, 48. 4. Gelling & Davidson, 92. 5. Davidson, G.M.V.A., 122.

Mascot

A mascot is still an animal symbol, the modern version of a totem or a witch's **familiar**. The word comes from French Provençal *masco*, a masked sorceress, and *mascoto*, "witchcraft."[1] In pagan civilizations the sacred animal **head** or **mask** represented the divine animal identified with the clan: a custom that gave Christian authorities an abundance of animal-headed **demons**. Today, mascots are generally seen at football games, on heraldic crests, in advertising, or on the banners and ensigns of military companies.

1. de Lys, 94.

*Monkey God of India,
Hanuman*

Monkey

When Rama, one of the ten incarnations (avatars) of the god Vishnu, lost his beautiful bride to a marauding **demon,** it was the monkey Hanuman who discovered her whereabouts and led the god to her rescue. As a reward, the monkey was made a god and allowed to grow as big as a mountain. So runs the classical Hindu story. But it is likely that primitive India worshiped the monkey as a divine animal, just as primitive Egypt worshiped the baboon or dog-headed ape. "The cult of the ape is very ancient, and is probably pre-dynastic, in which period dead apes were embalmed with great care and buried."[1]

The popular symbol of the three apes or monkeys with hands on their ears, mouth, and eyes, respectively, bears a strange resemblance to the formula of initiation into the famous Eleusinian Mysteries, which involved "things heard, things tasted, and things seen."[2] The usual interpretation of the figures as "Hear no evil, speak no evil, see no evil" might have been another way of adopting or adapting a pagan triadic image. The monkey was a common medieval symbol of paganism.[3]

1. Budge, G.E. 2, 365. 2. Walker, W.E.M.S., 239. 3. Hall, 118.

Mouse

The mouse was one of the animal symbols or embodiments of the god Apollo, who was sometimes called Mouse-Apollo (Apollo Smintheus). The mouse was also a **soul** symbol in medieval Europe. Wonder-tales were often told by witnesses to a death, saying that the soul of the deceased ran out of his **mouth** in the form of a mouse at the last breath. Alternatively, mice could carry souls into a woman's body for reconception and rebirth.

Small creatures like mice and insects were often believed to carry souls: a notion arising from the popular image of the soul as a small, distinct entity living somewhere within the human body. At the same time, it was often denied that such little creatures reproduced themselves in humanlike ways, by giving birth. Medieval authorities firmly believed and taught that "mice and other vermin" kept up their numbers by "spontaneous generation" out of the mud.[1] Thus, by a paradox that was never analyzed, carriers of souls were born directly from the substance of Mother Earth.

1. Trachtenberg, 182.

OX
*of Saint Luke, from
the Book of Kells*

PANTHER
wall painting, Pompeii

Ox

An ox is a castrated **bull**: another word for a steer. Oxen were much used as beasts of burden in Europe, because of their great strength, although their manner was so slow and plodding as to make the animal a synonym for dullness. In esoteric lore, the ox represented the **earth** element. This may be why it was chosen as the totem animal of Saint Luke when the four evangelists were assimilated to the elemental powers. Hard work slowly but conscientiously performed is the usual interpretation of the symbolic ox.

Panther

The panther (or leopard) was a totemic symbol of Dionysus, whose priests wore panther skins. Its name in Greek meant "All-beast," referring to the god as "the All," which was also another beast version of divinity, Pan. Panthers were much admired in Rome, and were imported from Africa for public displays and games in the arena.

Pig

Jewish authorities sometimes pretend that the biblical taboo on eating pigs' flesh was a sensible precaution against trichinosis or other illnesses. In fact, the biblical authors knew nothing about natural causes of disease and never associated any illness with eating "unclean" meats. The pig taboo was copied by the early Hebrews from their neighbors in Syria and Egypt, where pigs were sacred to the Goddess and were eaten only on ceremonial occasions. The pig was "unclean" in the sense of "set apart," or sacred; it was a primitive Jewish totem.[1] The custom was widely known throughout the Middle East. Lucian said the sacred pigs of Hierapolis were taboo in the usual dual manner: both "unclean" and "holy" at the same time.[2]

Pigs were also holy in Germanic and Irish mythology, both branches of the long-established Indo-Aryan worship of Vishnu as the **boar** god. The Celts associated pigs with the other world and believed them to be the most appropriate food for sacred feasts, not to be eaten at other times.[3] Today's Christmas pig with an apple in its mouth is the descendant of Norse Yule pig sacrifices, when the pig was offered to the gods at the turn of the year.

Another little-known connection

between the formerly holy and the porcine was the classic Greek term for female genitals, *choiros*, which also meant "pig." Greek playwrights made many puns and double entendres based on the interchangeable meanings of "pig" and "cunt."[4] Significantly, in modern English both words are pejorative when applied to a woman.

1. Reinach, 19–20.   2. Crawley 1, 114.
3. Green, 180.   4. Keuls, 353.

Ram

All over the world, the ram was one of the most popular animal incarnations of the phallic god. Egypt's ram god Amon was addressed as "the virile male, the holy phallus, which stirreth up the passions of love, the Ram of rams."[1] A common Middle Eastern metaphor for sexual intercourse was "the Ram Caught in the Thicket," of which some literal graphic examples were found in Sumeria. The phrase is repeated in the Bible (Genesis 22:13), where the ram after being "caught" serves as a sacrificial animal to replace Isaac, who was about to be ceremonially murdered by his father. A similar Greek myth had the ram of the Golden Fleece replace young Prince Phrixus on the altar.

Phallic gods were sacrificial victims especially at atonement festivals at the turn of the year, becoming "saviors" as they bore away the people's sins. Amon the Holy Ram played this part of sin bearer in Egypt. The ram Aries opens the zodiacal year in March because that used to be the time of atonement festivals in Rome. The ram's horn (Hebrew *shophar*) was blown to signal destruction of the old aeon and the institution of the new. The ram's horn used by Joshua to blow down the walls of Jericho was another example of such destructive magic.

Ultimate destruction was associated with the blowing of the Last Trump on the horn of the Norse god Heimdall, whose name means "ram."[2] He too was a sacrificial Horned God and a symbol of virility, begetter of all the Viking castes when he lay with all three aspects of the Triple Goddess Earth.[3] During the Middle Ages, men continued to believe earnestly in the virile powers of the ram, whose meat, horns, hooves, testicles, and other parts were often ingested as fertility charms.

1. Budge, G.E. 2, 64.   2. Davidson, G.M.V.A., 173.   3. Turville-Petre, 150–153.

Salamander

Alas for the poor salamander! These helpless, harmless, pretty little creatures have been burned to death in untold numbers only because of persistent human symbolism, which maintained for thousands of years that salamanders are born of the fire **element** and are therefore impervious to flames. Along with the **gnomes** that represented earth, the undines that represented water, and the **sylphs** that represented air, salamanders were called elemental spirits. Learned men wrote in textbooks that salamanders live happily in fire and suffer no injury, so of course they were often thrown into fire to demonstrate the miracle. The fact that they were invariably burned to a crisp seemed to make little impact on the durability of the belief.

Serpent

The letter S was one of the oldest symbols of serpenthood, both in its shape and in its sibilant sound; and the serpent was one of the oldest symbols of female power. Woman and serpent together were considered holy in preclassic Aegean civilization, since both seemed to embody the power of life. Serpents were considered immortal because they were believed

to renew themselves indefinitely by shedding old skins. It was the mother of all gods, the Earth Goddess Gaea, who first founded the Delphic ("Womb") **oracle** and inspired its original Pythonesses or divinatory serpent-priestesses, according to Homeric hymns. Hesiod referred to her as Gaea Pelope, the female serpent.[1]

The biblical Nehushtan was a deliberate masculinization of a similar oracular she-serpent, Nehushtah, Goddess of Kadesh (meaning "Holy"), a shrine like that of the Pythonesses. Israelites apparently violated the sanctuary and raped its priestesses, but "Moses and Yahweh had to placate the angry serpent goddess of Kadesh, now deposed, by erecting her brazen image. . . . Mythologically, the serpent is always a female divinity."[2]

In India, the "Mother of All that Moves" and Goddess of the Earth sometimes bore the title of Sarparajni, "Serpent Queen." As the female serpent Ananta the Infinite, she enveloped all gods during their death-sleep between incarnations. As the female serpent Kundalini, she represented the inner power of the human body, coiled in the pelvis like woman's organs of life-giving. It was—and still is—the aim of male Tantric sages to awaken the female Kundalini serpent in their own bodies, through physical, mystical, and sexual exercises and through meditation on the female principle.

Among the oldest predynastic Goddess figures in Egypt was the serpent-mother Iusaset, or Ua Zit, or Per-Uatchet, whom the Greeks called Buto. Pyramid Texts say she is the Celestial Serpent, giver of the food of eternal life.[3] Her symbol, the **uraeus,** meant both "serpent" and "Goddess." She was also Mehen the En-veloper, the female serpent like Ananta who enclosed the **phallus** of Ra the sun god every night. There are mythic indications that this nightly sexual communion with the serpent power of Mother Earth was at times considered the real source of Ra's renewed power to light up the world again each day.

The Middle East used to regard the female serpent as the embodiment of en-lightenment, or wisdom, because she understood the mysteries of life. In Arabic, the words for "snake," "life," and "teach-ing" are all related to the name of Eve—the biblical version of the Goddess with her serpent form, who gave the food of enlightenment to the first man.[4] Of course, in the Bible both Eve and her serpent were much diabolized; but Gnostic sects of the early Christian era retained some of the older ideas about their collaboration concerning the fruit of knowledge. Some sects worshiped the snake as a benevolent Female Spiritual Principle, who taught Adam and Eve what they needed to know about God's duplicity, saying, "You shall not die; for it was out of jealousy that he said this to you. Rather, your eyes shall open, and you shall become like gods, recognizing evil and good."[5] The "arrogant ruler" (God) cursed the woman and her snake, declaring that they must be enemies to one another instead of collaborators.[6] But the Gnostics honored Eve and the serpent for providing the essential knowl-edge that made human beings human.

Naturally, the serpent was also mascu-linized and often viewed as Eve's first consort. Gnostics called this serpent Ophion, or the Aeon of Light, or Helios, or Agathodemon, which meant the Great Serpent of Good, as opposed to Kakodemon, the Great Serpent of Evil.[7] His worshipers were sometimes known as the Brotherhood of the Serpent. Their writings said: "Thou who risest from the four winds, thou friendly good demon, glittering Helios, shining over the whole earth, thou art the great serpent who lead-est the gods."[8]

Several other mythologies also had the **Tree of Life** or Tree of Knowledge guarded by a serpent sacred to the God-dess, such as Ladon, the mighty serpent who guarded Mother Hera's life-giving **ap-ple** tree in the Garden of the Hesperides. The intimate relationship between the Goddess

SOW
from an Egyptian bronze

and her serpent consort was often believed to be the reason for his deathlessness. Gnostic mysticism turned the Great Serpent into **Ouroboros,** the great earth dragon living forever in the uterine underworld. A symbol of his cosmic world-creating seed was the round, spiny sea urchin, which the Celts called "serpent's egg."[9] Some showed the angel Raphael as a Wise Serpent.

Christians adopted the Great Serpent as a form of their devil; yet the life-giving powers of the serpent retained popularity in secret books of magic and *materia medica.* As late as the eighteenth century A.D., Arnold de Villanova declared that stags are known to reverse the effects of old age and restore their youth, simply "by feeding on vipers and serpents."[10]

1. La Barre, 69.   2. Beltz, 119.   3. Lindsay, 54.   4. Shah, 387.   5. Robinson, 153–155. 6. Pagels, 31.   7. Cirlot, 276.   8. Campbell, P.C.M., 29.   9. Cirlot, 269.   10. Spence, 140.

Sow

The White Sow was one of the most popular and widely distributed animal forms of the Goddess. **Astarte,** Cerridwen, and Demeter appeared as sows. One of Freya's numerous names was Sýr, "the Sow."[1] A carving at the Tarxien temple on Malta shows a sow with thirteen teats, a lunar animal symbolizing the thirteen annual lunations.[2] Thirteen became a "bad luck" number only because of its ancient association with lunar Goddess worship.

Buddhists still speak of Marici, the Diamond Sow, a Great Goddess seated on her lotus throne attended by seven pigs. She is called Glorious One, Sun of Happiness.[3] The brilliant whiteness of the divine sow was perceived in the white and shiny surface of the eminently female-symbolic **cowrie** shell, which the Romans named *porcella,* "little sow." From this word for whiteness and shininess came our word *porcelain.*[4]

The brilliance of the White Sow and her seven porcine attendants is prominent in the Celtic myth of the Princess Goleuddydd, "Bright Day," mother of Culhwch, whose name meant something like "womb, or hiding place, of the pig." Though the myth was partly Christianized, it retained the essential episode of

*stag dancer, Les Trois Frères,
ca. 14,000 B.C.*

Goleuddydd giving birth in a sow's
lair. "Obviously she is the sow-mother, the
sow Goddess, and Culhwch is the
young hog that she carries in her sow's
hiding-place, her womb." Later, Culhwch
stole a **comb** from the head of the
magic boar, Twrch Trwyth, who may have
been a sow originally; because "he"
lay in "his" lair with "his" seven piglets—
something that only a female pig would do. [5]

The Welsh saints Dyfrig, Kentigern,
Cadog, and Brynach all were said
to have founded monasteries at places
where they were led by a magic White
Sow. [6] This is fairly good evidence that all
of them were only pseudosaints, or
loosely Christianized versions of earlier
pagan heroes, the men of the Sow.

1. Turville-Petre, 168.   2. Pepper & Wilcock,
75.   3. Waddell, 218, 233, 361.   4. Leland,
102.   5. Markale, 94–96.   6. Cavendish, 200.

Stag

The stag was probably one of the earliest
versions of the Horned God as sacrificial
consort of the Goddess of woodland
creatures, such as Artemis/Diana. (See
Hind.) As Actaeon, he was killed by **dogs**
under the Goddess's orders, after he
was permitted to see her without her **veils:**
a mythic transformation of the sacred
marriage. Horned animals, especially
stags, were associated with male sexuality. [1]
Phallic amulets were often carved of
staghorn. Because of its treelike **horns** the
stag was also depicted as a male spirit of the
forest. [2] The famous stag-man of the
Les Trois Frères cave paintings hints at a
stag cult among forest-dwelling people more
than fourteen thousand years ago.

The Christianized version of the stag-
horned **devil** was modeled on festival costumes like those of the Scandinavian
Julebuk (Yule Buck), a typical Horned God
figure. Clergymen insisted that a girl
who danced with him at the annual festival had danced with the devil. [3] Nevertheless, the authors of Christian bestiaries often
made the stag symbolize Christ, because of
its association with pagan savior gods,
and also because the animal was hunted
and slain to give its **blood** for humanity—
that is, as food. The Christ image
led to an unaccountable but very widespread belief that stags will kill and eat

snakes: a belief having no foundation whatsoever in fact, but only a rather rickety foundation in an appealing analogy to Christ destroying the devil.[4] Further attempts to Christianize the stag god appeared in the legends of at least two phony **saints,** Eustace and Hubert, of whom the same story was told: each was converted while out hunting, upon meeting a white stag with a crucifix between its horns, from which the Christ figure spoke to each saint-to-be.[5] Eustace became the patron saint of hunters, Hubert of hunting dogs. Since neither saint ever really existed, it is likely that they were drawn from minor pagan deities of the hunt.

1. Walker, *W.E.M.S.*, 409. 2. Green, 182–184. 3. Miles, 202. 4. Williamson, 109–110. 5. Hall, 117, 158.

Toad

Unlike **frogs,** which are smooth-skinned, toads are knobby and "warty." This gave rise to one of the most durable sympathetic-magic superstitions about toads, namely, that handling them will cause warts or other bumps and knobs on human skin.

Like frogs, toads seem to have been linked with rebirth magic. Deep burial pits of the first century B.C. in France were found to contain the bones of toads, as if the deceased might find them necessary in the afterworld.[1] The Aztecs made the toad a death symbol, related to the underworld womb of regeneration. American Indians said the wife of the sun is a Toad Goddess. In China, she was a three-legged toad dwelling in the moon, causing eclipses.[2]

Toads acquired a malignant reputation in Europe because of presumed connections with witchcraft. Although toads are quite harmless, the skin secretions of some species contain a poison, bufotenine, supposedly used in witches' potions. In the fifteenth century, churchmen accused the witches of Arras of making flying ointment out of toads that were fed on holy wafers stolen from the church.[3] It was claimed, however, that toads burned to ashes would lose their poison and become medicinal.

The so-called "horned toad" of the American southwest is not a toad at all, but a lizard. It has the peculiar ability to squirt a thin stream of blood from the corners of its eyes when disturbed. Despite this unsettling habit, however, the "horned toad" is easily caught and tamed and makes an acceptable pet.

1. Green, 133. 2. G. Jobes 2, 1582. 3. Duerr, 139, 146.

Tortoise

One of the oldest and most durable
Oriental beliefs was that the earth was
supported on the back of a gigantic tortoise, an animal Atlas underlying all the
abysses of the seas and the roots of
mountains. Some Hindu myths speak of
"Old Tortoise Man" as the father of
all creatures and the mate of the primal
Goddess of the watery Deep.[1] Others
maintain that this world-supporting tortoise was one of the incarnations of
Vishnu. Western mythologies identified
him with the ubiquitous Underground
God. The Greek name for his realm, Tar-
tarus, was derived from the word for
a tortoise, *tartaruga*. The Greeks held that
the tortoise was sacred to **Hermes,** who
created the first **lyre** from tortoise shell.[2]
This was a magical lyre capable of echo-
ing the basic harmonies of the **spheres.**
As Hermes Trismegistus of the alchemists,
the same Underground God was
called *spiritus tartari*, spirit of the underworld, whose essence was tartaric acid.

The world-supporting tortoise was a
symbol of eternal life—and therefore of
human longevity—in Japan, where it was
called *kame*, the Shinto sacred-tortoise
emblem here reproduced.[3]

1. Zimmer, 104. 2. Green, 169.
3. Lehner, 44.

Whale

Jonah's whale is described in the Bible as
a "fish," because writers of that period (and
for many centuries afterward) were
unaware that whales are mammals. The
whale of the original Jonah story was the
Babylonian Sea Goddess Derceto, "The
Whale of Der," who swallowed and gave
rebirth to the god Oannes. The same
Derceto was the mythical mother of Babylon's founding queen, Semiramis (Sam-
muramat). In this story and other ancient
scriptures, the whale appears as a
symbol of "the world, the body and the
grave."[1]

Swallowing by the whale indicates an
initiation rite, leading to rebirth. The
Finnish hero Ilmarinen was similarly
swallowed by a giant fish to be reborn. A
variant of the story shows that the fish
was really a **womb,** for Ilmarinen was
swallowed by the giant Hag of Hiisi. Similarly, the Polynesian hero Nganaoa
went into the belly of a sea monster and
returned therefrom. Such imagery
depicts "the belly of a giantess, of a Goddess, of a sea monster, symbolizing
the chthonian womb, cosmic night, the
realm of the dead."[2] Significantly, a tenth-
century Bible plainly said that Jonah

lived three days in the *womb* of the whale.[3] Christian exegetes took this as a prophecy of Jesus' three days in the womb of the earth, and subsequent resurrection.

1. Cirlot, 350. 2. Eliade, 64. 3. Potter & Sargent, 180.

Wolf

The wolf was one of the most popular clan totems in pre-Christian Europe, as indicated even now by the prevalence of names like Wolf, Wolfe, Wulf, Wulfstan, Wolfram, Wolfburg, and so on. Many tribes "turned themselves into wolves" periodically at religious festivals, by wearing wolf **masks** and wolf skins.[1] Even in Renaissance times, certain Irish tribes were said to become wolf-people at Yuletide. In Livonia it was claimed that certain witches were regularly transformed into wolves when they passed through a magic pool.[2] It is easy to see where **werewolf** stories began, in legends about sacred wolves and their pious imitators. Just as Africans could "become" lions in their ritual dances, and American Indians could "become" coyotes or deer in theirs, so the people of old Europe "became" wolves, bears, deer, and other familiar wild animals.

Often the Goddess was herself the Great She-Wolf, as in the primitive Roman cult of Lupa or Feronia, inherited from Sabine matriarchy. Sometimes known as "Mother of Wolves," she was also the divine midwife and first of the Vestals, Acca Larentia, mother of the *lares* or ancestral spirits.[3] Her antique statue in the Lupercal grotto was later provided with images of the infants, Romulus and Remus, whom she was supposed to have nursed. She was annually honored at the Lupercalia (Festival of the She-Wolf), when youths dressed in wolf skins ritually purified the Palatine towns.[4]

In Egypt, either Horus or Anubis was identified with the archaic wolf god Up-Uat, offspring of **Isis**-Nephthys. His title was Opener of the Way or Opener of the Body, a customary designation for the Goddess's firstborn child.[5] The frequent connections between Goddess figures and totemic wolves may be taken as another indication that it was women rather than men who first established relationships with wolves and eventually domesticated them.

1. Herodotus, 244. 2. Scot, 72. 3. Rank, 45–46. 4. Wedeck, 174. 5. Frankfort, 26.

Worm

The word *worm* used to be applied to
many different kinds of creatures: snakes,
caterpillars, millipedes, maggots, and even
lizards with legs, as well as mythical
dragons, in addition to true worms such as
earthworms. "The Worm That Never
Dies" was a common symbol of the corpse-
eating earth, meaning both the mystic
subterranean **Ouroboros** serpent and the
real corpse-eating grave worm or mag-
got—which was not a worm at all, but the
larva of a fly.

A recurrent feature of medieval folk
ballads was the Laidly Worm (or Loathly
Worm), one of many incarnations
of the Great Serpent. Sometimes, **Lamia**-
like, the Worm put on the shape of a
female or male human lover bent upon
tempting a victim into the underworld. In
Norse mythology, the Ouroboros was
named Midgard-Worm. Midgard was the
plane of Earth, enfolded in the coils
of the Worm, who would fight against the
gods at Ragnarok (Doomsday). According
to the Priestess's Prophecy, the god
Thor and the mighty Worm would destroy
each other in the final battle.

15

BIRDS

Human beings have always watched and envied the flight of birds, longing to rise into the air of heaven as birds seem to do, to move with similar swiftness, to investigate the mysterious realms beyond the clouds. Therefore, many cultures made birds symbols of the departed soul, or messengers from heaven, or carriers of occult secrets. To learn the language of birds was a prominent metaphor for mystic enlightenment. To fly up like a bird, in the state of holy trance, was sometimes a prerequisite for initiation.[1] To the Romans, the word *aves* meant both "birds" and "ancestral spirits." Birds were generally regarded as givers of omens and enlightenment, just as the ghosts of ancestors did likewise.

Goddesses and gods, too, had many bird forms. Angels, of course, were always birdlike if not actual birds, like the vultures or ravens who took the dead to the sky. Celtic fairies were supposed to have bird wings. Norse Valkyries wore magic feather garments owned by the Goddess Freya. The feather garments and ornaments of priesthoods from Siberia to Central America were connected with birdlike flight as a symbol of spirituality. In occult lore, birds and bird feathers often represented the air element, which was also the home of invisible souls, gods of the winds, and in several traditions the very essence of the supreme deity.[2]

The best known, if least probable, of the stories about Saint Francis was that of his taming of all the wild birds through his preaching. When he commanded the birds to express their praise of God, they all flew up into the air in the formation of a great cross.[3] Undoubtedly this story was drawn from earlier images of the pagan psychopomp, such as Hermes, leading flocks of souls in the form of birds. The savior god Orpheus, too, was credited with the ability to charm birds and converse with them.

1. Lindsay. 191–192. 2. Guthrie, 136, 142. 3. Hall, 132.

Ba

The *ba* was one of each person's seven souls, according to Egyptian belief. Its usual form was that of a human-headed bird. This image is linked to the ancient, worldwide concept of ancestors and ancestral divinities in bird shapes. Egyptian tombs had small passageways from inner chambers to the upper air, not for ventilation, but for the presumed goings and comings of the *ba* in its birdlike life after death.

Divination by consulting birds (that is, the souls of the dead) was common throughout Greece, Rome, and northern Europe because of the belief that all birds once lived on earth in human form and gave omens to those presently living on earth who were able to understand them. For this reason, folklore in all these areas emphasized the importance of learning to comprehend the magical language of birds.

Cock

It is no coincidence that "cock" is slang for "penis." The cock was a phallic totem in Roman and medieval sculptures showing cocks somehow transformed into, or supporting, human penises. Roman carvings of disembodied **phalli** often gave them the legs or wings of cocks. Hidden in the treasury of the Vatican is a bronze image of a cock with the head of a penis on the torso of a man, the pedestal inscribed "The Savior of the World."[1] The cock was also a symbol of Saint Peter, whose name also meant a phallus or male principle (*pater*) and a phallic **pillar** (*petra*). Therefore the cock's image was often placed atop church towers.[2]

In Jewish tradition the cock was almost universally accepted as a substitute for a man. The Hebrew word for a cock, *gever*, also means "man." The *Kapparah* atonement offering involves killing a cock and passing its body around the head of the offender, with the words, "This fowl is my substitute, this is my surrogate, this is my atonement." Among Russian Jews it was considered bad luck to dig a grave and leave it empty overnight; so if burial could not take place until the next day, a cock was buried in the partly filled grave as a substitute for the human corpse.[3]

It is said in the *Zohar* that a cock crowing three times is an omen of death. Medieval superstition generally claimed that the crowing of the white cock, red cock, and black cock in turn signaled the departure of the dead from the earth.[4] (These were, of course, the **colors** of the Triple Goddess of Fate in former times.) The Gospel story of Peter's denial of Christ, three times before cockcrow, was related to older legends associating the crowing of the cock with the death and resurrection of the solar Savior. In Greek paganism the bird was sacred to Asclepius, the god who was able to resurrect the dead, and was always vaguely connected with phallic spirit in the process of dying and standing up again. As a bird supposedly in communication with the other world, the cock became the preferred medium of Roman alectromancers, who drew omens from the way the bird pecked scattered grains of corn.

1. Knight, pl. 2.   2. Whittick, 220.
3. Trachtenberg, 164, 176.   4. Wimberly, 104.

Crow

Because of its carrion-eating propensities, the crow shared with the **dog** and **vulture** many points of identification with the Goddess-as-Crone, the death-giver. "Crow" really means a family of closely related carrion-eating birds including the rook (*Corvus frugilegus*), **raven** (*Corvus corax*), and carrion crow (*Corvus corone*). One of the Goddess's archaic forms, the crone Coronis, was a "crow" who was transformed into the virgin mother of the physician-god Asclepius; but other, similar forms appeared in myths as harbingers of the hero's death. The Goddess Badb transformed herself into a crow, Badb Catha, to confront the Celtic hero Cu Chulainn and thereby announce his doom.[1] An Anglo-Danish version of the fateful Goddess was named Krake, "Crow," although she assumed human form long enough to become the mother of Sigurd.

The symbol known as crow's foot—also called Witch's Foot—carried dire meanings, as might be expected from a death sign. Medieval superstition claimed that witches used crow's feet to cast death spells.[2] The facial wrinkles known as crow's feet were probably so named because they were associated with old age and its implication of approaching death. Otherwise, on the basis of shape alone the wrinkles could have been named for the feet of any bird. Romans regarded the crow as a symbol of the future because it cries *Cras, cras* (Tomorrow, tomorrow).[3]

1. Green, 101, 136.   2. Koch, 83.   3. Hall, 156.

Cuckoo

The cuckoo used to be the sacred bird of May, the season of springtime revels and Wearing of the Green, in pagan Europe's imitation of Mother Earth's new garment. The bird was named after its call, which sounds like "cuckoo"; and a "cuckold" was named after the bird because of the traditional sexual license of the old May festivals, when marriage bonds were declared temporarily in abeyance.[1] In *Love's Labor's Lost* (act V, scene II), Shakespeare mentions the cuckoo who mocks married men: "Cuckoo, cuckoo, cuckoo—O word of fear, unpleasing to a married ear."

Another circumstance relating the bird to cuckoldry is its well-known habit

of laying its eggs in other birds' nests. Sometimes the cuckoo's image surmounted the **scepter** of the Goddess **Juno,** perhaps referring to her conception of some of her children (e.g., Mars) without any help from her spouse, the Heavenly Father.[2] As a rain bird, the cuckoo was sacred to Juno's Greek counterpart Hera. An iconic image of the cuckoo nestling in the Goddess's bosom gave rise to the myth that Father Zeus first wooed her by taking the form of the cuckoo. In India, the cuckoo was sacred to Kama, the spirit of love. In Japan, it was regarded as a guide to the underworld—perhaps as a symbolic triumph of love over death.[3]

1. Potter & Sargent, 80. 2. Hall, 274. 3. G. Jobes 1, 395, 794.

Dove

Doves represented the Great Goddess in Asia Minor, under several of her names such as Aphrodite and **Astarte.** They were raised in her temples, carved on her stelae, depicted on her jewels and coins. According to Homer, it was the Goddess's doves who brought Heavenly Father Zeus the ambrosia that kept him immortal.[1] According to Herodotus, seven women called Doves founded the great **oracles** of Dodona and Thebes.[2] The image of the dove reborn from the **mouth** of a **dolphin** (or *delphos,* "womb") seems to have represented the Goddess's Virgin aspect renewed out of the devouring Crone. Biblical writers masculinized the image as Jonah, whose name means "Dove." The word *ionah* or *ione* may have descended from *yoni,* for the dove was a primary symbol of female sexuality. In India, the name of the Dove-goddess meant "lust."

So vital was the dove symbol that patriarchal cults were constrained to absorb it, in many different ways. The holy Seven Sisters called Pleiades, or "Doves," were originally born from Pleione: Aphrodite as "Queen of the Sea." They were assimilated by the Christian image of the Holy Ghost, a dove with seven rays proceeding from it.[3] Seven was the number of the Goddess **Sophia,** the original Gnostic conception of the female Holy Ghost who descended on Jesus at his baptism and on Mary at her impregnation. Sophia was blatantly masculinized early in the Christian era but her dove, and all doves, were always called

"she" even in Christian writings. Christian souls of **saints** flying to heaven were represented by white doves in the canonization ceremony. Among the Slavs it is still claimed that the souls of the dead turn into doves.[4] This corresponds with the ancient belief that the essence of every soul is female.

The Gypsies claimed that only the souls of women can fly, as doves, in and out of the magic mountain where the dead dwell—like the *ba*-soul of an Egyptian flying in and out of the burial mound. Men's souls are transformed into snakes, so they cannot fly.[5] This vision of female and male soul, or Goddess and God, as dove and **serpent,** respectively, goes back to an ancient iconography. Even Jesus referred to it metaphorically: "Wise as serpents, and harmless as doves" (Matthew 10:16), though with a bias toward the male already perceptible. The idea that all souls were doves lived on in the Roman term for catacombs, *columbaria,* "dovecotes," sacred to the Goddess as **Venus** Columba.[6] The Goddess was even canonized as a mythical Saint Columba, or "Holy Dove," who was much revered in France although she was only one of the church's saintly fictions.[7] Both dove and olive branch originally meant "the peace of the Goddess."

In the same way that pork became taboo to the Jews, the meat of doves or pigeons was declared taboo in the Russian church, because it was viewed as an embodiment of the Holy Ghost, or at least of soul-stuff. Alchemists often used the symbol of a white dove enclosed in lead (the **Saturn** metal) to represent soul or spirit enclosed in matter.[8] In such ways the sign of female sexuality, as an expression of Goddess energy, was transformed into a sign of disembodied, purified, ethereal spirituality.

1. d'Alviella, 91–92, 165. 2. Herodotus, 106.
3. de Lys, 13. 4. Cirlot, 81. 5. Trigg,
196. 6. Bachofen, 21. 7. Attwater, 92.
8. Cirlot, 173.

Eagle

The eagle was sacred to ancient sky gods like Zeus and **Jupiter,** and thus became a totemic sign of Roman emperors and of imperial power generally. The soul of each Roman emperor was supposed to be incarnate in an eagle. At an emperor's funeral, an eagle was released above his pyre.[1] This was supposed to carry the imperial soul to heaven, just as the eagle carried the young god Ganymede up

to Zeus. Each Roman legion carried "eagles" as military standards. Germanic emperors of the Holy Roman Empire inherited the eagles of the Caesars, which became their heraldic signs.

The double-headed eagle became a symbol of Germany, Austria, Russia, and the Turkish rulers during the Crusades, because of a misunderstanding of an archaic prototype. On golden fibulae from Mycenae, two eagles leaned against one another and looked in opposite directions, like the Egyptian "Lions of Yesterday and Today" (**akeru**), representing the passage of time, past and future. Later confusion between the image and its meaning gave rise to a single eagle with two heads.[2]

Eagles were traditionally associated with **lightning, fire,** and the **sun,** as well as the hero who, like Prometheus, brought down fire from heaven for the benefit of humanity. Prometheus offended the Heavenly Father by so doing, and a similar story was told of one of his predecessors, Zu the Storm Bird, a Sumerian version of the lightning eagle. Ironically, this was probably also an earlier version of Zeus himself. The Greeks believed eagles could control the lightning, so they

nailed eagles to the peaks of temples to deflect lightning bolts. Thus their pediments were called *aetoi*, "eagles."[3] This may have inspired the mythic image of Prometheus chained to a mountain.

Ezekiel's four-faced creature composed of eagle, **lion, bull,** and man, was piously interpreted as prophesying the four evangelists; but the original biblical description was copied from the fabulous composite beasts of Assyria, who represented the four **seasons** of the year.[4] Each was sacred to an element, the eagle naturally standing for the realm of the **air.**

1. Campbell, *Oc.M.*, 334.   2. Whittick, 237.   3. Reinach, 90.   4. Whittick, 269.

Falcon

The falcon used to be another of the funerary birds, representing the **soul** flying away, when it was released at burial services. The bird's Greek name, *kirkos*, was the same as the name of the Death-goddess Circe, whose island was a funerary shrine. Its name, Aeaea, means "Wailing." Homer's story that Circe transformed men into **pigs** probably meant the institution of porcine substitutes for earlier human sacrifices on the occasions of important funerals.

Garuda

India's garuda bird, "the golden-winged
sun bird," was a mysterious figure
in many ways, very similar to the Persian
simurgh. Garuda was variously pictured as
a man, a bird, a man riding a bird,
or a curious combination of human and
avian characteristics; also, Garuda
could be one or many. Though probably
older than the religion of Vishnu,
Garuda is now regarded as a "vehicle"
(*vahana*) of Vishnu, bearing the spirit of
the god either within, or on his back.

The most likely interpretation of Garuda
is that he used to represent the sunny,
hot, dry season, as opposed to the rainy
season, which was symbolized by the **serpent,** emblem of **water.** Garuda was in
perpetual conflict with serpents and was
addressed as the bird who kills or devours
serpents: the hot sun drying up streams. In
the Indian province of Orissa, Garuda is
invoked to heal persons suffering from
snakebite. In the Great Temple, such persons embrace the Garuda **pillar** and
hope for relief.[1]

1. Zimmer, 75.

Goose

The Goose that Laid the Golden Egg
was originally the Egyptian Goddess
Hathor who gave birth to the sun, when
she took the form of the Nile goose.
The sun god was "the Egg of the Goose
appearing from out of the sycamore," that
is, the Goddess's sacred tree.[1] The hieroglyphic sign for the World Egg was the
same as the sign for an embryo in a
woman's womb.[2]

Caesar said the goose was sacred to
Celtic tribes and was not considered edible, because of her connection with
the Sun-Egg.[3] For similar reasons, medieval superstition forbade the killing of
a goose in midwinter, when the sun was
thought to be in need of maternal
care to gain strength for the new season.[4]
Later the superstitious rule was reversed, so
radically that a goose could even become a
traditional Christmas dinner by the
time Dickens wrote A *Christmas Carol.*
Like other formerly sacred creatures, geese
were said to contain souls of the unbaptized (pagans).[5]

1. Budge, E.M., 132.
2. Stone, A.M.W. 2, 61.
3. Green, 114.   4. Trachtenberg, 258.
5. G. Jobes 1, 620.

HAWK
hawk-headed Horus

IBIS
ibis-headed Thoth

KINGFISHER

Hawk

The hawk was the totemic form of the Egyptian god Horus, shown as a man's body with a hawk's head mask. Horus was particularly embodied in the pharaoh, whose funeral ceremonies often included the release of a live hawk to depict the dead king's soul flying away to its home in heaven. Likewise, the souls of Roman emperors flew to heaven as **eagles,** and those of Christian saints did their flying in the form of **doves.**

As conductor of souls, the hawk god was Khu-en-ua. Sometimes he served as the divine boatman ferrying the dead across the underground river. His name and function were hellenized as Charon, ferryman of the river Styx.

In Greece the hawk was sacred to Apollo; hence, like the eagle, a sun bird. Rome made it the totem of the god Quirinus, who was Christianized as a mythical Saint Quirinus, retaining the same totemic bird.[1]

1. G. Jobes 1, 733.

Ibis

The ibis was primarily the bird of Thoth, Egypt's god of magic, spells, writing, and record keeping. He was the spouse of the Goddess Maat who represented truth, law, and words of power, sometimes under her alternate name of Seshat, "Mistress of the House of Books." Like most gods intimately associated with some form of the Goddess, Thoth was endowed with a lunar nature. He became the guardian of the Moon Gates in heaven.[1]

Greeks identified this ibis god with **Hermes** and called his holy city Hermopolis.

1. *Larousse,* 27.

Kingfisher

The classic name of the kingfisher was halcyon; it was the "halcyon bird" of the legendary fourteen-day period of perfectly calm midwinter weather, when the winds and the sea kept still to facilitate the nesting of the magic bird. The name seems to have been derived from Alcyone, one of the Pleiades whose rising was important to the ancient navigational year. Another Alcyone was called daughter of Aegeale, "She Who Wards Off the Hurricane." The ancient writers believed (erroneously) that the kingfisher's nest must

float on the surface of the sea. Actually, kingfishers nest in shoreline burrows.

Robert Graves mentions his own experience of seeing "a halcyon skimming the surface of the same Mediterranean bay . . . about midsummer when the sea was without a ripple: its startlingly bright blue and white plumage made it an unforgettable symbol of the Goddess of calm seas."[1]

1. Graves, W.G., 193–195.

Magpie

The most "talkative" of birds, the magpie was often credited with oracular announcements and the communication of secrets to those who could understand the mystical bird language. Like other relatives of the **crow,** magpies could learn to imitate human speech when kept in captivity. For centuries the chattering of magpies was said to foreshadow the arrival of guests. Two or more magpies prophesied a happy occasion; one magpie meant sorrow.[1]

The bird used to be sacred to Magog ("Mother of Gog"), or to Aphrodite under her name of Pearl (Margarete). It was "pied" or "a pie" because of its black and white particolored plumage.[2]

1. Thomas, 625. 2. Potter & Sargent, 161.

Owl

The "wise owl" still appears with witches at **Halloween** (the Celtic feast of the dead), because of its past association with many forms of the Crone Goddess, who embodied wisdom as well as mortality. Lilith, **Athene,** Minerva, Blodeuwedd, Anath, and the staring owl-eyed Goddess Mari were closely associated with the owl or took the owl's shape. The wise-woman or witch had the same name in Latin as the owl: *strix*, plural *striges*, later the Italian *strega*, "witch."[1]

To the Algonquin Indians, the owl was a bird of death and of the winter, creator of the north wind. To the Babylonians, hooting owls were **ghosts** of women who died in childbirth, calling for their offspring.[2] The time-honored connection of the Midwife Goddess with owls may have contributed to this idea.

In medieval times the owl was sometimes called Night-hag, like the daughters of Lilith who had been reinterpreted as demonic succubae. Female spirits with owl wings were feared as potential kidnappers of infants: another manifestation of the mother-ghost.

Christian legend insisted that the owl was one of "three disobedient sisters" (the

Triple Goddess) who defied the Judeo-Christian God, and so was transformed into a bird that could never look at the sun.[3] This legend fostered a belief that owls are blind in daylight. Actually, owls' vision is keen in all conditions of light or dark. Other notable characteristics of the owl are its noiseless flight—muffled by thick, soft feathers—and its ability to turn its head almost all the way around on its shoulders, which popular superstition often attributed to **demons.**

1. Trigg, 96.   2. G. Jobes 2, 1222.   3. de Lys, 37.

Partridge

The name of the partridge descends from Middle English *pertriche*, Latin *perdix*, meaning "the Lost One." In Greek myth, a son of Perdix was thrown from a high peak of **Athene's** temple by his uncle Daedalus. Athene turned the youth's soul into a partridge as he flew through the air.[1] Some said Perdix was the name of the youth himself, not his mother. In any event, there was a sanctuary in honor of Perdix the partridge (or mother of the partridge) beside Athene's temple on the Acropolis. Since Athene also bore the name of Oncë, "Pear Tree," we seem to have here the origin of the puzzling phrase in the Christmas song

"A Partridge in a Pear Tree."[2]

Male priests of Athene used to perform hobbling dances in imitation of the hobbling mating dance of the male partridge hoping to outshine a rival and win the attention of the hen. The love call of a cock partridge so quickly attracts other male challengers that hunters used to cage one cock as a decoy to draw other cocks to the area.[3]

1. Potter & Sargent, 123.   2. Graves, G.M. 1, 252, 311–312.   3. G. Jobes 2, 1241.

Peacock

The peacock was sacred to the Roman Queen of Heaven, **Juno** (Greek Hera); and before her, to the Vedic Queen of Wisdom, Sarasvati, in whose honor peacocks still wander undisturbed in temple precincts. The eyed **feathers** of the peacock's tail stood for the Goddess's starry heavens, or her all-seeing awareness. One story said she took them from the hundred-eyed giant Argus to put in the feathers of her sacred bird; but the

hundred-eyed and hundred-handed giants of myth were usually symbols of the "college" of fifty priestesses who traditionally served each temple of the Goddess.[1] On Roman coins, Juno's peacock meant apotheosis for women.[2]

In her holy processions, Juno's priestesses carried tall peacock-feather fans called *flabelli*, signifying the presence of their Goddess. These were taken over by Christianity and annually displayed at papal Easter services. They are now described as symbols of "the many-eyed vigilance of the church."[3] The peacock itself has been declared a bad-luck sign because of its widely known association with the Great Goddess.[4] Buddhists still use peacock feathers to sprinkle holy water.

1. Hall, 182. 2. Cirlot, 239. 3. Brewster, 166. 4. Leland, 154.

Pelican

The pelican has become famous in Western iconography because of a truly silly superstition about pelican motherhood: a superstition solemnly enshrined in learned writings for thousands of years, endorsed by Saint Augustine and other fathers of the church.[1] The superstition maintained that every mother pelican "vulns" (wounds) her own breast with her bill, so as to feed her young on the **blood** that flows forth from her wound. Therefore the mother pelican was enthusiastically adopted as a symbol of the self-sacrificing Christ or the charitable church and was also depicted on many medieval coats of arms, banners, flags, and official seals. Dante spoke of "Christ our Pelican."[2]

The fact that no such behavior was ever observed on the part of a real pelican seemed to carry little weight against the accumulated "wisdom" of a received tradition of such hoary antiquity. The pelican might stand today as a symbol of the perennial viability of human nonsense and general lack of curiosity about the natural truth.

1. Potter & Sargent, 179. 2. Hall, 86.

PHOENIX
*sun disc, Assyrian
bas-relief*

Petrel

Applied to several varieties of sea birds, "petrel" is a diminutive form of "peter," just as "chicken" is a diminutive form of "cock."[1] It is usually assumed that the birds were named after Saint Peter, who was like them a water-walking fisher. There are reasons, though, to connect the birds with an older, pagan tradition. In France they were known as *les oiseaux de Notre Dame*, the birds of Our Lady. The Lady seems not to have been the Christian one. In England the birds were Mother Carey's chickens, the property of a wind-riding sea witch whose name came from Latin *Mater Cara*, "Beloved Mother," a title of the Goddess as Mistress of Earth and Sea. Certain stories described the birds as pagan spirits, who returned to the underworld **womb** (which Christians called hell) via "holes in the earth."[2] Though the petrels may have represented the Roman *petra, pater,* or phallic god, it seems unlikely that they were primarily associated with Christianity.

1. Potter & Sargent, 71, 117. 2. Walker, W.E.M.S., 790.

Phoenix

The periodic resurrection of the phoenix bird from its own **ashes** was often adduced as sure proof of the resurrection of the dead in general, according to authorities of the church.[1] In A.D. 386, Cyril of Jerusalem proclaimed that God had created the phoenix in order to help men believe in the resurrection of Christ.[2] Unfortunately for this argument, neither God nor nature had ever created the phoenix at all. It was a purely mythical pseudobird apparently evolved from primitive sun worship.

The name of the phoenix means a god of Phoenicia. The original "bird" was probably the horned, winged sun disc, which resembled that of Egypt but appeared more birdlike in Mesopotamian iconography.[3] It was the sun who flew on wings through heaven and was constantly immolated and reborn from the fires of sunset and sunrise. Egypt's phoenix was sometimes identified with the bennu bird, a heron sacred to **Osiris,** symbolizing both the human soul and the god's cycle of rebirth or resurrection. Sometimes the bird represented the morning star.[4]

Greeks gave the phoenix the name of *Kerkes* (Circe). In Turkey the legend of the phoenix was incorporated into that of the **simurgh.**[5] According to the *Haggadah,* the phoenix is a vast sun bird who

"spreads out his wings and catches the fiery rays of the sun." On these wings are enormous letters, saying, "Neither the earth produces me, nor the heavens, but only the wings of fire."[6]

In the most popular medieval version of the legend, the phoenix was supposed to live for several centuries and then build its own funeral pyre, light it with a burning twig, throw itself on the flames, burn up, and then arise newborn from the ashes.

1. Trachtenberg, 182.   2. Abelard, 38.
3. d'Alviella, 148.   4. Budge, G.E. 2, 97.
5. Cirlot, 242.   6. Barnstone, 25.

Raven

Like their relatives the **crows,** ravens were known throughout Europe as death birds and other-world messengers. **Valkyries** wore black raven **feathers** in their role of Choosers of the Slain. Dead warriors on the battlefield were called "feeders of ravens" in skaldic verse. Some of the skalds' *kennings* (metaphors) for the raven included "blood-swan" and "blood-goose."[1] Among the Celts, ravens were sacred to the other-world Birdgoddess Rhiannon, and also incarnations of the death-dealing Morrigan.[2] Ravens brought omens of death. It was often said that ravens could foretell outbreaks of the plague.[3]

Because of their association with the other world, ravens were viewed as **oracles** and teachers of magic. Ravens gave magical instruction to the Celtic god Lug and to his Norse counterpart Odin.[4] An adept in the first stage of Mithraic initiation took the title of Raven, which was linked with the lunar sphere.[5] Later stages carried the titles of Bridegroom, Warrior, Lion, Persian, Sunrunner, and Pater.[6] A fourteenth-century Italian manuscript said that high position and honor would surely come to a person who owned an amulet showing a raven standing on a **serpent's** tail.[7] Among the Eskimo, Siberians, and Indians of some northwestern American tribes, Raven was a major god who married the Great Mother, brought dry land out of the sea, and finally sacrificed himself to provide magical wisdom for men. In Christian tradition, however, ravens were often said to be the souls of wicked persons.

1. Turville-Petre, 59.   2. Green, 188.
3. Thomas, 625.   4. Gelling & Davidson, 175.
5. Campbell, Oc. M., 255.   6. Rose, 288.
7. Desautels, 23.

SIMURGH
Persian miniature,
6th century A.D.

STORK

Robin

Robin Redbreast, or "Cock Robin," was a bird form of Robin Goodfellow, one of the common names of the so-called god of the witches. He was also known as Robin Hood, Robin the Bobbin, Robin son of Art (Artio), and Puck. His red breast may have been connected with the "blood-runes" carved on the breast of a pagan hero, according to old Scandinavian poetry.[1] A revised, post-Christian legend attributed the robin's red breast to the blood of Christ: the bird tried to remove the thorns from Christ's crown, but only succeeded in piercing its own breast, which remained red ever afterward.[2]

The nursery rhyme says "Cock Robin" was slain by **arrows,** a common mode of sacrificial death for pagan heroes such as Cu Chulainn, for example. Robin Hood's death scene also featured an arrow. The rebirth of Robin—or the return of the robin to the greenwood—was and still is the classic harbinger of spring.

1. Walker, W.E.M.S., 870. 2. Bowness, 38.

Simurgh

The simurgh was depicted in Persian art as a strange amalgam of **lion** claws, **peacock** plumes, snake tails, and a head like a **griffin.** According to some myths, the simurgh was made up of thirty different birds, or it symbolized all the birds of the world, collectively. In the *Shah-Nameh* the simurgh was a benevolent **vulture,** foster-mother of the legendary hero Zal, who became the father of Rustem. When the infant Zal was exposed to die, the simurgh saved him and took him to its secret nest on the summit of Mount Elburz, where he grew up. The creature seems to have descended from many other Middle Eastern and Egyptian vulture-mother figures, who were thought to bestow life or immortality on chosen mortals.[1]

1. *Larousse,* 315, 322.

Stork

The image of the stork bringing babies dates back to dimmest antiquity. When it was observed that storks frequent ponds and marshes, many people still believed that the spirits of unborn children waited in such places, seeking passage to a new mother. Storks thus became soul-carriers (**psychopomps**) on behalf of mother and

child. Their name derives from Greek *storge*, meaning "powerful affection" or "mother-love."[1] On the other hand, the Hebrew word for a stork, *hasidah*, means "pious."[2]

The connection of the stork with fertility magic led to a popular belief that storks' nests on the roof of the house would provide the mother with plenty of easy births and healthy children. Therefore the storks' nests were encouraged, and many legends were invented to protect the nesting storks from interference. A German story, based on a tale told by Aelian, appealed to avarice as well as motherhood. A woman named Heracleis tended an injured stork, cured it, and let it go. Years later the same bird returned and dropped a precious stone into her lap by way of payment. According to the German version, the stone was called either *Storchstein* (stork stone) or *Donnerkeil* (lightning).[3] The latter name seems to recall the ubiquitous image of lightning as a fertilizing principle, and also as a male "jewel" (*vajra*) dropped into the lap of the Mother. (See **Lightning**.)

1. Brasch, 21. 2. Whittick, 323. 3. Kunz, 162.

Swallow

The fork-tailed swallow was a bird of springtime, flowering, and love, sacred to the May-maiden in northern Europe and to **Isis** and **Venus** in the south.[1] Therefore, the swallow was respected by all who retained any memory traces of the old rites of the Goddess. Among the common sayings of the wise-women was the unequivocal declaration that to kill swallows, or to rob their nests, was "a more fearful sacrilege than to steal a chalice out of a church."[2] Because of its forked tail, however, the clergy sometimes viewed the swallow as in some sense demonic. It was known as "witch-chick."[3]

1. Cirlot, 306. 2. Thomas, 624. 3. G. Jobes 2, 1687.

Swan

Swan Maidens abound in Indo-European myths. They are thought to derive from the Vedic heavenly **nymphs,** *apsaras,* symbolized by swans and perhaps seen in the feathery white clouds swimming across lakes of blue sky. The Vedic Brahma himself had the swan for his special vehicle (*vahana*) or bird incarnation.[1] He foreshadowed the Greek myth of Zeus in swan form impregnating Leda (or, "the Lady"), who then gave

birth to the Heavenly Twins, twilight and dawn, and Helen, another name for Selene, the **moon.**[2] But the swan also symbolized the **Muses,** and through them, Apollo; and it was one of the birds of Aphrodite. A Cyprian legend identified Leda with the "inescapable" Goddess Nemesis-Adrasteia, the implacable Fate whom even the gods feared.[3]

Both male and female swan spirits appeared in folktales derived from pagan mythology. The **Valkyries** wore swan-feather cloaks, which meant they turned into swans on occasion; the hero who could steal one of their feather garments could compel its owner to grant him a wish. The Valkyrie queen Kara had a swan incarnation, perhaps based on the Indo-Aryan Goddess Kauri as leader of the swan nymphs. A Saxon chronicler told of the Swan Knight, Lohengrin, who came from "the mountain where Venus lives in the Grail."[4] His function was to rescue women dispossessed by new patriarchal laws. His silver swan symbol became a special order of knighthood in fifteenth-century Cleves, where a special tournament was held in honor of "the Knight of the Swan, servant of women."[5]

1. Ross, 36.   2. Baring-Gould, 561–578.
3. Graves, G.M. 1, 126, 206–208.   4. Jung & von Franz, 121.   5. Baring-Gould, 600.

Thunderbird

The Navajo image of the thunderbird was an archetypal bird/savior similar to the **Garuda** bird of southeastern Asia, associated with **lightning,** fire-from-heaven, the **thunderbolt, rain,** and the bringing of forbidden divine gifts (such as enlightenment) to humanity. An early prototype can be found as far back as Sumerian civilization in Zu the Storm Bird who defied the gods. Ancestral divinities, culture heroes, animal totems, and nature spirits merged in such concepts. The Indians of the southwestern United States were particularly interested in the rain-bringing potential of this bird deity because their climate was dry and their need for water was ever present.

Vulture

Nekhbet or Mut, the archaic vulture mother of Egypt, represents "an ancient matriarchal stratum." The Egyptian word for *mother* was the sign of the vulture.[1] A hieroglyph for *grandmother* was the vulture bearing symbols of royal authority. It used to be generally believed that all vultures are female, and that they

conceive offspring from the air, without male assistance. In fact, early Christian fathers cited the example of the vulture mothers to defend the doctrine of the virgin birth.[2]

In the *Book of the Dead*, the Vulture Goddess guards the first **gate** of the underworld and represents Mut's taking back of the dead into her own maternal substance.[3] Vulture mothers were said to care for dead pharaohs, nursing them at their breasts forever.[4] Vulture carriers of the dead were worshiped also by the Persians, who required a corpse to be torn by vultures before burial.[5] Parsees still place the dead in Towers of Silence where they can be eaten by vultures, in order to bring about their rebirth.[6]

The *necropolis* or "city of the dead" derives from Nekhen, the sacred city of the ancient Vulture Goddess Nekhbet, who daily devoured the dying sun and gave him rebirth. Greeks named the city after their own childbirth Goddess, Aphrodite Ilithyia. To the Romans, it was the city of **Juno**.[7] All, apparently, recognized the vulture as a leading avian symbol of the Mother of death and rebirth.

1. Neumann, 12. 2. Budge, G.E. 1, 286; 2, 372; Neumann, 65. 3. *Book of the Dead*, 272. 4. Neumann, 13. 5. Herodotus, 56. 6. Cirlot, 343. 7. *Book of the Dead*, 493; Budge, G.E. 1, 438.

Wren

Druids considered the wren "supreme among all birds." It was the sacred bird of the Isle of Man, which used to be a shrine of the dead and a dwelling-place of the Moon Goddess who cared for pagan souls, until missionaries came to destroy her. Then, as the shape-shifting Fairy Queen, she took refuge in the form of the "Jenny Wren" of nursery rhymes. The more pious Manxmen instituted wren hunts at New Year, as if to catch the Fairy Queen. Captured birds were hung by one leg in the center of two hoops and carried about in an exorcistic ritual.[1] The two hoops may have represented the intersecting circles of the ecliptic and the **Milky Way**. In Devonshire the wren was known as Bran's Sparrow, a bird of prophecy; in Somersetshire it was hunted on the Twelfth Day of Christmas and enclosed in a box surmounted by a **wheel,** representing the wheel of the year.[2]

1. Hazlitt 2, 666. 2. Graves, W.G., 192–193.

16

INSECTS

L ike all other inhabitants of the natural world, insects were regarded by the ancients as mystically powerful, filled with magic energies and secrets. Their mysterious habits, their curious nests, their ability to fly, and their shape-changing metamorphoses were always matters for wonder. Burrowing insects were thought to have special rapport with the Earth. Flying insects were often viewed as soul-carriers or intermediate forms of human souls. Thread-spinning insects and arachnids were seen as servants of the thread-spinning Fate Goddesses. Destructive insects were much feared, because a plague of locusts could mean widespread famine, termites could shatter houses, scorpions could kill.

Because insects are mostly small, their activities often escaped notice and so there were many erroneous ideas about them. The ancient naturalists knew something about bees, which they domesticated, and such common pests as flies, ants, mosquitoes, and crop-eating caterpillars. But the true study of insects was initiated only in the nineteenth century, and many questions about their ways still remain unanswered. Naturally, such considerations never appreciably interfered with their use as symbols.

Ant

There was a tribe of ancient Pthiotis known as Myrmidons, "Ants," said to be "an Ant clan subject to the Goddess." The legendary hero Achilles became their sacred king, "presumably by marriage with the tribal representative of the Goddess."[1] Ants were generally sacred to the Harvest Mother, because they were seen busily carrying grains and seeds. Because it was believed that their comings and goings both underground and above ground would put them in touch with the secrets of both worlds, ants were often used in divination, and omens were taken from their movements.[2] Moslems placed the ant in heaven among the constellations, honoring it as the earthly teacher of Solomon, hence an embodiment of wisdom.

1. Graves, W.G., 128, 432.   2. Cirlot, 13.

Bee

Bees were greatly prized in the ancient world as makers of the honey that was simultaneously a desired food and one of the few important preservatives then known. According to Porphyry, all bees were the souls of **nymphs** (priestesses) who had been in the service of Aphrodite during their lifetimes, especially at her temple of Eryx where her symbol was a golden **honeycomb**.[1] Priestesses of the Goddess were called *melissae*, "bees." At the Ephesian temple of Artemis, the *melissae* were accompanied by eunuch priests known as *essenes*, meaning "drones."[2] The Goddess Demeter was also addressed as "the pure mother bee." A former matriarchal ruler of Israel was

Deborah, whose name means "queen bee."
The mother of Lemminkainen used
magic honey to restore her son's life in the
Kalevala, assisted by Mehilainen the
Bee.[3] Even the patriarchal Mithraic cult
revered the Moon Goddess as maker of "the
honey which was used in purifications."[4]

Bees are *hymenoptera*, "veil-winged,"
recalling the *hymen* or **veil** that covered the
inner shrine of the Goddess's temple,
and the officiating nymph (high priestess)
who bore the title of Hymen and ruled over
marriage rituals and the honey-moon.

In folklore, bees were always identified
with mortality. If bees left their hive, it was
taken as a sign that the hive's owner
would soon die.[5] It was also considered
important to "tell the bees" about a death
in the family, so they would not fly
away. In some sections of England it was
customary to turn beehives around
to face in the opposite direction when a
corpse was being carried out of the house.

1. de Lys, 50. 2. Gimbutas, 183. 3. *Larousse*,
301. 4. Cumont, *M.M.*, 112. 5. Pegg, 124.

Butterfly

Psyche was the Greek word for both "soul"
and "butterfly," dating from the belief
that human **souls** became butterflies while
searching for a new reincarnation.
The mythical romance of the maiden
Psyche, beloved by the god Eros, was really
an allegory of the soul's union with
the body and of their subsequent separation. The Celts also believed in **fly**-souls and
butterfly-souls which, like bird-souls,
flew about seeking a new mother. It was
thought that women became pregnant by
swallowing such creatures. In Irish
myth, Etain took the form of a butterfly
for seven years, then entered the drinking
cup of Etar (Etarre), who swallowed
her, and so brought her to rebirth. In her
second incarnation, Etain married
Eochy, the High King of Ireland.[1] It is still
said in Cornwall that the spirits of the
dead take the form of white butterflies.[2] It
is also said in Mexico and Siberia.

Butterflies were soul symbols in the Far
East as well as in Western Europe.
The Chinese considered a **jade** butterfly
the essential emblem of love, suggesting a
wedding of souls. The most appropriate gift
for a bridegroom to give his bride in
China was a jade butterfly.[3]

1. Spence, 150. 2. Evans-Wentz, 178.
3. Kunz, 84.

Cicada

"Rosy-fingered" Eos, Greek Goddess of the dawn, had a mortal lover named Tithonus for whom she obtained the precious gift of immortality. However, she did not give him eternal youth. So with the passing centuries he grew older, and grayer, and smaller, and his voice climbed to a higher and higher pitch, until he turned into a cicada. Eos locked him in her bedroom where he shrilled his greeting to her as she arose each morning.

This was another of the pleasant classical myths devised to explain an aspect of nature. The cicada's name Tithonus means "partner of the Queen of Day," and his former humanity was supposed to explain why all cicadas begin each morning to sing to the growing light of day.[1] Symbolically, the insect represents a discarded lover.

1. Graves, G.M. 1, 150.

Fly

Along with the **butterfly,** the fly was one of the common **soul** symbols of antiquity. Many myths tell of souls taking this form and seeking to enter a woman's body to be reclothed in human flesh. The Celtic hero Cu Chulainn was conceived when his mother-to-be swallowed him in the form of a fly. Perhaps the "Old Woman Who Swallowed a Fly" in the traditional folk song was one of these pre-Christian mothers.

The name of Beelzebub (Baal-zebub) meant "Lord of the Flies," because he was originally a Philistine god envisioned as a **psychopomp.** The title meant the same as "Lord of Souls." Beelzebub became a Christian **devil** only because he was mentioned in the Bible as one of the *other* gods (that is, not Yahweh); but his character seemed to be that of a healer and oracular deity. King Ahaziah of Israel sent messengers to Ekron to consult Beelzebub when he was in need of healing (2 Kings 1:2).

Intimate connections between flies and the souls of the dead undoubtedly arose for the same reasons that affected **vultures, dogs,** and carrion **crows.** That is, the creatures were seen clustering thickly around dead bodies. The ancients may not have known that the flies' purpose was not so much to eat the carrion as to lay their eggs in it.

Grasshopper (Locust)

Grasshoppers are eaten in Oriental countries, and according to the Bible they were the staple food of John the Baptist (Matthew 3:4). The family of grasshoppers known as Acrididae were the biblical "locusts" who sometimes came in great swarms, called *plagues*, to destroy crops. Still, the name of locust is often erroneously applied to the **cicada.**

The other biblical locusts of Revelation 9:3–11 were very peculiar insects indeed. They looked like horses with men's faces, women's hair, lions' teeth, and scorpions' tails; they wore gold crowns and iron breastplates. Their king was Apollyon (Abaddon), the **Black Sun,** otherwise known as the Angel of the Bottomless Pit. The humble grasshopper certainly would find it difficult to recognize any such ancestors as these.

In ancient Athens the grasshopper was a symbol of nobility, implying ownership of land (see **Grass**). Members of aristocratic clans used to wear golden grasshoppers as ornaments of rank.[1]

1. Whittick, 250.

Mantis

The praying (or preying) mantis is named after Mante, the priestess daughter of the Theban sage Teiresias. Her name means "Prophetess" or "One Inspired by the Moon." The Hellenic myth said that her father was turned into a woman by the **Goddess,** and lived for seven years as a temple harlot, which made him enormously wise because he understood everything from both male and female points of view. This myth allegorized the priestly takeover of priestesses' functions in Thebes, probably with ceremonies of castration and/or transvestism at first to make male priests into pseudowomen.[1] There are many other stories about early priesthoods attaining their spiritual powers by such means.

The Mantes were oracular clans descended from Mante, whose **souls** perhaps took on mantis form between incarnations. They came to be all male in classical times, though they had been mixed sexes earlier, and all female even earlier. The mantids are rather appropriate symbols for ancient female powers, since the female insects are larger and stronger than the males, and, like **spiders,** well-known husband-eaters. Among certain African tribes, such as the Bushmen, the mantis was regarded as the creator of the world.[2]

1. Graves, G.M. 1, 258; 2, 11.   2. G. Jobes 1, 269.

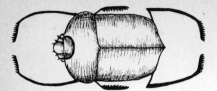

Scarab

The Egyptian *scarabaeus* beetle was the symbol of the god Khepera, a solar deity, said to roll the ball of the **sun** across the heavens as the beetles roll their balls of dung on the ground. Male priesthoods seized upon the notion that the *scarabaei* are never female, and that the male beetles hatch offspring incubated in their dung balls. (Actually, scarab beetles hatch from eggs laid by the females under the sand.) Khepera's priests claimed that he was the sole creator, who said, "There was no other being who worked with me." The sacred beetles were depicted on all kinds of amulets and seals. Carved scarabs replaced hearts within mummies. Large scarabs were worshiped in temples.[1] To this day, Egyptian and Sudanese women believe that the dried and powdered beetles, ingested in water, act as conception charms.[2] Medieval alchemists also used the scarab symbol in diagrams of the double spiral path to the "center of the universe."

Despite the scarab god's brief notoriety as a sole creator, scriptures soon began talking about his divine mother, and showing him emerging from the yonic **lotus** symbol.[3] It was found that the scarab beetle's purported masculine fertility depended on Mother **Moon**. Horapollo said the dung ball must be deposited in the earth "for the space of twenty-eight days (for in so many days the moon passes through the twelve signs of the zodiac). By thus remaining under the moon, the race of scarabaei is endued with life."[4]

The carved scarab is now a popular item of jewelry, a modification of the gemstone cut *en cabochon*. Worldwide interest in things Egyptian was generated by the discovery of the tomb of Tutankhamen with its treasures, including scarabs, which jewelers everywhere were quick to copy.

1. Whittick, 307.   2. Budge, G.E. 2, 381.
3. *Book of the Dead*, 435; d'Alviella, 29.
4. Brier, 147.

Scorpion

Indians of Central and South America say Mother Scorpion receives the souls of the dead in her house at the end of the **Milky Way.** Pawnee and Cherokee Indians said the star Antares—the Scorpion's Eye—is the spirit-star of the Old Goddess. These American versions resemble Egypt's scorpion-tailed Goddess Selket, or Serqet, and Babylon's Goddess Ishara Tamtim, or Ishara of the Sea, a

scorpion-tailed Mother in the same constellation that the whole world, apparently, named the Scorpion. The Goddess was identified with Siduri Sabitu, who "sits on the throne of the sea" in the *Epic of Gilgamesh*. To approach her dwelling, Gilgamesh had to pass her servants the Scorpion Men.[1] These creatures were "two-thirds divine" and related to the constellations of both **Scorpio** and **Sagittarius**.[2]

Scorpions are not really insects. They are arachnids, relatives of the **spiders**. Some species have poison glands in their jaws and/or poisonous stingers in their tails, and have been known to cause fatalities—which may be why the Scorpion Stars and their personifications were often associated with death.

1. de Santillana & von Dechend, 243–244, 295. 2. Cirlot, 265.

Spider

Association of the Great Goddess with the spider occurs in myths of both the Old World and the New. The pre-Hellenic **Athene**, spinner of fate, once bore the name of Arachne in a spider incarnation. Later Hellenic mythographers claimed that Arachne was Athene's rival, a mortal whom the Goddess transformed into a spider through jealousy of her spinning skill. However, this was a reinterpretation of older myths designating the triune Goddess as spinner, measurer, and cutter of life's **threads,** and spoke of souls as flies in her cosmic **web.** The six arms and two legs of ancient East Indian Goddess figures may have been associated with the eight-legged spider, as well as with Odin's eight-legged steed of universal fate. Surely the common concept of the Goddess's destroyer aspect, as the Crone devouring her consort in the moment of his love-death, was not unrelated to the known habits of spiders.

Pueblo Indians called Spider Woman the creator of the universe, with such names as Kokyangwuti, Tsitsicinako, and Sussistanako, Thought Woman, Thinking Woman. The world was her brainchild. She began creation by spinning two threads, east-west and north-south. She produced two daughters, who made the **sun** and **moon.** She made the people of the earth from white, red, yellow, and black **clay.** Several times she destroyed the world and remade it, as spiders do their webs, saving only those wise ones who keep contact with her via the invisible strands spun to the tops of their heads—a concept very like the "lotus light" *chakra* in Hindu belief.

Spider Woman was somewhat modified by Kiowa myth into Spider Grandmother, a Prometheus-like heroine who brought light to the world. She took **fire** and the sun from the eastern land of light. She tossed the sun up into the sky, keeping a small piece for the gift of fire to her people.[1]

In Ghana, the Spider Goddess was named Anansi. Transported to the New World, she became the Haitian voodoo Spider Woman known as Aunt Nancy.

1. Stone, A.M.W. 2, 92–107.

17

FLOWERS

There is an old maxim: the language of flowers is the language of love. It is true not only in a metaphorical sense, but also in the sense of botanical biology, since flowers are the genitalia of plants. Perhaps the beauty of flowers is not the only reason, then, that they so often symbolize human sexual relationships. Many lexicons of romantic flower language have been compiled. Flowers are used as messages, love charms, gifts, and ritual objects. Myths of lovers transformed into flowers are told and retold. According to a charming Chinese tradition, every woman has the form of a flower in the spirit world. Flowers in the sense of "language" appear more literally in the Buddhist claim that with every word spoken by the Enlightened One, flowers dropped from the sky.

Flowers still have extensive ceremonial uses in expressions of joy, affection, welcome, gratitude, sympathy, celebration, grief, friendship, marital union, or spiritual contemplation. Without even referring to any formal language of flowers, people "say it with flowers" often enough to keep florists in business everywhere.

Flowers in this section are not chosen from the usual romantic lists of flower language, however. Some of the most popular blooms in today's bouquets are missing from the older sources of flower tradition; therefore they are not included. Many other reference works are available that present the romantic type of symbolism, which has many variations in the hands of different authorities. Here we discover that flowers represent not only the language of love, but many other things as well.

Alchemical Rose

The red and white rose was adopted by alchemists as a symbol of the *vas spirituale*, the sacred **womb** from which the *filius philosophorum* would be born. This was an ancient female symbol of the virgin daughter (white) within the mother (red), formerly applied to such images as Kore/Demeter and **Mary**/Eve. The conglomerate rose was similar to the **apple** (the mother and the fruit), containing its five-lobed core (the daughter and the flower). Symbolism was drawn entirely from female creative powers. White and red were the sacred **colors** of the Virgin and Mother, respectively. In male-centered systems, however, the black of the destroying Crone was pointedly omitted.

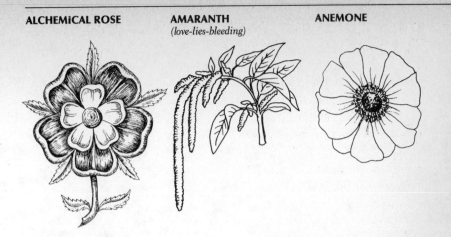

Amaranth

Greek *amarantos* means "unfading."[1] The amaranth was declared a flower of immortality because of its long-lasting blossom. It was sacred to Artemis and her priest-king and Lord of the Hunt named Amarynthus. He ruled a town of the same name and presided in the temple of Artemis Amarynthia. The flower was much used in Greco-Roman culture to decorate divine images and the tombs of savior-heroes, an expression of healing and external life.

Over fifty species of amaranth plants are now recognized. They include love-lies-bleeding, prince's-feather, Joseph's-coat, globe amaranth, wild beet, pigweed, and a tumbleweed.

1. Whittick, 195.

Anemone

The scarlet *Anemone coronaria* grows wild at Easter time in Syria, where it was identified with the **blood** of the dying god Adonis.[1] This god's title and several other attributes were inherited by Jesus, who was called *Adonai*, "the Lord," and worshiped in a former sanctuary of Adonis at Bethlehem.[2] The god's thorny **crown** of **myrrh** was also assimilated to the Christian legend; Adonis's mother was the virgin Myrrha, or "Myrrh of the Sea," whose name was applied by early Christians to the mother of Jesus.[3]

The springtime reddening of the landscape with anemone blossoms was said to demonstrate the fructification of the whole earth by the outpouring of the god's sacred blood.

1. Frazer, G.B., 390.
2. Briffault 3, 97.
3. Walker, W.E.M.S., 10.

Asphodel

A modest little flower with grayish leaves, the asphodel was a Greek symbol of the underworld, hence of death and/or immortality. Persephone, as queen of the dead, wore a garland of asphodel flowers. The souls in her underground realm of Hades wandered in meadows of asphodel. It was a popular saying that only asphodels can grow "in the meadow of the soul."[1]

1. Cirlot, 197.

Bluebell

The generic name of the bluebell, *Endymion*, shows that it was another of the flowers associated with a doomed lover of Aphrodite or some other aspect of the Goddess, just as the **anemone** was associated with Adonis, the **narcissus** with Narcissus, the **hyacinth** with Hyacinthus, and so on. Endymion was put into an eternal deathlike sleep by the Goddess under her name of Selene, the Moon. She wanted him to lie always in the same spot on a certain hillside, where she could kiss him each night as she arose. This concept of rootedness naturally applied to all the gods of the Greek Heroantheia, which meant the festival of "hero-flowering."

Columbine

The columbine was named after *columba*, the Dove, once a universally recognized symbol of the Goddess Aphrodite or **Venus** (see **Dove**). It retained a reputation for magical properties. Medieval doctors believed that columbine was a universal antitoxin. When powdered in a drink, it "driveth away all poisons," as one of their medical texts said.[1]

1. Williamson, 219.

Dandelion

The sixteenth-century herbalist Mattioli declared that dandelion juice is "useful for the flow of sperm," which may account for the popularity of dandelion wine.[1] In reality, dandelion juice has no such effect. The notion is one of sympathetic magic based on a vague resemblance between the dandelion's milky white juice and human semen.

1. Williamson, 219.

Enclosed Garden

"A garden enclosed is my sister, my spouse," says the Song of Solomon (4:12); "a spring shut up, a fountain sealed." We now understand that the whole poem is a work of sexual mysticism, modeled on traditional Sumero-Babylonian wedding songs that combined the erotic with metaphors of vegetable fertility—for this was the ultimate aim of the king's marriage to the priestess-queen who represented the earth and its fruits. The Song of Solomon was retained in the biblical canon only by a convoluted exegesis claiming that its lascivious double entendres represented the love of Christ for his church. The image of the enclosed garden—the Vulgate's *hortus conclusus*—was declared identical with the Virgin Mary, because it was a commonly accepted metaphor for physical virginity. The Garden of Paradise is the **vagina** in a number of ancient writings, or else the **womb,** from which each child "falls" at birth from a blissful environment into a considerably less comfortable world.

Therefore Christian iconography often depicted Mary within her enclosed garden, surrounded by a high circular wall, the **Tree of Life** in the center, or sometimes a **fountain** drawn from the oldest symbolism of all, which made woman's inner lunar blood the fount of life.

The flowers of the garden expressed the same symbolism. Menstrual blood was the "flower," in biblical terminology, that would produce the "fruit of the womb," a child. Thus if the enclosed garden was taken as a womb symbol, enclosed because it was as yet walled in by a maidenhead, then the presence of its flowers was quite comprehensible as anatomical simile.

The same ideas are obvious in the Hindu concept of the kula flower, blossoming within the "enclosed garden" of the virgin womb. (See **Blood**.) The Andaman Islanders follow the pattern by giving a new name to a girl at her first menstruation, the name being also that of a flower, "because she is, as it were, in blossom, and only when her body ripens to its fruit is she a complete woman."[1] Though the enclosed garden is a classic symbol of female virginity, it need not be restricted to the improbable ever-virgin mother of the Christian myth, but may be applied to womanhood in general. In the Song of Solomon it is no patriarchal deity that makes the decision to open the enclosure, but the priestess-queen herself who says, "Let my beloved come into his garden, and eat his pleasant fruits" (4:16).

1. Sanday, 99.

Fireflower

According to Slavonic myth, the fireflower bloomed on the fern, exactly at midnight on the festival of the Water Goddess, once each year. A hero who managed to get past the **demons** who guarded it and seize the flower would be able to understand the language of oracular trees ever afterward. The story was obviously connected with the numerous **groves** of oracular trees (usually **oaks**) that flourished in the pagan world. These groves were guarded by various pagan spirits (*daemones*), and any hero who could conquer them was hailed as the new King of the Wood and oracular priest. The grove itself was female, and the fireflower, or **rose,** or **lily,** or **lotus** represented the essential gift of the Goddess's love.

Fleur-de-lis

The fleur-de-lis or Lily of France descended from Gaulish symbols of the Lily Maid, another form of the Virgin **Juno** whose emblem was also a lily. The flower originally represented the Goddess's power of self-fertilization, when Juno used her magic lily to conceive her son **Mars** without any male assistance.[1] The same lily was inherited by the Virgin Mary, as a symbol of *her* impregnation in turn. Naturally, however, the patriarchal version took away her initiative and sent the lily to her in the hand of a male angel, Gabriel. Early churchmen insisted that God's semen was magically filtered through the lily to enter Mary's body through her ear.[2]

Still, the original pagan Lily Maid reappeared in medieval legends in many different guises including that of the Arthurian Elaine. The three-lobed lily seems to have represented the Triple Goddess from a remote era, like the **shamrock** in pagan Ireland. Because the people knew it as a sacred symbol, it was placed on many banners and coats of arms, and eventually came to represent French royalty in general.

1. *Larousse*, 202.   2. Walker, *W.E.M.S.*, 543.

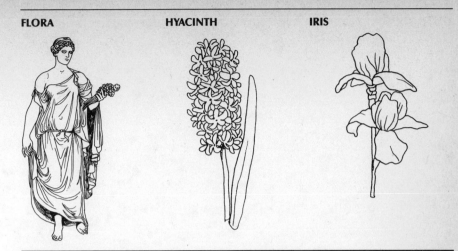

Flora

The Roman Goddess Flora ("Flourishing One") has bequeathed her name to modern science as a general designation of all the botanical world: flowers, plants, trees, vegetables, fruits, grasses, and fungi. As a Goddess, she represented much the same things, but in a more personalized, intimate way. Her annual festival the Floralia was the forerunner of our May Day, the beginning of the season of "wearing of the green," when the Earth put on her new green robe starred with flowers, and all people rejoiced in the return of spring. Flora was identified with the Greek Goddess Chloris, "the Green One."[1] Since her rites were attended by sexual license and lascivious behavior, early Christian fathers detested them and condemned the Goddess as a mere "Lady of Pleasure." But some Roman writers maintained that the mystic energy of Flora was the secret of all life for the Empire, and that Flora was the hidden soul-name of Rome itself.[2] A Welsh counterpart of Flora was the Goddess Blodeuwedd, whose body was made entirely of flowers.

1. *Larousse*, 217.   2. J. H. Smith, 225.

Hyacinth

The hyacinth flower was supposed to have been born from the **blood** of the slain Cretan flower-hero Hyacinthus, who seems to have been called Narcissus as well. The later, classical Greek story was that the god Apollo fell in love with Hyacinthus—thus becoming the first god to introduce homosexual romance—but Apollo's rival, the god of the west wind, became insanely jealous. Preferring to see Hyacinthus dead rather than beloved by another, the west wind caused a thrown discus to strike the young hero and kill him.[1]

In England, the hyacinth flower is known as the harebell.[2] The bulbs are poisonous.

1. Graves, G.M. 1, 78, 81.   2. Emboden, 36.

Iris

The iris was named after the Greek Goddess of the rainbow, because it can appear in many different colors. In Virgil's *Aeneid*, Iris is the messenger of heaven, sent to gather up the souls of women. She appears to the dying Queen Dido and carries away a lock of the queen's hair in order to free her soul from her body.[1]

The Latin name of the iris flower, *gladiolus*, means a little sword, because of its sword-shaped leaves. The flower that we now call gladiolus is actually a member of the iris family.

1. Williamson, 139, 188.

Lily

The so-called Easter lily was once the floral emblem of the Goddess **Juno** in her virgin aspect, and of the spring Goddess who was her northern counterpart, Eostre, whose name gave us "Easter." Worshipers of the Great Goddess insisted that the world's first lily sprang from the **milk** of her **breast**.[1] Roman pagans said the lily sprang from Juno's milk; Roman Christians naturally reassigned the honor to the milk of **Mary.**

The lily took over in Europe the role assigned to the **lotus** in Oriental sexual symbolism.[2] That is, it became the female "cup" holding the divine essence of life. In fact, the Christian *chalice* (cup) was derived from the *calyx* (cup) of the lily flower. In the Middle East, the lily was sacred to **Astarte,** who also bore the name of Lilith (the lily), from the Sumero-Babylonian *lilu,* a lotus.

The lily was always a symbol of the miraculous impregnation of the virgin Goddess. The "Blessed Virgin Juno"

conceived **Mars** with it; so of course the Blessed Virgin Mary followed suit.

The difference between the pagan and Christian stories was that in the latter, the lily appeared in a male hand, that of Gabriel, whose name means "divine husband."[3]

1. Whittick, 265; Guthrie, 71.　2. d'Alviella, 102.　3. Whittick, 208.

Lily of the Valley

Lily of the valley was widely known as a witches' herb and was said to attract **silver,** the moon metal. The flower contains convallatoxin, one of the most potent of all digitalislike drugs, and more than twenty other cardiac glycosides. It is also strongly diuretic and has been used to treat dropsy. Dried flowers have been used as snuff. Ointment of the root in lard was supposed to help heal burns. The flowers were described as fairy bells, and fanciful people sometimes claimed to hear them ringing.

Lotus

Before creation, the Hindus said, all the
world was a golden lotus, Matripadma, the
Mother Lotus, **womb** of nature. In
Egypt, the Great Goddess was called the
lotus from whom the **sun** was born
at his first rising. In China, the Golden
Flower of mystical quest was the same
female-symbolic lotus, just as in Western
Europe the lost female-symbolic **Grail** became an object of quest. The Egyptian lotus
was identified with Hathor; the Indian
lotus with Lakshmi, or the Goddess
Padma, whose name means lotus. Everywhere the Lotus Goddess was a **yoni**
that devoured the sun god, to become
his matrix and give him daily rebirth.[1]
It was said of an Egyptian pharaoh upon
his death that he was united with the
Lotus.[2] In the Middle East, the primal
lotus was Lilith, named from the *lilu* or
lotus. She could be identified with both
the Egyptian Goddess and with India's
Mother Kali, to whom the lotus was also
sacred. In fact, Kali was one of Lilith's other
names.[3] Bearing bud, bloom, and seed
pod together, a lotus is Virgin-Mother-
Crone.

The lotus was often taken as a symbol
of all four of the classical **elements,**
indicating the primal condition before
creation when all these elements were
united in the cosmic womb. **Earth** is the
mud in which the flower is rooted,
water the surrounding support of its stalk.
Its blossom is said to partake of the
essence of **air,** releasing its perfume into
the breezes; and its fertility is drawn from
the **fire** of the sun. The red lotus
stands for Mother India.

The illustration shows a stylized lotus
in the left hand of a Persian king,
who holds the **rod** or **scepter** of his own
virility in the right hand, representing his
own union with the Goddess. Later
rulers employed the same symbolism in
the combination of scepter and **orb.** On a
red-figured amphora of the fourth
century B.C., found in Apulia, the female
omphalos rises from an eight-petaled
base resembling the Saivite "lotus throne,"
which always represented the female
yoni.[4]

1. d'Alviella, 28.   2. Budge, G.E. 2,
32.   3. Patai, 215.   4. d'Alviella, 28.

Narcissus

The narcissus is a member of the amaryllis family and is named from Greek *narke,* "a drugged stupor." The bulb is very poisonous. The famous legend of the beautiful young hero Narcissus, captivated by his own reflection and unable to move away from the **nymph's** pool, was clearly based on an image of narcissi along a shoreline, reflecting themselves in the water. The water nymph faded away in the classical story until she became nothing but a **voice,** Echo; but older myths made the female personification of the Creative Word an "echo" (Sanskrit Vac, Hebrew Bath Kol, Greek Acco). Narcissus flowers were symbols of the underworld. Pausanias said that Persephone gathered narcissi before returning to Hades to become queen of the dead.[1]

There was a Christianized version of Narcissus, said to have been a bishop of Jerusalem in the second century A.D. He was credited with the usual long life (116 years) that early Christians claimed their religion could bring about. At the time of "Saint Narcissus," however, the Jerusalem temple was dedicated to **Venus** and her dying god Adonis, for whom Narcissus was an alternate name.[2] Jerusalem had no "bishops." It has been suggested that the six-petaled flowerets of narcissi stood for the six-lobed symbol of Venus and the sacred **hexagram** that used to imply sexual union between Goddess and God.

1. Whittick, 280.   2. Brewster, 467.

Orchid

The orchid is named from the Greek word for a testicle, *orchis,* because its twin bulbs resemble testicles. French vernacular calls it *testicule de prêtre,* "priest's testicle." In England it was "dog's stones." The Romans called the orchid *satyrion* and said that it grew from semen spilled on the ground by copulating **satyrs,** or else that the flowers grew from the scattered pieces of a satyr's son named Orchis, who was sacrificially killed and dismembered.[1]

Naturally, with all these associations with male sexuality, the orchid came to be regarded as a potency charm. Pliny said that holding the roots in one's hand would arouse sexual desire, and that the flower should be given to rams and billy goats when they are "too sluggish."[2] Parts of the orchid plant were common ingredients in love potions. When a man gave a woman an orchid as a gift,

in the language of flowers he expressed his intention to seduce her. Is it then so strange that in our own society the orchid has been considered the most desirable of floral gifts?

1. Emboden, 29.   2. Williamson, 210.

Pansy

Shakespeare's Ophelia says the pansy symbolizes "thoughts," because the French word for the flower was *pensée,* formerly spelled *pansé* or *pansée,* meaning thought.[1] The concept may have arisen from the pansy's resemblance to an elfin face crinkled up as if in deep thought.

The pansy was also commonly associated with the Goddess **Venus,** on whose "mounts" (Venusbergs) it grew. Some of the flower's other names were Love-in-Idleness, Cupid's Delight, and Kiss-me. When a sixteenth-century herbal, *The Book of Simples,* called the pansy "Herb of the Trinity," William Bullein angrily denounced the author's irreverence in comparing God's majesty to a "base, vain, venerous flower."[2]

1. Whittick, 291.   2. Williamson, 134.

Passion Flower

This plant was confused with the Easter **lily,** which was sometimes called pas-flower, pasch-flower, pasque flower, or Paschal flower, from Latin *passus,* to pass over, cognate of *pascha,* the Passover. It is possible that the passion flower originally symbolized sexual passion, because the blossom resembles genital structures in somewhat the same manner as a **lingam-yoni.** Yet, sixteenth-century Spanish friars made a great display of associating the flower with Christ's passion, describing its various parts as the crown of thorns, the five wounds, the twelve disciples, the three nails, and so on.[1]

Another name for the flower is maypop. An alkaloid derived from it, passiflorine, is said to have a tranquilizing or sedative effect.

1. Whittick, 292.

Peony

The peony was named after the physician to the Olympian gods, Paeon or Paean, "Giver of Light." This was sometimes a title of Apollo, or the name of a mortal bearing Apollo's spirit, as in the Christian sense of an "incarnation." Later, it became the title of the divine physician Asclepius. Followers of the god were known as *paeoni*, whose hymns of thanksgiving for his miracles of healing gave us the word *paeans*.

The famous doctor and medical writer Galen claimed that if a woman lost her menses, her normal function could be restored if she wore a piece of peony root as a neck pendant.

Periwinkle

The common periwinkle (*Vinca minor*) used to be called "sorcerer's violet" or "flower of death" because condemned criminals were forced to wear garlands of periwinkle on their way to execution.[1] The custom may have arisen from the garlands of blue or violet flowers that pagan Romans placed on sacrificial animals on their last journey to the **altar.**

A major alkaloid in periwinkle is vinca-mine, now used in some kinds of cancer therapy. It is mildly hallucinogenic and has been used as a substitute for mar-ijuana, although there are toxic side effects including hair loss and muscle de-bilitation. More than seventy alkaloids have been identified in the plant, including reserpine, which may account for its seda-tive effect and its purported ability to "exorcise evil spirits" from the body.[2]

Of all the thousands of plant products that have been isolated and tested as cancer treatments, vinca alkaloids from the periwinkle are among the very few that show any significant activity; and these will affect only certain types of cancer.

1. Emboden, 66. 2., Duke, 106, 509.

Poinsettia

Some authorities say the pretty Christmas poinsettia (*Euphorbia pulcherrima*) is so poisonous that a child may die from eating one leaf. Others claim that the colorful bracts may be eaten as a vegetable without ill effect.[1] In Central America the poinsettia has been used as a medicine; in China it was used as a fish poison and a source of red dye.

One fact that few people know about this "flower" is that it is not a flower. The red "petals" are leaf bracts; the actual flowers are small and insignificant.

1. Duke, 190.

Poppy

Since opium and its derivatives—
morphine, heroin—are extracted from the
opium poppy, it is hardly surprising
to find the flower associated with sleep,
inertia, numbness, and death. Demeter as
a death Goddess was often shown with
poppies. The Etruscans' Island of the
Souls of the Dead was pictured with decorations of poppy capsules.[1] On the
other hand, the poppy was also associated
with fertility because of its numerous
seeds. Poppy seeds contain no opium and
are a good food source. Poppy leaves,
sacred to Mother Hera, were used for
divination.

The scarlet ornamental poppy, *Papaver
bracteatum*, contains no opium either; but
it does have the alkaloid thebaine,
which can be converted into codeine, but
not readily into heroin. Thebaine
yields an important narcotic antagonist,
naloxone, which is given to infants
born of heroin addicts, to help soften the
shock of withdrawal that such infants must
go through.[2]

1. Duerr, 209. 2. Duke, 343.

Rose

No flower, with the possible exception of
the **lotus,** has borne so many connotations and interpretations as the rose.
Throughout the Orient, the "Flower of the
Goddess" was the red China rose, or scarlet hibiscus, five-petaled like the classical
rose, before modern multipetaled varieties were created by selective breeding.[1] Like
the five-petaled apple blossom and the
five-lobed **apple,** the rose formed a natural **pentacle.** Like the apple and its
pentacle, the rose was sacred to the Goddess everywhere. Romans knew it as
the Flower of **Venus,** worn as a badge
of office by her prostitute-priestesses.[2]
When the Great Mother of the Gods
(Cybele) passed in solemn procession
through Roman streets, her image was
showered with "a snow of roses."[3]
Gnostic scriptures said the first rose
sprouted from the menarchal blood of
Psyche, the virgin Soul, when she became
enamored of Eros, symbol of sexuality.[4]

Arab mystics spoke of a paradise
called Gulistan, the Rose Garden, perhaps

derived from the ancient Babylonian Goddess Gula. Like the magic garden of the Fairy Queen, paradise centered on "the rose of love." The same word was applied to female genitals. Arab poets spoke coyly of the attraction of the female-genital rose and the secrets connected with it: "I think of nothing but the Rose; I wish nothing but the ruby Rose."[5] French troubadours adopted the same symbolism, which was embodied in their love poetry. To this day, *la rose* is a common French metaphor for "maidenhead."[6]

Just as the **rosary**—or "rose-wreath"—was adopted from the Middle East for application to the Christian version of the Virgin Goddess, so the rose also was declared proper to the worship of **Mary,** despite its earlier, blatantly sexual symbolism. **Rose windows** in the western, "female" facade of the cathedral usually featured Mary in the center. Church authorities claimed that Mary's immaculate conception was brought about through the magic of a rose: Mary's mother Anne (or Hana) conceived her daughter while smelling a rose.[7] Like Aphrodite before her, Mary was addressed as the Holy

Rose, Rose Garden, Rose Bush, Rose Garland, Mystic Rose, or Wreath of Roses.[8] The similarly five-petaled apple blossom belonged to Eve; the rose to Mary who was called her reincarnation, "the second Eve." Rose and apple were likewise merged in the Oriental symbol of the paradise **island,** Land of the Rose-Apple Tree.[9]

Despite the abundant female symbolism of the rose, some medieval mystics insisted on identifying the red rose with Christ. Albertus Magnus wrote of "the rose made red by the blood of Christ in his passion," recalling the Syrian **anemone** made red by the blood of Adonis. Yet other writers remembered the old female symbolism and wrote verses with obvious double meaning:

> When I dislodged the bud, a little seed
> I spilled just in the center, as I spread
> The petals to admire their loveliness
> Searching the calyx to its inmost
>   depths.[10]

Roses of various kinds also became mystic symbols of alchemy and hermetic lore. The blue rose stood for impossibility. The golden rose meant absolute achievement, or perfection. A seven-petaled rose

meant seven days of the week, seven planets, and seven degrees of enlightenment. Like the eight-petaled lotus of the Goddess Kali, the eight-petaled rose signified regeneration.[11]

1. Avalon, 203.   2. Wilkins, 108, 136. 3. Vermaseren, 83.   4. Barnstone, 68. 5. Shah, 108.   6. Dunham, 250.   7. Mâle, 238.   8. Wilkins, 93, 106.   9. Tatz & Kent, 84.   10. Williamson, 117, 172. 11. Cirlot, 263.

Scarlet Pimpernel

This magic flower was credited with the power to counteract the spells of evil sorcerers, especially those who caused splinters to become embedded in the victim's flesh. As a rationale for this beneficent influence, the scarlet pimpernel was said to have sprung out of the

ground beneath Christ's cross, where his **blood** fell on the **earth**.[1] The myth was obviously copied from that of Adonis, from whose blood sprang the red **anemone.**

1. Emboden, 91.

Sunflower

The sunflower of the ancients was probably not the giant blossom on its five-foot stalk that now bears this name, but rather several flowers of the daisy or marigold type that turn themselves to face the sun during its east-to-west arc across the sky. Greeks called the sunflower Clytie or Kleite (Famous One). Classical writers made her a **nymph** who loved the sun god and followed his fructifying beams with her head. Since her name was also the root of the word *clitoris* (kleitoris), it seems that the myth may have begun with symbols of the divine marriage between Father Heaven and Mother Earth.

Violet

The modest "shrinking violet" was burdened with an evil reputation in Christian symbolism. Because of its earlier association with the Goddess Aphrodite, it was said to represent lust. In Chaucer's time, a lady-love was called Violet and "flower of desire."[1] Ophelia says she would have given violets to Hamlet, in token of love, but they "withered all" with the death of her father.

Candied violets became a popular confection during the Renaissance. It was also common to treat coughs with violet tea.

1. Williamson, 105, 132.

18

PLANTS

L ike all other animals, human beings have always depended on plants for their sustenance. Even meat-eaters depend on plants, because their food consists of herbivores. So in a real sense, every creature clings for its life to Mother Earth's green garment. Even in the oceans, the food chain begins with minute plants.

Human beings naturally understood that plants are essential to life. Through long ages of trial and error, they also discovered medicines, poisons, and recreational drugs in the plants they ate. By further trial and error, they learned to enhance some of these effects by steeping, baking, boiling, fermenting, drying, mixing, distilling, and otherwise treating plants and plant extracts.

Herb lore was a complex discipline in primitive societies, requiring great patience, prodigious memory, and considerable ingenuity in explaining away one's failures. The herbal healer almost inevitably became a sacred person because she held power over other people's lives. In prepatriarchal times, clan mothers were usually the herbalist-healers, because doctoring was a simple extension of their mothering behavior patterns.

A certain amount of disillusionment with modern, depersonalized, high-tech doctoring has led to a popular resurgence of interest in the subject of herbal healing. During the decades of the forties and fifties, inspired by the famous examples of quinine and curare, scientists spent much time, money, and effort on collecting exotic plants for drug tests, and sifting the plant lore of exotic populations for possible valid new information. With a few noteworthy exceptions like reserpine from Indian snakeroot (*Rauwolfia serpentina*), native plant lore yielded thousands of dead ends. It was found that as a rule, so-called healing herbs did not do what native herbalists for countless centuries had claimed they would do.

Almost every herb has been termed "good for" such diseases as cancer, syphilis, tuberculosis, heart disease, and impotence; has been touted as a stomachic, carminative, tonic, or "blood purifier," whatever that may mean; and has been used for a hundred different complaints because native witch doctors never really knew what might or might not work. The use of herbs for healing was actually symbolic, the healing accomplished by an act of faith and the natural regenerative capacities of the human body, rather than by any virtue of the plant.

These disappointing facts did not seem to filter down to the general public, however. A few decades later, many people still believe in a vast herbal pharmacopeia that is largely mythical. One of the most popular mass delusions is that herbal healing is "natural," as opposed to modern medicines, which are "chemicals." Herbal mixtures are said to be free of "chemicals," and natural means better. But one of the surprising truths uncovered by extensive scientific identification of natural products is the enormous number of real chemicals that compose the tissues and juices of plants.

For example, ordinary tea leaves contain the following chemicals in addition to caffeine, polyphenols, and reducing sugars: carotene, riboflavin, nicotinic acid, pantothenic acid, ascorbic acid, tannin, malic acid, oxalic acid, kaempferol, quercitin, theophylline, theobromine, xanthine, hypoxanthine, adenine, inositol, hexenal, hexenol, butyraldehyde, isobutyraldehyde, isovaleraldehyde, linalool, acetophenone, benzyl alcohol, citral, catechin, and epigallocatechin. For another example, the popular kitchen staple cinnamon has the following chemicals in its bark and leaves: resins, tannins, mucilage, calcium oxalate, cinnzelanin, coumarin, cinnamaldehyde, eugenol acetate, cinnamyl acetate, methyl eugenol, benzaldehyde, cuminal-dehyde, benzyl benzoate, linalool, caryophyllene, safrole, camphene, limonene, delta-3-carene, alpha-phellandrine, alpha- and beta-pinene, sa-biene, alpha-terpinene, borneol, camphor, 1:8-cineole, geraniol, piperitone, alpha-terpineol, para-cymene, ethyl cinnamate, beta-caryophyllene, cinna-myl alcohol, alpha gumulene, gamma-ylangene, carene, phellandrine, humulene, alpha-ylangene, and coniferaldehyde. And these lists are not complete. They are only some compounds that have been identified so far. Many plant products have yet to be completely analyzed.

Such lists are the rule, not the exception: Mother Nature is an indefatigable producer of chemicals. However, real medicinal herbs usually have only one strongly pharmacologically active ingredient, which can be isolated and purified in the laboratory, then administered in controlled doses. A great disadvantage of "natural" herbal remedies is that the concentration of active ingredient can vary from one locality to another, from one season to another, even from one plant to another. Thus the effect of any given dosage is unpredictable. The difficulties that were experienced in dosing malaria patients with natural cinchona bark provide a classic example.

For these and other reasons it is usually appropriate to regard plants as symbols, not only because they have been given religious and magical con-notations throughout human history, but also because their supposed pharmacological effects are more often mythical than real. For every true discovery, like the digitalis in foxglove or the "aspirin" in willow bark, there have been a thousand false ones that seem equally tenacious. Dangerously poisonous plants have often been used to treat sick people, with the predictable effect of making them sicker. Most herbal remedies, however, have been shown to be both inactive and innocuous. Therefore, their principal function is to act as symbols of human faith in herbal healing.

Arum

The arum plant, called Jack-in-the-pulpit in the United States, has many European names that identify it as a **lingam-yoni** symbol more than anything else. It is known as Adam-and-Eve, bulls-and-cows, ladies-and-gentlemen, stallions-and-mares, kings-and-queens, lords-and-ladies, dog's dibber, bull's pintle, priest's pintle, or parson's billycock; also cuckoopint and wake robin. Geoffrey Grigson wrote of it, "Here's the penis of the lecherous cuckoo, who cuckolds the birds, and here's the penis inside a hood, or in a cowl—that is to say, the penis of a priest, or monk, or friar, who goes round cuckolding husbands."[1]

Because of all these fancied sexual connotations, the arum was often touted as an aphrodisiac. In the first century A.D., Dioscorides praised its erotic properties. In 1601, John Lyly wrote again of its supposed virtue of stimulating the passions. Actually, the plant is poisonous. Its tissues contain sharp needles of calcium oxalate, which cause intense irritation of mucous membranes.

1. Williamson, 212.

Ayahuasca

Known as *yaje* in Colombia, ayahuasca is one of the mind-altering drug plants considered sacred by South American Indians. "The drinking of yaje represents a return to the maternal womb, to the source and origin of all things." Under the influence of the drug, the Indians suppose that they can witness creation and many mythological events. This return to the womb is also "an acceleration of time, and is equivalent to death." After the symbolic dying, rebirth follows, with awakening into a better and wiser life.[1]

The plant's psychedelic effects are mainly due to the alkaloids harmine and harmaline.

1. Duke, 75.

Belladonna (Deadly Nightshade)

Atropa belladonna is a member of the Solanaceae family and one of the most notorious of witch plants. Named perhaps for that "beautiful lady," the Goddess, belladonna contains a variety of powerful poisonous alkaloids including atropine, scopolamine, and hyoscyamine. Children have been known to die from eating only three berries, which are especially deadly when unripe. Lesser doses of belladonna produce various central nervous system effects like delirium, distorted vision, incoherence, vasodilation, giddiness, and hallucinations. Many scholars believe that the witches' "trips" to the Sabbat were often brought about through ingestion of this and similar drugs, while the actual body remained comfortably at home.

Bulrush

In England, the bulrush is the cattail plant. In Egypt and in the Old Testament, it means the papyrus, a water plant whose stems made the **basket** in which the infant Moses was set adrift on the Nile. The Moses tale was originally that of an Egyptian hero, Ra-Harakhti, the reborn sun god of Canopus, whose life story was copied by biblical scribes.[1] The same story was told of the sun hero fathered by Apollo on the virgin Creusa; of Sargon, king of Akkad in 2242 B.C.; and of the mythological twin founders of Rome, among many other baby heroes set adrift in rush baskets. It was a common theme. Another Egyptian version of the bulrush basket made it a dense mass of papyrus plants growing out of the water, where **Isis** placed the infant Horus.[2] In India, the Goddess Cunti gave birth to a hero-child and set him adrift in a similar basket of rushes on the river Ganges.[3]

1. Graves, W.G., 150.   2. Budge, G.E. 1, 487.
3. Rank, 18–19.

Cherry Laurel

Scholars believe that chewing the cherry laurel caused the famous oracular frenzies of Delphic priestesses. Cherry laurel is a narcotic and a poison. It contains 0.1 percent of hydrogen cyanide, which can produce a toxic delirium such as the Delphic Pythonesses seem to have demonstrated. In the Vale of Tempe, oracular priestesses received the name of Daphne, "Laurel," which may have referred to the cherry laurel.

Coca

The coca shrub is the source of cocaine, which the Incas considered divine because of its physiological effects. Cocaine was also one of the ingredients of Coca-Cola, up to 1904, when the U.S. government compelled the Coca-Cola Company to discontinue its use. Cocaine continued to serve in medicine as an anesthetic and narcotic. At present, its major use is as an illicit recreational euphoriant or hallucinogen. Sad to say, the etiology of cocaine addiction is all too well known in our society and thus needs no further description.

Dittany

The aromatic dittany was originally sacred to the Cretan Goddess, whose title Diktynna (She of Mount Dicte) produced the plant's Greek name, *diktamnon*.

Dittany aroused the awe of the ancients by the curious property that earned it the alternate name of gas plant. It produces small quantities of an inflammable gas and will make a flash when a match or some other little flame is held under the flower, near the stem.

Fennel

Giant fennel stalks used to be sacred to fire-maker gods, like Prometheus, whose icons showed him with a fire drill in his hand. Prometheus was said to have brought down fire from heaven in a fennel stalk, to give it as a gift to humanity. "Greek islanders still carry fire from one place to another in the pith of a giant fennel," evidently because the pith is fire-resistant.[1]

The fennel retained its association with paganism, and hence witchcraft, during medieval and Renaissance times. In northern Italy, witches calling themselves *benandanti* (walkers of good) fought great mock battles with "evil sorcerers" called *malandanti* (walkers of evil), lest the latter's magic should injure the crops. These battles seem to have been ceremonial methods of averting agricultural disasters. The weapons on both sides were fennel stalks.[2]

1. Graves, G.M. 1, 144, 149. 2. Duerr, 35.

Foxglove

Foxglove is a corrupt form of "the Folks' glove," meaning the Little Folks, or the **fairies**. It was also called goblin's gloves and dead man's bells.

This plant is the original source of the heart-stimulating medicine digitalis (from Latin *digitae*, "fingers"), one of today's most valuable drugs, used for all kinds of ailments for many centuries. The artist van Gogh is said to have taken digitalis as a treatment for epilepsy. Digitalis can cause yellow vision, hallucinatory yellow rings, and other visual disturbances such as can be seen in van Gogh's art.[1] In excessive doses, digitalis can be fatal.

1. Duke, 166.

Ginseng

The Chinese revered the ginseng plant for much the same reasons that Europeans revered **mandrake**: its curiously twisted, often man-shaped roots inspired awe and numerous sexual fantasies. Ginseng was called Wonder of the World, Manroot, Man-Essence, Thunderbolt Root, Seed of Earth, Holy Herb, Five Fingers, and Tartar's Root. In accord with the standard myth of the phallic **lightning** god, ginseng is said to be generated when lightning strikes clear water: the fire-and-water, father-mother symbolism known throughout the world. Ginseng has been touted as a cure for impotence (of course), anemia, diabetes, neurasthenia, gastritis, insomnia, general debility, and many other ills.

Despite its undiminished popularity as a tonic, ginseng contains no pharmacologically active alkaloids at all.[1] It is officially named Cure-All *(Panax)*, but as the old aphorism says, cure-alls usually cure nothing. Nonetheless, the rarity and priciness of ginseng maintain a worldwide market for it and the usual assortment of enthusiasts who "swear by" its effects.

1. Emboden, 159–171.

Grass

The highest accolade in the Roman army was a **crown** of grass, awarded only to superheroes who had managed to save an entire army. Pliny records only seven recipients of the crown of grass in Roman history up to his time. The great significance of the grass crown dated from the very old custom of presenting a handful of grass to the conqueror of a whole country, thereby symbolically turning over to him the land itself.

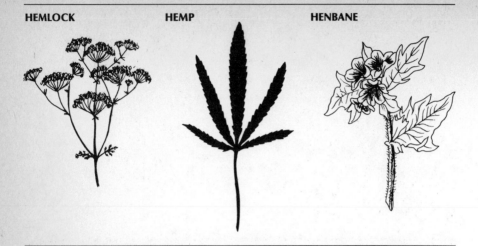

HEMLOCK　　　　**HEMP**　　　　　　**HENBANE**

Hemlock

The hemlock plant, which resembles a large wild carrot, is extremely poisonous. It was used in ancient Greece to execute condemned prisoners. The most famous victim of the hemlock was, of course, Socrates. Because of his story, "to drink the hemlock" became a symbol of suicide.

Hemp

Cannabis sativa, the hemp plant, has always been famous for its narcotic resin (hashish) as well as for its useful fibers, which still make excellent rope. In England, hemp was considered one of the sources of **broomsticks** that witches rode to the Sabbat. This was perhaps a metaphoric way of saying that the witches' experiences were simply hashish dreams.[1]

The now popular name of *Cannabis*, marijuana, is a female name originating in Central America, possibly because the plant was seen as having female characteristics.

1. Emboden, 76.

Henbane

Henbane is another "witches' herb," one of the Solanaceae, containing the usual mix of hyoscyamine, scopolamine, and so on. It is also called insane root, poison tobacco, hog's bean (or bane), and other names derived from its general nastiness. Pliny said four leaves of henbane in a drink would induce lunacy. He may have been right. Mania and convulsions have resulted from ill-advised attempts to smoke henbane. The Federal Drug Administration today classifies it as a poison.

Henna

Also known as Egyptian privet or mignon-ette, henna produces a red dye that was very important to the women of antiquity. Its red color was associated with their own life-giving "magic **blood**." They identified themselves with the **Goddess** by staining their hands and feet with henna. This was a custom of Greek women who worshiped Hecate, Syrian women who worshiped Anath, and Hindu women who worshiped any form of the Goddess. Egyptian mummies were wrapped in cloth dyed with henna, as a sign of re-birth from maternal blood. Indian

*leaf decoration, English,
17th century*

and Pakistani women still use the dye extensively, but Middle Eastern patriarchy took issue with it. Apocryphal scriptures mention "daughters of Cain"—that is, evil women—whose evil consisted of dying their hands and feet in the pagan manner.[1]

During the period of the Spanish Inquisition, women were arrested by the inquisitors for using henna to color their skin or nails, because such usage was equated with witchcraft.[2]

1. *Forgotten Books*, 78.   2. Walker, W.E.M.S., 391.

Ivy

Ivy was the letter *G*, *Gort*, in the druidic alphabet; it was said to represent intoxication, possibly because of the association of ivy with the Dionysian cult. Because of its traditional connection with the wine god, ivy was believed to cure as well as to cause drunkenness.[1] Romans used ivy leaves boiled in wine as a "hair of the dog" remedy for hangover. Plutarch said the Dionysian maenads (or bacchantes) were intoxicated as much by ivy as by wine. Certain varieties of ivy do contain toxic substances that "confuse the mind,"

as a sixteenth-century writer expressed it, and also make one sick. There have been occasional reports of death from poisonous ivy berries.[2]

1. de Lys, 63.   2. Duerr, 198.

Juniper

Juniper bushes used to be considered the domain of pagan spirits. Peasants in Waldeck made offerings to the juniper, calling on the **elves** and **fairies** that it harbored. A Swiss children's rhyme said, "Do not betray what the juniper bush has to protect." Many legends placed the entrance to the other world alongside a juniper bush. In Estonia it was said that Jesus rose to heaven out of a juniper bush.[1] Juniper was burned at funerals "to keep evil spirits away."[2]

Of course, the mystique associated with this plant suffered no detraction from the fact that the berries produced another kind of spirit: gin.

1. Duerr, 245–246.   2. G. Jobes 2, 895.

MANDRAKE
from an 18th-century engraving

Mandrake

Because it is mentioned in the Bible, medieval theologians went to great lengths to interpret the mandrake as a symbol of Christian faith. Its flowers represented the Holy Ghost, its root was Christ, the plant's growth demonstrated the growth of true piety, and so on. At the same time, ancient traditions and the use of mandrake in witches' recipes suggested quite different interpretations. It was called "phallus of the field," "Satan's apple," "devil's testicles," and "eggs of the genii" in Arabia. The French knew it as *main de gloire*, "hand of glory," sometimes contracted to Magloire, described as a little **fairy** spirit representing the plant. Old Testament Hebrew for mandrake fruit was *dudaim*, "love apples."

Josephus claimed that mandrakes could be taken from the ground only after being soaked with a woman's urine or menstrual **blood**. There seemed to be great difficulties involved in uprooting the plant. It was universally believed in the Middle Ages that when it was taken out of its mother the earth, the mandrake would emit a scream that would kill or drive insane anyone who heard it. The only way to obtain the plant was to tie a black **dog** (often identified as hell's creature) to its stem and run away with ears covered, so the dog would do the uprooting and suffer the consequences.[1] The twisted, often two-legged roots were so frequently viewed as an embryonic human being that Paracelsus maintained that he could create a new person by combining the mandrake with human semen and menstrual blood.[2]

Mandrake was much recommended in magic recipes, especially as a purgative, narcotic, and antispasmodic. Sometimes it was called the herb of beaten women, because mandrake berries were believed to remove the black and blue bruises inflicted by husbands' corrective admonitions.[3]

The original European mandrake is a member of the potato family, Solanaceae, indigenous to the Mediterranean area. In the United States, the name of mandrake was erroneously applied to the May apple (*Podophyllum peltatum*), and the name stuck. Therefore, this plant too is known as mandrake.

1. Simons, 67.   2. Emboden, 142–156.
3. Leek, 114.

MEADOWSWEET

MISTLETOE
(viscum album)

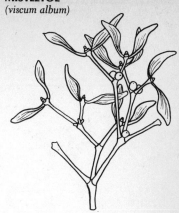

Meadowsweet

The meadowsweet herb was once a popular remedy for almost everything, from cancer, fevers, and melancholy to dropsy, rheumatism, and kidney ailments. In Scandinavia, it was added to beer and mead. It was also used for tea.

Like **willow** bark, meadowsweet was another of the witches' sources of "aspirin," that is, salicylic acid. This universal painkiller was first isolated from meadowsweet buds.[1]

1. Duke, 196.

Mistletoe

The North American mistletoe that we see at Christmastime, *Phoradendron serotinum*, bears both leaves and berries in clumps. The sacred mistletoe of ancient Europe, *Viscum album*, is a different plant whose leaves grow in winglike pairs, the berries in pairs or singly. Druids considered the plant's poisonous, pearly white berries to be drops of the **oak** god's semen, much as the red **holly** berries were drops of the life-giving lunar **blood** of the Goddess Hel (Holle). Thus the mistletoe acquired phallic significance. Druids "castrated" the oak god by cutting the mistletoe with a golden sickle, and catching it in a white cloth before it could touch the ground.

To Nordic pagans, the mistletoe was Guidhel, the same "guide to hell" that led Aeneas through the underworld as his Golden Bough.[1] The golden color of withered mistletoe was connected with its supposed ability to find buried treasure, through its magical familiarity with the underworld. The plant symbolized death (and eventual resurrection) for the "beautiful god" Balder, who was slain by a **spear** of mistletoe wielded by the blind Hod—actually, another version of the one-eyed Odin, supposed to be Balder's father. From this version of the dying and resurrected god arose the legend of the famous magic **sword** named Mistletoe.[2]

Because the mistletoe was the key to free access to the hidden places in the earth, Albertus Magnus and other authorities claimed that mistletoe can open every lock. Remembering also its phallic significance, some said the mistletoe was a love charm and an enhancer of potency; it "makes a man do often the act of generation."[3] Our present custom of kissing under the mistletoe is all that is left of earlier sexual orgies in honor of the earth and in hope of a fertile season.

The use of mistletoe at Christmastime encountered considerable opposition

from churchmen, who called it "the heathenish and profane plant, as having been of such distinction in the pagan rites of Druidism."[4] It continued anyway.

1. Hazlitt, 412.   2. Davidson, G.M.V.A., 187.
3. Wedeck, 189.   4. Hazlitt, 413.

Monkshood (Wolfbane, Aconite)

The monkshood plant was one of the most popular ingredients of witches' recipes. Its numerous potent alkaloids, including aconitine, can produce strange sensations, hallucinations, nervous excitement, dizziness, and even unconsciousness with weird dreams. Aconitine is very poisonous; one milligram can kill a human being. Nevertheless, this poisonous plant has been used often in medicine and is still a source of drugs for treating the inflammation of arthritis.

The classic mythological origin of aconite was the saliva of the three-headed underworld dog Cerberus. The plant sprang up where drops of slaver fell across the fields when Cerberus was dragged up to the earth's surface by Heracles. Because it was originally sacred to Hecate, the queen of the underworld, the plant used to be called hecateis.[1]

1. Graves, G.M. 2, 154.

Mugwort

Mugwort was also named *Artemisia vulgaris*, because like **wormwood** it used to be sacred to the Goddess Artemis. The old custom of gathering mugwort on Midsummer Eve led to another of its names, herb of Saint John, after the pagan festival of **Midsummer** was transformed into Saint John's Day. At Midsummer festivals, people wore mugwort **crowns** that were afterward hung up in the house or barn as protective talismans.[1] It was often claimed that divinational dreams could be had by adding a half kilo of mugwort to one's pillow stuffing, and clairvoyant trances could be brought on by drinking mugwort tea.[2] Large doses of this plant, however, could be toxic.

1. Williamson, 152.   2. Duke, 69.

Myrtle

Myrtle was sacred to the Goddess Aphrodite. The Greek word for myrtle meant also female genitals. The myrtle berry *(to myrton)* meant the clitoris.[1] Worshipers of Aphrodite's lover Adonis wore wreaths of myrtle and believed that myrtle wands could place them in communication with the god in the underworld. Thus, myrtle wands were usually recommended for getting in touch with the dead, either by listening over a grave, or by a necromantic invocation.[2]

Greek sailors invoked the blessing of Aphrodite by carrying myrtle on their voyages to new colonies. Among Hebrews, the Feast of Booths featured structures of cypress branches and myrtle, symbolizing happiness and fertility. In Rome, because the myrtle belonged to Venus, it represented union in marriage and specifically the union of Sabine and Roman tribes at the city's foundation. Therefore, as preservers of the city, successful Roman generals were awarded the crown of myrtle, known as the *ovation*.[3]

1. Keuls, 30.   2. Trachtenberg, 224.   3. G. Jobes 1, 389; 2, 1143.

Oleander (Dogbane)

In Spain, the oleander was called laurel. Some said that this, rather than **cherry laurel,** was the leaf chewed by Pythian priestesses to bring on their oracular frenzies.[1] Greeks knew the shrub as *rhododaphne*, from Daphne the laurel Goddess, and also as *rhododendron* (rosy branch) and *nerion*. A common modern name for the plant is rosebay. Like all members of the dogbane family it is extremely poisonous. Pliny commented on the virulence of its milky juice.

Some scholars believe the oleander was the biblical "willow of the brook" or Jericho rose, also called "rose of the waterbrooks" and "rose tree."[2]

1. Duerr, 206.   2. Duke, 327.

Ololiuqui

The ololiuqui herb with its trumpet-shaped, morning-glory-like flowers is a potent hallucinogen used by Mexican Indians, who inherited it from the Aztecs. Extracts were drunk in religious rites and to bring on divinatory visions. The Aztec name of the plant was *tlitliltzen*. The seeds contain amides of lysergic acid.

Pennyroyal

The pennyroyal plant was long used not only as a tea and an aromatic flavoring, but particularly for female reproductive problems such as menstrual cramps and uterine tumors. Pennyroyal oil is some-what ecbolic (produces uterine contractions), but practically useless for the medicinal purpose that was most often tried, that of an abortifacient. "While pennyroyal oil may indeed induce abortion, it does so only in lethal or near-lethal doses."[1] Less than one ounce can kill the patient.

Despite such potential toxicity, pennyroyal was widely favored as an aid to digestion. An Italian icon represents digestive health by a classic female figure crowned with a wreath of pennyroyal.[2]

1. Duke, 308.   2. G. Jobes 1, 444.

Peyote

Peyote is the holy herb of Mexico, ceremonially consumed in the form of "buttons" from the mescal cactus. The active alkaloid is mescaline, but peyote contains at least eight other alkaloids that have been isolated and identified.

Peyote intoxication, which may last several days, produces vivid hallucinations that the Indians regard as real experiences in another world. Worshipers believe the drug makes them braver, stronger, wiser, and immune to hunger and thirst. The hangover, however, is not at all pleasant.

Reed

The reed is called Syrinx, after the Greek **nymph** pursued by the god Pan. Syrinx turned herself into a reed and hid among the other reeds by the river Ladon. Pan, unable to distinguish her from the others, cut several of them together and made them into a Pan pipe.[1] This revised myth was meant to illustrate the use of reeds in such musical instruments as pipes and flutes. The reed was also a symbol of male divinity, a **scepter** of the sacred king in the Near East. When the vegetation deity Mot was sacrificed, his reed scepter was broken to symbolize his loss of virility and vitality. He was called Son of God and sacrificial **lamb.**[2] A similar reed scepter distinguished the sacrificed god Set in Egypt, and was adapted to the Christian myth also, when the same kind of scepter was presented to Jesus.[3] In the druidic alphabet, the reed is Ngetal, representing the death season of November.

Playing flutes and other reed instruments was a female prerogative, according

to the Fore people of New Guinea, until the men stole the flutes from the women and made new rules to keep women from seeing or touching them. Flutes became phallic symbols like the reed scepter. When a Fore man dies, his flute is broken, just as the ancient scepter of the sacred king was broken. The pieces are buried with him.[4]

1. Graves, G.M. 1, 101–102.   2. *Larousse*, 78.
3. Graves, G.M. 1, 283.   4. Sanday, 198.

Rosemary

Rosmarinus, the Latin name of this plant, means "rose of the sea," and was once a title of the Goddess **Venus.** It used to be called the Elfin Plant because it was sacred to the **fairies.**[1]

Shakespeare repeated the old belief that rosemary was a memory charm, perhaps because its scent lingers. For centuries it shared the honors of Christmas adornment with the **holly, ivy,** and **mistletoe;** but this usage declined. In England, rosemary is planted on graves as a symbolic pledge of remembrance.[2] It was formerly hung in churches at Christmas as a sign of welcome to fairies and elves.[3]

1. Wimberly, 350.   2. Whittick, 305.   3. G. Jobes 2, 1350.

Rue

Rue is a general name for any of a large family of plants, *Rutaceae*, that contain a variety of alkaloids. Syrian rue, *Peganum harmala*, contains the narcotic hallucinogen harmine, which was used as a truth serum by Nazi scientists during World War II.[1] Overdoses of this drug cause depression of the central nervous system.

Catholic priests used to sprinkle holy water by dipping it with sprigs of rue *(Ruta graveolens)*. The herb was considered effective against evil spirits, perhaps because of its noxious odor.[2]

1. Duke, 352.   2. Emboden, 79.

Rushes

There is an old belief, still extant in the more backward areas of France and the British Isles, that anyone who braids rushes into a **ring,** and looks through it, will be able to see the **fairies.** The only catch is that whichever eye looks through the ring will go blind afterward. For obvious reasons, few people have tested the hypothesis—which is probably why it still survives.

Saffron

Dioscorides mentions the use of saffron as a perfume, a religious **incense,** and a dye applied to the forehead for religious ceremonies. Saffron used to be a folk remedy for dozens of complaints, from tumors to diabetes. Now it is used principally as a cooking spice in Europe. East Indians still believe that it will heal menstrual difficulties and kidney ailments.[1] The dye made from saffron flowers is regarded as holy; it creates the regulation gold-orange coloring for monks' robes.

1. Duke, 148.

Sage

Named after the "wise-woman," *saga*, the sage was long regarded as a cure for paralysis and an aid to digestion.[1] Nowadays it is used chiefly as a food flavoring.

1. Trachtenberg, 207.

Shamrock

The shamrock or three-leaf clover is now claimed by the Irish as a symbol of their patron saint, Patrick, and of their country generally. However, worship of the shamrock vastly predated Christianity in Ireland and other Celtic lands. Its three heart-shaped leaves were supposed to be a natural reference to the Triple Mothers of Celtic lore, sometimes called Three Brigits or Three Morgans, the "mother-hearts" of Celtic tribes.

The symbol was not solely Irish, either. Its name came from the Arabic *shamrakh*, apparently an emblem of the triple lunar Goddess of pre-Islamic Arabia. The same **trefoil** decoration was common in the ancient Indus civilization and bore the same sacred connotation.

Despite the forced association with Saint Patrick's legend, the shamrock was not wholly liked by Christian authorities in Ireland. For this reason there arose the notion that a *four*-leaf clover was better—luckier—since four was usually taken to be a "masculine" number and the number of the cross. Also, the odd gene that produces four-leaf clovers among three-leaf ones is apparently rare and recessive, giving them the glamour of the uncommon.

Squill

Squill is the Mediterranean "sea onion" that grows half immersed on sandy shorelines. An Egyptian papyrus of 1500 B.C. recommended bulbs of squills for heart disease. Only in the twentieth century A.D. was it finally discovered that squill does indeed affect the heart in much the same way as digitalis, depending on dosage. Other effects of the plant are: emesis, diuresis, expectorant, and (in excess quantity) gastrointestinal poisoning.

In ancient times, squills were used for shamanistic purgings, trials by ordeal, and magical purifications. Squills rubbed on a gate or doorpost were said to be an infallible defense against evil forces seeking entrance. An Italian icon representing protection against enemies consists of a Goddess wearing a jeweled crown, holding a squill in her hand.[1]

1. G. Jobes 1, 425; 2, 1487.

Thistle

The thistle was declared symbolic of original sin, because of the biblical passage about God's curse on the land: "Cursed is the ground for thy sake. . . . Thorns also and thistles shall it bring forth to thee" (Genesis 3:17–18). Alcuin claimed on the strength of this passage that thistles were unknown on earth before the fall of Eve and Adam. Nevertheless, because the thistle was a sacred plant to pre-Christian Scottish clans, it remained the official emblem of Scotland. The plant had a martial symbolism, perhaps dating back to the belief expressed by Pliny that thistles affect the womb of an expectant mother so that she brings forth only male children.[1]

Some medieval herbalists believed that thistles could cure melancholia and plague. The "caroline thistle" was named after Charlemagne because of a certain legend: Charlemagne, on God's instructions, shot an **arrow** into the air to find a cure for such diseases as melancholia and plague, and it landed on that particular type of thistle, God's own revelation of the cure.[2]

Thistles were even credited with the ability to cure at long distance. Witches used to say that any sore on the body of a domestic animal could be cured by "gathering red thistles before daybreak and putting one at each corner of the compass with a stone in the middle," accompanying this performance with an incantation.[3]

1. Williamson, 194, 220. 2. Emboden, 83. 3. Leek, 29.

Thorn Apple (Jimsonweed)

The term *thorn apple* referred either to the **hawthorn** or to the intensely poisonous Jimsonweed (*Datura stramonium*), which was a frequent ingredient of witches' recipes. *Datura* contains a number of powerful alkaloids such as atropine and scopolamine. It has been responsible for more cases of plant poisoning than any other plant.

Its American name, Jimson, is a contraction of Jamestown, the first settlement in Virginia, where many colonists were accidentally poisoned by *Datura* when trying out the local "pot herbs." Jimsonweed in very small amounts has been successfully used to ease the choking attacks of asthma. Seeds have been deliberately taken for hallucinogenic effect, although this is a decidedly risky procedure because of their extreme toxicity. Symptoms of Jimsonweed poisoning include blurred vision, dry throat, dizziness, hallucinations, slurred speech, inability to urinate, and coma, generally followed by death.[1]

1. Duke, 161–162.

Thyme

The word *thyme* comes from the Greek, "to make a burnt offering," because the Greeks used it in temple **incense.**[1] Nowadays it is often used in cooking. Dried flowers are said to protect linens from insect damage. Thyme teas and ointments have long been used medicinally. Thymol, the oil of thyme, is deodorant and antiseptic and fungicidal, but also quite poisonous.[2]

1. Leek, 45.   2. Duke, 484.

Tobacco

Tobacco was unknown in Europe until it was discovered in use as a sacred plant among the Indians of the New World. The Indians did not take tobacco as a daily drug, but only in the solemn, formal tobacco-smoking ceremony. The calumet (pipe) was offered first to the sky, mouthpiece upward, so the heavenly deity could have the first puff; then to the earth, mouthpiece downward. Then, puffs of smoke were sent to the spirits of each of the four directions. Ritual decorations and tribal fetishes contributed to the solemnity of the tobacco ceremony.

Europeans, however, soon became addicted to tobacco after its introduction

VERBENA
(vervain)

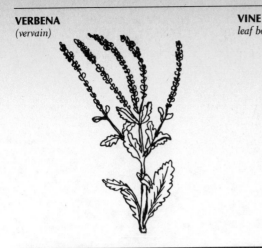

VINE
leaf border pattern

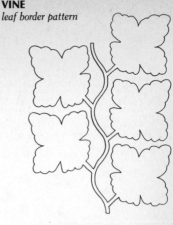

during the reign of Elizabeth I of England. People used it as a magic amulet, as a "clyster" (enema), and for other medicinal purposes, and they smoked it whenever they could. The sacredness that the Indians had found in tobacco was lost, to the regret of some afficionados. Christopher Marlowe wrote that Holy Communion would have been "much better being administered in a tobacco pipe."[1]

1. Thomas, 9, 20.

Verbena (Vervain)

Some varieties of *Verbenaceae* contain verbenalin (cornin), and others contain verbenone, a constituent of Spanish verbena oil. Although this plant has been prominent in the herbal pharmacopeia for centuries, its medicinal benefits are virtually nil.

The name *verbena* means "altar plant." Romans claimed it was sacred to **Venus** and had the power to inspire love. Under the English name of Saint John's wort, it was credited with many magical properties throughout European history. A charm that was repeated in the gathering of the plant demonstrates its Christianization in later centuries:

> Hallowed be thou Vervain, as thou growest on the ground
> For in the mount of Calvary there thou was first found.
> Thou healedst our Savior Jesus Christ, and staunchedst his bleeding wound,
> In the name of the Father, the Son, and the Holy Ghost,
> I take thee from the ground.[1]

1. Thomas, 181.

Vine

Although there are many kinds of vines, the usual reference in sacred art and symbolism is to the grapevine. This was preeminently an incarnation of Dionysus, or Bacchus, in his role of sacrificial savior. His immolation was likened to the pruning of the vine, necessary to its seasonal rebirth. A Syrian form of Dionysus was the "beautiful youth," Ampelus, who was sacrificed to sacred **bulls** and then "turned into a vine" (reborn in the grape harvest).

In Syria and Babylon the vine was a sacred **tree of life.** Old Testament writers

adopted it as an emblem of the chosen people, and New Testament writers made it an emblem of Christ (John 15:1, 5). When accompanied by wheat sheaves in sacred art, the vine signified the blood (wine) and body (bread) of the savior: an iconography that began in paganism and was soon adopted by early Christianity.

In the druidic alphabet the vine made the letter *M*, *Muin*, a sign of exaltation—probably through sacred drunkenness, like the wine-fired frenzies of the Dionysian maenads.

Wormwood

Wormwood's Latin name, *Artemisia absinthium*, reveals what Trevisa wrote in the fourteenth century A.D., that it was sacred to the Goddess Artemis, and was known as "mother of herbs." Its English name came from *wermod*, "spirit mother," the same as German *Wermut*, French *vermouth*.[1]

Wormwood was used in the manufacture of absinthe, from ancient witches' recipes, which became a commercial product in the eighteenth century. Soon, however, it became apparent to the

French government that absinthe was excessively addictive and dangerous, capable of destroying brain cells, causing blindness, and so on. During the nineteenth century, the drink was outlawed.

1. Potter & Sargent, 274–275.

Yarrow

The yarrow plant, *Achillea millefolium*, was named after Achilles, the hero of the Trojan war (ca. 1200 B.C.), who was said to have stopped the bleeding of his soldiers' wounds with yarrow leaves. Innumerable pharmacological effects, in addition to blood-clotting, have been attributed to yarrow. It is still used as an infusion for stomach and kidney troubles, and to reduce inflammation of the gums.

Yarrow stalks are sacred **wands** in China, having furnished the original divining sticks of the *I Ching*.

19

TREES

Trees have always been recognized as Nature's best gift to the human race. Trees provide food, houses, tools, medicines, boats, fire, containers, carts, weapons, even some types of clothing; also shade in summer, warmth in winter, and beauty the year round. Trees were to be approached with awe and circumspection, for they were obviously gigantic living entities, which primitive folk endowed with conscious spirit. It does not take too much imagination for any of us to see a thousand humanlike or animal-like faces and forms in tree foliage, especially in dim light. Our ancestors were certainly no less imaginative. If anything, they were more prone to anthropomorphize whatever their eyes saw.

Believing in the conscious tree spirit, then, people worshiped the tree for bestowing itself upon them, and hoped it would not resent being slain for human use. There were solemn ceremonies to be observed in cutting down a live tree. Even in historical times, lumberjacks of the Palatinate asked forgiveness of each tree before felling it.[1]

Tree worship was common, not only among the Druids who were famous for it, but also among many other peoples the world over. Middle Eastern nations all had sacred groves in which to practice phyllomancy: the art of divination by listening to the rustling of leaves.[2] Certain individual trees become oracular gods or goddesses, whose voices could be interpreted only by a sage or priestess dwelling beside her tree. Even the Bible has an example in Deborah, onetime ruler of Israel, who lived under the oracular tree that bore her own name (Judges 4:5).

In addition to worshiping real trees, the ancients sometimes envisioned the entire cosmos in the form of a tree, believing that earth's trees were tantalizing keys to the greatest of mysteries—which made their infinite variety all the more wonderful.

1. Duerr, 344.   2. d'Alviella, 159.

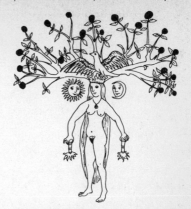

Acacia

The acacia furnished the holy "shittim wood" of which the **altar** of the Hebrew tabernacle and the **ark** of the covenant were made, according to the Bible. Because of this biblical tradition, acacia wood was frequently used in initiatory rituals by secret fraternities, such as the Freemasons. It was said to symbolize purity.

The tradition was older than the Bible, however. Nomadic tribes of the Arabian desert worshiped the tree for thousands of years. It was claimed that any person who broke a twig from a living acacia would die within the year. It was viewed as a Mother tree; its gum symbolized menstrual blood. In Egypt, the acacia was the residence of the Goddess Neith. Its thorns were said to represent repulsion of evil and may have been the original crowns of thorns worn by sacred kings at the time of their sacrificial deaths.[1]

1. G. Jobes 1, 21.

Alchemical Tree

This mysterious treelike symbol appeared in a number of alchemical texts, always as a crowned, naked woman with branches sprouting from her head, fruits and a **phoenix** bird on the branches, the **sun**
to her right, the **moon** to her left, and objects that might be roots or **wands** of power in her hands. Like the Tarot figure called The World (also a naked woman with wands in her hands), this seems to have been a late version of the primal mother tree, also called the **Tree of Life.** The implication was that the alchemist, through certain elemental manipulations, could understand the essence of this World Tree, which was almost the same as understanding the mystery of woman, and would give access to the Cosmic Mind and the secrets of creation.

Chinese alchemy identified the ailanthus as the Tree of Life, Tree of Heaven, or paradise tree. The graceful ailanthus was revered for its tenacious ability to flourish almost anywhere, even under the most adverse conditions. Also, the sacred tree has two sexes. One type could be considered definitely female (carrying the fertile flowers). The sacred ailanthus was imported into the United States, where it now grows exuberantly on city sidewalks, vacant lots, waste dumps, bad soil, in polluted air, and in similar conditions where no other tree could survive.[1]

1. G. Jobes 1, 55.

Alder

A tree associated with several pagan gods, the alder represented the letter *F (fearn)* in the druidic tree alphabet. It was known in medieval legend as the tree of the Erl King, or alternatively as the tree sacred to the god Bran, brother of Branwen who kept the **Cauldron** of Regeneration. Thus the tree stood for the idea of resurrection. It bore the same significance in the *Odyssey.* The beginning of the Celtic solar year was marked by the alder tree.[1] In the territory of Celtic druids there used to be a tribe known as Arverni, "People of the Alder."[2]

The Roman name of the alder was Vernostonus. It was associated with the Romano-Celtic god Cocidius, a form of Silvanus who was prince of **satyrs** in the Dionysian myth: an elder wine god, a wild man of the woods, and a disreputable orgiast.[3]

1. G. Jobes 1, 66.　2. Markale, 92.　3. Green, 112.

Ash

Yggdrasil, the World Ash Tree of Norse myth, had three huge roots. One root stretched to the underground spring of Urd (Earth), where the **Norns** live in their **cave** and perpetually decide the fates of human beings. Urd was the name of the eldest Norn. The Norns were the northern version of the Fortunae or Moerae, who were also called Meliae, "ash-tree nymphs," by the Greeks.

The second root of the World Ash Tree reached to the **well** of Mimir in the land of the frost **giants.** This well was the source of all wisdom. Odin sacrificed one of his eyes for a drink from its enlightening waters. In Cornwall he was remembered as Odin the Wanderer or the Troll of Tolcarne, whom one could summon by holding leaves of ash, oak, and thorn, while pronouncing a secret phrase that could be taught only by a woman to a man, or by a man to a woman, as in the "witches' circle" of alternating sexes.[1]

The third root of the World Ash Tree went to Niflheim, the underworld presided over by the goddess Hel.[2] To enter the underworld and learn its feminine secrets, such as the magic of the **runes,** Odin hung nine nights on the tree as a sacrifice to his own godhead. In the druidic tree alphabet the ash was *N* or *nion,* meaning knowledge.

The roots of Yggdrasil produced a magic fluid called *aurr,* never precisely defined, but most probably the same life-giving female lunar **blood** that lies secretly at the root of all universal-elixir myths. The tree was also the universal mother, "source of unborn souls," like the **Tree of Life** found in nearly all Asiatic myths.[3] One story said that the first man, Askr, was created from the ash tree: hence his name. The Latin name of the tree is Fraxinus, "firelight." Though this may have meant the light of knowledge, ash was a traditional wood for the Yule log.[4]

1. Evans-Wentz, 176.   2. d'Alviella, 167.
3. Davidson, G.M.V.A., 195.   4. Williamson, 88–89.

Aspen

Aspen was the letter *E, eadha,* in the druids' tree alphabet. Aspen wood, being light but tough, was much prized in medieval times for the manufacture of arrows. Aspen trees were also much used for phyllomancy (divination by leaf-rustlings) because the leaves are constantly tremulous and their friction creates soft sounds.

Birch

The birch tree stood for *beth,* the first letter of the druidic alphabet. It was the sacred *beth* of Cerridwen, representing beginnings and births, as did the corresponding *alpha* of the Greek alphabet. The whiteness of the tree's bark apparently suggested its connection with the White Goddess, who was both birth-giver and death-bringer in her Crone form as the carrion-eating white **sow**. Birch or *beorc* was also the runic letter *B*.

Cedar

The cedars of Lebanon were made world-famous by the high regard in which they were held by writers of the Bible. Much of the wood for Solomon's symbolic (and probably mythical) temple came from these fabulous cedars. Hebraic reverence for the cedar was evidently copied from the attitude of the Assyrians, who said "the cedar is the tree that produces the pure charm and drives away the unfriendly demons." They believed that the cone of a cedar tree could heal the sick, that the secret names of the gods were written on the sacred cedar, and that the tree itself, properly understood, was "the revelation of the oracles of heaven and earth."[1] Like the oak **groves** of Europe, the cedar groves were considered oracular shrines.

1. d'Alviella, 150, 158.

Christmas Tree

The Christmas tree is still one of the Western world's most beloved symbols, although it had no meaning in the Judeo-Christian context but was drawn almost entirely from pagan tree worship. Preserved through the centuries in central Europe, it was unknown in English-speaking countries until after 1840, when Prince Albert, the German bridegroom of Queen Victoria, brought the custom from his native land to England. The Teutonic Christmas tree dated back to Yule celebrations, along with the **candles**, gifts, and sacrificial **pig** with an **apple** in its mouth. But there were pagan elements from southern Europe also. Certain priests of Attis called *dendrophori*, "tree-bearers," annually selected a **pine** tree from the sacred **grove** (*pinea silva*) to carry the effigy of the god into his Roman temple. The *dendrophori* were charged with the duty of setting up and decorating the tree, upon which the god was presented for sacrifice.[1] Perhaps this was the origin of the custom of hanging small male effigies, such as gingerbread men, on the Christmas tree.

Like all evergreens, such as the **holly** and **ivy,** the pine tree stood for a promise of eternal life because it kept its vital appearance even when other plants died off during the winter. Naturally this applied only to the living pine tree, lighted and decorated in the woods where it stood. Trees that were cut and brought indoors would soon become brown and dead, thus contradicting the symbolic meaning.

1. Vermaseren, 115.

Cypress

According to Orphic descriptions of the afterlife, the first thing a newly arrived **soul** would see in the underworld was a white cypress tree leaning over the **fountain** of Lethe, the Waters of Oblivion. All souls would be very thirsty and would crave the water. But the enlightened one must not drink of Lethe, for that would erase all memory of past lives. The Orphic initiate, having been properly coached when alive, would seek out the fountain of Mnemosyne (Memory).

Since this information came from the savior Orpheus, who descended into Hades and rose again, the Maenads annually reenacted the event, showing how their foremothers had sacrificed Orpheus. Eventually the savior was identified with the dying god of May Day festivals, and with the cypress tree itself, which was often used for **Maypoles.** In modern

Epirus, shepherd girls continue the tradition of the maenads, dancing around the "May boy" as he lies in the grass, and singing, "Look what a youth has died here, what a young cypress."[1]

The Goddess herself used to be called "the Cypress" in Lebanon.[2] The son of **Venus** "in his mother's lap" was depicted in Rome as a child within the foliage of a cypress tree, peeking forth very much like the **Green Man** images of northern Europe. In Romanized Gaul, cypress was sacred to Dis, god of death.

1. Duerr, 195. 2. d'Alviella, 142.

Elder

Often confused with the **alder**, the elder tree had a separate letter in the druidic alphabet, *ruis (R)*, sacred to the Elder Goddess or Crone, the Caillech, who was Hel, queen of the underworld. Naturally, the elder became known as a witch tree. Spirits of the pagan dead, once called Helleder, were said to be imprisoned in elder wood. They would be transformed into avenging **demons** and would haunt and persecute anyone who cut down an elder tree to make furniture. Moreover, a man who fell asleep under an elder tree would have visions of Hel's under-world, which Christians converted into hell.[1] Elder made witches' "travel-broomsticks."

Yet the healing magic of Hel's tree was not entirely forgotten. Medieval folk believed that a wreath of elder leaves worn as a collar would cure every pain in the neck.[2]

1. Emboden, 71. 2. Trachtenberg, 207.

Elm

The name of the German city Ulm means "elm tree." Medieval historians said the city was founded by Goddess-worshiping Amazons who ruled the city for many centuries and worshiped their Great Mother in **groves** of sacred elm trees (Latin *ulmae*).[1] Northern Teutons believed the elm tree represented primordial female powers. The elm was said to be the source of the world's first woman.[2] Her name was Embla. Her male consort was produced from the ash tree. There are other mythological hints that the first couple in the primal garden were actually produced by the Tree of Life, which represented the birthgiving Goddess, rather than having been forbidden by a patriarchal god to get anywhere near it, as in our familiar Bible mythology.

1. Borchardt, 104. 2. Williamson, 89.

Fir

The silver fir was *ailm* or "A" in the druidic alphabet, perhaps because it was used as a Yule tree and so represented the rebirth of the **sun.** Evergreens in general were powerful symbols of ongoing life or immortality, because they seemed to keep themselves alive when everything else died during the winter. Fir branches are still popular decorations for the Christmas season. The Greeks used to have a fir-tree Goddess, connected with the woodland cult of Pan. Her name was Pitys. Satyrs wore fir twigs in her honor. Hellenic writers later demoted her into a mere nymph with the usual mythic transformation given to every ancient Goddess of trees: she was turned into "her" tree to prevent some god from raping her.[1] Forgotten were the older myths and icons showing the god either dying at the tree's foot, or hanging on it like the sacrificed satyr Marsyas.

1. Graves, G.M. 1, 103.

Grove

The sacred grove, Latin *nemus*, was the characteristic shrine of the Great Goddess Diana throughout the Roman empire: hence her titles, Diana of Nemi, Nemesis, Nemetona, and Nemorensis. In Ireland her **oak** groves were called *nemed*.[1] Her consorts among the Celtic gods were known to the Romans as Silvanus or Rigonemetis (King of the Grove).[2] She was still widely worshiped in sacred groves throughout Europe in the fifth century A.D., when a Christian writer complained that all the people "worship a cut branch and call a log Diana."[3] A century later, another Christian authority claimed that all the woods were inhabited by female **devils** called Dianas.[4]

In the Middle East, the Goddess of the Grove was **Asherah,** whose groves were made "on every high hill, and under every green tree" (1 Kings 14:23). Asherah was known as the Mother or Creator of all the gods, including the Heavenly Father, El, whose name was used as a synonym for "God" in biblical texts.[5] At times El even claimed to be her spouse. In the sacred grove of Asherah in Jerusalem, there were sacrificial feasts, according to Apion. Offerings of **goats,** sheep, or other animals were killed, devoured, and their remains buried in a special pit or *mundus*, a **womb** symbol for their rebirth.[6]

1. Joyce 1, 360.   2. Green, 112.   3. Graves, W.G., 273–274.   4. J. H. Smith, 240.   5. *Larousse*, 74, 76.   6. Barrett, 203.

Hawthorn

Also called the May tree, the hawthorn
represented the White Goddess Maia,
mother of both **Hermes** and Buddha as
separate versions of the Enlightened One.
She was the Goddess of love and death, both
the ever-young Virgin giving birth to
the god, and the Grandmother bringing
him to the end of his season. Therefore her
tree was associated with both female
sexuality and destructive spells.

Some English countryfolk had an
intense horror of sleeping in the same
house with hawthorn blossoms, thinking
this would bring great misfortune.
Yet hawthorn blossoms were gathered each
May Day, to place in a wreath around
the **Maypole.** In the perpetual style of the
lingam-yoni, the wreath served as the
female symbol surrounding the phallic
pole. The gathering of the hawthorn
blossoms for this occasion was known
as "going a-Maying."[1] In Celtic tradition the tree was sacred to Olwen. It
also represented fertility in the druidic
alphabet, where it formed the letter
H, *uath.*

The Goddess as death-bringing Crone
was connected with the hawthorn in the
legend of Cu Chulainn. After pronouncing her death curse on the hero, in her
carrion **crow** shape, she settled in
a hawthorn thicket on the plain of Muir-
themne. Therefore, the place is known as
"the hawthorn of the Crow."[2]

1. Williamson, 128–129.   2. Markale, 113.

Hazel

An important food tree, producing the
once-prized hazelnuts (filberts), the hazel
was sacred to witches and to the Celtic sea
god, Manannan. It was considered
symbolic of female wisdom. Bards used to
claim that their knowledge of rhymes,
epic tales, secrets of magic, and poetic inspiration came from eating "sacred
hazelnuts" that dropped from the tree of
wisdom—symbolically, the Goddess as in-
structress. The tree's alphabetical letter was
C *(coll).* Its wood came to be known
as "witch hazel" because it was the wood
of choice for witches' divining **rods.**[1]
It was believed that such rods could locate
buried treasure as well as underground
minerals and water. In Norway, hazel was
sacred to the god Thor. Its connection with
deities of the sea led to a custom of
European shipmasters, to wear "wishing
caps" woven with hazel twigs, which were
supposed to enable the ship to weather safely
even the most severe storm at sea.[2]

1. Trachtenberg, 225.   2. G. Jobes 1, 735.

Holly

The druidic alphabet named the holly *tinne* (*T*), the form of a **Tau cross,** which may be why the holly represented heroism and was dedicated to Cu Chulainn. According to the Teutonic tribes, holly belonged to the underground Goddess Holle (Hel), whose name was also rendered Halja, Hilde, Hulda, Holde, Helle, Hol, and Hella. The holly's red berries were seen as drops of her life-giving **blood,** in which lay the secret of the tree's immortality or year-round greenness.

Holle as universal mother was the patron of all newborn children and had charge of naming them—which used to be the symbolic equivalent of giving the child its soul. The Hollekreisch baptismal formula preserved the idea in Germany. Persons at the baptismal party would raise the cry of "Hollekreisch! Hollekreisch! What shall this child's name be?" Then the response came: "Holle! Holle! This child's name shall be . . . " whatever it was.[1]

According to Pliny, holly trees planted in the courtyard of a house would keep away all evil spells. An English herbal written in A.D. 1640 said the same thing, piously adding that it was "a superstition." Another notable holdover from

paganism was the medieval Holly King or Holly Knight, also known as the Green Knight or the Wild Man, who appeared at midwinter festivals in the guise of an ancient sacrificial god.[2]

1. Trachtenberg, 42. 2. Williamson, 62–63, 73.

Laurel

Also called Grecian laurel or green bay, laurel was the plant of divinity and prophecy, chewed by the Goddess's priestesses in the vale of Tempe, until Apollo's cult replaced hers. This was mythologized as Apollo's attempted rape of the Delphic priestess Daphne, who foiled him by turning into a laurel tree.[1] Despite the Hellenic takeover, the Goddess's laurel **crowns** continued to be awarded to victors in Olympic and Pythian games at Delphi and elsewhere.[2] Romans believed that the laurel consecrated its wearer to **Jupiter,** wielder of the lightning; thus arose the belief that the laurel is never struck by lightning. Roman priests used laurel twigs to sprinkle holy water or sacrificial blood, so the laurel was the forerunner of the Christian church's aspergillum.[3]

Because of its long association with pagan deities, an early Christian authority declared that wearing a laurel wreath was a

sin that could send a man directly to hell.[4] Nevertheless, the custom refused to die. The national poet of England still rejoices in the title of Laureate, meaning "Laurel-crowned one."

1. Graves, G.M. 1, 81.   2. Whittick, 264.
3. Hall, 34.   4. J. H. Smith, 241.

Linden

In Europe, the linden is called the lime tree. Its flowers make a pleasant-tasting tea that has been used for innumerable medicinal purposes, although its only verified effects are mild diuresis and diaphoresis (stimulating perspiration, which can also be accomplished by drinking plain hot water).

Ancient Scythian sorcerers regarded the linden tree as the source of their prophetic insight. To consult spirits concerning future events, they would go to the linden tree and twine its leaves around their fingers.[1]

1. Emboden, 69.

Myrrh

Myrrh is gum resin from the *Commiphora* species of trees, native to Arabia. Myrrh resin was much used by the Egyptians in the mummification process, which may help to account for its death symbolism. The Magi's gift of myrrh to the infant Jesus was supposed to prefigure his death; myrrh was offered to him on the cross (Mark 15:23). Some have surmised that the **crown** of thorns was made from the thorny twigs of the myrrh tree. Myrrh figured prominently in the rites of Adonis, who also died as a "savior" and gave his **blood** to the world.

Moreover, the mothers of both Adonis and Jesus were connected with myrrh. The virgin mother of Adonis was named Myrrha (myrrh tree), and the virgin mother of Jesus was called "Myrrh of the Sea" by early Christians.[1] In view of the ancient birth-and-death symbolism of the Mother as both giver and taker of life, this dual role becomes comprehensible and even inevitable. The three Marys at the crucifixion bore the same title as pagan death priestesses, *myrrhophores*, bearers of myrrh.[2]

1. Walker, W.E.M.S., 702.   2. Hall, 155.

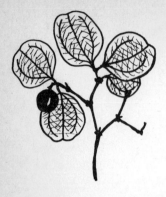

Nux Vomica

Nux vomica means "vomiting nut," from an Asiatic tree of the same name. The tree, *Strychnos nux-vomica*, is the source of brucine and strychnine. Though intensely poisonous, these substances do have medical uses. Nux vomica has been a folk remedy for centuries, although the margin between useful and life-threatening dosage is very narrow.[1]

Nux vomica is believed to cause abortion when introduced into the vagina. It has also been used as a "nerve tonic." Since the dosage in any untreated plant product is always problematical, such dangerous substances are to be avoided. The most active ingredient, strychnine, kills by stopping respiration through tetanic spasms.

1. Duke, 462.

Oak

Few trees have been so widely revered as the oak. The classic composition of the Dianic **grove** or *nemeton*, the residence of the heaven-god who controlled thunder and **lightning,** the deity of druids and **dryads,** the oak was *duir* (D) in the druidic alphabet and represented power. Irish churches used to be called *dair-thech*, "oak-house," an old druidic name for the sacred grove.[1]

The biblical mother-shrine Mamre at Hebron included a sacred oak in a female-symbolic grove. Old Testament scribes pretended it was the home of Abraham, although even in the fourth century A.D. it was still a pagan site, dedicated to the worship of "idols."[2] England similarly revered its famous "Herne's Oak."

The oak stood for Diana and her successive lovers, the Kings of the Wood, in Greco-Roman tradition and well into the Christian era. Any Roman soldier who saved the life of a citizen was awarded a most coveted **crown** made of oak leaves and acorns.[3]

Since nearly everyone believed that lightning-attracting oak trees were residences of the lightning god, medieval Europe universally credited the oak with magical influence over the weather. Magic books said thunderstorms could be raised by burning a chameleon's head with oak wood.[4]

In addition to the many practical uses of this tree's hard, strong wood, the bark contains 10 to 20 percent tannins, and has long been used in the process of tanning leather.

1. de Paor & de Paor, 60. 2. Frazer, *F.O.T.*, 335. 3. Whittick, 226. 4. Agrippa, 137.

PALM
from a Cretan pot,
ca. 2000 B.C.

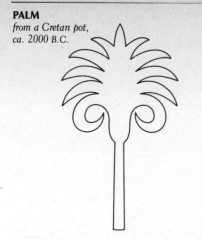

PINE

Palm

The palm branch was displayed not only in Jerusalem's sacred processions, but also in Roman celebrations of the savior **Osiris,** and Egyptian prototype of the sacrificed-and-resurrected Lord.[1] The palm branch signified the virility of the god in union with his mother-sister-wife, **Isis.** "Palm tree" was a metaphor for his penis, which was said to stand upright when he was reincarnated as Menu or Min, the "bull of his mother."[2] The palm tree had a similar meaning in the Phoenician cult of Baal-Peor, whose phallic emblem was a palm tree between two large **stones.**[3] This virile god also was worshiped in the Jewish tabernacle until reforming priests of Yahweh killed his followers (Numbers 25). The palm that represented him was apparently retained, however, in annual celebrations when a savior figure was welcomed into Jerusalem, as described in the Gospels. The waving of palm branches was associated also with processions in honor of the god

Tammuz, united with his mother-bride **Ishtar** in the Jerusalem temple when she was still the Hebraic "Queen of Heaven" (Ezekiel 8:14; Jeremiah 44:17). In Rome, the palm was awarded to victorious gladiators.

1. Budge, *G.E.* 2, 217. 2. *Book of the Dead,* 518. 3. Walker, *W.E.M.S.,* 86.

Pine

The pine was sacred to a number of savior gods including Attis, Dionysus, Marsyas, and **Osiris,** who was shown in his temple at Denderah enclosed in a pine tree. Pinecones generally were male genital symbols, especially in association with the female **lotus.** Assyrians utilized the sexual symbolism of pinecone and lotus by alternating them in ornamentation, after the manner of the classic **Egg and Dart Frieze.**[1] Pinecones appeared on the Dionysian **thyrsus,** on pillars (see **Perron**), on urns, tombs, and even Renaissance cathedral towers. As an evergreen, the pine was a natural symbol of immortality.

1. Whittick, 296.

Poplar

Some traditions identified the poplar as a
Tree of Life, because of its distinctly
bicolored leaves, dark green on the side
that faces heaven, pale green on the side
that faces earth.[1] The poplar seems
to have been the origin of the old country
tale of the tree that turns pale at the
approach of a thunderstorm. Rising wind
in advance of the storm would blow
the leaves upward and show their pale-
colored undersides.

1. Cirlot, 249.

Rowan

Also called quickbeam or mountain ash,
the rowan tree represented the second letter of the druidic tree alphabet, *luis*
(L). The tree stood for magic and was sacred to the Goddess Brigit. It was
thought efficacious in breaking evil enchantments. Medieval folk believed that the
sharpened stake to be driven through
the heart of a **vampire** should be made
from rowan.[1]

In Irish legends, "the rowan tree in the
north" bore the berries of immortality. The
tree was guarded by a Fomorian **giant**
with one fiery eye in the middle of his

forehead.[2] Perhaps he was identified with
the **Cyclops** of Homer's *Odyssey,* who was
conquered when his single eye was
blinded by a sharpened stake.

1. Emboden, 94.   2. G. Jobes 2, 1411.

Sycamore

The "holy sycamore" at Mataria in Egypt
was the Shrine of the Tree, sacred to
Isis-Hathor of Dendera. Later it was taken
over by Christians, who pretended
that the mother-and-child images associated with the tree were Mary and
the infant Jesus.[1] Long before Christianity,
however, the mother-tree of the Goddess was
called a receptacle for spirits of the
dead who sat in the branches. The wood
was used for mummy cases in which the
Goddess embraced the deceased.[2]

Actually, the Egyptian sycamore was
the wild fig tree, named from the Greek
sycos, "fig." In addition to fig wood,
dried figs were placed in the tombs of early
dynasties to serve as **womb** symbols
for the rebirth of the dead.[3] (See **Fig.**) The
fig tree was worshiped as a residence
of the Goddess throughout the Egyptian-
Mesopotamian culture complex and
the Indus valley during the third millennium B.C.[4] This may explain why
the Haggadah said the forbidden fruit in
the garden of Eden was the fig, not

SYCAMORE
of the Goddess Mut,
pouring
Water of Life

the **apple.**[5] Later identification of the primal tree with the sycamore led to the Greek story that Zeus and Hera (or Zeus and Europa), as primal couple, lay together under the sycamore tree. This event was annually reenacted at Knossos.[6]

1. Budge, *G.E.* 2, 220.   2. Duerr, 212.
3. Emboden, 194.   4. Campbell, *M.I.*, 266.
5. Barnstone, 34.   6. Duerr, 196.

Tamarisk

The tamarisk tree was especially sacred to Egyptian worshipers of **Osiris.** The myth said that when Osiris's body was enclosed in its sarcophagus and sent down the Nile to the sea, it washed ashore at Byblos and lodged in a growing tamarisk tree, which eventually grew up all around it. The king, Melcarthus, official consort of the Goddess **Astarte,** made the trunk of the tamarisk tree into a **pillar** to support the roof of his hall. Eventually, **Isis** learned about this, and so she traveled to Byblos to retrieve Osiris's body from its holy tomb of tamarisk wood and restore the god to life.

Tree Alphabet

Like the runic alphabet, the alphabet of the trees was used by European pagans for divination and for transmitting secret messages that would have been incomprehensible to anyone who did not know the system. Each letter was named for a tree or shrub, so messages could be spelled out by stringing the right sorts of leaves in the right order on a **cord** or a **wand,** with "blank" leaves not included in the alphabet to divide one word from the next. It has been suggested that nonletter leaves were sometimes inserted at random just to render the message more cryptic.

It has been claimed that the following version of the tree alphabet is "a genuine relic of Druidism orally transmitted down the centuries."[1]

THE CONSONANTS

B   Birch (Beth)
L   Rowan (Luis)
N   Ash (Nion)
F   Alder (Fearn)
S   Willow (Saille)
H   Hawthorn (Uath)
D   Oak (Duir)
T   Holly (Tinne)
C   Hazel (Coll)
M   Vine (Muin)
G   Ivy (Gort)
P   Dwarf Elder (Pethboc)
R   Elder (Ruis)

THE VOWELS

A   Silver Fir (Ailm)
O   Furze (Onn)
U   Heather (Ur)
E   White Poplar (Eadha)
I   Yew (Idho)

The consonantal letters have also been related to the lunar calendar, the pagan feast days and agricultural seasons, and various tutelary deities. Robert Graves points out that the letters of the modern Irish alphabet are similarly named after trees.

1. Graves, W.G., 168

Tree of Life

Many myths speak of the Tree of Life or World Tree that was somehow involved in the creation of the universe, the origin of humanity, and the divine gifts of nourishment and civilized skills. The Maya called it First Tree of the World, or Green Tree of Plenty, growing in their own territory on the Yucatan peninsula. Those who faithfully kept the rituals would go after death to the paradise shaded by the First Tree. It was represented in the form of a cross, and the savior-god was crucified on it as Our Lord of the Tree. His head wore a tree **crown** and his arms ended in branches.[1]

Martyrdom, an essential element in the myths of most major gods, was usually associated with some version of the Tree. Odin hung on the World Tree Yggdrasil to undergo death and resurrection before he could achieve full godhood—which, by the way, depended on his acquisition of

originally feminine knowledge. Krishna died on a tree. Attis died on a tree. **Osiris,** in his dead phase, was enclosed in a tree. Men embodying the Saxon god were sacrificed to the Goddess Andaste by hanging on trees.[2] The tradition continued into Christianity. Acts 5:30 and 1 Peter 2:24 say that Jesus hung on a tree, not a cross. Other Christian authorities insisted that Jesus' cross be identified with the biblical Tree of Life. The cross was planted in exactly the same spot and was made of the original tree's actual wood, which had been miraculously preserved for this very purpose. The church continued to claim the literal truth of this doctrine for many centuries.[3]

What is not often realized about this World Tree or Tree of Life is that it was assigned a female gender and was regarded as an all-nourishing, all-giving mother. Apparently, the **blood** shed on it in solemn sacrifice was intended to help maintain the life force of the tree, on which all other life depended. For example, the tree of Odin's sacrifice had alternate names like Mjotvidr or Mjodvidr, meaning either "mother tree" or "mead tree." Like the milk-giving mother tree of the Finns, it brought forth life, the first man and woman of the new universe. Moreover, its fruit magically facilitated childbirth, and the Triple Goddess dwelt in its roots in the form of the three **Norns.** This tree was "the source of unborn souls."[4]

In Persia and India, the World Tree was depicted with five branches holding the **elements** of creation: water, earth, air, fire, and ether.[5] A Goddess of the Tree was worshiped as early as 2000 B.C. in the Indus valley, where the tree was called the source of all mantras—hence, of creation.[6] The tree gave the gift of language to humanity, having a different letter or mantra written on each of its leaves. This concept was perhaps not unrelated to that of the druidic **tree alphabet.** Other myths credited the Goddess Kali with the invention of the Sanskrit alphabet, showing that she was in some sense interchangeable with the tree. Medieval Europeans believed in the continued existence of the wonderful Tree of Life in "a spot in the Orient" that was paradise, with a "fountain flowing forth in four rivers."[7]

To Indo-Europeans in general, the vision of paradise included the sacred tree with a spring at its root, like the obviously female rose-apple tree of Jambu Island, the Fairy Tree of Celtic tradition, or the Goddess's life-giving apple trees in Avalon, Hesperides, or Eden. It is possible that the whole Eden myth was falsely deduced from an icon showing the Goddess, personifying the Tree of Life, handing her **apple** to the first man while her **serpent** of wisdom twined in the branches. Such icons are not uncommon.

Tales of Goddesses or divine women becoming trees abound in classical mythology. There were Daphne, Myrrha, Dione, and the **dryads** (female druids). The mother tree was again personified as a fairy godmother in the Germanic Cinderella story, which began as an antiecclesiastical allegory. The fairy tree grew from the grave of Cinderella's dead mother (the submerged Goddess). This tree spirit provided her daughter (humanity) with fine clothes and golden apples, which were not given to the two greedy stepsisters (church and state).[8] Thus the maternal, all-giving tree became a fairy wishing-tree, especially for women, who had little more than wishes to sustain them in those virulently patriarchal times.

The wishing tree was a rather abject descendant of the mighty Tree of Life that had been the ancient Goddess. In Babylon it was **Ishtar,** as the cosmic fig tree known as "primeval mother at the central place of the earth." Her roots reached to the lowest abyss. Her branches ascended to heaven, with fruit shining like stars. According to the Haggadah, the

fruit of the Tree of Life in Eden was the **fig,** which makes another connection between the Tree of Life and Ishtar, and also Eve who inherited the Goddess's title, Mother of All Living.[9]

Southeastern Asia's Tree of Life continued as a Logos image, with a "destiny word" written on every leaf. Such words became personal mantras for all souls of the dead, each of whom must obtain one of the tree's leaves before rebirth to a new life on earth. It was claimed that the word on the leaf determines the character of each new life.[10] This image of the tree as identical with the Book of Life may show why we still refer to the pages of a book as "leaves."

1. Duerr, 214–215.   2. Briffault 3, 70.
3. Walker, W.E.M.S., 189.   4. Davidson,
G.M.V.A., 195.   5. Cirlot, 330.
6. Campbell, M.I., 266.   7. Baring-Gould,
259.   8. Jung & von Franz, 127.   9. Barnstone,
34.   10. G. Jobes 1, 454.

Walnut

Walnut trees used to be important to the pagan Goddess, for the Middle Ages had many stories about walnut trees harboring devils—especially she-devils—who whispered obscenities to passersby.

The church of Santa Maria del Popolo in Rome was built on the spot where a scandalous walnut tree once stood, making indecent propositions to all who listened to the rustlings of its leaves. According to legend, Saint Barbatus had the tree cut down and the ground exorcised and reconsecrated for the construction of the church.

Another offshoot of the pagan Goddess, the apocryphal Saint Agatha, was said to have sailed across the Mediterranean Sea in a walnut shell.[1] Walnuts were among the numerous tree fruits associated with female genitals.

1. Emboden, 67.

Willow

Medieval churchmen claimed that witches, or "daughters of Satan," go to the willow tree to forswear God; that the willow begets **serpents;** and that willows are the devil's trees, planted by streams to lure men into a watery grave. The legendary witch Kundry laughed at Christ, they said, but found comfort in a willow **grove.**[1]

All these disparaging remarks about willows stemmed from their notorious connection with ancient Goddess figures. Willow **wands** were used for divination by

the hermaphroditic Scythian priests called Ennarees, after the Goddess Inara, as she was called in several Indo-European and Hittite tongues.[2] The Greeks knew her as Helice, meaning "Willow." Helice was a virgin form of Hecate guarding Mount Helicon, the home of the **Muses.** Her willow wand was a cosmic symbol connected with the stars. The pole-encircling constellation of Ursa Major was sometimes known as Helice's Axle.[3] This constellation was also Artemis, one of whose names was Lygodesma, "The willow-bound one," because her arms were wound with willow branches.[4] A seventeenth-century herbal continued to insist that "the Moon owns the willow."[5]

The willow was sacred to the Goddess Arianrhod in Celtic tradition and was called the letter *S, saille,* in the tree alphabet. Willow bark was one of the world's oldest sources of pain relief, salicylic acid, which the world still uses in the form of aspirin (acetylsalicylic acid), thanks to the witches who never forgot their Goddess-inspired remedy.

Willows were sacred in Jerusalem, where the six-day Festival of the Willow Branch was annually celebrated with willow withes brought from a certain holy place known as Motza. The willows were set up around the **altar** in the central temple.[6] The weeping willow, which loves to grow on riverbanks, became a symbol of mourning because of biblical allusions to the Babylonian captivity, in a place where willows apparently were plentiful. "By the rivers of Babylon, there we sat down, yea, we wept, when we remembered Zion. We hanged our harps upon the willows in the midst thereof" (Psalm 137:1–2).

In England, where no **palm** trees were available, willow branches were traditionally used for the "palms" of Palm Sunday, not only because they were among the first to leaf out in the spring, but also because they had been revered by pagan populations of the British Isles and countryfolk still loved them.[7]

1. Emboden, 68. 2. Markale, 143.
3. Lindsay, 251. 4. Duerr, 12. 5. Pepper & Wilcock, 57. 6. Barrett, 157. 7. Scot, 574.

Wood

The illustration shows the alchemical symbol for wood: a stylized tree, topped by a **trefoil,** the black "trunk" bearing an odd resemblance to a witch's hat. Here may be seen the intermediate step between the wooden "club" or wand of

the Tarot suit—often shown in older deck designs as a real club—and the modern "club," which is simply a trefoil on a flat base and resembles a clover more than a club. Both designs originated, however, with the idea of wood.[1]

The former sacredness of wood is somewhat preserved in the modern custom of "knocking wood" to avert ill luck. This began as an invocation of a tree spirit and an expression of gratitude to the knocked-upon tree, in assurance that the source of good fortune was not forgotten.

1. Koch, 74.

Yew

Yew is the traditional cemetery tree because priests of the old Celtic religion regarded it as a symbol of immortality and planted it in their sacred **groves,** where Christian cemeteries were later situated.[1] In this way, the death-and-resurrection connotations of the yew were perpetuated. Druids also used **wands** of yew to foretell the future. There was a priestly tribe known as Eburovices, "people of the yew."[2] "Yew Valley" was the abode of Odin as a death god, in his winter aspect as Ullr.[3] The runic symbol of *eoh* meant yew, as did the letter *I*, *idho*, in the druidic alphabet.

Yew also symbolized hunting because yew wood was considered superior for the manufacture of bows.

Plutarch and Dioscurides claimed that sleeping in the shadow of a yew tree could be fatal, perhaps because in warm weather the trees give off the alkaloid taxine, which may have hallucinatory effects.[4] Needles and berries of yew trees are poisonous.

1. Whittick, 352.   2. Markale, 92, 143.
3. Duerr, 220.   4. Ibid., 30.

20

FRUIT AND FOODSTUFFS

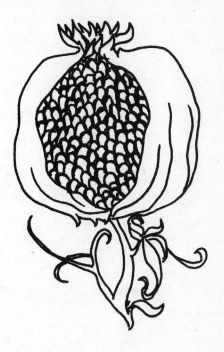

The day-to-day survival of every creature depends on finding and maintaining an adequate supply of food. There is no subject of more immediate, direct, and constant concern. Therefore, it is hardly surprising that human religious and magical symbolism—as well as practical skills—has been deeply involved with preservation of the food supply. If magical and religious ceremonies are acted-out wishes, as Freud maintained, then the wish for more and better food might well be expected to outrank all others in importance.

Especially significant in this context is the extent of identification between food and the feminine principle. The earth, giver of all foods, is always Mother. Conversely, Mother is always food-giver, in the basic childhood experience of nearly every human being who ever lived. The female body not only produces offspring; it also produces food to nourish the offspring. Even after the suckling period, in primitive village cultures it was maternal labor and thought that planted, gathered, stored, prepared, and dispensed food. The Neolithic matriarch, presiding over her gardens and her hearth, provided more than 80 percent of the average human diet. Other food came from mother-surrogates like cows, hens, and milch goats.

In addition to the Mother symbolism, a more generalized feminine-gender symbolism was attached to food. As the immature female was likened to a flower or a bud, so the nubile, ripe woman was herself symbolized by fruit, as if her potential motherhood made her somehow edible. Round-shaped fruits have always been likened to female breasts, and vice versa. Many fruits have been regarded as vulva or womb symbols. In the sexual context, women are often described as tasty, juicy, sweet, appetizing, tempting, delicious. Even today, women's nicknames and slang titles tend to sound edible: Candy, Peaches, Honey, Sugar, Cookie, Taffy; cupcake, honeybun, sweet potato, sweetie pie, tomato, pumpkin, gumdrop, jellybean, dumpling, cream puff, bonbon, little cabbage. Throughout most of the history of human art, idealized female forms have been solidly plump like fully ripe fruit. Until the twentieth century came along with its models of lean, bony feminine beauty, thin women were considered ugly. Even though fertility has nothing to do with fat, the Western world somehow always managed to connect fruitfulness with a round, ripe-fruit appearance.

A certain confusion exists, then, between woman-as-food-giver and woman-as-food. With the advent of patriarchal religions a new element was introduced: god-as-food. The numerous dying gods and devoured saviors of the past—Osiris, Dionysus, Orpheus, Aleyin, and many other spirits of grape and grain—prefigured the symbolic cannibalism of the Eucharist. The god's

eaten flesh and blood became the medium of salvation in various mystery cults of the early Christian era; and so they are still, in various sects of traditional Christianity.

In these several ways, food has been personified and deified. To human minds, food is more than mere nourishment. It often becomes a symbol that exerts a powerful attraction, just because food is always of interest to creatures that must eat daily to maintain optimum health and comfort. Our well-fed, affluent culture tends to forget how much hunger hurts; but the majority of the human race through the majority of its existence on earth has had direct experience of this kind of pain, one way or another. This alone would be quite enough to explain the widespread importance of food symbolism. People still eat together as a ritual of conviviality, because it was originally a means of establishing social kinship. To share food is to share flesh, literally as well as figuratively. It creates a bond. In myths, visitors to the other world—or to the land of the dead—were bound in kinship to that world if they ate of its food, and were thus compelled to return to it.

Food giving, food receiving, food growing and storing were and are some of the foremost, basic preoccupations of humans everywhere. It is only natural, then, that food is so widely invested with symbolic significances.

Apple

Magic apples of immortality, or of death-and-rebirth, are common to most Indo-European mythologies. The apples are usually dispensed by the **Goddess** to a man, hero, ancestor, or god. The Norse Goddess Idun kept all the gods alive with her magic apples. Influenced by this idea, Norsemen buried apples with the dead to serve as resurrection charms.[1] Mother Hera fed the gods on apples from the **Tree of Life** in her western garden of paradise. The Irish hero Connla received a magic apple of immortality from a woman of the Other World. King Arthur was taken by the Triple Goddess to Avalon, the "Apple-land" of eternal life.

It seems that the famous scene of three women, a man, and an apple, known as *The Judgment of Paris*, was "mistakenly deduced from the icon which showed

Heracles being given an apple-bough by the Hesperides—the naked Nymph-goddess in triad—[or] Adanus of Hebron being immortalized by the Canaanite Mother of All Living."[2] In similar iconography, the first man (Adam) was brought to life by the Mother of All Living, which was one of the titles of Eve (Genesis 3:20). The Triple Goddess created the world in the Greek myth of Eurynome, Eurybia, and Eurydice, three sisters ruling earth, sea, and the underworld.[3] The three Mothers of the World were always closely connected with apple trees in early Greek and in Celtic myth. The Goddess became the mistress of the paradise garden and greeted the hero Owein while she stood beside her apple tree, "which is the axis of the world, the centre of life."[4] The apple tree remained sacred to the Goddess in Romanian folklore, where she appeared as "the fairy Magdalina," sitting in a cosmic apple tree whose branches touched the sky, and whose roots reached into the bottom of the ocean.[5]

Much of the reverence paid to the apple arose not only from its value as food, but also from the secret, sacred sign in its core: the **pentacle,** which is revealed when the apple is transversely cut. Gypsies claimed this was the only proper way to cut an apple, especially when it was shared between lovers before and after sexual intercourse.[6] At Gypsy weddings it was customary for the bride and groom to cut the apple, revealing its pentacle, and eat half apiece.[7] Such marriage customs may suggest the real story behind Eve's

sharing of an apple with her spouse: an idea that developed quite apart from the biblical version, in which there is no mention of an apple, but only of a "fruit."

In the Volsung cycle, it is the poet's wife who provides "apples of Hel," that is, gifts from the underworld Goddess Hel, which will enable him to live under the earth.[8] Going down to the underworld (**womb**) was a common method for heroes and poets to discover secrets of nature, and not incidentally to acquire wealth—or, as the Gypsies called it, "earth." A fifteenth-century Book of Lismore, copied from earlier material, mentioned three Irish princes who had to marry three wives before they could find their "fortunes," another form of the three Fortunae. The three wives represented the Triple Goddess and her sacred apple trees: one in full bloom, a second shedding the blossom, and the third covered with ripe fruit.[9]

Apples figured prominently in the lore of magic, undoubtedly because of their ubiquitous connections with Goddess worship. It was said that a holy name written on an apple and eaten on three consecutive days would cure a fever. Abortion could be procured by writing the palindromic charm *sator arepo tenet opera rotas* on an apple and eating it.[10] Apples consumed on **Halloween** could show a young person the dream image of his or her future spouse; hence the bobbing-for-apples game. Christian lore

made the apple a symbol of original sin, but this never appreciably interfered with the popularity of the fruit that could "keep the doctor away."

1. Turville-Petre, 187.   2. Graves, G.M. 2, 277.   3. Beltz, 113.   4. Markale, 238.
5. Duerr, 162.   6. Derlon, 157.   7. Crawley 2, 133.   8. Davidson, G.M.V.A., 165.
9. Evans-Wentz, 412–413.
10. Trachtenberg, 202.

Apricot

Like the Oriental **peach,** the apricot was often used as a metaphor for female genitals. In medieval France, a slang word for "vulva" was *abricot*. Roman sculptures from the south of France show plump apricots in conjunction with stylized **phalli.**[1] Rabelais referred to a vulva as a "slit apricot" *(abricot fendu)*.[2]

There was a recent flurry of interest in laetrile derived from apricot pits, as a possible remedy for cancer. In 1980 the National Cancer Institute pronounced laetrile ineffective in cancer treatment, but some of the faithful continued to believe in it.

Laetrile research brought into general knowledge the fact that there are two varieties of apricot pits, sweet and bitter. The sweet kind are used as food and are called Chinese almonds. The bitter kind contain prussic acid and are poisonous.[3]

1. Knight,136.   2. Williamson,148.   3. Duke, 394.

Bean

The original Jack in the Beanstalk was the god Odin under one of his alternate names, Jalk, the "Giant-killer."[1] An ancient image of this ancestral deity was preserved in the popular **carnival** figure, "King of the Bean."[2] King of the Twelfth Night festival in England was the man who received a single bean in his piece of plum cake.[3] Like many of the old deities who became festival kings, the bean god owed his power to conjunction with the female principle, impersonated by the bean itself. The Romans believed that ancestral spirits lived in beans and had to be annually propitiated by each householder with a midnight bean-throwing ceremony.[4] These may have been female ancestors, the *manes* who descended from Moon Mother Mania. A modern Italian slang term for female genitals is *fava*, "bean." The sect of Pythagoreans laid a firm taboo on the eating of beans, because of their esoteric meanings.

1. MacKenzie, 170.   2. Cirlot, 266.
3. Hazlitt 2, 602.   4. *Larousse*, 213.

Bread

The plea for daily bread incorporated into the Lord's Prayer must have been a plea to the **Goddess** in earlier times, for she was always the giver of bread, the Grain Mother, the patron of bakers, mills, and ovens. The English word *lady* was derived from *hlaf-dig*, the "giver of daily bread," while *lord* descended from *hlaf-ward*, the guardian of her storehouses. [1]

The braided bread loaves of Germanic tradition were invented by the women of Teutonic tribes, who used to make offerings of their own **hair** to their Goddess. Eventually they learned to preserve their braids by substituting the imitative loaf, which was called Berchisbrod or Perchisbrod, bread offered to the Goddess Berchta, or Perchta. The name of the braided Sabbath loaf among German Jews, Berches or Barches, was copied from this tradition. [2]

Bread was long believed to be the one essential food. The rock-bottom minimal diet given to criminals or penitents was bread and water. A medieval health handbook, *Taquinum Sanitatis*, would have horrified a modern nutritionist by its recommendations: pasta and white bread were declared "very nourishing," and white sugar was a "purifier of the body." However, spinach, asparagus, cabbage, squash, melons, apricots, and plums were bad for the stomach and would cause vomiting or stomach damage; celery was the cause of headaches. [3]

Bread magic took many forms, from baking bread in all sorts of effigy shapes to speaking charms and exorcisms over bread about to be eaten; the modern "grace" is a relic of this. Saint Hildegard, a twelfth-century abbess of Bingen, wrote that bread could cure any person made witless by magic spells, provided the bread was first marked with a *jachant* stone (jacinth), with the words, "May God, who cast away all precious stones from the devil . . . cast away from thee all phantoms and all magic spells, and free thee from the pain of this madness." [4]

Of course, the bread most widely credited with well-nigh incredible powers of magic was the bread of the Host, which the church declared to be literally the flesh of Jesus. This bread used to be placed in the hands of communicants until the priests discovered that their congregations often carried it off for later use in magic charms, instead of eating it on the spot. So began the custom of placing the bread wafer in the communicant's mouth, a preventive measure that is still perpetuated today. If medieval texts and folktales are to be believed, the bread that was Jesus was able to put out fires, cure sick pigs, make fields fertile, increase the honey production of bees, keep caterpillars out of the garden, gain freedom for imprisoned criminals, and serve as a love charm, in addition

to many other wonderful effects. Official church literature complained that the bread of the Mass was much used by "witches, sorcerers, charmers, enchanters, dreamers, soothsayers, necromancers, conjurers, cross-diggers, devil-raisers, miracle-doers, dog-leeches and bawds."[5]

1. Brewster, 349.   2. Trachtenberg, 40.
3. Abelard, 61.   4. Kunz, 82.   5. Thomas, 34–35.

Bun

Hot cross buns were the traditional Easter cakes throughout the Middle Ages, another inheritance from paganism. The cross that marked them was interpreted as a Christian symbol, but it was originally **Wotan's cross.** The bun itself was female-symbolic and associated with the Goddess Eostre, after whom the Easter festival was named. April was Eostre-month to the Anglo-Saxons, Germans, and Franks. The Goddess Eostre "must have been one of the most highly honored of the Teutonic deities, and her festival must have been a very important one, and deeply implanted in the popular feelings."[1] So thoroughly was her worship expunged, however, that we no longer know what people thought about her, and little remains except her name, which Christian authorities carefully refrain from explaining at Easter time.

The Goddess remained associated with wild woodlands, like the Fairy Queens and wood nymphs of Celtic tradition. Her

priestesses become the *wudu-maer,* Wood Mothers or Little Wood Women, to whom buns or dumplings are still offered in some parts of Bavaria around Easter time.[2]

1. Wright, 86–87.   2. Frazer, *F.O.T.*, 312.

Cheese

As a **milk** product, cheese was long associated with the mysteries of birth and lactation. The Egyptians pictured the human body as a product of mother's milk "curdled" into solid matter as the child grew and put on new flesh. A remnant of this idea occurs in the Bible: "Hast thou not poured me out as milk, and curdled me like cheese?" (Job 10:10). One of an Egyptian's seven **souls** was the *ren* or milk name, given by the nursing mother, which also gave us the word *rennet,* a milk-curdling agent.

Cheese figured prominently in a traditional rite still practiced at rural British christening feasts. The newborn child was passed through a hole in the center of a large cheese known as the Groaning Cheese, which the rite obviously converted into a surrogate mother, "birthing" the child.[1]

1. Pegg, 112.

Cherry

The *Cherry Tree Carol* in Christmas
songbooks was composed from an old story
linking Maya, the virgin mother of
Buddha, with the sacred cherry tree Sala.
It was said that the tree recognized
her divinity and bent down to offer her its
fruit and to give her support while
she brought forth her holy child.[1] Cherries
were thus associated with virginity in
more ways than in modern slang. The
redness of the fruit, carrying its seed
within, made it an obvious uterine symbol. Gypsy girls used to use cherry
stones as love charms.[2]

Twigs and leaves of cherry trees contain
amygdalin, a compound that releases
cyanide when eaten, and may cause a state
of nervous excitement followed by
prostration.

1. *Larousse*, 348.   2. Bowness, 22.

Cloves

Commercial cloves are dried unopened
flower buds of the clove plant, consisting of
a nail-shaped calyx tube and four
calyx teeth. Because of their nail-like
shape, cloves were taken as symbols of
Christ's crucifixion.[1] Therefore, Christians believed them endowed by nature
with various kinds of healing magic, like
the "holy nails" themselves—of which there

were dozens in Europe's churches,
enough to have studded liberally the entire
cross.

Clove oil is antiseptic and has been
used as a local anesthetic for toothache.

1. Williamson, 51.

Fig

To "make the fig" by sticking the thumb
through the fingers of a closed fist
is still considered an obscene insult,
equivalent to "fuck you," in many parts of
Europe. In England it is called *to
fig*; in Italy, *far la fica*; in Spain, *hacer el
higo*; in France, *faire la figue*; in Germany, *die Feige weisen*.[1] Yet the gesture
was considered a powerful charm against
the evil eye and other threats. Thousands of
fig-making hands of carved ivory, metal,
bone, wood, and plastic are sold each year
as good-luck charms.[2]

The solution to the paradox is, of
course, the sexual connotation of the gesture, which used to be holy because
it is a **lingam-yoni**. According to Ovid, a
Roman afraid of meeting a **ghost** would
invoke the life-preserving power of
sex by making "a sign with his thumb in
the middle of his closed fingers."[3] Figs
were classified with **apricots** and **pomegranates** as female genital symbols.
Hence, Gaulish pagan gods were referred
to in medieval Latin texts as *ficarii*,
"fig-eaters," perhaps a reference to cunni-
lingus.[4] An archaic Roman festival
called Nonae Caprotinae connected Juno

Caprotina, Goddess of fig trees, with the lustful goat god.[5] Similarly in Greece, a euphemism for "vagina" was *sykon*, "fig." Fig trees were supposed to arouse lust and were favorite resting places for **satyrs.** Significantly, Tannhäuser was also resting under a fig tree when he was approached by the Goddess **Venus.** As in Rome, so in Greece general fertility was assured by invoking the power of sex through the fig, in an annual ceremony of touching the genitals of the king's wife with a **phallus** of fig wood.[6]

According to the Ananda Tantra, the fig leaf is "the conventional form of the yoni."[7] This may account for the common use of the fig tree as a symbol of man's enlightenment, which was formerly supposed to come through his connection with the female principle. Buddha attained "perfect illumination" by sitting under the sacred fig tree.[8] His *boddhi* or *bo* tree was identified as *ficus religiosa*, the Holy Fig.[9] Adam and Eve placed "aprons" of fig leaves over their genitals after they had become enlightened (Genesis 3:7), which seems to indicate a male imitation of female genital symbolism. According to the Haggadah, the forbidden fruit of the Tree of Knowledge in the Garden of Eden was not an **apple** but a fig.[10] This hints at the probability, never very deeply concealed, that the knowledge forbidden by the Judeo-Christian God was knowledge of specifically female sexuality, which patriarchal societies have always tried to suppress. The fig tree Ruminalis was worshiped as a symbol of the Goddess herself in the Palatine temple in Rome.[11]

1. Trachtenberg, 161. 2. Elworthy, 152. 3. Dumézil, A.R.R. 1, 367. 4. Knight, 149, 153. 5. Rose, 217. 6. Duerr, 189, 198. 7. King, 28. 8. d'Alviella, 162. 9. Wilkins, 45. 10. Barnstone, 34. 11. Grant, 104.

Garlic

According to a Talmudic tradition, garlic arouses sexual passion and "multiplies the semen." Therefore a Jewish husband was commanded to eat garlic on the **Sabbath** eve when he lay with his wife.[1] One cannot help wondering how the wives felt about it. Perhaps they ate garlic too, in self-defense, although the tradition says nothing about garlic multiplying female sexual juices.

Moslems disliked garlic and **onions.** Their claim was that when Satan first stepped out of the Garden of Eden, garlic sprang up from his left footprint, and onion from his right.[2] This was odd, in view of the fact that they also thought Satan had no feet at the time, having just been bidden by God to travel always on his belly like a snake (Genesis 3:14).

Balkan Christians used to believe that Moslem corpses were particularly prone to become **vampires,** which may account for the constant use of garlic as a vampire repellent.

1. Patai, 24. 2. Leek, 42.

Grain

Wheat, rye, oats, millet, barley—nearly all grains, except rice, could fall in the general category of "corn" according to European definitions. What Americans call corn was either Indian corn or maize to Europeans, which tends to confuse the many references to the "ancient corn-mother" of pagan Europe. But, to clarify, she was usually the Mother Earth who gave birth to all grains.

The son of this Mother was typically the dying-and-resurrected god who personified the grain. His "death" (reaping) brought life to humankind; he descended into the underworld (planting); and he rose again from the dead, only to be harvested and sacrificed again each season. According to Egyptian scriptures, man at the moment of his death is also a grain, "which falls into the earth in order to draw from her bosom a new life."[1] The metaphor was universally employed, and even copied into the Gospels: "Except a corn of wheat fall into the ground and die, it abideth alone; but if it die, it bringeth forth much fruit" (John 12:24).

Wheat was the "plant of truth" cultivated on the mummy-cases of **Osiris** and made into communion cakes, to be eaten by worshipers so they could partake of the god's divinity and become immortal like him. Egyptians were among the first to eat their god in the form of **bread,** instead of the flesh of sacrificial animals or human surrogates; but the cults of many other savior-gods followed

suit. Adonis too was worshiped as a savior-god and cultivated as sprouting grain in the famous "gardens of Adonis," where clay **pots** were used to symbolize the Mother's **womb**—a commonplace custom all the way up to the twentieth century A.D.[2] The flesh of Dionysus also was eaten in the form of wheat cakes, while his **blood** was drunk in the form of **wine.** Grain gods represented the wheat or barley crop at Eleusis and other pagan shrines, where the cycles of growth were controlled by the Great Mother (Demeter/Ceres/Ops/Terra Mater), who resurrected them from the underground tomb-womb, and who was shown crowned with sheaves.

A mythical English saint was created from a rather sloppy canonization of this same Earth Mother. She was Saint Milburga, whose name means simply the Place of the Mill. She was alleged to have lived in the eighth century, although there were no records of her before the twelfth. Her sacred spring still exists in Stoke Saint Milborough. The customary growth miracle—instant maturity upon the planting of the seed—marks her hagiographical fairy tale, and the oldest version of her feast day marked the spring sowing season.[3]

Christianity also took over the Roman festival of purification of the sprouting grain, originally an invocation of the Earth Mother to protect the crop from blight. In pagan times it was the Robigalia, transformed by the church into a pseudo-

Christian Rogation Day (April 25), which employed the same rituals but changed the name of the deity.[4]

The church's official doctrine of transubstantiation was also copied from pagan antiquity, for Christians and pagans alike declared that the communion bread was the god's flesh in fact, not only in imagination. When this doctrine was openly doubted in the thirteenth and fourteenth centuries, innumerable heresies were bred from it and the first Protestant churches were founded on its denial. The controversy dragged on for seven centuries and still continues today. Voltaire summed up the transubstantiation quarrels by saying that Catholics eat God but not bread; Calvinists eat bread but not God; and the Lutherans eat both.[5]

The rest of the world, presumably, is simply grateful for the existence of edible grains that form the staple food nearly everywhere. There was also a magical shrine that gave women particular cause for gratitude: that of Saint Wilgerfort, whose statue stood in Saint Paul's Cathedral in London. It was said that unhappy wives could visit this saint with offerings of a peck of grain, and their cruel husbands would soon drop dead. For this reason the saint was nicknamed Saint Uncumber. Since women of past centuries had little defense against abusive spouses, Uncumber was popular.[6]

1. Pepper & Wilcock, 50.   2. Frazer, G.B., 400–401.   3. Berger, 67–70.   4. Ibid., 22.
5. Abelard, 71.   6. Thomas, 26–27, 241.

Grape

The discovery that spoiled grape juice will ferment into wine was made so long ago that it is lost in prehistory; but because of it, the grape has been carefully cultivated for thousands of years. The grape has also been personified and deified, for example, as Dionysus-Bacchus, the Greco-Roman wine god. The name of his Greek festival, Oschophoria, meant literally "Carrying of the Grape Clusters."[1] The wine was worshiped not only for its sweet taste but also, most particularly, for its ability to cause drunkenness, which was regarded as possession by the god's spirit. (See **Wine**.)

According to the Gnostic gospel *On the Origin of the World*, the forbidden fruit of Eden was neither the **apple** nor the **fig**, but "clusters of white grapes."[2] The **serpent** deity who revealed the secret of the grapes to Eve, then, could have been the Hebraic Dionysus, who was still identified with Jehovah as late as the first century A.D. He was specifically the god of Noah, the first of the biblical patriarchs to get drunk.[3]

1. Keuls, 302.   2. Barnstone, 67.   3. Graves, W.G., 366–368.

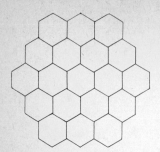

Honeycomb

Pythagoreans perceived the hexagon as an expression of the spirit of Aphrodite, whose sacred number was six (the dual Triple Goddess), and worshiped **bees** as her sacred creatures who understood how to create perfect hexagons in their honeycomb. In Aphrodite's temple at Eryx, the priestesses were *melissae*, "bees"; the Goddess herself was entitled Melissa, the queen bee "who annually killed her male consort"; and a golden honeycomb was on display as her symbol.[1] Seeking to understand the secrets of nature through geometry, the Pythogoreans meditated on the endless triangular lattice, all sixty-degree angles, that results from extending the sides of all hexagons in the honeycomb diagram until their lines meet in the centers of adjacent hexagons. It seemed to them a revelation of the underlying symmetry of the cosmos.

Moreover, since honey and **salt** were the only commonly known preservatives at the time, both were symbols of resurrection or reincarnation. The dead were often embalmed in honey, especially in the large *pithoi* or burial **vases,** where they were placed in fetal position for rebirth. Demeter was "the pure mother bee" who governed the cycles of life, as was the biblical Deborah whose name means "bee." Honey cakes formed like female genitals figured prominently in worship of the Goddess. The bee was usually looked upon as a symbol of the feminine potency of nature, because it created this magical, good-tasting substance and stored it in hexagonal cells of geometric mystery. (See **Bee.**) With so many ancient connections with the Goddess, it was inevitable that medieval hymns addressed the virgin Mary as a "nest of honey" and "dripping honeycomb."[2]

1. Graves, G.M. 1, 42, 72.   2. Duerr, 186.

Leek

The leek is a symbol of Wales because of the legend that the Welsh patron, Saint David, lived only on leeks and water during his period of retirement in the Vale of Ewias.[1] The story was apocryphal, as there was no Saint David. His "life" was composed by an eleventh-century bishop of Saint David's, to canonize what used to be the local deity, Dewi or Devi ("God"), a sea spirit who also became Davy Jones and the Welsh red **dragon.** This sea god bore the title of Waterman, which the monks took to mean that Saint David drank only water throughout his life; but in view of the fact that nothing was heard about his life until five hundred years after he was supposed to have lived it, he is one of the more improbable saints.[2] The leek was perhaps sacred to early Welsh tribes who used it as a staple vegetable.

1. Whittick, 265.   2. Attwater, 101–102.

Milk

Milk was the substance of creation in the Hindu myth of the Churning of the Sea of Milk. Movement in the primordial milky ocean produced all the world's solid material, the constellations, the earth and its creatures. According to the Sakta Sastra, the Great Mother thickens as she creates, like milk forming a curd; solid matter is produced as a "crust."[1] Creation stories based on milk are found throughout the Middle East, India, Japan, Egypt, and Homeric Greece.[2] A remnant exists even in the Bible: "Hast thou not poured me out as milk, and curdled me like cheese?" (Job 10:10). The eponymous Mother Goddess of pre-Roman Latium was the Goddess of Milk, Lat, who appeared in Greco-Roman mythology as Latona, Leto, or Leda; in Arabia as Al-Lat, the original feminine Allah; and in modern Italian as the word *latte*, "milk." In the language of Canaan, Lat meant "Goddess." The isle of Malta used to be sacred to her, under the earlier form of its name, Ma Lata.[3] One of her oldest shrines in Egypt was known to the Greeks as Latopolis.[4] She gave mother's milk as a baptismal fluid.

The association of the primordial **serpent** with the Great Goddess who was milk-giver to the universe led to curious superstitions connecting snakes and milk. It is widely believed even today that at least some species of snakes can suck the milk of women, cows, and other lactating mammals; so they are known as milk snakes. The belief is especially prevalent in Mexico where it probably dates back to the serpent god Quetzalcoatl, nourished by the Great Mother. The Welsh used to say that after drinking the milk of women spilt on the ground, certain snakes could sprout wings and fly.[5] All such superstitions naturally ignore the biological facts, which are that snakes cannot suck, cannot digest milk, and have no use for lactating mammals unless such mammals happen to be small enough to be swallowed whole.

1. Avalon, 305.   2. de Santillana & von Dechend, 383.   3. Stone, A.M.W. 1, 117.   4. *Larousse*, 29.   5. La Barre, 94–95.

Nuts

Like **grain,** nuts arouse human wonder by serving as food and seed simultaneously. Moreover, they seemed to pack mighty fertility magic into a very small space: "Great oaks from little acorns grow." In some European traditions it became customary always to finish a meal with nuts, as a symbol of ongoing fertility, to restore the supplies of all the food that had been consumed. Hence the expression, "From soup to nuts."

Scottish folk used to use nuts for divination before a marriage. Two nuts representing the bride and groom were placed on the **hearth.** If they burned gently, the match would be a happy one. If they flared and jumped apart, there would be strife and separation.[1]

The almond was especially revered as a fertility charm and a blessing for marriages. It was a custom in Italy to distribute almonds at every wedding in token of future fruitfulness for the union: an obvious holdover from ancient pagan symbolism of the **mandorla** ("almond") as a female genital symbol and a sign of virgin motherhood. Indeed, the almond was even adopted as another emblem of the Virgin Mary. A popular term for this birth-bringing nut was Womb of the World. On the other hand, the walnut reverted from a fertility symbol in ancient Greece and Rome to an antifertility charm in rural Romania. It is still believed that each roasted walnut secretly carried in the bodice of a young bride will prevent her from conceiving for a period of one year.[2]

A widely prescribed (if ineffective) fever remedy was to confine a **spider** in a nutshell and hang it on the neck of the sufferer. The rationale of this remains obscure.

1. Pegg, 113. 2. G. Jobes 1, 71; 2, 1663.

Olive

The olive was sacred to **Athene,** whose miracle placed Greece's first olive tree on the Acropolis at Athens. The city was the subject of dispute between Athene and the sea god Poseidon, who stuck his **trident** into the ground and produced a **well** of sea water on the site. Athene countered with her olive tree, a more useful gift in the opinion of all the goddesses as well as the Athenian people; so the city received her name and patronage.[1]

The olive was often associated with the **dove,** both symbolizing the Peace of the Goddess. An icon combining the two may have been the origin of Noah's dove, returning to the ark with an olive leaf in her beak as a sign that the flood-causing God had "made peace" with the world (Genesis 8:11). Still, the magic of the olive could be used in aggression. Odysseus put out the eye of the Cyclops with a bar of olive wood.[2] Olive crowns were awarded to Roman soldiers for bravery in battle.

The oil-rich olive was one of the few sources of lamp fuel, lubrication, and dietary fat among the ancients who ate meat on comparatively rare occasions and did not generally use inorganic oils. Therefore, cultivation of the olive was of primary importance.

1. Graves, G.M. 1, 60. 2. Campbell, Oc.M., 166.

FRUIT AND FOODSTUFFS

Onion

Roman mythology proposed that the onion served as a symbol for sacrificial human **heads** offered to the father-god **Jupiter.** The change was brought about by the legendary King Numa, who had been admitted "in celestial wedlock" to the "love and converse" of the Goddess Egeria (Diana). By the grace of his holy spouse, Numa acquired blessedness and godlike wisdom, whereby he was able to establish rites "most approved by the gods."[1] This was no more than a Roman version of the universal archaic belief that no king could rule unless he was married to the Goddess of the land.

King Numa argued with Jupiter in an attempt to stop the human sacrifices and save the heads of his people. So eloquent was he, that he managed to persuade the god to accept onion heads and the **blood** of **fish** as substitutes.

1. Perry, 180.

Orange

The custom of brides wearing or carrying orange blossoms was derived from Saracenic fertility rituals connected with weddings. The orange represented simultaneous virginity and fruitfulness— like virgin-mother-hood—because flowers and fruit can appear simultaneously on the same tree.[1] Therefore the orange blossom stood for the bride's virginity and served as a fertility charm in addition. Inevitably, the orange was also associated with the virgin Mary, "bearing at the same time the white flower of her virginity and the fruit of her chastity."[2]

The orange was not established in Europe until the twelfth century. Grown largely in southern France and the Iberian peninsula, it was soon identified with the golden apples of the Hesperides in Greek myth. Its name was *narang* in Persian, *naranj* in Arabic, *naranja* in Spanish. It lost its initial *n* due to confusion with the indefinite article in English: "a naranja" became corrupted to "an orange."

In the East, the orange was known as celestial fruit. It was frequently used as a cure for dyspepsia or heartburn. This may have been one reason why the orange became a heart symbol in European witchcraft.[3]

1. Whittick, 288. 2. Williamson, 145. 3. G. Jobes 2, 1212.

Parsley

Pagan Europe considered parsley a magic plant associated with the dead and capable of laying restless spirits. It was used as a garnish for meat to mollify the spirit of the butchered animal. Even the spoken name of parsley was thought an effective protection against vengeful **ghosts,** which is why it often occurs in charms and the choruses of folk songs.[1] The Greeks decorated tombs with parsley, possibly to keep the dead in place. Plutarch tells of an army that turned tail and fled from a battle upon seeing an ass carrying sacks of parsley, to them an omen of death.[2]

Crowns of parsley were worn by victors at the Nemean Games, which identifies parsley with the hero cult and may explain its connection with the martyred dead. It kept the same connotation in Christian tradition, which said parsley must not be planted on any day but Good Friday, the day of death not only for Jesus but also for his pagan counterparts, Attis and Adonis.

According to an English herbal, parsley seed was taken as a preventive for drunkenness. It "helpeth men that have weak brains to drink better."[3]

1. Wimberly, 350. 2. Emboden, 55.
3. Leek, 107.

Peach

Once thought to have originated in Persia, the peach is now known to have come from China where it was the Goddess's holy tree of life. Fruit of Mother Hsi Wang Mu's mystic Peach Garden appeared every 3,000 years and produced the gods' elixir of immortality. The peach was also a standard symbol of female genitalia and was connected with Taoist sexual mysticism. The symbol of human longevity was the old man, Shou Lu, always slyly shown with his finger stuck into the cleft of a fuzzy peach, to reveal the Way to his secret of long life.[1]
One of the old meanings of Tao is "peach." Peach Blossom meant a virgin in Taoist terminology. The peach was the yonic source of life. Magic **wands** were made from peach twigs in China, to partake of this female vitality.[2] A Japanese culture hero was born in typical mythological fashion from a peach while floating on a stream (birth waters), drawn forth by the midwife Goddess in the form of an old woman—recalling Rome's Acca Larentia, Akkad's "water-drawing" deity Akka, and their biblical counterpart, pharaoh's daughter of the Moses legend.[3]

Europeans remembered some of the sexual meanings of the peach. It was called a fruit of **Venus** or a fruit sacred to **Hymen.** Albertus Magnus claimed that peaches are aphrodisiac.[4] Yet their

former holiness was not entirely forgotten. A popular symbol of Sincerity or Truth was a peach with one attached leaf, representing the union of heart and tongue.[5]

1. Rawson, E.A.E., 19.   2. de Lys, 397.
3. G. Jobes 2, 1118.   4. Williamson, 148.
5. Hall, 238.

Pomegranate

The name of the pomegranate means "apple of many seeds," but its biblical name was *rimmon*, from *rim*, "to bear a child."[1] The fruit was almost universally known as a **womb** symbol, with its red juice and numerous "offspring." Pomegranates were carved on the pillars of Solomon's temple to represent fertility (1 Kings 7:18–20). Solomon himself impersonated Baal-Rimmon, the Lord of the Pomegranate, when he mated with his holy bride and drank the juice of her pomegranate (Song of Solomon 8:2).

In Europe, the pomegranate was always an attribute of the Queen of Heaven, Hera or **Juno**.[2] The shrine of Our Lady with the Pomegranate near Paestum still shows the Madonna with her child in one hand and her pomegranate in the other, and she is worshiped in the same way as the ancient statue of the Goddess who sat in the same shrine with her child in one hand and her pomegranate in the other.[3] Recognizing the tie between the fruit and the female principle of fertility, some nineteenth-century designers of **Tarot cards** substituted the pomegranate for the equally female-symbolic **pentacles** or discs. It was called Fruit of the Tree of Knowledge.

Naturally, so potent a symbol was assimilated to the image of Christ by the strenuous efforts of Christian iconographers like Bede and Cassiodorus, who insisted that its metaphorically uterine **blood** was really his. "Where such precious fragrant juice and scent flows forth, so must one also penetrate into the inner suffering of the Redeemer, in order to contemplate the boundless soul-suffering of the heart of God whose blood flows over all mankind."[4] Their flowery language, however, could not conceal the fact that it is woman's blood that flows over all humanity born of mothers.

1. Graves, W.G., 410.   2. Hall, 182.   3. J. H. Smith, 244.   4. Williamson, 102.

Potato

Many people are surprised to learn that
the staple vegetable potato belongs
to the family of Solanaceae, which includes **henbane,** deadly nightshade (belladonna), and other poisonous plants.
Potato foliage and green shoots contain
solanine and can cause fatalities.

It is said that Sir Walter Raleigh was
the first to plant the potato in Ireland.
However, he mistakenly ate the berries instead of the roots, which made him
so sick that he ordered all his plants
uprooted.[1]

In countries where the potato is a staple
crop, it has been customary to give
the name of a fertility deity to the first potato to be harvested, then to divide
and share it among all members of the
family. Among the names given to
the potato in South America was "Great
Life Mama."[2]

1. Duke, 453.   2. G. Jobes 1, 488; 2, 1289.

Quince

Ancient Greeks regarded the quince as a
symbol of female fertility. Their old
custom of giving a quince to a bride to eat
persisted into Christian times, becoming a
popular wedding-day ritual. The bridegroom did not eat the quince, which may
indicate an archaic origin of the custom in
times when only women were believed
capable of reproduction.[1]

Flowering quince has been cultivated
as a garden ornament. Its flowers are five-
petaled, somewhat resembling the old-
fashioned rose.

1. Whittick, 299.

Rhubarb

Rhubarb is one of those rare food plants
that can be extremely poisonous. The
leaves, raw or cooked, can kill—as opposed to the cooked stems, which
are tasty and nutritious. Rhubarb was cultivated in China as long ago as the
third millennium B.C., for use as a medicinal drug.

Seed

All seed was made synonymous with
semen in patriarchal agricultural societies
where the maternal body was likened
to the earth that incubated male "seeds" of
life. Planting was often compared to
a sexual encounter between the **grain** god
and the **earth** mother. Rome even
had a grain god named for the seed, Semo
Sancus; and India had a similar god
called Sukra, "Seed," who was born from
Shiva's penis. The name of Mother
Demeter's consort, Triptolemus, meant
"three plowings," because it was said that
he lay with her three times (casting

"seed" into the **furrow**). Like Semo San-cus, he died in the Mother's embrace in order to regenerate himself. The symbolic dying of the grain plants at harvest time, the symbolic dying of the penis after planting its "seed," and the dying of the savior god whose flesh and blood be-came food for his followers: all these were combined in a single sacred metaphor. Vegetation gods were also gods of "seed," and their sacred marriages and sacrificial deaths took place almost simultaneously.

There is no doubt that these ancient ag-ricultural images influenced medieval and Renaissance Christian theology, which insisted that male "seed" contained all the soul of the offspring, whereas the mother of a child was only passive "soil" in which the seed could grow.[1] Knowing nothing of the relatively huge, complex human egg—many of its most subtle functions not yet discovered—male authorities could only fall back on the simple agricultural metaphor that had given men their first notions of reproductive importance in a long-past age of unenlightenment.

1. Walker, W.E.M.S., 304.

Tomato

As a member of the Solanaceae family, which includes many poisonous plants, the succulent tomato was mistrusted when introduced into Europe in the sixteenth century. It was first cultivated in Central America, evidently as a yellow variety that the Italians later called *pomi d'oro*, "golden apple."

Elsewhere the tomato was called "love apple," because it was believed to be an aphrodisiac. For this reason, the church declared it a devilish plant. There was strong resistance against garden toma-toes for a century or so, until people discovered that the various bad names were unfounded.

The official name of the common tomato, *Lycopersicon esculentum*, means "succulent wolf peach," and probably dates from some of the early misapprehensions concerning it. It is still not wholly understood. The tomato is really a fruit, although it is classed as a vegetable.

Wine

Always symbolic of the Blood of Life, one way or another, wine was identified long ago in India with women's life-giving menstrual **blood** that flows gently without sacrificial killing. Scriptures said, "Wine is Tara herself in liquid form, the Savior of beings, the Mother of enjoyment and liberation."[1] Similar sentiments may have evolved the Goddess Libera, who was imported into Rome as a consort of Bacchus Liber, and whose festivals involved much drinking of wine.

The *Epic of Gilgamesh* disguises the Goddess of sacred blood as Siduri Sabitu, the Wine-bearer. She counseled the hero to live quietly in the love of his family, and to accept death when it came, instead of making himself and his loved ones miserable in a hopeless quest for immortality.[2] In southern Mesopotamia, the Wine Goddess was known as the Lady of the Vine: the same Goddess whom northern tribes called the Lady of Eden.[3] Later Sufi philosophers named her Saki, perhaps a derivative of Shakti, personifying "reality revealed."[4] Or, as the Romans said, *in vino veritas*. One of her Greek titles was Oenothea, "Wine Goddess."

Worshipers of Dionysus-Bacchus believed that their god's sacred blood was the wine, pouring out of his body at his sacrificial death, just as the juice poured out of the grapes. Before the Christian doctrine of transubstantiation, pagan saviors universally provided wine that was also blood and was supposed to bring about purification, spiritual regeneration, and a promise of immortality in those who drank it as a sacrament. Euripides said that the holy drunkenness caused by possession by the wine god's spirit enabled the drinker to prophesy the future.[5]

In addition to its many sacred meanings, wine has always been used as a drug to enhance good cheer and conviviality. There was a Jewish saying, "A man in whose home wine does not flow like water is not among the truly blessed."[6]

1. *Mahanirvanatantra*, 273.   2. *Larousse*, 72.
3. d'Alviella, 173.   4. *Epic of Gilgamesh*, 38.   5. d'Alviella, 165.   6. Trachtenberg, 167.

21

MINERALS, STONES AND SHELLS

At present there is an efflorescence of popular interest in minerals, not only for the sake of scientific curiosity but also for more esoteric reasons. Once again minerals are being viewed as embodiments of symbolic/spiritual qualities. Of course, the timeless beauty of gems has always attracted human beings. Philosophers have talked of the piquant contrast between ephemeral humanity and the relatively indestructible gem, rock, or fossil. Stones serve as aids to meditation.

In addition, romantic fancy has always perceived gems and minerals as the vital bones of Mother Earth, or the hidden flowers of her underworld gardens, or the silent keys to her secrets. Many people love to collect and contemplate choice specimens. Stones of all kinds have served as lucky charms, personal talismans, amulets, and treasures.

It is unfortunate that romantic fancy often tends to lose sight of its own creative genesis and begins to mistake its metaphors for facts. Mineralogical knowledge has come a long way since the time of the alchemists; yet its discoveries remain largely unnoticed by many modern "crystal mystics" who still base their views on concepts centuries out of date and long since proved wrong. Consequently, current literature on the subject of minerals includes much misinformation, some of which so firmly contradicts easily discernible facts as to achieve new heights (or depths) of human absurdity.

For example, it is claimed that a nonmagnetic, nonconductive mineral such as quartz "absorbs magnetism from the earth's core," and can be used to "magnify, store, focus, transmit, and direct" electrical current.[1] The actual piezoelectric, pyroelectric, and photoelectric properties of some minerals are misunderstood. Their terminology is taken out of context and misapplied to meaningless polysyllabic effusions designed to dazzle the ignorant. A prominent sourcebook for contemporary "mineral metaphysics" offers such mock-scientific gibberish as the following:

> By adjusting the etheric organizing field of tissues, organs, glands, and so on, the physiological functioning harmonizes with the more causal vibratory patterns. Within every level of every energy field of creation, magnetics creates the fundamental coordinates in which each unit of consciousness functions.
>
> Crystals, from this perspective, contain the code patterns of the electromagnetic (and gravitic) coordinates of Light-frequencies as they crystallize into the form of quartz. The molecular latticework holds this information code steady and functions as a "seed of wholeness" that can be stimulated in order to activate powerful force fields of specific parameters. This is basically a matter of activating the code patterns and extending them through the environment, thus recrystallizing the electromagnetic fields. The Oraxians and Atlanteans, for example, created energy domes that covered thousands of square miles.[2]

Popular attention has focused particularly on quartz (silicon dioxide), because it is relatively inexpensive, plentiful, and hard enough to be cut and polished; it forms large, attractive crystals as well as the basic substance of many rocks. Quartz is one of the vast family of silicates that constitute 80 percent of the earth's crust; a full 12 percent of the total is quartz alone. Crystal mystics often seem unaware of this, failing to recognize their favorite minerals in everyday dress. The same sourcebook declares: "Crushed quartz can be used in mortar in order to raise the general vibratory level of an entire building."[3] If so, then most of the world's buildings must be vibrating away at top speed already. Crushed quartz is routinely used in mortar. Its other name is sand.

Crystal mystics also tend to envision their favorite minerals even where they are not. The author of an egregiously unenlightened book entitled *Crystal Enlightenment* flatly states that "Human beings are also largely comprised [sic] of silicon dioxide,"[4] which would certainly astonish any biologist. Like all other living organisms, human beings use a number of minerals in their tissues; but silicon dioxide is not one of them.

Biologists would be surprised to learn also that "Quartz's DNA-like structure has a primary resonant affinity with human DNA and the blood crystals,"[5] or even that normal blood should contain "crystals" at all. Crystal mystics do tend to be vague about biological matters. One declares, without giving reasons, that crystals must never contact "animal-derived substances" like leather; but in the next sentence says with equal conviction that crystals should be wrapped in silk—another animal-derived substance.[6] A gem guru contributes this delicious chowder:

Rubies have qualities of amplification generally in a spectrum which relates to the pineal-pituitary. They are very largely used by entities whom [sic] have some sort of fluidic difficulties in terms of a talisman. . . . Can have some slight effect upon the electro-chemical pattern 'of the body, and can tend to reduce the enzymes found in the epidermal. And generally relate well to those of light or less dense vibrations in terms of their projections.[7]

Crystal mystics are responsible for the most recent manifestation of a widespread ancient belief that illness can be cured by touching—or even approaching—certain minerals or gems. Their modern books contain prescriptive lists of which minerals are "good for" which afflictions: in many instances, the same prescriptive lists that were being circulated a thousand or two thousand years ago.[8] The usual rationale of the ancients was based on sympathetic magic: that is, the principle of like affects like. Therefore red stones are good for the blood, stones that resemble eyes are good for the eyes, cool-colored stones are good for overheating and fevers, transparent yellow stones are good for urinary troubles, and so on.

The present rationales are not much more sophisticated; only their language has become fancier. The central theory involves "vibrations" emanating from the molecular structure of minerals, supposedly projecting themselves into human tissues, which respond by copying the same vibrational frequencies. Then, by some mechanism that is never explained, this fixes whatever ails them. "The ability of gemstones to heal is based on the transference of their stable form of molecular structure, permeating into the body physical down to the molecular level and bringing stability on the biomolecular level to where there is a sympathetic resonancy."[9] Or, in another equally cloudy description, "Crystal healing . . . employs the capabilities of quartz to receive, retain, modify, and transmit an extremely broad range of complex energy frequencies in conjunction with its sensitive responsiveness to thought-waves of Divine Intelligence and the human mind."[10] In other words, it is old-fashioned faith healing tricked out in a brand-new jargon.

This is not to say that faith healing doesn't work. Of course, it does work—sometimes. But it is usually preferable not to entrust any potentially serious condition to faith healing alone. The disappointment could be fatal.

For just such a reason as this, one might question the wisdom of one crystal mystic's advice to tape a crystal to the skin over any "pain area," and leave it there for three consecutive nights on the waning moon; then "after the third night, take the crystal and bury it outside in the ground."[11] Theoretically, the pain is buried along with the crystal. Should the pain arise from something like a hot appendix, however, after three nights of waiting it could be the patient who will be buried instead.

The jargon is easily recognized by its recurrent key words such as attuning, balancing, centering, cleansing, energizing, grounding, harmonizing, influencing, purifying, stabilizing, and stimulating. They are nearly always transitive verbs without objects. One is never told what is attuned to what else, or what is balanced with what else, or what kind of soil is removed by the cleansing or purifying, or what instability requires stabilizing, or how any of this is ascertained, let alone accomplished. Moreover, because crystal mystics love the aura of science even though they do not want to study it, they are also fond of words like precise, accurate, coherent, measurable, specific, exact, and technical—as, for example, in the following remarkable passage:

> The programming process, on the slightly more technical levels, is an interdimensional matrix transduction in which a higher dimensional causal energy-coding structure is superimposed within a receptive crystalline structure that enfolds it within the latticework supraholographically. To make a long and technical story shorter and simpler, the higher dimensional thought-pattern forms

dimensional membrane "stress" patterns that produce a matrix-pattern of interdimensional hyperLight/deltron firing patterns that transpose a holographic standing wave pattern into an ordered latticework. The responsive latticework enfolds the conformation of the causal energy pattern within the atomic-subatomic magneto-gravitational quantum valence levels.[12]

Of course none of this makes any sense. To make sense is not the object; nor is the acquisition of real mineralogical knowledge. Some writers do not even bother to learn how to spell the names of the minerals they talk about.[13] The real aim of crystal mysticism is the same as any fantasy, whether it be playful or serious: to retreat from a troublesome reality into a world of pure symbol. However difficult, uncontrollable, or indifferent the external universe may seem, symbolism is manipulatable and so provides at least the illusion of comfort.

Minerals, then, are true symbol-objects, numinous, filled with *mana*. Although the earth's mineral resources are essential to civilization, and even to life itself, people treat certain forms of those resources as if they were meaningful beyond any possible practical application. To attribute medicinal, divinatory, or mystical powers to minerals is an attempt to rationalize the feelings engendered by their very existence, just as natural human awe in the presence of a mountain once created a host of ancient deities (including Yahweh himself) dwelling in or personifying mountains.

"A gem can become an amazing form of life-giving energy,"[14] certain modern mystics say. Others orate, in their more flowery style of pseudo-explanation, "Gems serve as the mathematical-geometrical correspondents of higher plane vibratory patterns, supraholographic standing-wave patterns of rarefied energy-matter that hold the access lines of interdimensional energy exchange open and steady for receiving higher Light and for gaining amplified, coherent access to the Universal Energy Network."[15] However befuddled the language, it indicates an effort to express a sense of oneness with the rest of the organic and inorganic universe—a sense that Western religions have officially lacked, ever since their God was placed outside of perceptible reality and declared transcendent.

It is true enough that we and all our symbolic concepts are necessarily in and of the material world: the only world that we will ever be able to regard as in any sense self-evident. The usual qualities of minerals—density, solidity, heaviness, toughness, and relative immutability in comparison to organic life—remind us that matter (or Mater) is universal, and our own selves are but a few more among the multitude of its (or Her) diverse forms.

Perhaps the most significant element of human reverence for gems and other minerals is the poorly understood but universal capacity for esthetic emotional response. A sense of beauty seems to inhere in human beings, however they may disagree on its specifics; and this sense often proves to be a major route to what is called religious experience, a state of transcendence, the oceanic feeling, oneness with the Infinite, and so on. Who has not experienced intense, if indescribable, feelings about a sunset, a seascape, a cloud formation, the quality of light on a certain day, the interior of a temple, or a work of art?

As a power for psychological motivation, the field of esthetics has not received as much attention as it deserves. Esthetic responses can be as overwhelming as intense sexual stimuli and probably bear a profound unconscious relationship to them. Ardent human responses to crystals may arise largely from an awareness of their beauty, so keen that *esthetic* seems too mild a description. Therefore, other rationales must be devised to account for such vivid feeling.

Some who strongly respond to the beauty of minerals will channel that response into assiduous study and become mineralogists. Others, less able or less inclined to concentrate, will channel the same response into an unfocused mysticism that satisfies their emotion without making excessive demands on their intellect. In both cases the stimulus is the same; only the effects differ. The symbolism of minerals throughout history reveals a rich supply of both varieties of human behavior.

1. Stein, 175.   2. Baer & Baer, W.L., 37.   3. Ibid., 123.   4. Raphaell, 49.   5. Baer & Baer, C.C., 328.   6. Ibid., 80.   7. *Gems, Stones, & Metals*, 9.   8. Stein, 185–190.   9. *Lapidary Journal*, 40.   10. Baer & Baer, W.L., 94.   11. Stein, 180.   12. Baer & Baer, C.C., 122.   13. Raphaell, 3, 7, 48, 56, 101, 163, 164.   14. Lorusso & Glick, 13.   15. Baer & Baer, C.C., 29.

Agate

Marbodus, bishop of Rennes in the eleventh century, declared that the favor of God can be had by wearing agates. The stone was so frequently credited with divine attraction that in 1709 a Brazilian priest invented a bizarre airship supposedly powered by agates set into its roof. The idea was that the agates would be magnetized by the sunlight that fell on them and would automatically draw the airship upward toward God.

The orbicular type of agate is sometimes called Aleppo stone, because it was believed to heal the "Aleppo boil," a sore that forms a white ring like that of the agate's "eye." Obviously the theory of sympathetic magic underlay this belief, the principle of like cures like. It has been suggested, however, that some temporary relief may have been felt by laying the cool stone on the inflammation.[1]

The resemblance between orbicular agate and the human eye was inevitably noticed and applied to the supposed relief of eye diseases by agates of this type. They were also used as prophylactics against the evil eye.

Moss agate, perhaps because of its many "tongues," was prized by Orientals and gypsies as an aid to persuasive speech. Moslems drank agate powder in water to cure lunacy or melancholia. Romans claimed agates would bring good crops and protect sailors at sea.[2] Some sailors still carry an agate "lucky stone" on every voyage.

1. Kunz, 51–52, 149.   2. G. Jobes 1, 45.

Amber

Electricity was named after the Latin word for amber, *electrum*, because of amber's well-known ability to develop a static charge when rubbed: enough to pick up small bits of paper or to raise the hairs on the skin. Most modern plastics will do the same. The other word for amber was *lyncurius* or lynx stone, stemming from a widespread belief that amber was made of the solidified urine of the lynx. Pliny's *Historia Naturalis* denied this belief, but affirmed amber's reputed ability to cure fever, blindness, deafness, and other disorders.[1] A Greek myth, widely repeated through the Middle Ages, said that amber was formed from the tears of the sun **nymphs** called Heliads, when they wept for the downfall of their brother Phaethon.[2] In Baltic countries, amber beads were called the tears of Freya and were considered a sovereign remedy for arthritis.[3]

Germans named amber *Bernstein*, "burning stone," because it burns easily and gives off an aromatic scent. Of course it is not a stone at all, but a fossilized resin from the sap of primitive pine trees. Medieval alchemists considered it a **sun** symbol. The *Speculum Lapidum* of Camillus Leonardus (1502) said that amber will cure disorders of the throat and belly, counteract poison, and when laid on the breast of a sleeping woman will make her confess all her sins. Something like

the same idea of amber's healing properties is recorded still, in a book published in 1985: "By placing amber over the area of internal organs, these tissues can be revitalized."[4]

1. Desautels, 24, 31. 2. Hall, 244. 3. G. Jobes 1, 82. 4. Raphaell, 136.

Amethyst

Amethyst is the purple variety of **quartz.** Its name is Greek, meaning "not drunken." It was long considered a sure charm for remaining sober no matter how much wine one consumed. Some said it was necessary to hold an amethyst under the tongue when drinking; others considered it equally efficacious worn in a ring. Perhaps for the latter reason, amethyst became the traditional stone for bishops' and cardinals' rings. In medieval times it was known as "bishop's stone."[1]

The power of amethyst against alcoholic excess may have had a logical origin in the ancients' carved amethyst wine cups, which so well disguised the color of the wine that servants could water it down without being detected by their masters. A rich purple wine color could be imparted even to plain water by an amethyst cup.

Pagans also believed in the healing powers of amethysts; and despite their Christian faith, crusaders depended on pagan magic by wearing an amethyst attached to the rosary.[2]

One of the modern crystal mystics, typically uninformed on mineralogical matters, confuses amethyst with an entirely different mineral, beryl (beryllium aluminum silicate), then proceeds to explain its properties: "Other forms of amethyst as in beryl or beryl derivatives we would find to be significant in terms of a general or balancing nature. These can be used as amplification devices for energies in the midrange . . . of the energy spectrum."[3] Naturally, this would not have occurred to the Greeks or the Romans, even when in their cups.

1. Budge, A.T., 309. 2. Dake, Fleener, & Wilson, 17, 86. 3. *Gems, Stones, and Metals*, 5.

Bezoar Stone

The bezoar "stone" is an organic concretion from the alimentary tract of a cud-chewing animal. It may include mostly hair (German bezoar), resinous matter (Oriental bezoar), vegetable fiber (phytobezoar), or calcium phosphate (Western bezoar). Whatever its composition, the bezoar stone has always been much revered as an amulet. Mark Twain described one in *Huckleberry Finn*: "A hair-ball as big as your fist, which had been took out of the fourth stomach of an ox, and [Jim] used to do magic with it. He said there was a spirit inside of it, and it knowed everything."

Black Stone

The *Lapis Niger* (Black Stone) enshrined in the ancient Roman Forum was said to be engraved with the law of the **Goddess.** A similar black stone was worshiped by the Amazons on their sacred isle of Themiscyra, and another (or perhaps the same one) embodied the Goddess Cybele when she was brought to Rome in 204 B.C. by order of the Cumaean Sybil. The aniconic black stone represented an early Anatolian form of Cybele, whose variant names were Ku-Baba, Kuba, or Kube. She was listed as one of the ancestral queens of Sumeria, where she "reigned for a hundred years and founded the dynasty of Kish."[1]

This same black-stone Goddess was connected with the version of the sacred black stone that is still extant today, the Ka'aba (Cube) at Mecca, the central shrine of patriarchal Islam. Before the time of Mohammed, the shrine was devoted to "the Old Woman," a triple Goddess under three names, Manat, Al-Uzza, and Al-Lat (the feminine form of Allah).[2] Her priests seem to have taken over the shrine from an earlier order of priestesses, and they officially entitled themselves "Sons of the Old Woman."[3] Cybele-Kubaba-Kube-Ka'aba also had a place in the temple of Jerusalem. Her priests were the same as in Rome, men who had castrated themselves and assumed

CARBUNCLE

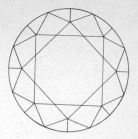

women's clothing.[4] The Bible rather inaccurately describes them as "sodomites" (1 Kings 15:12; 2 Kings 23:7), but the term originally meant "feminized ones."

1. Fisher, 275.   2. Vermaseren, 22.   3. Briffault 3, 80.   4. Beltz, 77–78.

Bloodstone

The name *bloodstone* has been given to almost any red or red-spotted minerals, including **ruby, garnet, carnelian,** and **hematite.** The usual reference, however, is to a variety of jasper (one of the chalcedony group) that is also known as heliotrope: a dark green opaque stone with red flecks. The Egyptians used to equate this stone with the blood of Isis, claiming that it would help pregnant women and cure "female complaints," especially menstrual difficulties.[1] Roman gladiators wore the bloodstone in the belief that it would retard bleeding of wounds.

Christians declared that the stone had been spotted with the **blood** of either Christ or Saint Stephen. Sometimes it was called "Saint Stephen's stone."[2]

In the Middle Ages, possession of a piece of bloodstone was believed to avert many disasters, such as drowning, chest diseases, and attacks by scorpions. According to the Leyden Papyrus, bloodstone had some truly miraculous properties: "The world has no greater thing; if any one have this with him he will be given whatever he asks for; it also

assuages the wrath of kings and despots, and whatever the wearer says will be believed. Whoever bears this stone . . . will find all doors open, while bonds and stone walls will be rent asunder."[3]

Apparently the powers of the bloodstone are no longer so sweeping; but it is still described as "a powerful cleanser for the physical body," able to purify the blood, "often creating a state of detoxification."[4] Another source claims that proximity to bloodstone can overcome iron deficiency.[5] It is certainly more effective, however, to eat a few raisins or take an iron pill from time to time.

1. Budge, A.T., 316.   2. Dake, Fleener, & Wilson, 144–147.   3. Kunz, 61.   4. Raphaell, 139.   5. Stein, 188–189.

Carbuncle

Although it is constantly mentioned in medieval poems, charms, and descriptions of real jewels, there is no such gem as a carbuncle. From Latin *carbunculus*, "a small burning coal," the word was applied indiscriminately to almost any red-colored gem, such as **ruby,** spinel, or the red **garnet** called pyrope (i.e., "burning" or "fiery"). Red gems were supposed to embody the spirit of **fire,** and so were used to treat fevers, diseases of the blood, and other "red" or "hot" conditions. The word *carbuncle* is also applied medically to any inflamed red spot or swelling such as a boil.

Carnelian

One of several red stones formerly known as **bloodstone,** the carnelian was supposed to suppress loss of blood from wounds or excessive menstrual flow, and to prevent blood from rising to the head. Carnelian is one of the many varieties of chalcedony. Its blood redness made it a highly favored stone for Egyptian heart amulets, which represented the *ab* or mother-given heart-soul. A carnelian amulet placed in the body cavity of a mummy was described as "the blood of Isis, the virtue of Isis, the magic power of Isis."[1]

Moslems called carnelian the Mecca stone, which could fulfill all desires and bring perfect happiness. Ancient Greeks supposed that it could grant the heart's desires. Some have derived its name from Latin *carne,* "flesh," though the European version is cornelian, perhaps from *cor,* "heart." Carnelian had the first position on Aaron's breastplate of magical stones. Persians imitated the Egyptians in burying carnelian with the dead, as a charm for new flesh to be put on in rebirth. The stone's association with flesh and blood persists in the folk belief that bleeding gums can be controlled by using a carnelian toothpick.[2]

Today, crystal mystics are still saying that carnelian is good for menstrual problems, and also that it "feeds energy molecules directly through the skin," despite the fact that there are no such things as energy molecules.[3]

1. Kunz, 38, 226. 2. G. Jobes 1, 292.
3. Lorusso & Glick, 69.

Cat's Eye

Other than the comparatively rare chrysoberyl cat's eye stones, most cat's eye or tigereye minerals consist of chatoyant quartz: that is, a translucent variety with inclusions of some other fibrous mineral capable of reflecting light in the characteristic straight ray resembling the slit pupil of a cat.

The Arabs assigned very peculiar properties to such a stone. They believed it could make its wearer invisible in battle. They also believed it could prevent an adulterous wife from conceiving children by her lover, provided her husband made her drink milk in which the stone had been dipped, before he went away on a journey.[1] Perhaps the stone, perceived as an eye, was thought to affect various phenomena of vision and watching.

1. Budge, A.T., 311.

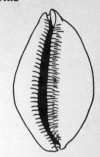

Chrysoprase

The green variety of cryptocrystalline quartz known as chrysoprase has been credited with many miraculous powers. In the Middle Ages it was thought that a piece of chrysoprase held in the mouth could make a person invisible and that a condemned thief could escape punishment by means of this stone.[1]

   1. Dake, Fleener, & Wilson, 141.

Copper

The alchemical sign for copper is the same as the sign for the Goddess **Venus** (Aphrodite), because one of the richest sources of copper known to the ancient world was the Goddess's sacred isle, Cyprus, whose very name means "copper." The metal dug from Cyprian mines and worked by Cyprian smiths became the Goddess's metal, associated with her in many different ways. Copper is the magic **mirror** of divination for Friday (Venus's day), for example, and is even symbolically linked with the planet Venus, like silver with the moon and gold with the sun.

   Venus-Aphrodite was often poetically called "the Cyprian" or "the Paphian," after the copper-isle or its major city of Paphos where her greatest temple stood, with her image decked out in copper ornaments. Healing miracles attributed to copper ornaments may well be traced back to archaic worship of the Goddess.

Coral

Red coral was greatly valued as a magical necklace for children throughout the Mediterranean world; it was supposed to protect them from the evil eye.[1] Coral was called the ocean's **Tree of Life,** its red color attributed to life-giving feminine **blood.** Greek legend said all red coral grew from the blood of the **Gorgon,** Medusa.[2]

   The mythic connections with female blood and fertility led to a conviction among Italian peasant women that their coral jewelry would change color in harmony with their menstrual cycles.[3] In addition to this, powdered coral was considered a cure for sterility and was added to many medicinal recipes.

   1. Trachtenberg, 133. 2. Cirlot, 59.
3. Kunz, 69.

Cowrie

The cowrie shell is probably one of the world's first yonic symbols, its resemblance to female **genitalia** being almost impossible to miss. Its very name is thought to be derived from Kauri, a pre-Vedic version of the Goddess in India. The shell is still revered in India as magical jewelry for averting the evil eye.[1] But the use of cowrie shells as rebirth

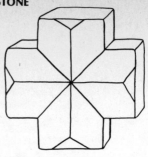

symbols—representing the female Gate of Life—dates as far back as 20,000 B.C.[2]

Cowries were used throughout the Middle East, Egypt, the South Pacific, and the Mediterranean countries as charms for healing, fertility, rebirth, magical power, or good luck. Romans called the shell *matriculus*, the "little matrix," or "little womb." It was also known as *porcella*, meaning both "vulva" and "little sow." Our word *porcelain* derives from this, since it was originally likened to the shiny white surface of the cowrie shell.[3]

Among the Greeks, the word *kteis* meant a vulva, a cowrie shell, a scallop shell, or a comb. Cowrie-shell magic persisted well into the Christian era, despite persistent efforts not to see its obvious symbolism. Gypsy women continued to value cowries above any other kind of amulet as a focus for their own feminine powers.[4] Christianized Sudanese accepted amulets made of strips of leather stamped with a cross, but regarded them as relatively useless unless they were decorated with nine cowries.[5]

1. Gifford, 79. 2. Campbell, *P.M.*, 376.
3. Leland, 102. 4. Trigg, 43. 5. Budge, A.T., 352.

Cross Stone

Cross stone is the common name of the mineral staurolite, which often forms cruciform twinned crystals, crossing either at sixty degrees in an X cross, or at ninety degrees in a Greek cross. Such twinned crystals are also known as fairy crosses. Italians call them *piedra della croce* and regard them as powerful amulets. In Britain, staurolite crystals were used as protection against shipwreck. The legend current in the United States is that cross stones were formed in the rocks by the tears that the **fairies** wept, when they first heard the news of Christ's crucifixion.[1] This legend seems to blend Christian and pagan elements more or less impartially.

1. Kunz, 271.

Crystal Ball

Abbot Tritheim, the teacher of Cornelius Agrippa von Nettesheim, wrote that a wizard's crystal ball should be perfectly clear and about "the bigness of a small orange." It should be mounted in **gold** on an ivory or ebony pedestal, with the **Tetragrammaton** engraved on it, as well as the names of the four Archangels, Michael, Gabriel, Uriel, and Raphael, "ruling over the Sun, Moon, Venus, and Mercury."

A crystal ball two and a half inches in diameter surmounts the Scottish **scepter.** The use of such balls has been traced back to the Druids. They were still known as

MINERALS, STONES, AND SHELLS

"stones of power" in Sir Walter Scott's day. Another sphere of smoky quartz, which the Scots called *cairngorm*, is now in the possession of the British Museum and is reputed to be the famous "shew-stone" of Dr. Dee, the court diviner to Queen Elizabeth I of England.[1] Crystal balls remain popular to this day, whether they are made of glass or of clear quartz. Museums contain some very large clear quartz balls created in the Orient by years of patient hand-polishing. In Japan, the crystal ball known as *tama* is regarded as a symbol of eternity.[2]

1. Kunz, 181, 183, 190.   2. G. Jobes 1, 527.

Diamond

Diamond descends from the Sanskrit *dyu*, a luminous being, a deity.[1] Though most dictionaries derive *diamond* from *adamas*, adamant, this older connection as well as many mythological figures point to a diamond as the stone of Dia, the Goddess. She is still known in the East as the Diamond Sow; her yonic shrine in paradise is the Diamond Seat; and *diamond* can easily be read as "Goddess of the World."[1]

Because diamonds were popularly supposed to have been deposited in the earth by **lightning,** the **thunderbolt** jewel, Sanskrit *vajra*, it was said in medieval Europe that thunder can "dissolve" diamonds, on the theory that whatever creates can also destroy. Sir John Mandeville insisted that diamonds were sexual

and could bring forth children like themselves. Owners of diamonds naturally craved mightily to know how they could encourage their diamonds to mate. Sir John also said that diamonds watered with May dew would grow bigger.[2]

Only about 20 percent of all the diamonds mined annually are useful as gemstones. The rest find industrial uses. There is still a long-standing tradition that the worldwide specialists in diamond marketing, cutting, and lapidary work are the Jews. A popular Renaissance aphorism said, "Pagans have faith in herbs; Christians have faith in words; Jews have faith in diamonds."[3] The Western custom of giving a diamond for betrothal was unknown, however, in China where diamonds were considered inferior to jade. The proper gift from a bridegroom to his bride was jade.

The most popular legend about any famous large diamond is its "curse." Tragic tales about the owners of such stones were told over and over, with a relish not unrelated to common envy of the rich. It was often said that women wearing diamond buttons on their clothing would surely court disaster.[4] Robbery, perhaps accompanied by physical harm, was probably the disaster that they risked most of all.

1. Cirlot, 77.   2. Kunz, 71–72.
3. Trachtenberg, 136.   4. G. Jobes 1, 441.

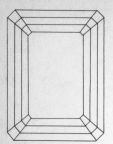

Emerald

"The Emerald is the very essence of the fifth ray of healing and science and was brought to earth in a minute seed particle by the Lords of the Flame from the planet Venus," according to certain present-day crystal mystics.[1] Some ancient beliefs about emeralds were almost as bizarre as this (Albertus Magnus said that all emeralds come from griffins' nests); but these might be excused on the ground that mineralogical knowledge was lacking, which is not the case today.

Emerald is a grass-green variety of beryl, typically much flawed, hard to find in gem quality. The emperor Nero evidently owned an unusually clear emerald, through which he watched his gladiators, believing that the green gem would protect his eyes. Centuries later, alchemical writings attributed to Hermes Trismegistus said that emeralds can cure ophthalmia, stop hemorrhages, and counteract poisons. Medieval physicians also said a sure cure for dysentery was an emerald dangling over the abdomen.[2]

Hermes Trismegistus was another incarnation of the ancient god Hermes who owned the famous Emerald Tablet, the ultimate book of magic. Made of *uat*, "matrix emerald," it was originally attributed to the corresponding Egyptian god Thoth, master of magic. Like the Philosopher's Stone and the Holy Grail, the Emerald Tablet became a perennial object of quest, drawing some of its legends from Arabian stories of the Preserved Tablet, Mother of the Book, a heavenly prototype of the Koran.

Emerald green was looked upon with suspicion by Christian authorities, because it used to be associated with the pagan **Hermes** and his Goddess, Aphrodite. As the color of springtime and fertility, it was considered unsuitable for ecclesiastical garments. Not only did the Goddess wear emerald green, but the pagan god Horus was called "Prince of the Emerald Stone." The Holy Grail itself was said to have been carved out of a huge emerald that once belonged to Satan and fell from his crown as he descended into the underworld.[3]

1. Lorusso & Glick, 37. 2. Kunz, 79, 227, 380–381. 3. G. Jobes 1, 508.

Garnet

Garnet is a collective term for a family of variously colored silicates, including andradite, almandine, pyrope, grossular, spessartine, and uvarovite, with subgroups demantoid, melanite, topazolite, hessonite, hyacinth, rosolite, tsavorite, and several others. These varieties come in many colors: black, green, yellow, brown, violet, orange, and colorless; but the

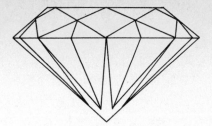

most familiar garnet color is a rich dark red like venous **blood.**

As might be expected, therefore, by the rules of sympathetic magic, garnet has always been associated with blood, bleeding, wounds, diseases of the blood, and blood bonds. The word *garnet* comes from *granatum,* the **pomegranate,** a traditional symbol of the womb and life-giving uterine blood. Perhaps for this reason, garnets usually have been considered more appropriate for women than for men. In the Middle Ages, red garnets were credited with the power to dry up and heal bleeding cuts and other wounds. On the other hand, Indian troops fighting the British in Kashmir used garnet bullets, because they believed that these bullets would cause exceptionally bloody wounds, difficult to heal.[1]

1. Desautels, 100.

Gemstones

According to rulings of the Council of Leodicea (A.D. 355), the early Christian church declared that precious stones were fetters of the **soul,** corrupted by the **sin** of Adam; and people who wore them must be cast out of the church.[1] Superstitions arising in the wake of this claimed that many gems were venomous and that **diamonds** were to be found in the jaws of poisonous snakes.[2] The ancient Goddess, in one of her new medieval diabolized forms as the Goddess Mari, was said to give her nocturnal worshipers gems

that turned into lumps of coal by the light of day.[3]

Because of ecclesiastical opposition, the old arts of gem cutting and engraving were forgotten in Europe's Middle Ages. Nevertheless, elaborately carved gems survived from antiquity and from the Gnostic period, to be covertly admired. The Spanish called the *piedras de rayo,* "stones of the light."[4] Christians began to pretend that these desirable jewels were not the works of ancient lapidarics but natural formations from the hand of God. Konrad von Megenburg wrote that he felt assured of God's grace despite his love of gems, for "God granted these stones their beauty and virtue for the help and comfort of the human race."[5]

The church eventually recognized the vast potential of jewels to augment its secular treasuries, just as priesthoods in India had done. Krishna's practical, acquisitive priests made lists of postmortem rewards for the donors of various gems. Givers of **rubies** would be reborn as kings and emperors. Givers of **emeralds** would receive Knowledge of the Soul and of the Eternal. Givers of **coral** would "subdue all the three worlds." Givers of **gold** would attain salvation (Nirvana) and "enjoy eternal life." Krishna commanded each follower to give "whatever is best and most valued in this world and that which is most dear to you," to receive the promise of riches in another life.[6]

Perceiving the advantage of such exchanges, Christian authorities discovered that jewels were acceptable after all, provided the church got them. Evil connotations were removed by saying three masses over them, with a benediction: "We humbly beseech Thy majesty since Thou has elected one of the stones to be a dwelling-place for the majesty of Thy heart, that Thou wilt deign to bless and sanctify these stones by the sanctification and incarnation of Thy name, so that they may be sanctified, blessed, and consecrated, and may receive from Thee the effect of the virtues Thou hast granted to them, according to their kinds, and which the experience of the learned has shown to have been given by Thee."[7]

It was newly discovered that Gnostic gems portrayed, not the pagan deities whose names were written on them, but Christian celebrities in disguise. It seemed that the god Mercury on a gem was really Saint Michael. Zeus and Athene before her olive tree were really Adam and Eve in Eden. Jupiter Serapis, it seemed, was the patriarch Joseph when his gem entered a church treasury. Soon, most of Europe's store of precious stones was in the hands of the church.[8]

Once the ban was lifted, Europeans became assiduous collectors of gems. Physicians insisted on a gemstone pharmacopeia: sapphires for eye disorders, infections, and evil spells; carnelian to stop bleeding; coral for nervous diseases;

topaz to halt nightmares, and to bring fame and wealth (to the doctor perhaps, not the patient).[9]

Because of their monetary value, gems have been connected with every kind of theft, fraud, and scam that human ingenuity could devise. Naturally, the current popularity of gemstones and other minerals has brought forth several new versions of the old con games. One of the oldest was the sale—for highly inflated prices—of water into which a gemstone had been dipped, on the pretense that contact with the stone had made the water medicinal.

Today it is still perfectly legal to sell such "prepared gemstone essence," as it is now called, though what the customer really buys is a small but pricey vial of plain water, without a single molecule of the mineral in it. Gemstones are not soluble in water. Most are not soluble even in strong acids. Yet "crystal mystics" freely sell and endorse this nonproduct, making such claims as "The water serves as a receptive medium that stores the energy of the crystal as it processes the energies of the sun, moon, and stars."[10] The believer is enjoined to drink such water every day, which could run into considerable expense. "Gem tinctures," says the sourcebook, "have their primary effect upon the gravito-magnetic crystallization patterns of the blood. Some of these tinctures have a strong magnetic reorientation effect upon the brain cells and brain-mind centers."[11] Perhaps this could be translated into a need to have one's head examined.

A less pernicious sales campaign was undertaken on behalf of the jewelers, to assign a gemstone to each month of the year (or sign of the zodiac), and encourage people to buy their "birthstones." The ancients used varying lists of zodiac stones. One such list provided the much-discussed twelve jewels on the breastplate of the Old Testament high priest (Exodus 28:17–20). Birthstone lists still vary, although jewelers' organizations have tried to standardize them. Despite the variations—which would certainly negate any specific interpretations—modern mystics also struggle to justify the idea of birthstones, describing them as "conductors of equilibrium through the doorways and gates of vibration that each cycle and season of the twelve Earth months brings to man."[12] Or, as another one hazily expresses it, "There are those vibrations which are found in the element, mineral which do relate to the time of entry because of the electro-magnetic matrix which is formed celestially or cosmically with the earth plane. So logically one can conceive that as these gradients are located, and as the cosmic alignment is calculated there can be those which vibrate best, or relate best, to entities whom [sic] entered at that time."[13]

1. Kunz, 42–44.   2. Cirlot, 155.   3. Baroja, 238.   4. Leland, 250.   5. Kunz, 141. 6. Ibid., 240–241.   7. Ibid., 45.   8. Ibid., 257.   9. G. Jobes 2, 1268, 1398, 1588. 10. Baer & Baer, W.L., 98.   11. Baer & Baer, C.C., 156.   12. Lorusso & Glick, 7. 13. Gems, Stones, & Metals, 26.

Gold

The alchemical sign for gold is the same as the symbol of the **sun.** Gold has always been equated with the sun because of its color and brightness and with the idea of immortality because of its impervious nature. Gold is never dimmed by corrosion or rust. It does not deteriorate in water or disintegrate in soil or mud. Fire can melt it but not impair its luster. As the unchangeable, untarnishable, "immortal" metal, gold symbolized human hopes of eternal life particularly in Egypt and the Orient, where honored dead were encased in gold caskets so the metal might confer its enduring qualities on them.

In the legendary temple of Heracles-Melkart, the sun god of Tyre, one pillar was made entirely of gold and probably represented the god himself. Hindus named gold the "mineral light," supposing it to come from a mysterious congealment of sunlight, buried underground.[1]

Gold has been the preferred material for wedding rings because of its symbolic suggestion of brightness (happiness) never to be dimmed by time.

In Oriental symbolism a golden cube commonly signifies the earth. One possible source of this symbol is the widespread substitution of pyrite or "fool's gold" for the real thing. Pyrite (iron disulfide) has a brilliant golden color and tends to crystallize in perfect cubes.

1. Cirlot, 58, 114.

Hematite

Hematite, an iron ore, can be scraped into a bright red powder (iron oxide), which is sometimes known as red ochre. This was used in antiquity for every medical and mystical representation of **blood**: hence the name *hematite*, which means bloodstone. Hematite powder was supposed to cure bloodshot eyes, to stop internal bleeding, and to relieve bladder infections that produce bloody urine. Stone Age graves were sometimes reddened throughout the entire excavation with hematite, to imitate a blood-filled womb that may give rebirth. The Romans made both hematite and iron sacred to **Mars,** their red god of war; so the stone was often used as an amulet of protection for warriors in battle.[1]

The alchemical symbol for hematite apparently combined the sigil of **Venus** (consort of Mars) with an inverted sigil of Venus, suggesting a birth-and-death sequence.[2]

1. Kunz, 81.   2. Koch, 69.

Jade

Jade is either of two minerals that are different, but hard to tell apart. They are (1) jadeite, a pyroxene silicate, and (2) nephrite, an amphibole silicate. The former is now considered the more valuable "imperial jade," but the latter was the important Chinese jade before the eighteenth century.

Nephrite was named from Latin *lapis nephriticus,* "kidney stone," because of a belief that it could cure kidney ailments. *Jade* comes from Spanish *piedras de ijada,* "stones of the loin," because of the same belief, held by the conquistadores who found jadeite in Mexico.[1]

The Chinese used jade for jewels, ornaments, weapons, tools, furniture, and medicine. Boiled with rice and dew water in a copper pot, jade made a "divine liquor" believed to cure many ills: an ancient Oriental version of the "gemstone essence."[2] Taken just before death, this decoction was thought to prevent decomposition of the body.

The Chinese love of jade was based on the idea that it was the congealed semen of the celestial **dragon,** deposited in the body of the earth. People valued it "for its profound symbolic significance," constantly touching and fondling their jade jewels not for "a mere sensuous pleasure but a symbolic contact with the seminal source of celestial vitality."[3] Some similarly exotic fancy might have inspired certain present-day American claims that jade is "not of the Earth but is a mutation from a planet outside of this solar system."[4] How this was discovered has not been explained.

1. Desautels, 23, 221.   2. Kunz, 385.
3. Rawson, *E.A.E.,* 230.   4. Lorusso & Glick, 44–45.

4

Jet

Jet is another name for anthracite coal that is hard enough to be cut and polished like a gemstone. Its glossy blackness often led to its association with underworld powers. Talismans of jet were supposed to control **demons,** avert the evil eye, combat witchcraft or demonic possession, cure snakebite, and prevent poisoning. The protective *mano cornuta* (**devil's horns** amulet) was often made of jet.[1]

1. Budge, A.T., 316.

Lapis Lazuli

Blue lapis lazuli traditionally symbolized **water** as the primordial element of creation.[1] Egyptians buried lapis lazuli amulets with mummies, to replace the heart, and bring about regeneration in the afterworld.[2] As the Stone of Truth, lapis was sacred to the Goddess Maat, Mother of the All-Seeing Eye, whose name meant both "truth" and "seeing eye."[3] This may account for the widespread belief that lapis lazuli could cure eye diseases.[4] It was also revered in China as one of the Seven Precious Things.

Lapis lazuli belongs to the same silicate family as the blue sodalite. Also known as *lazurite*, it was named from a Persian word for "heaven," *lazuward*, which also gave us *azure*. Confusingly, an entirely different blue mineral is named lazulite—a phosphate—while still another unrelated blue mineral is azurite, a carbonate of copper. Nomenclature through lazulite-lazuli-lazurite-azurite has led to many misunderstandings.

The alchemical symbol for lapis lazuli seems to be a reversal of the sign for **Jupiter** the heaven god, possibly to express the idea of a bit of blue heaven having descended to earth and looking upward from the rocks.[5]

1. Cirlot, 33. 2. Budge, E.M., 30. 3. Kunz, 119, 293. 4. G. Jobes 2, 973. 5. Koch, 72.

Lapis Manalis

"Stone of the Underworld" is the usual translation of *lapis manalis*, the sacred stone on Rome's Palatine Hill, covering the **pit** in which ancestral spirits were supposed to dwell. Actually, it means "Stone of the Ancestral Spirits," which were collectively *manes*, the children of the archaic Moon Goddess Mana, or Mania, who appeared as mother of all the dead, wearing a fearsome **mask,** at her own annual festivals. Each year at the festival of the Parentalia, Romans removed the *lapis manalis* from the top of the pit and invited the *manes* to come forth and attend the feasts held in their honor. In essence it was the Roman version of **Halloween,** which the Celts called Samhain, the feast of honoring the dead. These dead under the *lapis manalis* were even older than Rome itself.

Lodestone (Magnetite)

Lodestone is a natural magnet, and its power of attraction readily suggested its use in love charms and other operations where attraction was the goal. Lodestone was believed to attract **lightning,** so should not be carried during a thunderstorm. It also made the memory more retentive. Prostitutes prized lodestone for attracting customers. Some Mexican Indians still believe that the lodestone is alive and must be put in water every Friday so it can drink and that it must be given iron filings to eat.[1]

According to Pliny, magnetite was named after the shepherd Magnes, who discovered it while tending his flock on Mount Ida, when pieces of the stone clung to the nails in his shoes. The Roman poet Claudian in the fifth century A.D. described a miraculous marriage of **Venus** and **Mars** arranged by the priests of their joint temple. The statue of Mars was made of iron; the statue of Venus was made of lodestone; naturally, they would rush together. It was often said that in the same way, women draw men to them as the lodestone draws iron. In China the stone was called *t'su shi,* the loving stone.[2]

1. Budge, A.T., 318.   2. Kunz, 94–95.

Malachite

Renaissance physicians used malachite as "a powerful local anesthetic," which must have involved considerable power of suggestion, because the stone itself possesses no such property.[1]

Malachite was "peacock stone" in Italy. Its orbicular markings resemble the eyes in a peacock's tail; therefore the stone was sacred to **Juno,** whose totem was the **peacock.** Malachite was also considered a protection against the evil eye, especially when the amulet was cut in a triangular shape.[2] This notion might even date back to the original version of Juno as a Triple Goddess, the earlier, all-female Capitoline Triad.

One of the modern crystal mystics writes: "If someone is very evolved and dedicated to humanitarian purposes, Malachite assists in grounding higher energies onto the planet to be used for these purposes."[3] Presumably, however, the "higher energies" no longer come from Juno.

1. Desautels, 24.   2. Kunz, 137.   3. Raphaell, 143.

Millstone

The millstone used to be a symbol of the Goddess of **grain**, harvest, milling, and baking. Certain ancient icons of her with her millstone were converted into pictures of a wholly mythical Christian **saint**, Christina—whose name means simply a female Christian. Her revised legend made her the usual adamant virgin imprisoned and hideously tortured for retaining her virginity. Among other brutalities she was thrown into Lake Bolsena with a millstone around her neck, yet she refused to sink, but miraculously floated, millstone and all.[1] Yet somehow the God who thus preserved her from death soon abandoned her anyway, and she died of an overdose of arrows.

1. Hall, 67–68.

Opal

The opal may have been the **Philosopher's Stone** as it was described by certain Arabian alchemists, uniting in itself "all the colors: white, red, yellow, sky-blue and green."[1]

There was a belief that an opal ring would shine brighter on the finger of a sick person just before death. Mineralogists say this could be true. Opals are affected by heat, and a wearer with a high fever might intensify the stone's color.[2]

In the Middle Ages it was sometimes thought that opal could make the wearer invisible to the eyes of others, so it became known as the stone of thieves.[3]

Western Europeans have often called the opal a bad-luck stone. Like many other bad-luck symbols, this may have stemmed from a tenuous connection with ancient **Goddess** worship: namely, that of the pre-Roman Earth Mother Ops, whose annual festivals were known as Opalia. The stone's name, however, came from Sanskrit *upala*, "valuable stone."

1. Seligmann, 94. 2. Dake, Fleener, & Wilson, 244. 3. Kunz, 150.

Pearl

Pearls were sacred to Aphrodite Marina as Pearl of the Sea, who was vaguely Christianized as the mythical Saint Margaret ("Pearl") via several different legends. The most popular of these held that Margaret was a former priestess of Aphrodite, a wealthy sacred harlot who suddenly turned Christian and gave away all her property to the church. In other words, she was the **Goddess** converted. But Aphrodite's "pearly gate," the symbolic **yoni** leading to her sexual paradise, also became a Christian tradition.[1] In Moslem mythology, too, paradise is a pearl representing complete sexual fulfillment. Each blessed hero will live after death with his *houri* in a mass of pearls; male and female will join together as a perfect "spherical man," or **androgyne,** signifying the Pearls of Wisdom that used to mean perfect knowledge of the Goddess. [2]

Because of these connotations of male-female combination, it was often said that pearls are formed of male **fire** and female **waters.** Another, more poetic, tradition said pearls are formed by the merging of water and moonlight. [3]

The famous story of Cleopatra's pearl was repeated in folklore for centuries. She was said to have dropped a very valuable pearl into wine and when the pearl dissolved, drank it in Marc Antony's presence. It was another of those impossible tales beloved by the uninformed, easy to disprove but never checked. Pearls do not dissolve in wine. Any liquid capable of rapidly dissolving a pearl would equally rapidly have dissolved Cleopatra's insides. [4]

Pearl fishers of Borneo used to insist that a pearl placed with two grains of rice into a bottle stoppered by a dead man's finger would soon give birth to more pearls. [5] This too was improbable enough to be widely believed.

1. Walker, *W.E.M.S.*, 582. 2. Cirlot, 130, 239. 3. de Lys, 284–285. 4. Desautels, 17. 5. Kunz, 41.

Philosopher's Stone

No one was quite certain what the Philosopher's Stone was, except that most texts hinted at a substance of universal creation, capable of transforming every kind of matter, so that base metals might be converted into gold, and the alchemist could attain perfect knowledge of natural processes that formerly belonged only to deities. The Philosopher's Stone was variously described as a divine child, a hermaphroditic *rebis* or *lapis*, a dragon, tincture, elixir, water, urine, *filius*, *puer*, vinegar, or *menstruum universale*; its vessel was a virginal **womb** (sometimes even called the Womb of Mary) fertilized by the alchemists' god **Mercury,** or Hermes Trismegistus. [1] The Stone was the symbol of the whole alchemical art, which was sometimes called the Sophic Art; therefore its central goal was also known as the Sophistical Stone. [2]

Clearly, this "Stone" was not a stone at all, according to the texts. Yet it was always so described, and many different kinds of gems and minerals were identified with it. Beneath all the mystical rhetoric might lie the extremely ancient concept of the stuff of primal **chaos,** before the elements were differentiated from one another, and all things were blended "neither hot nor cold, wet nor dry"

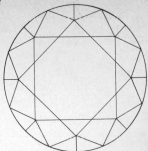

in the cosmic womb. In this context, *menstruum universale* would come closest to the original meaning. A more modern meaning might be *magma*: the mother of all "stones."

1. Campbell, C.M., 272–273.   2. Shah, 194.

Quartz

Ancient Greeks believed that quartz crystals were petrified ice, frozen so hard that it could never thaw; so they named the mineral *krystallos*, "ice." This notion survived all the way up to A.D. 1777 and was endorsed by the Swedish scientist Linnaeus.[1] Folk tradition holds that thirst can be quenched by holding a quartz crystal in the mouth, as if it might melt into water.[2] Robert Boyle finally pointed out that quartz cannot be ice, because quartz sinks in water, whereas ice floats.

In fact, the Greeks were closer to the truth than they knew. Crystallization is the same as freezing. Water is the mineral hydrogen oxide, that freezes into its solid crystalline state at 32 degrees F. Molten quartz freezes into its solid crystalline state at 3,115 degrees F.

Roman priestesses of Vesta used quartz crystals to "draw down fire from heaven" to light **altar** fires, which could be kindled in no other way. The altar fire that consumed the sons of Aaron was similarly engendered by "fire from the Lord" (Leviticus 10:2). Quartz has been used through the centuries for both practical and magical purposes of every kind. Mexican Indians believe that spirits of the dead live in quartz crystals. Christian authorities claimed that they represented the Immaculate Conception.[3] Modern crystal mystics especially revere quartz, but disagree about its properties. One says that quartz "works directly with the separations of layers of the disconnected mind, attempting to reintegrate the levels of consciousness."[4] Another claims that quartz crystals "are used by the Higher Evolution as fundamental building blocks to set up a measurable grid of a larger harmonic system which allows for different combinations of wave structures to unite and form myriads of gravitational wave combinations which, in turn, react with one another to transmit thought-forms to physical planetary realities."[5] Or perhaps the grid can be measured by the disconnected mind.

1. Dake, Fleener, & Wilson, 82, 110.   2. G. Jobes 1, 392.   3. Budge, A.T., 312.   4. Lorusso & Glick, 61.   5. Baer & Baer, W.L., 144.

Ruby

In India the ruby is *ratnaraj*, "lord of precious stones." Dark rubies are called male, lighter ones female. Rubies were associated with heat and passion. It was even claimed that the red heat of a ruby in water would make the water boil.[1] It

is hard to see how a notion so easy to disprove could have been so long perpetuated, unless it was simply the comparative rarity of rubies that made experimentation unlikely.

Another popular legend said a ruby or "carbuncle" could shine in darkness like a lamp. European bards insisted that the temple of the Holy **Grail** was surmounted by a huge ruby serving as a beacon, to guide Grail knights during the night.[2] The idea that gemstones can produce light, instead of merely reflecting or refracting it, is very common in mythology. According to Hindu tradition the entire underworld is illuminated by a great gem, *Kantha*, as if by a subterranean sun.[3]

Islamic legend said that Adam and Eve were reunited in the stone of the Ka'aba, which was carved from a gigantic ruby with a white stone set into its center: thus, a female (red) principle surrounding and enclosing the male (white) principle. Later, the stone turned entirely black—allegedly because sinful men touched it—making the third of the three sacred colors.[4]

Like other red stones, the ruby was often used as a charm to prevent bloodshed or to treat disorders of the blood. Technically, ruby is only the red variety of

corundum (aluminum oxide), the common form of which is emery. Corundum gems in every other color—blue, yellow, white, brown, violet, green—are known as **sapphire.**

1. Kunz, 101–102.   2. Walker, *W.E.M.S.*, 352. 3. G. Jobes 2, 908.   4. Cavendish, 114–115.

Salt

Not surprisingly, the alchemical symbol for salt was the same as the symbol for the **water** element: the straight sea horizon dividing upper and lower portions of the world.[1] Like the **sea** itself, salt was always revered as a symbol of purification and rebirth. Salt was probably the first discovered means of preserving foods, such as meat and fish. It also tastes like **blood** and seawater, both of these fluids being identified with the all-producing **womb.** The **thrones** of gods often had cubical shapes resulting from the observation that "the salt of the earth" forms cubical crystals. In the Orient, the three-dimensional sign of Earth was the cube.

The biblical God insisted that every offering on his **altars** must be made with an offering of salt (Leviticus 2:13) because nearly all Middle Eastern cultures used salt to consecrate altars and sacrifices. Egyptians dedicated altars by sprinkling them with salt, probably as a substitute for the blood that was formerly

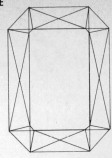

used for this purpose. Our word *immolate* comes from the Roman *mola*, sacred salted flour, prepared by the Vestal Virgins to sprinkle over each animal offered in sacrifice to the gods.[2] The biblical story of Lot's wife as a "pillar of salt" seems to have been derived from the Hebrew MLH, "salt," a sacred name of Queen Mother Earth (Malkuth), revered for having the same numerical value as three repetitions of the secret name of God—therefore, possibly an earlier manifestation of the Triple Goddess.[3]

Because of such ancient intimations of holiness, salt has always been used to repel **demons** and other evil influences. Christian altars, **bells,** reliquaries, and other religious articles were "blessed" with salt. The common practice of bringing salt into a house before the family moves in was based on salt's antidemon qualities. Salt consecrated on Saint Stephen's Day was considered a particularly efficacious protection charm. People ate some of it when a storm threatened, or when starting on a journey.[4] Throwing spilled salt over the shoulder is a death-repelling charm.

1. Koch, 65. 2. Walker, *W.E.M.S.*, 110, 666, 887. 3. Trachtenberg, 160; Budge, A.T., 323. 4. Miles, 311.

Sapphire

Sapphire is the English translation of the biblical *sappur*, said to be the substance of the **throne** of God (Ezekiel 1:26). In Egypt, however, *sappur* seems to have meant the holy **blood** of Isis, whose "lap" was the throne of God; and the Assyrian version, *sapuhru*, meant "a red paste" concocted to bring about magical purifications "in the eyes of the gods."[1] This indicates that ancient versions of sapphire were not the corundum jewel of today but some other stone, or a powdered stone, which may have been blood-colored.

Like all the more expensive gemstones, sapphire was often recommended as a medicine. Bartolomeus wrote that all witches love sapphire, because "they may work certain wonders by virtue of this stone." Star sapphires were called Stones of Destiny, because their three crossing rays invoked the Triple Goddess of Fate. Such stones were also supposed to cure diseases of the eye. The inventory of Charles V listed "an oval Oriental sapphire for touching the eyes."[2] Medieval medical texts declared that sapphires would cure boils.[3] Because sapphire was supposed to preserve both chastity and secrecy, it became a favorite ring stone for cardinals.[4]

1. Graves, *W.G.*, 290; Pritchard 2, 62.
2. Kunz, 105–107, 388. 3. Desautels, 24.
4. G. Jobes 2, 1398.

Scallop

The scallop shell was worn by Christians
to indicate completion of a pilgrimage to the
shrine of Saint James of Compostela in
northwestern Spain. Actually, this
popular shrine was taken over from the
Goddess Brigit, a Celtic version of
sea-born Aphrodite; its former name was
Brigantium.[1] The scallop was her yonic
symbol, as designated by the Greek word
kteis, which meant a scallop, a **cowrie**, or
a vulva. The English *scallop* comes
from Norse *skalpr*, meaning a sheath (or
vagina).[2] Botticelli chose the scallop shell
for his *Venus* with rather precise knowledge of its symbolism.

The absurd legend that converted the
shrine of the Goddess into that of Saint
James (Santiago) was that the body of the
saint had left Jerusalem by sea, floating alone
in a stone coffin, and came ashore in
northwestern Spain to donate its relics to
the shrine. Even Catholic scholars
now agree that the legend of Saint James
of Compostela was entirely faked,
although the shrine continues its operations undisturbed.[3]

1. Graves, G.M. 1, 296.   2. Potter & Sargent,
108.   3. Attwater, 182.

Serpentine

Serpentine is the name of a group of
greenish silicate minerals including an-
tigorite, lizardite, and chrysotile, the fibrous variety also known as asbestos. The
name serpentine arose from imagined re-
semblances to snakeskin. Inevitably,
therefore, serpentine amulets were supposed to heal snakebite and ward off the
poisonous stings of insects. It was often
claimed that a serpentine cup would begin to sweat as soon as any poisonous drink
was put in it.[1]

1. Budge, A.T., 324.

Silver

Silver has always been regarded as the
metal of the **moon**. Medieval superstition
said a woman should not pray to God for any
special favor, for she was not likely to get
it from that source. Instead, she should pray
to her own deity, the moon, by means
of a piece of silver. A direct descendant of
this is the belief, still prevalent in
some areas, that a woman should turn a
silver coin when making her wish
on the moon.[1]

Silver was a divinatory metal, even in
the Bible. The seer Joseph had as
his divinatory tool a silver **cup**, which
represented the moon as a source of
"waters of enlightenment" (Genesis 44:5).

1. de Lys, 458.

Stone

Many traditions and myths point to
humankind's long-established habit of
worshiping unusual stones as divine spirits, particularly the spirits of female
ancestors or Goddesses. The Hebrew *beth-
el*, house or embodiment of a deity,
was a cognate of Greek *baitulos* or *baetyl*,
a standing stone. Pausanias said the
three Charites or **Graces,** very old versions
of the Triple Goddess, were worshiped at
Orchomenos as three standing stones.[1]
Icelanders worshiped their Goddess Ar-
mathr, "Mother of Prosperity," in the form
of a stone.[2] "Holed stones" all over
the world symbolized the **womb** and birth.
In parts of Europe women still pray
to such stones, or crawl through them, as
conception charms.[3] In Aargau, midwives
used to invoke the Goddess before
each birth by circumambulating a certain
stone, whistling, then "opening" the
stone with a golden **key** to let the Mother-
spirit out.[4] Moabite Arabs used to call
themselves Beni Sahr, Sons of the Rock.
The prophet Jeremiah inveighed against his
contemporaries' custom of calling a
stone one's mother (Jeremiah 2:27).

Prepatriarchal records show that Yahweh
was worshiped in the Jerusalem temple as a
consort of the Goddess Anath, who
was combined with him as an androgynous deity Anathyahu. Two stone slabs within
the **Ark** were said to represent this
Goddess and God. One of the common
titles of the Semitic Anath was "Progeni-
tress of the Peoples."[5] Certain myths
even reveal that the people of the world
were thought to have been born of
stones in the beginning. According to
Greek tradition, after the Deluge the flood-
hero Deucalion and his spouse Pyrrha
were taught by the primal Goddess Themis
to raise up their children from stones
to repopulate the earth.[6]

Much hostility was shown by patriarchal
societies toward the ancient stone figures (or
nonfigures) that had been so long
revered as maternal spirits. The famous
Stone of Scone, which now rests under the
English coronation throne in Westminster
Abbey, was once a Hag of Scone,
that is, a Grandmother-Goddess, the same
as the Caillech, a queen of the **elves**
or Elder Deities. Legend said she became
a stone because she was cursed by a
Christian missionary; but it seems likely
that this Hag had always been a stone.[7] Her
function in resting under a coronation
throne is made clear by ancient pagan
tales about the Stone of Fal or Stone of
Sovereignty in Irish myth. A commentary
says this stone's name came from Fo-
all, meaning "rock under a king," and it
would cry out with a loud voice when the
rightful king of Tara was placed on
it: the usual magic signification by Mother
Earth that the king was acceptable to
her. Attempts have been made to connect
the Stone of Fal with *phallus,* and
some sources call it the Penis Stone;
"but it has no phallic characteristics

whatsoever, and its association with sovereignty suggests, on the contrary, that it is feminine."[8]

The famous Tarpeian Rock on Rome's Capitoline Hill was originally sacred to an Etruscan Goddess and evidently embodied her. In classical times a myth was invented about the treacherous maiden Tarpeia, who was crushed under the **shields** of warriors she had betrayed; but the point of this story was to explain the ancient custom of piling up shields as victory offerings to the Goddess of the Rock.[9]

Up to 1860, a stone Goddess image in an ancient shrine on the island of Guernsey continued to receive offerings of flowers and food, until the churchwarden had the stone broken up. Another stone Goddess near Baud, in Brittany, was worshiped until late in the seventeenth century. People were baptized in the stone trough at her feet. This was supposed to help cure the sick.[10] Many myths, such as that of Mithra, still speak of the Mother-stone, the *petra genetrix*, from whom heroes and saviors were born.

On the other hand, the magical powers so often attributed to stones made them objects of superstitious fear among the people of medieval and Renaissance Europe. Having seen that pathological conditions could be caused by "stones" in the kidneys or bladder, many laypeople and even doctors came to believe that a wide variety of diseases and pains were the result of stones inside the body, perhaps placed there by witchcraft. Headaches, blurred vision, hallucinations, or lunacy could be caused by "a stone in the head," according to popular belief. Quack doctors used to perform an operation for this condition. Palming a small pebble, the doctor would make a slight incision on the sufferer's brow or scalp, and when the wound was bleeding freely would pretend to draw forth the blood-covered pebble, thus "curing" the condition.[11] Sometimes it worked. There are modern practitioners of this same kind of quackery, who by sleight of hand perform "scarless operations" and pretend to draw out tumors and other messy-looking blobs, usually obtained beforehand from the local slaughterhouse.

1. Dumézil, A.R.R. 1, 166.   2. Turville-Petre, 230.   3. Cirlot, 142.   4. Duerr, 23.   5. Patai, 62, 135–136.   6. Graves, G.M. 1, 139.   7. Wimberly, 36.   8. Markale, 190.   9. Grant, 123–124.   10. Evans-Wentz, 404.   11. Hall, 229.

Stygian Stone

The Stygian Stone, or Stone of the Styx, was adopted into Hebrew mythology as the *Eben stijjah*, Stone of the Deeps. The Jews claimed that this stone had been found by King David when the foundation was dug for his temple, for it was buried deep in the ground on the sacred spot. The magical stone "unlocked the fountain of the great deep," because the secret magic-working name of God, the *Sem ha-mephoras*, was

inscribed on it.[1] Obviously the original reference was to the unlocking of the Fountains of the Deep in Hittite and Semitic creation myths generally, producing the "nether upsurge" from the **womb** of Earth, which gave the energy of living water or **blood** to make all things alive.

1. Silberer, 315.

Sulfur

Sulfur was sacred to the Goddess **Athene;** therefore its alchemical symbol was the same as her sign. Sulfur was also called brimstone, after another of her manifestations, the Goddess Brimo (the "angry" aspect of Athene), who was also identified with Demeter. Because of its association with the Virgin Goddess of the Parthenon ("Virgin-House"), sulfur was widely regarded as an agent of purification. Sickrooms and **demon**-haunted places were rendered pure by burning sulfur, possibly on the theory that anything with so bad a smell as burning sulfur would be powerful medicine.

By the same token, the bad-tasting waters of natural sulfur springs were always considered great curatives. To this day, sick people make pilgrimages to sulfur springs to "take the waters." Up to a generation or so ago, children were regularly dosed with sulfur and molasses each year as a spring tonic, or "blood purifier": the sulfur to do the purifying, the molasses to help mask the bad taste.

Touchstone

Although the word *touchstone* is still generally used to mean a testing standard, few people know its origin. Touchstone is a black, fine-grained variety of amorphous **quartz** called basanite, or "Lydian stone" to the ancients. It was and is used to determine the purity of precious metals. Different alloys leave streaks of different colors on this stone, and the colors can be readily seen against its blackness. By scraping the metal on the stone, it is possible "to determine the fineness of the metal to an accuracy of about one carat."[1]

1. Dake, Fleener, & Wilson, 155.

Turquoise

Turquoise means "Turkish stone." Turks greatly prized it as an amulet, calling it Fayruz, the lucky stone. It was perhaps identical with the Moslem *sakhrat*, a sacred stone from Mount Qaf, the residence of fairies and giants. This stone was "the color of an emerald reflecting the blue sky." Miracles could be worked with a single grain of it. This stone also had a tenuous connection with the ancient Goddess, for one of the ancient Egyptian titles of Isis was "Lady of Turquoise."[1] However, the original reference may have been to lapis lazuli; mineral names in old writings are often inaccurate and arbitrary.

Buddhists claimed that Buddha once destroyed a monster with the help of a magic turquoise.[2] In Arabia it was believed that the stone would warn of approaching danger by changing its color. The color of some varieties can in fact be changed by environmental factors such as heat, light, oil, perspiration, or dryness.

Turquoise was used as a horse amulet because it was believed to keep horses from foundering, and to protect both horses and their riders from falls. European writers insisted that turquoise would at least soften the effects of a fall: "Whoever owns the true turquoise set in gold will not injure any of his limbs when he falls, whether he be riding or walking, so long as he has the stone with him."[3]

1. G. Jobes 2, 963, 1389. 2. Budge, A.T., 325. 3. Kunz, 109.

Venus Hair Stone

"Venus hair" is a traditional name for clear **quartz** containing fine golden or silvery needles of the mineral rutile (titanium dioxide), a combination more precisely known as rutilated quartz. When the acicular crystals of rutile are very long and slender, they do greatly resemble hairs from a blond head, sparkling in sunbeams just as hair does. Stones with thicker, stiffer crystals of golden rutile were sometimes called Cupid's Arrows. In

any event, the stone was widely regarded as a love charm because of its titular association with the Love Goddess. Sometimes she was deliberately overlooked, however, and the stone received the alternate name of "maiden hair."

White Stone

It was a Roman custom to mark any happy event with a white stone. This became a universal symbol of pleasant memory.[1] For such reasons, memorial tombstones, cenotaphs, and other reminders of the dead were traditionally made of white marble or some other white stone.

White agate, called milk stone in Italy, was much prized for increasing the milk of nursing mothers: a prime example of magic attribution based on nothing but likeness of color.

An Armenian church preserved a white stone set into a cross, which stone was said to be part of the basin in which Jesus washed the disciples' feet. When laid on a dying person, the stone would turn black—or so it was claimed. After the death occurred, it would turn white again.[2] Over the centuries, many thousands whose faith was more perfect than their common sense have implicitly believed in this and similar claims. In eighteenth-century Wales, after the great **Halloween** bonfire, each person placed in the embers a white stone individually marked. If anyone's stone disappeared during the night, it was considered a sign that he or she would die before the Halloween Feast of the Dead came around again the following year.[3]

The Irish used to place white stones on graves, claiming that the dead would mistake them for offerings of precious gems and so would be propitiated. This may well have had a common source with the Buddhist belief that angels drop white or black stones into opposing pans of the scales of the spirit, according to the virtues or sins of the deceased, respectively.[4] White stones could be placed on graves in an effort to weight the scales favorably.

1. Whittick, 350.   2. Kunz, 260.   3. Pegg, 122.   4. G. Jobes 1, 669; 2, 1438.

BIBLIOGRAPHY

Abelard, Miles R. *Physicians of No Value: The Repressed Story of Ecclesiastical Flummery*. Winter Park, FL: Reality Publications, 1979.

Agrippa, Henry Cornelius. *The Philosophy of Natural Magic*. Secaucus, NJ: University Books, 1974.

Albright, William Powell. *Yahweh and the Gods of Canaan*. New York: Doubleday, 1968.

Angus, S. *The Mystery-Religions*. New York: Dover, 1975.

Arens, W. *The Man-Eating Myth*. New York: Oxford University Press, 1979.

Aries, Philippe. *The Hour of Our Death*. New York: Knopf, 1981.

Arnheim, Michael. *Is Christianity True?* Buffalo, NY: Prometheus Books, 1984.

Attwater, Donald. *The Penguin Dictionary of Saints*. Baltimore: Penguin Books, 1965.

Avalon, Arthur. *Shakti and Shakta*. New York: Dover, 1978.

Bachofen, J. J. *Myth, Religion and Mother Right*. Princeton, NJ: Princeton University Press, 1967.

Baer, Randall N., & Baer, Vicki V. *Windows of Light: Quartz Crystals and Self-Transformation*. San Francisco: Harper & Row, 1984.

Baer, Randall N., & Baer, Vicki V. *The Crystal Connection: A Guidebook for Personal and Planetary Ascension*. San Francisco: Harper & Row, 1987.

Bardo Thodol (W. Y. Evans-Wentz, trans.). London: Oxford University Press, 1927.

Baring-Gould, Sabine. *Curious Myths of the Middle Ages*. New York: University Books, 1967.

Barnstone, Willis, ed. *The Other Bible*. San Francisco: Harper & Row, 1984.

Baroja, Julio Caro. *The World of Witches*. Chicago: University of Chicago Press, 1965.

Barrett, C. K. *The New Testament Background*. New York: Harper & Row, 1961.

Beard, Mary R. *Woman as Force in History*. London: Collier-Macmillan, 1946.

Beltz, Walter. *God and the Gods: Myths of the Bible*. Harmondsworth, England: Penguin Books, 1983.

Benson, George Willard. *The Cross, Its History and Symbolism*. New York: Hacker Art Books, 1983.

Berger, Pamela. *The Goddess Obscured: Transformation of the Grain Protectress from Goddess to Saint*. Boston: Beacon, 1985.

Book of the Dead (E. A. Wallis Budge, trans.). New York: Bell, 1960.

Borchardt, Frank. *German Antiquity in Renaissance Myth*. Baltimore: Johns Hopkins University Press, 1971.

Boulding, Elise. *The Underside of History*. Boulder, CO: Westview Press, 1976.

Bowness, Charles. *Romany Magic*. New York: Samuel Weiser, 1973.

Branston, Brian. *Gods of the North*. London: Thames & Hudson, 1955.

Brasch, R. *How Did It Begin? Customs and Superstitions and Their Romantic Origins*. New York: Simon & Schuster, 1969.

Brennan, Martin. *The Stars and the Stones: Ancient Art and Astronomy in Ireland*. London: Thames & Hudson, 1984.

Brewster, H. Pomeroy. *Saints and Festivals of the Christian Church*. New York: Frederick A. Stokes, 1904.

Brier, Bob. *Ancient Egyptian Magic*. New York: Quill, 1980.

Briffault, Robert. *The Mothers*. 3 vols. New York: Macmillan, 1927.

Bromberg, Walter. *From Shaman to Psychotherapist*. Chicago: Henry Regnery, 1975.

Brown, Robert. *Semitic Influence in Hellenic Mythology*. New York: Arno, 1977.

Budge, Sir E. A. Wallis. *Amulets and Talismans*. New York: University Books, 1968.

———. *Gods of the Egyptians*. 2 vols. New York: Dover, 1969.

———. *Egyptian Magic*. New York: Dover, 1971.

———. *Dwellers on the Nile*. New York: Dover, 1977.

———. *Egyptian Language*. New York: Dover, 1977.

Campbell, Joseph. *The Hero with a Thousand Faces*. Princeton, NJ: Princeton University Press, 1949.

———. *The Masks of God: Primitive Mythology*. New York: Viking, 1959

———. *The Masks of God: Oriental Mythology*. New York: Viking, 1962.

———. *The Masks of God: Occidental Mythology*. New York: Viking, 1964.

———. *The Flight of the Wild Gander*. Chicago: Henry Regnery, 1969.

———. *The Masks of God: Creative Mythology*. New York: Viking, 1970.

———. *The Mythic Image*. Princeton, NJ: Princeton University Press, 1974.

———. *The Way of the Animal Powers*. San Francisco: Harper & Row, 1983.

Campbell, Joseph, ed. *Pagan and Christian Mysteries: Papers from the Eranos Yearbooks*. New York, Bollingen, 1955.

Cavendish, Richard. *Legends of the World*. New York: Schocken Books, 1982.

Chamberlain, Basil Hall, trans. *The Kojiki: Records of Ancient Matters*. Tokyo: Charles E. Tuttle, 1981.

Cirlot, J. E. *A Dictionary of Symbols*. New York: Philosophical Library, 1962.

Crawley, Ernest. *The Mystic Rose*. 2 vols. New York: Meridian Books, 1960.

Crowley, Aleister. *The Book of Thoth*. New York: Samuel Weiser, 1969.

Cumont, Franz. *The Mysteries of Mithra*. New York: Dover, 1956.

_____. *Astrology and Religion Among the Greeks and Romans*. New York: Dover, 1960.

Dake, H. C.; Fleener, Frank L.; and Wilson, Ben Hur. *Quartz Family Minerals*. New York: McGraw-Hill, 1938.

d'Alviella, Count Goblet. *The Migration of Symbols*. New York: University Books, 1956.

Dames, Michael. *The Silbury Treasure*. London: Thames & Hudson, 1976.

Daraul, Arkon. *A History of Secret Societies*. Secaucus, NJ: Citadel Press, 1961.

Darrah, John. *The Real Camelot: Paganism and the Arthurian Romance*. London: Thames & Hudson, 1981.

Davidson, H. R. Ellis. *Pagan Scandinavia*. New York: Frederick A. Praeger, 1967.

_____. *Gods and Myths of the Viking Age*. New York: Bell, 1981.

de Givry, Grillot. *Witchcraft, Magic and Alchemy*. New York: Dover, 1971.

de Lys, Claudia. *The Giant Book of Superstitions*. Secaucus, NJ: Citadel Press, 1979.

de Paor, Máire, and de Paor, Liam. *Early Christian Ireland*. London: Thames & Hudson, 1958.

de Riencourt, Amaury. *Sex and Power in History*. New York: Dell, 1974.

Derlon, Pierrre. *Secrets of the Gypsies*. New York: Ballantine Books, 1977.

de Santillana, Giorgio, and von Dechend, Hertha. *Hamlet's Mill: An Essay on Myth and the Frame of Time*. Boston: Gambit, Inc., 1969.

Desautels, Paul E. *The Gem Kingdom*. New York: Random House, n.d.

Douglas, Mary. *Natural Symbols: Explorations in Cosmology*. New York: Pantheon, 1970.

Duerr, Hans Peter. *Dreamtime: Concerning the Boundary Between Wilderness and Civilization* (Felicitas Goodman, trans.). Oxford, England: Basil Blackwell, 1985.

Duke, James A. *Handbook of Medicinal Herbs*. Boca Raton, FL: CRC Press, 1985.

Dumézil, Georges. *Archaic Roman Religion*. 2 vols. Chicago: University of Chicago Press, 1970.

_____. *From Myth to Fiction: The Saga of Hadingus*. Chicago: University of Chicago Press, 1973.

Dunham, Barrows. *Heroes and Heretics: A Political History of Western Thought*. New York: Knopf, 1964.

Eliade, Mircea. *Rites and Symbols of Initiation*. New York: Harper & Row, 1958.

Elworthy, Frederick. *The Evil Eye*. New York: Julian Press, 1958.

Emboden, William A. *Bizarre Plants: Magical, Monstrous, Mythical*. New York: Macmillan, 1974.

Epic of Gilgamesh. Harmondsworth, England: Penguin Books, 1960.

Evans-Wentz, W. Y. *The Fairy-Faith in Celtic Countries*. New York: University Books, 1966.

Fisher, Elizabeth. *Woman's Creation: Sexual Evolution and the Shaping of Society*. New York: Doubleday, 1979.

Forgotten Books of Eden. New York: Bell, 1980.

Frankfort, Henri. *Kingship and the Gods*. Chicago: University of Chicago Press, 1978.

Frazer, Sir James G. *The Golden Bough*. New York: Macmillan, 1922.

———. *Folk-Lore in the Old Testament*. New York: Macmillan, 1927.

French, Marilyn. *Beyond Power: On Women, Men, and Morals*. New York: Simon & Schuster, 1985.

Funk, Wilfred. *Word Origins and Their Romantic Stories*. New York: Bell, 1978.

Gage, Matilda Joslyn. *Woman, Church and State: A Historical Account of the Status of Woman Through the Christian Ages: With Reminiscences of the Matriarchate*. New York: Arno, 1972.

Gaster, Theodor. *Myth, Legend and Custom in the Old Testament*. New York: Harper & Row, 1969.

Gelling, Peter, and Davidson, Hilda Ellis. *The Chariot of the Sun*. New York: Frederick A. Praeger, 1969.

Gems, Stones, and Metals for Healing and Attunement: A Survey of Psychic Readings. Heritage Publications, 1977.

Gifford, Edward S., Jr. *The Evil Eye*. New York: Macmillan, 1958.

Gimbutas, Marija. *The Goddesses and Gods of Old Europe: Myths and Cult Images*. Berkeley: University of California Press, 1974.

Glover, T. R. *The Conflict of Religions in the Early Roman Empire*. New York: Cooper Square, 1975.

Goodrich, Norma Lorre. *Medieval Myths*. New York: New American Library, 1977.

Grant, Michael. *Roman Myths*. New York: Scribner, 1971.

Graves, Robert. *The Greek Myths*. 2 vols. New York: Penguin Books, 1955.

———. *The White Goddess*. New York: Vintage Books, 1958.

Green, Miranda. *The Gods of the Celts*. Totowa, NJ: Barnes & Noble, 1986.

Groome, Francis Hindes. *Gypsy Folk Tales*. London: Herbert Jenkins, 1963.

Guthrie, W. K. C. *The Greeks and Their Gods*. Boston: Beacon, 1955.

Hall, James. *Dictionary of Subjects and Symbols in Art*. New York: Harper & Row, 1974.

Halliday, William Reginald. *Greek and Roman Folklore*. New York: Cooper Square, 1963.

Hawkins, Gerald S. *Stonehenge Decoded*. New York: Dell, 1965.

Hazlitt, W. Carew. *Faiths and Folklore of the British Isles*. 2 vols. New York: Benjamin Blom, 1965.

Herodotus. *The Histories* (Henry Cary, trans.). New York: D. Appleton, 1899.

Hitching, Francis. *Earth Magic*. New York: Pocket Books, 1978.

Hornung, Clarence P. *Hornung's Handbook of Designs and Devices*. New York: Dover, 1959.

Howard, Michael. *The Magic of the Runes: Their Origins and Occult Power*. New York: Samuel Weiser, 1980.

Huson, Paul. *The Devil's Picturebook*. New York: Putnam, 1971.

Huxley, Francis. *The Way of the Sacred*. New York: Doubleday, 1974.

Hyde, Walter Woodburn. *Greek Religion and Its Survivals*. New York: Cooper Square, 1963.

Jobes, Gertrude. *Dictionary of Mythology, Folklore and Symbols*. 3 vols. New York: Scarecrow Press, 1962.

Jobes, Gertrude, and Jobes, James. *Outer Space*. New York: Scarecrow Press, 1964.

Johnson, Paul. *A History of Christianity*. New York: Atheneum, 1976.

Joyce, P. W. *A Social History of Ancient Ireland*. 2 vols. New York: Arno, 1980.

Jung, Carl Gustav. *Man and His Symbols*. New York: Doubleday, 1964.

Jung, Emma, and von Franz, Marie-Louise. *The Grail Legend*. New York: Putnam, 1970.

Keuls, Eva C. *The Reign of the Phallus: Sexual Politics in Ancient Athens*. New York: Harper & Row, 1985.

King, Francis. *Sexuality, Magic and Perversion*. Secaucus, NJ: Citadel Press, 1972.

Knight, Richard Payne. *A Discourse on the Worship of Priapus*. New York: University Books, 1974.

Koch, Rudolf. *The Book of Signs*. New York: Dover, 1955.

Kunz, George Frederick. *The Curious Lore of Precious Stones*. Philadelphia: Lippincott, 1913.

La Barre, Weston. *They Shall Take Up Serpents: Psychology of the Southern Snake-Handling Cult*. New York: Schocken Books, 1974.

Lapidary Journal. January 1987.

Larousse Encyclopedia of Mythology. London: Hamlyn Publishing Group, 1968.

Lederer, Wolfgang. *The Fear of Women*. New York: Harcourt Brace Jovanovich, 1968.

Leek, Sybil. *Sybil Leek's Book of Herbs*. New York: Thomas Nelson, 1973.

Lehner, Ernst. *Symbols, Signs and Signets*. New York: Dover, 1969.

Leland, Charles Godfrey. *Gypsy Sorcery and Fortune Telling*. New York: University Books, 1962.

Lethaby, W. R. *Architecture, Mysticism and Myth*. New York: George Braziller, 1975.

Lindsay, Jack. *The Origins of Astrology*. New York: Barnes & Noble, 1971.

Lorusso, Julia, & Glick, Joel. *Healing Stoned: The Therapeutic Use of Gems and Minerals*. Albuquerque, NM: Brotherhood of Life, 1985.

Luck, Georg. *Arcana Mundi*. Baltimore: Johns Hopkins University Press, 1985.

MacKenzie, Norman. *Secret Societies*. New York: Holt, Rinehart & Winston, 1967.

McLoughlin, Emmett. *Crime and Immorality in the Catholic Church*. New York: Lyle Stuart, 1962.

Mahanirvanatantra (Sir John Woodroffe, trans.). New York: Dover, 1972.

Mâle, Emile. *The Gothic Image*. New York: Harper & Row, 1958.

Malvern, Marjorie. *Venus in Sackcloth*. Carbondale: Southern Illinois University Press, 1975.

Markale, Jean. *Women of the Celts*. Rochester, VT: Inner Traditions International, 1986.

Martin, Walter. *The Kingdom of the Cults*. Minneapolis: Bethany House, 1985.

Miles, Clement A. *Christmas Customs and Traditions*. New York: Dover, 1976.

Moakley, Gertrude. *The Tarot Cards Painted by Bembo*. New York: New York Public Library, 1966.

Mollenkott, Virginia Ramey. *The Divine Feminine: The Biblical Imagery of God as Female*. New York: Crossroad, 1985.

Montagu, Ashley. *Sex, Man, and Society*. New York: Putnam, 1967.

Morton, Nelle. *The Journey Is Home*. Boston: Beacon, 1985.

Neumann, Erich. *Art and the Creative Unconscious*. Princeton, NJ: Princeton University Press, 1959.

Pagels, Elaine. *The Gnostic Gospels*. New York: Random House, 1979.

Patai, Raphael. *The Hebrew Goddess*. Ktav Publishing House, 1967.

Pegg, Bob. *Rites and Riots: Folk Customs of Britain and Europe*. Poole, Dorset, England: Blandford Press, 1981.

Pepper, Elizabeth, and Wilcock, John. *Magical and Mystical Sites*. New York: Harper & Row, 1977.

Perry, John Weir. *Lord of the Four Quarters*. New York: Macmillan, 1966.

Phillips, Guy Ragland. *Brigantia*. London: Routledge & Kegan Paul, 1976.

Potter, Stephen, and Sargent, Laurens. *Pedigree*. New York: Taplinger, 1974.

Pritchard, James B. *The Ancient Near East*. 2 vols. Princeton, NJ: Princeton University Press, 1958.

Rank, Otto. *The Myth of the Birth of the Hero*. New York: Vintage Books, 1959.

Raphaell, Katrina. *Crystal Enlightenment: The Transforming Properties of Crystals and Healing Stones*. New York: Aurora Press, 1985.

Rawson, Philip. *Erotic Art of the East*. New York: Putnam, 1968.

————. *The Art of Tantra*. Greenwich, CT: New York Graphic Society, 1973.

Rees, Alwyn, and Rees, Brinley. *Celtic Heritage*. New York: Grove, 1961.

Reinach, Salomon. *Orpheus*. New York: Horace Liveright, 1930.

Robertson, J. M. *Pagan Christs*. New York: University Books, 1967.

Robinson, James M., ed. *The Nag Hammadi Library in English*. San Francisco: Harper & Row, 1977.

Rose, H. J. *Religion in Greece and Rome*. New York: Harper & Bros., 1959.

Ross, Nancy Wilson. *Three Ways of Asian Wisdom*. New York: Simon & Schuster, 1966.

Sadock, B. J.; Kaplan, H. I.; and Freedman, A. M. *The Sexual Experience*. Baltimore: Williams & Wilkins, 1976.

Sanday, Peggy Reeves. *Female Power and Male Dominance: On the Origins of Sexual Inequality*. Cambridge: Cambridge University Press, 1981.

Schumann, Walter. *Gemstones of the World*. New York: Sterling, 1977.

Scot, Reginald. *Discoverie of Witchcraft*. Yorkshire, England: Rowmand & Littlefield, 1973.

Seligmann, Kurt. *Magic, Supernaturalism and Religion*. New York: Pantheon, 1948.

Shah, Idris. *The Sufis*. London: Octagon Press, 1964.

Silberer, Herbert. *Hidden Symbolism of Alchemy and the Occult Arts*. New York: Dover, 1971.

Simons, G. L. *Sex and Superstition*. New York: Harper & Row, 1973.

Sjöö, Monica, and Mor, Barbara. *The Great Cosmic Mother: Rediscovering the Religion of the Earth*. San Francisco: Harper & Row, 1987.

Smith, Homer. *Man and His Gods*. Boston: Little, Brown, 1952.

Smith, John Holland. *The Death of Classical Paganism*. New York: Scribner, 1976.

Smith, Morton. *Jesus the Magician*. San Francisco: Harper & Row, 1978.

Spence, Lewis. *An Encyclopedia of Occultism: A Compendium of Information on the Occult Sciences, Occult Personalities, Psychic Science, Magic, Demonology, Spiritism, Mysticism and Metaphysics*. New York: University Books, 1960.

Stanton, Elizabeth Cady. *The Original Feminist Attack on the Bible*. New York: Arno, 1974.

Steenstrup, Johannes C. H. R. *The Medieval Popular Ballad*. Seattle: University of Washington Press, 1968.

Stein, Diane. *The Women's Spirituality Book*. St. Paul, MN: Llewellyn, 1987.

Stewart, Bob. *The Waters of the Gap: The Mythology of Aquae Sulis*. Bath, England: Pitman, 1981.

Stone, Merlin. *When God Was a Woman*. New York: Dial, 1976.

————. *Ancient Mirrors of Womanhood: Our Goddess and Heroine Heritage*. 2 vols. New York: New Sibylline Books, 1979.

Tatz, Mark, and Kent, Jody. *Rebirth*. New York: Anchor/Doubleday, 1977.

Tennant, F. R. *The Sources of the Doctrines of the Fall and Original Sin*. New York: Schocken Books, 1968.

Teubal, Savina J. *Sarah the Priestess: The First Matriarch of Genesis*. Athens, OH: Swallow, 1984.

Thomas, Keith. *Religion and the Decline of Magic*. New York: Scribner, 1971.

Trachtenberg, Joshua. *Jewish Magic and Superstition: A Study in Folk Religion*. New York: Atheneum, 1984.

Trigg, Elwood B. *Gypsy Demons and Divinities*. Secaucus, NJ: Citadel Press, 1973.

Turville-Petre, E. O. G. *Myth and Religion of the North*. New York: Holt, Rinehart & Winston, 1964.

Upanishads. New York: New American Library, 1957.

Vermaseren, Maarten J. *Cybele and Attis*. London: Thames & Hudson, 1977.

von Hagen, Victor W. *World of the Maya*. New York: New American Library, 1960.

Waddell, L. Austine. *Tibetan Buddhism*. New York: Dover, 1972.

Walker, Barbara G. *The Woman's Encyclopedia of Myths and Secrets*. San Francisco: Harper & Row, 1983.

_____. *The Secrets of the Tarot: Origins, History, and Symbolism*. San Francisco: Harper & Row, 1984.

Warner, Marina. *Alone of All Her Sex: The Myth and Cult of the Virgin Mary*. New York: Knopf, 1976.

Watts, Alan W. *Myth and Ritual in Christianity*. New York: Grove, 1954.

Wedeck, Harry E. *A Treasury of Witchcraft*. Secaucus, NJ: Citadel Press, 1975.

Weston, Jessie L. *From Ritual to Romance*. New York: Peter Smith, 1941.

White, Andrew D. *A History of the Warfare of Science with Theology in Christendom*. 2 vols. New York: George Braziller, 1955.

Whittick, Arnold. *Symbols: Signs and Their Meaning and Uses in Design*. Newton, MA: Charles T. Branford, 1971.

Wilkins, Eithne. *The Rose-Garden Game*. London: Victor Gallancz, 1969.

Williamson, John. *The Oak King, the Holly King, and the Unicorn*. New York: Harper & Row, 1986.

Wimberly, Lowry Charles. *Folklore in the English and Scottish Ballads*. New York: Dover, 1965.

Woods, William. *A History of the Devil*. New York: Putnam, 1974.

Wright, Thomas. *The Worship of the Generative Powers During the Middle Ages of Western Europe*. New York: Bell, 1957.

Zimmer, Heinrich. *Myths and Symbols in Indian Art and Civilization*. Princeton, NJ: Princeton University Press, 1946.

INDEX

This index is both a general subject index and an alphabetical guide to all the symbols listed in this book. These symbols are set in boldface type, and the page number of their main entry is set in italics for easy reference.

Bujan, 342
Bull, 95, 170, 250, 264, 279, 284, 295, 366, 369, 385, 455
Bulrush, *441*
Bun, *483*
Buto, 109, 268, 388
Butterfly, 245, *415*, 416 ·
Byblos, 197, 471

C
Cabala, 56
Cabiria, 140
Caduceus, 26, *85*, 119, 274
Caer sidi, 16
Caillech, 40, 104, 130, 161, 251, 346, 463, 523
Cain, 15
Cairngorm, 509
Cale, 256
Calf, 207, 367
Calliope, 76
Calumet, 454
Calvary cross, 86
Calvin, 8, 38
Calypso, 320
Cancer, 284, 289
Candle, *123*, 315, 354
Candlemas, *171*
Cannibalism, 6, 281, 478
Capricorn, *290*, 376
Capstan, *124*
Carbuncle, 505
Carmenta, 117, 185
Carmentes, 185
Carna, 172
Carnelian, 107, 505, *506*, 512

Carnival, 17, 83, 116, 118, 145, *172*, 187, 218, 253, 325, 481
Carpho, 256
Carpocratians, 208
Cartomancy, 155
Caryatid, 76, 86
Cassiel, 98
Castor and Pollux, 271, 290
Castration, 92, 151, 173, 417, 447
Cat, 105, 180, 247, *367*
Cathedral, 11, 12, 20, **86,** 148, 249
Cat's eye, *506*
Cattail, 441
Caul, *305*, 352
Cauldron, 30, 57, 90, *124*, 199, 300, 341–42, 351, 355, 460
Cave, 15, 95, 144, 175, 257, 277, 330, 335, 346, 378, 460
Cecrops, 77
Cedar, *461*
Celtic cross, 47
Centaur, 30, 237, 293
Cerberus, 371, 448
Ceres, 90, 130, *198*, 210, 217, 295
Cernunnos, 125, 139, *199*, 253
Cerridwen, 330, 352, 389, 461
Cetus, 361

Chakras, 4, 26, 134, *306*, 420
Chalcedony, 505–6
Chalice, 90, 132, 134, 140
Changeling, 245–46, 260
Chaos, 84, 175, 210, 254, 300, 336, 518
Chariot, 17, 62, 103, *126*, 231, 259, 381
Charites, 256, 523
Charlemagne, 22, 28, 31, 278, 347, 453
Charon, 270, 350, 403
Chartres, 11
Cheese, *483*
Cheiron, 237
Cherry, *484*
Cherry laurel, *441*
Cherubim, 84, 232, 257
Chidambaram, 175
Chimera, *237*
Chloris, 427
Chomo-lung-ma, 346
Chrism, 25, 88
Chrismon, *199*
Christ, 11, 12, 38, 50, 54, 59, 78, 88, 95, 162, 169, 171, 196, 204, 270, 280, 338, 380, 390, 406, 409, 425, 434–35, 456, 493, 505
Christina, Saint, 517
Christmas tree, *462*
Christos, 25, 88
Chronos, 218
Chrysoprase, *507*
Chrysostom, John, 8, 287
Church, 11
Churching, 171, *172*, 314

Manger, 131
Manilius, 7
Mannaz, 37
Mano pantea, 315
Mansion, *144*
Mantis, 173, *417*
Mantramatrika, 99, 212
Mantras, 7, 190, 473–74
Mara, 247, 351
Mardi Gras, 118
Marduk, 51, 99, 191, 202, 212, 237, 336
Mare, 75, 280, *383*
Margaret, Saint, 517
Mari, 201, 222, 351, 374, 404, 511
Mari-anath, 84, 168
Mari-anna, 77, 129, 201, 219
Marica, 213
Marici, 222, 389
Marijuana, 432, 444
Marina, 129, 274, 351, 374, 517
Maris, 213
Marriage, 133, 180
Mars, 13, 20, 134, 171, 209, *213,* 224, 289, 294, 348, 399, 426, 428, 514, 516
Marsyas, 54, 213, 376, 464, 469
Martha, 88
Martyrdom, 132, 272, 472
Mary, 9, 29, 40, 56, 59, 87–88, 95, 123, 171, 190, 216, 222, 304, 338, 351, 364, 374, 423, 428, 434, 470

Mary Magdalene, 40, 88, 325, 480
Mascara, 145
Mascot, *383*
Mashu, 346
Mashya and Mashyoi, 217
Mask, 81, *145,* 154, 172, 250, 264, 281, 365, 383, 393, 516
Maskim, 13, 70
Matrika, 99, 117, 212
Matripadma, 429
Matronalia, 179
Matronit, 219
Matu, 330
Mau, 367
Maya, 63, 176, 205, 252, 349, 372, 484
May apple, 446
May Eve, 25, *186,* 379, 427
Maypole, 25, 30, 116, 186, 189, 253, 462, 465
Maypop, 431
Meadowsweet, *447*
Mecca, 345, 378, 504
Medea, 126
Medicine wheel, *11*
Medusa, 81, 161, 198, 231, 235, 245, 255, 261, 378, 507
Megaera, 249
Mehen, 268, 388
Mehilainen, 415
Mehit, 381
Meirothea, 330
Melanippe, 383
Meliae, 460
Melissae, 414, 488
Melpomene, 76
Melusine, 263

Mem-aleph, 96
Memnon, 119
Mena, 303
Menarche, 173, 299, 311
Menat, 97
Menorah, 97
Menos, 117
Menstruation, 173, 299, 323, 341, 493, 495
Menstruum universale, 518
Mercury, 13, 85, 92, 109, 204, *214,* 271, 291, 296, 310, 348, 512, 518
Mercy seat, 84
Merkabah, 103, 126
Merlin, 346, 352
Mermaid, 129, 259, 263, 266, 274, 278, 374
Merudanda, 26
Mescaline, 450
Meteor, 75, 338
Metis, 81, 198, 205, 255
Mezuzah, 98, 103
Michael, 51, 97, 119, 233, 508, 512
Microcosmic Man, 70
Midgard-worm, 268, 394
Midsummer, *187,* 192, 253, 282, 448
Midwife, 77, 137, 147, 349, 404
Mignonette, 444
Milburga, Saint, 486
Milk, 147, 169, 185, 323, 343, 346, 367–68, 428, 483, 489
Milk stone, 526
Milky Way, 140, 303, 343, 368, 419
Mill, 57

This book has been composed in Electra, with
Optima Black display, by Walker Graphics of
San Francisco, and printed and bound by
The Haddon Craftsmen, Inc., Scranton,
Pennsylvania.

Design and production under the direction of
Harper & Row, San Francisco,
by Editorial Design, San Francisco:

Joy Dickinson, design & production
Samuel Jennings, production assistance